THE ENDURING VISION

THE ENDURING VISION

A History of the American People

VOLUME TWO: From 1865

Dolphin Edition

Paul S. Boyer
University of Wisconsin

Clifford E. Clark, Jr.
Carleton College

Joseph F. Kett
University of Virginia

Neal Salisbury
Smith College

Harvard Sitkoff
University of New Hampshire

Nancy Woloch
Barnard College

Houghton Mifflin Company
Boston   New York

Publisher: Charles Hartford
Senior Sponsoring Editor: Sally Constable
Development Editor: Lisa Kalner Williams
Senior Project Editor: Bob Greiner
Editorial Assistant: Trinity Peacock-Broyles
Manufacturing Manager: Florence Cadran
Senior Marketing Manager: Sandra McGuire

Cover art: Alson Skinner Clark, American, 1876–1940, *The Coffee House, before 1906.* Oil on Canvas, 96.5 x 76.2 cm. Gift of Mr. and Mrs. Alson E. Clark, 1915.256, © The Art Institute of Chicago (1915.256 E19299)

Printed in the U.S.A.

Library of Congress Catalog Number: 2004105487

ISBN: 0-618-47312-2

1 2 3 4 5 6 7 8 9-CRW-07   06   05   04

Contents

21

THE PROGRESSIVE ERA, 1900–1917

764

23

THE 1920s: COPING WITH CHANGE, 1920–1929

844

24
THE GREAT DEPRESSION AND THE NEW DEAL, 1929–1939
883

30

SOCIETY, POLITICS,
AND WORLD EVENTS
FROM FORD TO
REAGAN, 1974–1989
1113

Preface

Much has changed in America and the world since we first began planning *The Enduring Vision* more than a decade ago. Some of these developments have been welcome and positive; others have been troubling and unsettling. In this new *Dolphin Edition,* based on the Fifth Edition of *The Enduring Vision,* we fully document the scope of these changes, for good or ill. But we have also taken care to stress the continuities that can provide assurance and inspire hope in troubled times.

Although the United States of today is profoundly different from the nation of even a few decades ago, the determination to live up to the values that give meaning to America—among them freedom, social justice, tolerance for diversity, and equality of opportunity—remains a strong and vibrant force in our life as a people. Our desire to convey the strength of this enduring vision in a world of change has guided our efforts throughout the writing of this book.

In this *Dolphin Edition* we have built on the underlying strategy that has guided us from the beginning. We want our version of U.S. history to be not only comprehensive and illuminating, but also lively, readable, and true to the actual lives of many earlier generations of Americans. We have maintained a clear political and chronological framework into which we integrate the best recent scholarship in all areas of American history. Our particular interest in social and cultural history, which looms large in the courses we ourselves teach at our various colleges and universities, has been a shaping force in *The Enduring Vision* from the outset, and it remains strongly evident in this *Dolphin Edition.* This edition expands and integrates coverage of the historical experience of women, African-Americans, Hispanic-Americans, Asian-Americans, and American Indians—in short, of men and women of all regions, ethnic groups, and social classes who make up the American mosaic.

Organization

In a few key instances we have reorganized the chapter sequence so the narrative flows more smoothly and to assure full coverage of recent events. Two chapters on the late-nineteenth-century era, "The Transformation of Urban America" and "Daily Life, Popular Culture, and the Arts, 1860–1900," have been combined into one: Chapter 19, "Immigration, Urbanization, and Everyday Life, 1860–1900." Similarly, the two chapters on the 1930s have been consolidated into one taut chapter, Chapter 24, "The Great Depression and the New Deal, 1929–1939." This allows us to convey more directly how the economic crisis and the reform energies of the 1930s played out not only in Washington, D.C., but across American society and culture as a whole.

We also decided to shift some material among chapters to promote clarity and coherence. We moved the discussion of early-twentieth-century foreign relations, including the Open Door notes to China and the building of the Panama Canal, into Chapter 22, "Global Involvements and World War I, 1902–1920," allowing us to trace America's expanding world role in those crucial years. Similarly, the diplomacy of the 1930s, which as the decade wore on focused heavily on the deepening foreign menace in Europe and Asia, formerly included in the chapter on the Great Depression and the New Deal, is now covered at the beginning of Chapter 25, "Americans and a World in Crisis, 1933–1945," which also deals with World War II.

Having restructured and tightened our treatment of earlier time periods, we were able to add a new concluding chapter, so that we now devote three full chapters to the eventful contemporary era, from Richard Nixon's resignation in 1974 to the present—a period of nearly thirty years. The energy crises of the 1970s, the ferment and controversies of the Reagan years, the end of the Cold War, new patterns of immigration, the economic transformation associated with the rise of the service economy and the revolution in information processing, the roller-coaster economy of the late 1990s and beyond, the deadly attack on America in September 2001, and even the corporate scandals and stock-market collapse of 2002 are now treated in full analytic detail.

New Interpretations, Expanded Coverage

In our planning we carefully assessed the coverage, interpretations, and analytic framework of the entire book, to be sure that it continues to incorporate the latest scholarship. We have been especially attentive to new work in social and cultural history, building on a strength of the book that instructors have long recognized.

As in earlier editions, our extensive coverage of environmental history, the land, and the West is fully integrated into the narrative, and treated analytically, not simply mechanically "tacked on" to a traditional account. We have incorporated the best of the new political history, stressing the social and economic issues at stake in politics, rather than simply recounting election results and party battles. We give close attention to America's emergence as a world power and the evolution of the nation's global role over time.

Building on a theme we have stressed from the beginning, this Dolphin Edition of *The Enduring Vision* pays even closer attention to the crucial role of science and technology in American history. From the hunting implements of the Paleo-Indians to the key inventions and manufacturing innovations of the industrial age and today's breakthroughs in information processing and genetic engineering, the applications of science and technology are central throughout the text. In addition, we have created a new feature, "Technology and Culture," to highlight key innovations in each stage of American history (see "Special Features" section, below).

Continuing one of the distinctive strengths of *The Enduring Vision*, Dolphin Edition we have also expanded coverage of the vital areas of medicine and disease.

From the devastating epidemics brought by the first European explorers and settlers and the appalling health conditions of the industrial city to the rise of the public-health movement, the controversies over health-care financing, the AIDS crisis, bioethics debates, and much else, this central and growing area of research receives the attention it deserves in *The Enduring Vision*, Dolphin Edition.

Revisions and Innovations in Each Chapter

A chapter-by-chapter glimpse of some of the changes in this edition highlights the depth of effort that went into its preparation.

Chapter 1 incorporates the latest archaeological findings relating to the earliest Native American peoples while a new section on Mesoamerica and South America places the discussion of North American Indians in a broader hemispheric perspective. Chapter 2 focuses more sharply on the emerging Atlantic world and offers revised discussions of West African and European societies and the Spanish invasions of Mexico and New Mexico.

Chapter 3 features a reorganized, more concise section on New England, a revised discussion of slavery and race in the Chesapeake, and an expanded treatment of the Pueblo Revolt. In Chapter 4 new material appears on patterns of consumption in colonial America and on slavery and African-American life, along with material from other chapters on the Tuscarora, Yamasee, and King George's Wars. A new section, "Public Life in British America," combines discussions of colonial politics, the Enlightenment, and the Great Awakening.

Chapter 5 has new material on the ideological underpinnings of colonial resistance to British rule and a discussion of African-Americans in the mid-eighteenth century, while Chapter 6 includes revised discussions of Native Americans and of state constitutions. In Chapter 7 we offer revised and expanded discussions of African-Americans and of white women, formerly discussed in Chapter 6.

In Chapter 8, we have added material on the Thomas Jefferson and Sally Hemings relationship and a greatly expanded discussion of Tecumseh and his reaction to the 1809 Treaty of Fort Wayne. In keeping with recent scholarship, Chapter 9 includes more on rural capitalism and how industrialization evolved out of a crisis in the New England countryside, as well as economic developments in the South. A section on northern free blacks and the A.M.E. church has been added as well.

To further the chronological flow of the work, the discussion of the Mormons in Chapter 10 ends with Joseph Smith's death in 1844, leaving the story of the great trek to Deseret for Chapter 13. In Chapter 11 we provide more attention to the development in the 1830s and 1840s of machine tools and the two industries that immediately benefited from them, the manufacture of guns and sewing machines. Chapter 13, which now starts with the Mormon trek, includes enhanced coverage of the Gold Rush.

Chapters 14, 15, and 16, on the Civil War and Reconstruction eras, include a new segment on the lives of Civil War soldiers, an expanded discussion of the experiences of Confederate women, new material on the start of woman-suffrage organizations during Reconstruction, and expanded treatment of postwar changes in plantation labor.

Chapter 17 incorporates new scholarship on the connections between western expansionism, Native Americans, and the environment in the trans-Mississippi West. In Chapter 18, on late-nineteenth-century industrialization, we have added a new section on the role of small manufacturers such as the furniture makers of Grand Rapids, Michigan, who could adapt quickly to new tastes and social trends.

Chapter 19, a melding of two chapters from the fourth edition, shows how industrialization, urbanization, and immigration transformed everyday life, sharpened racial and ethnic divisions, and made Americans more conscious of social class. Chapter 20 incorporates the latest scholarship on industrialization's impact on politics and foreign policy as well as new material on women's influence on the political ideology of the era. In Chapter 21, on the Progressive Era, we offer more coverage of urban popular culture; the woman-suffrage movement in the West; and the public-health aspects of Progressive reform, including more on the birth-control movement. Chapter 22 explores in greater analytic depth America's growing world role in the early twentieth century and World War I home-front developments, including the devastating influenza pandemic of 1918. The treatment of the 1920s in Chapter 23 offers more on the burgeoning consumer culture, including the importance of air conditioning, the growth of the cosmetics industry, the implications of the automobile for women, and the environmental impact of tourism. Republican domestic policy, the Immigration Act of 1924, the experience of Hispanic newcomers, and the larger impact of the terrible Mississippi River flood of 1927 all receive expanded coverage.

Chapter 24, on the 1930s, offers a newly integrated, single-chapter interpretive treatment of American life in the era of the depression and New Deal. The depression's human toll, with specific examples and quotations from ordinary Americans, is vividly evoked. The environmental consequences of New Deal public-works programs, particularly the great dams built in the West, are fully explored.

We have reorganized Chapter 25 to include the events of the 1930s leading up to World War II, as well as to expand the treatment of the Holocaust and American minorities during wartime. Chapter 26 includes a new section on the GI Bill of Rights, while Chapter 27 enlarges the discussions of the postwar development of the West and of political conservatism, and adds new sections on TV culture, rock-and-roll, Native Americans, and Latinos and Latinas.

A restructured Chapter 28 now treats the key developments of the struggle for black equality and the Vietnam War in separate, comprehensive narratives. In this chapter we have also expanded the discussion of the women's movement and added sections on Asian-Americans, Hispanic-Americans, and Native Americans. Chapter 29 greatly expands the discussion of the Youth Movement and adds new sections on Kent State–Jackson State, the legacy of student activism, hippies and drugs, the musical revolution, and gay liberation—all topics of great interest to today's students.

Chapters 30 and 31 now cover the period from Nixon's resignation through the era of Bill Clinton's first term. Chapter 30 offers expanded treatment of popular culture in the 1970s and 1980s; the environmental history of the period, including the Alaska Lands Bill and the Love Canal crisis; the shift of the South into the Republican camp; and the Democratic party's move to the center. In Chapter 31 we analyze the Welfare Reform Act of 1996 and other important measures; draw on the 2000 census to explore the social trends of the 1990s and beyond, including new immigration patterns, developments in rural America, and the experience of Hispanic-Americans, Asian-Americans, and other groups; and offer an interpretive perspective on the popular culture and religious trends of the contemporary era.

The final chapter, 32, presents an integrated narrative and preliminary assessment of recent events: the scandals and impeachment crisis of Clinton's second term; the speculative bubble of the later 1990s; the disputed 2000 presidential election; the domestic and international policies of the George W. Bush administration; the attack of September 11, 2001, and its aftermath; the worsening Middle East crisis, including the war in Iraq; the latest corporate scandals; and the race for the 2004 presidential election.

Special Features This *Dolphin Edition* features "Technology and Culture" essays that describe key innovations and their impact on American society and culture. In Chapter 5, "Technology and Culture" explains the role of engineering and public sanitation as Philadelphia grew during the 1700s. The feature in Chapter 15 examines the role of the camera and the Civil War.

These essays alternate with the popular "A Place in Time" feature. "A Place in Time" delves into experiences of a particular community. The feature in Chapter 29, for example, highlights the counterculture movement in the Haight-Ashbury district of San Francisco during the 1960s. A new "A Place in Time" in Chapter 17 focuses on the Phoenix Indian School from 1891 to 1918.

Student Website In addition to the main text, *The Enduring Vision, Dolphin Edition,* shares *The Enduring Vision,* Fifth Edition's redesigned and expanded website. On the interactive site, students will find ACE self-assessment quizzes, vocabulary flashcards, and other supplemental material including additional "A Place in Time" and "Technology and Culture" essays.

Paul S. Boyer

Clifford E. Clark, Jr.

Joseph F. Kett

Neal Salisbury

Harvard Sitkoff

Nancy Woloch

About the Authors

PAUL S. BOYER, Merle Curti Professor of History emeritus at the University of Wisconsin, Madison, earned his Ph.D. from Harvard University. An editor of *Notable American Women, 1607–1950* (1971), he also coauthored *Salem Possessed: The Social Origins of Witchcraft* (1974), for which, with Stephen Nissenbaum, he received the John H. Dunning Prize of the American Historical Association. His other works include *Urban Masses and Moral Order in America, 1820–1920* (1978), *By the Bomb's Early Light: American Thought and Culture at the Dawn of the Atomic Age* (1985), *When Time Shall Be No More: Prophecy Belief in Modern American Culture* (1992), and *Promises to Keep: The United States since World War II,* 2nd ed. (1999). He is also editor-in-chief of the *Oxford Companion to United States History* (2001). His articles and essays have appeared in the *American Quarterly, New Republic,* and other journals. He has been a visiting professor at the University of California, Los Angeles, Northwestern University, and the College of William and Mary.

CLIFFORD E. CLARK, JR., M.A. and A.D. Hulings Professor of American Studies and professor of history at Carleton College, earned his Ph.D. from Harvard University. He has served as both the chair of the History Department and director of the American Studies program at Carleton. Clark is the author of *Henry Ward Beecher: Spokesman for a Middle-Class America* (1978), *The American Family Home, 1800–1960* (1986), *The Intellectual and Cultural History of Anglo-America since 1789* in the *General History of the Americas,* and, with Carol Zellie, *Northfield: The History and Architecture of a Community* (1997). He also has edited and contributed to *Minnesota in a Century of Change: The State and Its People since 1900* (1989). A past member of the Council of the American Studies Association, Clark is active in the fields of material culture studies and historic preservation, and he serves on the Northfield, Minnesota, Historical Preservation Commission.

JOSEPH F. KETT, Commonwealth Professor of History at the University of Virginia, received his Ph.D. from Harvard University. His works include *The Formation of the American Medical Profession: The Role of Institutions, 1780–1860* (1968), *Rites of Passage: Adolescence in America, 1790–Present* (1977), *The Pursuit of Knowledge under Difficulties: From Self-Improvement to Adult Education in America, 1750–1990* (1994), and *The New Dictionary of Cultural Literacy* (2002), of which he is coauthor. A former History Department chair at Virginia, he also has participated on the Panel on Youth of the President's Science Advisory Committee, has served on the Board of Editors of the *History of Education Quarterly,* and is a past member of the Council of the American Studies Association.

NEAL SALISBURY, professor of history at Smith College, received his Ph.D. from the University of California, Los Angeles. He is the author of *Manitou and Providence: Indians, Europeans, and the Making of New England, 1500–1643* (1982), editor of *The Sovereignty and Goodness of God,* by Mary Rowlandson (1997), and coeditor, with Philip J. Deloria, of *The Companion to American Indian History* (2002). He also has contributed numerous articles to journals and edited collections. Formerly chair of the History Department at Smith, he is active in the fields of colonial and Native American history, has served as president of the American Society for Ethnohistory, and coedits a book series, *Cambridge Studies in North American Indian History.*

HARVARD SITKOFF, professor of history at the University of New Hampshire, earned his Ph.D. from Columbia University. He is the author of *A New Deal for Blacks* (1978), *The Struggle for Black Equality, 1954–1992* (1992), and *Postwar America: A Student Companion* (2000); coauthor of the National Park Service's *Racial Desegregation in Public Education in the United States* (2000) and *The World War II Homefront* (2003); and editor of *Fifty Years Later: The New Deal Reevaluated* (1984), *A History of Our Time,* 6th ed. (2002), and *Perspectives on Modern America: Making Sense of the Twentieth Century* (2001). His articles have appeared in the *American Quarterly, Journal of American History,* and *Journal of Southern History,* among others. A frequent lecturer at universities abroad, he has been awarded the Fulbright Commission's John Adams Professorship of American Civilization in the Netherlands and the Mary Ball Washington Professorship of American History in Ireland.

NANCY WOLOCH received her Ph.D. from Indiana University. She is the author of *Women and the American Experience* (1984, 1994, 1996, 2000, 2002), editor of *Early American Women: A Documentary History, 1600–1900* (1992, 1997, 2002), and coauthor, with Walter LaFeber and Richard Polenberg, of *The American Century: A History of the United States since the 1890s* (1986, 1992, 1998). She is also the author of *Muller v. Oregon: A Brief History with Documents* (1996). She teaches American history and American Studies at Barnard College, Columbia University.

THE ENDURING VISION

16

The Crises of Reconstruction, 1865–1877

66 "The war weren't so great as folks suppose," declared former slave Felix Heywood. "It was the endin' of it that made the difference. That's when we all wakes up that somethin' had happened." To Heywood, who was twenty years old at the Civil War's end, emancipation was breathtaking. "We was all walkin' on golden clouds," he recalled. "We all felt like heroes and nobody made us that way but ourselves. We was free! Just like that, we was free!"

Heywood's parents had been purchased in Mississippi by William Gudlow and brought to southern Texas, where the Gudlows ran a ranch. There, Heywood and his five brothers and sisters were born. As a teenager, Felix Heywood had been a sheepherder and cowpuncher, and the war, he claimed, left his routine intact. "The ranch went on just like it always had. . . . Church went on," he observed. But after the war, Heywood noticed an important change in the African-American community: the impulse among newly freed people to move somewhere else. "Nobody took our homes away," Heywood recalled. "But right off colored folks started on the move. They seemed to want to get closer to freedom so they'd know what it was—like it was a place or a city."

Felix Heywood did not change place at once. Instead, he "stuck close as a lean tick to a sick chicken." At the outset, the Gudlows provided Heywood and his father with ranch land, where they rounded up cattle that had wandered astray. Then local ranchers gave the two Heywoods a herd of seventy cattle, and they ran their own ranch. Eventually, however, like many other former slaves, Felix Heywood migrated to the nearest city. He moved to San Antonio, a booming cattle town, where he found a job with the waterworks.

In old age, after raising a family, Felix Heywood still lived in San Antonio, now with his youngest sister. Looking back on his long life, he dwelled on the era right after the war and on the instant that emancipation arrived. "We know'd freedom was on us, but we didn't know what was to come with it," he recalled. "We thought we was goin' to be richer and better off than the white folks; cose we was stronger and knowed how to work, and the whites didn't and they didn't have us to work for them anymore. Hallelujah! But it didn't turn out like that. We soon found out that freedom could make folks proud but it didn't make 'em rich."

For the nation, as for Felix Heywood, the end of the Civil War was a turning point and a moment of uncharted possibilities. It was also a time of unresolved conflicts. While former slaves exulted over freedom, the postwar mood of ex-Confederates was often as grim as the wasted southern landscape. Unable to face "southern Yankeedom," some planters considered emigrating to the American West or to Europe, Mexico, or Brazil, and a few thousand did. The morale of the vanquished rarely concerns the victors, but the Civil War was a special case, for the Union had sought not merely military triumph but the return of national unity. The questions that the federal government faced in 1865 were therefore unprecedented.

First, how could the Union be restored and the defeated South reintegrated into the nation? Would the Confederate states be treated as conquered territories, or would they quickly rejoin the Union with the same rights as other states? Who would set the standards for readmission—Congress or the president? Would Confederate leaders be punished for treason? Would their property be confiscated and their political rights curtailed? Most important, what would happen to the more than 3.5 million former slaves? The future of the freedmen constituted the crucial issue of the postwar era, for emancipation had set in motion the most profound upheaval in the nation's history. Before the war slavery had determined the South's social, economic, and political structure. What would replace it in the postwar South? The end of the Civil War, in short, posed two problems that had to be solved simultaneously: how to readmit the South to the Union and how to define the status of free blacks in American society.

Between 1865 and 1877, the nation met these challenges, but not without discord and turmoil. Conflict prevailed in the halls of Congress as legislators debated plans to readmit the South to the Union; in the former Confederacy where defeated southerners and newly freed former slaves faced an era of turbulence; and in the postwar North where economic and political clashes arose. Indeed, the crises of Reconstruction—the restoration of the former Confederate states to the Union—reshaped the legacy of the Civil War.

This chapter focuses on five major questions:

How did Radical Republicans gain control of Reconstruction politics?

What impact did federal Reconstruction policy have on the former Confederacy, and on ex-Confederates?

In what ways did newly freed southern slaves reshape their lives after emancipation?

What factors contributed to the end of Reconstruction in the 1870s, and which was most significant?

To what extent should Reconstruction be considered a failure?

RECONSTRUCTION POLITICS, 1865–1868

At the end of the Civil War, President Johnson might have exiled, imprisoned, or executed Confederate leaders and imposed martial law indefinitely. Demobilized Confederate soldiers might have continued armed resistance to federal occupation forces. Freed slaves might have taken revenge on former owners and the rest of the white community. But none of these drastic possibilities occurred. Instead, intense *political* conflict dominated the immediate postwar years. In national politics, unparalleled disputes produced new constitutional amendments, a presidential impeachment, and some of the most ambitious domestic legislation ever enacted by Congress, the Reconstruction Acts of 1867–1868. The major outcome of Reconstruction politics was the enfranchisement of black men, a development that few—black or white—had expected when Lee surrendered.

In 1865 only a small group of politicians supported black suffrage. All were Radical Republicans, a minority faction that had emerged during the war. Led by Senator Charles Sumner of Massachusetts and Congressman Thaddeus Stevens of Pennsylvania, the Radicals had clamored for the abolition of slavery and a demanding reconstruction policy. Any plan to restore the Union, Stevens contended, must "revolutionize Southern institutions, habits, and manners . . . or all our blood and treasure have been spent in vain." But the Radicals, outnumbered in Congress by other Republicans and opposed by the Democratic minority, faced long odds. Still, they managed to win broad Republican support for parts of their Reconstruction program, including black male enfranchisement. Just as civil war had led to emancipation, a goal once supported by only a minority of Americans, so Reconstruction policy became bound to black suffrage, a momentous change that originally had only narrow political backing.

Lincoln's Plan

Conflict over Reconstruction began even before the war ended. In December 1863 President Lincoln issued the Proclamation of Amnesty and Reconstruction, which outlined a path by which each southern state could rejoin the Union. Under Lincoln's plan a minority of voters (equal to at least 10 percent of those who had cast ballots in the election of 1860) would have to take an oath of allegiance to the Union and accept emancipation. This minority could then create a loyal state government. Lincoln's plan excluded some southerners from taking the oath: Confederate government officials, army and naval officers, as well as those military or civil officers who had resigned from Congress or from U.S. commissions in 1861. All such persons would have to apply for presidential pardons. Also excluded, of course, were blacks, who had not been voters in 1860. Lincoln hoped that his "10 percent plan" would undermine the Confederacy by establishing pro-Union governments within it. Characteristically, Lincoln had partisan goals, too. He wanted to win the allegiance of southern Unionists (those who had opposed secession), especially former Whigs, and to build a southern Republican party.

Radical Republicans in Congress, however, envisioned a slower readmission process that would bar even more ex-Confederates from political life. Most Republicans agreed that Lincoln's program was too weak. Thus, in July 1864 Congress passed the Wade-Davis bill, which provided that each former Confederate state would be ruled by a military governor. Under the Wade-Davis plan, after at least half the eligible voters took an oath of allegiance to the Union, delegates could be elected to a state convention that would repeal secession and abolish slavery. To qualify as a voter or delegate, a southerner would have to take a second, "ironclad" oath, swearing that he had never voluntarily supported the Confederacy. Like the 10 percent plan, the congressional plan did not provide for black suffrage, a measure then supported by only some Radicals. Unlike Lincoln's plan, however, the Wade-Davis scheme would have delayed the readmission process almost indefinitely.

Claiming that he did not want to bind himself to any single restoration policy, Lincoln pocket-vetoed the Wade-Davis bill (that is, he failed to sign the bill within ten days of the adjournment of Congress). The bill's sponsors, Senator Benjamin Wade of Ohio and Congressman Henry Winter Davis of Maryland, blasted Lincoln's act as an outrage. By the war's end, the president and Congress had reached an impasse. Arkansas, Louisiana, Tennessee, and parts of Virginia under Union army control moved toward readmission under variants of Lincoln's plan. But Congress refused to seat their delegates, as it had a right to do. Lincoln, meanwhile, hinted that a more rigorous Reconstruction policy might be in store. What Lincoln's ultimate policy would have been remains unknown. But after his assassination, on April 14, 1865, Radical Republicans turned with hope toward his successor, Andrew Johnson of Tennessee, in whom they felt they had an ally.

Presidential Reconstruction Under Johnson   The only southern senator to remain in Congress when his state seceded, Andrew Johnson had served as military governor of Tennessee from 1862 to 1864. He had taken a strong anti-Confederate stand, declaring that "treason is a crime and must be made odious." Above all, Johnson had long sought the destruction of the planter aristocracy. A self-educated man of humble North Carolina origins, Johnson had moved to Greenville, Tennessee, in 1826 and became a tailor. His wife, Eliza McCardle, had taught him how to write. He had entered politics in the 1830s as a spokesman for nonslaveowning whites and rose rapidly from local official to congressman to governor to senator. Once the owner of eight slaves, Johnson reversed his position on slavery during the war. When emancipation became Union policy, he supported it. But Johnson neither adopted abolitionist ideals nor challenged racist sentiments. He hoped mainly that the fall of slavery would injure southern aristocrats. Andrew Johnson, in short, had his own political agenda, which, as Republicans would soon learn, did not coincide with theirs. Moreover, he was a lifelong Democrat who had been added to the Republican, or National Union, ticket in 1864 to broaden its appeal and who had become president by accident.

Many Republicans voiced shock when Johnson announced a new plan for the restoration of the South in May 1865—with Congress out of session and not due to convene until December. In two proclamations, the president explained how the seven southern states still without reconstruction governments—Alabama, Florida, Georgia, Mississippi, North Carolina, South Carolina, and Texas—could return to the Union. Almost all southerners who took an oath of allegiance would receive a pardon and amnesty, and all their property except slaves would be restored. Oath takers could elect delegates to state conventions, which would provide for regular elections. Each state convention, Johnson later added, would have to proclaim the illegality of secession, repudiate state debts incurred when the state belonged to the Confederacy, and ratify the Thirteenth Amendment, which abolished slavery. (Proposed by an enthusiastic wartime Congress early in 1865, the amendment would be ratified in December of that year.) As under Lincoln's plan, Confederate civil and military officers could not take the oath needed to vote. Johnson also disqualified all well-off ex-Confederates—those with taxable property worth $20,000 or more. This purge of the plantation aristocracy, he said, would benefit "humble men, the peasantry and yeomen of the South, who have been decoyed . . . into rebellion." Poorer whites would now be in control.

Presidential Reconstruction took effect in the summer of 1865, but with unforeseen consequences. Southerners disqualified on the basis of wealth or high Confederate position applied for pardons in droves, and Johnson handed out pardons liberally—some thirteen thousand of them. He also dropped plans for the punishment of treason. By the end of 1865, all seven states had created new civil governments that in effect restored the status quo from before the war. Confederate army officers and large planters assumed state offices. Former Confederate congressmen, state officials, and generals were elected to Congress. Georgia sent Alexander Stephens, the former Confederate vice president, back to Washington as a senator. Some states refused to ratify the Thirteenth Amendment or to repudiate their Confederate debts.

Most infuriating to Radical Republicans, all seven states took steps to ensure a landless, dependent black labor force: they passed "black codes" to replace the slave codes, state laws that had regulated slavery. Because the ratification of the Thirteenth Amendment was assured by the terms of Johnson's Reconstruction plan, all states guaranteed the freedmen some basic rights. They could marry, own property, make contracts, and testify in court against other blacks. But the codes harshly restricted freedmen's behavior. Some established racial segregation in public places; most prohibited racial intermarriage, jury service by blacks, and court testimony by blacks against whites. All codes included provisions that effectively barred former slaves from leaving the plantations. South Carolina required special licenses for blacks who wished to enter nonagricultural employment. Mississippi prohibited blacks from buying and selling farmland. Most states required annual contracts between landowners and black agricultural workers and provided that blacks without lawful employment would be arrested as vagrants and their labor auctioned off to employers who would pay their fines.

The black codes left freedmen no longer slaves but not really liberated either. Although "free" to sign labor contracts, for instance, those who failed to sign them would be considered in violation of the law and swept back into involuntary servitude. In practice, many clauses in the codes never took effect: the Union army and the Freedmen's Bureau (a federal agency that assisted former slaves) swiftly suspended the enforcement of racially discriminatory provisions of the new laws. But the black codes revealed white southern intentions. They showed what "home rule" would have been like without federal interference.

Many northerners denounced what they saw as southern defiance. "What can be hatched from such an egg but another rebellion?" asked a Boston newspaper. Republicans in Congress agreed. When Congress convened in December 1865, it refused to seat the delegates of the ex-Confederate states. Establishing the Joint (House-Senate) Committee on Reconstruction, Republicans prepared to dismantle the black codes and lock ex-Confederates out of power.

Congress Versus Johnson   The status of the southern blacks now became the major issue in Congress. Radical Republicans like Congressman Thaddeus Stevens—who hoped to impose black suffrage on the former Confederacy and delay the readmission of the southern states into the Union—were still a minority in Congress. Conservative Republicans, who tended to favor the Johnson plan, formed a minority too, as did the Democrats, who also supported the president. Moderate Republicans, the largest congressional bloc, agreed with the Radicals that Johnson's plan was too feeble. But they thought that northern voters would oppose black suffrage, and they wanted to avoid a dispute with the president. Since none of the four congressional blocs could claim the two-thirds majority required to overturn a presidential veto, Johnson's program would prevail unless the moderates and the Radicals joined forces. Ineptly, Johnson alienated a majority of moderates and pushed them into the Radicals' arms.

The moderate Republicans supported two proposals drafted by one of their own, Senator Lyman Trumbull of Illinois, to invalidate the black codes. These measures won wide Republican support. In the first, Congress voted to continue the Freedmen's Bureau, established in 1865, whose term was ending. This federal agency, headed by former Union general O. O. Howard and staffed mainly by army officers, provided relief, rations, and medical care. It also built schools for the freed blacks, put them to work on abandoned or confiscated lands, and tried to protect their rights as laborers. Congress extended the bureau's life for three years and gave it new power: it could run special military courts to settle labor disputes and could invalidate labor contracts forced on freedmen by the black codes. In February 1866 Johnson vetoed the Freedmen's Bureau bill. The Constitution, he declared, did not sanction military trials of civilians in peacetime, nor did it support a system to care for "indigent persons."

In March 1866 Congress passed a second measure proposed by Trumbull, a bill that made blacks U.S. citizens with the same civil rights as other citizens and authorized federal intervention in the states to ensure black rights in court. Johnson vetoed the civil rights bill also. He argued that it would "operate in favor of the colored and against the white race." In April Congress overrode his veto; the Civil Rights Act of 1866 was the first major law ever passed over a presidential veto. In July Congress enacted the Supplementary Freedmen's Bureau Act over Johnson's veto as well. Johnson's vetoes puzzled many Republicans because the new laws did not undercut presidential Reconstruction. The president insisted, however, that both bills were illegitimate because southerners had been shut out of the Congress that passed them. His stance won support in the South and from northern Democrats. But the president had alienated the moderate Republicans, who began to work with the Radicals against him. Johnson had lost "every friend he has," one moderate declared.

Some historians view Andrew Johnson as a political incompetent who, at this crucial turning point, bungled both his readmission scheme and his political future. Others contend that he was merely trying to forge a coalition of the center, made up of Democrats and non-Radical Republicans. In either case, Johnson underestimated the possibility of Republican unity. Once united, the Republicans moved on to a third step: the passage of a constitutional amendment that would

King Andrew *This Thomas Nast cartoon, published in* Harper's Weekly *just before the 1866 congressional elections, conveyed Republican antipathy to Andrew Johnson. The president is depicted as an autocratic tyrant. Radical Republican Thaddeus Stevens, upper right, has his head on the block and is about to lose it. The Republic sits in chains.*

prevent the Supreme Court from invalidating the new Civil Rights Act and would block Democrats in Congress from repealing it.

The Fourteenth Amendment, 1866

In April 1866 Congress adopted the Fourteenth Amendment, which had been proposed by the Joint Committee on Reconstruction. To protect blacks' rights, the amendment declared in its first clause that all persons born or naturalized in the United States were citizens of the nation and citizens of their states and that no state could abridge their rights without due process of law or deny them equal protection of the law. This section nullified the *Dred Scott* decision of 1857, which had declared that blacks were not citizens. Second, the amendment guaranteed that if a state denied suffrage to any of its male citizens, its representation in Congress would be proportionally reduced. This clause did not guarantee black suffrage, but it threatened to deprive southern states of some legislators if black men were denied the vote. This was the first time that the word *male* was written into the Constitution. To the dismay of women's rights advocates, woman suffrage seemed a yet more distant prospect. Third, the amendment disqualified from state and national office *all* prewar officeholders—civil and military, state and federal—who had supported the Confederacy, unless Congress removed their disqualifications by a two-thirds vote. In so providing, Congress intended to invalidate Johnson's wholesale distribution of amnesties and pardons. Finally, the amendment repudiated the Confederate debt and maintained the validity of the federal debt.

The Fourteenth Amendment was the most ambitious step that Congress had yet taken. It revealed Republican legislators' growing receptivity to the Radicals' demands, including black male enfranchisement. Republicans now realized that southern states would not deal fairly with blacks unless forced to do so. The Fourteenth Amendment was the first national effort to limit state control of civil and political rights. Its passage created a firestorm. Abolitionists decried the second clause as a "swindle" because it did not explicitly ensure black suffrage. Southerners and northern Democrats condemned the third clause as vengeful. Southern legislatures, except for Tennessee's, refused to ratify the amendment, and President Johnson denounced it. His defiance solidified the new alliance between moderate and Radical Republicans, and turned the congressional elections of 1866 into a referendum on the Fourteenth Amendment.

Over the summer Johnson set off on a whistle-stop train tour from Washington to St. Louis and Chicago and back. But this innovative campaign tactic—the "swing around the circle," as Johnson called it—failed. Humorless and defensive, the president made fresh enemies and doomed his hope of creating a new National Union party that would sink the Fourteenth Amendment. Moderate and Radical Republicans defended the amendment, condemned the president, and branded the Democratic party "a common sewer . . . into which is emptied every element of treason, North and South."

Republicans carried the congressional elections of 1866 in a landslide, winning almost two-thirds of the House and almost four-fifths of the Senate. They had secured a mandate to overcome southern resistance to the Fourteenth Amendment and to enact their own Reconstruction program, even if the president vetoed every part of it.

Congressional
Reconstruction,
1866–1867

The congressional debate over reconstructing the South began in December 1866 and lasted three months. Radical Republican leaders called for black suffrage, federal support for public schools, confiscation of Confederate estates, and an extended period of military occupation in the South. Moderate Republicans, who once would have found such a plan too extreme, now accepted parts of it. In February 1867, after complex legislative maneuvers and many late-night sessions, Congress passed the Reconstruction Act of 1867. Johnson vetoed the law, and on March 2 Congress passed it over his veto. Later that year and in 1868, Congress passed three further Reconstruction acts, all enacted over presidential vetoes, to refine and enforce the first.

The Reconstruction Act of 1867 invalidated the state governments formed under the Lincoln and Johnson plans. Only Tennessee, which had ratified the Fourteenth Amendment and had been readmitted to the Union, escaped further reconstruction. The new law divided the other ten former Confederate states into five temporary military districts, each run by a Union general. Voters—all black men, plus those white men who had not been disqualified by the Fourteenth Amendment—could elect delegates to a state convention that would write a new state constitution granting black suffrage. When eligible voters ratified the new constitution, elections could be held for state officers. Once Congress approved the state constitution, once the state legislature ratified the Fourteenth Amendment, and once the amendment became part of the federal Constitution, Congress would readmit the state into the Union—and Reconstruction, in a constitutional sense, would be complete.

The Reconstruction Act of 1867 was far more radical than the Johnson program because it enfranchised blacks and disfranchised many ex-Confederates. It fulfilled a central goal of the Radical Republicans: to delay the readmission of former Confederate states until Republican governments could be established and thereby prevent an immediate rebel resurgence. But the new law was not as harsh toward ex-Confederates as it might have been. It provided for only temporary military rule. It did not prosecute Confederate leaders for treason or permanently exclude them from politics. Finally, it made no provision for the confiscation or redistribution of property.

During the congressional debates, Radical Republican congressman Thaddeus Stevens had argued for the confiscation of large Confederate estates to "humble the proud traitors" and to provide for the former slaves. He had proposed subdividing such confiscated property into forty-acre tracts to be distributed among the freedmen and selling the rest, some 90 percent of it, to pay off war debts. Stevens wanted to crush the planter aristocracy and create a new class of self-sufficient black yeoman farmers. His land-reform bill won the support of other Radicals, but it never

Major Reconstruction Legislation

Law and Date of Congressional Passage	Provisions	Purpose
Civil Rights Act of 1866 (April 1866)*	Declared blacks citizens and guaranteed them equal protection of the laws.	To invalidate the black codes.
Supplementary Freedmen's Bureau Act (July 1866)*	Extended the life of the Freedmen's Aid Bureau and expanded its powers.	To invalidate the black codes.
Reconstruction Act of 1867 (March 1867)*	Invalidated state governments formed under Lincoln and Johnson.	To replace presidential Reconstruction with a more stringent plan.
	Divided the former Confederacy into five military districts.	
	Set forth requirements for readmission of ex-Confederate states to the Union.	
Supplementary Reconstruction Acts		To enforce the First Reconstruction Act.
Second Reconstruction Act (March 1867)*	Required military commanders to initiate voter enrollment.	
Third Reconstruction Act (July 1867)*	Expanded military commanders' powers.	
Fourth Reconstruction Act (March 1868)*	Provided that a majority of voters, however few, could put a new state constitution into force.	
Army Appropriations Act (March 1867)*	Declared in a rider that only the general of the army could issue military orders.	To prevent President Johnson from obstructing Reconstruction.
Tenure of Office Act (March 1867)*	Prohibited the president from removing any federal official without the Senate's consent.	To prevent President Johnson from obstructing Reconstruction.

Major Reconstruction Legislation (cont.)

Law and Date of Congressional Passage	Provisions	Purpose
Omnibus Act (June 1868)†	Readmitted seven ex-Confederate states to the Union.	To restore the Union, under the term of the First Reconstruction Act.
Enforcement Act of 1870 (May 1870)‡	Provided for the protection of black voters.	To enforce the Fifteenth Amendment.
Second Enforcement Act (February 1871)	Provided for federal supervision of southern elections.	To enforce the Fifteenth Amendment.
Third Enforcement Act (Ku Klux Klan Act) (April 1871)	Strengthened sanctions against those who impeded black suffrage.	To combat the Ku Klux Klan and enforce the Fourteenth Amendment.
Amnesty Act (May 1872)	Restored the franchise to almost all ex-Confederates.	Effort by Grant Republicans to deprive Liberal Republicans of a campaign issue.
Civil Rights Act of 1875 (March 1875)§	Outlawed racial segregation in transportation and public accommodations and prevented exclusion of blacks from jury service.	To honor the late senator Charles Sumner.

*Passed over Johnson's veto.

†Georgia was soon returned to military rule. The last four states were readmitted in 1870.

‡Sections of the law declared unconstitutional in 1876.

§Invalidated by the Supreme Court in 1883.

made progress, for most Republicans held property rights sacred. Tampering with such rights in the South, they feared, would jeopardize those rights in the North. Moreover, Stevens's proposal would alienate southern ex-Whigs from the Republican cause, antagonize other white southerners, and thereby endanger the rest of Reconstruction. Thus land reform never came about. The "radical" Reconstruction acts were a compromise.

Congressional Reconstruction took effect in the spring of 1867, but it could not be enforced without military power. Johnson, as commander-in-chief, impeded the congressional plan by replacing military officers sympathetic to the Radical cause with conservative ones. Republicans seethed. More suspicious than ever of the president, congressional moderates and Radicals once again joined forces to block Johnson from obstructing Reconstruction.

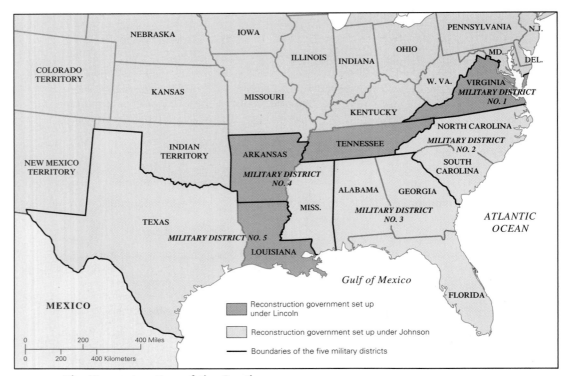

The Reconstruction of the South

The Reconstruction Act of 1867 divided the former Confederate states, except Tennessee, into five military districts and set forth the steps by which new state governments could be created.

The Impeachment Crisis, 1867–1868 In March 1867 Republicans in Congress passed two laws to limit presidential power. The Tenure of Office Act prohibited the president from removing civil officers without Senate consent. Cabinet members, the law stated, were to hold office "during the term of the president by whom they may have been appointed" and could be fired only with the Senate's approval. The goal was to bar Johnson from dismissing Secretary of War Henry Stanton, the Radicals' ally, whose support Congress needed to enforce the Reconstruction acts. The other law, a rider to an army appropriations bill, barred the president from issuing military orders except through the commanding general, Ulysses S. Grant, who could not be removed without the Senate's consent.

The Radicals' enmity toward Johnson, however, would not die until he was out of office. They began to seek grounds on which to impeach him. The House Judiciary Committee, aided by private detectives, could at first uncover no valid charges against Johnson. But Johnson again rescued his foes by providing the charges they needed.

In August 1867, with Congress out of session, Johnson suspended Secretary of War Stanton and replaced him with General Grant. In early 1868 the reconvened

Senate refused to approve Stanton's suspension, and Grant, sensing the Republican mood, vacated the office. Johnson then removed Stanton and replaced him with an aged general, Lorenzo Thomas. Johnson's defiance forced Republican moderates, who had at first resisted impeachment, into yet another alliance with the Radicals: the president had "thrown down the gauntlet," a moderate charged. The House approved eleven charges of impeachment, nine of them based on violation of the Tenure of Office Act. The other charges accused Johnson of being "unmindful of the high duties of office," of seeking to disgrace Congress, and of not enforcing the Reconstruction acts.

Johnson's trial, which began in the Senate in March 1868, riveted public attention for eleven weeks. Seven congressmen, including leading Radical Republicans, served as prosecutors or "managers." Johnson's lawyers maintained that he was merely seeking a court test by violating the Tenure of Office Act, which he thought was unconstitutional. They also contended, somewhat inconsistently, that the law did not protect Secretary Stanton, an appointee of Lincoln, not Johnson. Finally, they asserted, Johnson was guilty of no crime indictable in a regular court.

The congressional "managers" countered that impeachment was a political process, not a criminal trial, and that Johnson's "abuse of discretionary power" constituted an impeachable offense. Although Senate opinion split along party lines and Republicans held a majority, some of them wavered, fearing that the removal of a president would destroy the balance of power among the three branches of the federal government. They also distrusted Radical Republican Benjamin Wade, the president pro tempore of the Senate, who, because there was no vice president, would become president if Johnson were thrown out.

Intense pressure weighed on the wavering Republicans. Late in May 1868, the Senate voted against Johnson 35 to 19, one vote short of the two-thirds majority needed for conviction. Seven Republicans had risked political suicide and sided with the twelve Senate Democrats in voting against removal. In so doing, they set a precedent. Their vote discouraged impeachment on political grounds for decades to come. But the anti-Johnson forces had also achieved their goal: Andrew Johnson's career as a national leader would soon end. After serving out the rest of his term, Johnson returned to Tennessee, where he was reelected to the Senate five years later. Republicans in Congress, meanwhile, pursued their last major Reconstruction objective: to guarantee black male suffrage.

The Fifteenth Amendment and the Question of Woman Suffrage, 1869–1870

Black suffrage was the linchpin of congressional Reconstruction. Only with the support of black voters could Republicans secure control of the ex-Confederate states. The Reconstruction Act of 1867 had forced every southern state legislature to enfranchise black men as a prerequisite for readmission to the Union. But though black voting had begun in the South, much of the North rejected black suffrage at home. Congressional Republicans therefore had two aims. They sought to protect black suffrage in the South against future repeal by Congress or the states and to enfranchise northern and border-state blacks, who would presumably vote Republican. To achieve these goals, Congress in 1869 proposed the Fifteenth Amendment, which prohibited the denial of suffrage by the states to any citizen on account of "race, color, or previous condition of servitude."

Democrats argued that the proposed amendment violated states' rights by denying each state the power to determine who would vote. But Democrats did not control enough states to defeat the amendment, and it was ratified in 1870. Four votes came from those ex-Confederate states—Mississippi, Virginia, Georgia, and Texas—that had delayed the Reconstruction process and were therefore forced to approve the Fifteenth Amendment, as well as the Fourteenth, in order to rejoin the Union. Some southerners contended that the new amendment's omissions made it acceptable, for it had, as a Richmond newspaper pointed out, "loopholes through which a coach and four horses can be driven." What were these loopholes? The Fifteenth Amendment did not guarantee black officeholding, nor did it prohibit voting restrictions such as property requirements and literacy tests. Such restrictions might be used to deny blacks the vote, and indeed, ultimately they were so used.

The debate over black suffrage drew new participants into the political fray. Since the end of the war, a small group of abolitionists, men and women, had sought to revive the cause of women's rights. In 1866, when Congress debated the Fourteenth Amendment, women's rights advocates tried to join forces with their old abolitionist allies to promote both black suffrage and woman suffrage. Most Radical Republicans, however, did not want to be saddled with the woman-suffrage plank; they feared it would impede their primary goal, black enfranchisement.

This defection provoked disputes among women's rights advocates. Some argued that black suffrage would pave the way for the women's vote and that black men deserved priority. "If the elective franchise is not extended to the Negro, he is dead," explained Frederick Douglass, a longtime women's rights supporter. "Woman has a thousand ways by which she can attach herself to the ruling power of the land that we have not." But the women's rights leaders Elizabeth Cady Stanton and Susan B. Anthony disagreed. In their view, the Fourteenth Amendment had disabled women by including the word *male* and the Fifteenth Amendment compounded the injury by failing to prohibit the denial of suffrage on account of sex. Instead, Stanton contended, the Fifteenth Amendment established an "aristocracy of sex" and increased women's disadvantages.

The battle over black suffrage and the Fifteenth Amendment split women's rights advocates into two rival suffrage associations, both formed in 1869. The Boston-based American Woman Suffrage Association, endorsed by reformers such as Julia Ward Howe and Lucy Stone, retained an alliance with male abolitionists and campaigned for woman suffrage in the states. The New York–based and more radical National Woman Suffrage Association, led by Stanton and Anthony, condemned its leaders' one-time male allies and promoted a federal woman-suffrage amendment.

For the rest of the 1870s, the rival woman-suffrage associations vied for constituents. In 1869 and 1870, independent of the suffrage movement, two territories,

Stanton and Anthony, c. 1870
Women's rights advocates Susan B. Anthony and Elizabeth Cady Stanton began to promote woman suffrage in 1866 when the issue of black suffrage arose, and subsequently assailed the proposed Fifteenth Amendment for excluding women. By the end of the 1860s, activists had formed two competing suffragist organizations.

Wyoming and Utah, enfranchised women. But lacking support, suffragists failed to sway legislators elsewhere. In 1872 Susan B. Anthony mobilized about seventy women to vote nationwide and, as a result, was indicted, convicted, and fined. One of the women who tried to vote in 1872, Missouri suffragist Virginia Minor, brought suit with her husband against the registrar who had excluded her. The Minors based their case on the Fourteenth Amendment, which, they claimed, enfranchised women. In *Minor* v. *Happersett* (1875), however, the Supreme Court declared that a state could constitutionally deny women the vote. Divided and rebuffed, woman-suffrage advocates braced for a long struggle.

By the time the Fifteenth Amendment was ratified in 1870, Congress could look back on five years of momentous achievement. Since the start of 1865, federal legislators had broadened the scope of American democracy by passing three constitutional amendments. The Thirteenth Amendment abolished slavery, the Fourteenth expanded civil rights, and the Fifteenth prohibited the denial of suffrage on the basis of race. Congress had also readmitted the former Confederate states into the Union. But after 1868 congressional momentum slowed, and in 1869, when Ulysses S. Grant became president, enmity between Congress and the chief executive ceased. The theater of action now shifted to the South, where an era of tumultuous change was under way.

RECONSTRUCTION GOVERNMENTS

During the unstable years of presidential Reconstruction, 1865–1867, the southern states had to create new governments, revive the war-torn economy, and face the impact of emancipation. Social and economic crises abounded. War costs had cut into southern wealth, cities and factories lay in rubble, plantation-labor systems distintegrated, and racial tensions flared. Beginning in 1865, freedmen organized black conventions, political meetings at which they protested ill treatment and demanded equal rights. These meetings occurred in a climate of violence. Race riots erupted in major southern cities, such as Memphis in May 1866 and in New Orleans two months later. Even when Congress imposed military rule, ex-Confederates did not feel defeated. "Having reached bottom, there is hope now that we may rise again," a South Carolina planter wrote in his diary.

Congressional Reconstruction, supervised by federal troops, took effect in the spring of 1867. The Johnson regimes were dismantled, state constitutional conventions met, and voters elected new state governments, which Republicans dominated. In 1868 a majority of the former Confederate states rejoined the Union, and two years later, the last four states—Virginia, Mississippi, Georgia, and Texas—followed.

Readmission to the Union did not end the process of Reconstruction, for Republicans still held power in the South. But Republican rule was very brief, lasting less than a decade in all southern states, far less in most of them, and on average under five years. Opposition from southern Democrats, the landowning elite, thousands of vigilantes, and, indeed, most white voters proved insurmountable. Still, the governments formed under congressional Reconstruction were unique, because black men, including ex-slaves, participated in them. In no other society where slaves had been liberated—neither Haiti, where slaves had revolted in the 1790s, nor the British Caribbean islands, where Parliament had ended slavery in 1833—had freedmen gained democratic political rights.

A New Electorate   The Reconstruction laws of 1867–1868 transformed the southern electorate by temporarily disfranchising 10 to 15 percent of potential white voters and by enfranchising more than seven hundred thousand freedmen. Outnumbering white voters in the South by one hundred thousand, blacks held voting majorities in five states.

The new electorate provided a base for the Republican party, which had never existed in the South. In the eyes of the Democrats, southern Republicans comprised three types of scoundrels: northern "carpetbaggers," who had allegedly come south seeking wealth and power (with so few possessions that they could be stuffed into traveling bags made of carpet material); southern "scalawags," predominantly poor and ignorant whites, who sought to profit from Republican rule; and hordes of uneducated freedmen, who were ready prey for Republican manipulators. Although the "carpetbag" and "scalawag" labels were derogatory and the stereotypes that they conveyed inaccurate, they remain in use as a form of shorthand. Crossing class and racial lines, the hastily established Republican party was in fact a loose coalition of diverse factions with often contradictory goals.

To northerners who moved south after the Civil War, the former Confederacy was an undeveloped region, ripe with possibility. The carpetbaggers' ranks included many former Union soldiers who hoped to buy land, open factories, build railroads, or simply enjoy the warmer climate. Albion Tourgee, a young lawyer who had served with the New York and Ohio volunteers, for example, relocated in North Carolina after the war to improve his health. There he worked as a journalist, politician, and Republican judge. Perhaps no more than twenty thousand northern migrants like Tourgee—including veterans, missionaries, teachers, and Freedmen's Bureau agents—headed south immediately after the war, and many returned north by 1867. But those who remained played a disproportionate part in Reconstruction politics, for they held almost one out of three state offices.

Scalawags, white southerners who supported the Republicans, included some entrepreneurs who applauded party policies such as the national banking system and high protective tariffs as well as some prosperous planters, former Whigs who had opposed secession. Their numbers included a few prominent politicians, among them James Orr of South Carolina and Mississippi's governor James Alcorn, who became Republicans in order to retain influence and limit Republican radicalism. Most scalawags, however, were small farmers from the mountain regions of North Carolina, Georgia, Alabama, and Arkansas. Former Unionists who had owned no slaves and had no allegiance to the landowning elite, they sought to improve their economic position. Unlike carpetbaggers, they were not committed to black rights or black suffrage; most came from regions with small black populations and cared little whether blacks voted or not. Scalawags held the most political offices during Reconstruction, but they proved the least stable element of the southern Republican coalition: eventually, many drifted back to the Democratic fold.

Freedmen, the backbone of southern Republicanism, provided eight out of ten Republican votes. Republican rule lasted longest in states with the largest black populations—South Carolina, Mississippi, Alabama, and Louisiana. Introduced to politics in the black conventions of 1865–1867, the freedmen sought land, education, civil rights, and political equality and remained loyal Republicans. As an elderly freedman announced at a Georgia political convention in 1867, "We know our friends." Although Reconstruction governments would have collapsed without black votes, freedmen held at most one in five political offices. Blacks served in all southern legislatures and filled many high posts in Louisiana, Mississippi, and South Carolina. They constituted a majority, however, only in the legislature of South Carolina, whose population was more than 60 percent black. No blacks became governor, and only two served in the U.S. Senate, Hiram Revels and Blanche K. Bruce, both of Mississippi. In the House of Representatives, a mere 6 percent of southern members were black, and almost half of these came from South Carolina.

Black officeholders on the state level formed a political elite. They often differed from black voters in background, education, wealth, and complexion. A disproportionate number were literate blacks who had been free before the Civil War. (More former slaves held office on the local level than on the state level.) South Carolina's roster of elected officials illustrates some distinctions between high-level black officeholders and the freedmen who voted for them. Among those sent

Republicans in the South Carolina Legislature, c. 1868 *Only in South Carolina did blacks comprise a majority in the legislature and dominate the legislative process during Reconstruction. This photographic collage of "Radical" legislators, black and white, suggests the extent of black representation. In 1874, blacks won the majority of seats in South Carolina's state senate as well.*

RADICAL · MEMBERS
OF THE S°. C^. LEGISLATURE.

to Congress, almost all claimed some secondary education; some held advanced degrees. In the state legislature, most black members, unlike their constituents, came from large towns and cities; many had spent time in the North; and some were well-off property owners or even former slaveowners. Color differences were evident, too: 43 percent of South Carolina's black state legislators were mulattos (mixed race), compared to only 7 percent of the state's black population.

Black officials and black voters often had different priorities. Most freedmen cared mainly about their economic future, especially about acquiring land, whereas black officeholders cared most about attaining equal rights. Still, both groups shared high expectations and prized enfranchisement. "We'd walk fifteen miles in wartime to find out about the battle," a Georgia freedman declared. "We can walk fifteen miles and more to find how to vote."

Republican Rule   Large numbers of blacks participated in American government for the first time in the state constitutional conventions of 1867–1868. The South Carolina convention had a black majority, and in Louisiana half the delegates were freedmen. The conventions forged democratic changes in their state constitutions. Delegates abolished property qualifications for officeholding, made many appointive offices elective, and redistricted state legislatures more equitably. All states established universal manhood suffrage, and

Louisiana and South Carolina opened public schools to both races. These provisions integrated the New Orleans public schools as well as the University of South Carolina, from which whites withdrew.

But no state instituted land reform. When proposals for land confiscation and redistribution arose at the state conventions, they fell to defeat, as they had in Congress. Hoping to attract northern investment to the reconstructed South, southern Republicans hesitated to threaten property rights or to adopt land-reform measures that northern Republicans had rejected. South Carolina did set up a commission to buy land and make it available to freedmen, and several states changed their tax structures to force uncultivated land onto the market, but in no case was ex-Confederate land confiscated.

Once civil power shifted from the federal army to the new state governments, Republican administrations began ambitious programs of public works. They built roads, bridges, and public buildings; approved railroad bonds; and funded institutions to care for orphans, the insane, and the disabled. Republican regimes also expanded state bureaucracies, raised salaries for government employees, and formed state militia, in which blacks were often heavily represented. Finally, they created public-school systems, almost nonexistent in the South until then.

Because rebuilding the devastated South and expanding state government cost millions of dollars, state debts and taxes skyrocketed. State legislatures increased poll taxes or "head" taxes (levies on individuals); enacted luxury, sales, and occupation taxes; and imposed new property taxes. Before the war southern states had taxed property in slaves but had barely taxed landed property. Now state governments assessed even small farmers' holdings, and propertied planters paid what they considered an excessive burden. Although northern tax rates still exceeded southern rates, southern landowners resented the new levies. In their view, Reconstruction was punishing the propertied, already beset by labor problems and falling land values, in order to finance the vast expenditures of Republican legislators.

To Reconstruction's foes, Republican rule was wasteful and corrupt, the "most stupendous system of organized robbery in history." A state like Mississippi, which had an honest government, provided little basis for such charges. But critics could justifiably point to Louisiana, where the governor pocketed thousands of dollars of state funds and corruption permeated all government transactions (as indeed it had before the war). Or they could cite South Carolina, where bribery ran rampant. Besides government officials who took bribes, the main postwar profiteers were the railroad promoters who doled them out. Not all were Republicans. Nor did the Republican regimes in the South hold a monopoly on corruption. After the war bribery pervaded government transactions North and South, and far more money changed hands in the North. But critics assailed Republican rule for additional reasons.

Counterattacks   Ex-Confederates chafed at black enfranchisement and spoke with dread about the "horror of Negro domination."

As soon as congressional Reconstruction took effect, former Confederates began a clamorous campaign to undermine it. Democratic newspapers assailed delegates to North Carolina's constitutional convention as an "Ethiopian minstrelsy . . . baboons, monkeys, mules . . . and other jackasses," and demeaned Louisiana's constitution as "the work of ignorant Negroes cooperating with a gang of white adventurers."

The Democrats did not mobilize until the southern states were readmitted to the Union. Then they swung into action, calling themselves Conservatives in order to attract former Whigs. At first they sought to win the votes of blacks; but when that effort failed, they tried other tactics. In 1868–1869 Georgia Democrats challenged the eligibility of black legislators and expelled them from office. In response, the federal government reestablished military rule in Georgia, but determined Democrats still undercut Republican power. In every southern state, they contested elections, backed dissident Republican factions, elected some Democratic legislators, and made inroads among scalawags, siphoning some of their votes from the Republicans.

Vigilante efforts to reduce black votes bolstered the Democrats' campaigns to win white ones. Antagonism toward free blacks, long a motif in southern life, had resurged after the war. In 1865 Freedmen's Bureau agents itemized outrages against blacks, including shooting, murder, rape, arson, roasting, and "severe and inhuman beating." Vigilante groups sprang up spontaneously in all parts of the former Confederacy under names like moderators, regulators, and in Louisiana, Knights of the White Camelia. One group rose to dominance. In the spring of 1866, when the Johnson governments were still in power, six young Confederate war veterans in Tennessee formed a social club, the Ku Klux Klan, distinguished by elaborate rituals, hooded costumes, and secret passwords. New Klan dens spread through the state; within a year Democratic politicians and former Confederate officers took control of them. By the election of 1868, when black suffrage took effect, Klan dens existed in all the southern states. Klansmen embarked on night raids to intimidate black voters. No longer a social club, the Ku Klux Klan was now a widespread terrorist movement and a violent arm of the Democratic party.

The Klan sought to suppress black voting, reestablish white supremacy, and topple the Reconstruction governments. Its members attacked Freedmen's Bureau officials, white Republicans, black militia units, economically successful blacks, and black voters. Concentrated in areas where the black and white populations were most evenly balanced and racial tensions greatest, Klan dens adapted their tactics and timing to local conditions. In Mississippi the Klan targeted black schools; in Alabama it concentrated on Republican officeholders. In Arkansas terror reigned in 1868; in Georgia and Florida Klan strength surged in 1870. Some Democrats denounced Klan members as "cut-throats and riff-raff." But prominent ex-Confederates were also known to be active Klansmen, among them General Nathan Bedford Forrest, the leader of the 1864 Fort Pillow massacre, in which Confederate troops who captured a Union garrison in Tennessee murdered black soldiers after they had surrendered. Vigilantism united southern whites of different social classes and drew on the energy of many Confederate veterans. In areas where the Klan was inactive, other vigilante groups took its place.

Republican legislatures outlawed vigilantism through laws providing for fines and imprisonment of offenders. But the state militia could not enforce the laws, and state officials turned to the federal government for help. In May 1870 Congress passed the Enforcement Act to protect black voters, but witnesses to violations were afraid to testify against vigilantes, and local juries refused to convict them. The Second Enforcement Act, which provided for federal supervision of southern elections, followed in February 1871. Two months later Congress passed the Third Enforcement Act, or Ku Klux Klan Act, which strengthened punishments for those who prevented blacks from voting. It also empowered the president to use federal troops to enforce the law and to suspend the writ of habeas corpus in areas that he declared in insurrection. (The writ of habeas corpus is a court order requiring that the detainer of a prisoner bring that person to court and show cause for his or her detention.) President Grant, elected in 1868, suspended the writ in nine South Carolina counties that had been devastated by Klan attacks. The Ku Klux Klan Act generated thousands of arrests; most terrorists, however, escaped conviction.

By 1872 the federal government had effectively suppressed the Klan, but vigilantism had served its purpose. Only a large military presence in the South could have protected black rights, and the government in Washington never provided it. Instead, federal power in the former Confederacy diminished. President Grant steadily reduced troop levels in the South; Congress allowed the Freedmen's Bureau to die in 1869; and the Enforcement acts became dead letters. White southerners, a Georgia politician told congressional investigators in 1871, could not discard "a feeling of bitterness, a feeling that the Negro is a sort of instinctual enemy of ours." The battle over Reconstruction was in essence a battle over the implications of emancipation, and it had begun as soon as the war ended.

THE IMPACT OF EMANCIPATION

"The master he says we are all free," a South Carolina slave declared in 1865. "But it don't mean we is white. And it don't mean we is equal." Emancipated slaves faced extreme handicaps. They had no property, tools, or capital and usually possessed meager skills. Only a minority had been trained as artisans, and more than 95 percent were illiterate. Still, the exhilaration of freedom was overwhelming, as slaves realized, "Now I am for myself" and "All that I make is my own." At emancipation they gained the right to their own labor and a new sense of autonomy. Under Reconstruction the freed blacks asserted their independence by seeking to cast off white control and shed the vestiges of slavery.

Confronting Freedom

For the former slaves, liberty meant they could move where they pleased. Some moved out of the slave quarters and set up dwellings elsewhere on their plantations; others left their plantations entirely. Landowners found that one freed slave after another vanished, with house servants and artisans leading the way. "I have never in my life met with such ingratitude," one South Carolina mistress exclaimed when a former slave ran off. Field workers, who had less contact with whites, were more likely to stay behind or more reluctant to leave. Still, flight remained tempting. "The moment they see an opportunity to improve themselves, they will move on," diarist Mary Chesnut observed.

Emancipation stirred waves of migration within the former Confederacy. Some freed slaves left the Upper South for the Deep South and the Southwest— Florida, Mississippi, Arkansas, and Texas—where planters desperately needed labor and paid higher wages. Even more left the countryside for towns and cities, traditional havens of independence for blacks. Urban black populations sometimes doubled or tripled after emancipation. Overall during the 1860s, the urban black population rose by 75 percent, and the number of blacks in small rural towns grew as well. Many migrants eventually returned to their old locales, but they tended to settle on neighboring plantations rather than with their former owners. Freedom was the major goal. "I's wants to be a free man, cum when I please, and nobody say nuffin to me, nor order me roun'," an Alabama freedman told a northern journalist.

Freed blacks' yearnings to find lost family members prompted much movement. "They had a passion, not so much for wandering as for getting together," a Freedmen's Bureau official commented. Parents sought children who had been sold; husbands and wives who had been separated by sale, or who lived on different plantations, reunited; and families reclaimed youngsters from masters' homes. The Freedmen's Bureau helped former slaves get information about missing relatives and travel to find them. Bureau agents also tried to resolve entanglements over the multiple alliances of spouses who had been separated under slavery.

Reunification efforts often failed. Some fugitive slaves had died during the war or were untraceable. Other ex-slaves had formed new partnerships and could not revive old ones. "I am married," one husband wrote to a former wife (probably in a dictated letter), "and my wife [and I] have two children, and if you and I meet it would make a very dissatisfied family." But there were success stories, too. "I's hunted an' hunted till I track you up here," one freedman told his wife, whom he found in a refugee camp twenty years after their separation by sale.

Once reunited, freed blacks quickly legalized unions formed under slavery, sometimes in mass ceremonies of up to seventy couples. Legal marriage affected family life. Men asserted themselves as household heads; wives and children of able-bodied men often withdrew from the labor force. "When I married my wife, I married her to wait on me and she has got all she can do right here for me and the children," a Tennessee freedman explained.

Black women's desire to secure the privileges of domestic life caused planters severe labor shortages. Before the war at least half of field workers had been women; in 1866, a southern journal claimed, men performed almost all the field labor. Still, by the end of Reconstruction, many black women had returned to agricultural work as part of sharecropper families. Others took paid work in cities, as laundresses, cooks, and domestic servants. (White women often sought employment as well, for the war had incapacitated many white breadwinners, reduced the supply of future husbands, and left families destitute or in diminished circumstances.) However, former slaves continued to view stable, independent domestic life, especially the right to bring up their own children, as a major blessing of freedom. In 1870 eight out of ten black families in the cotton-producing South were two-parent families, about the same proportion as among whites.

Black Institutions   The freed blacks' desire for independence also led to the postwar growth of black churches. In the late 1860s, some freedmen congregated at churches operated by northern missionaries; others withdrew from white-run churches and formed their own. The African Methodist Episcopal church, founded by Philadelphia blacks in the 1790s, gained thousands of new southern members. Negro Baptist churches sprouted everywhere, often growing out of plantation "praise meetings," religious gatherings organized by slaves.

The black churches offered a fervent, participatory experience. They also provided relief, raised funds for schools, and supported Republican policies. From the outset black ministers assumed leading political roles, first in the black conventions of 1865–1866 and later in the Reconstruction governments. After southern Democrats excluded most freedmen from political life at Reconstruction's end, ministers remained the main pillars of authority within black communities.

Black schools played a crucial role for freedmen as well. The ex-slaves eagerly sought literacy for themselves and even more for their children. At emancipation blacks organized their own schools, which the Freedmen's Bureau soon supervised. Northern philanthropic societies paid the wages of instructors, about half of them women. In 1869 the bureau reported that there were more than four thousand black schools in the former Confederacy. Within three years each southern state

The Freedmen's School *Supported by the Freedmen's Bureau, northern freedmen's aid societies, and black denominations, freedmen's schools reached about 12 percent of school-age black children in the South by 1870. Here, a northern teacher poses with her students at a school in rural North Carolina.*

had a public-school system, at least in principle, generally with separate schools for blacks and whites. Advanced schools for blacks opened as well, to train tradespeople, teachers, and ministers. The Freedmen's Bureau and northern organizations like the American Missionary Association helped found Howard, Atlanta, and Fisk universities (all started in 1866–1867) and Hampton Institute (1868).

Despite these advances, black education remained limited. Few rural blacks could reach the freedmen's schools located in towns. Underfunded black public schools, similarly inaccessible to most rural black children, held classes only for very short seasons and were sometimes the targets of vigilante attacks. At the end of Reconstruction, more than 80 percent of the black population was still illiterate. Still, the proportion of youngsters who could not read and write had declined and would continue to fall.

School segregation and other forms of racial separation were taken for granted. Some black codes of 1865–1866 had segregated public-transit conveyances and public accommodations. Even after the invalidation of the codes, the custom of segregation continued on streetcars, steamboats, and trains as well as in churches, theaters, inns, and restaurants. On railroads, for example, whites could ride in the "ladies' car" or first-class car, whereas blacks had to stay in smoking cars or boxcars with benches. In 1870 Senator Charles Sumner of Massachusetts began promoting a bill to desegregate schools, transportation facilities, juries, and public accommodations. After Sumner's death in 1874, Congress honored him by enacting a new law, the Civil Rights Act of 1875, which encompassed many of his proposals, except for the controversial school-integration provision. But the law was rarely enforced, and in 1883, in the *Civil Rights Cases,* the Supreme Court invalidated it. The Fourteenth Amendment did not prohibit discrimination by individuals, the Court ruled, only that perpetrated by the state.

White southerners rejected the prospect of racial integration, which they insisted would lead to racial mixing. "If we have social equality, we shall have intermarriage," one white southerner contended, "and if we have intermarriage, we shall degenerate." Urban blacks sometimes challenged segregation practices, and black legislators promoted bills to desegregate public transit. Some black officeholders decried all forms of racial separatism. "The sooner we as a people forget our sable complexion," said a Mobile official, "the better it will be for us as a race." But most freed blacks were less interested in "social equality," in the sense of interracial mingling, than in black liberty and community. The newly formed postwar elite—teachers, ministers, and politicians—served black constituencies and therefore had a vested interest in separate black institutions. Rural blacks, too, widely preferred all-black institutions. They had little desire to mix with whites. On the contrary, they sought freedom from white control. Above all else, they wanted to secure personal independence by acquiring land.

Land, Labor, and Sharecropping

"The sole ambition of the freedman," a New Englander wrote from South Carolina in 1865, "appears to be to become the owner of a little piece of land, there to erect a humble home, and to dwell in peace and security, at his own free will and pleasure." Indeed, to freed blacks everywhere, "forty acres and a mule" (a phrase that originated in 1864 when Union General William T. Sherman set aside land on the South Carolina Sea Islands for black settlement) promised emancipation from plantation labor, from white domination, and from cotton, the "slave crop." Just as garden plots had provided a measure of autonomy under slavery, so did landownership signify economic independence afterward. "We want to be placed on land until we are able to buy it and make it our own," a black minister had told General Sherman in Georgia during the war. Some freedmen defended their right to the land they lived on by pointing out that they and their forebears had worked on it for decades without pay.

But freedmen's visions of landownership failed to materialize, for, as we have seen, neither Congress nor the southern states imposed large-scale land reform. Some freedmen did obtain land with the help of the Union army or the Freedmen's Bureau, and black soldiers sometimes pooled resources to buy land, as on the Sea Islands of South Carolina and Georgia. The federal government also attempted to provide ex-slaves with land. In 1866 Congress passed the Southern Homestead Act, which set aside 44 million acres of public land in five southern states for freedmen and loyal whites. This acreage contained poor soil, and few former slaves had the resources to survive even until their first harvest. About four thousand blacks resettled on homesteads under the law, but most were unable to establish farms. (White southern homesteaders fared little better.) By the end of Reconstruction, only a small minority of former slaves in each state owned working farms. In Georgia in 1876, for instance, blacks controlled a mere 1.3 percent of total acreage. Without large-scale land reform, the obstacles to black landownership remained overwhelming.

What were these obstacles? First, most freedmen lacked the capital to buy land and the equipment needed to work it. Furthermore, white southerners on the whole opposed selling land to blacks. Most important, planters sought to preserve a black labor force. They insisted that freedmen would work only under coercion, and not at all if the possibility of landownership arose. As soon as the war ended, the white South took steps to make sure that black labor would remain available where it was needed, on the plantations.

During presidential Reconstruction, southern state legislatures tried to limit black mobility and to preserve a captive labor force through the black codes. Under labor contracts in effect in 1865–1866, freedmen received wages, housing, food, and clothing in exchange for fieldwork. With cash scarce, wages usually took the form of a very small share of the crop, often one-eighth or less, divided among the entire plantation work force. Freedmen's Bureau agents promoted the new labor system; they urged freedmen to sign labor contracts and tried to ensure adequate wages. Imbued with the northern free-labor ideology, which held that wage workers could rise to the status of self-supporting tradesmen and property owners, bureau officials endorsed black wage labor as an interim arrangement that would lead to economic independence. "You must begin at the bottom of the ladder and climb up," Freedmen's Bureau head O. O. Howard exhorted a group of Louisiana freedmen in 1865.

But the freedmen disliked the new wage system, especially the use of gang labor, which resembled the work pattern under slavery. Planters had complaints, too. In some regions the black labor force had shrunk to half its prewar size or less, due to the migration of freedmen and to black women's withdrawal from field-work. Once united in defense of slavery, planters now competed for black workers. But the freedmen, whom planters often scorned as lazy and incorrigible, did not intend to work as long or as hard as they had labored under slavery. One planter estimated that workers accomplished only "two-fifths of what they did under the old system." As productivity fell, so did land values. Some planters considered importing white immigrant labor, but they doubted that whites would perform black fieldwork for long. To top off the planters' woes, cotton prices plummeted, for during the war northern and foreign buyers had found new sources of cotton in Egypt and India, and the world supply had vastly increased. Finally, the harvests of 1866 and 1867 were extremely poor. By then an agricultural impasse had been reached: landowners lacked labor and freedmen lacked land. But free blacks, unlike slaves, had the right to enter into contracts—or to refuse to do so—and thereby gained some leverage.

Planters and freedmen began experimenting with new labor schemes, includ-ing the division of plantations into small tenancies. Sharecropping, the most wide-spread arrangement, evolved as a compromise. Under the sharecropping system, landowners subdivided large plantations into farms of thirty to fifty acres, which they rented to freedmen under annual leases for a share of the crop, usually half. Freedmen preferred this system to wage labor because it represented a step toward independence. Heads of households could use the labor of family members. Moreover, a half-share of the crop far exceeded the fraction that freedmen had received as wages under the black codes. Planters often spoke of sharecropping as a concession to freedmen, but they gained as well. Landowners retained power over tenants, because annual leases did not have to be renewed; they could expel undesirable tenants at the end of the year. Planters also shared the risk of planting with tenants: if a crop failed, both suffered the loss. Most important, planters retained control of their land and in some cases extended their holdings. The most productive land, therefore, remained in the hands of a small group of owners, as before the war. Sharecropping forced planters to relinquish daily control over the labor of freedmen but helped to preserve the planter elite.

Sharecropping arrangements varied widely. On sugar and rice plantations, the wage system continued; strong markets for sugar and rice meant that planters of those crops could pay their workers in cash—cash that cotton planters lacked. Some freedmen remained independent renters. Some landowners leased areas to white tenants, who then subcontracted with black labor. But by the end of the 1860s, sharecropping prevailed in the cotton South, and the new system continued to expand. A severe depression in 1873 drove many black renters into sharecrop-ping. By then thousands of independent white farmers had become sharecroppers as well. Stung by wartime losses and by the dismal postwar economy, they sank into debt and lost their land to creditors. Many backcountry residents, no longer able to get by on subsistence farming, shifted to cash crops like cotton and suffered the same fate. At the end of Reconstruction, one-third of the white farmers in Mississippi, for instance, were sharecroppers.

By 1880, 80 percent of the land in the cotton-producing states had been sub-divided into tenancies, most of it farmed by sharecroppers, white and black. Indeed, white sharecroppers now outnumbered black ones, although a higher pro-portion of southern blacks, about 75 percent, were involved in the system. Changes in marketing and finance, meanwhile, made the sharecroppers' lot increasingly precarious.

Toward a Crop-Lien Economy   Before the Civil War, planters had depended on factors, or middlemen, who sold them supplies, extended credit, and marketed their crops through urban merchants. These long-distance credit arrangements were backed by the high value and liquidity of slave property. When slavery ended, the factorage system collapsed. The postwar South, with hundreds of thousands of tenants and sharecroppers, needed a far more localized network of credit.

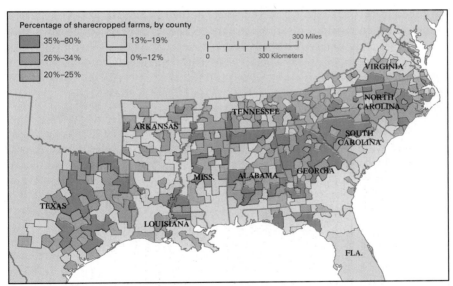

Southern Sharecropping, 1880

The depressed economy of the late 1870s caused poverty and debt, increased tenancy among white farmers, and forced many renters, black and white, into sharecropping. By 1880 the sharecropping system pervaded most southern counties, with the highest concentrations in the cotton belt from South Carolina to eastern Texas.

(*Source:* U.S. Census Office, Tenth Census, 1880, *Report of the Production of Agriculture* [Washington, D.C.: Government Printing Office, 1883], Table 5.)

Into the gap stepped the rural merchants (often themselves planters), who advanced supplies to tenants and sharecroppers on credit and sold their crops to wholesalers or textile manufacturers. Because renters had no property to use as collateral, the merchants secured their loans with a lien, or claim, on each farmer's next crop. Exorbitant interest rates of 50 percent or more quickly forced many tenants and sharecroppers into a cycle of indebtedness. Owing part of the crop to a landowner for rent, a sharecropper also owed a rural merchant a large sum (perhaps amounting to the rest of his crop, or more) for supplies. Illiterate tenants who could not keep track of their financial arrangements often fell prey to unscrupulous merchants. "A man that didn't know how to count would always lose," an Arkansas freedman later explained. Once a tenant's debts or alleged debts exceeded the value of his crop, he was tied to the land, to cotton, and to sharecropping.

By the end of Reconstruction, sharecropping and crop liens had transformed southern agriculture. They bound the region to staple production and prevented crop diversification. Despite plunging cotton prices, creditors—landowners and merchants—insisted that tenants raise only easily marketable cash crops. Short of capital, planters could no longer invest in new equipment or improve their land by such techniques as crop rotation and contour plowing. Soil depletion, land erosion, and agricultural backwardness soon locked much of the South into a cycle of poverty.

Trapped in perpetual debt, tenant farmers became the chief victims of the new agricultural order. Raising cotton for distant markets, for prices over which they

Sharecroppers during Reconstruction
By the end of the 1870s, about three out of four African-Americans in the cotton-producing states had become sharecroppers. Here, sharecroppers pick cotton in Aiken, South Carolina.

had no control, remained the only survival route open to poor farmers, regardless of race. But the low income thus derived often forced them into sharecropping and crop liens, from which escape was difficult. African-American tenants, who attained neither landownership nor economic independence, saw their political rights dwindle, too. As one southern regime after another returned to Democratic control, freedmen could no longer look to the state governments for protection. Nor could they turn to the federal government, for northern politicians were preoccupied with their own problems.

NEW CONCERNS IN THE NORTH, 1868–1876

The nomination of Ulysses S. Grant for president in 1868 launched an era of crises in national politics. Grant's two terms in office featured political scandals, a party revolt, a massive depression, and a steady retreat from Reconstruction policies. By the mid-1870s, northern voters cared more about the economic climate, unemployment, labor unrest, and currency problems than about the "southern question." Responsive to the shift in popular mood, Republicans became eager to end sectional conflict and turned their backs on the freedmen of the South.

Grantism   Republicans had good reason to pass over party leaders and nominate the popular Grant to succeed Andrew Johnson. A war hero, Grant was endorsed by Union veterans, widely admired in the North, and unscathed by the bitter feuds of Reconstruction politics. To oppose Grant in the 1868 election, the Democrats nominated New York governor Horatio Seymour, arch-critic of the Lincoln administration during the war and now a foe of Reconstruction. Grant ran on his personal popularity more than on issues. Although he carried all but eight states, the popular vote was very close; in the South, newly enfranchised freedmen provided Grant's margin of victory.

A strong leader in war, Grant proved a passive president. Although he lacked Johnson's instinct for disaster, he had little skill at politics. Many of his cabinet appointees—business executives, army men, and family friends—were mediocre if not unscrupulous; scandals plagued his administration. In 1869 financier Jay Gould and his partner Jim Fisk attempted to corner the gold market with the help of Grant's brother-in-law, a New York speculator. When gold prices tumbled, Gould salvaged his own fortune, but investors were ruined and Grant's reputation was tarnished. Then before the president's first term ended, his vice president, Schuyler Colfax, was found to be linked to the Crédit Mobilier, a fraudulent construction company created to skim off the profits of the Union Pacific Railroad. Using government funds granted to the railroad, the Union Pacific directors awarded padded construction contracts to the Crédit Mobilier, of which they were also the directors. Discredited, Colfax was dropped from the Grant ticket in 1872.

More trouble lay ahead. Grant's private secretary, Orville Babcock, was unmasked in 1875 after taking money from the "whiskey ring," a group of distillers who bribed federal agents to avoid paying millions of dollars in whiskey taxes.

And in 1876 voters learned that Grant's secretary of war, William E. Belknap, had taken bribes to sell lucrative Indian trading posts in Oklahoma. Impeached and disgraced, Belknap resigned.

Although uninvolved in the scandals, Grant loyally defended his subordinates. To his critics, "Grantism" came to stand for fraud, bribery, and political corruption, evils that spread far beyond Washington. In Pennsylvania, for example, the Standard Oil Company and the Pennsylvania Railroad controlled the legislature. Urban politics also provided rich opportunities for graft and swindles. The New York City press revealed in 1872 that Democratic boss William M. Tweed, the leader of Tammany Hall, led a ring that had looted the city treasury and collected an estimated $200 million in kickbacks and payoffs. When Mark Twain and coauthor Charles Dudley Warner published their satiric novel *The Gilded Age* (1873), readers recognized the book's speculators, self-promoters, and opportunists as familiar types in public life. (The term "Gilded Age" was subsequently used to refer to the decades from the 1870s to the 1890s.)

Grant had some success in foreign policy. In 1872 his competent secretary of state, Hamilton Fish, engineered the settlement of the *Alabama* claims with England. To compensate for damage done by British-built raiders sold to the Confederacy during the war, an international tribunal awarded the United States $15.5 million. But the Grant administration faltered when it tried to add nonadjacent territory to the United States, as the Johnson administration had done. In 1867 Johnson's secretary of state, William H. Seward, had negotiated a treaty in which the United States bought Alaska from Russia at the bargain price of $7.2 million. Although the press mocked "Seward's Ice Box," the purchase kindled expansionists' hopes. In 1870 Grant decided to annex the eastern half of the Caribbean island of Santo Domingo. Today called the Dominican Republic, the territory had been passed back and forth since the late eighteenth century among France, Spain, and Haiti. Annexation, Grant believed, would promote Caribbean trade and provide a haven for persecuted southern blacks. American speculators anticipated windfalls from land sales, commerce, and mining. But Congress disliked Grant's plan. Senator Charles Sumner denounced it as an imperialist "dance of blood." The Senate rejected the annexation treaty and further diminished Grant's reputation.

As the election of 1872 approached, dissident Republicans expressed fears that "Grantism" at home and abroad would ruin the party. Even Grant's new running mate, Henry Wilson, referred to the president privately as a burden on his fellow Republicans. The dissidents took action. Led by a combination of former Radicals and other Republicans left out of Grant's "Great Barbecue" (a disparaging reference to profiteers who feasted at the public trough), the president's critics formed their own party, the Liberal Republicans.

The Liberals' Revolt

The Liberal Republican revolt marked a turning point in Reconstruction history. By splitting the Republican party, the Liberals undermined support for Republican southern policy. (The label "liberal" at the time referred to those who endorsed economic doctrines such as free trade, the gold standard, and the law of supply and demand.) The Liberals attacked the "regular" Republicans on several key issues. Denouncing "Grantism" and "spoilsmen" (political hacks who gained party office), they demanded civil-service reform to bring the "best men" into government. Rejecting the usual Republican high-tariff policy, they espoused free trade. Most important, the Liberals condemned "bayonet rule" in the South. Even some Republicans once known for radicalism now claimed that Reconstruction had achieved its goal: blacks had been enfranchised and could manage for themselves from now on. Corruption in government, North and South, they asserted, posed a greater danger than Confederate resurgence. In the South, indeed, corrupt Republican regimes were *kept* in power, the Liberals said, because the "best men"—the most capable politicians—were ex-Confederates who had been barred from officeholding.

For president the new party nominated *New York Tribune* editor Horace Greeley, who had inconsistently supported both a stringent reconstruction policy and leniency toward former rebels. The Democrats endorsed Greeley as well, despite his long-time condemnation of them. Their campaign slogan explained their support: "Anything to Beat Grant." Horace Greeley proved so diligent a campaigner that he worked himself to death making speeches from the back of a campaign train. He died a few weeks after the election.

Grant, who won 56 percent of the popular vote, carried all the northern states and most of the sixteen southern and border states. But the division among Republicans affected Reconstruction. To deprive the Liberals of a campaign issue, Grant Republicans in Congress, the "regulars," passed the Amnesty Act, which allowed all but a few hundred ex-Confederate officials to hold office. The flood of private amnesty acts that followed convinced white southerners that any ex-Confederate save Jefferson Davis could rise to power. During Grant's second term, Republican desires to discard the "southern question" mounted as a depression of unprecedented scope gripped the whole nation.

The Panic of 1873 The postwar years brought accelerated industrialization, rapid economic expansion, and frantic speculation. Investors rushed to profit from rising prices, new markets, high tariffs, and seemingly boundless opportunities. Railroads provided the biggest lure. In May 1869 railroad executives drove a golden spike into the ground at Promontory Point, Utah, joining the Union Pacific and Central Pacific lines. The first transcontinental railroad heralded a new era. By 1873 almost four hundred railroad corporations crisscrossed the Northeast, consuming tons of coal and miles of steel rail from the mines and mills of Pennsylvania and neighboring states. Transforming the economy, the railroad boom led entrepreneurs to overspeculate, with drastic results.

Philadelphia banker Jay Cooke, who had helped finance the Union effort with his wartime bond campaign, had taken over a new transcontinental line, the

Northern Pacific, in 1869. Northern Pacific securities sold briskly for several years, but in 1873 the line's construction costs outran new investments. In September of that year, his vaults full of bonds he could no longer sell, Cooke failed to meet his obligations, and his bank, the largest in the nation, shut down. A financial panic began; other firms collapsed, as did the stock market. The Panic of 1873 triggered a five-year depression. Banks closed, farm prices plummeted, steel furnaces stood idle, and one out of four railroads failed. Within two years, eighteen thousand businesses went bankrupt, and 3 million employees were out of jobs by 1878. Those still at work suffered repeated wage cuts; labor protests mounted; and industrial violence spread. The depression of the 1870s revealed that conflicts born of industrialization had replaced sectional divisions.

The depression also fed a dispute over currency that had begun in 1865. The Civil War had created fiscal chaos. During the war, Americans had used both national bank notes, yellow in color, which would eventually be converted into gold, and greenbacks, a paper currency not "backed" by a particular weight in gold. To stabilize the postwar currency, greenbacks would have to be withdrawn from circulation. This "sound-money" policy, favored by investors, was implemented by Treasury Secretary Hugh McCulloch with the backing of Congress. But those who depended on easy credit, both indebted farmers and manufacturers, wanted an expanding currency; that is, more greenbacks. Once the depression began, demands for such "easy money" rose. The issue divided both major parties and was compounded by another one: how to repay the federal debt.

During the war the Union government had borrowed what were then astronomical sums, on whatever terms it could get, mainly through the sale of war bonds—in effect, short-term federal IOUs—to private citizens. By 1869 the issue of war-debt repayment afflicted the Republican party, whose support came from voters with diverse financial interests. To pacify bondholders, Senator John Sherman of Ohio and other Republican leaders obtained passage of the Public Credit Act of 1869, which promised to pay the war debt in "coin," a term that meant either gold or silver. Holders of war bonds expected no less, although many had bought their bonds with greenbacks!

With investors reassured by the Public Credit Act, Sherman guided legislation through Congress that swapped the old short-term bonds for new ones payable over the next generation. In 1872 another bill in effect defined "coin" as "gold coin" by dropping the traditional silver dollar from the official coinage. Through a feat of ingenious compromise, which placated investors and debtors, Sherman preserved the public credit, the currency, and Republican unity. In 1875 he engineered the Specie Resumption Act, which promised to put the nation on the gold standard in 1879, while tossing a few more immediate but less important bones to Republican voters who wanted "easy money."

Republican leaders had acted not a moment too soon because when the Democrats gained control of the House in 1875, with the depression in full force, a verbal storm broke out. Many Democrats and some Republicans demanded that the silver dollar be restored in order to expand the currency and relieve the depression.

These "free-silver" advocates secured passage of the Bland-Allison Act of 1878, which partially restored silver coinage. The law required the Treasury to buy \$2–4 million worth of silver each month and turn it into coin but did not revive the silver standard. In 1876 other expansionists formed the Greenback party, which adopted the debtors' cause and fought to keep greenbacks in circulation. But despite the election of fourteen Greenback congressmen, they did not get even as far as the free-silver people had. As the nation emerged from depression in 1879, the clamor for "easy money" subsided, only to resurge in the 1890s. The controversial "money question" of the 1870s, never resolved, gave politicians and voters another reason to forget about the South.

Reconstruction and the Constitution The Supreme Court of the 1870s also played a role in weakening northern support for Reconstruction. During the war, few cases of note had come before the Court. After the war, however, constitutional questions surged into prominence.

First, would the Court support congressional laws to protect freedmen's rights? The decision in *Ex parte* Milligan (1866) suggested not. In this case, the Court declared that a military commission established by the president or Congress could not try civilians in areas remote from war where the civil courts were functioning. Thus special military courts to enforce the Supplementary Freedmen's Bureau Act were doomed. Second, would the Court sabotage the congressional Reconstruction plan, as Republicans feared? Their qualms were valid, for if the Union was indissoluble, as the North had claimed during the war, then the concept of *restoring* states to the Union would be meaningless. In *Texas* v. *White* (1869), the Court ruled that although the Union was indissoluble and secession was legally impossible, the process of Reconstruction was still constitutional. It was grounded in Congress's power to ensure each state a republican form of government and to recognize the legitimate government in any state.

The 1869 decision protected the Republicans' Reconstruction plan. But in the 1870s, when cases arose involving the Fourteenth and Fifteenth amendments, the Court backed away from Reconstruction policy. In the *Slaughterhouse* cases of 1873, the Supreme Court began to chip away at the Fourteenth Amendment. The cases involved a business monopoly rather than freedmen's rights, but they provided an opportunity to interpret the amendment narrowly. In 1869 the Louisiana legislature had granted a monopoly over the New Orleans slaughterhouse business to one firm and closed down all other slaughterhouses in the interest of public health. The excluded butchers brought suit. The state had deprived them of their lawful occupation without due process of law, they claimed, and such action violated the Fourteenth Amendment, which guaranteed that no state could "abridge the privileges or immunities" of U.S. citizens. The Supreme Court upheld the Louisiana legislature by issuing a doctrine of "dual citizenship." The Fourteenth Amendment, declared the Court, protected only the rights of *national* citizenship, such as the right of interstate travel or the right to federal protection on the high seas. It did not protect those basic civil rights that fell to citizens by virtue of their *state* citizenship. Therefore, the federal government was not obliged to protect such rights against violation by the states. The *Slaughterhouse* decision came close to nullifying the intent of the Fourteenth Amendment—to secure freedmen's rights against state encroachment.

The Supreme Court again backed away from Reconstruction in two cases in 1876 involving the Enforcement Act of 1870, which had been enacted to protect black suffrage. In *U.S. v. Reese* and *U.S. v. Cruikshank,* the Supreme Court undercut the effectiveness of the act. Continuing its retreat from Reconstruction, the Supreme Court in 1883 invalidated both the Civil Rights Act of 1875 and the Ku Klux Klan Act of 1871. These decisions cumulatively dismantled the Reconstruction policies that Republicans had sponsored after the war and confirmed rising northern sentiment that Reconstruction's egalitarian goals could not be enforced.

Republicans in Retreat　　The Republicans did not reject Reconstruction suddenly but rather disengaged from it gradually. The withdrawal process began with Grant's election to the presidency in 1868. Although not one of the architects of Reconstruction policy, Grant defended it. But he shared with most Americans a belief in decentralized government and a reluctance to assert federal authority in local and state affairs.

In the 1870s, as the northern military presence shrank in the South, Republican idealism waned in the North. The Liberal Republican revolt of 1872 eroded what remained of radicalism. Although the "regular" Republicans, who backed Grant, continued to defend Reconstruction in the 1872 election, many held ambivalent views. Commercial and industrial interests now dominated both wings of the party, and Grant supporters had greater zeal for doing business in and with the South than for rekindling sectional strife. After the Democrats won control of the House in the 1874 elections, support for Reconstruction became a political liability.

By 1875 the Radical Republicans, so prominent in the 1860s, had vanished from the political scene. Chase, Stevens, and Sumner were dead. Other Radicals had lost office or abandoned their former convictions. "Waving the Bloody Shirt"—defaming Democratic opponents by reviving wartime animosity—now struck many Republicans, including former Radicals, as counterproductive. Party leaders reported that voters were "sick of carpet-bag government" and tiring of both the "southern question" and the "Negro question." It seemed pointless to continue the unpopular and expensive policy of military intervention in the South to prop up Republican regimes that even President Grant found corrupt. Finally, few Republicans shared the egalitarian spirit that had animated Stevens and Sumner. Politics aside, Republican leaders and voters generally agreed with southern Democrats that blacks, although worthy of freedom, were inferior to whites. To insist on black equality would be a thankless, divisive, and politically suicidal undertaking. Moreover, it would quash any hope of reunion between the regions. The Republicans' retreat from Reconstruction set the stage for its demise in 1877.

RECONSTRUCTION ABANDONED, 1876–1877

"We are in a very hot political contest just now," a Mississippi planter wrote to his daughter in 1875, "with a good prospect of turning out the carpetbag thieves by whom we have been robbed for the past six to ten years." Similar contests raged through the South in the 1870s, as the resentment of white majorities grew and Democratic influence surged. By the end of 1872, the Democrats had regained power in Tennessee, Virginia, Georgia, and North Carolina. Within three years they won control in Texas, Alabama, Arkansas, and Mississippi. As the 1876 elections approached, Republican rule survived in only three states—South Carolina, Florida, and Louisiana. Democratic victories in the state elections of 1876 and political bargaining in Washington in 1877 abruptly ended what little remained of Reconstruction.

Redeeming the South
The Republicans' collapse in the South accelerated after 1872. Congressional amnesty enabled ex-Confederate officials to regain office; divisions among the Republicans loosened their party's weak grip on the southern electorate; and attrition diminished Republican ranks. Some carpetbaggers gave up and returned North; others shifted to the Democratic party. Scalawags deserted in even larger numbers. Southerners who had joined the Republicans to moderate rampant radicalism tired of northern interference; once "home rule" by Democrats became a possibility, staying Republican meant going down with a sinking ship. Scalawag defections ruined Republican prospects. Unable to win new white votes or retain the old ones, the always-precarious Republican coalition crumbled.

Meanwhile, the Democrats mobilized formerly apathetic white voters. The resurrected southern Democratic party was divided: businessmen who envisioned an industrialized "New South" opposed an agrarian faction called the Bourbons, the old planter elite. But all Democrats shared one goal: to oust Republicans from office. Their tactics varied from state to state. Alabama Democrats won by promising to cut taxes and by getting out the white vote. In Louisiana the "White League," a vigilante organization formed in 1874, undermined the Republicans' hold. Intimidation also proved effective in Mississippi, where violent incidents— like the 1874 slaughter in Vicksburg of about three hundred blacks by rampaging whites—terrorized black voters. In 1875 the "Mississippi plan" took effect: local Democratic clubs armed their members, who dispersed Republican meetings, patrolled voter-registration places, and marched through black areas. "The Republicans are paralyzed through fear and will not act," the anguished carpetbag governor of Mississippi wrote to his wife. "Why should I fight a hopeless battle?" In 1876 South Carolina's "Rifle Clubs" and "Red Shirts," armed groups that threatened Republicans, continued the scare tactics that had worked so well in Mississippi.

New outbursts of intimidation did not completely squelch black voting, but the Democrats deprived the Republicans of enough black votes to win state elections.

In some counties they encouraged freedmen to vote Democratic at supervised polls where voters publicly placed a card with a party label in a box. In other instances employers and landowners impeded black suffrage. Labor contracts included clauses barring attendance at political meetings; planters used the threat of eviction to keep sharecroppers in line. Since the Enforcement acts could not be enforced, intimidation and economic pressure succeeded.

Redemption, the word Democrats used to describe their return to power, introduced sweeping changes. Some states called constitutional conventions to reverse Republican policies. All cut back expenses, wiped out social programs, lowered taxes, and revised their tax systems to relieve landowners of large burdens. State courts limited the rights of tenants and sharecroppers. Most important, the Democrats, or "redeemers," used the law to ensure a stable black labor force. Legislatures restored vagrancy laws, revised crop-lien statutes to make landowners' claims superior to those of merchants, and rewrote criminal law. Local ordinances in heavily black counties often restricted hunting, fishing, gun carrying, and ownership of dogs and thereby curtailed the everyday activities of freedmen who lived off the land. States passed severe laws against trespassing and theft; stealing livestock or wrongly taking part of a crop became grand larceny with a penalty of up to five years at hard labor. By the end of Reconstruction, a large black convict work force had been leased out to private contractors at low rates.

For the freedmen, whose aspirations had been raised by Republican rule, redemption was devastating. The new laws, Tennessee blacks contended at an 1875 convention, would impose "a condition of servitude scarcely less degrading than that endured before the late civil war." In the late 1870s, as the political climate grew more oppressive, an "exodus" movement spread through Mississippi, Tennessee, Texas, and Louisiana. Some African-Americans decided to become homesteaders in Kansas. After a major outbreak of "Kansas fever" in 1879, four thousand "exodusters" from Mississippi and Louisiana joined about ten thousand who had reached Kansas earlier in the decade. But the vast majority of freedmen, devoid of resources, had no migration options or escape route. Mass movement of southern blacks to the North and Midwest would not gain momentum until the twentieth century.

The Election of 1876

By the autumn of 1876, with redemption almost complete, both parties moved to discard the heritage of animosity left by the war and Reconstruction. The Republicans nominated Rutherford B. Hayes, three times Ohio's governor, for president. Untainted by the scandals of the Grant years and popular with all factions in his party, Hayes presented himself as a "moderate" on southern policy. He favored "home rule" in the South and a guarantee of civil and political rights for all—two planks that were clearly contradictory. The Democrats nominated Governor Samuel J. Tilden of New York, a millionaire corporate lawyer and political reformer. Known for his assaults on the Tweed Ring that had plundered New York City's treasury, Tilden campaigned against fraud and waste. Both candidates were fiscal conservatives, favored sound money, endorsed civil-service reform, and decried corruption, an irony since the 1876 election would be extremely corrupt.

Tilden won the popular vote by a 3 percent margin and seemed destined to capture the 185 electoral votes needed for victory. But the Republicans challenged the pro-Tilden returns from South Carolina, Florida, and Louisiana. If they could deprive the Democrats of these nineteen electoral votes, Hayes would triumph. The Democrats, who needed only one of the disputed electoral votes for victory, challenged the validity of Oregon's single electoral vote, which the Republicans had won, on a technicality. Twenty electoral votes, therefore, were in contention. But Republicans still controlled the electoral machinery in the three unredeemed southern states, where they threw out enough Democratic ballots to declare Hayes the winner.

The nation now faced an unprecedented dilemma. Each party claimed victory in the contested states, and each accused the other of fraud. In fact, both sets of southern results involved fraud: the Republicans had discarded legitimate Democratic ballots, and the Democrats had illegally prevented freedmen from voting. To resolve the conflict, Congress in January 1877 created a special electoral commission to decide which party would get the contested electoral votes. Made up of senators, representatives, and Supreme Court justices, the commission included seven Democrats, seven Republicans, and one independent, Justice David Davis of Illinois. When Davis resigned to run for the Senate, Congress replaced him with a Republican, and the commission gave Hayes the election by an 8 to 7 vote.

Congress now had to certify the new electoral vote. But since the Democrats controlled the House, a new problem loomed. Some Democrats threatened to

The Disputed Election of 1876

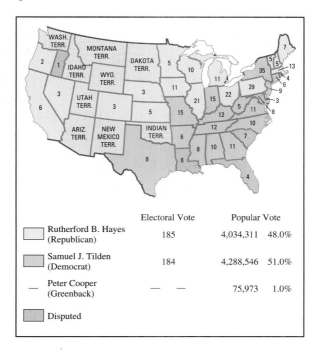

		Electoral Vote	Popular Vote	
	Rutherford B. Hayes (Republican)	185	4,034,311	48.0%
	Samuel J. Tilden (Democrat)	184	4,288,546	51.0%
—	Peter Cooper (Greenback)	— —	75,973	1.0%
	Disputed			

obstruct debate and delay approval of the electoral vote. Had they carried out their scheme, the nation would have been without a president on inauguration day, March 4. There remained room for compromise, for many southern Democrats accepted Hayes's election. Among them were former scalawags with commercial interests to protect, who still favored Republican financial policies, and railroad investors, who hoped that a Republican administration would help them build a southern transcontinental line. Other southerners cared mainly about Democratic state victories and did not mind conceding the presidency as long as the new Republican administration would leave the South alone. Republican leaders, although sure of eventual triumph, were willing to bargain as well, for candidate Hayes desired not merely victory but southern approval.

A series of informal negotiations ensued, at which politicians exchanged promises. Ohio Republicans and southern Democrats, who met at a Washington hotel, reached an agreement that if Hayes won the election, he would remove federal troops from South Carolina and Louisiana, and Democrats could gain control of those states. In other bargaining sessions, southern politicians asked for federal patronage, federal aid to railroads, and federal support for internal improvements. In return, they promised to drop the filibuster, to accept Hayes as president, and to treat freedmen fairly.

With the threatened filibuster broken, Congress ratified Hayes's election. Once in office, Hayes fulfilled some of the promises his Republican colleagues had made. He appointed a former Confederate as postmaster general and ordered federal troops who guarded the South Carolina and Louisiana statehouses back to their barracks. Although federal soldiers remained in the South after 1877, they no longer served a political function. The Democrats, meanwhile, took control of state governments in Louisiana, South Carolina, and Florida. When Republican rule toppled in these states, the era of Reconstruction finally ended, though more with a whimper than with a resounding crash.

But some of the bargains struck in the Compromise of 1877, such as Democratic promises to treat southern blacks fairly, were forgotten, as were Hayes's pledges to ensure freedmen's rights. "When you turned us loose, you turned us loose to the sky, to the storm, to the whirlwind, and worst of all . . . to the wrath of our infuriated masters," Frederick Douglass had charged at the Republican convention in 1876. "The question now is, do you mean to make good to us the promises in your Constitution?" The answer provided by the 1876 election and the 1877 compromises was "No."

IMPORTANT EVENTS, 1865–1877

1863   President Abraham Lincoln issues Proclamation of Amnesty and Reconstruction.

1864   Wade-Davis bill passed by Congress and pocket-vetoed by Lincoln.

1865   Freedmen's Bureau established.
Civil War ends.
Lincoln assassinated.
Andrew Johnson becomes president.
Johnson issues Proclamation of Amnesty and Reconstruction.
Ex-Confederate states hold constitutional conventions (May–December).
Black conventions begin in the ex-Confederate states.
Thirteenth Amendment added to the Constitution.
Presidential Reconstruction completed.

1866   Congress enacts the Civil Rights Act of 1866 and the Supplementary Freedmen's Bureau Act over Johnson's vetoes.
Ku Klux Klan founded in Tennessee.
Tennessee readmitted to the Union.
Race riots in southern cities.
Republicans win congressional elections.

1867   Reconstruction Act of 1867.
William Seward negotiates the purchase of Alaska.
Constitutional conventions meet in the ex-Confederate states.
Howard University founded.

1868   President Johnson is impeached, tried, and acquitted.
Omnibus Act.
Fourteenth Amendment added to the Constitution.
Ulysses S. Grant elected president.

1869   Transcontinental railroad completed.

1870   Congress readmits the four remaining southern states to the Union.
Fifteenth Amendment added to the Constitution.
Enforcement Act of 1870.

1871   Second Enforcement Act.
Ku Klux Klan Act.

1872   Liberal Republican party formed.
Amnesty Act.
Alabama claims settled.
Grant reelected president.

1873   Panic of 1873 begins (September–October), setting off a five-year depression.

1874   Democrats gain control of the House of Representatives.

1875   Civil Rights Act of 1875.
Specie Resumption Act.

1876   Disputed presidential election: Rutherford B. Hayes versus Samuel J. Tilden.

1877   Electoral commission decides election in favor of Hayes.
The last Republican-controlled governments overthrown in Florida, Louisiana, and South Carolina.

1879   "Exodus" movement spreads through several southern states.

17

The Transformation of the Trans-Mississippi West, 1860–1900

In spring 1871 fifteen-year-old Luna Warner began a diary as she ventured west with her family to a new homestead claim near the Solomon River in western Kansas. In it she carefully recorded her impressions of the vast western landscape that seemed so different from the countryside near her Massachusetts home. She was delighted by the rugged beauty of the local river and gathered wildflowers everywhere, but she was most impressed by the large numbers of birds and animals she saw: great shaggy bison, wild turkeys and ducks, antelope, and prairie chickens.

In her diary, which chronicled her family's struggle to build a cabin, break the sod, and plant crops, Luna singled out for special attention the bison hunt that her uncle participated in the following winter. She noted that her uncle, who eventually brought back six bison, initially lost his way, but was helped by an Indian who led him back to camp. The following summer Luna was out riding with her father and two younger cousins when they, too, encountered a bison. She vividly described what happened.

"Pa got off. He handed me the bridle while he went for the buffalo, revolver in hand. . . . He fired and then they [the buffalo] came right toward us. The horse sprang and snorted and whirled around me, but I kept fast hold and talked to her and she arched her neck. . . . Then he [the buffalo] fell dead in the ravine. [We] hitched the oxen to the buffalo and dragged him up where they could skin him . . . [and] they all went to skinning the buffalo with pocket knives."

Luna Warner and her family were part of one of the great human migrations in modern history. Lured by tales of the West as a region of free land and rare minerals, miners, farmers, land speculators, and railroad developers flooded onto the fertile prairies of Iowa, Minnesota, and Kansas, carving the land into farms and communities. Then, tempted by the discovery of gold in the Rocky Mountains, these same settlers, aided by the U.S. army, pushed aside the Indian inhabitants who lived there and swarmed onto the Great Plains and the semiarid regions beyond them. Scarcely a decade later, when Luna married and settled on her own farm, the trans-Mississippi West had been transformed into a contested terrain as Native peoples fought to preserve their homeland from being broken up into new settlements, reservations, mines, ranches, farmland, and national parks.

The transformation of the West left a mixed legacy. Although many white families like the Warners prospered on the High Plains, the heedless pursuit of land and profit proved destructive to the Native Americans, to the environment, and often to the settlers themselves. Under the banner of civilization and progress, industrious western entrepreneurs exploited white, Native American, Chinese, and Mexican laborers alike. They slaughtered millions of bison for their hides, skinned the mountainsides in search of minerals, and tore up the prairie sod to build farms even in areas west of the ninety-eighth meridian, where limited rainfall made farming problematic.

Although entrepreneurs attributed their economic achievements to American individualism and self-reliance, the West's development depended heavily on the federal government. The government sent troops to pacify the Indians, promoted the acquisition of farm land through the Homestead Act (1862), and subsidized the construction of the transcontinental railroad. Eastern banks and foreign capitalists provided investment capital and eased access to international markets. Yet westerners clung to their ideal of the self-reliant individual who could handle any obstacle. That ideal, though often sorely tested, survived to form the bedrock of western Americans' outlook even today.

This chapter will focus on five major questions:

How was Indian life on the Great Plains transformed in the second half of the nineteenth century?

What roles did the army and the railroads play in the settlement of the West?

To what extent did the Homestead Act succeed in making free land available to those who settled in the West?

How was the Wild West image of cowboys and Indians created? Why has it remained so popular?

How did some Americans become more aware of the need to conserve natural resources by setting them aside in national parks?

NATIVE AMERICANS AND THE TRANS-MISSISSIPPI WEST

No aspect of the transformation of the West was more visible and dramatic than the destruction of the traditional Indian way of life. Even before settlers, ranchers, and miners poured onto the Great Plains at midcentury, Indian life in the trans-Mississippi West was changing. In the Southwest earlier in the century, the Spanish had forcibly incorporated pueblo peoples such as the Hopis and Zuñis into their Mexican trading networks. Other tribes, such as the Navajos, had gradually given up migratory life in favor of settled agriculture. To the North, the Cheyenne and the Lakota Sioux, already expelled from the Great Lakes region by the expansion of white settlement, had moved onto the grasslands of the Great Plains and had seized hunting grounds from their enemies, the Pawnees and the Crows. These and other nomadic warrior tribes, dispersed in small bands and moving from place to place to follow the bison herds, had developed a resilient culture adapted to the harsh environment.

When white pioneers invaded their territory at midcentury, it was the resistance of these nomadic Indians that most captured the public's attention and spurred debate. Caught between a stampede of miners and settlers who took their land and depleted their natural resources and the federal government that sought to force them onto reservations, Native Americans desperately fought back. By the 1890s relocation to distant, often inferior lands had become the fate of almost every Indian nation. Beaten and victimized, resilient Native Americans struggled to preserve their traditions and rebuild their numbers.

The Plains Indians   The Indians of the Great Plains inhabited three major subregions. The northern Plains, from the Dakotas and Montana southward to Nebraska, were dominated by several large tribes such as the Lakota who spoke Siouan languages, as well as by the Flatheads, Blackfeet, Assiniboins, northern Cheyennes, Arapahos, and Crows. Some of these were allies, but others were bitter enemies perpetually at war. In the central region the so-called Five Civilized Tribes, who had been driven there from the Southeast in the 1830s, pursued an agricultural life in the Indian Territory (present-day Oklahoma). The Pawnees in Nebraska maintained the older, more settled tradition characteristic of Plains river valley culture before the introduction of horses, spending at least half the year in villages of earthen lodges along watercourses. Surrounding these to the South were the migratory tribes of western Kansas, Colorado, eastern New Mexico, and Texas—the Comanches, Kiowas, southern Arapahos, and Kiowa Apaches.

Considerable diversity flourished among the Plains peoples, and customs varied even within subdivisions of the same tribe. For example, the easternmost branch of the great Sioux Nation, the Dakota Sioux of Minnesota who inhabited the wooded edge of the prairie, led a semisedentary life based on small-scale agriculture, deer and bison hunting, wild-rice harvesting, and maple-sugar production. In contrast, many Plains tribes—not only the Lakota Sioux, but also the Blackfeet, Crows, and Cheyennes—using horses obtained from the Spanish and guns obtained from traders, roamed the High Plains to the west, and followed the bison migrations.

For all the Plains Indians, life revolved around extended family ties and tribal cooperation. Within the various Sioux-speaking tribes, for example, children were raised without physical punishment and were taught to treat each adult clan member with the respect accorded to relatives. Families and clans joined forces to hunt and farm and reached decisions by consensus.

For the various Sioux bands, religious and harvest celebrations provided the cement for village and camp life. Sioux religion was complex and entirely different from the Judeo-Christian tradition. The Lakota Sioux thought of life as a series of circles. Living within the daily cycles of the sun and moon, Lakotas were born into a circle of relatives, which broadened to the band, the tribe, and the Sioux Nation. The Lakotas also believed in a hierarchy of plant and animal spirits whose help could be invoked in the Sun Dance. To gain access to spiritual power and to benefit the weaker members of the community, young men would "sacrifice" themselves by suffering self-torture. For example, some fastened skewers to their chest from which they dragged buffalo skulls; others suspended themselves from poles or cut pieces of their flesh and placed them at the foot of the Sun Dance pole. Painter George Catlin, who recorded Great Plains Indian life before the Civil War, described such a ceremony. "Several of them, seeing me making sketches, beckoned me to look at their faces, which I watched through all this horrid operation, without being able to detect anything but the pleasantest smiles as they looked me in the eye, while I could hear the knife rip through the flesh, and feel enough of it myself, to start involuntary and uncontrollable tears over my cheeks."

On the semiarid High Plains where rainfall averaged less than twenty inches a year, both the bison and the Native peoples adapted to the environment. The huge herds, which at their peak contained an estimated 30 million animals, broke into small groups in the winter and dispersed into river valleys where they sought protection from harsh storms and bone-numbing cold. In the summer, they returned to the High Plains in vast herds to feed on the nutritious short grasses and mate. Like the bison, the Indians dispersed across the landscape to minimize their impact on any one place, wintering in the river valleys and returning to the High Plains in summer. When their herds of horses consumed the grasses near their camps, they moved. Hunting the bison not only supplied the Native peoples with food, clothing, and teepee covers, but also created a valuable trading commodity, buffalo robes. To benefit from this trade, Indians themselves, as the nineteenth century progressed, dramatically increased their harvest of animals.

The movement of miners and settlers onto the eastern High Plains in the 1850s began to erode the bison's habitat and threaten the Native American way of life. As the pioneers trekked westward, they occupied the river valley sites where the buffalo had wintered and exhausted the tall grasses upon which the animals depended. In the 1860s whites began systematically to hunt the animals, often with Indian help, to supply the eastern market with carriage robes and industrial belting. William F. "Buffalo Bill" Cody, a famous scout, Indian fighter, and organizer of Wild West shows, killed nearly forty-three hundred bison in 1867–1868 to feed construction crews building the Union Pacific Railroad. Army commanders also encouraged the slaughter of buffalo to undermine Indian resistance to the encroachment of miners and settlers. The carnage that resulted was almost inconceivable in its scale. Between 1872 and 1875, hunters killed 9 million buffalo, taking only the skin and leaving the carcasses to rot. By the 1880s the once-thundering herds had been reduced to a few thousand animals, and the Native American way of life dependent on the buffalo had been ruined.

The Destruction of Nomadic Indian Life

As early as the 1850s, the seeds of the impending crisis were apparent. The Indians who felt pressure from the declining bison herds and deteriorating grasslands now faced the onslaught of thousands of pioneers lured by the discovery of gold and silver in the Rocky Mountains. The federal government's response was to reexamine its Indian policies. Abandoning the previous position that treated much of the West as a vast Indian reserve, the federal government sought to introduce a system of smaller, separate, bounded areas—tribal reservations—where the Indians were to be concentrated, by force if necessary, and where they were expected to exchange their nomadic ways for a settled agricultural life. To achieve this goal, the army established outposts along well-traveled trails and stationed troops that could be mobilized at a moment's notice.

Some Native Americans, like the Pueblos of the Southwest, the Crows of Montana, and the Hidatsas of North Dakota, peacefully accepted their fate. Others, among them the Navajos of Arizona and New Mexico and the Dakota Sioux, opposed the new policy to no avail. By 1860 eight western reservations had been established.

Significant segments of the remaining tribes on the Great Plains, more than a hundred thousand people, fought against removal for decades. From the 1860s through the 1890s, many bands from these tribes—the western Sioux, Cheyennes, Arapahos, Kiowas, and Comanches on the Great Plains; the Nez Percés and Bannocks in the northern Rockies; and the Apaches in the Southwest—faced the U.S. army in a series of final battles for the West.

Misunderstandings, unfulfilled promises, brutality, and butchery marked the conflict. Nowhere was this more evident than in the eroding relationship between the Cheyennes and Arapahos and the settlers near Sand Creek, Colorado, in 1864. During the gold rush six years earlier, more than a hundred thousand people (more than twice the number who went to California in 1849) had stampeded into the area. The Indians, facing starvation because of unfulfilled treaties that had promised food, support, and farm equipment, slipped away from the reservation areas to hunt bison and steal livestock from nearby settlers.

In the spring of the year, local militia troops (replacements for soldiers fighting in the Civil War) attacked Cheyenne and Arapaho camps. The Indians retaliated with a flurry of attacks on travelers. The governor, in a panic, issued an extraordinary proclamation, authorizing Colorado's white citizenry to seek out and kill all hostile Indians on sight. He then activated a regiment of troops under Colonel John M. Chivington, a Methodist minister. At dawn on November 29, under orders to "remember the murdered women and children on the Platte [River]," Chivington's troops massacred a peaceful band of Indians, including terrified women and children, camped at Sand Creek, who believed that they would be protected by the nearby fort.

This massacre and others that followed rekindled public debate over federal Indian policy. In response, in 1867 Congress sent a peace commission to end the fighting, and set aside two large districts, one north of Nebraska, the other south

Indian Wars and Reservations in the West

Although they were never recognized as such in the popular press, the battles between Native Americans and the U.S. army on the Great Plains amounted to a major undeclared war.

of Kansas. There, it was hoped, the tribes would take up farming and convert to Christianity. Behind the federal government's persuasion lay the threat of force. Any Native Americans who refused to "locate in [the] permanent abodes provided for them," warned Commissioner of Indian Affairs Ely S. Parker, himself a Seneca Indian, "would be subject wholly to the control and supervision of military authorities, [and] . . . treated as friendly or hostile as circumstances might justify."

At first the plan appeared to work. Representatives of sixty-eight thousand southern Kiowas, Comanches, Cheyennes, and Arapahos signed the Medicine Lodge Treaty of 1867 and pledged to live on land in present-day Oklahoma. The following year, scattered bands of Sioux, representing nearly fifty-four thousand northern Plains Indians, signed the Fort Laramie Treaty and agreed to move to reservations on the so-called Great Sioux Reserve in the western part of what is now South Dakota in return for money and provisions.

But Indian dissatisfaction with the treaties ran deep. As a Sioux chief, Spotted Tail, told the commissioners, "We do not want to live like the white man. . . . The Great Spirit gave us hunting grounds, gave us the buffalo, the elk, the deer, and the antelope. Our fathers have taught us to hunt and live on the Plains, and we are contented." Rejecting the new system, many bands of Indians refused to move to the reservations or to remain on them once there.

In August 1868 war parties of defiant Cheyennes, Arapahos, and Sioux raided settlements in Kansas and Colorado, burning homes and killing whites. In retaliation, army troops attacked Indians, even peaceful ones, who refused confinement. That autumn Lieutenant Colonel George Armstrong Custer's raiding party struck a sleeping Cheyenne village, killing more than a hundred warriors, shooting more than eight hundred horses, and taking fifty-three women and children prisoner. Other hostile Cheyennes and Arapahos were pursued, captured, and returned to the reservations.

In 1869, spurred on by Christian reformers, Congress established a Board of Indian Commissioners drawn from the major Protestant denominations to reform the reservation system. But the new and inexperienced church-appointed Indian agents quickly encountered obstacles in trying to implement the board's policies. The pacifist Quaker agent Lawrie Tatum, a big-boned Iowa farmer, for example, failed to persuade the Comanches and Kiowas to stay on their reservations in Oklahoma rather than raid Texas settlements. Two Kiowa chiefs, Satanta and Big Tree, insisted that they could be at peace with the federal government while remaining at war with Texans. Other agents were unable to restrain scheming whites who fraudulently purchased reservation lands from the Indians. By the 1880s the federal government, frustrated with the churches, ignored their nominations for Indian agents and made its own appointments.

Caught in the sticky web of an ambiguous and deceptive federal policy, and enraged by continuing non-Indian settlement of the Plains, defiant Native Americans struck back in the 1870s. On the southern Plains, Kiowa, Comanche, and Cheyenne raids in the Texas panhandle in 1874 set off the so-called Red River War. In a fierce winter campaign, regular army troops destroyed Indian supplies and slaughtered a hundred Cheyenne fugitives near the Sappa River in Kansas. With the exile of seventy-four "ringleaders" to reservations in Florida, Native American independence on the southern Plains came to an end. In the Southwest, in present-day Arizona and New Mexico, the Apaches fought an intermittent guerrilla war until their leader, Geronimo, surrendered in 1886.

Custer's Last Stand, 1876   Of all the acts of Indian resistance against the new reservation policy, none aroused more passion or caused more bloodshed than the battles waged by the western Sioux tribes in the Dakotas, Montana, and Wyoming. The 1868 Treaty of Fort Laramie had set aside the Great Sioux Reserve "in perpetuity." But not all the Sioux bands had fought in the war or signed the treaty.

Indian Chiefs *Early photographs of the Indian leaders Chief Joseph (left) and Sitting Bull (right) captured both their pride and the frustration they felt after years of alternately negotiating and battling with the U.S. army. "I don't want a white man over me," Sitting Bull insisted. "I want to have the white man with me, but not to be my chief. I ask this because I want to do right by my people. . . ."*

In 1873, skillfully playing local officials against the federal government, Chief Red Cloud's Oglala band and Chief Spotted Tail's Brulé band won the concession of staying on their traditional lands. To protect their hunting grounds, they raided encroaching non-Indian settlements in Nebraska and Wyoming, intimidated federal agents, and harassed miners, railroad surveyors, and any others who ventured onto their lands.

Non-treaty Sioux found a powerful leader in the Hunkpapa Lakota Sioux chief and holy man Sitting Bull. Broad-shouldered and powerfully built, Sitting Bull led by example and had considerable fighting experience. "You are fools," he told the reservation Indians, "to make yourselves slaves to a piece of fat bacon, some hardtack, and little sugar and coffee."

Pressured by would-be settlers and developers and distressed by the Indian agents' inability to prevent the Sioux from entering and leaving the reservations at will, the federal government took action. In 1874 General William Tecumseh Sherman sent a force under Colonel George Armstrong Custer into the Black Hills of South Dakota, near the western edge of the Great Sioux Reserve. Lean and mustachioed, with shoulder-length reddish-blond hair, the thirty-four-year-old Custer had been a celebrity since his days as an impetuous young Civil War officer, when he was known for the black velvet uniform embellished with gold braid he wore on the battlefield. Now he had switched to a fringed buckskin uniform set off by a crimson scarf.

Custer's ostensible purpose was to find a location for a new fort and to keep an eye on renegade Indians. But his real objective was to confirm rumors about the existence of gold in the Black Hills. In this he was spurred on by the Northern Pacific Railroad, which wanted to attract settlers to the area. While Custer's troops mapped the lush meadows and chose a site for the fort, two "practical miners" panned the streams for gold. In a report that he telegraphed to the *New York World,* Custer described the region as excellent farm country and casually mentioned finding "gold among the roots of the grass." The gold stampede that predictably followed gave the army a new justification for interceding against the Indians.

Custer had in fact become part of a deliberate army plan to force concessions from the Sioux. In November 1875 negotiations to buy the Black Hills broke down because the Indians' asking price was deemed too high. President Grant and his generals then decided to remove all roadblocks to the entry of miners. Indians still outside the reservations after January 31, 1876, the government announced, would be hunted down by the army and taken in by force.

The army mobilized for an assault. In June 1876, leading 600 troops of the Seventh Cavalry, Custer proceeded to the Little Bighorn River area of present-day Montana, a hub of Indian resistance. On the morning of June 25, underestimating the Indian enemy and unwisely dividing his force, Custer, with 209 men, recklessly advanced against a large company of Cheyenne and Sioux warriors led by Chief Sitting Bull who had encamped along the Little Bighorn. Custer and his outnumbered troops were wiped out. Two days later, another company of cavalry came upon the carnage and buried the bodies where they lay. A single creature was found alive: a horse that had belonged to one of Custer's captains.

Americans reeled from this unexpected Indian victory. Newspaper columnists groped to assess the meaning of "Custer's last stand." Some went beyond criticism of Custer's leadership to question the wisdom of current federal policy toward the Indians. Others worried that an outraged public would demand retaliation and the extermination of the Sioux. Most, however, endorsed the federal government's determination to quash the Native American rebellion. "It is inconsistent with our civilization and with common sense," trumpeted a writer in the *New York Herald,* "to allow the Indian to roam over a country as fine as that around the Black Hills, preventing its development in order that he may shoot game and scalp his neighbors. That can never be. This region must be taken from the Indian."

Defeat at Little Bighorn made the army more determined. In Montana troops harassed various Sioux bands for more than five years, attacking Indian camps in the dead of winter and destroying all supplies. Even Sitting Bull, who had led his band to Canada to escape the army, surrendered in 1881 for lack of provisions: the slaughter of the buffalo had wiped out his tribe's major food supply. Ever resourceful, Sitting Bull joined Buffalo Bill's Wild West show for a time after his surrender and earned enough money to bring additional supplies to his people.

Similar measures were used elsewhere in the West against Chief Joseph and his Nez Percés of Oregon and against the Northern Cheyennes, who had been forcibly transported to Oklahoma after the Battle of Little Bighorn. Chief Dull Knife led some 150 survivors, including men, women, and children, north in September 1878 to join the Sioux. But the army chased them down and imprisoned them in Fort Robinson, Nebraska. When the army denied their request to stay nearer to their traditional northern lands, tribal leaders refused to cooperate. The post commander then withheld all food, water, and fuel. On a frigid night in January 1879, a desperate Dull Knife and his followers, in a suicidal escape attempt, shot the guards and broke for freedom. Members of the startled garrison chased the Indians and gunned down half of them in the snow, including women and children as well as Dull Knife himself. The Atlanta *Constitution* condemned the incident as "a dastardly outrage upon humanity and a lasting disgrace to our boasted civilization." But although sporadic Indian resistance continued until the end of the century, these brutal tactics had sapped the Indians' will to resist.

"Saving" the Indians
A growing number of Americans were outraged not only by bloody atrocities like the Fort Robinson massacre but also by the federal government's flagrant violation of its Indian treaties. The Women's National Indian Rights Association, founded in 1883, and other groups took up the cause. Helen Hunt Jackson, a Massachusetts writer who had recently moved to Colorado, published *A Century of Dishonor* in 1881 to rally public opinion against the government's record of broken treaty obligations. "It makes little difference . . . where one opens the record of the history of the Indians," she wrote; "every page and every year has its dark stain."

Well-intentioned humanitarians concluded that the Indians' interests would be best served by breaking up the reservations, ending all recognition of the tribes, and propelling individual Native Americans into mainstream society. In short, they proposed to eliminate the "Indian problem" by eliminating the Indians as a culturally distinct entity. Inspired by this vision, they threw their support behind a plan that resulted in the passage in 1887 of the Dawes Severalty Act.

The Dawes Act was designed to reform what well-meaning whites perceived to be the weaknesses of Indian life—the absence of private property and the Native peoples' nomadic tradition—by turning Indians into landowners and farmers. The law emphasized severalty, or the treatment of Indians as individuals rather than as members of tribes, and called for the distribution of 160 acres of reservation land for farming, or 320 acres for grazing, to each head of an Indian family who accepted the law's provisions. The remaining reservation lands (often the richest) were to be sold to speculators and settlers, and the income thus obtained would go toward purchase of farm tools. To prevent unscrupulous people from gaining control of the lands granted to individual Indians, the government would hold the property of each tribal member in trust for twenty-five years. Those Indians who at that point had accepted allotments would also be declared citizens of the United States.

Speculators who coveted reservation lands, as well as military authorities who wanted to break up the reservations for security reasons, had lobbied heavily for the Dawes Act. But the bill's strongest support had come from the "friends of the

Indian" like Helen Hunt Jackson. Convinced that citizenship would best protect the Indians and that full assimilation into society would enable them to get ahead, the reformers systematically tried to "civilize" the Indian peoples and wean them from their traditional culture (see A Place in Time: The Phoenix Indian School).

The Dawes Act did not specify a timetable for the breakup of the reservations. Few allotments were made to the Indians until the 1890s. The act eventually proved to be a boon to speculators, who commonly evaded its safeguards and obtained the Indians' most arable tracts. By 1934 the act had slashed the total Indian acreage by 65 percent. Much of what remained in Indian hands was too dry and gravelly for farming. In the twentieth century, ironically, periodic droughts and the fragile, arid High Plains landscape would push many white farmers back off the land.

Although some Native Americans who received land under the Dawes Act prospered enough to expand their holdings and go into large-scale farming or ranching, countless others struggled just to survive. Hunting restrictions on the former reservation lands prevented many Indians from supplementing their limited farm yields. Alcoholism, a continuing problem exacerbated by the prevalence of whiskey as a trade item (and by the boredom that resulted from the disruption of hunting and other traditional pursuits), became more prevalent as Native Americans strove to adapt to the constraints of reservation life.

The Ghost Dance and the End of Indian Resistance on the Great Plains, 1890

Living conditions for the Sioux worsened in the late 1880s. The federal government reduced their meat rations and imposed more and more restrictions. When disease killed a third of their cattle, they became desperate. The Sioux, who still numbered almost twenty-five thousand, turned to Wovoka, a new prophet popular among the Great Basin Indians in Nevada. Wovoka promised to restore the Sioux to their original dominance on the Plains if they performed the Ghost Dance.

Wearing sacred Ghost Shirts—cotton or leather vestments decorated to ward off evil—the dancers moved in a circle, accelerating until they reached a trancelike state and experienced visions of the future. Many believed that the Ghost Shirts would protect them from harm.

In the fall of 1890, as the Ghost Dance movement spread among the Sioux in the Dakota Territory, Indian officials and military authorities grew alarmed. The local reservation agent, Major James McLaughlin, decided that Chief Sitting Bull, whose cabin on the reservation had become a rallying point for the Ghost Dance movement, must be arrested. On a freezing, drizzly December morning, McLaughlin dispatched a company of forty-two Indian policemen from the agency to take Sitting Bull into custody. When two policemen pulled the chief from his cabin, his bodyguard Catch-the-Bear shot one of them. As the policeman fell, he in turn shot Sitting Bull at point-blank range. Bloody hand-to-hand fighting immediately broke out. As bullets whizzed by, Sitting Bull's horse began to perform the tricks it

The Phoenix Indian School, 1891–1918

Ten-year-old Chehia Red Arrow was scared when she left her home on the Gila River Reservation in 1908 for the Phoenix Indian School. Raised in a traditional Pima Indian family, Chehia, or Anna Moore Shaw, as she would later be called, had heard rumors that children at the school were whipped when they disobeyed. Would that happen to her? Would she have any friends? How would she be treated?

Chehia had good cause for concern. Founded in 1891, the Phoenix Indian School had been modeled after Richard Henry Pratt's famous military-style, off-reservation boarding school in Carlisle, Pennsylvania, which was designed to "Americanize" and "uplift" the Indian. Pratt believed that the Indians' culture, customs, and languages had halted their progress toward white civilization. His motto therefore became "Kill the Indian in him and save the man."

Opening in a converted hotel and nearby farm in 1891, the Phoenix Indian School was a joint product of local boosters and the federal Indian Office. Nestled between mountain ranges in the Salt River Valley, the city of Phoenix had been founded in 1868. The early settlers had restored the ancient Hohokam Indian irrigation system and had begun to create a bustling desert oasis. Although Phoenix in 1890 had a population of only three thousand, local promoters had also persuaded the legislature to place the territorial capital there. They now campaigned for an industrial training school that might provide "cheap and efficient" labor for local families and for the production of fruit

and cotton. The city's citizens joined with the federal government to purchase 160 acres of land located three miles north of the city for a school farm. In support of the school, federal Indian Commissioner Thomas Morgan visited Phoenix and delivered a speech entitled "Cheaper to Educate Indians Than to Kill Them."

The school, which enrolled both Indian and Mexican-American students, was run along strict military lines. Upon arrival, students were washed, given a haircut, and issued a military uniform. Forbidden to speak their native languages, they were assigned "civilized" Christian names. Often lonely or homesick, some ran away. Twelve-year-old James McCarthy, a Papago Indian, surprised his mother when he showed up at her doorstep after walking 115 miles.

Other runaways were caught. Helen Sekaquaptewa, a Hopi student, noted that boys who returned were placed in detention, or had their heads shaved and were forced to march in the schoolyard wearing girl's clothing. Girls might have to cut grass with scissors or wear a sign saying "I ran away." Although many school superintendents avoided physical punishment, some of their subordinates beat the students. Occasionally, measles, influenza, and mumps swept through the school and students died.

The academic program at the Phoenix Indian School, like that at Booker T. Washington's Tuskegee Institute, focused primarily on vocational training that was designed to change traditional Indian gender roles.

Boys, who were traditionally hunters, could learn carpentry, blacksmithing, tailoring, shoemaking, harness making, and farming; girls, who in Indian society did the farming, were now viewed as "the uplifter of the home." They studied home economics, dressmaking, and nursing. The students kept the school solvent. The boys ran the school farm; the girls sewed, washed, and ironed their own clothes, cleaned the buildings, and cooked and served the food.

To gain additional practical experience, students participated in the "outing" system that sent them into the community to work for local farmers or to serve as domestic help for families. As long as they behaved properly, students experienced little discrimination and were often pleased by the income made possible by their jobs. Eventually, however, the "outing" system, originally designed to promote assimilation, primarily became a method of supplying cheap labor to white employers.

Despite the strict discipline of school life, many students enjoyed their life there. Music was particularly popular. As Chehia remembered, "They had a boys' and a girls battalion. . . . The students were taught to keep in step to the music of the school band. . . . A snare drummer always beat his rhythms in front of the academic building, and we had to keep in step." Like other off-reservation boarding schools, the Phoenix Indian School was well known for its marching band, which was often invited to play for civic occasions in town. Tourists and townspeople frequently visited the school, and the Christmas pageant became an annual city event.

Sports, particularly football and baseball, were also popular. At the turn of the century, teams at Carlisle and other Indian schools competed against Harvard, Notre Dame, and Michigan State. The most famous Indian athlete, Jim Thorpe, captained the football and basketball teams at Carlisle and won gold medals at the 1912 Olympic games in Stockholm.

By the mid-1890s many Native American families acknowledged the value of boarding school education, and Phoenix and other schools were overwhelmed with requests for admission. By 1899 more than seven hundred Indians were attending the Phoenix school, making it second only to Carlisle. In 1900 the federal government was operating 153 boarding schools attended by more than seventeen thousand pupils.

Ironically, although many students valued the discipline and education of boarding school life, the attempt to stamp out Indian identity often resulted in resistance. Forming friendships with Indians from many different tribes, boarding school students forged their own sense of Indian identity. As Mitch Walking Elk, a Cheyenne-Arapaho-Hopi singer put it, "They put me in the boarding school and they cut off all my hair, gave me an education, but the Apache's still in there."

After graduating, Chehia Red Arrow moved back to the reservation and married Ross Shaw, a classmate. One month later, "with mixed emotions," they returned to Phoenix. "Our hearts ached for them [Shaw's parents] in their difficult existence," she admitted, "but both Ross and I knew that laboring beside his parents in the fields each day was not the best way to help. The educations they had strived so hard to give us had prepared us to bring in money from the white man's world: it would be wrong to waste all those years on a life of primitive farming. . . .

"True," she admitted, "we had been educated in the white man's ways, but we were still traditional Pimas with strong feelings of duty to our families and an intense love of our land." Decades later, after raising a family, she helped establish a Pima Indian museum, edited the tribal newsletter, and, to reaffirm and preserve her Indian identity, published her own book, *Pima Indian Legends*.

remembered from its days in the Wild West show. Some observers were terrified, convinced that the spirit of the dead chief had entered his horse.

Two weeks later, one of the bloodiest episodes of Indian-white strife on the Plains occurred. On December 29, the Seventh Cavalry was rounding up 340 starving and freezing Sioux at Wounded Knee, South Dakota, when an excited Indian fired a gun hidden under a blanket. The soldiers retaliated with cannon fire. Within minutes 300 Indians, including 7 infants, were slaughtered. Three days later, a baby who had miraculously survived was found wrapped in a blanket under the snow. She wore a buckskin cap on which a beadwork American flag had been embroidered. Brigadier General L. W. Colby, who adopted the baby, named her Marguerite, but the Indians called her Lost Bird.

As the frozen corpses at Wounded Knee were dumped into mass graves, a generation of Indian-white conflict on the Great Plains shuddered to a close. Lost Bird, with her poignantly patriotic beadwork cap, highlights the irony of the Plains Indians' response to white expansion. Many did try to adapt to non-Indian ways, but few succeeded fully, and many others were devastated at being forced to abandon deeply held religious beliefs and a way of life rooted in hunting, cooperative living, and nomadism. Driven onto reservations, the Plains Indians were reduced to almost complete dependency. By 1900 the Plains Indian population had shrunk from nearly a quarter-million to just over a hundred thousand. Nevertheless, the population began to increase slowly after 1900. Against overwhelming odds, the pride, group memory, and cultural identity of the Plains Indians survived all efforts at eradication.

Unlike the nomadic western Sioux, the more settled Navajos of the Southwest adjusted more successfully to the reservation system, preserving traditional ways while incorporating elements of the new order in a complex process of cultural adaptation. By 1900 the Navajos had tripled their reservation land, dramatically increased their numbers and their herds, and carved out for themselves a distinct place in Arizona and New Mexico.

These extraordinary changes were forced on the Indian population by the advance of non-Indian settlement. In the name of civilization and progress, non-Indians in the generation after the Civil War pursued a course that involved a mixture of sincere (if misguided) benevolence, coercion wrapped in an aura of legality, and outbursts of naked violence. Many white Americans felt toward the

Indians only contempt, hatred, and greed for their land. Others viewed themselves as divinely chosen instruments for uplifting and Christianizing the Indians. Both groups, however, were blind to the value of Native American life and traditions. And both played their part in shattering a proud people and an ancient culture. The Indians' fate would weigh on the American conscience for generations.

SETTLING THE WEST

The successive defeats of the Native Americans transformed the western landscape by opening up for settlement a vast territory that reached from the Great Plains to the Sierra Nevada and Cascade Mountains. In the 1840s, when nearly a quarter-million Americans had trudged overland to Oregon and California, they had typically endured a six- to eight-month trip in ox-drawn wagons. After 1870 railroad expansion made the trip faster and considerably easier. In the next three decades, more land was parceled out into farms than in the previous 250 years of American history combined, and agricultural production doubled.

The First Transcontinental Railroad

Passed in 1862, the Pacific Railroad Act authorized the construction of a new transcontinental link. The act provided grants of land and other subsidies to the railroads for each mile of track laid, which made them the largest landholders in the West. Over the next half-century, nine major routes, which ran from the South or Midwest to the West, were built. More than any other factor, the expansion of these railroads accelerated the transformation of everyday life west of the Mississippi.

Building the railroad took backbreaking work. Searching for inexpensive labor, the railroads turned to immigrants. The Central Pacific employed Chinese workers to chip and blast rail bed out of solid rock in the Sierra Nevada. The railroad preferred the Chinese laborers because they worked hard for low wages, did not drink, and furnished their own food and tents. Nearly twelve thousand Chinese graded the roadbed while Irish, Mexican-American, and black workers put down the track.

On May 10, 1869, Americans celebrated the completion of the first railroad spanning North America. As the two sets of tracks—the Union Pacific's, stretching westward from Omaha, Nebraska, and the Central Pacific's, reaching eastward from Sacramento, California—met at Promontory Point, Utah, beaming officials drove in a final ceremonial golden spike. The nation's vast midsection was now far more accessible than it had ever been.

The railroads quickly proved their usefulness. In the battles against Native Americans, the army shipped horses and men west in the dead of winter to attack the Indians when they were most vulnerable. From the same trains, hunters gained quick access to the bison ranges and increased their harvest of the animals. Once Indian resistance had been broken, the railroads not only expedited the shipment of new settlers and their supplies; they also provided fast access for the shipment of cattle and grain to eastern urban markets. In short, the railroads influenced much of the development of the West.

Settlers and the
Railroad

During the decade after the passage of the Pacific Railroad Act, Congress awarded the railroads 170 million acres, worth over half a billion dollars. By 1893 the states of Minnesota and Washington had also deeded to railroad companies a quarter of their state lands; Wisconsin, Iowa, Kansas, North Dakota, and Montana had turned over a fifth of their acreage. As mighty landowners, the railroads had a unique opportunity to shape settlement in the region—and to reap enormous profits.

The railroads used several different tactics to attract inhabitants. They created land sales offices and sent agents to the East Coast and Europe to recruit settlers. While the agents glorified the West as a new Garden of Eden, the land bureaus offered prospective buyers long-term loans and free transportation. Acknowledging that life on the Great Plains could be lonely, the promoters advised young men to bring their wives (because "maidens are scarce") and to emigrate as entire families and with friends.

One unintended consequence of these land promotions was to make land available to single women, or "girl homesteaders" as they were known at the time, to establish farms near other family members. In Wyoming single women made up more than 18 percent of the claimants.

In addition to the millions of Americans who migrated from nearby states, the railroads helped bring nearly 2.2 million foreign-born settlers to the trans-Mississippi West between 1870 and 1900. Some agents recruited whole villages of Germans and eastern Europeans to relocate to the North Dakota plains. Irish laborers hired to lay track could be found in every town along the rail lines. By 1905 the Santa Fe Railroad alone had transported sixty thousand Russian Mennonites to the fertile Kansas plains where black pioneers called exodusters had preceded them in the 1870s.

The railroads influenced agriculture as well. To ensure quick repayment of the money owed to them, the railroads urged new immigrants to specialize in cash crops—wheat on the northern Plains, corn in Iowa and Kansas, cotton and tobacco in Texas. Although these crops initially brought in high revenues, many farmers grew dependent on income from a single crop and became vulnerable to fluctuating market forces.

Homesteading on
the Great Plains

Liberalized land laws were another powerful magnet pulling settlers westward. The Homestead Act passed in 1862 reflected the Republican party's belief that free land would enable the poor to achieve economic independence. It offered 160 acres of land to any individual who would pay a ten-dollar registration fee, live on the land for five years, and cultivate and improve it. Because getting to the Great Plains was costly, most settlers migrated from nearby states.

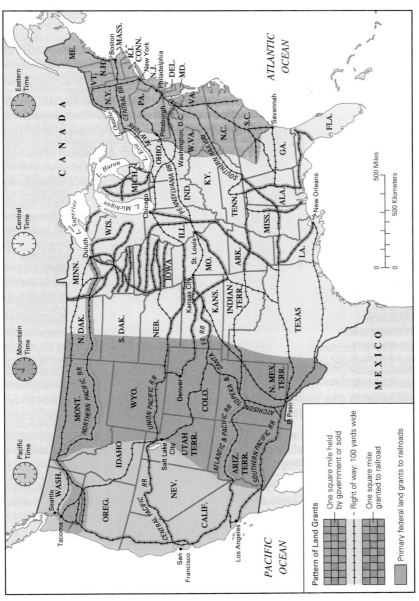

Transcontinental Railroads and Federal Land Grants, 1850–1900

Despite the laissez-faire ideology that argued against government interference in business, Congress heavily subsidized American railroads and gave them millions of acres of land. As illustrated in the box, belts of land were reserved on either side of a railroad's right of way. Until the railroad claimed the exact one-mile-square sections it chose to possess, all such sections within the belt remained closed to settlement.

An African-American Homestead Near Guthrie, Oklahoma Territory, 1889
Seated proudly in front of their sod house and barn, the two generations of this black family were part of the more than 56,000 blacks who had moved to Oklahoma by 1900.

The Homestead Act also proved attractive to immigrants from the British Isles as well as from Scandinavia and other regions of Europe where good-quality land was prohibitively expensive. Urged on by land promoters, waves of English, Irish, Germans, Swedes, Danes, Norwegians, and Czechs immigrated to the United States in the 1870s and 1880s and formed their own communities.

Although nearly four hundred thousand families claimed land under the provisions of the Homestead Act between 1860 and 1900, the law did not function as Congress had envisioned. Advance agents representing unscrupulous speculators filed false claims for the choicest locations, and railroads and state governments acquired huge landholdings. The result was that only one acre in every nine went to the pioneers for whom it was intended.

A second problem resulted from the 160-acre limit specified by the Homestead Act. On the rich soils of Iowa or in the fertile lands in California, Oregon, and Washington, a 160-acre farm was ample, but in the drier areas west of the hundredth meridian, a farmer needed more land. In 1873, to rectify this problem, Congress passed the Timber Culture Act, which gave homesteaders an additional 160 acres if they planted trees on 40 acres. For states with little rainfall, Congress enacted the Desert Land Act in 1877, which made 640 acres available at $1.25 an acre on condition that the owner irrigate part of it within three years. However, this act, along with the Timber and Stone Act of 1878, which permitted the purchase of up to 160 acres of forest land for $2.50 an acre, was abused by grasping speculators, lumber-company representatives, and cattle ranchers seeking to expand their holdings. Yet, even though families did not receive as much land as Congress had intended, federal laws kept alive the dream of the West as a place for new beginnings.

In addition to problems faced by those who bought from unscrupulous speculators or chose property in areas that lacked sufficient rainfall to grow crops, almost all settlers faced difficult psychological adjustments to frontier life. The first years of settlement were the most difficult. Toiling to build a house, plow the fields, plant the first crop, and drill a well, the pioneers put in an average of sixty-eight hours of tedious, backbreaking work a week in isolated surroundings. Howard Ruede, a Pennsylvania printer who migrated to Kansas to farm, wrote home in 1877 complaining about the mosquitoes and bedbugs infesting his house, which was cut out of thick grass sod and dug into the ground. He and countless others coping with the severe Plains conditions saw their shining vision of Edenic farm life quickly dim. For blacks who emigrated from the South to Kansas and other parts of the Plains after the Civil War, prejudice compounded the burdens of adjusting to a different life (see Chapter 16).

Many middle-class women, swept up in the romantic conventions of the day, found adaptation to Plains frontier life especially difficult. At least initially, some were enchanted by the haunting landscape, and in letters they described the open Plains as arrestingly beautiful. But far more were struck by the "horrible tribes of Mosquitoes"; the violent weather-drenching summer thunderstorms with hailstones as "big as hen's eggs" and blinding winter blizzards; and the crude sod huts that served as their early homes because of the scarcity of timber. One woman burst into tears upon first seeing her new sod house. The young bride angrily informed her husband that her father had built a better house for his hogs.

The high transience rate on the frontier in these years reflected the difficulty that newcomers faced in adjusting to life on the Great Plains. Nearly half of those who staked homestead claims in Kansas between 1862 and 1890 relinquished their rights to the land and moved on. However, in places like Minnesota and the Pacific Northwest that were populated largely by Germans, Norwegians, and other immigrants with a tradition of family prosperity tied to continuous landownership, the persistence rate (or percentage of people staying for a decade or more) could be considerably higher.

Many who weathered the lean early years eventually came to identify deeply with the land. Within a decade, the typical Plains family that had "stuck it out" had moved into a new wood-framed house and had fixed up the front parlor. Women worked particularly hard on these farms and took pride in their accomplishments. "Just done the chores," wrote one woman to a friend. "I went fence mending and getting out cattle . . . and came in after sundown. I fed my White Leghorns [chickens] and then sat on the step to read over your letter. I forgot my wet feet and shoes full of gravel and giggled joyously."

New Farms,
New Markets

Farmers on the Plains took advantage of advances in farm mechanization and the development of improved strains of wheat and corn to boost production dramatically. Efficient steel plows; spring-tooth harrows that broke up the dense prairie soil more effectively than earlier models; specially designed wheat planters; and improved grain binders, threshers, and windmills all allowed the typical Great Plains farmer of the late nineteenth century to increase the land's yield tenfold.

Barbed wire, patented in 1874, was another crucial invention that permitted farmers who lived where few trees grew to keep roving livestock out of their crops. But fencing the land touched off violent clashes between farmers and cattle ranchers, who demanded the right to let their herds roam freely until the roundup. Generally the farmers won.

The invention of labor-saving machinery together with increased demand for wheat, milk, and other farm products created the impression that farming was entering a period of unparalleled prosperity. But few fully understood the perils of pursuing agriculture as a livelihood. The cost of the land, horses, machinery, and seed needed to start up a farm could exceed twelve hundred dollars, far more than the annual earnings of the average industrial worker. Faced with substantial mortgage payments, many farmers had to specialize in a crop such as wheat or corn that would fetch high prices. This specialization made them dependent on the railroads for shipping and put them at the mercy of the international grain market's shifting prices.

Far from being an independent producer, the western grain grower was a player in a complex world market economy. Railroad and steamship transport enabled the American farmer to compete in the international market. High demand could bring prosperity, but when world overproduction forced grain prices down, the heavily indebted grower faced ruin. Confronted with these realities, many Plains farmers quickly abandoned the illusion of frontier independence and easy wealth.

Unpredictable rainfall and weather conditions further exacerbated homesteaders' difficulties west of the hundredth meridian, where rainfall averaged less than twenty inches a year. Farmers compensated through "dry farming"—plowing deeply to stimulate the capillary action of the soils and harrowing lightly to raise a covering of dirt that would retain precious moisture after a rainfall. They also built windmills and diverted creeks for irrigation. But the onset of unusually dry years in the 1870s, together with grasshopper infestations and the major economic depression that struck the United States between 1873 and 1878 (see Chapter 16), made the plight of some midwesterners desperate.

Building a Society
and Achieving
Statehood

Despite the hardships, many remote farm settlements often blossomed into thriving communities. Churches and Sunday schools among the first institutions to appear became humming centers of social activity as well as of worship. Farmers gathered for barn raisings and group threshings, and families pooled their energies in quilting and husking bees. Neighbors readily lent a hand

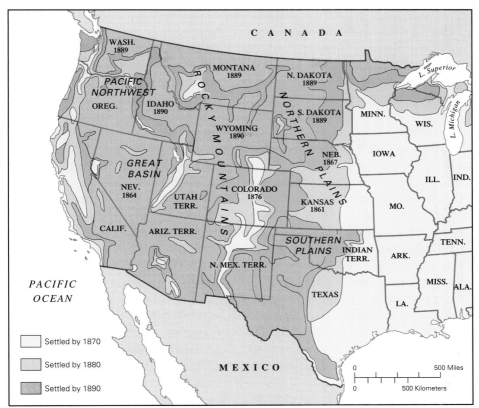

The Settlement of the Trans-Mississippi West, 1860–1890

The West was not settled by a movement of peoples gradually creeping westward from the East. Rather, settlers first occupied California and the Midwest and then filled up the nation's vast interior.

to the farmer whose barn had burned or whose family was sick. Cooperation was a practical necessity and a form of insurance in a rugged environment where everyone was vulnerable to instant misfortune or even disaster.

As settlements grew into small towns, their inhabitants labored to reverse easterners' images of rural life as unrefined and backward. They eagerly established lyceums and libraries to uplift local residents. Masonic lodges, temperance clubs, and a wide variety of social associations followed. Larger communities established fashionable hotels, the symbol of sophistication and culture, and brought in entertainers to perform at their new "opera houses."

When the population increased, local boosters lobbied to turn the territory into a state. Achieving statehood required the residents of the territory to petition Congress to pass an enabling act establishing the territory's boundaries and authorizing an election to select delegates for a state constitutional convention. Once the state constitution had been drawn up and ratified by popular vote, the territory applied to Congress for admission as a state.

Under these procedures, Kansas entered the Union in 1861, followed by Nevada in 1864 and Nebraska in 1867. Colorado joined in 1876. Not until 1889 did North Dakota, South Dakota, Montana, and Washington gain statehood. Wyoming and Idaho came into the Union the following year. Utah, long prevented from joining because of the Mormon practice of polygamy, finally declared plural marriages illegal and entered in 1896. With Oklahoma's admission in 1907 and Arizona's and New Mexico's in 1912, the process of creating permanent political institutions in the trans-Mississippi West was complete.

Although generally socially conservative, the new state governments supported woman suffrage. As territories became states, pioneer women, encouraged by women's rights activists like Susan B. Anthony and Elizabeth Cady Stanton, battled for the vote. Seven western states held referenda on this issue between 1870 and 1910. Success came first in the Wyoming Territory, where the tiny legislature enfranchised women in 1869 in the belief that the vote would give women equal political rights and would make them more effective moral caretakers on the rowdy frontier. The Utah Territory followed in 1870 and reaffirmed its support for woman suffrage when it became a state. Nebraska in 1867 and Colorado in 1876 permitted women to vote in school elections. Although these successes were significant, by 1910 only four states—Idaho, Wyoming, Utah, and Colorado—had granted women full voting rights. The very newness of their place in the Union may have sensitized legislators in these states to women's important contributions to settlement and made them open to experimentation, but by and large, familiar practices persisted.

THE SOUTHWESTERN FRONTIER

In 1848 the Treaty of Guadalupe Hildalgo that had ended the Mexican War ceded to the United States an immense territory, part of which became California, Arizona, and New Mexico. At the time, Mexicans had controlled vast expanses of the Southwest. They had built their own churches, maintained large ranching operations, and had traded with the Indians. Although the United States had pledged to protect the liberty and property of Mexicans who remained on American soil, in the next three decades, American ranchers and settlers took control of the territorial governments and forced the Spanish-speaking population off much of the land. Mexicans who stayed behind adapted to the new Anglo society with varying degrees of success.

In Texas the struggle for independence from Mexico had left a legacy of bitterness and misunderstanding. After 1848 Texas cotton planters confiscated Mexican lands and began a racist campaign to label Mexicans as nonwhite. Only white people, the Texans assumed, deserved economic and legal rights. Angered by their loss of land and discriminatory treatment, Mexican bandits retaliated by raiding American communities. Tensions peaked in 1859 when Juan Cortina, a Mexican rancher, attacked the Anglo border community of Brownsville, Texas, and freed all the prisoners in jail. Pursued by the U.S. army, Cortina battled the Americans for

Santa Fe Plaza, New Mexico, in the 1880s, by Francis X. Grosshenney
After the railroad went through in 1878, Santa Fe became a popular tourist attraction known for its historic adobe buildings. Although the town retained a large Spanish-speaking population with their own newspaper, by the 1880s American and German immigrants monopolized most positions in business, government, the professions, and the skilled trades.

years until the Mexican government, fearing a U.S. invasion, imprisoned him in 1875.

Mexican-Americans in California in the 1850s and 1860s faced similar exclusionary pressures. A cycle of flood and drought, together with a slumping cattle industry at midcentury, had ruined many of the large southern California ranches owned by the *Californios,* the Spanish-speaking descendants of the original Spanish settlers. The collapse of the ranch economy forced many of these Mexican-Americans to retreat into socially segregated urban neighborhoods called barrios. Spanish-surnamed citizens made up nearly half the 2,640 residents of Santa Barbara, California, in 1870; they comprised barely a quarter of the population ten years later. Maintaining a tenacious hold on their traditions, Spanish-speaking people in Santa Barbara and other towns survived by working as low-paid day laborers.

In California, the pattern of racial discrimination, manipulation, and exclusion was similar for Mexicans, Native Americans, and Chinese. As the number of Anglo newcomers increased, they identified minority racial, cultural, and language differences as marks of inferiority. White state legislators passed laws that made ownership of property difficult for non-Anglos. Relegated to a migratory labor force, non-Anglos were tagged as shiftless and irresponsible. Yet their labor made possible increased prosperity for the farmers, railroads, and households that hired them.

The cultural adaptation of Spanish-speaking Americans to Anglo society unfolded more smoothly in Arizona and New Mexico, where initial Spanish settlement had been sparse and a small class of wealthy Mexican landowners had long dominated a poor, illiterate peasantry. Moreover, beginning in the 1820s, well-to-do Mexicans in Tucson, Arizona, had educated their children in the United States and formed trading partnerships and business alliances with Americans. One of the most successful was Estevan Ochoa, who began a long-distance freighting business in 1859 with a U.S. partner and then expanded it into a lucrative merchandising, mining, and sheep-raising operation.

The success of hard-working businessmen such as Ochoa, who became mayor of Tucson, helped moderate American settlers' antagonistic attitudes toward the indigenous Mexican-American population. So, too, did the work of popular writers like Bret Harte and Helen Hunt Jackson. By sentimentalizing an older, gracious Spanish-Mexican past, these authors increased public sympathy for Spanish-speaking Americans. Jackson's 1884 romance *Romona,* a tale of doomed love set on a California Spanish-Mexican ranch overwhelmed by the onrushing tide of Anglo civilization, was enormously popular. Moreover, over time, Mexican and Spanish revival architecture, with its white adobe-style walls and red-clay tile roofs, which was associated with this romantic past, fused with Anglo building traditions to create a distinctive Southwest regional building style.

Even in Arizona and New Mexico, not all interactions between Mexican-Americans and Anglos were harmonious. In the 1880s, Mexican-American and Anglo ranchers became embroiled in fiery land disputes. Organizing themselves as Las Gorras Blancas (the White Caps) in 1888, Mexican-American ranchers tore up railroad tracks and intimidated and attacked both Anglo newcomers and those Hispanics who had fenced acreage in northern New Mexico previously considered public grazing land. But this vigilante action gained them little, as Anglo-dominated corporate ranching steadily reduced their resources. Relations changed in the urban centers as well, as Mexican-American businessmen increasingly restricted their business dealings to their own people, and the Spanish-speaking population as a whole became more impoverished. Even in Tucson, where the Mexican-American elite enjoyed considerable economic and political success, 80 percent of the Mexican-Americans in the work force were laborers in 1880, taking jobs as butchers, barbers, cowboys, and railroad workers.

As increasing numbers of Mexican-American men lost title to their lands and were forced to search for seasonal migrant work, Mexican-American women took responsibility for holding families and communities together. Women managed the households when their husbands were away, and fostered group identification through their emphasis on traditional customs, kinship, and allegiance to the Catholic Church. They served as *madrinas,* or godmothers, for one another's children; tended garden plots; and traded food, soap, and produce with other women. This economy, invisible to those outside the village, stabilized the community in times of drought or persecution by Anglos.

Violence and discrimination against Spanish-speaking citizens of the Southwest escalated in the 1890s, a time of rising racism in the United States. Riots against Mexican-Americans broke out in the Texas communities of Beeville and Laredo in 1894 and 1899. Expressions of anti-Catholicism, as well as verbal attacks on Mexican-Americans as violent and lazy, increased among hostile Anglos. For Spanish-speaking citizens, the battle for fair treatment and cultural respect would continue into the twentieth century.

EXPLOITING THE WESTERN LANDSCAPE

The domination of Mexican-Americans and the removal of Native peoples opened the way for the transformation and exploitation of the natural environment in the trans-Mississippi West. White publicists, developers, and boosters had long promoted the region as a land of boundless opportunity. Between 1860 and 1900, a generation of Americans sought to strike it rich by joining the ranks of miners, ranchers, and farmers intent on making a fortune. Although the mining, ranching, and farming "bonanzas" promised unheard-of wealth, in reality they set in motion a boom-and-bust economy in which many people went bankrupt or barely survived and others were bought out by large-scale enterprises that have continued to dominate production until today. Of all the groups that surged into the nation's mid-continent in the late nineteenth century, none had to revise their expectations more radically than the speculators and adventurers thirsting for quick fortunes.

The Mining Frontier   In the half-century that began with the California gold rush in 1849, a series of mining booms swept from the Southwest northward into Canada and Alaska. Sensational discoveries in California's Sierra Nevada produced more than $81 million worth of gold bullion in 1852. The following year, Henry Comstock, an illiterate prospector, stumbled on the rich Comstock Lode along Nevada's Carson River. Months later, feverishly pursuing rumors of new strikes, prospectors swarmed into the Rocky Mountains and uncovered deep veins of gold and silver near present-day Denver. Over the next five decades, gold was discovered in Idaho, Montana, Wyoming, South Dakota, and, in 1896, the Canadian Klondike. Although the popular press clearly exaggerated reports of miners scooping up gold by the panful, by 1900 more than a billion dollars' worth of gold had been mined in California alone.

The early discoveries of "placer" gold, panned from streams, attracted a young male population thirsting for wealth and reinforced the myth of mining country as "a poor man's paradise." In contrast to the Great Plains, where ethnic groups recreated their own ethnic enclaves, western mining camps became ethnic melting pots. In the California census of 1860, more than thirty-three thousand Irish and thirty-four thousand Chinese had staked out early claims.

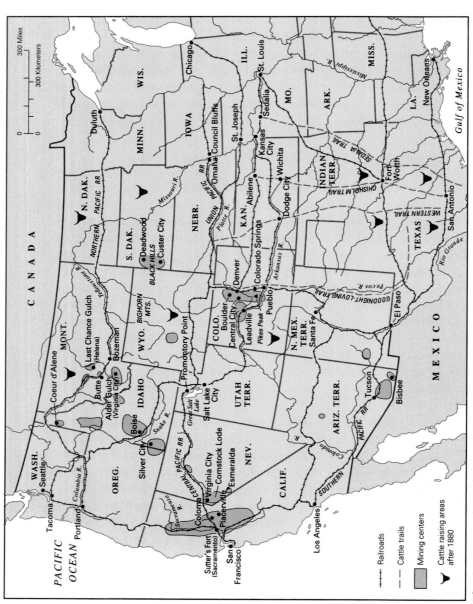

The Mining and Cattle Frontiers, 1860–1890

The western mining and ranching bonanzas lured thousands of Americans hoping to get rich quick.

Although a few prospectors became fabulously wealthy, the experience of Henry Comstock, who sold out one claim for eleven thousand dollars and another for two mules, was more typical. Because the larger gold and silver deposits lay embedded in veins of quartz deep within the earth, extracting them required huge investments in workers and expensive equipment. Deep shafts had to be blasted into the rock. Once lifted to the surface, the rock had to be crushed, flushed with mercury or cyanide to collect the silver, and smelted into ingots. No sooner had the major discoveries been made, therefore, than large mining companies backed by eastern or British capital bought them out and took them over.

Life in the new mining towns was vibrant but unpredictable. During the heyday of the Comstock Lode in the 1860s and 1870s, Virginia City, Nevada, erupted in an orgy of speculation and building. Started as a shantytown in 1859, it swelled by 1873 into a thriving metropolis of twenty thousand people complete with elaborate mansions, a six-story hotel, an opera house, 131 saloons, 4 banks, and uncounted brothels. Men outnumbered women three to one. Money quickly earned was even more rapidly lost.

The boom-and-bust cycle evident in Virginia City was repeated in towns across the west. Mark Twain captured the thrill of the mining "stampedes" in *Roughing It* (1872). "Every few days," wrote Twain, "news would come of the discovery of a brand-new mining region: immediately the papers would teem with accounts of its richness, and away the surplus population would scamper to take possession. By the time I was fairly inoculated with the disease, 'Esmeralda' had just had a run and 'Humboldt' was beginning to shriek for attention. 'Humboldt! Humboldt!' was the new cry, and straightway Humboldt, the newest of the new, the richest of the rich, the most marvelous of the marvelous discoveries in silverland, was occupying two columns of the public prints to 'Esmeralda's' one."

One unintended consequence of the gold rush mania was the growth of settlement in Alaska. Small strikes were made there in 1869, two years after the United States had purchased the territory from Russia. More miners arrived in the 1880s after prospector Joe Juneau, for whom the town of Juneau was named, and others developed the Treadwell Mine. But it was the discovery of gold in the Canadian Klondike in 1897 that brought thousands of prospectors into the area and eventually enabled Alaska to establish its own territorial government in 1912.

Word of new ore deposits like the ones in Alaska lured transient populations salivating to get rich. Miners who worked deep within the earth for large corporations typically earned about $2,000 a year at a time when teachers made $450 to $650 and domestic help $250 to $350. But most prospectors at best earned only enough to go elsewhere, perhaps buy some land, and try again. Nevertheless, the production of millions of ounces of gold and silver stimulated the economy, lured new foreign investors, and helped usher the United States into the mainstream of the world economy.

Progress came at a price. The long-term cost to the environment to extract these metals was high. Hydraulic mining, which used water cannons to dislodge minerals, polluted rivers, turned creeks brown, and flushed millions of tons of silt into valleys. The scarred landscape that remained was littered with rock and gravel filled with traces of mercury and cyanide, and nothing would grow on it. Smelters spewed dense smoke containing lead, arsenic, and other carcinogenic chemicals on those who lived nearby and often made them sick. The destruction to the environment is still evident today.

Cowboys and the Cattle Frontier   As Mark Twain so colorfully related, accounts of gold strikes in the popular press had helped fuel the feverish expansion of the mining frontier during the 1860s and 1870s. Similar stories romanticizing the life of the hardy cowboy, driving dusty herds of longhorns northward from Texas through Oklahoma to markets in Dodge City and Abilene, Kansas, sparked the transformation of the cattle industry in these same decades. In this case, astute businessmen and railroad entrepreneurs, eager to fund their new investments in miles of track, promoted cattle herding as the new route to fame and fortune, and the eastern press took up the theme. The cowboy, once scorned as a ne'er-do-well and drifter, was now glorified as a man of rough-hewn integrity and self-reliant strength.

In 1868 Joseph G. McCoy, a young cattle dealer from Springfield, Illinois, shrewdly combined organizational and promotional skills to turn the cattle industry into a new money-maker. With the relocation of the Plains Indians onto reservations and the extension of the railroads into Kansas in the post–Civil War period, McCoy realized that cattle dealers could now amass enormous fortunes by raising steers cheaply in Texas and bringing them north for shipment to eastern urban markets.

Forming a partnership with his brothers, McCoy built a new stockyard in Abilene, Kansas. By guaranteeing to transport his steers in railcars to hungry eastern markets, he obtained a five-dollar kickback from the railroads on each cattle car shipped. To make the overland cattle drives from Texas to Abilene easier, McCoy also helped survey and shorten the Chisholm Trail in Kansas. Finally, in a clever feat of showmanship, he organized the first Wild West show, sending four Texas cowboys to St. Louis and Chicago, where they staged roping and riding exhibitions that attracted exuberant crowds. At the end of his first year in business, thirty-five thousand steers were sold in Abilene; the following year the number more than doubled.

The great cattle drives of the 1860s and 1870s turned into a bonanza for herd owners. Steers purchased in Texas at nine dollars a head could be sold in Abilene, after deducting four dollars in trail expenses, for twenty-eight dollars. A herd of two thousand head could thus bring a tidy thirty-thousand-dollar profit. But the cattlemen, like the grain growers farther north on the Great Plains, lived at the mercy of high interest rates and an unstable market. During the financial panic of 1873, cattle drovers, unable to get extensions on their loans, fell into bankruptcy by the hundreds.

Little of the money made by the large-scale cattle ranchers found its way into the pockets of the cowboys themselves. The typical cowpunchers who drove herds through the dirt and dust from southern Texas to Abilene earned a mere thirty dollars a month, about the same as common laborers. They also braved the gangs of cattle thieves that operated along the trails. The most notorious of the cattle rustlers, William H. Bonney, better known as Billy the Kid, may have murdered as many as eleven men before he was killed by a sheriff in 1881 at the age of twenty-one. The long hours, low pay, and hazardous work discouraged older ranch hands from applying. Most cowboys were men in their teens and twenties who worked for a year or two and then pursued different livelihoods.

Of the estimated 35,000 to 55,000 men who rode the trails in these years, nearly one-fifth were black or Mexican. Barred by discrimination from many other trades, blacks enjoyed the freedom of life on the trail. Although they were excluded from the position of trail boss, they distinguished themselves as resourceful and shrewd cowpunchers. Nat Love, the son of Tennessee slaves, left for Kansas after the Civil War to work for Texas cattle companies. As chief brander, he moved through Texas and Arizona "dancing, drinking, and shooting up the town." By his own account, he was "wild, reckless, free," and "afraid of nothing." On July 4, 1876, when the Black Hills gold rush was in full swing, Love delivered three thousand head of cattle to a point near the hills and rode into Deadwood to celebrate. Local miners and gamblers had raised prize money for roping and shooting contests, and Nat Love won both, as well as a new title, Deadwood Dick.

Ned Huddleston, Alias Isom Dart *Outlaws and gunfighters, although small in number, created an image of the trans-Mississippi West as lawless and dangerous. Isom Dart, a member of Brown's Park outlaw faction in Colorado and Wyoming, here poses with his six-shooters.*

Close relationships sometimes developed between black and white cowboys. Shortly before Charles Goodnight, a white pioneer trailblazer, died in 1929, he recalled of the black cowboy Bose Ikard, a former slave, that "he was my detective, banker, and everything else in Colorado, New Mexico, and the other wild country I was in. The nearest and only bank was at Denver, and when we carried money I gave it to Bose." Goodnight revealed much about the economic situation of blacks on the Plains, however, when he added that "a thief would never think of robbing him [Ikard]—never think of looking in a Negro's bed for money."

Although the typical cowboy led a lonely, dirty, and often boring existence, a mythic version of the frontier cowboy who might with equal ease become a gun-slinging marshal or a dastardly villain was glamorized in the eastern press as early as the 1870s. The image of the West as a wild and lawless land fired easterners' imaginations. In 1877 Edward L. Wheeler, a writer for the publishing house of Beadle and Adams, penned his first dime novel, *Deadwood Dick, The Prince of the Road: or, the Black Rider of the Black Hills*. Over the next eight years, Wheeler turned out thirty-three Deadwood Dick novels relating the adventures of the muscular young hero who wore black clothes and rode a black horse. Cast alternately as outlaw, miner, gang leader, and cowboy, Deadwood Dick turned his blazing six-shooters on ruthless ruffians and dishonest desperadoes. He had much in common with the real-life Deadwood Dick except that Wheeler, to please his white readership, made him a white man.

The reality was a good deal less picturesque. Although Abilene, for example, went through an early period of violence that saw cowboys pulling down the walls of the jail as it was being built, the town quickly established a police force to maintain law and order. City ordinances forbade carrying firearms and regulated saloons, gambling, and prostitution. James B. ("Wild Bill") Hickok served as town marshal in 1871, but his tenure was less eventful than legend had it. Dime novelists described him as "a veritable terror to bad men on the border," but during his term as Abilene's lawman, Hickok killed just two men, one of them by mistake. Transient, unruly types certainly gave a distinctive flavor to cattle towns like Abilene, Wichita, and Dodge City, but the overall homicide rates there were not unusually high.

More typical of western conflicts were the range wars that pitted "cattle kings" (who thought that the open range existed for them alone to exploit) against farmers. Gaining the upper hand in state legislatures, farming interests sought to cripple the freewheeling cattlemen with quarantine laws and inspection regulations. Ranchers retaliated against the spread of barbed-wire farm fencing, first by cutting the settlers' fences and then by buying up and enclosing thousands of acres of their own. Meanwhile, dozens of small-scale shooting incidents broke out between inhabitants of isolated farms and livestock drovers, as well as between rival cattlemen and sheep ranchers.

Despite these range wars, the cattle bonanza, which peaked between 1880 and 1885, produced more than 4.5 million head of cattle for eastern markets. Prices began to sag as early as 1882, however, and many ranchers, having expanded too rapidly, plunged heavily into debt. When President Grover Cleveland, trying to improve federal observance of Indian treaties, ordered cattlemen to remove their stock from the Cheyenne-Arapaho reservation in 1885, two hundred thousand more cattle were crowded onto already overgrazed ranges. That same year and the following, two of the coldest and snowiest winters on record combined with summer droughts and Texas fever destroyed nearly 90 percent of the cattle in some regions, pushing thousands of ranchers into bankruptcy. The cattle industry lived on, but railroad expansion, which enabled ranchers to ship their steers north, brought the days of the open range and the great cattle drives to an end. As had the mining frontier, the cattle frontier left behind memories of individual daring, towering fortunes for some, and hard times for many.

Bonanza Farms The enthusiasm that permeated mining and ranching in the 1870s and 1880s also percolated into agriculture. Like the gold rushes and cattle bonanzas, the wheat boom in the Dakota Territory started small but rapidly attracted large capital investments that produced the nation's first agribusinesses.

The boom began during the Panic of 1873, when the failure of numerous banks caused the price of Northern Pacific Railroad bonds to plummet. The railroad responded by exchanging land for its depreciated bonds. Speculators, including the railroad's own president, George W. Cass, jumped at the opportunity and purchased more than three hundred thousand acres in the fertile Red River valley of North Dakota for between fifty cents and a dollar an acre.

Operating singly or in groups, the speculators established factorylike ten-thousand-acre farms, each run by a hired manager, and invested heavily in labor and equipment. On the Cass-Cheney-Dalrymple farm near Fargo, North Dakota, which covered an area six miles long by four miles wide, fifty or sixty plows rumbled across the flat landscape on a typical spring day. The New York *Tribune* reported that Cass, who had invested fifty thousand dollars for land and equipment, paid all his expenses plus the cost of the ten thousand acres with his first harvest alone.

The publicity generated by the tremendous success of a few large investors like Cass and Oliver Dalrymple led to an unprecedented wheat boom in the Red River valley in 1880. Eastern banking syndicates and small farmers alike rushed to buy land. North Dakota's population tripled in the 1880s. Wheat production skyrocketed to almost 29 million bushels by the end of the decade. But the profits so loudly celebrated in the eastern press soon evaporated. By 1890 some Red River valley farmers were destitute.

The wheat boom collapsed for a variety of reasons. Overproduction, high investment costs, too little or too much rain, excessive reliance on one crop, and depressed grain prices on the international market all undercut farmers' earnings. Large-scale farmers who had invested in hopes of getting rich felt lucky just to survive. Oliver Dalrymple lamented in 1889 that "it seems as if the time has come when there is no money in wheat raising."

Large-scale farms proved most successful in California's Central Valley. Using canals and other irrigation systems to water their crops, farmers were growing higher-priced specialty crops and had created new cooperative marketing associations for cherries, apricots, grapes, and oranges by the mid-1880s. Led by the California Citrus Growers' Association, which used the "Sunkist" trademark for their oranges, large-scale agribusinesses in California were shipping a variety of fruits and vegetables in refrigerated train cars to midwestern and eastern markets by 1900.

The Oklahoma Land Rush, 1889   As farmers in the Dakotas and Minnesota were enduring poor harvests and falling prices, hard-pressed would-be homesteaders greedily eyed the enormous Indian Territory, as present-day Oklahoma was then known. The federal government, considering much of the land in this area virtually worthless, had reserved it for the Five Civilized Tribes since the 1830s. Because these tribes (except for some Cherokees) had sided with the Confederacy during the Civil War, Washington had punished them by settling thousands of Indians from other tribes on lands in the western part of the territory. By the 1880s, land-hungry non-Indians argued that the Civilized Tribes' betrayal of the Union justified further confiscation of their land.

In 1889, over the Native Americans' protests, Congress transferred to the federally owned public domain nearly 2 million acres in the central part of the Oklahoma Territory that had not been specifically assigned to any Indian tribe. At noon on April 22, 1889, thousands of men, women, and children in buggies and wagons stampeded into the new lands to stake out homesteads. (Other settlers, the so-called Sooners, had illegally arrived earlier and were already plowing the fields.) Before nightfall tent communities had risen at Oklahoma City and Guthrie near stations on the Santa Fe Railroad. Nine weeks later, six thousand homestead claims had been filed. The next decade, the Dawes Severalty Act broke up the Indian reservations into individual allotments and opened the surplus to non-Indian settlement.

The Oklahoma land rush demonstrated the continuing power of the frontier myth, which tied "free" land to the ideal of economic opportunity. Despite early obstacles—the 1889 rush occurred too late in the season for most settlers to plant a full crop, and a drought parched the land the following year—Oklahoma farmers remained optimistic about their chances of making it on the last frontier. Most survived because they were fortunate enough to have obtained fertile land in an area where the normal rainfall was thirty inches, ten inches more than in the semi-arid regions farther west. Still, within two generations a combination of exploitative farming, poor land management, and sporadic drought would place Oklahoma at the desolate center of what in the 1930s would be called the dust bowl (see Chapter 24).

THE WEST OF LIFE AND LEGEND

In 1893, four years after the last major tract of western Indian land, the Oklahoma Territory, was opened to non-Indian settlement, a young Wisconsin historian, Frederick Jackson Turner, delivered a lecture entitled "The Significance of the Frontier in American History." "[T]he frontier has gone," declared Turner, "and with its going has closed the first period of American history." Although Turner's assertion that the frontier was closed was based on a Census Bureau announcement, it was inaccurate (more western land would be settled in the twentieth century than in the nineteenth). But his linking of economic opportunity with the transformation of the trans-Mississippi West caught the popular imagination and launched a new school of historical inquiry into the effects of the frontier on U.S. history.

Scholars now recognize that many parts of Turner's "frontier thesis," particularly its ethnocentric omission of Native Americans' claims to the land, were inaccurate. Yet his idealized view of the West did reflect ideas popular among his contemporaries in the 1890s. As farmers, miners, ranchers, Indian agents, and prostitutes had pursued their varied activities in the real West, a parallel legendary West had taken deep root in the American imagination. In the nineteenth century, this mythic West was a product of novels, songs, and paintings. In the twentieth century, it would be perpetuated by movies, radio programs, and television shows. The legend merits attention, for its evolution is fascinating and its influence has been far-reaching.

The American Adam and the Dime-Novel Hero

In the early biographies of frontiersmen like Daniel Boone and in the wilderness novels of James Fenimore Cooper, the western hero's personal development sometimes parallels, but more often runs counter to, the interests of society. Mid-nineteenth-century writers, extending the theme of the western wilderness as an alternative to society, presented the frontiersman as a kind of mythic American Adam—simple, virtuous, and innocent, untainted by a corrupt social order. For example, an early biographer of Kit Carson, the Kentucky-born guide who made one of the first recorded crossings of California's Mojave Desert in 1830, depicted him as a perfect antidote to the evils of refined society, an individual of "genuine simplicity, . . . truthfulness . . . [and] bravery." At the end of Mark Twain's *Huckleberry Finn*, Huck rejects the constraints of settled society as represented by Aunt Sally and heads west with the declaration, "I reckon I got to light out for the territory ahead of the rest, because Aunt Sally she's going to adopt me and sivilize me, and I can't stand it. I been there before." In this version of the legend, the West is a place of adventure, romance, or contemplation where one can escape from society and its pressures.

But even as this conception of the myth was being popularized, another powerful theme had emerged as well. The authors of the dime novels of the 1860s and

1870s offered the image of the western frontiersman as a new masculine ideal, the tough guy who fights for truth and honor. In *Buffalo Bill: King of the Border Men* (1869), a dime novel loosely based on real-life William F. ("Buffalo Bill") Cody, Edward Judson (who published under the name Ned Buntline) created an idealized hero who is a powerful moral force as he drives off treacherous Indians and rounds up villainous cattle rustlers.

So enthusiastically did the public welcome this new fictional frontiersman that Cody was inspired in 1883 to start his Wild West show. A former army scout and buffalo hunter, Cody was a natural showman, and his exhibitions proved immensely popular. Cody presented mock battles between army scouts and Indians that were, in effect, morality dramas of good versus evil. Along with entertainment, in short, the Wild West show reinforced the dime-novel image of the West as an arena of moral encounter where virtue always triumphed.

Revitalizing the Frontier Legend   Eastern writers and artists eagerly embraced both versions of the myth—the West as a place of escape from society and the West as a stage on which the moral conflicts confronting society were played out. Three young members of the eastern establishment, Theodore Roosevelt, Frederic Remington, and Owen Wister, spent much time in the West in the 1880s, and each was intensely affected by the adventure.

Each man found precisely what he was looking for in the West. The frontier that Roosevelt glorified in such books as *The Winning of the West* (four volumes, 1889–1896), and that Remington portrayed in his work, was a stark physical and moral environment that stripped away all social artifice and tested each individual's character. Drawing on a popular version of English scientist Charles Darwin's evolutionary theory, which characterized life as a struggle in which only the fittest survived, Roosevelt and Remington exalted the disappearing frontier as the proving ground for a new kind of virile manhood and the last outpost of an honest and true social order.

This version of the frontier myth reached its apogee in Owen Wister's enormously popular novel *The Virginian* (1902), later reincarnated as a 1929 Gary Cooper movie and a 1960s television series. In Wister's tale, the elemental physical and social environment of the Great Plains produces individuals like his unnamed cowboy hero, "the Virginian," an honest, strong, and compassionate man, quick to help the weak and fight the wicked. The Virginian is one of nature's aristocrats—ill-educated and unsophisticated but tough, steady, and deeply moral. The Virginian sums up his own moral code in describing his view of God's justice: "He plays a square game with us." For Wister, as for Roosevelt and Remington, the cowboy was the Christian knight on the Plains, indifferent to material gain as he upheld virtue, pursued justice, and attacked evil.

Needless to say, the western myth was far removed from the reality of the West. Critics delighted in pointing out that not one scene in *The Virginian* showed the hard physical labor of the cattle range. The idealized version of the West also glossed over the darker underside of frontier expansion—the brutalities of Indian warfare, the forced removal of the Indians to reservations, the racist discrimination against Mexican-Americans and blacks, the risks and perils of commercial agriculture and cattle growing, and the boom-and-bust mentality rooted in the selfish exploitation of natural resources.

Further, the myth obscured the complex links between the settlement of the frontier and the emergence of the United States as a major industrialized nation increasingly tied to a global economy. Eastern and foreign capitalists controlled large-scale mining, cattle, and agricultural operations in the West. The technical know-how of industrial America underlay the marvels of western agricultural productivity. Without the railroad, that quintessential symbol of the new industrial order, the transformation of the West would have been far slower.

Beginning a Conservation Movement   Despite its one-sided and idealized vision, Owen Wister's celebration of the western experience reinforced a growing recognition that many unique features of the western landscape were being threatened by overeager entrepreneurs. One important by-product of the western legend was a surge of public support for creating national parks and the beginning of an organized conservation movement.

Those who went west in the 1860s and 1870s to map the rugged terrain of the High Plains and the Rocky Mountains were often awed by the natural beauty of the landscape. Major John Wesley Powell, the one-armed veteran of the Civil War who charted the Colorado River through the Grand Canyon in 1869, waxed euphoric about its towering rock formations and powerful cataracts. "A beautiful view is presented. The river turns sharply to the east, and seems enclosed by a wall, set with a million brilliant gems. . . . On coming nearer, we find fountains bursting from the rock, high overhead, and the spray in the sunshine forms the gems which bedeck the way."

In his important study, *Report on the Lands of the Arid Regions of the United States* (1878), Powell argued that settlers needed to change their pattern of settlement and readjust their expectations about the use of water in the dry terrain west of the hundredth meridian. Recognizing that incoming farmers had often mistakenly believed that rain would miraculously follow the plow, Powell called for public ownership and governmental control of watersheds, irrigation, and public lands, a request that went largely unheeded.

Around the time Powell was educating Congress about the arid nature of the far West, a group of adventurers led by General Henry D. Washburn visited the hot springs and geysers near the Yellowstone River in northwestern Wyoming and eastern Montana. They were stunned by what they saw. "You can stand in the valley of the Yosemite [the California park land protected by Congress in 1864]," wrote one of the party, "and look up its mile of vertical granite, and distinctly recall its minutest feature; but amid the canyon and falls, the boiling springs and sulphur mountain, and, above all, the mud volcano and the geysers of the Yellowstone, your memory becomes filled and clogged with objects new in experience, wonderful in extent, and possessing unlimited grandeur and beauty." Overwhelmed by the view, the Washburn explorers abandoned their plan to claim the area for the Northern Pacific Railroad and instead petitioned Congress to protect it from settlement, occupancy, and sale. Congress responded in 1872 by creating Yellowstone National Park to "provide for the preservation . . . for all time, [of] mineral deposits, natural curiosities, or wonders within said park . . . in their natural condition." In doing so, they excluded the Native Americans who had long considered the area a prime hunting range.

These first steps to conserve a few of the West's unique natural sites reflected the beginning of a changed awareness of the environment. In his influential study *Man and Nature* in 1864, George Perkins Marsh, an architect and politician from Vermont, had attacked the view that nature existed to be tamed and conquered. Cautioning Americans to curb their destructive use of the landscape, he warned the public to change its ways. "Man," he wrote, "is everywhere a disturbing agent. Wherever he plants his foot, the harmonies of nature are turned to discords."

Marsh's plea for conservation found its most eloquent support in the work of John Muir, a Scottish immigrant who had grown up in Wisconsin. Temporarily blinded by an accident, Muir left for San Francisco in 1869 and quickly fell in love with the redwood forests. For the next forty years he tramped the rugged mountains of the West and campaigned for their preservation. A romantic at heart, he struggled to experience the wilderness at its most elemental level. Once trekking high in the Rockies during a summer storm, he climbed the tallest pine he could find and swayed back and forth in the raging wind.

Muir became the late nineteenth century's most articulate publicist for wilderness protection. "Climb the mountains and get their good tidings," he advised city dwellers. "Nature's peace will flow into you as the sunshine into the trees. The winds will blow their freshness into you, and the storms their energy, while cares will drop off like autumn leaves." Muir's spirited campaign to protect the wilderness contributed strongly to the establishment of Yosemite National Park in 1890. Two years later, the Sierra Club, an organization created to encourage the enjoyment and protection of the wilderness in the mountain regions of the Pacific Coast, made Muir its first president.

The precedent established by the creation of Yellowstone National Park remained ambiguous well into the twentieth century. Other parks that preserved the high rugged landforms of the West were often chosen because Congress viewed the sites as worthless for other purposes. Awareness of the need for biological conservation would not emerge until later in the twentieth century (see Chapter 21).

Ironically, despite the crusades of Muir, Powell, and Marsh to educate the public about conservation, the campaign for wilderness preservation reaffirmed the image of the West as a unique region whose magnificent landscape produced tough individuals of superior ability. Overlooking the senseless violence and ruthless exploitation of the land, contemporary writers, historians, and publicists proclaimed that the settlement of the final frontier marked a new stage in the history of civilization, and they kept alive the legend of the western frontier as a seedbed of American virtues.

IMPORTANT EVENTS, 1860–1900

1858	Henry Comstock strikes gold on the Carson River in Nevada. Gold discovered at Clear Creek, Colorado.
1862	Homestead Act. Pacific Railroad Act.
1864	Nevada admitted to the Union. Massacre of Cheyennes at Sand Creek, Colorado. George Perkins Marsh, *Man and Nature*.
1867	Joseph McCoy organizes cattle drives to Abilene, Kansas. New Indian policy of smaller reservations adopted. Medicine Lodge Treaty. The purchase of Alaska.
1868	Fort Laramie Treaty.
1869	Board of Indian Commissioners established to reform Indian reservation life. Wyoming gives women the vote.
1872	Mark Twain, *Roughing It*. Yellowstone National Park established.
1873	Panic allows speculators to purchase thousands of acres in the Red River valley of North Dakota cheaply. Timber Culture Act. Biggest strike on Nevada's Comstock Lode.
1874	Invention of barbed wire. Gold discovered in the Black Hills of South Dakota. Red River War pits the Kiowas, Comanches, and Cheyennes against the United States Army.
1875	John Wesley Powell, *The Exploration of the Colorado River*.
1876	Colorado admitted to the Union, gives women the right to vote in school elections. Massacre of Colonel George Armstrong Custer and his troops at Little Bighorn.
1877	*Munn* v. *Illinois*. Desert Land Act.
1878	Timber and Stone Act. John Wesley Powell, *Report on the Lands of the Arid Regions of the United States*.
1879	Massacre of northern Cheyennes at Fort Robinson, Nebraska.
1881	Helen Hunt Jackson, *A Century of Dishonor*.
1883	William ("Buffalo Bill") Cody organizes Wild West show.
1886	Severe drought on the Plains destroys cattle and grain. *Wabash* v. *Illinois*.
1887	Dawes Severalty Act.
1888	Las Gorras Blancas (the White Caps) raid ranchers in northern New Mexico.

1889	Oklahoma Territory opened for settlement.
1889–1896	Theodore Roosevelt, *The Winning of the West*.
1890	Ghost Dance movement spreads to the Black Hills. Massacre of Teton Sioux at Wounded Knee, South Dakota. Yosemite National Park established.
1892	John Muir organizes the Sierra Club.
1893	Frederick Jackson Turner, "The Significance of the Frontier in American History."

18

The Rise of Industrial America, 1865–1900

On October 21, 1892, before a crowd of more than two hundred thousand onlookers, presidential candidate Grover Cleveland proudly opened the World's Columbian Exposition in Chicago. Grasping a small electric key connected to a two-thousand-horsepower engine, he proclaimed, "As by a touch the machinery that gives life to this vast Exposition is now set in motion, so in the same instant let our hopes and aspirations awaken forces which in all time to come shall influence the welfare, the dignity, and the freedom of mankind." A moment later, electric fountains shot streams of water high into the air, officially marking the exposition's start.

The Chicago world's fair represented the triumph of fifty years of industrial development. The country's largest corporations displayed their newest products: Westinghouse Company's dynamos mysteriously lit a tower of incandescent light bulbs; American Bell Telephone offered the first long-distance telephone calls to the East Coast; and inventor Thomas A. Edison exhibited his latest phonograph. The fair dazzled its more than 25 million visitors. But Isabelle Garland, mother of writer Hamlin Garland, who visited the fair from a small midwestern farm community, was simply stunned. "[M]y mother sat in her chair, visioning it all yet comprehending little of its meaning," Garland later observed. "Her life had been spent among homely small things, and these gorgeous scenes dazzled her, . . . letting in upon her in one mighty flood a thousand stupefying suggestions of art and history and poetry of the world. . . . At last utterly overcome, she leaned her head against my arm, closed her eyes and said, 'Take me home, I can't stand any more of it.'"

Isabelle Garland's emotional reaction captured the ambivalence of many late-nineteenth-century Americans who found themselves both unsettled and exhilarated as the nation was transformed by industrialization. At midcentury, the United States had played a minor role in world economy. Five decades later, innovations in management, technology, production, and transportation had expanded manufacturing output fivefold. The United States now produced 35 percent of the world's manufactured goods—more than England, Germany, and France combined. It had become the world's greatest industrial power.

Although the hallmark of this prodigious growth had been the rise of giant corporations that brought mass production and national distribution of oil, steel, and a variety of other products, important though less visible strides forward were made in numerous other areas of the economy. In countless small industries, new technologies were developed, manufacturing output soared, and innovative advertising and marketing techniques were created. By 1900 new enterprises both large and small, supported by investment bankers and using a nationwide railroad distribution system, offered a dazzling array of goods for national and international markets.

This stunning industrial growth came at a high cost to all involved. New manufacturing processes transformed the nature of work, undercutting skilled labor and creating mind-numbing assembly-line routines. Large-scale manufacturing companies often polluted their immediate environment, spewing noxious smoke into the air and dumping toxic waste into nearby streams and rivers. The challenges of new business practices made the American economy difficult to control. Rather than smoothly rolling forward, it lurched between booms and busts in business cycles that produced labor unrest and crippling depressions in 1873–1879 and 1893–1897.

This chapter will focus on five major questions:

What innovations in technology and business practices helped launch vast increases in industrial production in the post–Civil War period?

How were Andrew Carnegie, John D. Rockefeller, and other corporate leaders able to dominate their rivals and consolidate control over their industries?

Why did the South's experience with industrialization differ from that of the North and the Midwest?

How did workers respond to the changing nature of work and the growth of national corporations?

In the clash between industry and labor, what tactics enabled corporate executives in the 1890s to undercut labor's bargaining power?

THE RISE OF CORPORATE AMERICA

In the early nineteenth century, the corporate form of business organization had been used to raise large amounts of start-up capital for transportation enterprises such as turnpikes and canals. By selling stocks and bonds to raise money, the corporation separated the company's managers, who guided its day-to-day operation, from the owners—those who had purchased the stocks and bonds as investments. After the Civil War, American business leaders pioneered new forms of corporate organization that combined innovative technologies, creative management structures, and limited liability should the enterprise fail. The rise of corporate America in this period is a story of risk-taking and innovation as well as of rapacity and ruthlessness.

The Character of Industrial Change   Six features dominated the world of large-scale manufacturing after the Civil War: first, the exploitation of immense coal deposits as a source of cheap energy; second, the rapid spread of technological innovation in transportation, communication, and factory systems; third, the need for enormous numbers of new workers who could be carefully controlled; fourth, the constant pressure on firms to compete tooth-and-nail by cutting costs and prices, as well as the impulse to eliminate rivals and create monopolies; fifth, the relentless drop in price levels (a stark contrast to the inflation of other eras); and finally, the failure of the money supply to keep pace with productivity, a development that drove up interest rates and restricted the availability of credit.

All six factors were closely related. The great coal deposits in Pennsylvania, West Virginia, and Kentucky provided the cheap energy that fueled the railroads, the factories, and explosive urban growth. Exploiting these inexpensive energy sources, new technologies stimulated productivity and catalyzed breathtaking industrial expansion. Technology also enabled manufacturers to cut costs and hire cheap unskilled or semiskilled labor. This cost cutting enabled firms to undersell one another, destroying weaker competitors and prompting stronger, more efficient, and more ruthless firms to consolidate. At least until the mid-1890s, cost reduction, new technology, and fierce competition forced down overall price levels.

But almost everyone suffered terribly during the depression years, when the government debated whether it should get involved but did nothing to relieve distress. "The sufferings of the working classes are daily increasing," wrote a Philadelphia worker in 1874. "Famine has broken into the home of many of us, and is at the door of all." Above all, business leaders' unflagging drive to maximize efficiency both created colossal fortunes at the top of the economic ladder and forced millions of wage earners to live near the subsistence level.

Out of the new industrial system poured dismal clouds of haze and soot, as well as the first tantalizing trickle of what would become an avalanche of consumer goods. In turn, mounting demands for consumer goods stimulated heavy industry's production of capital goods—machines to boost farm and factory output even further. Together with the railroads, the corporations that manufactured capital goods, refined petroleum, and made steel became driving forces in the nation's economic growth.

Railroad Innovations   Competition among the aggressive and innovative capitalists who headed American heavy industry was intense. As the post–Civil War era opened, nowhere was it more intense than among the nation's railroads, which to many Americans most symbolized industrial progress. By 1900, 193,000 miles of railroad track crisscrossed the United States—more than in all of Europe including Russia. These rail lines connected every state in the Union and opened up an immense new internal market. Most important, railroad companies pioneered crucial aspects of large-scale

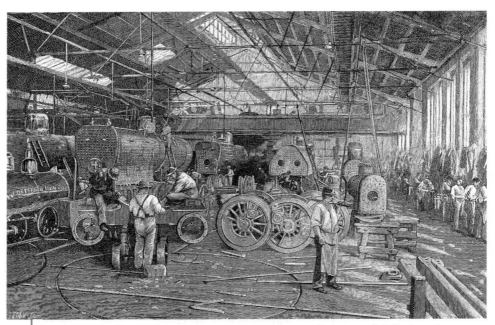

In the shop of the Baldwin Locomotive Works, small teams of skilled workers custom built each engine to the specifications of the purchaser.

corporate enterprise. These included the issuance of stock to meet their huge capital needs, the separation of ownership from management, the creation of national distribution and marketing systems, and the formation of new organizational and management structures.

Railroad entrepreneurs such as Collis P. Huntington of the Central Pacific Railroad, Jay Gould of the Union Pacific, and James J. Hill of the Northern Pacific faced enormous financial and organizational problems. To raise the staggering sums necessary for laying track, building engines, and buying out competitors, railroads at first appealed for generous land and loan subsidies from federal, state, and local governments (see Chapter 17). Even so, the larger lines had to borrow heavily by selling stocks and bonds to the public. Bond holders earned a fixed rate of interest; stockholders received dividends only when the company earned a profit. By 1900 the yearly interest repayments required by the combined debt of all U.S. railroads (which stood at an astounding $5.1 billion—nearly five times that of the federal government) cut heavily into their earnings.

In addition to developing ways to raise large amounts of capital, the railroads created new systems for collecting and using information. To coordinate the complex flow of cars across the country, railroads relied heavily on the magnetic telegraph, invented in 1837. To improve efficiency, the railroads set up clearly defined, hierarchical organizational structures and divided their lines into separate geographic units, each with its own superintendent. Elaborate accounting systems documented the cost of every operation for each division, from coal consumption to the repair of engines and cars. Using these reports, railroad officials could set rates and accurately predict profits as early as the 1860s, a time when most businesses had no idea of their total profit until they closed their books at year's end. Railroad management innovations thus became a model for many other businesses seeking a national market.

Consolidating the Railroad Industry The expansion and consolidation of railroading reflected both the ingenuity and the dishonesty flourishing on the corporate management scene. Although by the 1870s railroads had replaced the patchwork of canal and stagecoach operations that dominated domestic transportation before the Civil War, the industry itself was in a state of chaos. Hundreds of small companies used widely different standards for car couplers, rails, track width, and engine size. Financed by large eastern and British banks, Huntington, Gould, and others devoured these smaller lines to create large, integrated track networks. In the Northeast four major trunk lines were completed. West of the Mississippi five great lines—the Union Pacific (1869); the Northern Pacific (1883); the Atchison, Topeka, and Santa Fe (1883); the Southern Pacific (1883); and the Great Northern (1893)—controlled most of the track by 1893.

Huntington, Gould, and the other larger-than-life figures who reorganized and expanded the railroad industry in the 1870s and 1880s were often depicted by their contemporaries as villains and robber barons who manipulated stock markets and company policies to line their own pockets. For example, newspaper publisher Joseph Pulitzer called Jay Gould, the short, secretive president of the Union Pacific, "one of the most sinister figures that have ever flitted batlike across the vision of the American people." Recent historians, however, have pointed out that the great industrialists were a diverse group. Although some were ironfisted pirates who engaged in fraudulent practices, others were upstanding businessmen who managed their companies with sophistication and innovation. Indeed, some of their ideas were startling in their originality and inventiveness.

The massive trunk systems created by these entrepreneurs became the largest business enterprises in the world, towering over state and federal governments in the size and scale of their operations. As they consolidated a hodgepodge of small railroads into a few interlocking systems, these masterminds pioneered the most advanced methods of accounting and large-scale organization. They also standardized all basic equipment and facilities, from engines and cars to automatic couplers, air brakes, signal systems, and outhouses (now provided in standard one-, two-, and three-hole sizes). In 1883, independently of the federal government, the railroads corrected scheduling problems by dividing the country into four time zones. In May 1886 all railroads shifted simultaneously to the new standard 4'8 1/2"-gauge track. Finally, cooperative billing arrangements enabled the railroads to ship cars from other roads, including dining and sleeping cars owned by the Pullman Palace Car Company, at uniform rates nationwide.

But the systemization and consolidation of the railroads had its costs. Heavy indebtedness, overextended systems, and crooked business practices forced the railroads to compete recklessly with each other for traffic. They cut rates for large shippers, offered special arrangements for handling bulk goods, showered free passes on politicians who supported their operations, and granted substantial rebates and kickbacks to favored clients. None of these tactics, however, shored up the railroads' precarious financial position. And the continuous push to expand drove some overbuilt lines into bankruptcy.

Caught in the middle of the railroads' tug-of-war and stung by exorbitant rates and secret kickbacks, farmers and small business owners turned to state governments for help. In the 1870s many midwestern state legislatures responded by outlawing rate discrimination. Initially upheld by the Supreme Court, these and other decisions were negated in the 1880s when the Court ruled that states could not regulate interstate commerce. In response in 1887, Congress, persuaded by Illinois Senator Shelby M. Cullom's detailed study of devious railroad practices, passed the Interstate Commerce Act. A five-member Interstate Commerce Commission (ICC) was established to oversee the practices of interstate railroads. The law banned monopolistic activity like pooling, rebates, and discriminatory short-distance rates.

The railroads challenged the commission's rulings in the federal courts. Of the sixteen cases brought to the Supreme Court before 1905, the justices found in favor of the railroads in all but one, essentially nullifying the ICC's regulatory clout. The Hepburn Act (see Chapter 21), passed in 1906, strengthened the ICC by finally empowering it to set rates.

The railroads' vicious competition did not abate until a national depression that began in 1893 forced a number of roads into the hands of J. Pierpont Morgan and other investment bankers. Morgan, a massively built man with piercing eyes and a commanding presence, took over the weakened systems, reorganized their administration, refinanced their debts, and built intersystem alliances. By 1906, thanks to the bankers' centralized management, seven giant networks controlled two-thirds of the nation's rail mileage.

Applying the Lessons of the Railroads to Steel   The close connections between railroad expansion, which absorbed millions of tons of steel for tracks, and the growth of corporate organization and management are well illustrated in the career of Andrew Carnegie. A diminutive dynamo of a man, only 5'3" tall, Carnegie was born in Scotland and immigrated to America in 1848 at the age of twelve, in the company of his father, a skilled hand-loom weaver who never found steady employment once the industry mechanized.

Ambitious and hard-working, Carnegie took a job at $1.20 a week as a bobbin boy in a Pittsburgh textile mill. Although he worked a sixty-hour week, the aspiring youngster also enrolled in a night course to learn bookkeeping. The following year, Carnegie became a Western Union messenger boy. Taking over when the telegraph operators wanted a break, he soon became the city's fastest telegraph operator.

Because he had to decode the messages for every major business in Pittsburgh, Carnegie gained an insider's view of their operations.

Carnegie's big break came in 1852 when Tom Scott, superintendent of the Pennsylvania Railroad's western division, hired him as his secretary and personal telegrapher. When Scott became vice president of the Pennsylvania Railroad seven years later, the twenty-four-year-old Carnegie took over as head of the line's western division. A daring innovator, Carnegie, in his six years as division chief, used the complex cost-analysis techniques developed by Scott to more than double the road's mileage and quadruple its traffic. He slashed commuter fares to keep ridership at capacity and developed various cost-cutting techniques. Having invested his earnings in the railroads, by 1868 Carnegie was earning more than $56,000 a year from his investments, a substantial fortune in that era.

In the early 1870s Carnegie decided to build his own steel mill. His connections within the railroad industry, the country's largest purchaser of steel, made this a logical choice. Starting with his first mill, he introduced a production technology named after its English inventor, Henry Bessemer, which shot a blast of air through an enormous crucible of molten iron to burn off carbon and impurities. Combining this new technology with the cost-analysis approach learned from his railroad experience, Carnegie became the first steelmaker to know the actual production cost of each ton of steel.

Carnegie's philosophy was deceptively simple: "Watch the costs, and the profits will take care of themselves." From the start he priced his rails below the competition. Then, through rigorous cost accounting and by limiting wage increases to his workers, he lowered his production costs even further. Moreover, he was not above asking for favors from his railroad-president friends or giving "commissions" to railroad purchasing agents.

As output climbed, Carnegie discovered the benefits of vertical integration—that is, controlling all aspects of manufacturing from extracting raw materials to selling the finished product. In Carnegie's case, this control embraced every stage from the mining and smelting of ore to the selling of steel rails. Carnegie Steel thus became the classic example of how sophisticated new technology might be combined with innovative management (and brutally low wages) to create a mass-production system that could slash consumer prices.

The management of daily operations by his close associates left Carnegie free to pursue philanthropic activities. While still in his early thirties, Carnegie resolved to donate his money to charitable projects. (He knew full well that such actions would buttress his popularity.) Carnegie set up foundations and eventually gave more than $300 million to libraries, universities, and international-peace causes.

By 1900 Carnegie Steel, employing twenty thousand people, had become the world's largest industrial corporation. Carnegie's competitors, worried about the wily Scot's domination of the market, decided to buy him out. In 1901 J. Pierpont Morgan, who controlled Federal Steel, asked Charles Schwab, Carnegie Steel's president, to inquire what Carnegie wanted for his share of Carnegie Steel. The next day Carnegie gave Schwab a penciled note asking for nearly half a billion dollars.

Iron and Steel Production, 1875–1915

New technologies, improved plant organization, economies of scale, and the vertical integration of production brought a dramatic spurt in iron and steel production.

Note: short ton = 2,000 pounds.

Source: Historical Statistics of the United States.

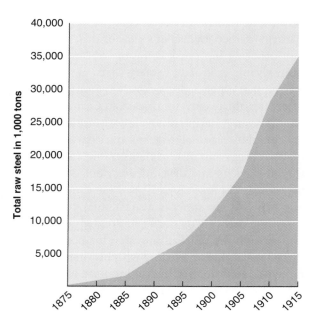

Morgan's response was simple: "Tell Carnegie I accept his price." Combining Carnegie's companies with Federal Steel, Morgan set up the United States Steel Corporation, the first business capitalized at more than $1 billion. The corporation, made up of two hundred member companies employing 168,000 people, marked a new scale in industrial enterprise.

Throughout his chain of corporate-world triumphs, Carnegie consistently portrayed his success as the result of self-discipline and hard work. The full story was more complex. Carnegie did not mention his uncanny ability to see the larger picture, his cleverness in hiring talented associates who would drive themselves (and the company's factory workers) mercilessly, his ingenuity in transferring organizational systems and cost-accounting methods from railroads to steel, and his callousness in keeping wages as low as possible. To a public unaware of corporate management techniques, however, Carnegie's success reaffirmed the openness of the American economic system. For the new immigrants flooding the nation's shores, Carnegie's career gave credence to the idea that anyone might rise from rags to riches.

The Trust: Creating New Forms of Corporate Organization

Between 1870 and 1900, the same fierce competition that had stimulated consolidation in the railroad and steel industries also swept the oil, salt, sugar, tobacco, and meatpacking industries. Like steel, these highly competitive businesses required large capital investments. Entrepreneurs in each industry therefore raced to reduce costs, lower prices, and drive their rivals out of the market. Chicago meatpackers Philip Armour and Gustavus Swift, for

Industrial Consolidation: Iron and Steel Firms, 1870 and 1900		
	1870	1900
No. of firms	808	669
No. of employees	78,000	272,000
Output (tons)	3,200,000	29,500,000
Capital invested	$121,000,000	$590,000,000

Source: Robert L. Heilbroner and Aaron Singer, The Economic Transformation of America: 1600 to Present, 2d ed. (San Diego: Harcourt Brace Jovanovich, 1984), 92.

example, raised the process of making bacon, pork chops, and steak from hogs and cattle to a high level of efficiency by using every part of the animal. Hides were tanned into leather, bones became fertilizer, and hooves were turned into gelatin. When lowering costs failed to drive out rivals, new organizational methods were pioneered to control competition and preserve market share.

The evolution of the oil industry illustrates the process by which new corporate structures evolved. After Edwin L. Drake drilled the first successful petroleum (or "crude-oil") well in 1859 near Titusville in northwestern Pennsylvania, competitors rushed into the business, sinking wells and erecting small refineries nearby. Petroleum was distilled into oil, which soon replaced animal tallow as the major lubricant, and into kerosene, which became the leading fuel for household and public lighting. By the 1870s the landscape near Pittsburgh and Cleveland, the sites of the first discoveries, was littered with rickety drilling rigs, assorted collection tanks, and ramshackle refineries. Oil spills were a constant problem. "So much oil is produced," reported one Pennsylvania newspaper in 1861, "that it is impossible to care for it, and thousands of barrels are running into the creek; the surface of the river is covered with oil for miles."

In this rush for riches, John D. Rockefeller, a young Cleveland merchant, gradually achieved dominance. Although he did not share Andrew Carnegie's outgoing personality, the solemn Rockefeller resembled the opportunistic steelmaker in other respects. Having gotten his start as a bookkeeper and opened his first refinery in 1863, Rockefeller, like Carnegie, had a passion for cost cutting and efficiency. When he became the head of the Standard Oil Company in 1873, he scrutinized every aspect of its operation. In one case he insisted that a manager find 750 missing barrel stoppers. He realized that in a mass-production enterprise, small changes could save thousands of dollars.

Rockefeller resembled Carnegie, too, in his ability to understand the inner workings of an entire industry and the benefits of vertical integration. The firm that controlled the shipment of oil between the well and the refinery and between the refinery and the retailers, he realized, could dominate the industry. In 1872 he purchased his own tanker cars and obtained not only a 10 percent rebate from the railroads for hauling his oil shipments but also a kickback on his competitors' shipments. When new pipeline technology became available, Rockefeller set up his own massive interregional pipeline network.

Like Carnegie, Rockefeller aggressively forced out his competitors. When local refineries rejected his offers to buy them out, he priced his products below cost and strangled their businesses. When rival firms teamed up against him, Rockefeller set up a pool—an agreement among several companies—that established production quotas and fixed prices. By 1879 Rockefeller had seized control of 90 percent of the country's oil-refining capacity.

Worried about competition, Rockefeller in 1882 decided to eliminate it by establishing a new form of corporate organization, the Standard Oil Trust. In place of the "pool" or verbal agreement among companies to control prices and markets, which lacked legal status, the trust created an umbrella corporation that ran them all. To implement his trust, Rockefeller and his associates persuaded the stockholders of forty companies to exchange their stock for trust certificates. Under this arrangement, stockholders retained their share of the trust's profits while enabling the trust to control production. Within three years the Standard Oil Trust had consolidated crude-oil buying throughout its member firms and slashed the number of refineries in half. In this way Rockefeller integrated the petroleum industry both vertically, by controlling every function from production to local retailing, and horizontally, by merging the competing oil companies into one giant system.

Taking a leaf from Rockefeller's book, companies in the copper, sugar, whiskey, lead, and other industries established their own trust arrangements. By limiting the number of competitors, the trusts created an oligopoly, the market condition that exists when the limited number of sellers can greatly influence price and other market factors. But their rapacious tactics, semimonopolistic control, and sky-high earnings provoked a public outcry. Beginning in New York State in 1879 and progressing to the federal level, legislative committees exposed the unscrupulous practices of the trusts, and both parties denounced them in the presidential election of 1888.

Fearful that the trusts would stamp out all competition, Congress, under the leadership of Senator John Sherman of Ohio, passed the Sherman Anti-Trust Act in 1890. The Sherman Act outlawed trusts and any other monopolies that fixed prices in restraint of trade and slapped violators with fines of up to five thousand dollars and a year in jail. But the act failed to define clearly either *trust* or *restraint of trade*. The government prosecuted only eighteen antitrust suits between 1890 and 1904. When Standard Oil's structure was challenged in 1892, its lawyers simply reorganized the trust as an enormous holding company. Unlike a trust, which literally owned other businesses, a holding company simply owned a controlling share of the stock of one or more firms. The new board of directors for Standard Oil (New Jersey), the new holding company, made more money than ever.

The Supreme Court further hamstrung congressional antitrust efforts by interpreting the Sherman Act in ways sympathetic to big business. In 1895, for example, the federal government brought suit against the sugar trust in *United States* v. *E. C. Knight Company*. It argued that the Knight firm, which controlled more than 90 percent of all U.S. sugar refining, operated in illegal restraint of trade. Asserting that manufacturing was not interstate commerce and ignoring the company's vast distribution network that enabled it to dominate the market, the Court threw out the suit. Thus vindicated, corporate mergers and consolidations surged ahead at the turn of the century. By 1900 these mammoth firms accounted for nearly two-fifths of the capital invested in the nation's manufacturing sector.

STIMULATING ECONOMIC GROWTH

Although large-scale corporate enterprise significantly increased the volume of manufactured goods in the late nineteenth century, it alone did not account for the colossal growth of the U.S. economy in this period. Other factors proved equally important, including new inventions, specialty production, and innovations in advertising and marketing. In fact, the resourcefulness of small enterprises, which combined innovative technology with new methods of advertising and merchandising, enabled many sectors of the economy to grow dramatically by adapting quickly to changing fashions and consumer preferences.

The Triumph of Technology   New inventions not only streamlined the manufacture of traditional products but also frequently stimulated consumer demand by creating entirely new product lines. The development of a safe, practical way to generate electricity, for example, made possible a vast number of electrical motors, household appliances, and lighting systems.

Many of the major inventions that stimulated industrial output and underlay mass production in these years were largely hidden from public view. Few Americans had heard of the Bessemer process for manufacturing steel or of the improved technologies that facilitated bottle making and glassmaking, canning, flour milling, match production, and petroleum refining. Fewer still knew much about the refrigerated railcars that enabled Gustavus Swift's company to slaughter beef in Chicago and ship it east or about the Bonsack cigarette-making machine that could roll 120,000 cigarettes a day, replacing sixty skilled handworkers.

The inventions that people did see were ones that changed the patterns of everyday life and encouraged consumer demand. Inventions like the sewing machine, mass-produced by the Singer Sewing Machine Company beginning in the 1860s; the telephone, developed by Alexander Graham Bell in 1876; and the light bulb, perfected by Thomas A. Edison in 1879 eased household drudgery and, in some cases, reshaped social interactions. With the advent of the sewing machine, many women were relieved of the tedium of sewing the family's apparel by hand; inexpensive mass-produced clothing thus led to a considerable expansion in personal wardrobes. The spread of telephones—by 1900 the Bell Telephone Company had installed almost eight hundred thousand in the United States—not only transformed communication but also undermined social conventions for polite behavior that had been premised on face-to-face or written exchanges. The light bulb, by further freeing people from dependence on daylight, made it possible to shop after work.

In the eyes of many, Thomas A. Edison epitomized the inventive impulse and the capacity for the creation of new consumer products. Born in 1847 in Milan, Ohio, Edison, like Andrew Carnegie, had little formal education and got his start in the telegraphic industry. Also like the shrewd Scot, Edison was a born salesman and self-promoter. When he modestly said that "genius is one percent inspiration and ninety-nine percent perspiration," he tacitly accepted the popular identification of himself as an inventing "wizard." Edison moreover shared Carnegie's vision of a large, interconnected industrial system resting on a foundation of technological innovation.

In his early work, Edison concentrated on the telegraph. His experimentation led to his first major invention, a stock-quotation printer, in 1868. The money earned from the patents on this machine enabled Edison to set up his first "invention factory" in Newark, New Jersey, a research facility that he moved to nearby Menlo Park in 1876. Assembling a staff that included university-trained scientists, Edison boastfully predicted "a minor invention every ten days, and a big one every six months."

Buoyed by the success and popularity of his invention in 1877 of a phonograph, or "sound writer" (*phono:* "sound"; *graph:* "writer"), Edison set out to develop a new filament for incandescent light bulbs. Characteristically, he announced his plans for an electricity-generation process before he perfected his inventions and then worked feverishly, testing hundreds of materials before he found a carbon filament that would glow dependably in a vacuum.

Edison realized that practical electrical lighting had to be part of a complete system containing generators, voltage regulators, electric meters, and insulated wiring and that the system needed to be easy to install and repair. It also had to be cheaper and more convenient than kerosene or natural gas lighting, its main competitors. In 1882, having built this system with the support of banker J. Pierpont Morgan, the Edison Illuminating Company opened a power plant in the heart of New York City's financial district, furnishing lighting for eighty-five buildings.

On the heels of Edison's achievement, other inventors rushed into the electrical field. Edison angrily sued many of his competitors for patent violations. Embittered by the legal battles that cost him more than $2 million, Edison relinquished control of his enterprises in the late 1880s. In 1892, with Morgan's help, Edison's company merged with a major competitor to form the General Electric Company (GE). Four years later, GE and Westinghouse agreed to exchange patents under a joint Board of Patent Control. Such corporate patent-pooling agreements became yet another mechanism of market domination.

In the following years, Edison and his researchers pumped out invention after invention, including the mimeograph machine, the microphone, the motion-picture camera and film, and the storage battery. By the time of his death in 1931, he had patented 1,093 inventions and amassed an estate worth more than $6 million. Yet

Edison's greatest achievement remained his laboratory at Menlo Park. A model for the industrial research labs later established by Kodak, General Electric, and Du Pont, Edison's laboratory demonstrated that the systematic use of science in support of industrial technology paid large dividends. Invention had become big business.

Custom-Made Products

Along with inventors, manufacturers of custom and specialized products such as machinery, jewelry, furniture, and women's clothes dramatically expanded economic output. Using skilled labor, these companies crafted one-of-a-kind or small batches of articles that ranged in size from large steam engines and machine tools to silverware, furniture, and custom-made dresses. Keenly attuned to innovations in technology and design, they constantly created new products tailored to the needs of individual buyers.

Although they were vastly different in terms of size and number of employees, Philadelphia's Baldwin Locomotive Works and small dressmaking shops were typical of flexible specialization displayed by small batch processors. Both faced sharp fluctuations in the demand for their products as well as the necessity of employing skilled workers to make small numbers of specialized items. Founded before the Civil War, by the 1890s the Baldwin Locomotive Works employed two thousand workers and produced about nine hundred engines a year. Each machine was custom designed to meet the needs of its purchaser. Construction was systematized through precision plans for every part of an engine, but standardization was not possible since no single engine could meet the needs of every railroad.

Until the turn of the twentieth century, when ready-to-wear clothes came to dominate the market, most women's apparel was custom produced in small shops run by women proprietors. Unlike the tenement sweatshops that produced men's shirts and pants, dressmakers and milliners (a term derived from fancy goods vendors in sixteenth- and seventeenth-century Milan, Italy) paid good wages to highly skilled seamstresses. The small size of the shops together with the skill of the workers enabled them to shift styles quickly to follow the latest fashions.

Thus, alongside of the increasingly rationalized and bureaucratic big businesses like steel and oil in the late nineteenth century, American productivity was also stimulated by custom and batch producers who provided a variety of goods that supplemented the bulk-manufactured staples of everyday life.

Advertising and Marketing

As small and large factories alike spewed out a dazzling array of new products, business leaders often discovered that their output exceeded what the market could absorb. This was particularly true in two kinds of businesses—those that manufactured devices for individual use such as sewing machines and farm implements, and those that mass-produced consumer goods such as matches, flour, soap, canned foods, and processed meats. Not surprisingly, these industries were trailblazers in developing advertising and marketing techniques. Strategies for whetting consumer demand and for differentiating one product from another represented a critical component of industrial expansion in the post–Civil War era.

The growth of the flour industry illustrates both the spread of mass production and the emergence of new marketing concepts. In the 1870s the nation's flour mills adopted the most advanced European manufacturing technologies and installed continuous-process machines that graded, cleaned, hulled, ground, and packaged the product in one rapid operation. These companies, however, soon produced more flour than they could sell. To unload this excess, the mills thought up new product lines such as cake flours and breakfast cereals and sold them using easy-to-remember brand names like Quaker Oats.

Through the use of brand names, trademarks, guarantees, slogans, endorsements, and other gimmicks, manufacturers built demand for their products and won enduring consumer loyalty. Americans bought Ivory Soap, first made in 1879 by Procter and Gamble of Cincinnati, because of the absurdly overprecise but impressive pledge that it was "99 and 44/100ths percent pure." James B. ("Buck") Duke's American Tobacco Company used trading cards, circulars, box-top premiums, prizes, testimonials, and scientific endorsements to convert Americans to cigarette smoking.

In the 1880s in the photographic field, George Eastman developed a paper-based photographic film as an alternative to the bulky, fragile glass plates then in use. Manufacturing a cheap camera for the masses, the Kodak, and devising a catchy slogan ("You press the button, we do the rest"), Eastman introduced a system whereby customers returned the one-hundred-exposure film and the camera to his Rochester factory. There, for a charge of ten dollars, the film was developed and printed, the camera reloaded, and everything shipped back. In marketing a new technology, Eastman had revolutionized an industry and democratized a visual medium previously confined to a few.

Economic Growth: Costs and Benefits By 1900 the chaos of early industrial competition, when thousands of companies had struggled to enter a national market, had given way to the most productive economy in the world, supported by a legion of small, specialized companies and dominated by a few enormous ones. An industrial transformation that had originated in railroading and expanded to steel and petroleum had spread to every nook and cranny of American business and raised the United States to a position of world leadership.

For those who fell by the wayside in this era of spectacular economic growth, the cost could be measured in bankrupted companies and shattered dreams. John D. Rockefeller put things with characteristic bluntness when he said he wanted "only the big ones, only those who have already proved they can do a big business" in the Standard Oil Trust. "As for the others, unfortunately they will have to die."

The cost was high, too, for millions of American workers, immigrant and native-born alike. The vast expansion of new products was built on the backs of an army of laborers who were paid subsistence wages and who could be fired on a moment's notice when hard times or new technologies made them expendable.

Industrial growth often devastated the environment as well. Rivers fouled by oil or chemical waste, skies filled with clouds of soot, and a landscape littered with reeking garbage and toxic materials bore mute witness to the relentless drive for efficiency and profit.

To be sure, the vast expansion of economic output brought social benefits as well, in the form of labor-saving products, lower prices, and advances in transportation and communications. The benefits and liabilities sometimes seemed inextricably interconnected. The sewing machine, for example, created thousands of new factory jobs, made available a wider variety of clothing, and eased the lives of millions of housewives. At the same time, it encouraged avaricious entrepreneurs to operate sweatshops in which the immigrant poor—often vulnerable young women—toiled long hours for pitifully low wages (see Chapter 21).

Whatever the final balance sheet of social gains and costs, one thing was clear: the United States had muscled its way onto the world stage as an industrial titan. The ambition and drive of countless inventors, financiers, managerial innovators, and marketing wizards had combined to lay the groundwork for a new social and economic order in the twentieth century.

THE NEW SOUTH

The South entered the industrial era far more slowly than the Northeast. As late as 1900, total southern cotton-mill output, for example, remained little more than half that of the mills within a thirty-mile radius of Providence, Rhode Island. Moreover, the South's $509 average per capita income was less than half that of northerners.

The reasons for the South's late economic blossoming are not hard to discern. The Civil War's physical devastation, the scarcity of southern towns and cities, lack of capital, illiteracy, northern control of financial markets and patents, and a low rate of technological innovation crippled efforts by southern business leaders to promote industrialization. Economic progress was also impeded by the myth of the Lost Cause, which, through its nostalgic portrayal of pre–Civil War society, perpetuated an image of the South as traditional and unchanging. As a result, southern industrialization inched forward haltingly and was shaped in distinctive ways.

Obstacles to Economic Development Much of the South's difficulty in industrializing arose from its lack of capital and the devastation of the Civil War. So many southern banks failed during the Civil War that by 1865 the South, with more than a quarter of the nation's population, possessed just 2 percent of its banks.

Federal government policies adopted during the war further restricted the expansion of the southern banking system. The Republican-dominated wartime Congress, which had created a national currency and banking structure, required anyone wishing to start a bank to have fifty thousand dollars in capital. Few southerners could meet this standard.

With banks in short supply, country merchants and storekeepers became bankers by default, lending supplies rather than cash to local farmers in return for a lien, or mortgage, on their crops (see Chapter 16). As farmers sank in debt, they increased their production of cotton and tobacco in an effort to stay afloat, and became trapped on the land. As a result, the labor needed for industrial expansion remained in short supply.

The shift from planting corn to specializing in either cotton or tobacco made small southern farmers particularly vulnerable to the fluctuations of commercial agriculture. When the price of cotton tumbled in national and international markets from eleven cents per pound in 1875 to less than five cents in 1894, well under the cost of production, many southern farmers grew desperate.

The South also continued to be the victim of federal policies designed to aid northern industry. High protective tariffs raised the price of machine technology imported from abroad; the demonetization of silver (see Chapter 20) further limited capital availability; and discriminatory railroad freight rates hiked the expense of shipping finished goods and raw materials.

The South's chronic shortage of funds affected the economy in indirect ways as well, by limiting the resources available for education. During Reconstruction northern philanthropists together with the Freedmen's Bureau, the American Missionary Association, and other relief agencies had begun a modest expansion of public schooling for both blacks and whites. But Georgia and many other southern states operated segregated schools and refused to tax property for school support until 1889. As a result, school attendance remained low, severely limiting the number of educated people able to staff technical and managerial positions in business and industry.

Southern states, like those in the North, often contributed the modest funds they had to war veterans' pensions. In this way, southern state governments built a white patronage system for Confederate veterans and helped reinforce southerners' idealization of the old Confederacy—the South's Lost Cause. As late as 1911, veterans' pensions in Georgia ate up 22 percent of the state's entire budget, leaving little for economic or educational development.

The New South Creed and Southern Industrialization   Despite the limited availability of private capital for investment in industrialization, energetic southern newspaper editors such as Henry W. Grady of the Atlanta *Constitution* and Henry Watterson of the Louisville *Courier Journal* championed the doctrine that became known as the New South creed. The South's rich coal and timber resources and cheap labor, they proclaimed in their papers, made it a natural site for industrial development. As one editor declared, "The El Dorado [the fabled land of riches] of the next half century is the South. The wise recognize it; the dull and the timid will ere long regret their sloth or their hesitancy."

The movement to industrialize the South gained momentum in the 1880s. To attract northern capital, southern states offered tax exemptions for new businesses, set up industrial and agricultural expositions, and leased prison convicts to serve as cheap labor. Florida, Texas, and other states gave huge tracts of lands to railroads, which expanded dramatically throughout the South and in turn stimulated the birth of new towns and villages. Other states sold forest and mineral rights on nearly 6 million acres of federal lands to speculators, mostly from the North, who significantly expanded the production of iron, sulfur, coal, and lumber.

Following the lead of their northern counterparts, the southern iron and steel industries expanded as well. Birmingham, Alabama, founded in 1871 in the heart of a region blessed with rich deposits of coal, limestone, and iron ore, grew in less than three decades to a bustling city with noisy railroad yards and roaring blast furnaces. By 1900 it was the nation's largest pig-iron shipper. In these same years, Chattanooga, Tennessee, housed nine furnaces, seventeen foundries, and numerous machine shops.

As large-scale recruiters of black workers, the southern iron and steel mills contributed to the migration of blacks to the cities. By 1900, 20 percent of the southern black population was urban. Many urban blacks toiled as domestics or in similar menial capacities, but others entered the industrial work force. Southern industry reflected the patterns of racial segregation in southern life. Tobacco companies used black workers, particularly women, to clean the tobacco leaves while white women, at a different location, ran the machines that made cigarettes. The burgeoning textile mills were lily-white. In the iron and steel industry, blacks, who comprised 60 percent of the unskilled work force by 1900, had practically no chance of advancement. Nevertheless, in a rare reversal of the usual pattern, southern blacks in the iron and steel industry on average earned more than did southern white textile workers.

The Southern Mill Economy

Unlike the urban-based southern iron and steel industry, the textile mills that mushroomed in the southern countryside in the 1880s often became catalysts for the formation of new towns and villages. (This same pattern had occurred in rural New England in the 1820s.) In those southern districts that underwent the gradual transition from an agricultural to a mill economy, country ways and values suffused the new industrial workplace.

The cotton-mill economy grew largely in the Piedmont, a beautiful highland country of rolling hills and rushing rivers stretching from central Virginia to northern Georgia and Alabama. The Piedmont had long been the South's backcountry, a land of subsistence farming and limited roads. But postwar railroad construction opened the region to outside markets and sparked a period of intense town building and textile-mill expansion. Between 1880 and 1900 track mileage in North Carolina grew dramatically; the number of towns and villages jumped, quickening the pulse of commerce; and the construction of textile mills accelerated. Between 1860 and 1900 cotton-mill capacity shot up 1,400 percent, and by 1920 the South was the nation's leading textile-mill center. Augusta, Georgia, with 2,800 mill workers, became known as the Lowell of the South, named after the mill town in Massachusetts where industrialization had flourished since the 1820s. The expansion of the textile industry nurtured promoters' visions of a new, more prosperous, industrialized South.

Even sharecroppers and tenant farmers at first hailed the new cotton mills as a way out of rural poverty. But appearances were deceptive. The chief cotton-mill promoters were drawn from the same ranks of merchants, lawyers, doctors, and bankers who had profited from the commercialization of southern agriculture (and from the misfortunes of poor black and white tenant farmers and sharecroppers enmeshed in the new system). R. R. Haynes, a planter and merchant from North Carolina's Rutherford County, was typical of the new entrepreneurs. Starting out as a storekeeper, he purchased land and water rights on Second Broad Creek in 1884 and formed a company to finance construction of the Henrietta Mills. By 1913 Haynes owned not only one of the South's largest gingham-producing operations but also banks, railroads, lumber businesses, and general stores.

To run the mills, mill superintendents commonly hired poor whites from impoverished nearby farms. They promised that textile work would free these farming families from poverty and instill in them the virtues of punctuality and industrial discipline. The reality was different. Cotton-mill entrepreneurs shamelessly exploited their workers, paying just seven to eleven cents an hour, 30 percent to 50 percent less than what comparable mill workers in New England were paid.

The mills dominated most Piedmont textile communities. The mill operator not only built and owned the workers' housing and the company store but also supported the village church, financed the local elementary school, and pried into the morals and behavior of the mill hands. To prevent workers from moving from one mill to another seeking better opportunities, the mill owner usually paid them just once a month, often in scrip—a certificate redeemable only in goods from the company store. Since few families had enough money to get through a month, they usually overspent and fell behind in their payments. The charges were deducted from workers' wages the following month. In this way, the mill drew workers and their families into a cycle of indebtedness very much like that faced by sharecroppers and tenant farmers.

Since farm families had shared farm responsibilities together, southern mill superintendents accommodated themselves to local customs and hired whole families, including the children. Mothers commonly brought babies into the mills and kept them in baskets nearby while tending their machines. Little children who were visiting older siblings in the mills sometimes learned to operate the machines themselves. Laboring a twelve-hour day, the mill hands relieved their tedium by stationing themselves near friends so that they might talk as they worked. Ties among the workers were strong. One employee put it simply, "The mill community was a close bunch of people . . . like one big family. We just loved one another."

To help make ends meet, mill workers kept their own garden patches and raised chickens, cows, and pigs. Southern mill hands thus brought communal farm values, nurtured through cooperative planting and harvesting, into the mills and mill villages. Although they had to adapt to machine-paced work and received barely enough pay to live on, the working poor in the mill districts, like their prewar counterparts in the North, eased the shift from rural to village-industrial life by clinging to a cooperative country ethic.

As northern cotton mills did before the Civil War, southern textile companies exploited the cheap rural labor around them, settling transplanted farm people in paternalistic company-run villages. Using these tactics, the industry underwent a period of steady growth.

The Southern Industrial Lag Industrialization occurred on a smaller scale and at a slower rate in the South than in the North and also depended far more on outside financing, technology, and expertise. The late-nineteenth-century southern economy remained essentially in a colonial status, subject to control by northern industries and financial syndicates. U.S. Steel, for example, controlled the foundries in Birmingham, and in 1900 its executives began to price Birmingham steel according to the "Pittsburgh plus" formula based

"Pig Iron Scene, Birmingham, Alabama," by Charles Graham, 1886 *Although Birmingham, Alabama's, extensive foundries turned out inexpensive iron ingots, the northern owners forced factory operators to price their products at the same rate as ingots produced in Pittsburgh.*

on the price of Pittsburgh steel, plus the freight costs of shipping from Pittsburgh. As a result, southerners paid higher prices for steel than did northerners, despite the cheaper production costs.

An array of factors thus combined to retard industrialization in the South. Banking regulations requiring large reserves, scarce capital, absentee ownership, unfavorable railroad rates, cautious state governments, wartime debts, lack of industrial experience, and control by profit-hungry northern enterprises all hampered the region's economic development. Dragged down by a poorly educated white population unskilled in modern technology and by an equally poorly trained, indigent black population excluded from skilled jobs, southern industry languished. Not until after the turn of the century did southern industry undergo the restructuring and consolidation that had occurred in northern business enterprise two decades earlier.

As in the North, industrialization brought significant environmental damage, including polluted rivers and streams, decimated forests, grimy coal-mining towns, and soot-infested steel-making cities. Although Henry Grady's vision of a New South may have inspired many southerners to work toward industrialization, economic growth in the South, limited as it was by outside forces, progressed in its own distinctly regional way.

Factories and the Work Force

Industrialization proceeded unevenly nationwide, and most late-nineteenth-century Americans still worked in small shops. But as the century unfolded, large factories with armies of workers sprang onto the industrial scene in more and more locales. The pattern of change was evident. Between 1860 and 1900, the number of industrial workers jumped from 885,000 to 3.2 million, and the trend toward large-scale production became unmistakable.

From Workshop to Factory   The transition to a factory economy came not as a major earthquake but rather as a series of jolts varying in strength and duration. Whether they occurred quickly or slowly, the changes in factory production had a profound impact on artisans and unskilled laborers alike, for they involved a fundamental restructuring of work habits and a new emphasis on workplace discipline. The impact of these changes can be seen by examining the boot and shoe industry. As late as the 1840s, almost every shoe was custom-made by a skilled artisan who worked in a small, independent shop. Shoemakers were aristocrats in the world of labor. Taught in an apprentice system, they took pride in their work and controlled the quality of their products. In some cases they hired and paid their own helpers.

A distinctive working-class culture subdivided along ethnic lines evolved among these shoemakers. Foreign-born English, German, and Irish workers set up ethnic trade organizations and joined affiliated benevolent associations. Bound together by their potent religious and ethnic ties, they observed weddings and funerals according to old-country traditions and relaxed together at the local saloon after work. Living in tenements and boardinghouses within the same tight-knit ethnic neighborhood, they developed a strong ethnic and community pride and helped one another weather accidents or sicknesses.

As early as the 1850s, even before the widespread use of machinery, changes in the ready-made shoe trade had eroded the status of skilled labor. The manufacturing process was broken down into a sequence of repetitive, easily mastered tasks. Skilled shoe artisans now worked in "teams" of four men, each responsible for one function: putting the shoe on the last (a form shaped like a person's foot), attaching the heel, trimming the sole, "finishing" the leather with stain and polish, and so forth. Thus instead of crafting a pair of shoes from start to finish, each team member specialized in only one part of the process.

Under the new factory system of shoe manufacture, workers also lost the freedom to drink on the job and to take time off for special occasions. A working-class culture that had reinforced group solidarity was now dismissed by owners and shop foremen as wasteful and inefficient.

In the 1880s, shoe factories became larger and more mechanized, and traditional skills largely vanished. Sophisticated sewing and buffing machines allowed shoe companies to replace skilled operatives with lower-paid, less-skilled women and children. By 1890 women made up more than 35 percent of the work force in an industry once dominated by men. In many other industries, skilled artisans found their responsibilities and relation to the production process changing. With the exception of some skilled construction crafts such as carpentry and bricklaying, artisans no longer participated in the production process as a whole. Like the laborer whose machine nailed heels on 4,800 shoes a day, even "skilled" workers in the new factories specializing in consumer goods found themselves performing numbingly repetitive tasks.

The Hardships of Industrial Labor   The expansion of the factory system spawned an unprecedented demand for unskilled labor. By the 1880s nearly one-third of the 750,000 workers employed in the railroad and steel industries, for example, were common laborers.

In the construction trades, the machine and tool industries, and garment making, the services of unskilled laborers were procured under the so-called contract system. To avoid the problems of hiring, managing, and firing their own workers, large companies negotiated an agreement with a subcontractor who took responsibility for employee relations. A foreman or boss employed by the subcontractor supervised gangs of unskilled day laborers. These common workers were seasonal help, hired in times of need and laid off in slack periods. The steel industry employed them to shovel ore in the yards and to move ingots inside the mills. The foremen drove the gangs hard; in the Pittsburgh area, the workers called the foremen "pushers."

Notoriously transient, unskilled laborers drifted from city to city and from industry to industry. In the late 1870s unskilled laborers earned $1.30 a day, while

Textile Workers *Young children like this one were often used in the textile mills because their small fingers could tie together broken threads more easily than those of adults.*

bricklayers and blacksmiths earned more than $3. Only unskilled southern mill workers, whose wages averaged a meager eighty-four cents a day, earned less.

Unskilled and skilled workers alike not only worked up to twelve-hour shifts but also faced grave hazards to their health and safety. The alarming incidence of industrial accidents stemmed from a variety of circumstances, including dangerous factory conditions, workers' inexperience, and the rapid pace of the production process. Author Hamlin Garland described the perilous environment of a steel-rail mill at Carnegie's Homestead Steel Works in Pittsburgh. One steelworker recalled that on his first day at the mill, "I looked up and a big train carrying a big vessel with fire was making towards me. I stood numb, afraid to move, until a man came to me and led me out of the mill." Under such conditions the accident rate in the steel mills was extremely high.

In the coal mines and cotton mills, child laborers typically entered the work force at age eight or nine. These youngsters not only faced the same environmental hazards as adults but were especially prone to injury because of the pranks and play that they engaged in on the job. When supervision was lax in the cotton mills, for example, child workers would grab the belts that powered the machines and see who could ride them farthest up toward the drive shaft in the ceiling before letting go and falling to the floor. In the coal industry, children were commonly employed as slate pickers. Sitting at a chute beneath the breakers that crushed the coal, they removed pieces of slate and other impurities. The cloud of coal dust that swirled around them made them vulnerable to black lung disease—a disorder that could progress into emphysema and tuberculosis. Children and others who toiled in the cotton mills, constantly breathing in cotton dust, fell ill with brown lung, another crippling disease.

For adult workers, the railroad industry was one of the most perilous. In 1889, the first year that the Interstate Commerce Commission compiled reliable statistics, almost two thousand rail workers were killed on the job and more than twenty thousand were injured.

Disabled workers and widows received only minimal financial aid from employers. Until the 1890s the courts considered employer negligence to be one of the normal risks borne by employees. Railroad and factory owners regularly fought against the adoption of state safety and health standards on the grounds that the economic costs would be excessive. For sickness and accident benefits, workers joined fraternal organizations and ethnic clubs, part of whose monthly dues benefited those in need. But in most cases, the amounts set aside were too low to be of much help. When a worker was killed or maimed in an accident, the family became dependent on relatives or kindly neighbors for assistance and support.

Immigrant Labor　In their search for cheap labor, factory owners turned to unskilled immigrant workers for the muscle needed in the booming factories, mills, and railroads and in heavy-construction industries. In Philadelphia, where native-born Americans and recent German immigrants dominated the highly skilled metalworking trades, Irish newcomers remained mired in unskilled horse-carting and construction occupations until the 1890s, when the "new immigrants" from southern and eastern Europe replaced them (see Chapter 19). Poverty-stricken French Canadians filled the most menial positions in the textile mills of the Northeast. On the West Coast, Chinese immigrants performed the dirtiest and most physically demanding jobs in mining, canning, and railroad construction.

Writing home in the 1890s, eastern European immigrants described the hazardous and draining work in the steel mills. "Wherever the heat is most insupportable, the flames most scorching, the smoke and soot most choking, there we are certain to find compatriots bent and wasted in toil," reported one Hungarian. Yet those immigrants disposed to live frugally in a boardinghouse and to work an eighty-four-hour week could save fifteen dollars a month, far more than they could have earned in their homeland.

Although most immigrants worked hard, few adjusted easily to the frantic pace of the factory. Rural peasants from southern and eastern Europe who immigrated after 1890 found it especially difficult to abandon their irregular work habits for the unrelenting factory schedules. Where farm routines had followed a seasonal pace, slowing in the winter, factory operations were relentless, dictated by the invariable speed of the machines. A brochure that the International Harvester

Corporation used to teach English to its Polish workers attempted to instill the "proper" values. Lesson 1 read:

I hear the whistle. I must hurry.
I hear the five minute whistle.
It is time to go into the shop.
I take my check from the gate board and hang it on the department board.
I change my clothes and get ready to work.
The starting whistle blows.
I eat my lunch.
It is forbidden to eat until then.
The whistle blows at five minutes of starting time.
I get ready to go to work.
I work until the whistle blows to quit.
I leave my place nice and clean.
I put all my clothes in the locker.
I must go home.

As this "lesson" reveals, factory work tied the immigrants to a rigid timetable very different from the pace of farm life.

When immigrant workers resisted the tempo of factory work, drank on the job, or took unexcused absences, employers used a variety of tactics to enforce discipline. Some sponsored temperance societies and Sunday schools to teach punctuality and sobriety. Others cut wages and put workers on the piecework system, paying them only for the items produced. Employers sometimes also provided low-cost housing to gain leverage against work stoppages; if workers went on strike, the boss could simply evict them.

In the case of immigrants from southern Europe whose skin colors were often darker than northern Europeans, employers asserted that the workers were nonwhite and thus did not deserve the same compensation as native-born Americans. Because the concept of "whiteness" in the United States bestowed a sense of privilege and the automatic extension of the rights of citizenship, Irish, Greek, Italian, Jewish, and a host of other immigrants, although of the Caucasian race, were also considered nonwhite. Rather than being a fixed category based on biological differences, the concept of race was thus used to justify the harsh treatment of foreign-born labor.

Women and Work in Industrial America Women's work experiences, like those of men, were shaped by marital status, social class, and race. White married women in all classes widely accepted an ideology of "separate spheres" (see Chapter 19) and remained at home, raised children, and looked after the household. The well-to-do hired maids and cooks to ease their burdens. Working-class married women, in contrast, not only lacked such assistance but also often had the added responsibility of earning money at home to make ends meet.

For working-class married women, working for wages at home by sewing, button-making, taking in boarders, or doing laundry had predated industrialization.

In the late nineteenth century, urbanization and economic expansion enabled unscrupulous entrepreneurs to exploit this captive work force. Cigar manufacturers would buy or lease a tenement and require their twenty families to live and work there. In the clothing industry, manufacturers hired out finishing tasks to lower-class married women and their children, who labored long hours in crowded apartments.

Young, working-class single women often viewed factory work as an opportunity. In 1870, 13 percent of all women worked outside the home, the majority as cooks, maids, cleaning ladies, and laundresses. But most working women intensely disliked the long hours, dismally low pay, and social stigma of being a "servant." When jobs in industry expanded in the last quarter of the century, growing numbers of single white women abandoned domestic employment for better-paying work in the textile, food-processing, and garment industries. Discrimination barred black working women from following this path. Between 1870 and 1900, the number of women of all races working outside the home nearly tripled, and by the turn of the century, women made up 17 percent of the country's labor force.

A variety of factors propelled the rise in the employment of single women. Changes in agriculture prompted many young farmwomen to seek employment in the industrial sector (see Chapter 19), and immigrant parents often sent their daughters to the factories to supplement meager family incomes. Plant managers welcomed young immigrant women as a ready source of inexpensive unskilled labor. But factory owners assumed that many of these women would marry within a short time and thus treated them as temporary help and kept their wages low. Late in the century, young women in the clothing industry were earning as little as five dollars for seventy hours of work.

Despite their paltry wages, long hours, and often unpleasant working conditions, many young women relished earning their own income and joined the work force in increasing numbers. Although the financial support that these working women contributed to their families was significant, few working women were paid enough to provide homes for themselves. Rather than fostering their independence, industrial work enmeshed them more deeply in a family economy that depended on their earnings.

When the typewriter and the telephone came into general use in the 1890s, office work provided new employment opportunities, and women with a high-school education moved into clerical and secretarial jobs earlier filled primarily by men. They were attracted by the clean, safe working conditions and relatively good pay. First-rate typists could earn six to eight dollars a week, which compared favorably with factory wages. Even though women were excluded from managerial positions, office work carried higher prestige and was generally steadier than work in the factory or shop.

Despite the growing number of women workers, the late-nineteenth-century popular press portrayed women's work outside the home as temporary. Few people even considered the possibility that a woman could attain local or even national prominence in the emerging corporate order.

Hard Work and
the Gospel of
Success

Although women were generally excluded from the equation, influential opinion molders in these years preached that any man could achieve success in the new industrial era. In *Ragged Dick* (1867) and scores of later tales, Horatio Alger, a Unitarian minister turned dime novelist, recounted the adventures of poor but honest lads who rose through ambition, initiative, and self-discipline. In his stories shoeshine boys stopped runaway horses and were rewarded by rich benefactors who gave them a start in business. The career of Andrew Carnegie was often offered as proof that the United States remained the land of opportunity and "rags to riches."

Not everyone embraced this belief. In an 1871 essay, Mark Twain chided the public for its naïveté and suggested that business success was more likely to come to those who lied and cheated. In testimony given in 1883 before a Senate committee investigating labor conditions, a New Yorker named Thomas B. McGuire dolefully recounted how he had been forced out of the horse-cart business by larger, better-financed concerns. Declared McGuire, "I live in a tenement house, three stories up, where the water comes in through the roof, and I cannot better myself. My children will have to go to work before they are able to work. Why? Simply because this present system . . . is all for the privileged classes, nothing for the man who produces the wealth." Only with starting capital of ten thousand dollars—then a large sum—said McGuire, could the independent entrepreneur hope to compete with the large companies.

What are the facts? Certainly Carnegie's rise from abject poverty to colossal wealth was the rare exception, as studies of nearly two hundred of the largest corporations reveal. Ninety-five percent of the industrial leaders came from middle- and upper-class backgrounds. However, even if skilled immigrants and native-born working-class Americans had little chance to move into management in the largest corporations, they did have considerable opportunity to rise to the top in small companies. Although few of them reaped immense fortunes, many attained substantial incomes.

The different fates of immigrant workers in San Francisco show the possibilities and perils of moving up within the working class. In the 1860s the Irish-born Donahue brothers grew wealthy from the Union Iron Works they had founded, where six hundred men built heavy equipment for the mining industry. In contrast, the nearly fifteen thousand Chinese workers who returned to the city after the Central Pacific's rail line was completed in 1869 were consigned by prejudice to work in cigar, textile, and other light-industry factories. Even successful Chinese entrepreneurs faced discrimination. When a Chinese merchant, Mr. Yung, refused to sell out to the wealthy Charles Crocker, a dry-goods merchant turned railroad entrepreneur who was building a mansion on Nob Hill, Crocker built a thirty-foot-high "spite fence" around Yung's house so that it would be completely sealed from view.

Thus, while some skilled workers became owners of their own companies, the opportunities for advancement for unskilled immigrant workers were considerably more limited. Some did move to semiskilled or skilled positions. Yet most immigrants, particularly the Irish, Italians, and Chinese, moved far more slowly than the sons of middle- and upper-class Americans who began with greater educational advantages and family financial backing. The upward mobility possible for such unskilled workers was generally mobility within the working class. Immigrants who got ahead in the late nineteenth century went from rags to respectability, not rags to riches.

One positive economic trend in these years was the rise in real wages, representing gains in actual buying power. Average real wages climbed 31 percent for unskilled workers and 74 percent for skilled workers between 1860 and 1900. Overall gains in purchasing power, however, were often undercut by injuries and unemployment during slack times or economic slumps. The position of unskilled immigrant laborers was particularly shaky. Even during a prosperous year like 1890, one out of every five nonagricultural workers was unemployed at least one month of the year. During the depressions of the 1870s and 1890s, wage cuts, extended layoffs, and irregular employment pushed those at the bottom of the industrial work force to the brink of starvation.

Thus the overall picture of late-nineteenth-century economic mobility is complex. At the top of the scale, a mere 10 percent of American families owned 73 percent of the nation's wealth in 1890, while less than half of industrial laborers earned more than the five-hundred-dollar poverty line annually. In between the very rich and the very poor, skilled immigrants and small shopkeepers swelled the ranks of the middle class. So although the standard of living for millions of Americans rose, the gap between the poor and the well-off remained a yawning abyss.

LABOR UNIONS AND INDUSTRIAL CONFLICT

The rapid growth of large corporations in the late nineteenth century transformed the working conditions for millions of Americans and drove them to seek new forms of organization and support. Aware that the expansion of regional markets and their integration into national and world markets gave industrial leaders unprecedented power to control the workplace, labor leaders searched for ways to create broad-based, national organizations that could protect their members and resist corporate power.

From the outset, the drive to create a nationwide labor movement faced many problems. Ethnic and racial divisions within the work force, including competition between immigrant groups, hampered unionizing efforts. Skilled craftsworkers, moreover, felt little kinship with low-paid common laborers. Divided into different trades, they often saw little reason to work together. Thus, unionization efforts moved forward slowly and experienced many setbacks.

Two groups, the National Labor Union and the Knights of Labor, struggled to build a mass labor movement that would unite skilled and unskilled workers regardless of their specialties. After impressive initial growth, however, both efforts collapsed. Far more effective was the American Federation of Labor (AFL), which represented an amalgamation of powerful independent craft unions. The AFL survived and grew, but it still represented only a small portion of the total labor force.

With unions so weak, labor unrest reached crisis proportions. When working conditions became intolerable, laborers walked off the job. These actions, born of desperation, often exploded into violence. The labor crisis of the 1890s, with its strikes and bloodshed, would reshape the legal environment, increase the demand for state regulation, and eventually contribute to a movement for progressive reform.

Organizing the Workers   The Civil War marked a watershed in the development of labor organizations. From the eighteenth century on, skilled workers had organized local trade unions to fight wage reductions and provide benefits for their members in times of illness or accident. By the 1850s some tradesmen had even organized national associations along craft lines. But the effectiveness of these organizations was limited. The main challenge that labor leaders faced in the postwar period was how to boost the unions' clout. Some believed that this goal could be achieved by forming one big association that would transcend craft lines and pull in a mass membership.

One person inspired by this vision was Philadelphian William H. Sylvis, who in 1863 was elected president of the Iron Molders' International Union, an organization of iron-foundry workers. Strongly built and bearded, with a "face and eyes beaming with intelligence," Sylvis traveled the country exhorting iron molders to organize. Within a few years, Sylvis had built his union from "a mere pygmy" to a membership of eighty-five hundred.

In 1866, acting on his dream of a nationwide association to represent all workers, Sylvis called a convention in Baltimore that formed a new organization, the National Labor Union (NLU). Reflecting the lingering aura of pre–Civil War utopianism, the NLU endorsed the eight-hour-day movement, which insisted that labor deserved eight hours for work, eight hours for sleep, and eight hours for personal affairs. Leaders also called for an end to convict labor, for the establishment of a federal department of labor, and for currency and banking reform. To push wage scales higher, they endorsed restriction on immigration, especially of Chinese migrants, whom native-born workers blamed for undercutting prevailing wage levels. The NLU under Sylvis's leadership supported the cause of working women and elected a woman as one of its national officers. It urged black workers to organize as well, though in racially separate unions.

In the winter of 1866–1867, Sylvis's own union became locked in a harrowing strike against the nation's foundry owners. When the strike failed miserably, Sylvis turned to national political reform. He invited a number of reformers to the 1868 NLU convention, including woman-suffrage advocates Susan B. Anthony and Elizabeth Cady Stanton who, according to a reporter, made "no mean impression on the bearded delegates." But the NLU suffered a shattering blow when Sylvis suddenly died in 1869. Despite a claim of three hundred thousand members, it faded quickly. After a brief incarnation in 1872 as the National Labor Reform party, it vanished from the scene.

The dream of a national labor movement lived on in a new organization, the Noble and Holy Order of the Knights of Labor, founded in 1869 by nine Philadelphia tailors led by Uriah H. Stephens, head of the Garment Cutters of Philadelphia. A secret society modeled on the Masonic order, the Knights welcomed all wage earners or former wage earners; they excluded only bankers, doctors, lawyers, stockbrokers, professional gamblers, and liquor dealers. Calling for a great association of all workers, the Knights demanded equal pay for women, an end to child labor and convict labor, and the cooperative employer-employee ownership of factories, mines, and other businesses. At a time when no federal income tax existed, they called for a tax on all earnings, graduated so that higher income earners would pay more.

The Knights grew slowly at first. But membership rocketed in the 1880s after Terence V. Powderly replaced Stephens as the organization's head. A young Pennsylvania machinist of Irish-Catholic immigrant origins, Powderly was an unlikely labor leader. He was short and slight, with a blond drooping mustache, elegant attire, and a fastidious, somewhat aloof manner. One journalist expressed surprise at finding such a fashionable man as the leader of "the horny-fisted sons of toil." But Powderly's eloquence, coupled with a series of successes in labor clashes, brought in thousands of new members.

During its growth years in the early 1880s, the Knights of Labor reflected both its idealistic origins and Powderly's collaborative vision. Powderly opposed strikes, which he considered "a relic of barbarism," and organized producer and consumer cooperatives. A teetotaler, he also urged temperance upon the membership. Powderly advocated the admission of blacks into local Knights of Labor assemblies, although he recognized the strength of racism and allowed local assemblies to be segregated in the South. Under his leadership the Knights welcomed women members; by 1886 women organizers such as the feisty Irish-born Mary Harris Jones, known as Mother Jones, had recruited thousands of workers, and women made up an estimated 10 percent of the union's membership.

Powderly supported restrictions on immigration and a total ban on Chinese immigration. Union members feared that immigrants would work so cheaply that they would steal their jobs. In the West such fears were directed particularly against the Chinese, and they were heightened when California railroad magnate Leland Stanford declared, "[O]pen the door and let everybody come who wants to come . . . until you get enough [immigrants] here to reduce the price of labor to such a point that its cheapness will stop their coming." In 1877 San Francisco workers demonstrating for an eight-hour workday destroyed twenty-five Chinese-run laundries and terrorized the local Chinese population. In 1880 both major party platforms included anti-Chinese immigration plans. Two years later, Congress passed the Chinese Exclusion Act, placing a ten-year moratorium on Chinese immigration. The ban was made permanent in 1902.

The Eight-Hour-Day Movement *Striking artisans from more than three hundred companies filled New York streets for weeks in 1872 in a campaign to reduce the workday from ten hours to eight hours. As is evident in this illustration, the eight-hour movement gained additional support from local saloons catering to German immigrants.*

Although inspired by Powderly's vision of a harmonious and cooperative future, most rank-and-file Knights of Labor strongly disagreed with Powderly's antistrike position. In 1883–1884 local branches of the Knights led a series of spontaneous strikes that elicited only reluctant support from the national leadership. In 1885, however, when Jay Gould tried to eradicate the Knights of Labor from his Wabash railroad by firing active union members, Powderly and his executive board instructed all Knights employed by the Wabash line to walk off the job and those working for other lines to refuse to handle Wabash cars. This highly effective action crippled the Wabash's operations. To the nation's amazement, the arrogant Jay Gould met with Powderly and cancelled his campaign against the Knights of Labor. "The Wabash victory is with the Knights," declared a St. Louis newspaper; "no such victory has ever before been secured in this or any other country."

With this apparent triumph, membership in the Knights of Labor soared. By 1886 more than seven hundred thousand workers were organized in nearly six thousand locals. Turning to political action that fall, the Knights mounted campaigns in nearly two hundred towns and cities nationwide, electing several mayors and judges (Powderly himself had served as mayor of Scranton since 1878), and claimed a role in electing a dozen congressmen. In state legislatures they secured passage of laws banning convict labor, and at the national level they lobbied successfully for a law against the importation of foreign contract labor. Business executives warned darkly that the Knights could cripple the economy and take over the country if they chose.

But the organization's strength soon waned. Workers became disillusioned when a series of unauthorized strikes failed in 1886. The national reaction to the Haymarket riot (see below) also contributed to the decline. By the late 1880s, the Knights of Labor was a shadow of its former self. Nevertheless, the organization had served as a major impetus to the labor movement and had awakened in thousands of workers a sense of group solidarity and potential strength. Powderly, who survived to 1924, always remained proud of his role "in forcing to the forefront the cause of misunderstood and downtrodden humanity."

As the Knights of Labor weakened, another national labor organization, pursuing more immediate and practical goals, was gaining strength. The skilled craft unions had long been uncomfortable with labor organizations like the Knights that welcomed skilled and unskilled alike. They were also concerned that the Knights' emphasis on broad reform goals would undercut their own commitment to better wages and protecting the interests of their particular crafts. The break came in May 1886 when the craft unions left the Knights of Labor to form the American Federation of Labor (AFL).

The AFL replaced the Knights' grand visions with practical tactics aimed at bread-and-butter issues. This philosophy was vigorously pursued by Samuel Gompers, the immigrant cigar maker who became head of the AFL in 1886 and led it until his death in 1924. Gompers believed in "trade unionism, pure and simple." For Gompers, higher wages were not simply an end in themselves but were rather the necessary base to enable working-class families to exist decently, with respect and dignity. The stocky, mustachioed labor leader had lost faith in utopian social reforms and recognized that "the poor, the hungry, have not the strength to engage in a conflict even when life is at stake." To stand up to the corporations, Gompers asserted, labor would have to harness the bargaining power of skilled workers, whom employers could not easily replace, and concentrate on the practical goals of raising wages and reducing hours.

A master tactician, Gompers believed that the trend toward large-scale industrial organization necessitated a comparable degree of organization by labor. He also recognized, however, that the skilled craft unions that made up the AFL retained a strong sense of independence. He knew that he had to persuade craftsworkers from the various trades to join forces without violating their sense of craft autonomy. Gompers's solution was to organize the AFL as a federation of trade unions, each retaining control of its own members but all linked by an executive council that coordinated strategy during boycotts and strike actions. "We want to make the trade union movement under the AFL as distinct as the billows, yet one as the sea," he told a national convention.

Focusing the federation's efforts on short-term improvements in wages and hours, Gompers at first sidestepped divisive political issues. The new organization's platform did, however, demand an eight-hour workday, employers' liability for workers' injuries, and mine-safety laws. Although women participated in many craft unions, the AFL did little to recruit women workers after 1894 because Gompers and others believed that women's place was in the home. By 1904, under Gompers's careful tutelage, the AFL had grown to more than 1.6 million strong.

Although the unions held up an ideal toward which many might strive, labor organizations before 1900 remained weak. Less than 5 percent of the work force joined union ranks. Split between skilled artisans and common laborers, separated along ethnic and religious lines, and divided over tactics, the unions battled with only occasional effectiveness against the growing power of corporate enterprise. Lacking financial resources, they typically watched from the sidelines when unorganized workers launched wildcat strikes that sometimes turned violent.

Strikes and Labor Violence   Americans had lived with a high level of violence from the nation's beginnings, and the nineteenth century, with its international and civil wars, urban riots, and Indian-white conflict, was no exception. Terrible labor clashes toward the end of the century were part of this continuing pattern, but they nevertheless shocked and dismayed contemporaries. From 1881 to 1905, close to 37,000 strikes erupted, in which nearly 7 million workers participated.

The first major wave of strikes began in 1873 when a Wall Street crash triggered a stock market panic and a major depression. Six thousand businesses closed the following year, and many more cut wages and laid off workers. Striking Pennsylvania coal miners were fired and evicted from their homes. Tramps roamed the streets in New York and Chicago. The tension took a deadly turn in 1877 during a wildcat railroad strike. Ignited by a wage reduction on the Baltimore and Ohio Railroad in July, the strike exploded up and down the railroad lines, spreading to New York, Pittsburgh, St. Louis, Kansas City, Chicago, and San Francisco. Rioters in Pittsburgh torched Union Depot and the Pennsylvania Railroad roundhouse. By the time newly installed President Rutherford B. Hayes had called out the troops and quelled the strike two weeks later, nearly one hundred people had died, and two-thirds of the nation's railroads stood idle.

The railroad strike stunned middle-class America. The religious press responded hysterically. "If the club of the policeman, knocking out the brains of the rioter, will answer, then well and good," declared one Congregational journal, "[but if not] then bullets and bayonets . . . constitute the one remedy. . . . Napoleon was right when he said that the way to deal with a mob was to exterminate it." The same middle-class Americans who worried about corporate abuse of power at the top echelons grew terrified of mob violence from the bottom ranks of society.

Employers capitalized on the public hysteria to crack down on labor. Many required their workers to sign "yellow dog" contracts in which they promised not to strike or join a union. Some hired Pinkerton agents to serve as their own private police force and, when necessary, turned to the federal government and the U.S. army to suppress labor unrest.

Although the economy had recovered, more strikes and violence followed in the 1880s. On May 1, 1886, 340,000 workers walked off their jobs in support of the campaign for an eight-hour workday. Strikers in Cincinnati virtually shut down the city for nearly a month. Also in 1886, Chicago police shot and killed four strikers at the McCormick Harvester plant on May 3. At a protest rally the next evening in the city's Haymarket Square, someone threw a bomb from a nearby building, killing or fatally wounding seven policemen. In response, the police fired wildly into the crowd and killed four demonstrators.

Public reaction was immediate. Business leaders and middle-class citizens lashed out at labor activists and particularly at the sponsors of the Haymarket meeting, most of whom were associated with a German-language anarchist newspaper that advocated the violent overthrow of capitalism. Eight men were arrested. Although no evidence connected them directly to the bomb throwing, all were convicted of murder, and four were executed. One committed suicide in prison. In Haymarket's aftermath, still more Americans became convinced that the nation was in the grip of a deadly foreign conspiracy, and animosity toward labor unions intensified.

Confrontations between capital and labor became particularly violent in the West. When the Mine Owners' Protective Association cut wages at work sites along Idaho's Coeur d'Alene River in 1892, the miners, who were skilled in the use of dynamite, blew up a mill and captured the guards sent to defend it. Mine owners responded by mustering the Idaho National Guard to round up more than three hundred men and cripple their union.

Back east that same year, armed conflict broke out at the Carnegie Steel Company plant in Homestead, Pennsylvania, when managers cut wages and locked out the workers to destroy their union. When workers responded by firing on the armed men from the Pinkerton Detective Agency who came to protect the plant, a battle broke out. Seven union members and three Pinkertons died. A week later the governor sent eight thousand National Guardsmen to restore order. The union crushed, the mills resumed full operation a month later.

The most systematic use of troops to smash union power came in 1894 during a strike against the Pullman Palace Car Company. In 1880 George Pullman, a manufacturer of elegant dining, parlor, and sleeping cars for the nation's railroads, had constructed a factory and town, called Pullman, ten miles south of Chicago. The carefully planned community provided solid brick houses for the workers, beautiful parks and playgrounds, and even its own sewage-treatment plant. Pullman also closely policed workers' activities, outlawed saloons, and insisted that his properties turn a profit.

When the depression of 1893 hit, Pullman slashed workers' wages without reducing their rents. In reaction thousands of workers joined the newly formed American Railway Union and went on strike. They were led by a fiery young organizer, Eugene V. Debs, who vowed "to strip the mask of hypocrisy from the pretended philanthropist and show him to the world as an oppressor of labor." Union members working for the nation's largest railroads refused to switch Pullman cars, paralyzing rail traffic in and out of Chicago, one of the nation's premier rail hubs.

In response, the General Managers' Association, an organization of top railroad executives, set out to break the union. The General Managers imported strikebreakers from among jobless easterners and asked U.S. attorney general Richard Olney, who sat on the board of directors of three major railroad networks, for a federal injunction (court order) against the strikers for allegedly refusing to move railroad cars carrying U.S. mail.

In fact, union members had volunteered to switch mail cars onto any trains that did not carry Pullman cars, and it was the railroads' managers who were delaying the mail by refusing to send their trains without the full complement of cars. Nevertheless, Olney, supported by President Grover Cleveland and citing the Sherman Anti-Trust Act, secured an injunction against the leaders of the American Railway Union for restraint of commerce. When the union refused to order its members back to work, Debs was arrested, and federal troops poured in. During the ensuing riot, seven hundred freight cars were burned, thirteen people died, and fifty-three were wounded. By July 18 the strike had been crushed.

By playing upon a popular identification of strikers with anarchism and violence, crafty corporate leaders persuaded state and federal officials to cripple organized labor's ability to bargain with business. When the Supreme Court (in the 1895 case *In re Debs*) upheld Debs's prison sentence and legalized the use of injunctions against labor unions, the judicial system gave business a potent new weapon with which to restrain labor organizers.

Despite successive attempts by the National Labor Union, Knights of Labor, American Federation of Labor, and American Railway Union to build a strong working-class movement, aggressive employer associations and conservative state and local officials hamstrung their efforts. In sharp contrast to Great Britain and Germany, where state officials often mediated disputes between labor and capital, federal and state officials in the United States increasingly sided with manufacturers. Ineffective in the political arena, blocked by state officials, and frustrated by court decisions, American unions failed to expand their base of support. Post–Civil War labor turmoil had sapped the vitality of organized labor and given it a negative public image that it would not shed until the 1930s.

Social Thinkers Probe for Alternatives   Widespread industrial violence was particularly unsettling when examined in the context of working-class poverty. In 1879, after observing three men rummaging through garbage to find food, the poet and journalist Walt Whitman wrote, "If the United States, like the countries of the Old World, are also to grow vast crops of poor, desperate, dissatisfied, nomadic, miserably-waged populations, such as we see looming upon us of late years . . . , then our republican experiment, notwithstanding all its surface-successes, is at heart an unhealthy failure." Whitman's bleak speculation was part of a general public debate over the social meaning of the new industrial order. At stake was a larger issue: should government become the mechanism for helping the poor and regulating big business?

Defenders of capitalism preached the laissez-faire ("hands-off") argument, insisting that government should never attempt to control business. They buttressed their case by citing Scottish economist Adam Smith, who had argued in *The Wealth of Nations* (1776) that self-interest acted as an "invisible hand" in the marketplace, automatically regulating the supply of and demand for goods and services. In "The Gospel of Wealth," an influential essay published in 1889, Andrew Carnegie justified laissez-faire by applying the evolutionary theories of British scientist Charles Darwin to human society. "The law of competition," Carnegie argued, "may be sometimes hard for the individual, [but] it is best for the race, because it insures the survival of the fittest in every department." Ignoring the scramble among businesses in the late nineteenth century to eliminate competition, Carnegie praised an unregulated competitive environment as a source of positive long-term social benefits.

Tough-minded Yale professor William Graham Sumner shared Carnegie's disapproval of government interference. In his combative book *What Social Classes Owe to Each Other* (1883), Sumner asserted that inexorable natural laws controlled the social order: "A drunkard in the gutter is just where he ought to be. . . . The law of survival of the fittest was not made by man, and it cannot be abrogated by man. We can only, by interfering with it, produce the survival of the unfittest." The state, declared Sumner, owed its citizens nothing but law, order, and basic political rights.

This conservative, laissez-faire brand of Social Darwinism (as such ideas came to be called) did not go unchallenged. In *Dynamic Sociology* (1883), Lester Frank Ward, a geologist with the U.S. Geological Survey, argued that contrary to Sumner's claim, the supposed "laws" of nature could be circumvented by human will. Just as scientists had applied their knowledge to breeding superior livestock, government experts could use the power of the state to regulate big business, protect society's weaker members, and prevent the heedless exploitation of natural resources.

Henry George, a self-taught San Francisco newspaper editor and economic theorist, proposed to solve the nation's uneven distribution of wealth through what he called the single tax. In *Progress and Poverty* (1879), he noted that speculators reaped huge profits from the rising price of land that they neither developed nor improved. By taxing this "unearned increment," the government could obtain the funds necessary to ameliorate the misery caused by industrialization. The result would bring the benefits of socialism—a state-controlled economic system that distributed resources according to need—without socialism's great disadvantage, the stifling of individual initiative. George's program was so popular that he lectured around the country and only narrowly missed being elected mayor of New York in 1886.

The vision of a harmonious industrialized society was vividly expressed in the utopian novel *Looking Backward* (1888) by Massachusetts newspaper editor Edward Bellamy. Cast as a glimpse into the future, Bellamy's novel tells of Julian

West, who falls asleep in 1888 and awakens in the year 2000 to find a nation without poverty or strife. In this future world, West learns, a completely centralized, state-run economy and a new religion of solidarity have combined to create a society in which everyone works for the common welfare. Bellamy's vision of a conflict-free society where all share equally in industrialization's benefits so inspired middle-class Americans fearful of corporate power and working-class violence that nearly five hundred local Bellamyite organizations, called Nationalist clubs, sprang up to try to turn his dream into reality.

Ward, George, and Bellamy did not deny the benefits of the existing industrial order; they simply sought to humanize it. These utopian reformers envisioned a harmonious society whose members all worked together. Marxist socialists advanced a different view. Elaborated by German philosopher and radical agitator Karl Marx (1818–1883) in *Das Kapital* (1867) and other works, Marxism rested on the proposition (which Adam Smith had also accepted) that the labor required to produce a commodity was the only true measure of that commodity's value. Any profit made by the capitalist employer was "surplus value" appropriated from the exploited workers. As competition among capitalists increased, Marx predicted, wages would decline to starvation levels, and more and more capitalists would be driven out of business. At last society would be divided between a shrinking bourgeoisie (capitalists, merchants, and middle-class professionals) and an impoverished proletariat (the workers). At this point the proletariat would revolt and seize control of the state and of the economy. Although Marx's thought was dominated by an insistence on class struggle as the essence of modern history, his eyes were also fixed on the shining vision of the communist millennium that the revolution would eventually usher in—a classless utopia in which the state would "wither away" and all exploitation would cease. To lead the working class in its coming showdown with capitalism, Marx and his collaborator Friedrich Engels helped found socialist parties in Europe, whose strength grew steadily beginning in the 1870s.

Despite Marx's keen interest in the United States, Marxism proved to have little appeal in late-nineteenth-century America other than for a tiny group of primarily German-born immigrants. The Marxist-oriented Socialist Labor party (1877) had attracted only about fifteen hundred members by 1890. More alarming to the public at large was the handful of anarchists, again mostly immigrants, who rejected Marxist discipline and preached the destruction of capitalism, the violent overthrow of the state, and the immediate introduction of a stateless utopia. In 1892 Alexander Berkman, a Russian immigrant anarchist, attempted to assassinate Henry Clay Frick, the manager of Andrew Carnegie's Homestead Steel Works. Entering Frick's office with a pistol, Berkman shot him in the neck and then tried to stab him. A carpenter working in Frick's office overpowered the assailant. Rather than igniting a workers' insurrection that would usher in a new social order as he had hoped, Berkman came away with a long prison sentence, and his act confirmed the middle-class stereotype of "labor agitators" as lawless and violent.

IMPORTANT EVENTS, 1865–1900

1859 First oil well drilled in Titusville, Pennsylvania.

1866 National Labor Union founded.

1869 First transcontinental railroad completed.
Knights of Labor organized.

1870 John D. Rockefeller establishes Standard Oil Company.

1873 Panic of 1873 triggers a depression lasting until 1879.

1876 Alexander Graham Bell invents and patents the telephone.
Thomas A. Edison opens research laboratory at Menlo Park, New Jersey.

1877 Edison invents the phonograph.
Railway workers stage the first nationwide strike.

1879 Henry George, *Progress and Poverty.*
Edison perfects the incandescent lamp.

1881 Standard Oil Trust established.

1882 Edison opens the first electric power station on Pearl Street in New York City.
Chinese Exclusion Act.

1883 Railroads divide the country into time zones.
William Graham Sumner, *What Social Classes Owe to Each Other.*
Lester Frank Ward, *Dynamic Sociology.*

1886 American Federation of Labor (AFL) formed.
Police and demonstrators clash at Haymarket Square in Chicago.

1887 Interstate Commerce Act establishes the Interstate Commerce Commission.

1888 Edward Bellamy, *Looking Backward.*

1889 Andrew Carnegie, "The Gospel of Wealth."

1890 Sherman Anti-Trust Act.

1892 Standard Oil of New Jersey and General Electric formed.
Steelworkers strike at Homestead, Pennsylvania.
World's Columbian Exposition opens in Chicago.
Miners strike at Coeur d'Alene, Idaho.

1893 Panic of 1893 triggers a depression lasting until 1897.

1894 Pullman Palace Car workers strike, supported by the National Railway Union.

1901 J. Pierpont Morgan organizes United States Steel.

19

Immigration, Urbanization, and Everyday Life, 1860–1900

On a sweltering day in August 1899, Scott Joplin, a young, black pianist and composer, signed an unusual contract with his music publisher in Sedalia, Missouri. Instead of receiving an outright payment for his new sheet music composition, "Maple Leaf Rag," Joplin would earn one cent for every copy sold. At a time when most composers were paid a small fixed fee per composition, the contract signaled a new era in the popular-music industry. Over the next two decades, "Maple Leaf Rag" would sell more than half a million copies a year and make Joplin the king of ragtime, the popular, syncopated dance music that had become a national sensation.

Scott Joplin's transformation from unknown saloon piano player to renowned composer sheds light not only on the extraordinary expansion and commercialization of the entertainment industry at the turn of the nineteenth century but also on the class and racial tensions that pervaded popular culture. Although Joplin would publish more than seventy-five songs or piano rags in the next decade and a half, his success was undercut by white competitors who stereotyped his compositions as "Negro music" and "Coon songs." Joplin, who dreamed of gaining national recognition as an opera composer, remained frustrated by publishers' refusal to accept his classical compositions. Opera was considered serious music, a high art form controlled by the upper classes; blacks, even those with Joplin's talent, could not enter the field. Scott Joplin died in 1917, an admired leader in the entertainment industry whose genius for serious music would not be recognized for another half century. As Joplin's experience revealed, racial discrimination could reinforce the barriers of social class.

Scott Joplin's struggle to be accepted was not unusual. Countless others faced similar difficulties in moving up the economic ladder and adjusting to the changes taking place at the turn of the century. American society was slowly shifting from a rural producer economy that stressed work and thrift to an urban consumer economy in which new forms of entertainment, leisure activities, and material possessions were becoming the hallmarks of personal identity.

Nevertheless, Joplin's success as a ragtime composer mirrored the upward mobility of many Americans who could now enjoy unheard-of levels of comfort and convenience. Industrialization had opened up new jobs and destroyed older ones, rearranging the occupational structure, altering the distribution of income within society, and sharpening class divisions. These changes, together with the expansion of white-collar occupations, created new expectations for family life and fostered a growing class awareness.

While the middle and upper classes prospered, immigrants, farmers, and the urban working classes—the overwhelming majority of the population—improved their families' economic position only slowly and slightly. The growth of consumer products and leisure activities actually widened the gulf between the haves and the have-nots and intensified the sense of class consciousness among rich and poor. Nowhere were these divisions more visible than in the cities teeming with immigrants.

While the very rich lived in a world apart and the middle class embraced its particular behavior code and cultural pursuits, the working class to whom Joplin had first appealed created its own vigorous culture of dance halls, saloons, vaudeville theaters, social clubs, and amusement parks in the bustling cities. Middle-class reformers who strove to remake this working-class culture into their own image of propriety were soon frustrated. In the long run, the culture of the masses would prove more influential in shaping modern America.

This chapter will focus on five major questions:

How did the growth of cities and the influx of immigrants create a new awareness of ethnic and class differences? How were racial stereotypes used to reinforce these distinctions?

What was Victorian morality, and in what ways did it influence social conventions and patterns of everyday life?

How did women's educational opportunities change in this period, and why did women pioneer new approaches to social welfare?

How did the conflict between the working classes and those above them help reshape attitudes toward leisure and recreation at the turn of the century?

Why did Americans of different social classes grow disenchanted with Victorian social and intellectual ideals?

EVERYDAY LIFE IN FLUX: THE NEW AMERICAN CITY

Nowhere were the changes in everyday life more visible than in cities. During the late nineteenth century, American cities grew spectacularly. Not only on the East Coast but also in the South, cities swelled at an astonishing pace. Between 1870 and 1900 New Orleans's population nearly doubled, Buffalo's tripled, and Chicago's increased more than fivefold. By the start of the new century, Philadelphia, New York, and Chicago all had more than a million residents, and 40 percent of all Americans lived in cities. (In the census, cities were defined as having

Urban Growth: 1870–1900

City	1870 Population	1900 Population	Percent Increase
Boston	250,525	560,892	123.88
Chicago	298,977	1,698,575	468.12
Cincinnati	216,239	325,902	50.71
Los Angeles	5,728	102,479	1,689.08
Milwaukee	74,440	285,315	299.37
New Orleans	191,418	287,104	49.98
New York	1,478,103	3,437,202	132.54
Philadelphia	1,293,697	647,022	99.94
Pittsburgh	321,616	86,075	273.64
Portland	90,426	8,293	990.38
Richmond	51,038	85,050	66.64
San Francisco	149,473	342,782	129.32
Seattle	1,107	237,194	21,326.73

Source: *Thirteenth Census of the United States* (Washington, D.C.: U.S. Government Printing Office, 1913).

more than twenty-five hundred inhabitants.) In 1900 New York's 3.4 million inhabitants almost equaled the nation's entire 1850 urban population.

This spectacular urban growth, fueled by migration from the countryside and the arrival of nearly 11 million foreign immigrants between 1870 and 1900, created a dynamic new environment for economic development. Mushrooming cities created new jobs and markets that in turn dramatically stimulated national economic expansion. Like the frontier, the city symbolized opportunity for all comers.

The city's unprecedented scale and diversity threatened traditional expectations about community life and social stability. Rural America had been a place of face-to-face personal relations where most people shared the same likes and dislikes. In contrast, the city was a seething cauldron where a medley of immigrant groups contended with one another and with native-born Americans for jobs, power, and influence. Moreover, the same rapid growth that energized manufacturing and production strained city services, generated terrible housing and sanitation problems, and accentuated class differences.

Native-born city dwellers complained about the noise, stench, and congestion of this transformed cityscape. They fretted about the newcomers' squalid tenements, fondness for drink, and strange social customs. When native-born reformers set about cleaning up the city, they sought not only to improve the physical environment but also to destroy the distinctive customs that made immigrant culture different from their own. The late nineteenth century thus witnessed an intense struggle to control the city and benefit from its economic and cultural potential. The stakes were high, for America was increasingly becoming an urban nation.

Migrants and Immigrants

The growing concentration of industries in urban settings produced demands for thousands of new workers. The promise of good wages and a broad range of jobs (labeled by historians as "pull factors") drew men and women from the countryside and small towns. So great was the migration from rural areas, especially New England, that some farm communities vanished from the map.

Young farmwomen led the exodus to the cities. With the growing mechanization of farming in the late nineteenth century, farming was increasingly male work. At the same time, rising sales of factory-produced goods through mail-order catalogs serving country areas reduced rural needs for women's labor on subsistence tasks. So young farmwomen flocked to the cities, where they competed for jobs with immigrant, black, and city-born white women.

Scott Joplin Music
Despite Scott Joplin's desire to be recognized for his talent as an opera composer, publishers of his music preferred his popular ragtime compositions, such as his 1902 piano rag, "The Entertainer."

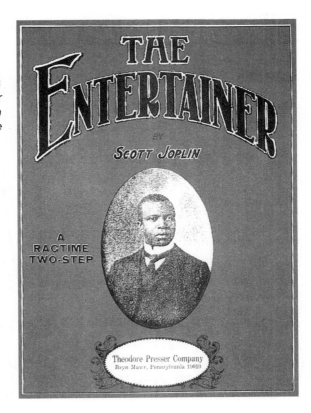

From 1860 to 1890, the prospect of a better life also attracted nearly 10 million northern European immigrants to East Coast and midwestern cities, where they joined the more than 4 million who had settled there in the 1840s and 1850s. Germans made up the largest group, numbering close to 3 million, followed by nearly 2 million English, Scottish, and Welsh immigrants and almost 1.5 million Irish. Moreover, by 1900 more than eight hundred thousand French-Canadians had migrated south to work in the New England mills, and close to a million Scandinavian newcomers had put down roots in the rich farmlands of Wisconsin and Minnesota. On the West Coast, despite the Chinese Exclusion Act of 1882 (see Chapter 18), more than eighty-one thousand Chinese remained in California and nearby states in 1900.

In the 1890s these "old immigrants" from northern and western Europe were joined by swelling numbers of "new immigrants"—Italians, Slavs, Greeks, and Jews from southern and eastern Europe, Armenians from the Middle East, and, in Hawaii, Japanese from Asia. In the next three decades, these new immigrants, many from peasant backgrounds, would boost America's foreign-born population by more than 18 million.

The Changing Face of U.S. Immigration, 1860–1930

Between 1865 and 1895, the majority of newcomers to America hailed from northern and western Europe. But the early twentieth century witnessed a surge of immigration from southern and eastern Europe.

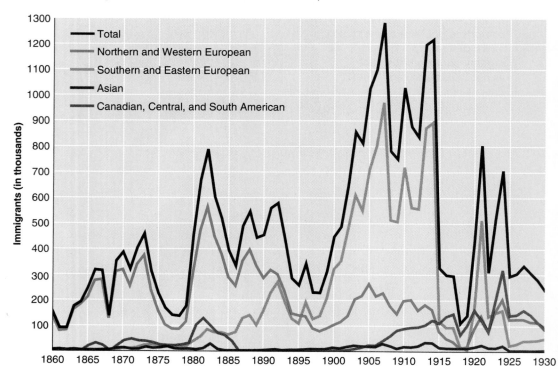

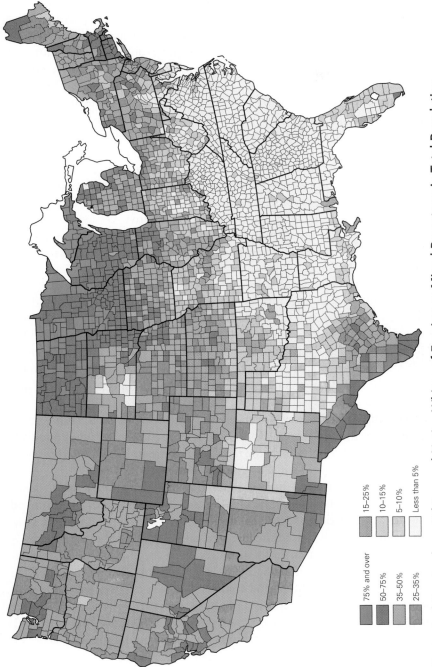

Percent of Foreign-born Whites and Native Whites of Foreign or Mixed Parentage in Total Population, by Countries, 1910

As this map indicates, new immigrants rarely settled in the South.

Source: D. W. Meinig, The Shaping of America—A Geographical Perspective of 500 Years of History. Yale University Press, Volume 3.

75% and over	15–25%
50–75%	10–15%
35–50%	5–10%
25–35%	Less than 5%

The overwhelming majority of immigrants settled in cities in the northeastern and north-central states, with the Irish predominating in New England and the Germans in the Midwest. The effect of their numbers was staggering. In 1890 New York City (including Brooklyn, still a legally separate municipality) contained twice as many Irish as Dublin, as many Germans as Hamburg, half as many Italians as Naples, and 2 1/2 times the Jewish population of Warsaw. That same year four out of five people living in New York had been born abroad or were children of foreign-born parents.

Some recent immigrants had been forced out of their home countries by overpopulation, crop failure, famine, religious persecution, violence, or industrial depression. (Historians call these reasons for immigration "push factors," since they drove immigrants out of their homelands.) Emigration from England, for example, spurted during economic downturns in 1873 and 1883. German peasants, squeezed by overpopulation and threatened by church reorganizations that they opposed, left in large numbers in the 1880s.

Many others came voluntarily in search of better opportunities. More than one hundred thousand Japanese laborers, for example, were lured to Hawaii in the 1890s to work on the lucrative sugar plantations by promises of high wages.

A large number of immigrants were single young men. Birger Osland, an eighteen-year-old Norwegian, explained his reasons for leaving to a friend: "as I now probably have a foundation upon which I can build my own further education, I have come to feel that the most sensible thing I can do is to emigrate to America." Although significant numbers of young men remained in the United States after they had become successful, large numbers, especially Italians and Chinese, returned home as well.

Although single women were less likely to come on their own, Irish women often did so and sent their earnings back home. Most commonly, wives and children waited in the old country until the family breadwinner had secured a job and saved enough money to pay for their passage to America.

Would-be immigrants first had to travel to a port—Hamburg was a major embarkation point—where they boarded a crowded steamship. The cramped ocean journey was noted for its poor food, lack of privacy, and rudimentary sanitary facilities. Immigrants arrived tired, fearful, and in some cases very sick.

Further complications awaited the travelers when they reached their destination, most often New York City or San Francisco. Customs officials inspected the newcomers for physical handicaps and contagious diseases. After 1892 those with "loathsome" infections such as leprosy, trachoma (a contagious viral disease of the eye), or sexually transmitted diseases were refused admittance and deported. Immigrants who passed the physical examination then had their names recorded. If a customs inspector had difficulty pronouncing a foreign name, he often Anglicized it. One German Jew became flustered when asked for his name and mumbled, "Schon vergessen [already forgotten]," meaning that he could not recall it. The inspector, who did not understand Yiddish, wrote "Sean Ferguson" on the

New York's Lower East Side *In the era before automobiles, the streets pulsed with life as shops, vendors, and shoppers spilled out on the streets.*

man's roster. In this manner, many immigrants ended up with Americanized names.

In 1855 New York State had established a special facility for admitting immigrants at Castle Garden on the tip of Manhattan Island. Later, when the numbers swelled, the federal government took control and built a new station on Ellis Island in New York harbor in 1892. Angel Island in San Francisco Bay on the West Coast served a similar purpose after 1910. At the immigrant processing centers, America's newest residents exchanged foreign currency for U.S. dollars, purchased railroad tickets, and arranged lodgings. In other cities immigrants were hounded by tavernkeepers, peddlers, and porters who tried to exploit their ignorance of the English language and American ways. "When you land in America," wrote one Swedish resident to friends back home, "you will find many who will offer their services, but beware of them because there are so many rascals who make it their business to cheat the immigrants."

Those who arrived with sufficient cash, including many German artisans and Scandinavian farmers, commonly traveled west to Chicago, Milwaukee, and the rolling prairies beyond. Most of the Irish, and later the Italians, who hailed largely from poor peasant backgrounds, remained in eastern cities like Boston, New York, and Philadelphia. The Irish and Italians who did go west typically made the trip in stages, moving from job to job on the railroad and canal systems.

Adjusting to an Urban Society

For many immigrants the stress of adjusting to a new life was eased by the fact that they could settle among compatriots who had preceded them. (Historians call this tendency to relocate near friends or relatives from one's original town "chain migration.") If a map of New York City's streets and neighborhoods were colored in by nationality, Jacob Riis observed in 1890, it "would show more stripes than on the skin of a zebra, and more colors than any rainbow." The streets of Manhattan between the West Side Irish neighborhoods and the East Side German neighborhoods teemed with Poles, Hungarians, Russians, Italians, and Chinese.

Late-nineteenth-century social commentators often assumed that each nationality clumped together for reasons of national clannishness. But settlement patterns were far more complex. Most immigrants preferred to live near others not merely from their own country but also from their own village or region. On New York's Lower East Side, for example, Italians divided into many different subgroups: Neapolitans and Calabrians at Mulberry Bend, Genoese on Baxter Street, northern Italians west of Broadway, and Tyrolese Italians on Sixty-ninth Street near the Hudson River.

In the competition to get ahead, some immigrant groups adjusted more easily than others. Those with a background in the skilled trades and a familiarity with Anglo-American customs had relatively few problems. English-speaking immigrants from the British Isles, particularly those from mill, mining, and manufacturing districts, found comparable work and encountered relatively little discrimination. Ethnic groups that formed a substantial percentage of a city's population also had a major advantage. The Irish, for example, who by the 1880s made up nearly 16 percent of New York's population, 8 percent of Chicago's, and 17 percent of Boston's, facilitated Irish immigrants' entry into the American mainstream by dominating Democratic party politics and controlling the hierarchy of the Catholic church in all three cities.

Ironically, domination of urban institutions by members of the larger immigrant groups often made adjustment to American society more difficult for members of smaller groups. Germans and other well-organized and skilled immigrants tended to exclude less-skilled newcomers from desirable jobs. English and German dominance of the building trades, for example, enabled those nationalities to limit the numbers of Italians hired.

The diversity of immigrants, even those from the same country, was remarkable. Nevertheless, the experience of being labeled a foreigner and of being discriminated against helped create a new common ethnic identity for many groups. Immigrants from the same home country forged a new sense of ethnic distinctiveness as Irish-American, German-American, or Jewish-American that helped them downplay internal divisions, compete for political power, and eventually assimilate into mainstream society.

Not all immigrants were interested in assimilation or intended to remain permanently in the United States. Young Chinese and Italian men often journeyed to American shores to earn enough money to return home and buy land or set

Chinatown *As is evident in this photograph of San Francisco at the turn of the century, Chinese immigrant workers often retained their traditional ways of dress and lived in the most congested part of town.*

themselves up in business. Expecting only a brief stay, they made little effort to learn English or understand American customs. Of the Italians who immigrated to New York before 1914, nearly 50 percent went back to Italy. Although the rate of return migration was greatest among Chinese and Italians, significant numbers of immigrants of other nationalities eventually returned to their homelands as well.

Various factors thus influenced the ability of immigrants to adapt to urban society in America. Nevertheless, as the number of foreigners in U.S. cities ballooned toward the turn of the century, all immigrant groups faced increasing hostility from white native-born Americans who not only disliked the newcomers' social customs but also feared their growing influence. Fearing the loss of the privileges and status that were associated with their white skin color, native-born whites began to stigmatize immigrants as racially different and inferior, even when they were of the same race. Only gradually, and with much effort, did Irish, Jews, Slavs, and Mediterranean people, although they were biologically Caucasian, come to be considered "white."

Slums and Ghettos

Every major city had its share of rundown, overcrowded slum neighborhoods. Generally clustered within walking distance of manufacturing districts, slums developed when landlords subdivided old buildings and packed in too many residents. The poorer the renters, the worse the slum. Slums became ghettos when laws, prejudice, and community pressure prevented the tenement inhabitants from renting elsewhere. During the 1890s Italians in New York, blacks in Philadelphia and Chicago, Mexican-Americans in Los Angeles, and Chinese in San Francisco increasingly became locked in segregated ghettos.

Life in the slums was particularly difficult for children. Juvenile diseases such as whooping cough (pertussis), measles, and scarlet fever took a fearful toll, and infant mortality was high. In one immigrant ward in Chicago in 1900, 20 percent of infants died in their first year of life.

Since tenements often bordered industrial districts, residents had to put up with the noise, pollution, and foul odors of tanneries, foundries, factories, and packing houses. Because most factories used coal-fired steam engines as their energy source, and because coal was also the preferred fuel for heating most apartment houses and businesses, vast quantities of soot and coal dust drifted skyward daily.

Most immigrants stayed in the shabbiest tenements only until they could afford better housing. Blacks, in contrast, were trapped in segregated districts. Driven out of the skilled trades and excluded from most factory work, blacks took menial jobs whose low pay left them little income for housing (see Chapter 18). Racist city-dwellers used high rents, real-estate covenants (agreements not to rent or sell to blacks), and neighborhood pressure to exclude them from areas inhabited by whites. Because the numbers of northern urban blacks in 1890 remained relatively small—for example, they composed only 1.2 percent of Cleveland's population and 1.3 percent of Chicago's—they could not overcome whites' concerted campaigns to shut them out. Nevertheless, as W. E. B. Du Bois, a black sociologist, pointed out in *The Philadelphia Negro* (1899), wealthy black entrepreneurs within these neighborhoods built their own churches, ran successful businesses, and established charitable organizations to help their people.

Fashionable Avenues and Suburbs   As remains true today, the same cities that harbored slums, suffering, and violence also boasted neighborhoods of dazzling opulence. Wealthy Americans such as John D. Rockefeller and Jay Gould built monumental residences near exclusive streets just outside the downtown area. Rockefeller and Gould lived near Fifth Avenue in New York; others lived on Commonwealth Avenue in Boston, Euclid Avenue in Cleveland, and Summit Avenue in St. Paul. In the 1870s and 1880s wealthy city-dwellers began moving to new suburbs to distance themselves farther from the crowded tenement districts. Promoters of the suburban ideal, playing on the romantic rural nostalgia popular at the time, contrasted the rolling lawns and stately houses on the city's periphery with the teeming streets, noisy saloons, and mounds of garbage and horse excrement downtown. Soon many major cities could boast of their own stylish suburbs: Haverford, Ardmore, and Bryn Mawr outside Philadelphia; Brookline near Boston; and Shaker Heights near Cleveland.

Middle-class city-dwellers followed the precedents set by the wealthy. Skilled artisans, shopkeepers, clerks, accountants, and sales personnel moved either to new developments at the city's edge or to outlying suburban communities (although those at the lower fringe of the middle class typically rented apartments in neighborhoods closer to the city center). Lawyers, doctors, small businessmen, and other professionals moved farther out along the main thoroughfares served by the street railway, where they purchased homes on large lots. By the twentieth century, this process would result in suburban sprawl.

In time, a pattern of informal residential segregation by income took shape in the cities and suburbs. Built up for families of a particular income level, certain neighborhoods and suburbs developed remarkably similar standards for lot size and house design. (Two-story houses with front porches, set back thirty feet from the sidewalk, became the norm in many neighborhoods.) Commuters who rode the new street railways out from the city center could identify the social class of the suburban dwellers along the way as readily as a geologist might distinguish different strata on a washed-out riverbank.

By 1900 whirring trolley cars and hissing steam-powered trains had burst the boundaries of the compact midcentury city. As they expanded, cities often annexed the contingent suburbs. Within this enlarged city, sharp dissimilarities in building height and neighborhood quality set off business sectors from fashionable residential avenues and differentiated squalid manufacturing districts from parklike suburban subdivisions. Musing about urban America in 1902, James F. Muirhead, a popular Scottish guidebook author, wrote that New York and other U.S. cities reminded him of "a lady in a ball costume, with diamonds in her ears, and her toes out at her boots." To Muirhead, urban America had become a "land of contrasts" in which the spatial separations of various social groups and the increasingly dissimilar living conditions for rich and poor had heightened ethnic, racial, and class divisions. Along with the physical change in American cities, in short, had come a new awareness of class and cultural disparities.

MIDDLE-CLASS SOCIETY AND CULTURE

Spared the struggle for survival that confronted most Americans after the Civil War, society's middle and upper ranks faced a different challenge: how to rationalize their enjoyment of the products of the emerging consumer society. To justify the position of society's wealthier members, ministers such as Brooklyn preacher Henry Ward Beecher and advice-book writers appealed to Victorian morality, a set of social ideas embraced by the privileged classes of England and America during the long reign (1837–1901) of Britain's Queen Victoria.

E. L. Godkin, the editor of *The Nation*, Phillips Brooks, minister to Boston's Trinity Church, and other proponents of Victorian morality argued that the financial success of the middle and upper classes was linked to their superior talent, intelligence, morality, and self-control. They also extended the antebellum ideal of separate spheres by arguing that women were the driving force for moral improvement.

While men were expected to engage in self-disciplined, "manly" dedication to the new industrial order, women would provide the gentle, elevating influence that would lead society in its upward march. While Beecher, Godkin, and others defended the superiority of America's middle and upper classes, a network of institutions, from elegant department stores and hotels to elite colleges and universities, reinforced the privileged position of these groups.

Manners and Morals

The Victorian world view, which first emerged in the 1830s and 1840s, rested on a number of assumptions. One was that human nature was malleable: people could improve themselves. Hence, Victorian Americans were intensely moralistic and eager to reform practices they considered evil or undesirable. A second assumption emphasized the social value of work. Proponents of Victorian morality believed that a commitment to working hard not only developed personal self-discipline and self-control, but also helped advance the progress of the nation. Finally, Victorian Americans stressed the importance of good manners and the value of literature and the fine arts as marks of a truly civilized society. Although this genteel outlook set a standard that was often violated in practice, particularly by the middle classes and the rich, it remained an ideal that was widely preached as the norm for all society.

Before the Civil War, reformers such as Henry Ward Beecher had energized the crusades to abolish slavery and alcoholism by appealing to the ethical standards of Victorian morality. (Both slavery and intemperance threatened feminine virtue and family life.) After the war, Beecher and other preachers became less interested in social reform and more preoccupied with the importance of manners and social protocol. Following their advice, middle- and upper-class families in the 1870s and 1880s increasingly defined their own social standing in terms not only of income but also of behavior. Good manners, especially a knowledge of dining and entertaining etiquette, and good posture became important badges of status.

In her popular advice book *The American Woman's Home* (1869), Catharine Beecher (the sister of Henry Ward Beecher) reflected typical Victorian self-consciousness about proper manners. The following list of dinner-table behaviors, she said, should be avoided by those of "good breeding":

> Reaching over another person's plate; standing up to reach distant articles, instead of asking to have them passed; . . . using the table-cloth instead of napkins; eating fast, and in a noisy manner; putting large pieces in the mouth; . . . [and] picking the teeth at the table.

For Beecher and other molders of manners, meals became important rituals that differentiated the social classes. Not only were they occasions for displaying the elaborate china and silver that wealthy families exclusively possessed, but they also provided telltale clues to a family's level of refinement and sophistication.

The Victorian code—with its emphasis on morals, manners, and proper behavior—thus served to heighten the sense of class differences for the post–Civil

War generation. Prominent middle- and upper-class Americans made bold claims about their interest in helping others improve themselves. More often than not, however, their self-righteous, intensely moralistic outlook simply widened the gap that income disparities had already opened.

The Cult of
Domesticity

Victorian views on morality and culture, coupled with rising pressures on consumers to make decisions about a mountain of domestic products, had a subtle but important effect on middle-class expectations about women's role within the home. From the 1840s on, many architects, clergymen, and other promoters of the so-called cult of domesticity had idealized the home as "the woman's sphere." They praised the home as a protected retreat where females could express their special maternal gifts, including sensitivity toward children and an aptitude for religion. "The home is the wife's province," asserted one writer; "it is her natural field of labor . . . to govern and direct its interior management."

During the 1880s and 1890s a new obligation was added to the traditional woman's role as director of the household: to foster an artistic environment that would nurture her family's cultural improvement. For many Victorian Americans of the comfortable classes, houses became statements of cultural aspiration. Excluded from the world of business and commerce, many middle- and upper-class women devoted considerable time and energy to decorating their homes, seeking to make the home, as one advice book suggested, "a place of repose, a refuge from the excitement and distractions of outside . . . , provided with every attainable means of rest and recreation."

Not all middle-class women pursued this domestic ideal. For some, housework and family responsibilities overwhelmed the concern for artistic accomplishment. For others the artistic ideal was not to their taste. Sixteen-year-old Mary Putnam complained privately to a friend that she played the piano because of "an abstract general idea . . . of a father coming home regularly tired at night (from the plow, I believe the usual legend runs), and being solaced by the brilliant yet touching performance of a sweet only daughter upon the piano." She then confessed that she detested the piano. Increasingly, middle- and upper-class women in the 1880s and 1890s sought other outlets for their creative energies in settlement house work and social reform.

Department
Stores

Although Victorian social thought justified the privileged status of the well-to-do, many thrifty people who had grown up in the early nineteenth century found it difficult to accept the new preoccupation with accumulation and display. To dull their pangs of guilt, merchandisers in the 1880s stressed the high quality and low cost of the objects they sold, encouraging Americans to loosen their purse strings and enjoy prosperity without reservations.

A key agent in modifying attitudes about consumption was the department store. In the final quarter of the nineteenth century, innovative entrepreneurs led by Rowland H. Macy in New York, John Wanamaker in Philadelphia, and Marshall Field in Chicago built giant department stores that became urban institutions and transformed the shopping experience for the millions of middle- and upper-class consumers who were their greatest patrons.

Merchants like Wanamaker and Macy helped overcome the middle and upper classes' reluctance to spend by advertising their products at "rock-bottom" prices and engaging in price wars. To avoid keeping their stock too long, they held giant end-of-the-season sales at drastically marked-down prices.

The major department stores tried to make shopping an exciting activity. Not only did rapid turnover of merchandise create a sense of constant novelty, but the mammoth stores themselves were designed as imitation palaces, complete with stained-glass skylights, marble staircases, brilliant chandeliers, and plush carpets. The large urban department store functioned as a kind of social club and home away from home for comfortably fixed women. Shopping became an adventure, a form of entertainment, and a way to affirm their place in society.

The Trans-formation of Higher Education   At a time when relatively few Americans had even a high-school education, U.S. colleges and universities represented another institutional stronghold of the business and professional elite and the moderately well-to-do middle class. In 1900, despite enrollment increases in the preceding decades, only 4 percent of the nation's eighteen- to twenty-one-year-olds were enrolled in institutions of higher learning.

Wealthy capitalists gained status and a measure of immortality by endowing colleges and universities. Leland Stanford and his wife, Jane Lathrop Stanford, launched Stanford University in 1885 with a bequest of $24 million in memory of their dead son; John D. Rockefeller donated $34 million to the University of Chicago in 1891. Industrialists and businessmen dominated the boards of trustees of many educational institutions and forced their probusiness views on administrators. Sardonic economist Thorstein Veblen called these business-oriented academic managers "Captains of Erudition."

Not only the classroom experience but also social contacts and athletic activities—especially football—prepared affluent young men for later responsibilities in business and the professions. Adapted by American college students in 1869 from English rugby, football was largely an elite sport. But the game, initially played without pads or helmets, was marred by violence. In 1905 eighteen students died of playing-field injuries. Many college presidents dismissed football as a danger-ous waste of time and money. In 1873, when the University of Michigan challenged Cornell to a game in Ann Arbor, Cornell's president Andrew D. White huffily telegraphed back, "I will not permit thirty men to travel four hundred miles merely to agitate a bag of wind."

But eager alumni and coaches strongly defended the new sport. Some—among them Henry Lee Higginson, the Civil War veteran and Boston banker who gave Harvard "Soldiers' Field" stadium as a memorial to those who had died in

Cigar-Box Label, c. 1910 *Vassar College promoted the new image of womanhood by stressing the interconnections among education, athletics, and ethics.*

battle—praised football as a character-building sport. Others, including famed Yale coach Walter Camp, insisted that football could function as a surrogate frontier experience in an increasingly urbanized society. By 1900 collegiate football had become a popular fall ritual, and team captains were campus heroes.

Although postsecondary education remained confined to a small minority, more than 150 new colleges and universities were founded between 1880 and 1900, and enrollments more than doubled. While wealthy capitalists endowed some institutions, others, such as the state universities of the Midwest, were financed largely through public funds generated from state sales of public lands under the Morrill Land Grant Act (1862). Many colleges were also founded and funded by religious denominations.

On the university level, innovative presidents such as Cornell's Andrew D. White and Harvard's Charles W. Eliot sought to change the focus of higher education. New discoveries in science and medicine sparked the reform. In the 1850s most physicians had attended medical school for only two sixteen-week terms. They typically received their degrees without ever having visited a hospital ward or examined a patient. The Civil War exposed the abysmal state of American medical education. Twice as many soldiers died from infections as from wounds. Doctors were so poorly trained and ignorant about sanitation that they often infected soldiers' injuries when they probed wounds with hands wiped on pus-stained aprons. "The ignorance and general incompetency of the average graduate of American medical schools, at the time when he receives the degree which turns him loose upon the community," wrote Eliot in 1870, "is something horrible to contemplate."

In the 1880s and 1890s the public's well-justified skepticism about doctors encouraged leading medical professors, many of whom had studied in France and

Germany, to begin restructuring American medical education. Using the experimental method developed by German scientists, they insisted that all medical students be trained in biology, chemistry, and physics, including laboratory experience. By 1900 graduate medical education had been placed on a firm professional foundation. Similar reforms took place in undergraduate and graduate programs in architecture, engineering, and law.

These changes were part of a larger transformation in higher education after the Civil War that gave rise to a new institution, the research university. Unlike the best of the mid-nineteenth-century colleges, whose narrow, unvarying curriculum focused on teaching Latin and Greek, theology, logic, and mathematics, the new research universities offered courses in a wide variety of subject areas, established professional schools, and encouraged faculty members to pursue basic research. For President Andrew D. White of Cornell University, the objective was to create an environment "where any person can find instruction in any study." At Cornell, the University of Wisconsin at Madison, Johns Hopkins, Harvard, and other institutions, this new conception of higher education laid the groundwork for the central role that America's universities would play in the intellectual, cultural, and scientific life of the twentieth century.

Despite these significant changes, higher education remained largely the privilege of a few as the nineteenth century ended. The era when college attendance would become the norm rather than the rare exception lay many years ahead.

WORKING-CLASS POLITICS AND REFORM

The contrast between the affluent world of the college-educated middle and upper classes and the gritty lives of the working class was most graphically displayed in the nation's growing urban centers, where immigrant newcomers reshaped political and social institutions to meet their own needs. If fancy department stores and elegant hotels furnished new social spaces for the middle and upper classes, saloons became the poor man's club, and dance halls became single women's home away from home. While the rich and the wellborn looked askance at lower-class recreational activities and sought to force the poor to change their ways, working-class Americans, the immigrant newcomers in particular, fought to preserve their own distinctive way of life. Indeed, the late nineteenth century witnessed an ongoing battle to eradicate social drinking, reform "boss" politics, and curb lower-class recreational activities.

Political Bosses and Machine Politics Earlier in the century the swelling numbers of urban poor had given rise to a new kind of politician, the "boss," who listened to his urban constituents and lobbied to improve their lot. The boss presided over the city's "machine"—an unofficial political organization designed to keep a particular party or faction in office. Whether officially serving as mayor or not, the boss, assisted by local ward or precinct captains, wielded enormous influence in city government. Often a former saloonkeeper or labor leader, the boss knew his constituents well.

For better or worse, the political machine was America's unique contribution to municipal government in an era of pell-mell urban growth. Typified by Tammany Hall, the Democratic organization that dominated New York City politics from the 1830s to the 1930s, machines emerged in Baltimore, Philadelphia, Atlanta, San Francisco, and a host of other cities during the Gilded Age.

By the turn of the century, many cities had experienced machine rule. Working through the local ward captains to turn out unusually high numbers of voters (see Chapter 20), the machine rode herd on the tangle of municipal bureaucracies, controlling who was hired for the police and fire departments. It rewarded its friends and punished its enemies through its control of taxes, licenses, and inspections. The machine gave tax breaks to favored contractors in return for large payoffs and slipped them insider information about upcoming street and sewer projects.

At the neighborhood level, the ward boss often acted as a welfare agent, helping the needy and protecting the troubled. It was important to the boss that he be viewed as generous to his constituents. To spend three dollars to pay a fine for a juvenile offense meant a lot to the poor, but it was small change to a boss who raked in millions from public-utility contracts and land deals. While the machine helped alleviate some suffering, it entangled urban social services with corrupt politics and often prevented city government from responding to the real problems of the city's neediest inhabitants.

Under New York City's boss William Marcy Tweed, the Tammany Hall machine revealed the slimy depths to which extortion and contract padding could sink. Between 1869 and 1871, Tweed gave $50,000 to the poor and $2,250,000 to schools, orphanages, and hospitals. In these same years, his machine dispensed sixty thousand patronage positions and pumped up the city's debt by $70 million through graft and inflated contracts. The details of the Tweed ring's massive fraud and corruption were brilliantly satirized in *Harper's Weekly* by German immigrant cartoonist Thomas Nast. In one cartoon Nast portrayed Tweed and his cronies as vultures picking at the city's bones. Tweed bellowed in fury. "I don't care a straw for your newspaper articles—my constituents don't know how to read," he told *Harper's*, "but they can't help seeing them damned pictures." Convicted of fraud and extortion, Tweed was sentenced to jail in 1873, served two years, escaped to Spain, was reapprehended and reincarcerated, and died in jail in 1878.

By the turn of the century the bosses were facing well-organized assaults on their power, led by an urban elite whose members sought to restore "good government" (see Chapter 21). In this atmosphere the bosses increasingly forged alliances with civic organizations and reform leagues. The results, although never entirely satisfactory to any of the parties involved, paved the way for new sewer and transportation systems, expanded parklands, and improved public services—a record of considerable accomplishment, given the magnitude of the problems created by urban growth.

Battling Poverty   Impatient with the political bosses' piecemeal attempts to help the urban poor, middle-class city leaders sought comprehensive solutions for relieving poverty. Jacob Riis and the first generation of reformers believed that the basic cause of urban distress was the immigrants' lack of self-discipline and self-control. Consequently, Riis and his peers focused on moral improvement. Only later would Jane Addams, Florence Kelley, and other settlement house workers examine the crippling impact of low wages and dangerous working conditions. Although many reformers genuinely sympathized with the suffering of the lower classes, the humanitarians often turned their campaigns to help the destitute into missions to Americanize the immigrants and eliminate customs that they perceived as offensive and self-destructive.

Poverty-relief workers first targeted their efforts at the young, who were thought to be most impressionable. Energized by the religious revivals of the 1830s and 1840s, Protestant reformers started charitable societies to help transient youths and abandoned street children. In 1843 Robert M. Hartley, a former employee of the New York Temperance Society, organized the New York Association for Improving the Condition of the Poor to urge poor families to change their ways.

Hartley's voluntaristic approach was supplemented by the more coercive tactics of Charles Loring Brace, who founded the New York Children's Aid Society in 1853. Brace admired "these little traders of the city . . . battling for a hard living in the snow and mud of the street" but worried that they might join the city's "dangerous classes." Brace established dormitories, reading rooms, and workshops where the boys could learn practical skills; he also swept orphaned children off the streets, shipped them to the country, and placed them with families to work as farm hands.

Where Brace's Children's Aid Society gave adolescents an alternative to living in the slums, the Young Men's Christian Association (YMCA), founded in England in 1841 and exported to America ten years later, provided housing and wholesome recreation for country boys who had migrated to the city. The Young Women's Christian Association (YWCA) similarly provided housing and a day nursery for young women and their children. In the Protestant tradition of moral improvement, both organizations subjected their members to curfews and expelled them for drinking and other forbidden behavior.

By 1900 more than fifteen hundred YMCAs and YWCAs served as havens for nearly a quarter-million young men and women. But YMCA and YWCA leaders reached only a small portion of the young adult population. Some whom they sought to help were put off by the organizations' close supervision and moralistic stance. Others, eager to assert their independence, preferred not to ask for help. Although charity workers made some progress in their efforts to aid youth, the strategy was too narrowly focused to stem the rising tide of urban problems.

New Approaches
to Social Work
The inability of the Children's Aid Society, YMCA, YWCA, and other relief organizations to cope with the explosive growth of the urban poor in the 1870s and 1880s convinced some reformers to search for other ways to fight poverty. One of the earliest and most effective agencies was the Salvation Army. A church established along pseudomilitary lines in England in 1865 by Methodist minister "General" William Booth, the Salvation Army sent its uniformed volunteers to the United States in 1880 to provide food, shelter, and temporary employment for families. Known for its rousing music and attention-getting street meetings, the group ran soup kitchens and day nurseries and dispatched its "slum brigades" to carry the message of morality to the immigrant poor. The army's strategy was simple. Attract the poor with marching bands and lively preaching; follow up with offers of food, assistance, and employment; and then teach them the solid middle-class virtues of temperance, hard work, and self-discipline.

A similar approach to poor relief was implemented by the New York Charity Organization Society (COS), founded in 1882 by Josephine Shaw Lowell. Of a prominent Boston family, the strong-willed Lowell had been widowed when her husband of a few months was killed during the Civil War, and she wore black for the rest of her life. Adopting what they considered a scientific approach to make aid to the poor more efficient, Lowell and the COS leaders divided New York City into districts, compiled files on all aid recipients, and sent "friendly visitors" into the tenements to counsel families on how to improve their lives. Convinced that moral deficiencies lay at the root of poverty and that the "promiscuous charity" of overlapping church welfare agencies undermined the desire to work, the COS tried to foster self-sufficiency in its charges. In 1891, Lowell helped found the Consumers' League of New York.

Although the COS did serve as a useful coordinator for relief efforts and developed helpful statistics on the extent of poverty, critics justly accused the society of being more interested in controlling the poor than in alleviating their suffering. One of the manuals, for example, stressed the importance of introducing "messy housekeepers" to the "pleasures of a cheery, well-ordered home." Unable to see slum problems from the vantage point of the poor, they failed, for the most part, in their underlying objective: to convert the poor to their own standards of morality and decorum.

The Moral-Purity
Campaign
The failure of Josephine Shaw Lowell and other like-minded social disciplinarians to eradicate urban poverty prompted other reformers to push for even tougher measures against sin and immorality. In 1872 Anthony Comstock, a pious young dry-goods clerk, founded the New York Society for the Suppression of Vice. The organization demanded that municipal authorities close down gambling and lottery operations and censor obscene publications.

Nothing symbolized the contested terrain between middle- and lower-class culture better than the fight over prostitution. Considered socially degenerate by some and a source of recreation by others, prostitution both exploited women and offered them a steady income and a measure of personal freedom. After the Civil War, the number of brothels—specialized houses controlled by women known as madams where prostitutes plied their trade—expanded rapidly. In the 1880s saloons, tenements, and cabarets, often controlled by political machines, hired prostitutes of their own. Even though immigrant women do not appear to have made up the majority of big-city prostitutes, reformers often labeled them as the major source of the problem.

In 1892 brothels, along with gambling dens and saloons, became targets for the reform efforts of New York Presbyterian minister Charles Parkhurst. Blaming the "slimy, oozy soil of Tammany Hall" and the New York City police—"the dirtiest, crookedest, and ugliest lot of men ever combined in semi-military array outside of Japan and Turkey"—for the city's rampant evils, he organized the City Vigilance League to clean up the city. Two years later a nonpartisan Committee of Seventy elected a new mayor who pressured city officials to enforce the laws against prostitution, gambling, and Sunday liquor sales.

The purity campaign lasted scarcely three years. The reform coalition quickly fell apart. New York City's population was too large, and its ethnic constituencies too diverse, for middle- and upper-class reformers to curb all the illegal activities flourishing within the sprawling metropolis.

The Social Gospel   In the 1870s and 1880s a handful of Protestant ministers began to explore several radical alternatives for aiding the poor. Instead of focusing on their alleged moral flaws and character defects, these ministers argued that the rich and the wellborn deserved part of the blame for urban poverty and thus had a responsibility to do something about it.

William S. Rainsford, the Irish-born minister of New York City's Saint George's Episcopal Church, pioneered the development of the so-called institutional church movement. Large downtown churches in once-elite districts that had been overrun by immigrants would provide their new neighbors with social services as well as a place to worship. With the financial help of J. Pierpont Morgan, a warden of his church, Rainsford organized a boys' club, built church recreational facilities for the destitute on the Lower East Side, and established an industrial training program.

Another effort within Protestantism to right contemporary social wrongs was the Social Gospel movement launched in the 1870s by Washington Gladden, a Congregational minister in Columbus, Ohio. Gladden insisted that true Christianity commits men and women to fight social injustice wherever it exists. Thus, in response to the wave of violent strikes in 1877, he urged church leaders to mediate the conflict between business and labor. Their attempt to do so was unsuccessful.

If Gladden set the tone for the Social Gospel, Walter Rauschenbusch, a minister at a German Baptist church in New York's notorious "Hell's Kitchen" neighborhood, articulated the movement's central philosophy. Educated in Germany, Rauschenbusch argued that a truly Christian society would unite all churches, reorganize the industrial system, and work for international peace. Rauschenbusch's appeal for Christian unity led to the formation of the Federal Council of Churches in 1908, but his other goals were never achieved. The Social Gospel's attack on what its leaders blasted as the complacent Christian support of the status quo attracted only a handful of Protestants. Nevertheless, their earnest voices blended with a growing chorus of critics bemoaning the nation's urban woes.

The Settlement House Movement By the 1880s many thoughtful Americans had become convinced that reform pressures applied from the top by the Charity Organization Society and the purity crusaders, however well intentioned, were not only ineffective but were also wrongheaded. A new approach to social work was needed. Relief workers would have to take up residence in poor neighborhoods where, in the words of Jane Addams, an early advocate of the movement, they could see firsthand "the struggle for existence, which is so much harsher among people near the edge of pauperism." A new institution—the settlement house—was born.

The youngest daughter of a successful Illinois businessman, Jane Addams purchased a dilapidated mansion on Chicago's South Halsted Street in 1889. After overseeing extensive repairs, she and her coworkers opened it as Hull House, the first experiment in the settlement house approach. Drawing on the middle-class domestic ideal of true womanhood as supportive and self-sacrificing, the indefatigable Addams turned Hull House into a social center for recent immigrants. She and her coworkers invited them to plays; sponsored art projects; held classes in English, civics, cooking, and dressmaking; and encouraged them to preserve their traditional crafts. She set up a kindergarten, a laundry, an employment bureau, and a day nursery for working mothers. Hull House also sponsored recreational and athletic programs and dispensed legal aid and health care.

In the hope of upgrading the filthy and overcrowded housing in its environs, Addams and her coworkers made studies of city housing conditions and pressured politicians to enforce sanitation regulations. For a time, demonstrating her principle of direct engagement with the lives of the poor, Addams even served as garbage inspector for her local ward.

By 1895 at least fifty settlement houses had opened in cities around the nation. Settlement house leaders trained a generation of young college students, mostly women, many of whom would later serve as state and local government officials. Florence Kelley, for example, who had worked at Hull House, became the chief factory inspector for Illinois in 1893. For Kelley as for other young female settlement workers, settlement houses functioned as a supportive sisterhood of reform through which they developed skills in working with municipal governments. Many settlement house veterans would later draw on their experience to play an influential role in the regulatory movements of the Progressive Era (see Chapter 21). Through their sympathetic attitudes toward the immigrants and their systematic publication of data about slum conditions, settlement house workers gave turn-of-the-century Americans new hope that the city's problems could be overcome.

But in their attempt to promote class cooperation and social harmony, settlement houses had mixed success. Although many immigrants appreciated the settlement houses' resources and activities, they felt that the reformers were uninterested in increasing their political power. Settlement house workers did tend to overlook immigrant organizations and their leaders. In 1894 Hull House attracted two thousand visitors per week, but this was only a fraction of the more than seventy thousand people who lived within six blocks of the building. "They're like the rest," complained one immigrant, "a bunch of people planning for us and deciding what is good for us without consulting us or taking us into their confidence."

WORKING-CLASS LEISURE IN THE IMMIGRANT CITY

In colonial America preachers had linked leisure time to "idleness," a dangerous step on the road to sin and wickedness. In the overwhelmingly rural culture of the early nineteenth century, the unremitting routines of farm labor left little time for relaxation. Family picnics, horse races, county fairs, revival meetings, and Fourth of July and Christmas celebrations had provided occasional permissible diversions. But most Americans continued to view leisure activities skeptically. Henry Clay Work's popular song "My Grandfather's Clock" (1876), which praised the ancient timepiece for "wasting no time" and working "ninety years, without slumbering," bore witness to the tenacity of this deep-seated reverence for work and suspicion of leisure.

After the Civil War, as immigration soared, urban populations shot up, and a new class of wealthy entrepreneurs arose, striking new patterns of leisure and amusement emerged, most notably among the urban working class. Middle-class educators and moralists continued to ponder the distinction between "wholesome" and "unwholesome" recreation, but they were little heeded by immigrants in the throbbing cities. After spending long hours in factories, in mills, behind department-store counters, or working as domestic servants in the homes of the wealthy, working-class Americans sought relaxation and diversion. Scorning the museums and concert halls favored by the wealthy, they thronged the streets, patronized saloons and dance halls, cheered at boxing matches and baseball games, and organized group picnics and holiday celebrations. As amusement parks, vaudeville theaters, sporting clubs, and racetracks provided further outlets for workers' need for entertainment, leisure became a big business catering to a mass public rather than to a wealthy elite.

For millions of working-class Americans, leisure time took on increasing importance as factory work became ever more routinized and impersonal. Although many recreational activities involved both men and women, others attracted one gender in particular. Saloons offered an intensely male environment where patrons could share good stories, discuss and bet on sporting events, and momentarily put aside pressures of job and family. Young working women preferred to share confidences with friends in informal social clubs, tried out new fashions in street promenading, and found excitement in neighborhood dance halls and amusement parks.

Streets, Saloons, and Boxing Matches   No segment of the population had a greater need for amusement and recreation than the urban working class. Hours of tedious, highly disciplined, and physically exhausting labor left workers tired and thirsting for excitement and escape at the end of the day. A banner carried by the Worcester, Massachusetts, carpenters' union in an 1889 demonstration for the eight-hour workday summed up the importance of workers' leisure hours: "EIGHT HOURS FOR WORK, EIGHT HOURS FOR REST, AND EIGHT HOURS FOR WHAT WE WILL."

City streets provided recreation that anyone could afford. Relaxing after a day's work, shop girls and laborers clustered on busy corners, watching shouting push-cart peddlers and listening to organ grinders and buskers (street musicians) play familiar melodies. For a penny or a nickel, they could buy bagels, baked potatoes, soda, and other foods and drinks. In the summer, when the heat and humidity in tenement apartments reached unbearable levels, the streets became a hive of neighborhood social life. One immigrant fondly recalled his boyhood on the streets of New York's Lower East Side, "Something was always happening, and our attention was continually being shifted from one excitement to another."

The streets were open to all, but other leisure institutions drew mainly a male clientele. For example, in cities with a strong German immigrant presence like Baltimore, Milwaukee, and Cincinnati, gymnastic clubs (called *Turnverein*) and singing societies (*Gesangverein*) provided both companionship and the opportunity to perpetuate old-world cultural traditions.

For workmen of all ethnic backgrounds, saloons offered companionship, conviviality, and five-cent beer, often with a free lunch thrown in. New York City had an estimated ten thousand saloons by 1900 and Denver nearly five hundred. As neighborhood gathering places, saloons reinforced group identity and became centers for immigrant politics. Saloonkeepers, who often doubled as local ward bosses, performed small services for their patrons, including finding jobs and writing letters for illiterate immigrants. Sports memorabilia and pictures of prominent prizefighters adorned saloon walls. With their rich mahogany bars, etched glass, shiny brass rails, and elegant mirrors, saloons provided patrons with a taste of high-toned luxury. Although working-class women rarely joined their husbands at the saloon, they might send a son or daughter to the corner pub to fetch a "growler"—a large tin pail of beer.

The conventions of saloon culture thus stood in marked contrast to both the socially isolating routines of factory labor and the increasingly private and family-centered social life of the middle class. Nevertheless, it would be a mistake to view the old-time saloon through a haze of sentimental nostalgia. Prostitution and crime flourished in the rougher saloons. Moreover, drunken husbands sometimes beat their wives and children, squandered their limited income, and lost their jobs. The pervasiveness of alcoholism was devastating. Temperance reformers, in their attack on saloons, targeted a widespread social problem.

For working-class men, bare-knuckled prizefighting became one of the most popular amusements. Drawing its heroes from the poorer ranks of society, the ring became an arena where lower-class men could assert their individuality and physical prowess. In East Coast cities, blacks, Irish, and Germans formed their own "sporting clubs" and used athletics to bolster their self-confidence and reaffirm their racial or ethnic identity.

The Rise of Professional Sports

Contrary to the prevailing myth, schoolboy Abner Doubleday did not invent baseball in Cooperstown, New York, in 1839. As an English game called rounders, the pastime had existed in one form or another since the seventeenth century. But if Americans did not create baseball, they unquestionably took this informal children's game and turned it into a major professional sport. The first organized baseball team, the New York Knickerbockers, was formed in 1845. In the 1860s the rules were codified, and the sport assumed its modern form. Overhand pitches replaced underhand tosses. Fielders, who now wore gloves, had to catch the ball on the fly to make an out instead of fielding it on one bounce. Games were standardized at nine innings, and bases were spaced ninety feet apart, as they are today.

In that same decade, promoters organized professional clubs and began to charge admission and compete for players. The Cincinnati Red Stockings, the first team to put its players under contract for the whole season, gained fame in 1869 by touring the country and ending the season with fifty-seven wins and no losses. Team owners organized the National League in 1876, took control from the players by requiring them to sign contracts that barred them from playing for rival organizations, and limited each city to one professional team. Soon the owners were filling baseball parks with crowds of ten to twelve thousand fans and earning enormous profits. By the 1890s baseball had become big business.

Although baseball attracted a national following from all social levels, the working class particularly took the sport to heart. The most profitable teams were those in major industrial cities with a large working-class population. Workers attended the games when they could and avidly followed their team's progress when they could not. Some saloons reported scores on blackboards. In Cleveland just after the turn of the century, Mayor Tom Johnson erected a bulletin board downtown that recorded game results.

Newspapers thrived on baseball. Joseph Pulitzer introduced the first separate sports page when he bought the *New York World* in 1883, and much of the sporting news in the *World* and other papers was devoted to baseball. For the benefit of German immigrants, the New York *Staats Zeitung* published a glossary of German equivalents of baseball terms; for example, *umpire* was *Unparteiischer*. Baseball, declared novelist Mark Twain in a burst of hyperbole, had become "the very

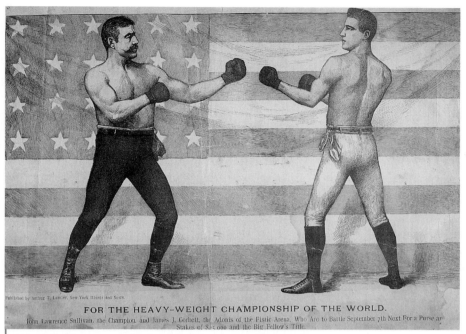

FOR THE HEAVY-WEIGHT CHAMPIONSHIP OF THE WORLD.

John Lawrence Sullivan, the Champion, and James J. Corbett, the Adonis of the Fistic Arena, Who Are to Battle September 7th Next For a Purse and Stakes of $25,000 and the Big Fellow's Title.

World's Heavyweight Boxing Championship, 1892 *In dethroning ring champion John L. Sullivan, "Gentleman Jim" Corbett demonstrated that speed and finesse were more than a match for brute strength.*

symbol . . . and visible expression of the drive and push and rush and struggle of the raging, tearing, booming nineteenth century."

Although no organized sport attracted as large a following as baseball, horse racing and boxing contests were also widely covered in the popular press and drew big crowds of spectators and bettors. Whereas races like Louisville's Kentucky Derby became important social events for the rich, professional boxing aroused more passionate devotion among the working class. By far the most popular sports hero of the nineteenth century was heavyweight fighter John L. Sullivan, "the Boston Strong Boy." Of Irish immigrant stock, Sullivan began boxing in 1877 at the age of nineteen. His first professional fight came in 1880 when he knocked out John Donaldson, "the Champion of the West," in a Cincinnati beer hall. With his massive physique, handlebar mustache, and arrogant swagger, Sullivan was enormously popular among immigrants. Barnstorming across the country, he vanquished a succession of local strong men, invariably wearing his trademark green tights with an American flag wrapped around his middle. Cleverly, Sullivan also refused to fight blacks, in deference, he said, to the wishes of his fans. This policy conveniently allowed him to avoid facing the finest boxer of the 1880s, the Australian black, Peter Jackson.

Sullivan loved drink and high living, and by the end of the eighties he was sadly out of shape. But when the editor of the *Police Gazette*, a sensational tabloid, designed a new heavyweight championship belt—allegedly containing two hundred ounces of silver and encrusted with diamonds and pure gold—and awarded it to Sullivan's rival Jake Kilrain, the champion had to defend himself. The two met on a sweltering, hundred-degree day in New Orleans in July 1889 for the last bare-knuckles championship match. After seventy-five short but grueling rounds, Kilrain's managers threw in the towel. Newspapers around the nation banner-headlined the story. Contemptuously returning the championship belt to the *Police Gazette* after having had it appraised at $175, Sullivan went on the road to star in a melodrama written specifically for him. Playing the role of a blacksmith, he (in the words of a recent historian of bare-knuckles boxing) "pounded an anvil, beat a bully, and mutilated his lines." But his fans did not care; he was one of them, and they adored him. As one admirer wrote,

> His colors are the Stars and Stripes,
> He also wears the green,
> And he's the grandest slugger that
> The ring has ever seen.

Vaudeville, Amusement Parks, and Dance Halls

In contrast to the male preserve of saloons and prizefights, the world of vaudeville, amusement parks, and neighborhood dance pavilions welcomed all comers regardless of gender. Some of them proved particularly congenial to working-class women.

Vaudeville evolved out of the pre–Civil War minstrel shows in which white comedians made up as blacks had performed songs and comic sketches. Vaudeville performances offered a succession of acts, all designed for mass appeal. The shows typically opened with a trained animal routine or a dance number. This was followed by a musical interlude featuring sentimental favorites such as "On the Banks of the Wabash Far Away" or new hits such as "Meet Me in St. Louis, Louis," a jaunty spoof of a young wife's frustration with her stick-in-the-mud husband. Comic skits followed, ridiculing the trials of urban life, satirizing the ineptitude of the police and municipal officials, poking fun at the babel of accents in the immigrant city, and mining a rich vein of broad ethnic humor and stereotypes. After more musical numbers and acts by ventriloquists, pantomimes, and magicians, the program ended with a "flash" finale such as flying-trapeze artists swinging against a black background.

By the 1880s vaudeville was drawing larger crowds than any other form of theater. Not only did it provide an inexpensive evening of lighthearted entertainment, but in the comic sketches, immigrant audiences could also laugh at their own experience as they saw it translated into slapstick and caricature.

The white working class's fascination with vaudeville's blackface acts has been the subject of considerable recent scrutiny by historians. Some have interpreted it as a way for the white working class to mock middle-class ideals. By pretending to act like the popular stereotypes of blacks, white working-class youths could challenge traditional family structures, the virtue of sexual self-denial, and adult expectations about working hard. In this view popular culture was making fun of the ideals of thrift and propriety being promoted in marketplace and domestic ideology. Other historians have argued that blackface buffoonery, with its grotesque, demeaning caricatures of African-Americans, reinforced prejudice against blacks and restricted their escape from lower-class status. Paradoxically, therefore, the popularity of blackface vaudeville acts reinforced white racial solidarity and strengthened the expanding wall separating whites and African-Americans.

Where vaudeville offered psychological escape from the stresses of working-class life by exploiting its comic potential, amusement parks provided physical escape, at least for a day. The prototype of the sprawling urban amusement park was New York's Coney Island, a section of Brooklyn's oceanfront that evolved into a resort for the masses in the 1870s. At Coney Island young couples went dancing, rode through the dark Tunnel of Love, sped down the dizzying roller coaster in Steeplechase Park, or watched belly dancers in the carnival atmosphere of the sideshows. Customers were encouraged to surrender to the spirit of play, forget the demands of the industrial world, and lose themselves in fantasy.

By the end of the nineteenth century, New York City had well over three hundred thousand female wage earners, most of them young, unmarried women working as seamstresses, laundresses, typists, domestic servants, and department-store clerks. For this army of low-paid young working women and their counterparts in other cities, amusement parks exerted a powerful lure. Here they could meet friends, spend time with young men beyond the watchful eyes of their parents, show off their new dresses, and try out the latest dance steps. As a twenty-year-old German immigrant woman who worked as a servant in a wealthy household observed,

> I have heard some of the high people with whom I have been living say that Coney Island is not tony. The trouble is that these high people don't know how to dance. I have to laugh when I see them at their balls and parties. If only I could get out on the floor and show them how—they would be astonished.

For such women, the brightly decorated dance pavilion, the exciting music, and the spell of a warm summer night could seem a magical release from the drudgery of daily life.

Ragtime   Since the days of slavery, black Americans had developed a strong, creative musical culture, and thus it is not surprising that blacks made a major contribution to the popular music of the late nineteenth century in the form of ragtime. Nothing could illustrate more sharply the differences between middle- and working-class culture than the contrasting styles of popular music they favored. The middle class preferred hymns or songs that conveyed a moral lesson. The working class delighted in ragtime, which originated in the 1880s with black musicians in the saloons and brothels of the South and Midwest and was played strictly for entertainment (see A Place in Time: New Orleans, Louisiana, 1890s).

Ragtime developed out of the rich tradition of sacred and secular songs through which African-Americans had long eased the burdens of their lives. Like spirituals, ragtime used syncopated rhythms and complex harmonies, but it blended these with marching-band musical structures to create a distinctive style. A favorite of "honky-tonk" piano players, ragtime was introduced to the broader public in the 1890s and became a national sensation.

The reasons for the sudden ragtime craze were complex. Inventive, playful, with catchy syncopations and an infectious rhythm in the bass clef, the music displayed an originality that had an appeal all its own. Part of ragtime's popularity also came from its origin in brothels and its association with blacks, who were widely stereotyped in the 1890s as sexual, sensual, and uninhibited by the rigid Victorian social conventions that restricted whites. The "wild" and complex rhythms of ragtime were widely interpreted to be a freer and more "natural" expression of elemental feelings about love and sex.

Ragtime's great popularity proved a mixed blessing for blacks. It testified to the achievements of brilliant composers like Scott Joplin, helped break down the barriers faced by blacks in the music industry, and contributed to a spreading rebellion against the repressiveness of Victorian standards. But ragtime simply confirmed some whites' stereotype of blacks as primitive and sensual, a bias that underlay the racism of the period and helped justify segregation and discrimination.

CULTURES IN CONFLICT

In the late nineteenth century the United States was embroiled in class conflict and cultural unrest. Part of this turmoil raged within the middle class itself. Victorian morality and genteel cultural standards were never totally accepted even within the elite and middle classes; and as the century ended, ethical questionings and new cultural stirrings intensified. Women stood at the center of the era's cultural turbulence. Thwarted by a restrictive code of feminine propriety, middle-class women made their dissatisfactions heard. Developments as diverse as the rise of women's clubs, the growth of women's colleges, and an 1890s bicycle fad contributed to the emergence of what some began to call the "new woman."

Although Victorian culture was challenged from within the middle class, a widening chasm divided the well-to-do from urban working-class immigrants. In no period of American history have class conflicts—cultural as well as economic—been more open and raw. As middle-class leaders nervously eyed the rambunctious and sometimes disorderly culture of city streets, saloons, boxing clubs, dance halls, and amusement parks, they saw a massive if unconscious challenge to their own cultural and social standing. Some middle-class reformers promoted the public school as a way to impose middle-class values on the urban masses. Others battled the hydra-headed manifestations of urban "vice" and "immorality." But ultimately it was the polite mores of the middle class, not urban working-class culture, that proved more vulnerable. By 1900 the Victorian social and moral ethos was crumbling on every front.

The Genteel Tradition and Its Critics

What was this genteel culture that aroused such opposition? In the 1870s and 1880s a group of upper-class writers and magazine editors, led by Harvard art history professor Charles Eliot Norton and New York editors Richard Watson Gilder of *The Century* magazine and E. L. Godkin of *The Nation,* codified Victorian standards for literature and the fine arts. They joined forces with artistic allies in Boston and New York in a campaign to improve American taste in interior furnishings, textiles, ceramics, wallpaper, and books. By fashioning rigorous criteria for excellence in writing and design, they hoped to create a coherent national artistic culture.

In the 1880s Norton, Godkin, and Gilder, joined by the editors of other highbrow periodicals such as the *Atlantic Monthly* and *North American Review,* set up new guidelines for serious literature. They lectured the middle class about the value of high culture and the insights to be gained from the fine arts. They censored their own publications to remove all sexual allusions, vulgar slang, disrespectful treatments of Christianity, and unhappy endings. Expanding their combined circulation to nearly two hundred thousand copies and opening their magazines to a variety of new authors, Godkin and the other editors of "quality" periodicals created an important forum for serious writing. Novelists Henry James, who published virtually all of his work in the *Atlantic,* and William Dean Howells, who served as editor of the same magazine, helped lead this elite literary establishment. James believed that "it is art that makes life. . . . [There is] no substitute whatever for [its] force and beauty. . . ."

This interest in art for art's sake paralleled a broader crusade called the "aesthetic movement," led in England by William Morris, Oscar Wilde, and other art critics, who sought to bring art into every facet of life. In America, Candace Wheeler and other reformers made its influence felt through the work of architects, jewelers, and interior decorators.

Although the magazines initially provided an important forum for new writers, their editors' elitism and desire to control the nation's literary standards soon aroused opposition. Samuel Langhorne Clemens, better known as Mark Twain, spoke for many young writers when he declared that he was through with "literature and all that bosh." Attacking aristocratic literary conventions, Twain and other authors who shared his concerns explored new forms of fiction and worked to broaden its appeal to the general public.

These efforts to chart new directions for American literature rested on fundamental changes taking place in the publishing industry. To compete with elite periodicals costing twenty-five to thirty-five cents, new magazines like *Ladies' Home Journal, Cosmopolitan,* and *McClure's* lowered their prices to a dime or fifteen cents and tripled or quadrupled their circulation. Supporting themselves through

New Orleans, Louisiana, 1890s

New Orleans was a unique city in the 1890s. Its popular culture fused elements from the culinary and musical traditions of the varied groups in its population, especially its free blacks and Creoles of color. The latter were the offspring of Africans and eighteenth-century Spanish and French immigrants who had settled along the swampy bayous of the Mississippi Delta south of the city. During the early nineteenth century, New Orleans's large free-black and "colored" Creole population had enjoyed a degree of independence people of color found nowhere else in the South. Free blacks had established their own churches and fraternal societies, formed their own militia, and borne arms. Both wealthy and poor free blacks had created a distinctive culture melding African and French customs. In the Vieux Carré, the old French part of the city, slaves and free blacks joined together on Sunday afternoons to play drums, banjos, and violins. Young people danced and sang, mingling African voodoo rhythms with Roman Catholic liturgical melodies.

During the Civil War and Reconstruction, however, the humiliating occupation of New Orleans by federal troops had left a legacy of southern white bitterness against the black population. Then in the 1880s and 1890s, when Italian immigrants swelled the city's population, racial tensions were rekindled. Despite the discord, festivals like Mardi Gras, with its riotous parades and boisterous balls, continued. The city won notoriety for racetrack betting, gambling, and prostitution. Sightseers flocked to New Orleans to savor spicy Creole food, drink in smoky bars, and visit seedy bordellos and raunchy dance halls. The sidewalks thronged with commercial travelers, longshoremen, country folk in the city for a day, and racetrack bettors. "One is apt to see here at some hour of the day anybody from a St. Louis capitalist to the man who came the night before with no change of linen, and seven dollars sewn in his waistcoat," wrote a visiting journalist. Appropriately, promoters chose New Orleans as the site of the September 1892 championship boxing match in which "Gentleman Jim" Corbett defeated John L. Sullivan.

Among the city's liveliest traditions was the marching band. A product of the eighteenth-century military whose drummers and fifers helped identify regiments' locations amidst battlefield chaos, by the mid-nineteenth century the marching band had become a fixture in cities and towns across America, and prominently so in New Orleans. On Saturday nights, young and old alike ambled to the city-park bandstand to hear local groups belt out the stirring marches of John Philip Sousa and other composers.

New Orleans's black brass bands pioneered new playing styles that captured national attention. Having snapped up the affordable used musical instruments piled high in pawn shops after the Civil War, blacks in New Orleans—unfettered by written scores and formal music lessons—developed innovative styles for bugles, trombones, and the newly invented piston-valve trumpets. Every black social organization, club, fire station, and lodge boasted its own twelve-member brass marching band. The bands played at picnics, parades, dances, church socials, circuses, minstrel shows, athletic contests, and holiday gatherings. By the 1880s many brass bands gained fame for playing in the new "ratty," "raggy," unscored, syncopated style, with its echoes of the older call-and-response African-American singing in which one person shouted a phrase and was answered by the group. Brass bands were also known for playing religious hymns "straight" on the way to the cemetery and "jazzing them up" on the way home. Within the bands, which often played in bars and brothels, individual soloists such as coronetist Charles "Buddy" Bolden became famous for improvisational blues solos. These soulful performances were the forerunners of a new musical style, "jazz," that emerged in the 1890s and became a national rage after the turn of the century.

Although the popularity of these musicians—who were later immortalized in Irving Berlin's song "Alexander's Ragtime Band"—increasingly attracted middle-class white audiences and seemed to imply a growing general acceptance of black musicians, racial prejudice continued to shape local practices. If a black band marched into a white neighborhood, the residents commonly pelted the musicians with rocks.

In 1897, seeking to isolate and regulate prostitution, city administrators created a special district, named Storyville after Sydney Story, the councilman who proposed the new quarter. Storyville's glittering saloons and ubiquitous houses of prostitution hired some of the best black ragtime piano players. Other black musicians, excluded from some white establishments, could find jobs only in the racially segregated bars and cabarets of the two-block "Tango Belt" surrounding Storyville. Musically talented Creoles of color—the proud descendants of free-black mulattos whose musical training had assured them positions in local orchestras and opera houses—could secure employment only in these districts, where they worked alongside criminals and prostitutes.

For all its uniqueness, New Orleans typified larger strands in the turn-of-the-century American fabric. (The city's cultural diversity also anticipated trends that in the twentieth century would make the United States a truly multicultural society.) And the complex history of early jazz in New Orleans paralleled the ironic relationship of popular culture and racism in the larger society. White middle-class America, like the middle class in New Orleans, would soon embrace this African-American musical contribution. Captivated by New Orleans "Dixieland" jazz, they would idolize its best practitioners, including the great trumpeter Louis Armstrong, a veteran of the New Orleans brass marching bands. Yet these middle-class Americans, like their counterparts in New Orleans, would see no contradiction in harboring deep prejudices against the very people from whose culture this vital new music had emerged.

advertising, these magazines encouraged new trends in fiction while mass-marketing new products. Their editors sought writers who could provide accurate depictions of the "whirlpool of real life" and create a new civic consciousness to heal the class divisions of American society.

Some of these authors have been called regionalists because they captured the distinctive dialect and details of local life in their environs. In *The Country of the Pointed Firs* (1896), for example, Sarah Orne Jewett wrote of the New England village life that she knew in South Berwick, Maine. Others, most notably William Dean Howells, have been called realists because of their focus on the truthful depiction of the commonplace and the everyday, especially in urban areas. Still others have been categorized as naturalists because their novels and stories deny free will and stress the ways in which life's outcomes are determined by economic and psychological forces. Stephen Crane's *Maggie: A Girl of the Streets* (1892), a bleak story of an innocent girl's exploitation and ultimate suicide in an urban slum, is generally considered the first naturalistic American novel. Yet in practice, these categories are imprecise and often overlap. What many of these writers shared was a skepticism about literary conventions and an intense desire to understand the society around them and portray it in words.

The careers of Mark Twain and Theodore Dreiser highlight the changes in the publishing industry and the evolution of new forms of writing. Both authors grew up in the Midwest, outside the East Coast literary establishment. Twain was born near Hannibal, Missouri, in 1835, and Dreiser in Terre Haute, Indiana, in 1871. As young men both worked as newspaper reporters and traveled widely. Both learned from direct and sometimes bitter experience about the greed, speculation, and fraud that figured centrally in Gilded Age life.

Of the two, Twain more incessantly sought a mass-market audience. With his drooping mustache, white hair, and white suits, Twain turned himself into a media personality, lecturing from coast to coast, founding his own publishing house, and using door-to-door salesmen to sell his books. The name Mark Twain became his trademark, identifying him to readers as a literary celebrity much as the labels Coca-Cola and Ivory Soap won instant consumer recognition. Although Dreiser possessed neither Twain's flamboyant personality nor his instinct for salesmanship, he, too, learned to crank out articles.

Drawing on their own experiences, Twain and Dreiser wrote about the human impact of the wrenching social changes taking place around them: the flow of people to the cities and the relentless scramble for power, wealth, and fame. In the *Adventures of Huckleberry Finn* (1884), Twain presents a classic narrative of two runaways, the rebellious Huck and the slave Jim, drifting down the Mississippi in search of freedom. Their physical journey, which contrasts idyllic life on the raft with the tawdry, fraudulent world of small riverfront towns, is a journey of identity that brings with it a deeper understanding of contemporary American society.

Dreiser's *Sister Carrie* (1900) also tells of a journey. In this case, the main character, Carrie Meeber, an innocent girl on her way from her Wisconsin farm home to Chicago, is first seduced by a traveling salesman and then moves in with the married proprietor of a fancy saloon. Driven by her desire for expensive department-store clothes and lavish entertainment, Carrie is an opportunist incapable of feeling guilt. She follows her married lover to New York, knowing that he has stolen the receipts from his saloon, abandons him when his money runs out, and pursues her own career in the theater.

Twain and Dreiser broke decisively with the genteel tradition's emphasis on manners and decorum. *Century* magazine readers complained that *Huckleberry Finn* was coarse and "destitute of a single redeeming quality." The publisher of *Sister Carrie* was so repelled by Dreiser's novel that he printed only a thousand copies (to fulfill the legal terms of his contract) and then stored them in a warehouse, refusing to promote them.

Growing numbers of scholars and critics similarly challenged the self-serving certitudes of Victorian mores, including assumptions that moral worth and economic standing were closely linked and that the status quo of the 1870s and 1880s represented a social order decreed by God and nature alike. Whereas Henry George, Lester Ward, and Edward Bellamy elaborated their visions of a cooperative and harmonious society (see Chapter 18), economist Thorstein Veblen in *The Theory of the Leisure Class* (1899) offered a caustic critique of the lifestyles of the new capitalist elite. Raised in a Norwegian farm community in Minnesota, Veblen looked at the captains of industry and their families with a jaundiced eye, mercilessly documenting their "conspicuous consumption" and lamenting the widening economic gap between "those who worked without profit" and "those who profited without working."

Within the new discipline of sociology, Annie MacLean exposed the exploitation of department-store clerks, Walter Wyckoff uncovered the hand-to-mouth existence of unskilled laborers, and W. E. B. Du Bois documented the suffering and hardships faced by blacks in Philadelphia. The publication of these social scientists' writings, coupled with the economic depression and seething labor agitation of the 1890s, made it increasingly difficult for turn-of-the-century middle-class Americans to accept the smug, self-satisfied belief in progress and gentility that had been a hallmark of the Victorian outlook.

Modernism in Architecture and Painting   The challenge to the genteel tradition also found strong support among architects and painters. By the 1890s Chicago architects William Holabird, John Wellborn Root, and others had tired of copying European designs. Breaking with established architects such as Richard Morris Hunt, the designer of French chateaux for New York's Fifth Avenue, these Chicago architects followed the lead of Louis Sullivan, who argued that a building's form should follow its function. In their view, banks should look like the financial institutions they were, not like Greek temples. Striving to evolve functional American design standards, the Chicago architects looked for inspiration to the future—to modernism—not to the past.

Frank Lloyd Wright's "prairie-school" houses, first built in the Chicago suburb of Oak Park in the 1890s, represented a typical modernist break with past styles.

Wright scorned the bulky Victorian house with its large attic and basement. His designs, which featured broad, sheltering roofs and low silhouettes, used interconnecting rooms to create a sense of spaciousness.

The call of modernism, with its rejection of Victorian refinement, influenced late-nineteenth-century American painting as well. The watercolors of Winslow Homer, a magazine illustrator during the Civil War, revealed nature as brutally tough and unsentimental. In Homer's grim, elemental seascapes, lone men struggle against massive waves that constantly threaten to overwhelm them. Thomas Eakins's canvases of swimmers, boxers, and rowers (such as his well-known *Champion Single Sculls,* painted in 1871) similarly captured moments of vigorous physical exertion in everyday life.

The revolt by architects and painters against Victorian standards was symptomatic of a larger shift in middle-class thought. This shift resulted from fundamental economic changes that had spawned a far more complex social environment than that of the past. As Protestant minister Josiah Strong perceptively observed in 1898, the transition from muscle to mechanical power had "separated, as by an impassable gulf, the simple, homespun, individualistic world of the . . . past, from the complex, closely associated life of the present." The increasingly evident gap between rural or small-town life—a world of quiet parlors and flickering kerosene lamps—and life in the big, glittering, electrified cities of iron and glass made nineteenth-century Americans acutely aware of differences in upbringing and wealth. Given the disparities between rich and poor, between rural and urban, and between native-born Americans and recent immigrants, it is no wonder that pious Victorian platitudes about proper manners and graceful arts seemed out of touch with the new social realities.

Distrusting the idealistic Victorian assumptions about social progress, middle-class journalists, novelists, artists, and politicians nevertheless remained divided over how to replace them. Not until the Progressive Era would social reformers draw on a new expertise in social research and an enlarged conception of the federal government's regulatory power to break sharply with their Victorian predecessors' social outlook.

From Victorian Lady to New Woman   Although middle-class women figured importantly in the revolt against Victorian refinement, their role was complex and ambiguous. Dissatisfaction with the cult of domesticity did not necessarily lead to open rebellion. Many women, although chafing against the constraints of deference and the assumption that they should limit their activities to the home, remained committed to playing a nurturing and supportive role within the family. In fact, early advocates of a "widened sphere" for women often fused the traditional Victorian ideal of womanhood with a firm commitment to political action.

The career of temperance leader Frances Willard illustrates how the cult of domesticity, with its celebration of special female virtues, could evolve into a broader view of women's social and political responsibilities. Like many of her contemporaries, Willard believed that women were compassionate and nurturing by nature. She was also convinced that drinking encouraged thriftlessness and profoundly threatened family life. Resigning as dean of women and professor of English at Northwestern University in 1874, Willard devoted her energies full-time to the temperance cause. Five years later she was elected president of the newly formed Woman's Christian Temperance Union (WCTU).

Willard took the traditional belief that women had unique moral virtues and transformed it into a rationale for political action. The domestication of politics, she asserted, would protect the family and improve public morality. Choosing as the union's badge a bow of white ribbon, symbolizing the purity of the home, she launched a crusade in 1880 to win the franchise for women so that they could vote to outlaw liquor. Willard soon expanded WCTU activities to include welfare work, prison reform, labor arbitration, and public health. Under her leadership the WCTU, with a membership of nearly 150,000 by 1890, became the nation's first mass organization of women. Through it, women gained experience as lobbyists, organizers, and lecturers, in the process undercutting the assumption of "separate spheres."

An expanding network of women's clubs offered another means by which middle- and upper-class women could hone their skills in civic affairs, public speaking, and intellectual analysis. In the 1870s many well-to-do women met weekly to study topics of mutual interest. These clubwomen soon became involved in social-welfare projects, public library expansion, and tenement reform. By 1892 the General Federation of Women's Clubs, an umbrella organization established that year, boasted 495 affiliates and a hundred thousand members.

Another major impetus to an expanded role for women came from a younger generation of college women. Following the precedent set by Oberlin College in 1836, coeducational private colleges and public universities in the Midwest enrolled increasing numbers of women. Columbia, Brown, and Harvard universities in the East admitted women to the affiliated but separate institutions of Barnard (1889), Pembroke (1891), and Radcliffe (1894), respectively. Nationally, the percentage of colleges admitting women jumped from 30 percent to 71 percent between 1880 and 1900. By the turn of the century, women made up more than one-third of the total college-student population.

Initially, female collegiate education reinforced the prevailing concepts of femininity. The earliest women's colleges—Mount Holyoke (1837), Vassar (1865), Wellesley and Smith (1875), and Bryn Mawr (1884)—were founded to prepare women for marriage, motherhood, and Christian service. But participation in college organizations, athletics, and dramatics enabled female students to learn traditionally "masculine" strategies for gaining power. The generation of women educated at female institutions in the late nineteenth century developed the self-confidence to break with the Victorian ideal of passive womanhood and to compete on an equal basis with men by displaying the strength, aggressiveness, and intelligence popularly considered male attributes. By 1897 the U.S. commissioner of education noted, "[I]t has become an historical fact that women have made rapid strides, and captured a greater number of honors in proportion to their numbers than men."

Victorian constraints on women were further loosened at the end of the century when a bicycling vogue swept urban America. Fearful of waning vitality, middle- and upper-class Americans explored various ways to improve their vigor. Some used health products such as cod liver oil and sarsaparilla for "weak blood." Others played basketball, invented in 1891 by a physical education instructor at Springfield College in Massachusetts to keep students in shape during the winter months. But bicycling, which could be done individually or in groups, quickly became the most popular sport for those who wished to combine exercise with recreation.

Bicycles of various designs had been manufactured since the 1870s, but bicycling did not become a national craze until the invention in the 1880s of the so-called safety bicycle, with smaller wheels, ball-bearing axles, and air-filled tires. By the 1890s over a million Americans owned bicycles.

Bicycling especially appealed to young women who had chafed under the restrictive Victorian attitudes about female exercise, which held that proper young ladies must never sweat and that the female body must be fully covered at all times. Pedaling along in a shirtwaist or "split" skirt, a woman bicyclist made an implicit feminist statement suggesting that she had broken with genteel conventions and wanted to explore new activities beyond the traditional sphere.

Changing attitudes about femininity and women's proper role also found expression in gradually shifting ideas about marriage. Charlotte Perkins Gilman, a suffrage advocate and speaker for women's rights, asserted that women would make an effective contribution to society only when they won economic independence from men through work outside the home (see Chapter 21). One very tangible indicator of women's changing relationship to men was the substantial rise in the divorce rate between 1880 and 1900. In 1880 one in every twenty-one marriages ended in divorce. By 1900 the rate had climbed to one in twelve. Women who brought suit for divorce increasingly cited their husbands' failure to act responsibly and to respect their autonomy. Accepting such arguments, courts frequently awarded the wife alimony, a monetary settlement payable by the ex-husband to support her and their children.

Women writers generally welcomed the new female commitment to independence and self-sufficiency. In the short stories of Mary Wilkins Freeman, for example, women's expanding role is implicitly compared to the frontier ideal of freedom. Feminist Kate Chopin pushed the debate to the extreme by having Edna Pontellier, the married heroine of her 1899 novel *The Awakening*, violate social conventions. First Edna falls in love with another man; then she takes her own life when his ideas about women prove as narrow and traditional as those of her husband.

Despite the efforts of these and other champions of the new woman, attitudes changed slowly. The enlarged conception of women's role in society exerted its greatest influence on college-educated, middle-class women who had leisure time and could reasonably hope for success in journalism, social work, and nursing. For female immigrant factory workers and for shop girls who worked sixty hours a week to try to make ends meet, however, the ideal remained a more distant goal. Although many women were seeking more independence and control over their lives, most still viewed the home as their primary responsibility.

| Public Education as an Arena of Class Conflict | While the debate over women's proper role remained largely confined to the middle class, a very different controversy, over the scope and function of public education, engaged Americans of all socioeconomic levels. This debate starkly |

highlighted the class and cultural divisions in late-nineteenth-century society. From the 1870s on, viewing the public schools as an instrument for indoctrinating and controlling the lower ranks of society, middle-class educators and civic leaders campaigned to expand public schooling and bring it under centralized control. Not surprisingly, the reformers' efforts aroused considerable opposition from ethnic and religious groups whose outlook and interests differed sharply from theirs.

Thanks to the crusade for universal public education started by Horace Mann and other antebellum educational reformers, most states had public school systems by the Civil War, and more than half the nation's children were receiving some formal education. But most attended school for only three or four years, and few went on to high school.

Concerned that many Americans lacked sufficient knowledge to participate wisely in public affairs or function effectively in the labor force, reformers such as William Torrey Harris worked to increase the number of years that children spent in school. First as superintendent of the St. Louis public schools in the 1870s and later as the federal commissioner of education, Harris urged teachers to instill in their students a sense of order, decorum, self-discipline, and civic loyalty. Believing that modern industrial society depended on citizens' conforming to the timetables of the factory and the train, he envisioned the schools as models of punctuality and precise scheduling: "The pupil must have his lessons ready at the appointed time, must rise at the tap of the bell, move to the line, return; in short, go through all the evolutions with equal precision."

To achieve these goals and to wrest control of the schools from neighborhood leaders and ward politicians, reform-minded educators like Harris elaborated a philosophy of public education stressing punctuality, centralized administration, compulsory-attendance laws, and a tenure system to insulate teachers from political favoritism and parental pressure. By 1900 thirty-one states required school attendance of all children from eight to fourteen years of age.

The steamroller methods used by Harris and like-minded administrators to systematize public education quickly prompted protests. New York pediatrician Joseph Mayer Rice, who toured thirty-six cities and interviewed twelve hundred teachers in 1892, scornfully criticized an educational establishment that stressed singsong memorization and prisonlike discipline.

Rice's biting attack on public education overlooked the real advances in reading and computation made in the previous two decades. Nationally, despite the influx of immigrants, the illiteracy rate for individuals ten years and older dropped from 17 percent in 1880 to 13 percent in 1890, largely because of the expansion of urban educational facilities. American high schools were also coeducational, and girls made up the majority of the students by 1900. But Rice was on target in assailing many teachers' rigid emphasis on silence, docility, and unquestioning obedience to the rules. When a Chicago school inspector found a thirteen-year-old boy huddled in the basement of a stockyard building and ordered him back to school, the weeping boy blurted out, "[T]hey hits ye if yer don't learn, and they hits ye if ye whisper, and they hits ye if ye have string in yer pocket, and they hits ye if yer seat squeaks, and they hits ye if ye don't stan' up in time, and they hits ye if yer late, and they hits ye if ye ferget the page."

By the 1880s several different groups found themselves in opposition to centralized urban public-school bureaucracies. Although many working-class families valued education, those who depended on their children's meager wages for survival resisted the attempt to force their sons and daughters to attend school past the elementary grades. Although some immigrant families made great sacrifices to enable their children to get an education, many withdrew their offspring from school as soon as they had learned the rudiments of reading and writing, and sent them to work.

Furthermore, Catholic immigrants objected to the overwhelmingly Protestant orientation of the public schools. Distressed by the use of the King James translation of the Bible and by the schools' failure to observe saints' days, Catholics set up separate parochial school systems. In response, Republican politicians, resentful of the Catholic immigrants' overwhelming preference for the Democratic party, tried unsuccessfully to pass a constitutional amendment cutting off all public aid to church-related schools in 1875. Catholics in turn denounced federal aid to public schools as intended "to suppress Catholic education, gradually extinguish Catholicity in this country, and to form one homogeneous American people after the New England Evangelical type."

At the other end of the social scale, upper-class parents who did not wish to send their children to immigrant-thronged public schools enrolled their daughters in female seminaries such as Emma Willard's in Troy, New York, and their sons in private academies and boarding schools like St. Paul's in Concord, New Hampshire. The proliferation of private and parochial schools, together with the controversies over compulsory education, school funding, and classroom decorum, reveals the extent to which public education had become entangled in ethnic and class differences. Unlike Germany and Japan, which standardized and centralized their national education systems in the late nineteenth century, the United States, reflecting its social heterogeneity, created a diverse system of locally run public and private institutions that allowed each segment of society to retain some influence over the schools attended by its own children. Amid the disputes, school enrollments dramatically expanded. In 1870 fewer than seventy-two thousand students attended the nation's 1,026 high schools. By 1900 the number of high schools had jumped to more than 5,000 and the number of students to more than half a million.

IMPORTANT EVENTS, 1860–1900

1843 Robert M. Hartley founds the New York Association for Improving the Condition of the Poor.

1851 The American branch of the Young Men's Christian Association (YMCA) opens.

1852 Charles Loring Brace founds the New York Children's Aid Society.

1855 New York opens its Castle Garden immigrant center.

1865 Vassar College founded.

1869 Boss William Marcy Tweed gains control of New York's Tammany Hall political machine.
First intercollegiate football game.

1871 Thomas Eakins, *The Champion Single Sculls.*

1872 Anthony Comstock founds the New York Society for the Suppression of Vice and leads a "purity" campaign.

1873 John Wanamaker opens his Philadelphia department store.

1874 Smith College founded.
Frances Willard joins the Woman's Christian Temperance Union.
Henry Clay Work, "My Grandfather's Clock."

1876 National League of baseball players organized.

1880 William Booth's followers establish an American branch of the Salvation Army.

1881 Josephine Shaw Lowell founds the New York Charity Organization Society (COS).

1884 Mark Twain, *Huckleberry Finn.*
Bryn Mawr College founded.

1889 Jane Addams and Ellen Gates Starr open Hull House.

1891 Stanford University founded.
University of Chicago founded.
Columbia University adds Barnard College as a coordinate institution for women.
Basketball invented at Springfield College in Massachusetts.

1892 Joseph Mayer Rice writes his exposé of public education in *Forum* magazine.
General Federation of Women's Clubs organized.

1895 Coney Island amusement parks open in Brooklyn.

1899 Scott Joplin, "Maple Leaf Rag."
Kate Chopin, *The Awakening.*
Thorstein Veblen, *The Theory of the Leisure Class.*
W. E. B. Du Bois, *The Philadelphia Negro.*

1900 Theodore Dreiser, *Sister Carrie.*

1910 Angel Island Immigration Center opens in San Francisco.

20

Politics and Expansion in an Industrializing Age, 1877–1900

July 2, 1881, was a muggy summer day in Washington, D.C., and President James A. Garfield was leaving town for a visit to western Massachusetts. At 9:30 A.M., as he strolled through the railroad station, shots rang out. Garfield fell, a bullet in his back. The shooter, Charles Guiteau, immediately surrendered.

At first, doctors thought the president would recover. But Garfield, a veteran who had seen the long-term effects of gunshot wounds, knew better. "I am a dead man," he told them. His doctors tried everything. But as the doctors probed the wound with bare hands and unsterilized instruments, blood poisoning set in. On September 19, Garfield died.

The nation mourned. An Ohio farm boy, Will Boyer, was shocked to hear the news from another farmer as he walked along a country road. Garfield embodied the American dream of the self-made man. Born in a log cabin in Ohio (he was the last log-cabin president), he had worked his way through Williams College, preached in the Disciples of Christ Church, taught at Hiram College, practiced law, and won election to the Ohio senate. He fought in the Civil War, went to Congress in 1863, and was elected president in 1880—thereby sealing his death warrant. As for Guiteau, the jury rejected his insanity plea, and in June 1882 he was hanged.

A decent, well-meaning man, Garfield also embodied a political generation that seemed more preoccupied with the spoils of office than with the problems of ordinary people. In Congress Garfield had been tainted by the 1873 Crédit Mobilier scandal and other corruption charges. His presidential nomination in 1880 had resulted from a split in the Republican party between two rival factions, the Stalwarts and the Half-Breeds, that vied with each other over the distribution of patronage jobs.

The obscure Guiteau, a Stalwart who had supported Garfield, expected to be rewarded with a high diplomatic post. When this failed to materialize, his delusionary mental state worsened. Viewing Garfield's death as "a political necessity," he believed that the Stalwarts would hail him as a hero. (Indeed, he had selected as his gun a .44-caliber "British Bulldog" pistol because it would look good in a museum.)

While contemporary critics like Henry Adams viewed Garfield's assassination as an example of the absurdity of late-nineteenth century politics—a time, Adams sneered, of "little but damaged reputations"—historians today see it as a sign of how closely contested and highly emotional political battles were. The phenomenal expansion of large corporations, the settlement of the trans-Mississippi West, and the surge in urban growth put intense pressure on the political process. At stake was not only the government's proper role in the stimulation and regulation of America's explosive industrial growth, but also the thorny issues of how to assimilate the new immigrants, control chaotic urban life, gain access to new markets, and encourage territorial expansion.

These intense debates over economic and social policy involved nothing less than contending visions of how industrial growth should or should not be regulated and who should benefit financially. The struggle to control economic expansion reached its peak in the 1890s when a new third party, the Populists, joined with the Democrats to challenge corporate control of the economy. The Populist campaign for "free silver," a monetary policy that would back currency with silver reserves instead of gold, implied strong support for reforms that would have relieved the exploitation of labor and the abysmal working conditions that accompanied the surging industrialization of this period. Representing the opposite position, the Republican party's support for high tariffs and the gold standard represented a commitment to encouraging the growth of large corporations, to freeing industry to expand without regulation, and to developing new markets.

From the mid-1870s to the mid-1890s, power seesawed back and forth between the political parties. No party was able to control the political process. But in 1896, the election of President William F. McKinley, who would also die from an assassin's bullet, brought the bitter battle over economic standards to an end and ushered in a generation of Republican domination of national politics. Having been elected in a campaign focused on the restoration of prosperity, McKinley stumbled into war with Spain, substantially increased U.S. territorial holdings, and established new outposts from which American corporations could gain access to overseas markets. Why it took twenty years to resolve the debate over economic policy and achieve a realignment in national politics, how the Republicans triumphed over the protests of farmers and laborers, and what effect the Republican vision had on territorial expansion are the subjects of this chapter.

This chapter focuses on four major questions:

How did the Democratic and Republican parties build coalitions of loyal followers out of their diverse ethnic and regional constituencies?

How did environmental factors influence the rise of the Grange and the Farmers' Alliance movements?

Why was the election of 1896 a watershed event? Why did William Jennings Bryan fail to win the presidency?

Why did the United States go to war with Spain and become an imperial power?

PARTY POLITICS IN AN ERA OF SOCIAL AND ECONOMIC UPHEAVAL, 1877–1884

Between 1877 and 1894 four presidents squeezed into office by the narrowest of margins; control of the House of Representatives changed hands five times; and seven new western states were admitted into the Union. Competition between political parties was intense. No one party could muster a working majority.

To meet these challenges, Republicans, Democrats, and third-party leaders sought desperately to reshape their political organizations to win over and cement the loyalty of their followers. While the Democrats rebuilt their strength in the South and mounted new challenges, Republicans struggled to maintain the loyalties of the working class, to strengthen their support from business, and to fight off the threat of new third parties. Not until 1896, in the aftermath of a massive depression that hit when the Democrats and a new third party, the Populists, were in office, did the Republicans consolidate their power and build a coalition that would control Congress and the presidency for the next fifteen years.

Between 1876 and 1896, the intense competition between parties produced an incredible turnout of voters. Although most women did not yet have the vote and blacks were increasingly being disenfranchised, more than 80 percent of eligible white males often voted, and in particularly hard-fought state and local elections, the percentage could rise to 95 percent. Voter participation a century later would equal scarcely half that level.

Higher voter turnout resulted in part from the attempts of the major parties to navigate the stormy economy created by postwar industrial and geographic expansion, the influx of millions of immigrants, and the pell-mell growth of cities (see Chapters 18 and 19). At the same time that voter turnout shot up, however, political parties sidestepped many of the issues created by industrialization such as taxation of corporations, support for those injured in factory accidents, and poverty relief. Nor was the American labor movement, unlike its counterparts in Europe, able to organize itself effectively as a political force (see Chapter 18). Except for the Interstate Commerce Act of 1887 and the largely symbolic Sherman Anti-Trust Act of 1890, Washington generally ignored the social consequences of industrialization and focused instead on encouraging economic growth.

How can we explain this refusal and, at the same time, account for the enormous popular support for parties? The answer lies in the political ideology of the period and the two major symbolic and economic issues that preoccupied lawmakers nationally. The first involved the economic issues of the tariff and the money supply. The second issue focused on civil-service reform, aimed at awarding government jobs on the basis of merit rather than political connections.

Contested
Political Visions

Political parties in the late nineteenth century energized voters not only by appealing to economic self-interest, as was evident in support for industrialization and pensions for Civil War veterans and their widows, but also by linking their programs to deeply held beliefs about the nature of the family and the proper role of government. In its prewar years, the Republican party had enhanced economic opportunities for common people by using governmental authority to expand railroads, increase tariff protection for industry, and provide land subsidies to farmers. With encouragement from evangelical ministers, it had also espoused a belief in female moral superiority and a willingness to use government as an instrument to protect family life. Hostility to slavery was based in part on the assumption that slaveholding corroded family values. The Democrats, in contrast, had viewed emancipation as a threat to patriarchal order and racial control.

After the Civil War, these positions hardened into political ideologies. Republicans justified their support for the tariff and defended their commitment to Union widows' pensions as a protection for the family home and female wage earners. Men, in particular, associated loyalty to party with a sense of masculinity. Democrats countered, using metaphors of the seduction and rape of white women by external forces and labeling Republican programs as classic examples of the perils of using excessive government force. High tariffs imperiled the family and threatened economic disaster.

Despite their differences over the tariff and monetary policy, neither Republicans nor Democrats believed that the national government had any right to regulate corporations or to protect the social welfare of workers. Many members of the dominant parties, particularly among the middle and upper classes, embraced the doctrine of laissez-faire—the belief that unregulated competition represented the best path to progress. According to this view, the federal government should promote economic development but not regulate the industries that it subsidized.

Rather than looking to Washington, people turned to local or state authorities. On the Great Plains, angry farmers demanded that their state legislatures regulate railroad rates. In the cities, immigrant groups competed for political power while native-born reformers periodically attempted to oust the political machines.

Moreover, city and state governments vied with each other for control. Cities often could not change their system of government, alter their tax structure, or regulate municipal utilities without state approval. When Chicago wanted to issue permits to street popcorn vendors, for example, the Illinois legislature had to pass a special act.

Party loyalty for both Republicans and Democrats was reinforced by a sense of personal grievance that resulted from the belief, often true, that the other party had engaged in election fraud to steal elections. Although both parties, in both the North and the South, practiced fraud by rigging elections, throwing out opposition votes, and paying for "floaters" who moved from precinct to precinct to vote, each developed a sense of moral outrage at the other's behavior that invigorated party spirit.

By linking economic policy to family values, both national parties reinforced the appeal of their platforms and, in the process, encouraged the participation of women in the political process. Although most women could not vote, they played an active role in politics in this period. Frances Willard and her followers in the Woman's Christian Temperance Union (WCTU), for example, helped create a Prohibition and Home Protection Party in the 1880s. A decade later western women Populists won full suffrage in Colorado, Idaho, and Utah.

Patterns of Party Strength   In the 1870s and 1880s each party had its own ideological appeal and centers of regional strength. The Democrats ruled the South; southern sections of border states like Ohio; and northern cities with large immigrant populations. In the South the white Democratic party elite viewed Republicans as villains who had devastated their lands and set up fraudulent carpetbag governments in the defeated Confederacy. The Democrats campaigned for minimal government expenditures, opposed tariff increases, and generally attacked what they considered to be "governmental interference in the economy."

In addition to resisting government support for the economy, Democrats staunchly defended their immigrant followers. On the state and local levels, they fiercely opposed prohibition and other attempts to limit alcohol use and license saloons. They also advocated support for parochial schools and opposed attempts to require immigrant children to attend only those schools that taught in English.

The Republicans, who reigned in rural and small-town New England, Pennsylvania, and the upper Midwest and who drew support from the Grand Army of the Republic (GAR), a social and political lobbying organization of northern Civil War veterans, often "waved the bloody shirt," reminding voters that their party had led the nation during the Civil War. "The Democratic Party," wrote one Republican, "may be described as a common sewer and loathsome receptacle, into which is emptied every element of treason North and South." To solidify their followers, the Republicans ran a series of former Union army generals for president and voted generous veterans' benefits.

State and local party leaders managed campaigns. They chose the candidates, raised money, organized rallies, and—if their candidate won—distributed public jobs to party workers. Chieftains like the former saloonkeepers "Big Jim" Pendergast of Kansas City, a Democrat, and George B. Cox of Cincinnati, a Republican, turned out the vote by taking care of constituents, handing out municipal jobs, and financing campaigns with "contributions" extracted from city employees.

Although the struggle to define the legitimate use of governmental authority shaped the general debate between the two major parties on the federal level, family tradition, ethnic ties, religious affiliation, and local issues often determined an individual's vote. Outside the South, ethnicity and religion were the most reliable predictors of party affiliation. Catholics, especially Irish Catholics, and Americans of German ancestry tended to vote Democratic. Old-stock northerners, in contrast, including 75 percent of Methodists and Congregationalists, 65 percent of Baptists, and 60 percent of Presbyterians voted Republican. Among immigrant groups, most British-born Protestants and 80 percent of Swedish and Norwegian Lutherans voted Republican, as did African-Americans, North and South. Although intolerant of racial differences, the Democrats were generally more accepting of religious diversity than were the Republicans.

As a result of the effect of ethnicity on politics, electoral skirmishes between groups often centered on cultural differences, as native-born Protestants tried to force on the immigrants their own views on gambling, prostitution, temperance, and Sabbath observance. No issue on the local level aroused more conflict than prohibition. Irish whiskey drinkers, German beer drinkers, and Italian wine drinkers were equally outraged by antiliquor legislation. State and local prohibition proposals always aroused passionate voter interest.

The Hayes White House: Virtue Restored

In this era of locally based politics and a diminished presidency, the state leaders who ran party politics tended to favor appealing but pliable presidential candidates. Rutherford B. Hayes fit the mold perfectly. A lawyer and Civil War general wounded in action, Hayes had won admiration as an honest governor of Ohio. His major presidential achievement was to restore respect for the office after the Grant scandals. With his flowing beard, the benevolent Hayes brought dignity and decorum to the White House. In part, this reflected the influence of his wife, Lucy, an intelligent, college-educated woman of great moral earnestness. The Hayeses and their five children often gathered after dinner for hymns and family prayers.

In contrast to the bibulous Grant, Hayes drank only moderately. He also recognized the political strength of the temperance movement. "Lemonade Lucy" Hayes supported the Woman's Christian Temperance Union. After one White House dinner, Hayes's secretary of state grumbled, "It was a brilliant affair. The water flowed like champagne."

Regulating the Money Supply

In the 1870s politicians confronted a tough problem of economic policy: how to create a money supply adequate for a growing economy without producing inflation. Americans' almost superstitious reverence for gold and silver added to the difficulty of establishing a coherent monetary policy. The only trustworthy money, many believed, was gold or silver, or certificates exchangeable for these precious metals. Reflecting this notion, all the federally issued currency in circulation in 1860 consisted of gold or silver coins or U.S. Treasury notes redeemable for gold or silver. (Currency from some sixteen hundred state banks was also in circulation, worsening a chaotic monetary situation.)

To complicate matters, opposing groups clashed over the money question. Bankers and creditors, most business leaders, economists, and politicians believed that economic stability required a strictly limited currency supply. Debtors, especially southern and western farmers, favored expanding the money supply to make it easier for them to pay off their debts. The monetary debate focused on a specific question: should the Civil War paper "greenbacks" that were still in circulation be retained and even expanded, or phased out, leaving only a currency backed by gold (see Chapter 15). The hard times associated with the Panic of 1873 sharpened this dispute.

The Greenback party (founded 1877) advocated an expanded money supply, health and safety regulations for the workplace, and other measures to benefit workers and farmers. In the 1878 midterm elections, with the support of labor organizations angered by the government's hostility in the labor unrest of 1877, Greenback candidates won fourteen seats in Congress.

As prosperity returned, the Greenback party faded, but the money issue did not. The debate now focused on the coinage of silver. In 1873, with little silver being mined, Congress instructed the U.S. mint to stop making silver coins. Silver had been "demonetized." But new discoveries in Nevada (see Chapter 17) soon increased the silver supply, and debtor groups now demanded that the government resume the coinage of silver.

Enthusiastically backed by the silver-mine owners, silver forces won a partial victory in 1878, when Congress required the Treasury to buy up to $4 million worth of silver each month and mint it into silver dollars. But the Treasury, dominated by monetary conservatives, sabotaged the law's intent by refusing to circulate the silver dollars that it minted.

Frustrated silver advocates tried a new approach in the Sherman Silver Purchase Act of 1890. This measure instructed the Treasury to buy, at current market prices, 4.5 million ounces of silver monthly—almost precisely the output of the nation's silver mines. The act further required the government to issue Treasury notes, redeemable in gold or silver, equivalent to the cost of these purchases. This law did slightly increase the money supply; but as silver prices fell in 1893 and after, the government paid far less for its monthly purchases and therefore issued fewer Treasury notes. The controversy over silver dragged on.

The Spoils System For decades successful candidates in national, state, and local elections had rewarded supporters and contributors with jobs ranging from cabinet seats and ambassadorships to lowly municipal posts. To its defenders, this system, originally called rotation in office, seemed the most democratic means of filling government positions, and it provided upward mobility for lucky appointees. But unqualified and incompetent applicants often got jobs simply because of their party loyalty. Once in office, these appointees had to contribute to the reelection campaigns of their political patrons. Because of such abuses, this mode of filling public jobs came to be called the spoils system after the old expression, "To the victor belong the spoils."

For years, a small but influential group of upper-class reformers, including Missouri Senator Carl Schurz and editor E. L. Godkin of the *Nation*, had campaigned for a professional civil service based on merit. Well bred, well educated, and well heeled, these reformers favored a civil service staffed by "gentlemen." Whatever their class biases, the reformers had a point. A professional civil service was needed as government grew more complex.

NY DEN

TRUSTS

"PROTECTION"

WHERE IS THE DIFFERENCE?

"Where Is the Difference?" 1894 *By equating criminal payoffs to the police to corporate contributions to senators, this cartoon suggests that corruption pervades society and needs to be stopped.*

Cautiously embracing the civil-service cause, President Hayes launched an investigation of the corruption-riddled New York City customs office in 1877 and ordered the resignation of two high officials. Both men had ties to Conkling, the leader of the Stalwart faction; one, Chester A. Arthur, was Conkling's top lieutenant in passing out jobs. When the two ignored Hayes's order, the president suspended them. Hayes's action won praise from civil-service reformers, but Conkling simply ridiculed "snivel service" and "Rutherfraud B. Hayes."

Civil-Service Reform Succeeds   When Congressman James A. Garfield, who had ties to the Half-Breed faction, won the 1880 Republican presidential nomination, the delegates, to soften the blow to Conkling, chose Chester A. Arthur, the Conkling loyalist Hayes had recently fired, as Garfield's running mate. Since Garfield enjoyed excellent health, the choice of the totally unqualified Arthur seemed safe.

The Democrats nominated a career army officer from Pennsylvania, Winfield Scott Hancock, and the Greenbackers gave the nod to Congressman James B. Weaver of Iowa. Garfield's managers stressed his Civil War record and his log-cabin birth. By a razor-thin margin of under forty thousand votes (of 9.2 million cast), Garfield edged out Hancock; Weaver trailed far behind.

When Garfield chose Blaine as secretary of state and named a Conkling opponent as the New York City customs collector, Conkling, in a political maneuver, resigned from the Senate. He hoped that the New York legislature would reelect him and thereby strengthen his political power. But Conkling miscalculated. The legislature chose another senator and ended Conkling's career.

Garfield's assassination in 1881, which brought to the White House Vice President Arthur, the very symbol of patronage corruption, gave a powerful emotional thrust to the cause, as civil-service reformers portrayed the fallen president as a spoils-system martyr. In 1883 Congress enacted a civil-service law introduced by Senator George Pendleton of Ohio (Garfield's home state) and drafted by the Civil Service Reform League that had been created two years earlier. The Pendleton Civil Service Act set up a commission to prepare competitive examinations and establish standards of merit for a variety of federal jobs; it also forbade political candidates from soliciting contributions from government workers. The Pendleton Act initially covered only about 12 percent of federal employees but was gradually expanded. The creation of a professional civil service helped bring the federal government in step with the modernizing trends transforming society.

As for Chester A. Arthur, the fact that he proved to be a mediocre president pleasantly surprised those who had expected him to be an utter disaster. Some feared that Roscoe Conkling would be "the power behind the throne," but Arthur supported civil-service reform and proved quite independent. Fed up with the feuding Republicans, in 1882 the voters gave the Democrats a strong majority in the House of Representatives. In 1884, for the first time since the 1850s, they would put a Democrat in the White House: Grover Cleveland.

POLITICS OF PRIVILEGE, POLITICS OF EXCLUSION, 1884–1892

The stalemate between the two major parties in their battle to establish the standards for economic growth continued under President Cleveland. Although no radical, Cleveland challenged powerful interests by calling for cuts in the tariff and in veterans' pensions. In 1888 aroused business groups and the veterans' lobby rallied to defeat Cleveland and elect Benjamin Harrison of Indiana, a former Civil War general, in one of the most corrupt campaigns in American history. Harrison further alienated voters by passing a high tariff and an expanded pension law that increased the number of pensioners by 43 percent.

Fed up with both the Democrats' and Republicans' fraud and inattention to the needs of rural Americans, debt-ridden, drought-stricken farmers mounted a spirited protest. While the Grange and Farmers' Alliance movements condemned the monopolistic practices of grain and cotton buyers, in the post-Reconstruction South the white majority took steps to consolidate their political power by denying the region's black citizens their most basic rights.

1884: Cleveland Victorious At a tumultuous Chicago convention in 1884, the Republicans nominated their best-known leader, James G. Blaine. A gifted orator with a keen memory for names and faces, Blaine spoke for the younger, more dynamic wing of the Republican party eager to shed the taint of "Grantism," promote economic development, and take a greater interest in foreign policy.

But Blaine's name had been smirched in the tawdry politics of the Gilded Age. In Blaine's 1876 senatorial campaign, his opponents had published letters in which Blaine, as Speaker of the House, offered political favors to a railroad company in exchange for stock. For civil-service reformers, Blaine epitomized the hated patronage system. To E. L. Godkin, he "wallowed in spoils like a rhinoceros in an African pool."

Sensing Blaine's vulnerability, the Democrats chose a sharply contrasting nominee, Grover Cleveland of New York. In a meteoric political rise from reform mayor of Buffalo to governor, Cleveland had fought the bosses and spoilsmen. Short, rotund, and resembling a bulldog, Cleveland was his own man.

The shrewdness of the Democrats' choice became apparent when Godkin, Carl Schurz, and other Republican reformers bolted to Cleveland. They were promptly nicknamed Mugwumps, an Algonquian term for a renegade chief.

But Cleveland had liabilities, including the fact that as a young man he had fathered an illegitimate child. Cleveland admitted the indiscretion, but the Republicans still jeered at rallies: "Ma, Ma, where's my pa?" Cleveland also faced opposition from Tammany Hall, the New York City Democratic machine that he had fought as governor. If Tammany's immigrant voters stayed home on election day, Cleveland could lose his own state. But in October a New York City clergyman denounced the Democrats as the party of "Rum, Romanism, and Rebellion." Blaine failed to immediately repudiate the remark. The Cleveland campaign managers widely publicized this triple insult to Catholics, to patriotic Democrats tired of the "bloody shirt," and to drinkers. This blunder and the Mugwumps' defection allowed Cleveland to carry New York State by twelve hundred votes, and with it the election.

Tariffs and
Pensions

In some respects, Cleveland fits the passive image of Gilded Age presidents. He had early embraced the belief that government must not meddle in the economy. In Andrew Jackson's day, laissez-faire had been a radical idea endorsed by ambitious small entrepreneurs who wanted business conditions favorable to competition; by the 1880s it had become the rallying cry of a corporate elite opposed to any public regulation or oversight. Sharing this outlook, Cleveland asserted the power of the presidency mostly through his vetoes and displayed a limited grasp of industrialization's impact. Vetoing a bill that would have provided seeds to drought-stricken farmers in Texas, he warned that people should not expect the government to solve their problems.

One public matter did arouse Cleveland's energies: the tariff, an issue involving a tangle of conflicting economic and political interests. Tariff duties were a major source of revenue in the era before a federal income tax, so the tariff was really a form of taxation. But which imported goods should be subject to duties, and how much? Opinions differed radically.

The producers of such commodities as coal, hides, timber, and wool demanded tariff protection against foreign competition, and industries that had prospered behind tariff walls—iron and steel, textiles, machine tools—wanted protection to continue. Many workers in these industries agreed, convinced that high tariffs meant higher wages. Other manufacturers, however, while seeking protection for their finished products, wanted low tariffs on the raw materials they required. Massachusetts shoe manufacturers, for example, urged high duties on imported shoes but low duties on imported hides. Most farmers, by contrast, hated the protective tariff, charging that it inflated farm-equipment prices and, by impeding trade, made it hard to sell American farm products abroad.

Cleveland's call for lower tariffs arose initially from the fact that in the 1880s the high tariff, generating millions of dollars in federal revenue, was feeding a growing budget surplus. This surplus tempted legislators to distribute the money in the form of veterans' pensions or expensive public-works programs, commonly called pork-barrel projects, in their home districts. With his horror of paternalistic government, Cleveland viewed the budget surplus as a corrupting influence. In his annual message to Congress in 1887, Cleveland argued that lower tariffs would not only cut the federal surplus but would also reduce prices and slow the development of trusts. Although the Democratic campaign of 1888 gave little attention to the issue, Cleveland's talk of lowering the tariff struck many corporate leaders as highly threatening.

Cleveland stirred up another hornet's nest when he took on the Grand Army of the Republic. Veterans' disability pensions cost the government millions of dollars annually. No one opposed pensions for the deserving, but by the 1880s fraudulent claims had become a public scandal. Unlike his predecessors, Cleveland investigated these claims and rejected many of them. In 1887 he vetoed a bill that would have pensioned all disabled veterans (even if their disability had nothing to do with military service) and their dependents. The pension list should be an honor roll, he declared, not a refuge for frauds.

1888: Big Business and the GAR Strike Back By 1888 some influential interest groups had concluded that Cleveland must go. When Blaine decided not to challenge him, the Republicans turned to Benjamin Harrison of Indiana, the grandson of William Henry Harrison. A corporation lawyer and former senator, Harrison was so aloof that some ridiculed him as the human iceberg. His campaign managers learned to whisk him away after speeches before anyone could talk with him or experience his flabby handshake.

Harrison's managers also developed a new style of electioneering. They brought delegations to Indianapolis and hammered at the tariff issue. Falsely portraying Cleveland as an advocate of "free trade"—the elimination of all tariffs—they warned of the bad effects of such a step. The high protective tariff, they argued, ensured prosperity, decent wages for industrial workers, and a healthy home market for farmers.

The Republicans amassed a $4 million campaign fund from worried business leaders. (Because the Pendleton Civil Service Act had outlawed campaign contributions by government workers, political parties depended more than ever on corporate donors.) This war chest purchased not only posters and buttons but also votes.

Despite such chicanery, Cleveland got almost a hundred thousand more votes than Harrison. But Harrison carried the key states of Indiana and New York and won in the electoral college. The Republicans held the Senate and regained the House. When Harrison piously observed that Providence had aided the Republican cause, his campaign chairman snorted, "Providence hadn't a damn thing to do with it. . . . [A] number of men . . . approach[ed] the gates of the penitentiary to make him president."

Harrison swiftly rewarded his supporters. He appointed as commissioner of pensions a GAR official who, on taking office, declared "God help the surplus!" The pension rolls soon ballooned from 676,000 to nearly a million. This massive pension system (which was coupled with medical care in a network of veterans' hospitals) became America's first large-scale public-welfare program. In 1890 the triumphant Republicans also enacted the McKinley Tariff, which pushed rates to an all-time high.

Rarely has the federal government been so subservient to entrenched economic interests and so out of touch with the plight of the disadvantaged as during the 1880s. But discontent was rising. The midterm election of 1890, when the Democrats gained sixty-six congressional seats to win control of the House of Representatives, awakened the nation to a tide of political activism engulfing the agrarian South and West. This activism, spawned by chronic problems in rural America, had a long history.

The Grange Movement   As discussed in Chapter 17, Great Plains farming proved far riskier than many had anticipated. Terrible grasshopper infestations consumed nearly half the midwestern wheat crop between 1873 and 1877. Although overall production surged after 1870, the abundant harvests undercut prices. Wheat tumbled from $2.95 a bushel in 1866 to $1.06 in 1880. Countless farmers who had borrowed heavily to finance homesteads and expensive new machinery went bankrupt or barely survived. One struggling Minnesota farmer wrote the governor in 1874, "[W]e can see nothing but starvation in the future if relief does not come."

When relief did not come, the farmers responded by setting up cooperative ventures. In 1867, under the leadership of Oliver H. Kelley, a Department of Agriculture clerk, midwestern farmers formed the Grange, or "Patrons of Husbandry," as it was officially called. Membership climbed to more than 1.5 million in the trying years of the early 1870s. Patterned after the Masonic Order, the Grange offered information, emotional support, and fellowship. For the inexperienced homesteader, it made available a library of the latest findings on planting and livestock raising.

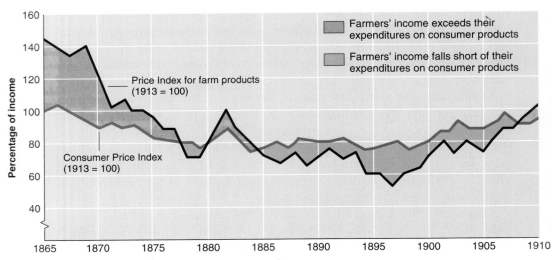

Consumer Prices and Farm-Product Prices, 1865–1913

As cycles of drought and debt battered Great Plains wheat growers, a Kansas farmer wrote, "At the age of 52, after a long life of toil, economy, and self-denial, I find myself and family virtually paupers."

For the lonely farm family, the Grange organized biweekly social gatherings, including cooperative meals and lively songfests.

But the Grange's central concern was farmers' economic plight. An 1874 circular announced the organization's primary purpose: to help farmers "buy less and produce more, in order to make our farms more self-sustaining." Grangers embraced the Jacksonian belief that the products of the soil were the basis of all honorable wealth and that the producer classes—people who worked with their hands—formed the true backbone of society. Members sought to restore self-sufficiency to the family farm. Ignoring the contradiction in farmers' banding together to help individuals become more independent, they negotiated special discounts with farm-machinery dealers and set up "cash-only" cooperative stores and grain-storage elevators to cut out the "middlemen"—the bankers, grain brokers, and merchants who made money at their expense.

Grangers vehemently attacked the railroads, which routinely gave discounts to large shippers, bribed state legislators, and charged higher rates for short runs than for long hauls. These practices stung hard-pressed farmers. Although professing to be nonpolitical, Grangers in Illinois, Wisconsin, Minnesota, and Iowa lobbied state legislatures in 1874 to pass laws fixing maximum rates for freight shipments.

The railroads appealed to the Supreme Court to declare these "Granger laws" unconstitutional. But in *Munn* v. *Illinois* (1877) the Court not only rejected the railroads' appeal but also upheld an Illinois law setting a maximum rate for the storage of grain. The regulation of grain elevators, declared the Court's majority, was legitimate under the federal Constitution's grant of police powers to states. When the Court in *Wabash* v. *Illinois* (1886) modified this position by prohibiting states from regulating interstate railroad rates, Congress passed the Interstate Commerce Act (1887), reaffirming the federal government's power to investigate and oversee railroad activities and establishing a new agency, the Interstate Commerce Commission (ICC), to do just that. Although the commission failed to curb the railroads' monopolistic practices, it did establish the principle of federal regulation of interstate transportation.

Despite promising beginnings, the Grange movement soon faltered. The railroads, having lost their battle on the national level, lobbied state legislatures and won repeal of most of the rate-regulation laws by 1878. Moreover, the Grange system of cash-only cooperative stores failed because few farmers had ample cash. Ultimately, the Grange ideal of complete financial independence proved unrealistic. Under the conditions that prevailed on the Plains, it was impossible to farm without borrowing money.

How valid was the Grangers' analysis of the farmers' problems? The Grangers blamed greedy railroads and middlemen for their difficulties, but the situation was not that simple. The years 1873–1878 saw the entire economy in a depression; railroad operators and merchant middlemen, no less than farmers, had to scramble to survive. Farm commodity prices did fall between 1865 and 1900, but so, too, did the wholesale prices of manufactured goods, including items needed on the farm. Even the railroads' stiff freight charges could be justified in part by the scarcity of western settlement and the seasonality of grain shipments.

Still, the farmers and the Grange leaders who voiced their grievances had reason to complain. Farmers who had no control over the prices of their crops were at the mercy of local merchants and farm-equipment dealers who exercised monopolistic control over the prices that they could charge. Similarly, railroads sometimes would transport wheat to only one mill. Some even refused to stop at small towns to pick up local wheat shipments. Policies like these struck the farmers as completely arbitrary and made them feel powerless. Hamlin Garland captured farmers' despair in his *Main-Travelled Roads* (1891) and *Son of the Middle Border* (1917), describing barely surviving families who "rose early and toiled without intermission, till the darkness fell on the plain, then tumbled into bed, every bone and muscle aching with fatigue."

When the prices of corn, wheat, and cotton briefly revived after 1878, many farmers deserted the Grange. Although the Grange lived on as a social and educational institution, it lost its economic clout because it was ultimately unable to improve its members' financial position. For all its weaknesses, the Grange movement did lay the groundwork for an even more powerful wave of agrarian protest.

The Alliance Movement

While the Grange was centered in the Midwest and the Great Plains, the Farmers' Alliance movement first arose in the South and West, where farmers grappled with many of the same problems. In the cotton South, small planters found themselves trapped by the crop-lien system, mortgaging future harvests to cover current expenses. Mired in debt, many gave up their land and became tenants or sharecroppers.

About a third of southern farmers were tenants by 1900. One historian has aptly called the South in these years "a giant pawnshop."

The Farmers' Alliance movement began in Texas in the late 1870s as poor farmers gathered to discuss their hardships. Soon an organization took shape, promoted by activists who organized hundreds of local alliances. The alliance idea advanced eastward across the lower South, especially after Texan Charles W. Macune, a self-trained lawyer and a physician, assumed leadership in 1887. By 1889 Macune had merged several regional organizations into the National Farmers' Alliance and Industrial Union, or Southern Alliance. A parallel black organization, the National Colored Farmers' Alliance, had meanwhile emerged in Arkansas and spread to other southern states.

Like the Grange, the Farmers' Alliance initially advocated farmers' cooperatives to purchase equipment and supplies and to market their cotton. These cooperatives mostly failed, however, because farmers lacked the capital to finance them. Still, by 1890 the Southern Alliance boasted 3 million members, with an additional 1.2 million claimed by the National Colored Farmers' Alliance. Alliance members generally comprised not only the poorest farmers but also those most dependent on a single crop and most geographically isolated. As they attended alliance rallies and picnics, read the alliance newspaper, and listened to alliance speakers, hard-hit farm families felt less cut off and increasingly aware of their political potential. An Arkansas member wrote in 1889, "Reform never begins with the leaders, it comes from the people."

Meanwhile, alliance fever hit the Great Plains as well. In the drought-plagued years of 1880 and 1881, alliances sprang up in Kansas, Nebraska, Iowa, and Minnesota. But the protest spirit faded as renewed rainfall revived confidence and lured thousands of settlers to the northern plains. The boom triggered frenzied land speculation. Kansas farms that had sold for $6.25 an acre in the 1860s went for $270 an acre in 1887. Railroads promoting settlement along their routes fed the boom mentality.

In 1886–1887, however, drought returned. From 1887 to 1897, only two Great Plains wheat crops were worth harvesting. Searing winds shriveled the half-ripe grain as locusts and chinch bugs gnawed away the rest. To make matters worse, wheat prices fell as world production increased.

Many settlers returned East. "In God we trusted, in Kansas we busted," some scrawled on their wagons. Western Kansas lost 50 percent of its population between 1888 and 1892. But others hung on, and the Northwestern Alliance grew rapidly. By 1890 the Kansas Alliance claimed 130,000 members, followed closely by alliances in Nebraska, the Dakotas, and Minnesota. Like the Southern Alliance, the Northwestern Alliance first experimented with cooperatives and gradually turned to politics.

Southern Alliance leaders Tom Watson of Georgia and Leonidas Polk of North Carolina urged southern farmers, black and white, to act together. For a time, this message of racial cooperation in the interest of reform offered promise. In Kansas, meanwhile, Jerry Simpson, a rancher who lost his stock in the hard winter of

1886–1887, became a major alliance leader. Mary E. Lease, a Wichita lawyer, burst on the scene in 1890 as a fiery alliance orator.

Other women, veterans of the Granger or prohibition cause, also rallied to the new movement, founding the National Women's Alliance (NWA) in 1891. Declared the NWA, "Put 1,000 women lecturers in the field and revolution is here." By no coincidence, a strong feminist strain pervades Ignatius Donnelly's *The Golden Bottle* (1892), a novel portraying the agrarian reformers' social vision.

As the movement swelled, the opposition turned nasty. When Jerry Simpson mentioned the silk stockings of a conservative politician in his district and noted that he had no such finery, a hostile newspaper editor labeled him "Sockless Jerry" Simpson, the nickname he carried to his grave. When Mary Lease advised Kansas to "raise less corn and more hell," another editor sneered: "[Kansas] has started to raise hell, as Mrs. Lease advised, and [the state] seems to have an overproduction. But that doesn't matter. Kansas never did believe in diversified crops."

From all this activity, a political agenda took form. In 1889 the Southern and Northwestern Alliances loosely merged and adopted a political litmus test for candidates in the 1890 midterm elections. Their overall goal was to reform the American economic system. Their objectives, which focused on increasing government action on behalf of farmers and workers, included tariff reduction, a graduated income tax, public ownership of the railroads, federal funding for irrigation research, a ban on landownership by aliens, and "the free and unlimited coinage of silver."

The 1890 elections revealed the depth of agrarian disaffection. Southern Democrats who endorsed alliance goals won four governorships and control of eight state legislatures. On the Great Plains, alliance-endorsed candidates secured control of the Nebraska legislature and gained the balance of power in Minnesota and South Dakota. In Kansas the candidates of the alliance-sponsored People's party demolished all opposition. Three alliance-backed senators, together with some fifty congressmen (including Watson and Simpson), went to Washington as angry winds from the hinterlands buffeted the political system.

But differences soon surfaced. Whereas Northwestern Alliance leaders favored a third party, the Southern Alliance, despite Watson's and Polk's advice, rejected such a move, fearing it would weaken the southern Democratic party, the bastion of white supremacy. By 1892, however, some Southern Alliance leaders had reluctantly adopted the third-party idea, since many Democrats whom they had backed in 1890 had ignored the alliance agenda once in office. In February 1892 alliance leaders organized the People's Party of the United States, generally called the Populist party. At the party convention that August, cheering delegates nominated for president the former Civil War general and Greenback nominee James B. Weaver of Iowa. Courting the South, they chose as Weaver's running mate the Virginian James Field, who had lost a leg fighting for the Confederacy.

The Populist platform restated the alliance goals while adding a call for the direct popular election of senators and other electoral reforms. It also endorsed a plan devised by alliance leader Charles Macune by which farmers could store their nonperishable commodities in government warehouses, receive low-interest loans using the crops as collateral, and then sell the stored commodities when market prices rose. Ignatius Donnelly's ringing preamble pronounced the nation on "the verge of moral, political, and material ruin" and called for a return of the government "to the hands of 'the plain people' with which class it originated."

African-Americans After Reconstruction
As the Populists geared up for the 1892 campaign, another group of citizens with far more profound grievances found themselves pushed even farther to the margins of American public life. The end of Reconstruction in 1877 and the restoration of power to the southern white elites, the so-called redeemers (see Chapter 16), spelled bad news for southern blacks. The redeemer coalition of large landowners, merchants, and "New South" industrialists had little interest in the former slaves except as a docile labor force or as political pawns. However, southern white opinion demanded an end to the hated "Negro rule," and local Democratic party officials pursued this objective. Suppressing the black vote was a major goal. At first, black disfranchisement was achieved by intimidation, terror, and vote fraud, as blacks were either kept from the polls or forced to vote Democratic. Then in 1890 Mississippi amended its state constitution in ways that effectively excluded most black voters, and other southern states soon followed suit.

Because the Fifteenth Amendment (1870) guaranteed all male citizens' right to vote, disfranchisement had to be accomplished indirectly by such means as literacy tests, poll taxes, and property requirements. The racist intent of these devices became obvious when procedures were introduced to ensure that they affected only black voters. One stratagem, the so-called grandfather clause, exempted from these electoral requirements anyone whose ancestor had voted in 1860. Black disfranchisement proceeded erratically over the South, but by the early twentieth century, it was essentially complete.

Disfranchisement was only one part of the system of white supremacy laboriously erected in the South. In a parallel development that culminated in the early twentieth century, state after state passed laws imposing strict racial segregation in many realms of life (see Chapter 21).

Black caterers, barbers, bricklayers, carpenters, and other artisans lost their white clientele. Blacks who went to prison—sometimes for minor offenses—faced the convict-lease system, by which cotton planters, railroad builders, coal-mine operators, and other employers "leased" prison gangs and forced them to work under slave-labor conditions.

The convict-lease system not only enforced the racial hierarchy but also played an important economic role as industrialization and agricultural change came to the South. The system brought income to hard-pressed state governments and provided factories, railroads, mines, and large-scale farms with a predictable, controllable, and cheap labor supply. The system also intimidated free laborers. One observer commented, "[O]n account of the convict employment, strikes are of rare occurrence." Recognizing this danger, free miners in Tennessee successfully agitated against the employment of convict labor in their state in the 1890s. Thousands died under the brutal convict-labor system. It survived into the early decades of the twentieth century, ultimately succumbing to humanitarian protest and to economic changes that made it unprofitable.

The ultimate enforcer of southern white supremacy was the lynch rope. Through the 1880s and 1890s, about a hundred blacks were lynched annually in the United States, mainly in the South. The stated reasons, often the rape of a white woman, frequently arose from rumor and unsubstantiated accusations. (The charge of "attempted rape" could cover a wide range of behaviors unacceptable to whites.)

The lynch mob demonstrated whites' absolute power. In *Festival of Violence,* their 1995 computer-assisted study of 2,805 southern lynchings, Stewart E. Tolnay and E. M. Beck found that more than 80 percent involved black victims. Lynchings most commonly occurred in the Cotton Belt, and they tended to peak at times of economic distress when cotton prices were falling and job competition between poor whites and poor blacks was most intense. By no coincidence, lynching peaked in 1892 as many poor blacks embraced the Farmers' Alliance movement and rallied to the Populist party banner. Fifteen black Populists were killed in Georgia alone, it has been estimated, during that year's acrimonious campaign.

The relationship between southern agrarian protest and white racism was complex. Some Populists, like Georgia's Tom Watson, sought to build an interracial movement. Watson denounced lynching and the convict-lease system. When a black Populist leader pursued by a lynch mob took refuge in his house during the 1892 campaign, Watson summoned two thousand armed white Populists to defend him. But most white Populists, abetted by rabble-rousers like "Pitchfork Ben" Tillman of South Carolina, clung to racism. Watson complained that most poor whites "would joyously hug the chains of . . . wretchedness rather than do any experimenting on [the race] question."

The white elite, eager to drive a wedge in the protest movement, inflamed lower-class white racism. The agricultural crisis of the period, which included a precipitous decline in cotton prices, had driven poor white tenant farmers in the South to the brink of despair. Those who lost control of their farms felt that they not only faced economic ruin, but that they also risked loss of their manhood. Conscious of themselves as a racial group, they feared that if they fell further down the economic ladder they would lose the racial privileges that came from their "whiteness" and be treated like blacks, Mexicans, and the foreign born. Hence, they were swayed by conservative Atlanta editor Henry W. Grady when he warned against division among white southerners: the region's only hope, he said, was "the clear and unmistakable domination of the white race."

Even as they raised the bugaboo of "Negro rule," the white elite manipulated the urban black vote as a weapon against agrarian radicalism, driving Tom Watson to despair. On balance, the rise of southern agrarian protest deepened racial hatred and ultimately worsened blacks' situation.

While southern blacks suffered racist oppression, the federal government stood aside. A generation of northern politicians paid lip service to egalitarian principles but failed to apply them to blacks.

The Supreme Court similarly abandoned blacks. The Fourteenth Amendment (1868) had granted blacks citizenship and the equal protection of the laws, and the Civil Rights Act of 1875 outlawed racial discrimination on juries, in public places such as hotels and theaters, and on railroads, streetcars, and other such conveyances. But the Supreme Court soon ripped gaping holes in these protective laws.

In the *Civil Rights Cases* (1883), the Court declared the Civil Rights Act of 1875 unconstitutional. The Fourteenth Amendment protected citizens only from governmental infringement of their civil rights, the justices ruled, not from acts by private citizens such as railroad conductors. In *Plessy* v. *Ferguson* (1896), the justices upheld a Louisiana law requiring segregated railroad cars. Racial segregation was constitutional, the Court held, if equal facilities were made available to each race. (In a prophetic dissent, Associate Justice John Marshall Harlan observed, "Our Constitution is color blind." Segregation, he added, violated the constitutional principle of equality before the law.) With the Supreme Court's blessing, the South segregated its public school system, ignoring the caveat that such separate facilities must be equal. White children studied in nicer buildings, used newer equipment, and were taught by better-paid teachers. Not until 1954 did the Court abandon the "separate but equal" doctrine. Rounding out their dismal record, in 1898 the justices upheld the poll tax and literacy tests by which southern states had disfranchised blacks.

Few northerners protested the South's white-supremacist society. Until the North condemned lynching outright, declared the aged abolitionist Frederick Douglass in 1892, "it will remain equally involved with the South in this common crime." The restoration of sectional harmony, in short, came at a high price: acquiescence by the North in the utter debasement of the South's African-American citizenry. Further, the separatist principle endorsed in *Plessy* had a pervasive impact, affecting blacks nationwide, Mexicans in Texas, Asians in California, and other groups.

Blacks responded to their plight in various ways. The nation's foremost black leader from the 1890s to his death in 1915 was Booker T. Washington. Born in slavery in Virginia in 1856, the son of a slave woman and her white master, Washington attended a freedman's school in Hampton, Virginia, and in 1881 organized a black state vocational school in Alabama that eventually became Tuskegee University. Although Washington secretly contributed to lawyers who challenged segregation, his public message was accommodation to a racist society. In a widely publicized address in Atlanta in 1895, he insisted that the first task of America's blacks must be to acquire useful skills such as farming and carpentry. Once blacks proved their economic value, he predicted, racism would fade; meanwhile, they must patiently accept their lot. Washington lectured widely, and his autobiography, *Up From Slavery* (1901), recounted his rise from poverty thanks to honesty, hard work, and kindly patrons—themes familiar to a generation reared on Horatio Alger's self-help books.

Other blacks responded resourcefully to the racist society. Black churches provided emotional support, as did black fraternal lodges like the Knights of Pythias. Some African-Americans started businesses to serve their community. Two black-owned banks, in Richmond and Washington, D.C., were chartered in 1888. The North Carolina Mutual Insurance Company, organized in 1898 by John Merrick, a prosperous Durham barber, evolved into a major enterprise. Bishop Henry M. Turner of the African Methodist Episcopal church urged blacks to return to Africa and build a great Christian nation. Turner made several trips to Africa in pursuit of his proposal.

African-American protest never wholly died out. Frederick Douglass urged that blacks press for full equality. "Who would be free, themselves must strike the first blow," he proclaimed in 1883. Blacks should meet violence with violence, insisted militant New York black leader T. Thomas Fortune.

Other blacks answered southern racism by leaving the region. In 1879 several thousand moved to Kansas (see Chapter 16). Some ten thousand migrated to Chicago between 1870 and 1890. Blacks who moved north soon found, however, that although white supremacy was not official policy, public opinion sanctioned many forms of de facto discrimination. Northern black laborers, for example, encountered widespread prejudice. The Knights of Labor welcomed blacks and by the mid-1880s had an estimated sixty thousand black members.

The Knights of Labor
Black delegate Frank J. Farrell introduces Terence V. Powderly, head of the Knights of Labor, at the organization's 1886 convention. The Knights were unusual in accepting both black and female workers.

Its successor, the American Federation of Labor, officially forbade racial discrimination, but in practice many of its member unions excluded blacks.

The rise of the so-called solid South, firmly established on racist foundations, had important political implications. For one thing, it made a mockery of the two-party system in the South. For years, the only meaningful election south of the Potomac was the Democratic primary. Only in the 1960s, in the wake of sweeping social and economic changes, would a genuine two-party system emerge there. The large bloc of southern Democrats elected to Congress each year, accumulating seniority and power, exerted a great and often reactionary influence on public policy. Above all, they mobilized instantly to quash any threat to southern white supremacy. Finally, southern Democrats wielded enormous clout in the national party. No Democratic contender for national office who was unacceptable to them stood a chance.

Above all, the caste system that evolved in the post-Reconstruction South shaped the consciousness of those caught up in it, white and black alike. White novelist Lillian Smith described her girlhood in turn-of-the-century Florida and Georgia: "From the day I was born, I began to learn my lessons. . . . I learned it is possible to be a Christian and a white southerner simultaneously; to be a gentle-woman and an arrogant callous creature at the same moment; to pray at night and ride a Jim Crow car the next morning; . . . to glow when the word democracy was used, and to practice slavery from morning to night."

THE 1890S: POLITICS IN A DEPRESSION DECADE

Discontent with the major parties and their commitment to supporting unrestricted business enterprise, which had smoldered during the 1870s and 1880s, burst into flames in the 1890s. As banks failed and railroads went bankrupt, the nation slid into a grinding depression. The crises of the 1890s laid bare the paralysis of the federal government—dominated by a business elite—when confronted by the new social realities of factories, urban slums, immigrant workers, and desperate farmers. In response, irate farmers, laborers, and their supporters created a new party, the Populists, to change the system.

1892: Populists Challenge the Status Quo
The Populist party platform adopted in July 1892 offered an angry catalog of agrarian demands. That same month, thirteen people died in a gun battle between strikers and strikebreakers at the Homestead steel plant near Pittsburgh, and President Harrison sent federal troops to Coeur d'Alene, Idaho, where a silver-mine strike had turned violent. Events seemed to justify the Populists' warnings of chaos ahead.

Faced with domestic turmoil and fearful that the powerful European socialist movement would spread to the United States, both major parties acted cautiously. The Republicans renominated Harrison and adopted a platform that ignored escalating unrest. The Democrats turned again to Grover Cleveland, who in four years out of office had made clear his growing conservatism and his opposition to the Populists. Cleveland won by more than 360,000 votes, a decisive margin in this era of close elections. A public reaction against labor violence and the McKinley Tariff hurt Harrison, while Cleveland's support for the gold standard won conservative business support.

Populist strength proved spotty. James B. Weaver got just over a million votes—8.5 percent of the total—and the Populists elected five senators, ten congressmen, and three governors. The new party carried Kansas and registered some appeal in the West and in Georgia, Alabama, and Texas, where the alliance movement had taken deep root. But it made no dent in New England, the urban East, or the traditionally Republican farm regions of the Midwest. It even failed to show broad strength in the upper Great Plains. "Beaten! Whipped! Smashed!" moaned Minnesota Populist Ignatius Donnelly in his diary.

Throughout most of the South, racism, ingrained Democratic loyalty, distaste for a ticket headed by a former Union general, and widespread intimidation and vote fraud kept the Populist vote under 25 percent. This failure killed the prospects for interracial agrarian reform in the region. After 1892, as Populism began to revive in the South and Midwest, many southern politicians seeking to appeal to poor whites—including a disillusioned Tom Watson—stayed within the Democratic fold and laced their populism with racism.

The Panic of 1893: Capitalism in Crisis
Cleveland soon confronted a major crisis, an economic collapse in the railroad industry that quickly spread. In the economic boom of the 1880s, railroads had led the way, triggering speculation among investors. Some railroads had fed the speculative mania by issuing more stock (and enticing investors with higher dividends) than their business prospects warranted. Weakened by agricultural stagnation, railroad growth slowed in the early 1890s, affecting many related industries, including iron and steel. The first hint of trouble ahead came in February 1893 with the failure of the Philadelphia and Reading Railroad.

This bankruptcy came at a time of weakened confidence in the gold standard, the government's pledge to redeem paper money for gold on demand. This diminished confidence had several sources. First, when a leading London investment bank collapsed in 1890, hard-pressed British investors sold millions of dollars' worth of stock in American railroads and other corporations and converted their dollars to gold, draining U.S. gold reserves. Second, Congress's lavish veterans' benefits and pork-barrel appropriations during the Harrison administration drained government resources just as tariff revenues were dropping because of the high McKinley Tariff. Third, the 1890 Sherman Silver Purchase Act further strained the gold reserve. This measure required the government to pay for its monthly silver purchases with treasury certificates redeemable for either silver or gold, and many certificate holders chose to convert them to gold. Finally, the election of Grover Cleveland in 1892 further eroded confidence in the dollar. Although Cleveland endorsed the gold standard, his party harbored many advocates of inflationary policies.

Between January 1892 and March 1893, when Cleveland took office, the gold reserve had fallen sharply to around $100 million, the minimum considered necessary to support the dollar. This decline alarmed those who viewed the gold standard as the only sure evidence of the government's financial stability.

The collapse of a railroad early in 1893 thus triggered an economic crisis whose preconditions already existed. Fear fed on itself as panicky investors converted their stock holdings to gold. Stock prices plunged in May and June; gold reserves sank; by the end of the year, seventy-four railroads and more than fifteen thousand commercial institutions, including six hundred banks, had failed. After the Panic of 1893 came four years of hard times.

The Depression of 1893–1897

By 1897 about a third of the nation's railroad mileage was in bankruptcy. Just as the railroad boom had spurred the industrial prosperity of the 1880s, so had the railroad crisis of the early 1890s battered the entire economy as banks and other businesses failed. A full-scale depression gripped the nation.

The crisis took a heavy human toll. Industrial unemployment soared into the 20 to 25 percent range, leaving millions of factory workers with no money to feed their families and heat their homes. Recent immigrants faced disaster. Jobless men tramped the streets and rode freight trains from city to city seeking work.

The unusually harsh winters of 1893 and 1894 made matters worse. In New York City, where the crisis quickly swamped local relief agencies, a minister reported actual starvation. Amid the suffering, a rich New Yorker named Bradley Martin threw a lavish costume ball costing several hundred thousand dollars. Popular outrage over this flaunting of wealth in a prostrate city forced Martin and his family to move abroad.

Rural America, already hard-hit by declining agricultural prices, faced ruin. Farm prices dropped by more than 20 percent between 1890 and 1896. Corn plummeted from fifty cents to twenty-one cents a bushel; wheat, from eighty-four cents to fifty-one cents. Cotton sold for five cents a pound in 1894.

Some desperate Americans turned to protest. In Chicago workers at the Pullman factory reacted to successive wage cuts by walking off the job in June 1894 (see Chapter 18). In Massillon, Ohio, self-taught monetary expert Jacob Coxey proposed as a solution to unemployment a $500 million public-works program funded with paper money not backed by gold but simply designated "legal tender" (just as it is today). A man of action as well as ideas, Coxey organized a march on Washington to lobby for his scheme. Thousands joined him en route, and several hundred actually reached Washington in late April 1894. Police arrested Coxey and other leaders when they attempted to enter the Capitol grounds, and his "army" broke up. Although some considered Coxey eccentric, his proposal closely resembled programs that the government would adopt during the depression of the 1930s.

As unrest intensified, fear clutched middle-class Americans. A church magazine demanded that troops put "a pitiless stop" to outbreaks of unrest. To some observers, a bloody upheaval seemed imminent.

Business Leaders Hunker Down In the face of suffering and turmoil, Cleveland retreated into a laissez-faire fortress. Boom-and-bust economic cycles were inevitable, he insisted, echoing the conventional wisdom of the day; the government could do nothing. Failing to grasp the larger picture, Cleveland focused on a single peripheral issue: defending the gold standard. As the gold reserve dwindled, he blamed the Sherman Silver Purchase Act, and in August 1893 he called on Congress to repeal it. Silver advocates protested, but Congress followed Cleveland's wishes.

Nevertheless, the gold drain continued. In early 1895, with the gold reserve down to $41 million, Cleveland turned to Wall Street. Bankers J. P. Morgan and August Belmont agreed to lend the government $62 million in exchange for U.S. bonds at a special discount. With this loan, the government purchased gold to replenish its reserve. Meanwhile, Morgan and Belmont resold the bonds for a substantial profit. This complicated deal did help restore confidence in the government's economic stability. The gold drain stopped, and when the Treasury offered $100 million in bonds early in 1896, they sold quickly.

Cleveland saved the gold standard, but at a high price. His dealings with Morgan and Belmont, and the bankers' handsome profits on the deal, confirmed radicals' suspicions of an unholy alliance between Washington and Wall Street. Cleveland's readiness to use force against the Pullman strikers and against Jacob Coxey's peaceful marchers deepened such suspicions.

In the ongoing maneuverings of competing interest groups, corporate interests held the whip hand, as a battle over the tariff made clear. Although Cleveland favored tariff reform, the Congress of 1893–1895—despite its Democratic majorities—generally yielded to high-tariff lobbyists. The Wilson-Gorman Tariff of 1894 lowered duties somewhat, but made so many concessions to protectionist interests that Cleveland disgustedly allowed it to become law without his signature.

Hinting at changes ahead, the Wilson-Gorman Tariff imposed a modest income tax of 2 percent on all income over $4,000 (about $40,000 in purchasing power today). But in *Pollock* v. *Farmers' Loan & Trust Co.* (1895), the Supreme Court narrowly held the law unconstitutional, ruling that the federal government could impose such a direct tax on personal property only if it were apportioned according to the population of each state. Whether one looked at the executive, the legislature, or the judiciary, Washington's subordination to a single interest group, the moneyed class, seemed absolute.

Cleveland's policies split the Democratic party. Farm leaders and silver Democrats condemned his opposition to the Sherman Silver Purchase Act. South Carolina's Ben Tillman, running for the Senate in 1894, proclaimed, "[T]his scoundrel Cleveland . . . is an old bag of beef and I am going to Washington with a pitchfork and prod him in his fat old ribs." This split in the Democratic ranks affected the elections of 1894 and 1896 and reshaped politics as the century ended.

The depression also helped reorient social thought. Middle-class charitable workers, long convinced that individual character flaws caused poverty, now realized—as socialists proclaimed and as the poor well knew—that even sober and hardworking people could succumb to economic forces beyond their control. As the social work profession took form in the early twentieth century, its members spent less time preaching to the poor and more time investigating the social sources of poverty.

Laissez-faire ideology weakened in the 1890s as many depression-worn Americans adopted a broadened view of the government's role in dealing with the social consequences of industrialization. In the early twentieth century, this new view would activate powerful political energies. The depression, in short, not only brought suffering; it also taught lessons.

THE WATERSHED ELECTION OF 1896

Republican gains in the 1894 midterm election revealed the depths of revulsion against Cleveland and the Democrats, who were blamed for the hard times. As 1896 approached, the monetary question became the overriding symbolic issue. Conservatives clung to the gold standard; agrarian radicals rallied to the banner of "free silver." At the 1896 Democratic convention, the nomination went to a young champion of the silver cause, William Jennings Bryan. Despite Bryan's eloquence, Republican William McKinley emerged victorious. His triumph laid the groundwork for a major political realignment that would influence American politics for a generation.

1894: Protest Grows Louder   With the depression at its worst and President Grover Cleveland deeply unpopular, the midterm election of 1894 spelled Democratic disaster. The Republicans, gaining 5 seats in the Senate and 117 in the House, won both houses of Congress. They also secured control of several key states—including New York, Illinois, and Wisconsin—as immigrant workers, battered by the depression, abandoned their traditional Democratic allegiance.

Populist candidates garnered nearly 1.5 million votes in 1894, an increase of more than 40 percent over their 1892 total. Populism's most impressive gains occurred in the South. Although several western states that had voted Populist in 1892 returned to their traditional Republican allegiance in 1894, the overall results heartened Populist leaders.

The serious economic divisions that split Americans in the mid-1890s focused especially on a symbolic issue: free silver. Cleveland's rigid defense of the gold standard forced his opponents into an equally exaggerated obsession with silver, obscuring the genuine issues that divided rich and poor, creditor and debtor, and farmer and city dweller. Whereas conservatives tirelessly upheld the gold standard, agrarian radicals extolled silver as a universal panacea. They were urged on and sometimes financed by western silver-mine owners who stood to profit if silver again became a monetary metal.

Each side had a point. Gold advocates recognized that a nation's paper money must be based on more than a government's ability to run printing presses and

The Election of 1896

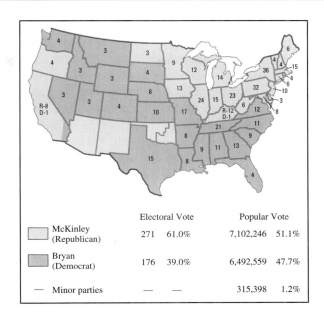

		Electoral Vote		Popular Vote	
☐	McKinley (Republican)	271	61.0%	7,102,246	51.1%
▨	Bryan (Democrat)	176	39.0%	6,492,559	47.7%
—	Minor parties	—	—	315,398	1.2%

that uncontrolled inflation could be catastrophic. The silver advocates knew from experience how tight-money policies depressed prices and devastated farmers. Unfortunately, these underlying realities were rarely expressed clearly. The silverites' most influential propaganda, William H. Harvey's widely distributed *Coin's Financial School* (1894), explained the monetary issue in simplified partisan terms, denounced "the conspiracy of Goldbugs," and insisted that the free coinage of silver would banish debt and end the depression.

Silver Advocates Capture the Democratic Party At the 1896 Democratic convention in Chicago, western and southern delegates adopted a platform—including a demand for the free and unlimited coinage of silver at the ratio to gold of sixteen to one—that in effect repudiated the Cleveland administration. The front-running candidate was Congressman Richard Bland of Missouri, a silverite. But behind the scenes, the groundwork was being laid for the nomination of a dark horse, William Jennings Bryan, a thirty-six-year-old Nebraska lawyer and politician. During two terms in Congress (1891–1895), he championed western agrarian interests.

Joining Christian imagery with economic analysis, Bryan delivered his major convention speech in the debate over the platform. In an era before electronic amplification, his booming voice easily reached the upper gallery of the cavernous hall. Bryan praised western farmers and scorned advocates of the gold standard. By the time he reached his rousing conclusion—"You shall not press down upon the brow of labor this crown of thorns, you shall not crucify mankind upon a cross of gold"—the wildly cheering delegates had identified their candidate.

The silverites' capture of the Democratic party presented a dilemma to the Populists. They, too, advocated free silver, but only as one reform among many. To back Bryan would be to abandon the broad Populist program. Furthermore, fusion with the Democrats could destroy their influence as a third party. Yet the Populist leaders recognized that a separate Populist ticket would likely siphon votes from Bryan and ensure a Republican victory. Reluctantly, the Populists endorsed Bryan, while preserving a shred of independence (and confusing voters) by naming their own vice-presidential candidate, Tom Watson of Georgia. The Populists were learning the difficulty of organizing an independent political movement in a nation wedded to the two-party system.

The Republicans, meanwhile, had nominated former governor William McKinley, who as an Ohio congressman had given his name to the McKinley Tariff of 1890. The Republican platform embraced the high protective tariff and endorsed the gold standard.

1896: Republicans Triumphant Bryan tried to sustain the momentum of the Chicago convention. Crisscrossing the nation by train, he delivered his free-silver campaign speech to hundreds of audiences in twenty-nine states. One skeptical editor compared him to Nebraska's notoriously shallow Platte River: six inches deep and a mile wide at the mouth.

McKinley's campaign was shrewdly managed by Mark Hanna, a Cleveland industrialist. Dignified and aloof, McKinley could not match Bryan's popular touch. Accordingly, Hanna built the campaign not around the candidate but around posters, pamphlets, and newspaper editorials that warned of the dangers of free silver, caricatured Bryan as a rabid radical, and portrayed McKinley and the gold standard as twin pillars of prosperity.

Drawing on a war chest possibly as large as $7 million, Hanna spent lavishly. J. P. Morgan and John D. Rockefeller together contributed half a million dollars, far more than Bryan's total campaign contributions. Like Benjamin Harrison in 1888, McKinley stayed home in Canton, Ohio, emerging from time to time to read speeches to visiting delegations. Carefully orchestrated by Hanna, McKinley's deceptively bucolic "front-porch" campaign involved elaborate organization. All told, some 750,000 people trekked to Canton that summer.

On election day, McKinley beat Bryan by over six hundred thousand votes. He swept the Northeast and the Midwest and even carried three farm states beyond the Mississippi—Iowa, Minnesota, and North Dakota—as well as California and Oregon. Bryan's strength was limited to the South and the sparsely settled Great Plains and mountain states. The Republicans retained control of Congress.

Why did Bryan lose despite the depression and the protest spirit abroad in the land? Certainly, Republican scare tactics played a role. But Bryan's candidacy carried its own liabilities. His core constituency, while passionately loyal, was limited. Seduced by free silver and Bryan's oratory, the Democrats had upheld a platform and a candidate with little appeal for factory workers, the urban middle class, or the settled family farmers of the midwestern corn belt. Urban voters, realizing that higher farm prices, a major free-silver goal, also meant higher food prices, went heavily for McKinley. Bryan's weakness in urban America reflected cultural differences as well. To urban Catholics and Jews, this moralistic, teetotaling Nebraskan thundering like a Protestant revival preacher seemed utterly alien.

Finally, despite their telling critique of laissez-faire capitalism, the Populists' effort to define a humane and democratic alternative relied heavily on visions of a premodern economic order of independent farmers and entrepreneurs. Although appealing, this vision bore little relationship to the new corporate order taking shape in America.

The McKinley administration quickly translated its conservative platform into law. The Dingley Tariff (1897) pushed rates to all-time high levels, and the Currency Act of 1900 officially committed the United States to the gold standard. With returning prosperity, rising farm prices after 1897, and the discovery of gold in Alaska and elsewhere, these measures aroused little protest. Bryan won renomination in 1900, but the fervor of 1896 was missing. The Republican campaign theme of prosperity easily won McKinley a second term.

The elections of 1894 and 1896 produced a Republican majority that, except for Woodrow Wilson's two presidential terms (1913–1921), would dominate national politics until the election of Franklin D. Roosevelt in 1932. Bryan's defeat and the Republicans' emergence as the party of prosperity and the sound dollar

William McKinley's "Front-Porch" Campaign, 1896 *McKinley (front row, fifth from left) poses with an Italian-American brass band from Buffalo, New York, in front of his home in Canton, Ohio.*

killed the Populist party and drove the Democrats back to their regional base in the South. But although populism collapsed, a new reform movement called progressivism was emerging. Many of the Populists' reform proposals would be enacted into law in the progressive years.

EXPANSIONIST STIRRINGS AND WAR WITH SPAIN, 1878–1901

The same corporate elite that dominated late-nineteenth-century domestic politics influenced U.S. foreign policy as well, contributing to surging expansionist pressures. Not only business leaders but also politicians, statesmen, and editorial writers insisted that national greatness required America to match Europe's imperial expansion. Fanned by sensationalistic newspaper coverage of a Cuban struggle for independence and by elite calls for greater American international assertiveness, war between the United States and Spain broke out in 1898.

Roots of Expansionist Sentiment   Since the first European settlers colonized North America's Atlantic coast, the newcomers had been an expansionist people. By the 1840s the push westward had acquired a name: Manifest Destiny. The expansionist impulse had faded as the Civil War and then industrialization absorbed American energies, but it revived strongly after 1880 as politicians and opinion molders proclaimed America's global destiny.

The example set by other nations encouraged this expansionist sentiment. By the 1890s Great Britain, France, Belgium, Italy, Germany, and Japan were busily collecting colonies from North Africa to the Pacific islands. National greatness, it appeared, demanded an empire.

In corporate circles, meanwhile, the opinion spread that continued prosperity required overseas markets. With industrial capacity expanding and the labor force growing, foreign markets offered a "safety valve" for potentially explosive pressures in the U.S. economy. Secretary of State James Blaine warned in 1890 that U.S. productivity was outrunning "the demands of the home market" and insisted that American business must look abroad.

Advocates of a stronger navy further fueled the expansionist mood. In *The Influence of Sea Power upon History* (1890), Alfred T. Mahan equated sea power with national greatness and urged a U.S. naval buildup. Since a strong navy required bases abroad, Mahan and other naval advocates supported the movement to acquire foreign territories, especially Pacific islands with good harbors. Military strategy, in this case and others, often masked the desire for access to new markets.

Religious leaders proclaimed America's mission to spread Christianity. This expansionist argument sometimes took on a racist tinge. As Josiah Strong put it in his 1885 work *Our Country,* "God is training the Anglo-Saxon race for its mission"—a mission of Christianizing and civilizing the world's "weaker races."

A group of Republican expansionists, led by Senator Henry Cabot Lodge of Massachusetts, diplomat John Hay, and Theodore Roosevelt of New York, preached imperial greatness and military might. "I should welcome almost any war," declared Roosevelt in 1897, ". . . this country needs one." Advocates of expansionism, like Roosevelt and Lodge, built upon the social Darwinist rhetoric of the day and argued that war, as a vehicle for natural selection, would test and refurbish American manhood, restore chivalry and honor, and create a new generation of civic-minded Americans. This gendered appeal to renew American masculinity both counterbalanced concerns about women's political activism and helped forge the disparate arguments for expansionism into a simpler, more visceral plea for international engagement that had a broad appeal.

A series of diplomatic skirmishes between 1885 and 1895 revealed the newly assertive American mood and paved the way for the war that Roosevelt desired. In the mid-1880s, quarrels between the United States and Great Britain over fishing rights in the North Atlantic and in the Bering Sea off Alaska reawakened Americans' latent anti-British feelings as well as the old dream of acquiring Canada. A poem published in the *Detroit News* (adapted from an English music-hall song) supplied the nickname that critics would apply to the promoters of expansion—jingoists:

> We do not want to fight,
> But, by jingo, if we do,
> We'll scoop in all the fishing grounds
> And the whole dominion too!

The fishing-rights dispute was resolved in 1898, but by then attention had shifted to Latin America. In 1891, as civil war raged in Chile, U.S. officials seized a Chilean vessel that was attempting to buy guns in San Diego. Soon after, a mob in Valparaiso, Chile, killed two unarmed sailors on shore leave. President Harrison practically called for war. Only when Chile apologized and paid an indemnity was the incident closed.

Another Latin American conflict arose from a boundary dispute between Venezuela and British Guiana in 1895. The disagreement worsened after gold was discovered in the contested territory. When the British rejected a U.S. arbitration offer and condescendingly insisted that America's revered Monroe Doctrine had no standing in international law, a livid Grover Cleveland asked Congress to set up a commission to settle the disputed boundary even without Britain's approval. As patriotic fervor pulsed through the nation, the British in 1897 accepted the commission's findings.

Pacific Expansion   Meanwhile, the U.S. navy focused on the Samoan Islands in the South Pacific, where it sought access to the port of Pago Pago as a refueling station. Britain and Germany had ambitions in Samoa as well, and in March 1889 the United States and Germany narrowly avoided a naval clash when a hurricane wrecked both fleets. Secretary of State Blaine's wife wrote to one of their children, "Your father is now looking up Samoa on the map." Once he found it, negotiations began, and the United States, Great Britain, and Germany established a three-way "protectorate" over the islands.

Attention had by that time shifted to the Hawaiian Islands, which had both strategic and economic significance for the United States. New England trading vessels had visited Hawaii as early as the 1790s, and Yankee missionaries had come in the 1820s. By the 1860s American-owned sugar plantations worked by Chinese and Japanese laborers dotted the islands. Under an 1887 treaty (negotiated after the planters had forcibly imposed a new constitution on Hawaii's native ruler, Kalākaua), the United States built a naval base at Pearl Harbor, near Honolulu. American economic dominance and the influx of foreigners angered Hawaiians. In 1891 they welcomed Liliuokalani, a strong-willed woman hostile to Americans, to the Hawaiian throne.

Meanwhile, in 1890, the framers of the McKinley Tariff, pressured by domestic sugar growers, eliminated the duty-free status enjoyed by Hawaiian sugar. In

U.S. Territorial Expansion in the Late Nineteenth Century

The major period of U.S. territorial expansion abroad came in a short burst of activity in the late 1890s, when newspapers and some politicians beat the drums for empire.

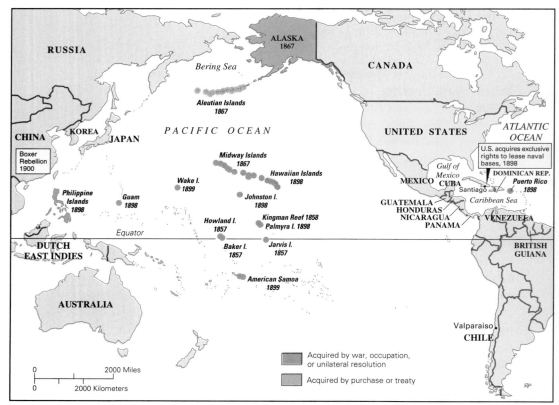

January 1893, facing ruin as Hawaii's wholesale sugar prices plunged 40 percent, the planters deposed Queen Liliuokalani, proclaimed the independent Republic of Hawaii, and requested U.S. annexation. The U.S. State Department's representative in Hawaii cabled Washington, "The Hawaiian pear is now fully ripe, and this is the golden hour for the United States to pluck it." But the grab for Hawaii troubled Grover Cleveland, who sent a representative to investigate the situation. This representative's report questioned whether the Hawaiian people actually desired annexation.

Cleveland's scruples infuriated expansionists. When William McKinley succeeded Cleveland in 1897, the acquisition of Hawaii rapidly moved forward. In 1898 Congress proclaimed Hawaii an American territory. Sixty-one years later, it joined the Union as the fiftieth state.

Crisis over Cuba

By 1898 American attention had shifted to the Spanish colony of Cuba, ninety miles off Florida, where in 1895 an anti-Spanish rebellion had broken out. This revolt, organized by the Cuban writer José Martí and other Cuban exiles in New York City, won little support from U.S. business, which had $50 million invested in Cuba and annually imported $100 million worth of sugar and other products from the island. Nor did the rebels initially secure the backing of Washington, which urged Spain to grant Cuba a degree of autonomy.

But the rebels' cause aroused popular sympathy in the United States. This support increased with revelations that the Spanish commander in Cuba, Valeriano Weyler, was herding vast numbers of Cubans into concentration camps. Malnutrition and disease turned these camps into hellholes in which perhaps two hundred thousand Cubans died.

Fueling American anger was the sensationalized reporting of two competing New York City newspapers, William Randolph Hearst's *Journal* and Joseph Pulitzer's *World*. The *Journal*'s color comic strip, "The Yellow Kid," provided a name for Hearst's debased editorial approach: yellow journalism. The Hungarian immigrant Pulitzer normally had higher standards, but in the cutthroat battle for readers, Pulitzer's *World* matched the *Journal*'s sensationalism. Both editors exploited the Cuban crisis. Headlines turned rumor into fact, and feature stories detailed "Butcher" Weyler's atrocities. When a young Cuban woman was jailed for resisting a rape attempt by a Spanish officer, a Hearst reporter helped the woman escape and brought her triumphantly to New York.

In 1897 a new, more liberal Spanish government sought a peaceful resolution of the Cuban crisis. But Hearst and Pulitzer continued to inflame the public. On February 8, 1898, Hearst's *Journal* published a private letter by Spain's minister to the United States that described McKinley as "weak" and "a bidder for the admiration of the crowd." Irritation over this incident turned to outrage when on February 15 an explosion rocked the U.S. battleship *Maine* in Havana harbor and killed 266 crewmen. A painstaking review of the evidence in 1976 concluded that a shipboard ammunition explosion, set off by a fire in a coal bunker, had caused the blast. But at the time neither Washington nor the yellow press was in any mood to view the tragedy as accidental. Newspaper headlines screamed of a "Spanish mine," and war spirit flared high.

Despite further Spanish concessions, McKinley sent a war message to Congress on April 11, and legislators enacted a joint resolution recognizing Cuba's independence and authorizing force to expel the Spanish. An amendment introduced by Senator Henry M. Teller of Colorado renounced any U.S. interest in "sovereignty, jurisdiction, or control" in Cuba and pledged that America would leave the island alone once independence was assured.

The Spanish-American War, 1898

The war with Spain involved only a few days of actual combat. The first action came on May 1, 1898, when a U.S. fleet commanded by George Dewey steamed into Manila Bay in the Philippines and destroyed or captured all ten Spanish ships anchored there, at the cost of 1 American and 381 Spanish lives. In mid-August U.S. troops occupied the capital, Manila.

In Cuba the fighting centered on the military stronghold of Santiago de Cuba on the southeastern coast. On May 19 a Spanish battle fleet of seven aging vessels sailed into the Santiago de Cuba harbor, where five U.S. battleships and two cruisers blockaded them. On July 1, in the war's only significant land action, American troops seized two strongly defended Spanish garrisons on El Caney Hill and San Juan Hill overlooking Santiago de Cuba. Leading the volunteer "Rough Riders" unit in the capture of San Juan Hill was Theodore Roosevelt, who at last got his taste of war.

On July 3 the Spanish attempted to pierce through the American blockade to the open sea. U.S. naval fire raked and sank their archaic vessels. Spain lost 474 men in this gallant but doomed show of the flag. Americans might have found a cautionary lesson in this sorry end to four hundred years of Spanish rule in the New World, but few had time for somber musings. The *Washington Post* observed, "A new consciousness seems to have come upon us—the consciousness of strength—and with it a new appetite, the yearning to show our strength . . . , [t]he taste of empire. . . ." John Hay was more succinct. It had been, he wrote Roosevelt, "a splendid little war."

Many who served in Cuba found the war far from splendid. Ill trained and poorly equipped, the troops went into summer combat in the tropics wearing heavy woolen uniforms. While 379 American soldiers died in combat, more than 5,000 succumbed to food poisoning, yellow fever, malaria, and other diseases during and after the war.

Several thousand black troops fought in Cuba. Some, such as the twenty-fourth infantry and tenth cavalry, were seasoned regular-army veterans transferred from bases in the West. Others were volunteers from various states. At assembly points in Georgia, and then at the embarkation port of Tampa, Florida, these troops encountered the racism of a Jim Crow society. Tampa restaurants and bars refused them service; Tampa whites disparaged them. On June 6, after weeks of racist treatment, some black troops exploded in riotous rage, storming into restaurants, bars, and other establishments that had barred them. White troops from Georgia restored order. Although white and black troops sailed to Cuba on the same transport ships (actually, hastily converted freighters), the ships themselves were segregated, with black troops often confined to the lowest quarters in the stifling heat, denied permission to mingle on deck with the other units, and in other ways discriminated against.

Despite the racism, African-Americans served with distinction once they reached Cuba. Black troops played key roles in the taking of both San Juan Hill and El Caney Hill. Of the total U.S. troops involved in the latter action, some 15 percent were black.

The Spanish sought an armistice on July 17. In the peace treaty signed that December in Paris, Spain recognized Cuba's independence and, after a U.S. payment of $20 million, ceded the Philippines, Puerto Rico, and the Pacific island of Guam to the United States. Americans now possessed an island empire stretching from the Caribbean to the Pacific.

From 1898 to 1902 the U.S. army governed Cuba under the command of General Leonard Wood. Wood's administration improved public health, education, and sanitation but nevertheless violated the spirit of the 1898 Teller Amendment. The troops eventually withdrew, though under conditions that limited Cuban sovereignty. The 1901 Platt Amendment, attached to an army appropriations bill offered by a Connecticut senator at the request of the War Department, authorized American withdrawal only after Cuba agreed not to make any treaty with a foreign power limiting its independence and not to borrow beyond its means. The United States also reserved the right to intervene in Cuba when it saw fit and to maintain a naval base there. With U.S. troops still occupying the island, the Cuban constitutional convention of 1901 accepted the Platt Amendment, which remained in force until 1934. Under its terms the United States established a naval base at Guantánamo Bay, near Santiago de Cuba, which it still maintains. U.S. investments in Cuba, some $50 million in 1898, soared to half a billion dollars by 1920.

Critics of Empire   The victories of the expansionists in Cuba and the Philippines did not bring universal praise. Some Americans, who had opposed imperialism for more than a decade, were dismayed by the results. Although few in number, the critics, like the Mugwumps who had challenged the spoils system, were influential. Indeed, some of them, like Carl Schurz and E. L. Godkin, were former Mugwumps. Other anti-imperialists included William Jennings Bryan, settlement house founder Jane Addams, novelist Mark Twain, and Harvard philosopher William James. Steel king Andrew Carnegie gave thousands of dollars to the cause. In 1898 these critics of empire had formed the Anti-Imperialist League.

For the United States to rule other peoples, the anti-imperialists believed, was to violate the principles of the Declaration of Independence and the Constitution.

As one of them wrote, "Dewey took Manila with the loss of one man—and all our institutions." The military fever that accompanied expansionism also dismayed the anti-imperialists. Some labor leaders feared that imperial expansion would lead to competition from cheap foreign labor and products.

In February 1899 the anti-imperialists failed by one vote to prevent Senate ratification of the expansionist peace treaty with Spain. McKinley's overwhelming reelection victory in 1900 and the defeat of expansionist critic William Jennings Bryan eroded the anti-imperialists' cause. Nevertheless, at a time of jingoistic rhetoric and militaristic posturing, they had upheld an older and finer vision of America.

Guerrilla War in the Philippines, 1898–1902

The worst fears of the anti-imperialists were subsequently borne out by events in the Philippines. When the Spanish-American War ended, President McKinley was faced with the urgent problem of what to do about this group of Pacific islands that had a population of more than 5 million people. At the war's outset, few Americans knew that the Philippines belonged to Spain or even where they were. Without a map, McKinley later confessed, "I could not have told where those darn islands were within two thousand miles."

But the victory over Spain whetted the appetite for expansion. To the U.S. business community, the Philippines offered a stepping-stone to the China market. McKinley, reflecting the prevailing mood as always, reasoned that the Filipinos were unready for self-government and would be gobbled up if set adrift in a world of imperial rivalries. McKinley further persuaded himself that American rule would enormously benefit the Filipinos, whom he called "our little brown brothers." A devout Methodist, he explained that America's mission was "to educate the Filipinos, and to uplift and civilize and Christianize them, and by God's grace do the very best we could by them." (In fact, most Filipinos were already Christian, a legacy of centuries of Spanish rule.) Having prayerfully reached his decision, McKinley instructed the American peace negotiators in Paris to insist on U.S. acquisition of the Philippines.

Uplifting the Filipinos required a struggle. In 1896 young Emilio Aguinaldo had organized a Filipino independence movement to drive out Spain. In 1898, with arms supplied by George Dewey, Aguinaldo's forces had captured most of Luzon, the Philippines' main island. When the Spanish surrendered, Aguinaldo proclaimed Filipino independence and drafted a democratic constitution. Feeling betrayed when the peace treaty ceded his country to the United States, Aguinaldo ordered his rebel force to attack Manila, the American base of operations. Seventy thousand more U.S. troops were shipped to the Philippines, and by the end of 1899 this initial Filipino resistance had been crushed.

These hostilities became the opening phase of a long guerrilla conflict. Before it ended, over 125,000 American men had served in the Philippines, and 4,000 had been killed. As many as 20,000 Filipino independence fighters died. As in the later Vietnam War, casualties and suffering ravaged the civilian population as well.

The Philippines Quagmire *Anticipating the Vietnam War, the U.S. suppression of the Philippines' independence struggle involved American troops in a long and nasty guerrilla campaign. One of the men in this 1900 photograph scrawled on the back: "27 hours on march, mud and rain, 24 hours without food."*

Aguinaldo was captured in March 1901, but large-scale guerrilla fighting went on through the summer of 1902.

In 1902 a special Senate committee heard testimony from veterans of the Philippines war about the execution of prisoners, the torture of suspects, and the burning of villages. The humanitarian mood of 1898, when Americans had rushed to save Cuba from the cruel Spaniards, seemed remote indeed. In retrospect, the American troops' ambivalent attitudes about the peoples of the Philippines, while deplorable, are not hard to understand. Despite America's self-image as a beacon of liberty and a savior of the world's peoples, many Americans in the 1880s and 1890s had been deeply troubled by the new immigrants from southern and eastern Europe and had expressed concerns over "backward" and "useless" races. As American nationalism was reformulated in this cauldron of immigration, imperialism, and the "winning of the West," racist attitudes about Native peoples and foreigners intermixed with rhetorical pleas for supervision and stewardship. In the process, as was evident in the treatment of American Indians (see Chapter 17), well-meaning paternalism often degenerated into deadly domination.

The subjugation of the Philippines followed years of expansionism that proclaimed America's debut on the world stage and underscored the global reach of U.S. capitalism. Nevertheless, most Americans remained ambivalent about the acquisition of territory. While anti-imperialist Mark Twain could acidly condemn "the Blessings of Civilization Trust," labor leader Samuel Gompers warned that "an inundation of Mongolians" might steal jobs from white labor. From the debate over the annexation of Hawaii in 1898 to the end of the war against Philippine independence in 1902, white Americans recoiled from making these "barbarian peoples" a part of the United States. Not fit to manage their own affairs, Cuban, Puerto Rican, Hawaiian, and Filipino peoples were placed in a protective status that denied their independence but kept them under U.S. control.

To stabilize relations in the Philippines, Congress passed the Philippine Government Act in 1902, which vested authority in a governor general to be appointed by the president. The act also provided for an elected Filipino assembly and promised eventual self-government. Progress toward this goal inched forward, with intervals of semimilitary rule. In 1946, nearly half a century after Admiral Dewey's guns had boomed in Manila Bay, independence finally came to the Philippines.

IMPORTANT EVENTS, 1877–1900

1878	Congress requires U.S. Treasury to purchase silver.
1880	James Garfield elected president.
1881	Assassination of Garfield; Chester A. Arthur becomes president.
1883	Pendleton Civil Service Act.
1884	Grover Cleveland elected president. *Wabash* v. *Illinois*.
1887	Interstate Commerce Act.
1888	Benjamin Harrison elected president.
1889	National Farmers' Alliance formed.
1890	Sherman Silver Purchase Act. Sherman Anti-Trust Act. McKinley Tariff pushes tariffs to all-time high.
1893	Panic of 1893; depression of 1893–1897 begins. Drain of Treasury's gold reserve. Repeal of the Sherman Silver Purchase Act. Overthrow of Queen Liliuokalani of Hawaii. Chicago World's Fair.
1894	"Coxey's Army" marches on Washington. Pullman strike. Wilson-Gorman Tariff.
1895	Supreme Court declares federal income tax unconstitutional. Bankers' loans end drain on gold reserves. United States intervenes in Venezuela–British Guiana boundary dispute.
1896	Free-silver forces capture Democratic party and nominate William Jennings Bryan. William McKinley elected president.
1898	Spanish-American War.
1898–1902	Guerrilla uprising in Philippines.
1900	Currency Act officially places United States on gold standard.
1901	Platt Amendment retains U.S. role in Cuba. Assassination of McKinley; Theodore Roosevelt becomes president.
1902	Philippine Government Act.

21

The Progressive Era, 1900–1917

I t was late Saturday afternoon on March 25, 1911, but at the Triangle Shirtwaist factory in New York City, hundreds of young women and a few men were still at work. In the eighth- and ninth-floor workrooms, the clatter of sewing machines filled the air. Suddenly fire broke out. Feeding on bolts of cloth, the fire soon turned the upper floors into an inferno. Panicked workers rushed for the doors, only to find some of them locked. Other doors opened inward (a fire-law violation) and were jammed shut by the crush of people trying to get out.

There were a few miraculous escapes. Young Pauline Grossman crawled to safety across a narrow alleyway when three male employees formed a human bridge. As others tried to cross, however, the weight became too great, and the three men fell to their deaths. Dozens of workers leaped from the windows to certain death on the sidewalk below.

Immigrant parents searched all night for their daughters; newspaper reporters could hear "a dozen pet names in Italian and Yiddish rising in shrill agony above the deeper moan of the throng." Sunday's headlines summed up the grim count: 141 dead.

The Triangle fire offered particularly horrifying evidence of what many citizens had recognized for years. Industrialization, for all its benefits, had taken a heavy toll on American life. For immigrants in unsafe factories and unhealthy slums, life often meant a desperate cycle of poverty, exhausting labor, and early death. In the aftermath of the Triangle Shirtwaist factory tragedy, New York passed a series of laws regulating factories and protecting workers.

Industrialization, urban growth, and the rise of great corporations affected all Americans. A new middle class of white-collar workers and urban professionals gained political influence. As middle-class women joined clubs and reform organizations, they became powerful voices in addressing the social issues of the day.

From this volatile social stew erupted a wave of reformist energy that came to be called the progressive movement. Historians once portrayed this movement rather simplistically as a triumph of "the people" over evil corporations. More recent historians have complicated this picture, noting the role of special-interest

The Triangle Fire *The bodies of young women workers lie on the sidewalk after they jumped from the burning building.*

groups (including big business) in promoting specific reforms, as well as the movement's darker side, its failures, and, above all, its rich diversity.

The progressive movement was a response to vast changes after the Civil War that had obliterated the familiar contours of an older, simpler America. Whatever their specific agendas, all progressives grappled with the new world of corporations, factories, cities, and immigrants. In contrast to the agrarian-based populists (see Chapter 20), progressives concentrated on the social effects of the new urban-industrial order.

Emerging in the 1890s at the city and state levels, a dizzying array of organizations, many led by women, pursued varied reform objectives. Under the influence of journalists, novelists, religious leaders, social thinkers, and politicians, these grass-roots efforts evolved into a powerful national movement. At the federal level, the reform spirit gripped Congress and the White House. By 1917, when reform gave way to war, America's political and social landscape had been transformed. New organizations, new laws, and new regulatory agencies had arisen to grapple with the consequences of helter-skelter urbanization, industrial expansion, and corporate growth. The progressives could be maddeningly moralistic. They had their blind spots (especially on such subjects as immigration and race), and their reforms didn't always work out as planned. But, on balance, their imposing record of achievement left a powerful legacy for future generations to build upon.

This chapter focuses on five major questions:

How did intellectuals, novelists, and journalists help lay the groundwork for the progressive movement?

What problems of the new urban-industrial order particularly disturbed progressives, and how did they address these problems?

How did progressive reform affect ordinary Americans, including workers, women, immigrants, city dwellers, and African-Americans?

As progressivism emerged as a national movement, which politicians and issues proved most important?

How did progressivism change Americans' view of the proper role of government?

PROGRESSIVES AND THEIR IDEAS

As the twentieth century dawned, local groups across the nation grappled with the problems of the new urban-industrial order. Workers protested unsafe and exhausting jobs. Expert commissions investigated social and economic conditions. Women's clubs turned from cultural uplift to reform. Intellectuals challenged the ideological foundations of a business-dominated social order, and journalists publicized municipal corruption and industrialism's human toll. Reform gained momentum as activists tried to make government more democratic, eradicate dangerous conditions in cities and factories, and curb corporate power.

Looking back on all these efforts, historians grouped them under a single label: "the progressive movement." In fact, "progressivism" was never a single movement. It is perhaps best understood as a widespread yearning for reform and an exciting sense of new social possibilities. This yearning found many outlets and focused on a wide array of issues.

The Many Faces of Progressivism   Who were the progressives, and what reforms did they pursue? To answer these questions, we need to look at the pattern of urban growth in the early twentieth century. Along with immigration, a rapidly growing middle class transformed U.S. cities. From the men and women of this class—most of whom were native-born, white, and Protestant—came many of the leaders and foot soldiers of the progressive movement.

From 1900 to 1920, the white-collar work force jumped from 5.1 million to 10.5 million—more than double the growth rate of the labor force as a whole. As industry grew, the number of secretaries, civil engineers, and people in advertising increased phenomenally. This white-collar class included corporate technicians and desk workers; the owners and managers of local businesses; and professionals such as lawyers, physicians, and teachers. Existing professional societies such as the American Bar Association grew rapidly. Scores of new professional groups arose, from the American Association of Advertising Agencies (1917) to the American Association of University Professors (1915). The age of organization had dawned, bringing new professional allegiances, a new emphasis on certification and licensing, and in general a more standardized, routinized society. For many middle-class Americans, membership in a national professional society provided a sense of identity that might earlier have come from neighborhood, church, or political party affiliations. Ambitious, well educated, and valuing social stability, the members of this new middle class were eager to make their influence felt.

For middle-class women, the city offered both opportunities and frustrations. Young unmarried women often became schoolteachers, secretaries, typists, clerks, and telephone operators. The number of women in such white-collar jobs surged from 949,000 in 1900 to 3.4 million in 1920. The ranks of college-educated women, although still small, more than tripled in this twenty-year period.

But for middle-class married women caring for homes and children, city life could mean isolation and frustration. The divorce rate crept up from one in twelve marriages in 1900 to one in nine by 1916. As we shall see, many middle-class women joined female white-collar workers and college graduates in leading a resurgent women's movement. Cultural commentators wrote nervously of the "New Woman."

The progressive reform impulse drew on the energies of men and women of this new urban middle class. The initial reform impetus came not from political parties but from women's clubs, settlement houses, and private groups with names like the Playground Association of America, the National Child Labor Committee, the National Consumers' League, and the American League for Civic Improvement. In this era of organizations, the reform movement, too, drew strength from organized interest groups.

Important as it was, the native-born middle class was not the only force behind progressivism. On issues affecting factory workers and slum dwellers, the urban-immigrant political machines—and workers themselves—provided critical support and often took the initiative. Some corporate leaders helped shape regulatory measures in ways to serve their interests.

What, then, was progressivism? At the most basic level, it was a series of political and cultural responses to industrialization and its by-products: immigration, urban growth, the rise of corporate power, and widening class divisions. In contrast to populism, progressivism's strength lay in the cities, and it enlisted many more journalists, academics, social theorists, and urban dwellers generally. Finally, most progressives were reformers, not radicals. They wished to remedy the social ills of industrial capitalism, not uproot the system itself.

But which parts of the urban-industrial order most needed attention, and what remedies were required? These key questions stirred deep disagreements, and the progressive impulse spawned an array of activities that sometimes overlapped and sometimes diverged. Many reformers wanted stricter regulation of business, from local transit companies to the almighty trusts. Others focused on protecting workers and the urban poor. Still others tried to reform the structure of government, especially at the municipal level. Finally, some reformers, viewing immigration, urban immorality, and social disorder as the central problems, fought for immigration restriction or various social-control strategies. All this contributed to the mosaic of progressive reform.

Central to progressivism was the confidence that all social problems could be solved through careful study and organized effort. Progressives had a high regard for science and expert knowledge. Scientific and technological expertise had produced the new industrial order, and progressives tended to believe that such expertise would also solve the social problems spawned by industrialism. Progressives marshaled research data, expert opinion, and statistics to support their various causes.

Some historians have portrayed progressivism as an organizational stage that all modernizing societies pass through. This is a useful perspective, provided we remember that it was not an automatic process unfolding independently of human will. Eloquent leaders, gifted journalists, activist workers, and passionate reformers all played a role. Human emotion—whether indignation over child labor, intense moralism, fear of the alien, hatred of unbridled corporate power, or raw political ambition—drove the movement forward.

Intellectuals Offer New Social Views A group of early-twentieth-century thinkers helped build progressivism's ideological scaffolding. As we have seen, some Gilded Age intellectuals had argued that Charles Darwin's theory of evolution justified brutal, unrestrained economic competition. In the 1880s and 1890s, sociologist Lester Ward, utopian novelist Edward Bellamy, and leaders of the settlement house and Social Gospel movements had all attacked this harsh version of Social Darwinism (see Chapters 18 and 19). This attack intensified as the twentieth century opened.

One of the sharpest critics of the new business order was economist Thorstein Veblen, who was reared by frugal Norwegian-American parents on a farm in Minnesota. In *The Theory of the Leisure Class* (1899), Veblen mercilessly satirized the lifestyle of the newly rich captains of industry. Dissecting their habits the way an anthropologist might study the customs of an exotic tribal people, he argued that they built showy mansions, threw elaborate parties, and otherwise engaged in "conspicuous consumption" to flaunt their wealth and assert their claims to superiority.

While Veblen scorned the "wastemanship" of the business class, he shared the era's admiration for efficiency, science, and technical expertise. In later works, he argued that workers and engineers, shaped by the discipline of the machine, were better fitted to lead society than the nation's corporate leaders.

Other intellectuals built a case for reform. Harvard philosopher William James, in an influential 1907 essay called "Pragmatism," argued that truth emerges not from abstract theorizing but from the experience of coping with life's realities. James emphasized the fluidity of knowledge and the importance of practical action. In this way, he contributed to the progressives' skepticism toward the conventional wisdom of conservatives, and to their confidence that social conditions could be bettered through intelligent and purposeful action.

No thinker better captured this faith in the power of new ideas to transform society than Herbert Croly. The son of New York journalists and reformers, Croly grew up in a cosmopolitan world where social issues were hotly debated.

In *The Promise of American Life* (1909), he called for an activist government of the kind advocated by Alexander Hamilton, the first secretary of the Treasury, in the 1790s. But rather than serving only the interests of the business class, as Hamilton had proposed, Croly argued that this activist government should promote the welfare of all citizens.

To build support for this enlarged view of government, Croly argued, intellectuals must play a key role. In 1914 he founded the *New Republic* magazine to promote progressive ideas.

Few intellectuals argued more effectively for organized efforts to address the social by-products of industrialization than the settlement house leader Jane Addams. In her books *Democracy and Social Ethics* (1902) and *Twenty Years at Hull House* (1910), Addams rejected the idea that unrestrained competition offered the best path to social progress. Instead, she argued, in a complex, modern industrial society, each individual's well-being depends on the well-being of all. Addams urged privileged middle-class men and women to recognize their common interests with the laboring masses, and to take the lead in demanding better conditions in factories and immigrant slums. Teaching by example, Addams made her Chicago social settlement, Hull House, a center of social activism and legislative-reform initiatives.

For philosopher John Dewey, the key social institution that could bring about a more humane and cooperative social order was the public school. With public-school enrollment growing from about 7 million in 1870 to more than 23 million in 1920, Dewey saw schools as potent engines of social change. Banishing bolted-down chairs and desks from his model school at the University of Chicago, he encouraged pupils to interact with one another. The ideal school, he said in *Democracy and Education* (1916), would be an "embryonic community" where children would learn to live as members of a social group.

For other thinkers, the key to social change lay in transforming the nation's courts. Conservative judges citing ancient precedents had upheld corporate interests and struck down reform legislation for decades. A few jurists, however, had argued for a more flexible view. In *The Common Law* (1881), law professor Oliver Wendell Holmes, Jr., had insisted that law must evolve as society changes. In a phrase much quoted by progressives, he had declared, "The life of the law has not been logic; it has been experience." Appointed to the Supreme Court in 1902, Holmes wrote a series of eloquent opinions dissenting from the conservative Court majority. Under the influence of the new social thinking, the courts slowly became more receptive to reform legislation.

Novelists, Journalists, and Artists Spotlight Social Problems

While intellectuals and social thinkers reoriented American social thought, novelists and journalists roused the reform spirit by chronicling corporate wrongdoing, municipal corruption, slum conditions, and industrial abuses. Advances in printing and photo reproduction ensured a mass audience and sharpened the emotional impact of their message.

In his popular novel *The Octopus* (1901), the young San Francisco writer Frank Norris portrayed the epic struggle between California railroad owners and the state's wheat growers. Basing his fiction on the actual practices of Gilded Age railroad barons, Norris described the bribery, intimidation, rate manipulation, and other means they used to promote their interests.

Theodore Dreiser's novel *The Financier* (1912) featured a hard-driving business tycoon utterly lacking a social conscience. Like Norris, Dreiser modeled his story on the career of an actual tycoon, Charles Yerkes, a railway financier with a reputation for underhanded practices. Like Veblen's *Theory of the Leisure Class,* such works undermined the reputation of the industrial elite and stimulated pressures for tougher regulation of business.

Also influential in forging the progressive spirit were articles exposing urban political corruption and corporate wrongdoing published in mass magazines such as *McClure's* and *Collier's*. President Theodore Roosevelt criticized the authors as "muckrakers" obsessed with the seamier side of American life, but the name became a badge of honor. Journalist Lincoln Steffens began the exposé vogue in October 1902 with a *McClure's* article documenting municipal corruption in St. Louis and the efforts of a crusading district attorney to fight it.

The muckrakers emphasized facts rather than abstractions. To gather material, some worked as factory laborers or lived in slum tenements. In a 1903 series, journalist Maria Van Vorst described her experiences working in a Massachusetts shoe factory where women's fingernails rotted away from repeated immersion in caustic dyes.

The muckrakers awakened middle-class readers to conditions in industrial America. The circulation of *McClure's* and *Collier's* soared. Some magazine exposés later appeared in book form, including Lincoln Steffens's *The Shame of the Cities* (1904), Ida Tarbell's damning *History of the Standard Oil Company* (1904), and David Graham Phillips's *Treason of the Senate* (1906).

Artists and photographers played a role as well. A group of New York painters dubbed the Ashcan School portrayed the harshness of life in the city's crowded slums. The Wisconsin-born photographer Lewis Hine captured images of immigrants and factory laborers. As official photographer for the National Child Labor Committee from 1911 to 1916, Hine took photographs of child workers with stunted bodies and worn expressions that helped build support for national legislation outlawing child labor.

STATE AND LOCAL PROGRESSIVISM

While they read novels, magazine articles, and works of social analysis on the problems besetting urban-industrial America, middle-class citizens also observed these problems firsthand in their own communities. In fact, the progressive movement began with grass-roots campaigns from New York to San Francisco to end urban political corruption, regulate corporate behavior, and improve conditions in factories and city slums. Eventually, these state and local movements came together in a powerful national surge of reform.

Reforming the Political Process   In a series of grass-roots campaigns beginning in the 1890s, native-born elites and middle-class reformers battled corrupt city governments. New York City experienced a succession of reform spasms in which Protestant clergy rallied the forces of righteousness against Tammany Hall, the city's entrenched Democratic organization. In Detroit the reform mayor Hazen Pingree (served 1890–1897) brought honesty to city hall, lowered transit fares, adopted a fairer tax structure, and provided public baths and other services for the poor. Pingree once slapped a health quarantine on a brothel, holding a prominent business leader hostage until he promised to back Pingree's reforms.

In San Francisco, a courageous newspaper editor led a 1907 crusade against the city's corrupt boss, Abe Reuf. Thanks to attorney Hiram Johnson, who took over the case when the original prosecutor was gunned down in court, Reuf and his cronies were convicted. Sternly self-righteous and full of reform zeal—one observer called him "a volcano in perpetual eruption"—Johnson rode his newly won fame to the California governorship and the U.S. Senate.

In Toledo, Ohio, a colorful eccentric named Samuel M. ("Golden Rule") Jones led the reform crusade. A self-made businessman converted to the Social Gospel (see Chapter 19), Jones introduced profit sharing in his factory, and as mayor he established playgrounds, free kindergartens, and lodging houses for homeless transients.

The political reform movement soon moved beyond simply "throwing the rascals out" to probing the roots of urban misgovernment, including the private monopolies that ran municipal water, gas, electricity, and transit systems. Reformers passed laws regulating the rates these utilities could charge, raising their taxes, and curbing their political influence. (Some even advocated public ownership of these companies.) This new regulatory structure would remain the rule for a century, until an equally strong deregulatory movement swept the nation in the 1990s.

Reflecting the Progressive Era vogue of expertise and efficiency, some municipal reformers advocated substituting professional managers and administrators, chosen in citywide elections, for mayors and aldermen elected on a ward-by-ward basis. Natural disasters sometimes gave a boost to this particular reform. Dayton, Ohio, went to a city-manager system after a ruinous flood in 1913. Supposedly above politics, these experts were expected to run the city like an efficient business.

Municipal reform attracted different groups depending on the issue. The native-born middle class, led by clergymen, editors, and other opinion molders, provided the initial impetus and core support. Business interests often pushed for citywide elections and the city-manager system, since these changes tended to reduce immigrants' political clout and increase the influence of the corporate elite.

Reforms that addressed the immediate needs of ordinary city dwellers, such as improved city services, won support from immigrants and even from political bosses who realized that explosive urban growth was swamping the old, informal system of meeting constituents' needs.

The electoral-reform movement soon expanded to the state level. By 1910, for example, all states had replaced the old system of voting, which involved preprinted ballots bearing the names of specific candidates, with the secret ballot, which made it harder to rig elections. An electoral reform introduced in Wisconsin in 1903, the direct primary, enabled rank-and-file voters rather than party bosses to select the candidates who would run in the general election.

To restore government by the people rather than by moneyed interests, some western states inaugurated electoral reforms known as the *initiative, referendum, and recall.* By an initiative, voters can instruct the legislature to consider a specific bill. In a referendum, they can actually enact a law or (in a nonbinding referendum) express their views on a proposed measure. By a recall petition, voters can remove a public official from office if they muster enough signatures.

While these reforms aimed to democratize voting, party leaders and interest groups soon learned to manipulate the new electoral machinery. Ironically, the new procedures may have weakened party loyalty and reduced voter interest. Voter-participation rates dropped steeply in these years, while political activity by organized interest groups increased.

Regulating Business, Protecting Workers

The late-nineteenth-century corporate consolidation that produced giants like Carnegie Steel and Standard Oil (see Chapter 18) continued after 1900. The United States Steel Company created by J. P. Morgan in 1901 controlled 80 percent of all U.S. steel production. A year later Morgan combined six competing companies into the International Harvester Company, which dominated the farm-implement business. The General Motors Company, formed in 1908 by William C. Durant with backing from the Du Pont Corporation, bought various independent automobile manufacturers, from the inexpensive Chevrolet to the luxury Cadillac, and consolidated their operations under one corporate umbrella.

Many workers benefited from this corporate growth. Industrial workers' average annual real wages (defined, that is, in terms of actual purchasing power) rose from $532 in the late nineteenth century to $687 by 1915. In railroading and other unionized industries, wages climbed still higher. But even though the cost of living was far lower than today, such wages could barely support a family and provided little cushion for emergencies.

To survive, entire families went to work. Two-thirds of young immigrant women entered the labor force in the early 1900s, working as factory help or domestics or in small establishments like laundries and bakeries. Even children worked. In 1910 the nonfarm labor force probably included at least 1.6 million children aged ten to fifteen who were working in factories, mills, tenement sweatshops,

Children in the Labor Force,* 1880–1930	1880	1890	1900	1910	1920	1930
Total number of children aged 10–15 (in millions)	6.6	8.3	9.6	10.8	12.5	14.3
Total number of children employed (in millions)	1.1	1.5	1.7	1.6	1.4	0.7
Percentage of children employed	16.8	18.1	18.2	15.0	11.3	4.7

*Nonagricultural workers.

Source: *The Statistical History of the United States from Colonial Times to the Present* (Stamford, Conn.: Fairfield Publishers, 1965).

and street trades such as shoe shining and newspaper vending. The total may have been higher, since many "women workers" listed in the census were in fact young girls. One investigator found a girl of five working at night in a South Carolina textile mill.

Most laborers faced long hours and great hazards. Despite the eight-hour movement of the 1880s, in 1900 the average worker still toiled 9 1/2 hours a day. Some southern textile mills required workdays of 12 or 13 hours. In one typical year (1907), 4,534 railroad workers and more than 3,000 miners were killed on the job. Few employers accepted responsibility for work-related accidents and illnesses. Vacations and retirement benefits were practically unheard of.

New industrial workers accustomed to the rhythms of farm labor faced the discipline of the time clock and the machine. Efficiency experts used time-and-motion studies to increase production and make human workers as predictable as machines. In *Principles of Scientific Management* (1911), Frederick W. Taylor explained how to increase output by standardizing job routines and rewarding the fastest workers. "Efficiency" became a popular catchword, but most workers deeply resented the pressures to speed up output.

For Americans troubled by the social implications of industrialization, the expansion of corporate power and the hazards of the workplace stirred urgent concern. The drive to regulate big business, inherited from the populists, thus became a vitally important impetus for progressivism. Since corporations had benefited from the government's economic policies, such as high protective tariffs, reformers reasoned, they should also be subject to government supervision.

Of the many states that passed laws regulating railroads, mines, and other businesses, none did so more avidly than Wisconsin under Governor Robert ("Fighting Bob") La Follette. As a Republican congressman, La Follette had feuded with the state's conservative party leadership, and in 1900 he won the governorship as an independent. Challenging the state's long-dominant business interests, La Follette and his administration adopted the direct-primary system, set up a railroad regulatory commission, increased corporate taxes, and limited campaign spending. Reflecting progressivism's faith in experts, La Follette met regularly with reform-minded professors at the University of Wisconsin. He also set up a legislative reference library so lawmakers would not be solely dependent on corporate lobbyists for factual information. La Follette's reforms gained national attention as the "Wisconsin Idea."

If electoral reform and corporate regulation represented the brain of progressivism, the impulse to improve conditions in factories and mills represented its heart. This movement, too, began at the local and state level. By 1907, for example, some thirty states had outlawed child labor. A 1903 Oregon law limited women in industry to a ten-hour workday.

Campaigns to improve industrial safety and otherwise better conditions for the laboring masses won support from political bosses in cities with large immigrant populations, such as New York, Cleveland, and Chicago. New York state senator Robert F. Wagner, a leader of Tammany Hall, headed the investigating committee set up after the 1911 Triangle fire. Thanks to the committee's efforts, New York legislators passed fifty-six worker-protection laws, including required fire-safety inspections of factories. By 1914, spurred by the Triangle disaster, twenty-five states had passed laws making employers liable for job-related injuries or deaths.

Florence Kelley was a leader in the drive to remedy industrial abuses. The daughter of a conservative Republican congressman, Kelley became a Hull House resident in 1891. Investigating conditions in factories and sweatshops, in 1893 she helped secure passage of an Illinois law prohibiting child labor and limiting working hours for women. In 1899 she became general secretary of the National Consumers' League, which mobilized consumer pressure for improved factory conditions. Campaigning for a federal child-labor law, Kelley pointedly asked, "Why are seals, bears, reindeer, fish, wild game in the national parks, buffalo, [and] migratory birds all found suitable for federal protection, but not children?"

Like many progressive reforms, the crusade for workplace safety relied on expert research. Alice Hamilton, for example, a pioneer in the new field of "industrial hygiene," taught bacteriology at Northwestern University while also working with Jane Addams at Hull House. In 1910, fusing her scientific training and her reformist impulses, she conducted a major study of lead poisoning among industrial workers. Appointed as an investigator by the U.S. Bureau of Labor in 1911, Hamilton became an expert on—and public campaigner against—work-related medical hazards.

Workers, who understood the hazards of their jobs better than anyone, provided further pressure for reform. For example, when the granite industry introduced new power drills that created a fine dust that workers inhaled, the *Granite Cutters' Journal* warned of "stone cutters' consumption" and called the new drills "widow makers." Sure enough, investigators soon linked the dust to a deadly respiratory disease, silicosis. This, too, became another industrial hazard that worker-safety advocates sought to remedy.

Making Cities
More Livable

In the early twentieth century, America became an urban nation. By 1920 the urban population passed the 50 percent mark, and sixty-eight U.S. cities boasted more than a hundred thousand inhabitants. New York City grew by 2.2 million from 1900 to 1920, and Chicago by 1 million.

Political corruption was only one of many problems plaguing these burgeoning urban centers. As manufacturing and businesses grew, a surging tide of immigrants and native-born newcomers engulfed the cities. Overwhelmed by this rapid growth, many cities became dreary, sprawling human warehouses. They lacked adequate parks, municipal services, public-health resources, recreational facilities, and other basic civic amenities. Unsurprisingly, as the progressive movement took shape, this worrisome tangle of urban problems loomed large.

Drawing on the efforts of Frederick Law Olmsted and others (see Chapter 19), reform-minded men and women campaigned for parks, boulevards, and street lights and proposed laws against billboards and unsightly overhead electrical wires. An influential voice for city planning and beautification was Daniel Burnham, chief architect of the 1893 Chicago world's fair. Burnham led a successful 1906 effort to revive a plan for Washington, D.C., first proposed by Charles L'Enfant in 1791. He also developed city plans for Cleveland, San Francisco, and other cities.

Burnham's 1909 plan for Chicago offered a seductive vision of a city both more efficient and more beautiful. He recommended lakefront parks and museums, wide boulevards to improve traffic flow, and a redesign of Chicago's congested major thoroughfare, Michigan Avenue. The focal point of Burnham's dream city was a majestic domed city hall and vast civic plaza. Although not all of Burnham's plan was adopted, Chicago spent more than $300 million on projects reflecting his ideas. Many Progressive Era urban planners shared Burnham's faith that more beautiful cities and imposing public buildings would ensure a law-abiding and civic-minded urban populace.

Beyond urban beautification, the municipal reform impulse also included such practical goals as decent housing and better garbage collection and street cleaning. Providing a model for other cities and states, the New York legislature passed laws imposing strict health and safety regulations on tenements in 1911.

Public health loomed large as well. With the discovery in the 1880s that germs cause diseases such as cholera and typhoid fever, municipal hygiene and sanitation became high priorities. Progressive reformers called for improved water and sewer systems, regulation of milk suppliers and food handlers, school medical examinations and vaccination programs, and informational campaigns to spread public-health information to the urban masses.

All these efforts bore fruit. From 1900 to 1920, infant mortality (defined as death in the first year of life) dropped from 165 per 1,000 population to around 75, and the tuberculosis death rate fell by nearly half. The municipal health crusades had a social-class dimension. Middle-class reformers set the "sanitary agenda," and the campaigns often targeted immigrants and the poor as the sources of contagion. When Mary Mallon, an Irish-immigrant cook in New York, was found to be a healthy carrier of the typhoid bacillus in 1907, she was confined for years by the city health authorities and demonized in the press as "Typhoid Mary."

Urban reformers also shared the heightened environmental consciousness of these years (see Chapter 17). The battle against air pollution illustrates both the promise and the frustrations of municipal environmentalism. Coal-fueled steam boilers, the major energy source for factories, produced massive amounts of soot and smoke. Factory chimneys belching smoke had once inspired pride, but by the early 1900s physicians had linked factory smoke to respiratory problems, and civic reformers were deploring the resulting air pollution.

As with other progressive reforms, the antismoke campaign combined expertise with activism. Civil engineers formed the Smoke Prevention Association in 1906, and researchers at the University of Pittsburgh—one of the nation's smokiest cities with its nearby steel mills—documented the hazards and costs of air pollution. Chicago merchant Marshall Field declared that the "soot tax" he paid to clean his stores was larger than his real-estate taxes. As women's clubs and other civic groups embraced the cause, many cities passed smoke-abatement laws.

Success proved elusive. Railroads and corporations fought back in the courts and often won. With coal still providing 70 percent of the nation's energy as late as 1920, cities remained smoky. Not until years later, with the shift from coal to other energy sources, did the battle against municipal air pollution make significant headway.

Progressivism and Social Control Progressives' belief that they could improve society through research, legislation, and aroused public opinion sprang from their confidence that they knew what was best for other people. While municipal corruption, unsafe factories, and corporate abuses captured their attention, so, too, did issues of personal behavior, particularly the behavior of immigrants. The problems they addressed deserved attention, but their self-righteous rhetoric and the remedies they proposed also betrayed an impulse to impose their own moral standards by force of law.

Moral Control in the Cities Early-twentieth-century urban life was more than crowded slums and exhausting labor. For all their problems, cities also offered fun and diversion. Department stores, vaudeville, music halls, and amusement parks (see Chapter 19) continued to flourish. While some vaudeville owners strove for respectability, raucous and bawdy routines full of sexual innuendo, including those of the comedienne Mae West, were popular with working-class audiences. New York City's amusement park, Coney Island, drew more patrons than ever. A subway ride from the city, it attracted as many as a million visitors a day by 1914.

For families, amusement parks provided escape from tenements. For female garment workers or department-store clerks, they provided an opportunity to spend time with friends, meet young men, and show off new outfits. With electrification, simply riding the streetcars or taking an evening stroll on well-lit downtown streets became leisure activities in themselves. News of Orville and Wilbur Wright's successful airplane flight in 1903, and the introduction of Henry Ford's Model T in 1908, which transformed the automobile from a toy of the rich to a vehicle for the masses, heightened the sense of exciting changes ahead, with cities at the heart of the action.

Jaunty popular songs, introduced in the music halls and produced in a district of lower Manhattan called Tin Pan Alley, added to the vibrancy of city life. The blues, rooted in the chants of southern black sharecroppers, reached a broader public with such songs as W. C. Handy's classic "St. Louis Blues" (1914). Ragtime, another import from the black South (see Chapter 19), enjoyed great popularity in early-twentieth-century urban America. Both the black composer Scott Joplin, with such works as "Maple Leaf Rag" (1899), and the white composer Irving Berlin, with his hit tune "Alexander's Rag-Time Band" (1911), contributed to this vogue.

These years also brought a new medium of mass entertainment—the movies. Initially a part of vaudeville shows, movies soon migrated to five-cent halls called "nickelodeons" in immigrant neighborhoods. At first featuring brief comic sequences like *The Sneeze* or *The Kiss,* the movies began to tell stories with *The Great Train Robbery* (1903). *A Fool There Was* (1914), with its famous line, "Kiss me, my fool!," made Theda Bara (really Theodosia Goodman of Cincinnati) the first female movie star. The British music-hall performer Charlie Chaplin emigrated to America in 1913 and appeared in some sixty short two-reel comedies between 1914 and 1917. Like amusement parks, the movies allowed immigrant youth to briefly escape parental supervision. As a New York garment worker recalled, "The one place I was allowed to go by myself was the movies. My parents wouldn't let me go anywhere else."

Ironically, the diversions that made city life more bearable for the poor struck some middle-class reformers as moral traps no less dangerous than the physical hazards of the factory or the slum tenement. Fearful of immorality and social disorder, reformers campaigned to regulate amusement parks, dance halls, and the movies. The early movies, in particular, struck many middle-class men and women as degenerate, and the darkened nickelodeons were seen as potential dens of vice. Warning of "nickel madness," reformers demanded film censorship. Several states and cities set up censorship boards, and the Supreme Court upheld such measures in 1915.

Building on the moral-purity crusade of the Woman's Christian Temperance Union (WCTU) and other groups in the 1890s (see Chapter 19), reformers also targeted prostitution, a major urban problem. Male procurers lured young women into the business and then took a share of their income. The paltry wages paid women for factory work or domestic service attracted many to this more-lucrative occupation. One prostitute wrote that she was unwilling "to get up at 6:30 . . . and work in a close stuffy room . . . until dark for $6 or $7 a week" when an afternoon with a man could bring in more.

Addressing the issue in the usual progressive fashion, investigators gathered statistics on what they called "the social evil." The American Social Hygiene

Association (1914), financed by John D. Rockefeller, Jr., sponsored medical research on sexually transmitted diseases, paid for "vice investigations" in various cities, and drafted model municipal statutes against prostitution.

As prostitution came to symbolize the larger moral dangers of cities, a "white slave" hysteria gripped the nation. Novels, films, and muckraking articles warned of farm girls' being kidnapped and forced into urban brothels. The Mann Act (1910) made it illegal to transport a woman across a state line "for immoral purposes." Amid much fanfare, reformers shut down the red-light districts of New Orleans, Chicago, and other cities.

Racism, anti-immigrant prejudice, fear of the city, and anxieties about changing sexual mores all fueled the antiprostitution crusade. Tipped off by neighbors and angry spouses, authorities employed the new legislation to pry into private sexual behavior. Scam artists entrapped men into Mann Act violations and blackmailed them. In 1913 the African-American boxer Jack Johnson, who had won the heavyweight championship five years earlier, was convicted under the Mann Act for traveling with a (white) woman across state lines for "immoral purposes." Johnson went abroad to escape imprisonment.

Battling Alcohol and Drugs Temperance had long been part of the American reform agenda, but reformers' tactics and objectives changed in the Progressive Era. Most earlier campaigns had urged individuals to give up drink. The powerful Anti-Saloon League (ASL), founded in 1895, shifted the emphasis to legislating a ban on the sale of alcoholic beverages. The ASL was a typical progressive organization. Full-time professionals ran the national office, while Protestant ministers staffed a network of state committees. The ASL presses in Westerville, Ohio, produced propaganda documenting alcohol's role in many social problems and touting prohibition as the answer. As the ASL added its efforts to those of the WCTU and various church bodies, many localities banned the sale of alcoholic beverages and the campaign for national prohibition gained strength.

This was a heavy-drinking era, and alcohol abuse did indeed contribute to domestic abuse, health problems, and work injuries. But like the antiprostitution crusade, the prohibition campaign became a symbolic battleground pitting native-born citizens against the new immigrants. The ASL, while it raised legitimate issues, also embodied Protestant America's impulse to control the immigrant city.

These years also saw the first sustained campaign against drug abuse—and for good reason. Physicians, patent-medicine peddlers, and legitimate drug companies freely prescribed or sold opium (derived from poppies) and its derivatives morphine and heroin. Cocaine, extracted from coca leaves, was widely used as well. Coca-Cola contained cocaine until about 1900.

As reformers focused on the problem, the federal government backed a 1912 treaty aimed at halting the international opium trade. The Narcotics Act of 1914, also known as the Harrison Act, banned the distribution of heroin, morphine, cocaine, and other addictive drugs except by licensed physicians or pharmacists. In

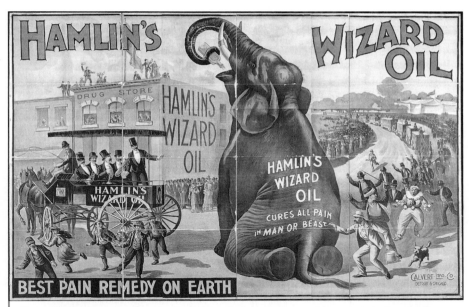

Patent Medicines *Progressive Era reformers targeted unregulated and often dangerous nostrums. Hamlin's Wizard Oil, a pain remedy marketed by traveling shows and musical groups, contained alcohol, ammonia, chloroform, and turpentine, among other ingredients.*

their battle against drugs, as in their environmental concerns, the progressives anticipated an issue that would remain important into the twenty-first century. But this reform, too, had racist undertones. Antidrug crusaders luridly described Chinese "opium dens" and warned that "drug-crazed Negroes" imperiled white womanhood.

Immigration Restriction and Eugenics

While many of the new city dwellers came from farms and small towns, the main source of urban growth continued to be immigration. More than 17 million newcomers arrived from 1900 to 1917 (many passing through New York's immigration center, Ellis Island), and most settled in cities. As in the 1890s (see Chapter 19), the influx came mainly from southern and eastern Europe, but more than two hundred thousand Japanese and forty thousand Chinese also arrived between 1900 and 1920, as well as thousands of Mexicans seeking railroad work. Some immigrants prospered, but many sank into poverty or survived precariously on the economic margins.

The dismay that middle-class Americans felt about appalling conditions in the urban slums stimulated support not only for protective legislation, but also for immigration restriction. If the immigrant city was a morass of social problems, some concluded, then immigrants should be excluded. Prominent Bostonians formed the Immigration Restriction League in 1894. The American Federation of Labor, fearing job competition, also endorsed restriction.

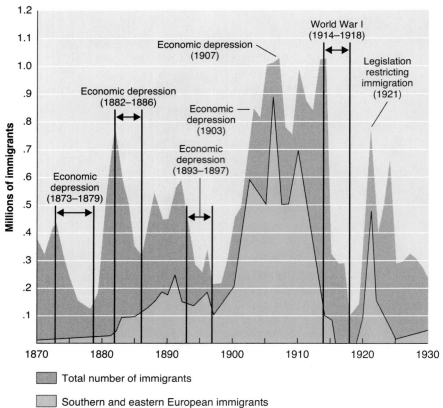

Total number of immigrants

Southern and eastern European immigrants

Immigration to the United States, 1870–1930

With the end of the depression of the 1890s, immigrants from southern and eastern Europe poured into American cities, spurring an immigration-restriction movement, urban moral-purity campaigns, and efforts to improve the physical and social conditions of immigrant life.

Sources: Statistical History of the United States from Colonial Times to the Present (Stamford, Conn.: Fairfield Publishers, 1965); and report presented by Senator William P. Dillingham, Senate document 742, 61st Congress, 3rd session, December 5, 1910: Abstracts of Reports to the Immigration Commission.

Progressives who supported this reform characteristically documented their case with claims of scientific expertise. In 1911 a congressional commission produced a massive statistical study allegedly proving the new immigrants' innate degeneracy. Sociologist Edward A. Ross, a prominent progressive, described the recent immigrants as "low-browed, big-faced persons of obviously low mentality."

Led by Massachusetts senator Henry Cabot Lodge, Congress passed literacy-test bills in 1896, 1913, and 1915, only to see them vetoed. These measures would have excluded would-be immigrants over sixteen years old who were unable to read, either in English or in some other language, thus discriminating against persons lacking formal education. In 1917 one such bill became law over President Woodrow Wilson's veto. Immigrants also faced physical examinations and tests in which legitimate public-health concerns became mixed up with stereotypes of entire ethnic groups as mental or physical defectives. This, too, was part of progressivism's mixed legacy.

Anti-immigrant fears helped fuel the eugenics movement. Eugenics is the control of reproduction to alter a plant or animal species, and some U.S. eugenicists believed that human society could be improved by this means. A leading eugenicist, the zoologist Charles B. Davenport, urged immigration restriction to keep America from pollution by "inferior" genetic stock.

In *The Passing of the Great Race* (1916), Madison Grant, a prominent progressive and eugenics advocate, used bogus data to denounce immigrants from southern and eastern Europe, especially Jews. He also viewed African-Americans as inferior. Anticipating the program of Adolf Hitler in the 1930s (see Chapter 25), Grant called for racial segregation, immigration restriction, and the forced sterilization of the "unfit," including "worthless race types." The vogue of eugenics gave "scientific" respectability to anti-immigrant sentiment, as well as the racism that pervaded white America in these years. Inspired by eugenics, many states legalized the sterilization of criminals, sex offenders, and persons adjudged mentally deficient. In the 1927 case *Buck* v. *Bell*, the Supreme Court upheld such laws.

Racism and
Progressivism

Progressivism arose at a time of significant changes in African-American life, and also of intense racism in white America. These racial realities are crucial to a full understanding of the movement.

Most of the nation's 10 million blacks lived in the South as sharecroppers and tenant farmers in 1900. As devastating floods and the cotton boll weevil, which spread from Mexico in the 1890s, worsened their lot, many southern blacks left the land. By 1910 over 20 percent of the black population lived in cities, mostly in the South, but many in the North as well. Black men in the cities took jobs in factories, mines, docks, and railroads or became carpenters, plasterers, or bricklayers. Many black women became domestic servants, seamstresses, or workers in laundries and tobacco factories. By 1910, 54 percent of America's black women held jobs.

Across the South, legally enforced racism peaked in the early twentieth century. Local "Jim Crow" laws segregated streetcars, schools, parks, and even cemeteries. The facilities for blacks, including the schools, were invariably inferior. Many southern cities imposed residential segregation by law until the Supreme Court restricted it in 1917. Most labor unions excluded black workers. Disfranchised and trapped in a cycle of poverty, poor education, and discrimination, southern blacks faced bleak prospects.

Fleeing poverty and racism and drawn by job opportunities, two hundred thousand blacks migrated North between 1890 and 1910. Wartime opportunities drew still more in 1917–1918 (see Chapter 22), and by 1920, 1.4 million African-Americans lived in the North. They found conditions only slightly better than in the South. In northern cities, too, racism worsened after 1890 as hard times and immigration heightened social tensions. (Immigrants, competing with blacks for jobs and housing, sometimes exhibited the most intense racial prejudice.) Segregation, though not imposed by law, was enforced by custom and sometimes by violence. Blacks lived in run-down "colored districts," attended dilapidated schools, and worked at the lowest-paying jobs.

Their ballots—usually cast for the party of Lincoln—brought little political influence. The only black politicians tolerated by Republican politicians were those willing to distribute low-level patronage jobs and otherwise keep silent. African-Americans in the segregated army faced hostility not only from white soldiers and officers, but also from civilians near the bases. Even the movies preached racism. D. W. Griffith's *The Birth of a Nation* (1915) disparaged blacks and glorified the Ku Klux Klan.

Smoldering racism sometimes exploded in violence. Antiblack rioters in Atlanta in 1906 murdered twenty-five blacks and burned many black homes. From 1900 to 1920 an average of about seventy-five lynchings occurred yearly. Some lynch mobs used trumped-up charges to justify the murder of blacks whose assertive behavior or economic aspirations angered whites. Some lynchings involved incredible sadism: with large crowds on hand, the victim's body was mutilated, and graphic postcards were sold later. Authorities rarely intervened. At a 1916 lynching in Texas, the mayor warned the mob not to damage the hanging tree, since it was on city property.

In the face of such hostility, blacks developed strong social institutions and a vigorous culture. Black religious life, centered in the African Methodist Episcopal church, proved a bulwark of support. Working African-American women, drawing on strategies dating to slavery days, relied on relatives and neighbors to provide child care. Dedicated teachers and administrators at a handful of black higher-education institutions such as Fisk in Nashville and Howard in Washington, D.C., carried on against heavy odds. John Hope, a university-trained classics scholar who became president of Atlanta's Morehouse College in 1906, assembled a distinguished faculty, championed African-American education, and fought racial segregation. His sister Jane (Hope) Lyons was dean of women at Spelman College, another black institution in Atlanta.

The urban black community included several black-owned insurance companies and banks, a small elite of entrepreneurs, teachers, ministers, and sports figures like Jack Johnson. Although major-league baseball excluded blacks, a thriving Negro League attracted many black fans.

In this racist age, progressives compiled a mixed record on racial issues. Lillian Wald, director of New York's Henry Street Settlement, protested racial injustice. Muckraker Ray Stannard Baker documented racism in his 1908 book, *Following the Color Line*. Settlement house worker Mary White Ovington helped found the National Association for the Advancement of Colored People (see below) and wrote *Half a Man* (1911) about the emotional scars of racism.

But most progressives kept silent as blacks were lynched, disfranchised, and discriminated against. Many saw African-Americans, like immigrants, not as potential allies but as part of the problem. Viewing blacks as inferior and prone to immorality and social disorder, white progressives generally supported or tolerated segregated schools and housing, restrictions on black voting rights, the strict moral oversight of African-American communities, and, at best, paternalistic efforts to "uplift" this supposedly backward and childlike people. Viciously racist southern politicians like Governor James K. Vardaman of Mississippi and Senator Ben Tillman of South Carolina also supported progressive reforms. Southern woman-suffrage leaders argued that granting women the vote would strengthen white supremacy.

BLACKS, WOMEN, AND WORKERS ORGANIZE

The organizational impulse so important to progressivism generally also proved a useful strategy for groups that found themselves discriminated against or exploited. African-Americans, middle-class women, and wage workers all had ample reason for dissatisfaction in these years, and all three groups organized to address those grievances.

African-American Leaders Organize Against Racism With racism on the rise, Booker T. Washington's accommodationist message (see Chapter 20) seemed increasingly unrealistic, particularly to educated northern blacks. In 1902 William Monroe Trotter, the editor of the *Boston Guardian,* a black newspaper, called Washington's go-slow policies "a fatal blow . . . to the Negro's political rights and liberty." Another opponent was black journalist Ida Wells-Barnett. Moving to Chicago from Memphis in 1892 after a white mob destroyed her offices, she mounted a national antilynching campaign, in contrast to Booker T. Washington's public silence on the subject. Washington's self-help theme would appeal to later generations of African-Americans, but in the early twentieth century, many blacks confronting lynching, blatant racism, and rising segregationist pressures tired of his cautious approach.

Washington's most potent challenger was W. E. B. Du Bois (1868–1963). After earning a Ph.D. in history from Harvard in 1895, Du Bois taught at Atlanta University. Openly criticizing Washington in *The Souls of Black Folk* (1903), he rejected Washington's call for patience and his exclusive emphasis on manual skills. Instead, Du Bois demanded full racial equality, including the same educational opportunities open to whites, and called on blacks to resist all forms of racism.

Du Bois's militancy signaled a new era of African-American activism. In 1905, under his leadership, blacks who favored vigorous, sustained resistance to racism held a conference at Niagara Falls. For the next few years, participants in the "Niagara Movement" met annually. Meanwhile, a group of white reformers had also grown dissatisfied with Washington's cautiousness. Their leader was newspaper publisher Oswald Garrison Villard, grandson of abolitionist William Lloyd Garrison. In 1909 Villard and his allies, Du Bois, and other blacks from the Niagara Movement formed the National Association for the Advancement of Colored

People (NAACP). This new organization called for vigorous activism, including legal challenges, to achieve political equality for blacks and full integration into American life. Attracting the urban black middle class, by 1914 the NAACP had six thousand members in fifty branches.

Revival of the Woman-Suffrage Movement

As late as 1910, women could vote in only four thinly populated western states: Wyoming, Utah, Colorado, and Idaho. Woman suffrage failed in six state referenda after 1896. But the progressive reform movement, in which women played a leading role, gave the cause fresh vitality. Middle-class women found disfranchisement especially galling when recently arrived immigrant men could vote. A vigorous suffrage movement in Great Britain reverberated in America as well. Like progressivism itself, this revived campaign started at the grass roots. A suffrage campaign in New York State in 1915, though unsuccessful, underscored the movement's new momentum.

So, too, did events in California. Indeed, the California campaign, as recounted by historian Gayle Gullett, illustrates both the strengths and the limitations of the revived movement. In the 1880s California's women's clubs focused mainly on cultural and domestic themes. By the early 1900s they had evolved into a potent statewide organization actively pursuing municipal reforms and public-school issues. This evolution convinced many members that full citizenship meant the right to vote. A state woman-suffrage referendum lost in 1896, but the leaders bounced back to form alliances with labor leaders and male progressives, built on a shared commitment to "good government" and opposition to municipal corruption. But while joining forces with male reformers, these woman-suffrage strategists always insisted on the unique role of "organized womanhood" in building a better society. Success came in 1911 when California voters approved woman suffrage.

"Organized womanhood" had its limits. The California campaign was led by elite and middle-class women, mainly based in Los Angeles and San Francisco. Working-class women and farmwomen played little role in this campaign, while African-American, Mexican-American, and Asian-American women were almost totally excluded.

New leaders translated the momentum in California and other states into a revitalized national movement. When Susan B. Anthony retired from the presidency of the National American Woman Suffrage Association (NAWSA) in 1900, Carrie Chapman Catt of Iowa succeeded her. Under Catt's shrewd direction, NAWSA adopted the so-called Winning Plan: grass-roots organization with tight central coordination.

Suffragists shrewdly deployed techniques drawn from the new urban consumer culture. They not only lobbied legislators, but also organized parades in open cars; devised catchy slogans; ran newspaper ads; put up posters; waved eye-catching banners; held fundraisers; arranged photo opportunities for the media; and distributed fans, playing cards, and other items emblazoned with the suffrage

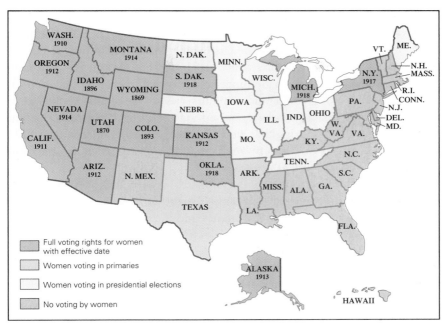

WASH.
1910

MONTANA
1914

N. DAK.

MINN.

VT. ME.

OREGON
1912

IDAHO
1896

WYOMING
1869

S. DAK.
1918

WISC.

N.Y.
1917

N.H.
MASS.

NEVADA
1914

UTAH
1870

COLO.
1893

NEBR.

IOWA

MICH.
1918

PA.

R.I.
CONN.

CALIF.
1911

KANSAS
1912

ILL. IND. OHIO

MO.

W.
VA. VA.

KY.

N.J.
DEL.
MD.

ARIZ.
1912

N. MEX.

OKLA.
1918

ARK.

TENN.

N.C.

S.C.

TEXAS

MISS. ALA. GA.

LA.

FLA.

ALASKA
1913

HAWAII

Full voting rights for women
with effective date

Women voting in primaries

Women voting in presidential elections

No voting by women

Woman Suffrage Before the Nineteenth Amendment

Beginning with Wyoming in 1869, woman suffrage made steady gains in western states before 1920. Farther east, key victories came in New York (1917) and Michigan (1918). But much of the East remained an anti-woman-suffrage bastion throughout the period.

message. Gradually, state after state fell into the suffrage column. A key victory came in 1917 when New York voters approved a woman-suffrage referendum.

As in California (and like progressive organizations generally), NAWSA's membership remained largely white, native born, and middle class. Few black, immigrant, or working-class women joined. Some upper-class women opposed the reform. The leader of the "Antis," the wealthy Josephine Dodge of New York, argued that women already had behind-the-scenes influence, and that to invade the male realm of electoral politics would tarnish their moral and spiritual role.

Not all suffragists accepted Catt's strategy. Alice Paul, who had observed the British suffragists' militant tactics while studying in England, grew impatient with NAWSA's state-by-state approach. In 1913 Paul founded the Congressional Union, later renamed the Woman's party, to pressure Congress to enact a woman-suffrage amendment. Targeting "the party in power"—in this case, the Democrats—Paul and her followers picketed the White House round the clock in the war year of 1917 and posted large signs accusing President Wilson of hypocrisy in championing democracy abroad while opposing woman suffrage at home. Several protesters were jailed and, when they went on a hunger strike, force-fed. At both the state and federal level, the momentum of the organized woman-suffrage movement had become well-nigh irresistible.

Enlarging "Woman's Sphere"

As the careers of such women as Florence Kelley, Alice Hamilton, and Ida Wells-Barnett make clear, the suffrage cause did not exhaust women's energies in the Progressive Era. Women's clubs, settlement house residents, and individual female activists joined a wide range of reform efforts. These included the campaigns to bring playgrounds and day nurseries to the slums, abolish child labor, help women workers, and ban unsafe foods and quack remedies. As Jane Addams observed, the nurturing that women gave their own children could also draw them into broader political activism in an industrial age when hazards came from outside the home as well as inside.

Cultural assumptions about "woman's sphere" weakened as women became active on many fronts. Penologist Katherine Bement Davis served as the innovative superintendent of a woman's reformatory and then as New York City's commissioner of corrections. Anarchist Emma Goldman crisscrossed the country lecturing on politics, feminism, and modern drama while coediting a radical monthly, *Mother Earth*. A vanguard of pioneering women in higher education included Marion Talbot, first dean of women at the University of Chicago.

In *Women and Economics* (1898) and other works, feminist intellectual Charlotte Perkins Gilman explored the historical and cultural roots of female subordination and gender stereotyping, and linked women's inferior status to their economic dependence on men. Confining women to the domestic sphere, Gilman argued, was an evolutionary throwback that had become outdated and inefficient.

Parading for Woman Suffrage *Suffrage leaders built support for the cause by using modern advertising and publicity techniques, including automobiles festooned with flags, bunting, banners, posters, and—in this case—smiling little girls.*

She advocated economic independence for women through equality in the workplace; the collectivization of cooking, cleaning, and other domestic tasks; and state-run day-care centers. In the novel *Herland* (1915), Gilman wittily critiqued patriarchal assumptions by injecting three naïve young males into a utopian society populated exclusively by women.

No Progressive Era reform raised the issue of women's rights more directly than the campaign challenging federal and state laws banning the distribution of contraceptives and birth-control information. Although countless women, particularly the poor, suffered exhaustion and health problems from frequent pregnancies, artificial contraception was widely denounced as immoral. In 1914 Margaret Sanger of New York, a practical nurse and socialist whose mother had died after bearing eleven children, began her crusade for birth control, a term she coined. When the authorities prosecuted her journal *The Woman Rebel* on obscenity charges, Sanger fled to England. She returned in 1916 to open the nation's first birth-control clinic in Brooklyn. In 1918 she founded a new journal, the *Birth Control Review,* and three years later she founded the American Birth Control League, the ancestor of today's Planned Parenthood Federation.

Meanwhile, another New Yorker, Mary Ware Dennett, a feminist and activist, had also emerged as an advocate of birth control and sex education. (Her 1919 pamphlet for youth, *The Sex Side of Life,* discussing human reproduction in clear, straightforward terms, was long banned as obscene.) Dennett founded the National Birth Control League (later the Voluntary Parenthood League) in 1915. While Sanger championed direct action, Dennett urged lobbying efforts to amend obscenity laws. More importantly, while Sanger insisted that contraceptives should be supplied only by physicians, Dennett argued that they should be freely available. Sanger's inability to tolerate any other leaders in the movement made for bad relations between the two women.

In retrospect, the emergence of the birth-control movement stands as one of progressivism's most important and little-recognized legacies. At the time, however, it stirred bitter resistance among conservatives and many religious leaders. Indeed, not until 1965 did the Supreme Court fully legalize the dissemination of contraceptive materials and information.

Workers Organize;
Socialism
Advances
In this age of organization, labor unions continued to expand. The American Federation of Labor (AFL) grew from fewer than half a million members in 1897 to some 4 million by 1920. This was still only about 20 percent of the industrial work force. With recent immigrants hungry for jobs, union activities could be risky. The boss could always fire an "agitator" and hire a docile newcomer. Judicial hostility also plagued the movement. In the 1908 *Danbury Hatters* case, for example, the Supreme Court forbade unions from organizing boycotts in support of strikes. Such boycotts were a "conspiracy in restraint of trade," said the high court, and thus a violation of the Sherman Anti-Trust Act. The AFL's strength remained in the skilled trades, not in the factories and mills where most immigrants and women worked.

A few unions did try to reach these laborers. The International Ladies' Garment Workers' Union (ILGWU), founded in 1900 by immigrants working in New York City's needle trades, conducted a successful strike in 1909 and another after the 1911 Triangle fire. The women on the picket lines found these strikes both exhilarating and frightening. Some were beaten by police; others fired. The 1909 strike began when young Clara Lemlich jumped up as speechmaking droned on at a protest rally and passionately called for a strike. Thousands of women garment workers stayed off the job the next day. Through such strikes, workers gained better wages and improved working conditions.

Another union that targeted the most exploited workers was the Industrial Workers of the World (IWW), nicknamed the Wobblies, founded in Chicago in 1905. The IWW's colorful leader was William "Big Bill" Haywood, a compelling orator. Utah-born Haywood became a miner as a boy and joined the militant Western Federation of Miners in 1896. In 1905 he was acquitted of complicity in the assassination of an antilabor former governor of Idaho. IWW membership peaked at around thirty thousand, and most members were western miners, lumbermen, fruit pickers, and itinerant laborers. But it captured the imagination of young cultural rebels in New York City's Greenwich Village, where Haywood often visited.

The IWW led mass strikes of Nevada gold miners; Minnesota iron miners; and timber workers in Louisiana, Texas, and the Northwest. Its greatest success came

IWW Journalism *On April 28, 1917, three weeks after the United States entered World War I, the IWW periodical* Solidarity *pictured a heroic IWW worker battling against an array of evils, including "militarism."*

in 1912 when it won a bitter textile strike in Massachusetts. This victory owed much to two women: the birth-control reformer Margaret Sanger, and Elizabeth Gurley Flynn, a fiery Irish-American orator who publicized the cause by sending strikers' children to sympathizers in New York City for temporary care. Although the IWW's reputation for violence was much exaggerated, it faced government harassment, especially during World War I, and by 1920 its strength was broken.

Other workers, as well as some middle-class Americans, turned to socialism. All socialists advocated an end to capitalism and backed public ownership of factories, utilities, railroads, and communications systems, but they differed on how to achieve these goals. The revolutionary ideology of German social theorist Karl Marx won a few converts, but the vision of democratic socialism achieved at the ballot box proved more appealing. In 1900 democratic socialists formed the Socialist Party of America (SPA). Members included Morris Hillquit, a New York City labor organizer; Victor Berger, the leader of Milwaukee's German socialists; and Eugene V. Debs, the Indiana labor leader. Debs, a popular orator, was the SPA's presidential candidate five times between 1900 and 1920. Many cultural radicals of New York's Greenwich Village embraced socialism as well and supported the radical magazine *The Masses,* founded in 1911.

Socialism's high-water mark came around 1912 when SPA membership stood at 118,000. Debs won more than 900,000 votes for president that year (about 6 percent of the total), and the Socialists elected a congressman (Berger) and hundreds of municipal officials. The Intercollegiate Socialist Society carried the message to college campuses. The party published over three hundred daily and weekly newspapers, many in foreign languages for immigrant members.

NATIONAL PROGRESSIVISM PHASE I: ROOSEVELT AND TAFT, 1901–1913

By around 1905 local and state reform activities were coalescing into a national movement. Symbolically, in 1906 Wisconsin governor Robert La Follette went to Washington as a U.S. senator. Five years earlier, progressivism had found its first national leader, Theodore Roosevelt, nicknamed "TR."

Bombastic, self-righteous, and jingoistic—but also brilliant, politically savvy, and endlessly interesting—Roosevelt became president in 1901 and at once made the White House a cauldron of activism. Skillfully orchestrating public opinion, the popular young president pursued his goals—labor mediation, consumer protection, conservation, business virtue, and engagement abroad (see Chapter 20)—while embracing and publicizing progressives' ideas and objectives.

Roosevelt's activist approach to the presidency permanently enlarged the powers of the office. TR's hand-picked successor, William Howard Taft, lacked the master's political genius, however, and his administration floundered amid sniping among former allies.

In the exciting election of 1912, voters faced a choice among four major presidential candidates: the conservative Taft; the socialist Eugene V. Debs; Theodore

Roosevelt; and political newcomer Woodrow Wilson, who offered differing visions of progressive reform.

Roosevelt's Path to the White House

On September 6, 1901, in Buffalo, anarchist Leon Czolgosz shot William McKinley. At first the president seemed likely to recover, and Vice President Theodore Roosevelt proceeded with a hiking trip in New York's Adirondack Mountains. But on September 14, McKinley died. At age forty-two, Theodore Roosevelt became president of the United States.

Many politicians shuddered at the thought of the impetuous Roosevelt as president. Republican kingmaker Mark Hanna exclaimed, "My God, that damned cowboy in the White House!" Roosevelt did, indeed, display many traits associated with the West. The son of an aristocratic New York family of Dutch origins, he was sickly as a child. But a bodybuilding program and summers in Wyoming transformed him into a model of physical fitness. When his young wife died in 1884, he stoically carried on. Two years on a Dakota ranch (1884–1886) further toughened him and deepened his enthusiasm for what he termed "the strenuous life."

Plunging into politics at a time when his social peers considered it unfit for gentlemen, he served as a state assemblyman, New York City police commissioner, and a U.S. civil-service commissioner. In 1898, fresh from his Cuban exploits (see Chapter 20), he was elected New York's governor. Two years later, the state's Republican boss, eager to be rid of him, arranged for Roosevelt's nomination as vice president.

As was the case with everything he did, TR found the presidency energizing. "I have been President emphatically . . . ," he boasted; "I believe in a strong executive." He enjoyed public life and loved the limelight. "When Theodore attends a wedding he wants to be the bride," his daughter observed, "and when he attends a funeral he wants to be the corpse." With his toothy grin, machine-gun speech, and amazing energy, he dominated the political landscape. When he refused to shoot a bear cub on a hunting trip, a shrewd toy maker marketed a cuddly new product, the Teddy Bear.

Labor Disputes, Trustbusting, Railroad Regulation

The new president's political skills were quickly tested. In May 1902 the United Mine Workers Union (UMW) called a strike to gain not only higher wages and shorter hours but also recognition as a union. The mine owners refused even to talk with the UMW leaders. After five months, with winter looming, TR acted. Summoning the two sides to the White House and threatening to take over the mines, he won their reluctant acceptance of an arbitration commission to settle the dispute. The commission granted the miners a 10 percent wage increase and reduced their working day from ten to nine hours.

TR's approach to labor disputes differed from that of his predecessors, who typically sided with management, sometimes using troops as strikebreakers. Though not consistently prolabor, he defended workers' right to organize. When a mine owner insisted that the miners' welfare be left to those "to whom God in his infinite wisdom has given control of the property interests of the country," Roosevelt derided such "arrogant stupidity."

With his elite background, TR neither feared nor much liked business tycoons. The prospect of spending time with "big-money men," he once wrote a friend, "fills me with frank horror." While he believed that big corporations contributed to national greatness, he also embraced the progressive conviction that business behavior must be regulated. A strict moralist, he held corporations, like individuals, to a high standard.

At the same time, Roosevelt the political realist also understood that many Washington politicians abhorred his views—among them Senator Nelson Aldrich of Rhode Island, a wily defender of business interests. Roosevelt's progressive impulses and his grasp of power realities in capitalist America remained in continuing tension.

Another test of Roosevelt's political skill came in 1901 when J. P. Morgan formed the United States Steel Company, the nation's first billion-dollar corporation. As public distrust of big corporations deepened, TR dashed to the head of the parade. His 1902 State of the Union message gave high priority to breaking up business monopolies, or "trustbusting." Roosevelt's attorney general soon filed suit against the Northern Securities Company, a giant holding company that had recently been formed to control railroading in the Northwest, for violating the Sherman Anti-Trust Act of 1890—a law that hitherto had seemed pathetically ineffective. On a speaking tour that summer, TR called for a "square deal" for all Americans and denounced special treatment for capitalists. "We don't wish to destroy corporations," he said, "but we do wish to make them . . . serve the public good." In 1904, on a 5 to 4 vote, the Supreme Court ordered the Northern Securities Company dissolved.

The Roosevelt administration filed forty-three other antitrust lawsuits. In two key cases decided in 1911, the Supreme Court ordered the breakup of the Standard Oil Company and the reorganization of the American Tobacco Company to make it less monopolistic.

As the 1904 election neared, Roosevelt made peace with his party's business wing, writing cordial letters to J. P. Morgan and other magnates. When the convention that unanimously nominated Roosevelt in Chicago adopted a probusiness platform, $2 million in corporate contributions poured in. The Democrats, meanwhile, eager to erase the taint of radicalism, embraced the gold standard and nominated a conservative New York judge, Alton B. Parker.

Winning easily, Roosevelt turned to one of his major goals: railroad regulation. He now saw corporate regulation as a more promising long-term strategy than antitrust lawsuits. This shift underlay his central role in the passage of the Hepburn Act of 1906. This measure empowered the Interstate Commerce Commission to set maximum railroad rates and to examine railroads' financial records. It also curtailed the railroads' practice of distributing free passes to ministers and other influential shapers of public opinion.

The Hepburn Act displayed TR's knack for political bargaining, as he skillfully fenced with Senator Aldrich and other conservatives. In one key compromise, he agreed to delay tariff reform in return for railroad regulations. Although the Hepburn Act did not fully satisfy reformers, it did significantly increase the government's regulatory powers.

Consumer Protection and Racial Issues

No progressive reform proved more popular than the campaign against unsafe and falsely labeled food, drugs, and medicine. Upton Sinclair's *The Jungle* (1906) graphically described the foul conditions in some meatpacking plants. Wrote Sinclair in one vivid passage, "[A] man could run his hand over these piles of meat and sweep off handfuls of dried dung of rats. These rats were nuisances, and the packers would put poisoned bread out for them, they would die, and then rats, bread, and meat would go into the hoppers together." (The socialist Sinclair also detailed the exploitation of immigrant workers, but this message proved less potent. "I aimed at the nation's heart, but hit it in the stomach," he later lamented.) Women's organizations and consumer groups rallied public opinion on this issue, and an Agriculture Department chemist, Harvey W. Wiley, helped shape the proposed legislation. Other muckrakers exposed useless or dangerous patent medicines, many laced with cocaine, opium, or alcohol. One tonic "for treatment of the alcohol habit" contained 26.5 percent alcohol. Peddlers of these nostrums freely claimed that they could cure cancer, grow hair, and restore sexual vigor.

Sensing the public mood, Roosevelt supported the Pure Food and Drug Act and the Meat Inspection Act, both passed in 1906. The former outlawed the sale of adulterated foods or drugs and required accurate ingredient labels; the latter imposed strict sanitary rules on meatpackers and set up a federal meat-inspection system. The more reputable food-processing, meatpacking, and medicinal companies, eager to regain public confidence, supported these regulatory measures.

On racial matters, Roosevelt's record was marginally better than that of other politicians in this dismally racist age. He appointed a black to head the Charleston customhouse despite white opposition, and closed a Mississippi post office rather than yield to demands that he dismiss the black postmistress. In a symbolically important gesture, he dined with Booker T. Washington at the White House. The worst blot on his record came in 1906 when he approved the dishonorable discharge of an entire regiment of black soldiers, including Congressional Medal of Honor winners, in Brownsville, Texas, because some members of the unit, goaded by racist taunts, had killed a local civilian. The "Brownsville Incident" incensed black Americans. (In 1972, when most of the men were long dead, Congress removed the dishonorable discharges from their records.)

Environmentalism Progressive-Style

With Theodore Roosevelt in the White House, environmental concerns ranked high on the national agenda. Singling out conservation in his first State of the Union message as "the most vital internal question" facing America, he highlighted an issue that still reverberates.

By 1900 decades of urban-industrial growth and western expansion had taken a heavy toll on the land. In the West, land-use disputes raged as mining and timber interests, farmers, ranchers, sheep growers, and preservationists advanced competing claims.

While business interests and boosters preached exploitation of the West's resources and agricultural groups sought government aid for irrigation projects, organizations such as the Sierra Club battled to preserve the unspoiled beauty of wilderness areas. Socially prominent easterners also embraced the wilderness cause. Under an act passed by Congress in 1891, Presidents Harrison and Cleveland had set aside some 35 million acres of public lands as national forests.

In the early twentieth century, a wilderness vogue swept America. Amid cities and factories, the wilderness promised tranquillity and solace. As Sierra Club president John Muir observed, "I never saw a discontented tree." Popular writers evoked the tang of the campfire and the lure of the primitive. Summer camps, which began in the 1890s, as well as the Boy Scouts (founded in 1910) and Girl Scouts (1912), gave city children a taste of wilderness living.

Between the wilderness enthusiasts and the developers stood government professionals like Gifford Pinchot who saw the public domain as a resource to be managed wisely. Appointed by President Roosevelt in 1905 to head the new U.S. Forest Service, Pinchot stressed not preservation but conservation—the planned, regulated use of forest lands for public and commercial purposes.

Wilderness advocates viewed Pinchot's Forest Service warily. They welcomed his opposition to mindless exploitation but worried that the multiple-use approach would despoil wilderness areas. As a Sierra Club member wrote, "It is true that trees are for human use. But there are . . . uses for the spiritual wealth of us all, as well as for the material wealth of some." Conservationists, in turn, dismissed the wilderness advocates as hopeless romantics.

By temperament Theodore Roosevelt was a preservationist. In 1903 he spent a blissful few days camping in Yosemite National Park with John Muir. He once compared "the destruction of a species" to the loss of "all the works of some great writer." But TR the politician backed the conservationists' call for planned development. He supported the National Reclamation Act of 1902 that designated the money from public-land sales for water management in arid western regions, and set up the Reclamation Service to plan and construct dams and irrigation projects.

As historian William Cronon notes, this measure (also known as the Newlands Act for its sponsor, a Nevada congressman) ranks in importance with the Northwest Ordinance of 1787 for promoting the development of a vast continental region. Under director Frederick Newell, the Reclamation Service undertook projects that sped settlement and productivity between the Rockies and the Pacific. The Roosevelt Dam in Arizona spurred the growth of Phoenix, and a complex of dams and waterways in the Snake River valley watered thousands of barren acres in Idaho, stimulating the production of potatoes and other commodities.

The law required farmers who benefited from these projects to repay the construction costs, creating a revolving federal fund for further projects. The Newlands Act and other measures of these years helped transform the West from a series of isolated "island settlements" into a thriving, interconnected region.

The competition for scarce water resources in the West sometimes led to bitter political battles. The Los Angeles basin, for example, with 40 percent of California's population in 1900, found itself with only 2 percent of the state's available surface water. In 1907 the city derailed a Reclamation Service project intended for the farmers of California's Owens Valley, more than 230 miles to the north, and diverted the precious water to Los Angeles.

Meanwhile, President Roosevelt, embracing Pinchot's multiple-use land-management program, set aside 200 million acres of public land (85 million of them in Alaska) as national forests, mineral reserves, and water-power sites. But this, too, provoked opposition in the West, and in 1907 Congress revoked the president's authority to create national forests in six timber-rich western states. Roosevelt signed the bill, but only after he had designated 16 million acres in the six states as national forests.

With Roosevelt's blessing, Pinchot organized a White House conservation conference for the nation's governors in 1908. There experts discussed the utilitarian benefits of resource management. John Muir and other wilderness preservationists were not invited. But the struggle between wilderness purists and multiple-use advocates went on (see A Place in Time: Hetch Hetchy Valley, California). Rallying support through magazine articles, preservationists won key victories. For example, campaigns by private groups, including women's organizations, saved a large grove of California's giant redwoods and a lovely stretch of the Maine coastline from logging.

While expanding the national forests, TR also created fifty-three wildlife reserves, sixteen national monuments, and five new national parks. As the parks drew more visitors, Congress created the National Park Service in 1916 to manage them. Earlier, the Antiquities Act (1906) had protected archaeological sites, especially in the Southwest, some of which eventually became national parks.

Taft in the White House, 1909–1913

Roosevelt had pledged not to run for a third term, and to the sorrow of millions, he kept his promise as the 1908 election approached. The Republican party's most conservative elements easily regained party control. They nominated TR's choice, Secretary of War William Howard Taft, for president but chose a conservative vice-presidential nominee. The party platform, influenced by the National Association of Manufacturers, was deeply conservative. The Democrats, meanwhile, nominated William Jennings Bryan for a third and final time. The Democratic platform called for a lower tariff, denounced the trusts, and embraced the cause of labor.

With Roosevelt's endorsement, Taft coasted to victory. But the Democrats made gains—Bryan bested Alton B. Parker's 1904 vote total by 1.3 million—and progressive Republican state candidates outran the national ticket. Overall, the outcome suggested a lull in the reform movement, not its end.

Republican conservatives, increasingly unhappy with Roosevelt's policies, were delighted when he departed to hunt big game in Africa. Quipped Senator Aldrich, "Let every lion do its duty." But even with TR an ocean away, his presence remained vivid. "When I am addressed as 'Mr. President,' " Taft wrote him, "I turn to see whether you are not at my elbow."

Taft, from an old political family in Cincinnati, was no Roosevelt. Whereas TR kept in fighting trim, the sedentary Taft was obese. Roosevelt had set up a boxing ring in the White House; Taft preferred golf. TR loved speechmaking and battling the forces of evil; Taft disliked controversy. His happiest days would come later, as chief justice of the United States.

Pledged to carry on TR's program, Taft supported the Mann-Elkins Act (1910), which beefed up the Interstate Commerce Commission's rate-setting powers and extended its regulatory authority to telephone and telegraph companies. The Taft administration actually prosecuted more antitrust cases than had Roosevelt. But Taft characteristically proceeded without much publicity; and to the public TR remained the mighty trustbuster.

The reform spotlight, meanwhile, shifted from the White House to Congress. During the Roosevelt administration, a small group of reform-minded Republicans nicknamed the Insurgents, who included Senators La Follette and Albert Beveridge of Indiana and Congressman George Norris of Nebraska, had challenged their party's conservative congressional leadership. In 1909 the Insurgents turned against President Taft after a bruising battle over the tariff.

Taft at first backed the Insurgents' call for a lower tariff. But in 1909, when high-tariff advocates in Congress pushed through the Payne-Aldrich Tariff, raising duties on hundreds of items, Taft not only signed it but praised it extravagantly. The battle between conservative and progressive Republicans was on.

A major Insurgent target was Speaker of the House Joseph G. Cannon of Illinois. Wielding near-absolute power, the arch-conservative Cannon kept most reform bills from even reaching a vote. In March 1910 the Insurgents joined with the Democrats to remove Cannon from the pivotal Rules Committee. This was a direct slap at Taft, who supported Cannon.

The so-called Ballinger-Pinchot affair widened the rift between Taft and the progressive Republicans. Taft's interior secretary, Richard Ballinger, was a Seattle lawyer who disliked federal controls and favored the private development of natural resources. In one of several decisions galling to conservationists, Ballinger approved the sale of several million acres of public lands in Alaska containing coal deposits to a group of Seattle businessmen in 1909. They in turn sold the land to a consortium of New York bankers including J. P. Morgan. When a Department of the Interior official protested, he was fired. In true muckraking style, he immediately published an article in *Collier's* blasting Ballinger's actions. When Gifford Pinchot of the Forestry Service publicly criticized Ballinger, he too got the ax. TR's supporters seethed.

Upon Roosevelt's return to America in June 1910, Pinchot met the boat. In the 1910 midterm election, Roosevelt campaigned for Insurgent candidates. In a speech that alarmed conservatives, he attacked judges who struck down progressive laws and endorsed the radical idea of reversing judicial rulings by popular vote. Borrowing a term from Herbert Croly's *The Promise of American Life,* TR proposed a "New Nationalism" that would powerfully engage the federal government in reform.

The Democrats captured the House in 1910, and a coalition of Democrats and Insurgent Republicans controlled the Senate. As the reform tide rose, TR sounded more and more like a presidential candidate.

The Four-Way Election of 1912   In February 1912 Roosevelt announced his candidacy for the Republican nomination, openly opposing Taft. But Taft wanted a second term, and a Republican battle loomed. For a time, Senator Robert La Follette's candidacy attracted reform-minded Republicans, but when TR entered the race, La Follette's support collapsed.

In a series of Republican state primaries and conventions, Roosevelt generally walloped Taft. But Taft controlled the party machinery, and the Republican convention in Chicago disqualified many of Roosevelt's hard-won delegates. Outraged, TR's backers bolted the convention and reassembled to form the Progressive party. What had been a general term for a broad reform movement became the official name of a political organization.

Woodrow Wilson and William Howard Taft *Having just squared off in the 1912 election campaign, the two politicians share a light moment before Wilson's inauguration on March 4, 1913.*

The Election of 1912

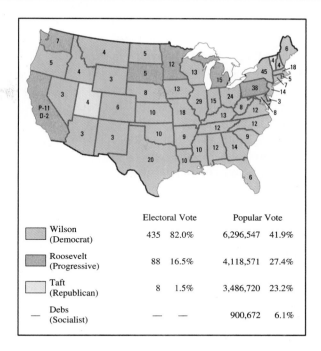

	Electoral Vote		Popular Vote	
Wilson (Democrat)	435	82.0%	6,296,547	41.9%
Roosevelt (Progressive)	88	16.5%	4,118,571	27.4%
Taft (Republican)	8	1.5%	3,486,720	23.2%
Debs (Socialist)	—	—	900,672	6.1%

"I feel fit as a bull moose," Roosevelt trumpeted, thereby giving his organization its nickname, the Bull Moose party. Riding an emotional high, the cheering delegates nominated their hero and designated California senator Hiram Johnson as his running mate. The convention platform endorsed practically every reform cause of the day, including tariff reduction, woman suffrage, business regulation, the abolition of child labor, the eight-hour workday, workers' compensation, the direct primary, and the popular election of senators. The new party attracted a highly diverse following, united in admiration for the charismatic Roosevelt.

Meanwhile, the reform spirit had also infused the Democratic party at the local and state levels. In New Jersey in 1910, voters had elected a political novice, Woodrow Wilson, as governor. A "Wilson for President" boom soon arose, and when the Democrats assembled in Baltimore in June 1912, Wilson won the nomination, defeating several established party leaders.

In the campaign, Taft more or less gave up, happy to have kept his party safe for conservatism. The Socialist party candidate Eugene Debs proposed an end to capitalism and a socialized economic order. Roosevelt and Wilson offered less radical prescriptions. TR preached his New Nationalism. The new corporate order was here to stay, he acknowledged, but big business must be strictly regulated in the public interest. The welfare of workers and consumers should be safeguarded, and the environment protected.

Wilson, by contrast, called his political vision the "New Freedom." Warning that the new corporate order was choking off opportunity for ordinary Americans,

Hetch Hetchy Valley, California, 1913

In 1900 one of the loveliest spots in California was Hetch Hetchy Valley, where glaciers and the Tuolumne River had carved deep, sharp-edged gorges of spectacular beauty. The Indian name referred to the valley's grassy meadows. But when officials of San Francisco, 150 miles away, visited Hetch Hetchy, they saw a solution to their city's water problems. A dam at the valley's mouth would create a vast reservoir that could supply water for San Francisco and pay for itself as a hydroelectric power source.

Because Hetch Hetchy was in Yosemite National Park, the secretary of the interior at first rejected San Francisco's application to dam the Tuolumne. But the city applied again in 1908, two years after an earthquake and fire had devastated San Francisco, and this time the secretary approved. The application needed congressional approval as well, and opponents of the plan confidently geared up to defeat it.

The Sierra Club and its president, John Muir, led the opposition. Muir and his associates alerted wilderness groups across the nation and published magazine articles describing the beauty of the valley that would be forever hidden under the waters of the reservoir.

Muir compared flooding Hetch Hetchy to the willful destruction of a great cathedral. Amid rampant urban growth, he argued, Americans needed wilderness for their spiritual well-being. He wrote bitterly, "These temple destroyers, devotees of ravaging commercialism, seem to have a perfect contempt for Nature, and instead of lifting their eyes to the God of the Mountains, lift them to the Almighty Dollar."

But the project had attracted powerful backers, including Gifford Pinchot, head of the U.S. Forest Service, who advocated a multiple-use approach to national forests and wilderness areas. San Francisco authorities also pushed hard for the plan. The reservoir, they argued, could support a variety of recreational activities. The *San Francisco Chronicle* called the dam's critics "hoggish and mushy esthetes." San Francisco's chief engineer ridiculed them as "short-haired women and long-haired men."

At first President Theodore Roosevelt endorsed the plan. As opposition grew he vacillated. In the national parks, he said in 1908, "all wild things should be protected and the scenery kept wholly unmarred."

The battle culminated in 1913 with hearings before the Public Lands Committee of the U.S. House of Representatives. Opponents rallied public opinion through more magazine articles; backers lobbied members of Congress. Pinchot, testifying in support of the application, offered his own utilitarian definition of conservation: "The fundamental principle . . . is that of use, to take every part of the land and its resources and put it to that use . . . which . . . will serve the most people." A California congressman pointed out that the "old barren rocks" of Hetch Hetchy Valley had a market value of only about three hundred thousand dollars, whereas the proposed dam would be worth many times that amount. Another legislator posed the issue in dramatic terms: "We all love the sound of whispering winds amid the trees," he said, but "the wail of a hungry baby will make us forget it."

Late in 1913, both houses of Congress passed the Hetch Hetchy dam bill by large margins. Within a year John Muir was dead of pneumonia. Some said he had died of a broken heart.

The dam project proceeded slowly, at twice the estimated cost. The first water reached San Francisco in 1934. The vision of Hetch Hetchy reservoir as a vacation paradise remained unfulfilled. Writes environmental historian Stephen Fox, "As the water level rose and fell with the changing seasons the shoreline was marred by slimy mud and decaying vegetation. Nothing could grow at the edge of the artificial lake. Under moonlight, with tree trunks scattered around like so many bodies, it resembled a battlefield one day after the fight: a wasteland bearing stark testimony to man's befuddled ingenuity."

Although the dam's opponents lost this battle, historians point out that the struggle had a larger meaning. For the first time, over a five-year period, the American public debated the aesthetic implications of a major public-works project. In the nineteenth century such a debate would have been unthinkable. Hetch Hetchy helped put wilderness preservation on the public agenda.

The battle also underscored tensions in Progressive Era environmental thought. Both sides considered themselves progressives, but while one group fought for wilderness preservation, the other advocated the "wise use" of natural resources for human purposes.

Hetch Hetchy retains its power to stir emotions. In 1987 Secretary of the Interior Donald Hodel proposed draining the reservoir and restoring the valley to its natural state. This, Hodel said, would relieve overcrowding in nearby Yosemite Valley. While environmentalists expressed interest, San Francisco officials reacted with the same outrage their predecessors had shown seventy-five years before. Meanwhile, Hetch Hetchy Valley lies under three hundred feet of water, submerged but not forgotten.

he nostalgically evoked an era of small government, small businesses, and free competition. "The history of liberty," he said, "is the history of the limitation of governmental power, not the increase of it."

Roosevelt garnered 630,000 more votes than Taft, but the divided Republicans proved no match for the united Democrats. Wilson won the presidency, and the Democrats also took both houses of Congress. More than 900,000 voters opted for Debs and socialism.

The 1912 election linked the Democrats firmly with reform (except on the issue of race)—a link on which Franklin D. Roosevelt would build in the 1930s. The breakaway Progressive party demonstrated the strength of the reform impulse among grass-roots Republicans while leaving the national party itself in the grip of conservatives.

National Progressivism Phase II: Woodrow Wilson, 1913–1917

The son and grandson of Presbyterian ministers, Wilson grew up in southern towns in a churchly atmosphere that shaped his oratorical style and moral outlook. Although slow in school (probably because of the learning disorder dyslexia), Wilson graduated from Princeton and earned a Ph.D. in political science from Johns Hopkins. He taught at Princeton and became its president in 1902. He lost support because of an unwillingness to compromise, and in 1910 left the academic world to enter politics. Three years later he was president of the United States.

Impressive in bearing, with piercing gray eyes, Wilson was an eloquent orator. But the idealism that inspired people could also alienate them. At his best, he excelled at political dealmaking. "He can walk on dead leaves and make no more noise than a tiger," declared one awed politician. But he could also retreat into a fortress of absolute certitude that tolerated no opposition. During his years as president, all these facets of his personality would come into play.

In his first term, Wilson played a key leadership role as Congress enacted an array of reform measures. Despite the nostalgia for simpler times evoked in some of his campaign speeches, he proved ready to use government to address the problems of the new corporate order. Under Wilson, the national progressive movement gained powerful new momentum.

Tariff and Banking Reform Tariff reform—long a goal of southern and agrarian Democrats—headed Wilson's agenda. Breaking a precedent dating from Thomas Jefferson's presidency, on April 8, 1913, Wilson appeared before Congress in person to read his tariff message. A low-tariff bill quickly passed the House but bogged down in the Senate. Showing his flair for drama, Wilson denounced the tariff lobbyists flooding into Washington. His censure led to a Senate investigation of lobbyists and of senators who profited from high tariffs. Stung by the publicity, the Senate slashed tariff rates even more than the House had done. The Underwood-Simmons Tariff reduced rates an average of 15 percent.

In June 1913 Wilson addressed Congress again, this time to call for banking and currency reform. The nation's banking system clearly needed overhauling. Totally decentralized, it lacked a strong central institution, a "lender of last resort" to help banks survive fiscal crises. The Panic of 1907, when many banks had failed, remained a vivid memory.

But no consensus existed on specifics. Many reformers wanted a publicly controlled central banking system. But the nation's bankers, whose Senate spokesman was Nelson Aldrich, favored a privately controlled central bank similar to the Bank of England. The large banks of New York City advocated a strong central bank, preferably privately owned, so they could better compete with London banks in international finance. Others, including influential Virginia congressman Carter Glass, opposed any central banking authority, public or private.

No banking expert, Wilson listened to all sides. He did insist that the monetary system ultimately be publicly controlled. As the bargaining went on, Wilson played a crucial behind-the-scenes role. The result was the Federal Reserve Act of December 1913. A compromise measure, this law created twelve regional Federal Reserve banks under mixed public and private control. Each regional bank could issue U.S. dollars, called Federal Reserve notes, to the banks in its district to make loans to corporations and individual borrowers. Overall control of the system was assigned to the heads of the twelve regional banks and a Washington-based Federal Reserve Board (FRB), whose members were appointed by the president for fourteen-year terms. (The secretary of the Treasury and the comptroller of the currency were made ex officio members.)

The Federal Reserve Act stands as Wilson's greatest legislative achievement. Initially, the Federal Reserve's authority was diffuse, but eventually the FRB, nicknamed "the Fed," grew into the strong central monetary institution it remains today, adopting fiscal policies to prevent financial panics, promote economic growth, and dampen inflationary pressures.

Regulating Business; Aiding Workers and Farmers   In 1914 Wilson and Congress turned to that perennial progressive cause, business regulation. Two key laws were the result: the Federal Trade Commission Act and the Clayton Antitrust Act. Though both sought a common goal, they embodied significantly different approaches.

The Federal Trade Commission Act took an administrative approach. This law created a new "watchdog" agency, the Federal Trade Commission (FTC), with power to investigate suspected violations of federal regulations, require regular reports from corporations, and issue cease-and-desist orders (subject to judicial review) when it found unfair methods of competition.

The Clayton Antitrust Act, by contrast, took a legal approach. It listed specific corporate activities that could lead to federal lawsuits. The Sherman Act of 1890, although outlawing business practices in restraint of trade, had been vague about details. The Clayton Act spelled out a series of illegal practices, such as selling at a loss to undercut competitors.

Because some of the watchdogs Wilson appointed to the FTC were conservatives with big-business links, this agency proved ineffective. But under the Clayton Act, the Wilson administration filed antitrust suits against nearly a hundred corporations.

Leading a party historically identified with workers, Wilson supported the American Federation of Labor and defended workers' right to organize. He also endorsed a Clayton Act clause exempting strikes, boycotts, and picketing from the antitrust laws' prohibition of actions in restraint of trade.

In 1916 (a campaign year) Wilson and congressional Democrats enacted three important worker-protection laws. The Keating-Owen Act barred from interstate commerce products manufactured by child labor. (This law was declared unconstitutional in 1918, as was a similar law enacted in 1919.) The Adamson Act established an eight-hour day for interstate railway workers. The Workmen's Compensation Act provided accident and injury protection to federal workers.

Other 1916 laws helped farmers. The Federal Farm Loan Act and the Federal Warehouse Act enabled farmers, using land or crops as security, to get low-interest federal loans. The Federal Highway Act, providing matching funds for state highway programs, benefited not only the new automobile industry but also farmers plagued by bad roads.

Like many progressives, Wilson's sympathies for the underdog stopped at the color line. A Virginia native reared in Georgia, he displayed a patronizing attitude toward blacks, praised the racist movie *The Birth of a Nation,* and allowed southerners in his cabinet and in Congress (some of them powerful committee chairmen) to impose rigid segregation on all levels of the government.

Progressivism and the Constitution The probusiness bias of the courts in the late nineteenth century softened a bit in the Progressive Era. Evidence of the changing judicial climate came in *Muller* v. *Oregon* (1908), in which the Supreme Court upheld an Oregon ten-hour law for women laundry workers. Defending the constitutionality of the Oregon law was Boston attorney Louis Brandeis, who offered economic, medical, and sociological evidence of how long hours harmed women workers. Rejecting a legal claim long made by business, the high court held that such worker-protection laws did not violate employers' rights under the due-process clause of the Fourteenth Amendment. *Muller* v. *Oregon* marked a breakthrough in making the legal system more responsive to new social realities.

In 1916 Woodrow Wilson nominated Brandeis to the Supreme Court. Disapproving of Brandeis's innovative approach to the law, the conservative American Bar Association protested, as did the *New York Times,* the president of Harvard, and Republican leaders in Congress. Anti-Semites opposed Brandeis because he was a Jew. But Wilson stood by his nominee, and after a fierce battle, the Senate confirmed him.

These years also produced four amendments to the Constitution, the first since 1870. The Sixteenth (ratified in 1913) granted Congress the authority to tax income, thus ending a long legal battle. A Civil War income tax had been phased out in 1872. Congress had authorized an income tax in an 1894 tariff act, but in *Pollock* v. *Farmers' Loan and Trust* (1895) the Supreme Court had not only ruled this measure unconstitutional, but also blasted it as "communistic." This ruling, denounced by populists and then by progressives, had spurred the campaign for a constitutional amendment. Quickly exercising its new authority, in 1913 Congress imposed a graduated federal income tax with a maximum rate of 7 percent on incomes in excess of five hundred thousand dollars. Income-tax revenues helped the government pay for the expanded regulatory activities assigned to it by various progressive reform measures.

The Seventeenth Amendment (1913) mandated the direct election of U.S. senators by the voters, rather than their selection by state legislatures as provided by Article I of the Constitution. This amendment brought to fruition a reform first advocated by the Populists as a way of making the Senate less subject to corporate influence and more responsive to the popular will.

The next two amendments, although coming after World War I, culminated reform campaigns that we have already examined. The Eighteenth (1919) established nationwide prohibition of the manufacture, sale, or importation of "intoxicating liquors." The Nineteenth (1920) granted women the vote. This remarkable wave of amendments underscored how profoundly the progressive impulse had transformed the political landscape.

1916: Wilson Edges Out Hughes

Wilson easily won renomination in 1916. The Republicans turned to Charles Evans Hughes, a Supreme Court justice and former New York governor. The Progressive party again courted Theodore Roosevelt, but TR's reform interests had given way to an obsession with drawing the United States into the war that had broken out in Europe in 1914 (see Chapter 22). At his urging, the Progressives endorsed Hughes and effectively committed political suicide.

With the Republicans now more or less reunited, the election was extremely close. War-related issues loomed large. Wilson won the popular vote, but the electoral college outcome remained in doubt for several weeks as the California tally seesawed back and forth. Ultimately, Wilson carried the state by fewer than four thousand votes and, with it, the election.

Following the flurry of worker-protection laws in 1916, the progressive movement lost momentum as the nation's attention turned from reform to war. A few reform measures enacted in the 1920s and a 1924 presidential campaign by an aging Senator La Follette under a revived Progressive party banner offered reminders of the progressive agenda. But the movement's zest and drive clearly waned with the coming of World War I.

IMPORTANT EVENTS, 1900–1917

1895 Anti-Saloon League founded.

1898 Charlotte Perkins Gilman, *Women and Economics.*

1899 Thorstein Veblen, *The Theory of the Leisure Class.*

1900 International Ladies' Garment Workers' Union (ILGWU) founded.
Socialist Party of America organized.
Theodore Dreiser, *Sister Carrie.*
Carrie Chapman Catt becomes president of the National American Woman Suffrage Association (NAWSA).

1901 Assassination of McKinley; Theodore Roosevelt becomes president.
J. P. Morgan forms United States Steel Company.
Frank Norris, *The Octopus.*

1902 Roosevelt mediates coal strike.
Jane Addams, *Democracy and Social Ethics.*

1903 W. E. B. Du Bois, *The Souls of Black Folk*.
The Great Train Robbery (movie).
Wright Brothers' flight.

1904 Roosevelt elected president.
Lincoln Steffens, *The Shame of the Cities*.
Ida Tarbell, *History of the Standard Oil Company*.

1905 Industrial Workers of the World (IWW) organized.
Niagara Movement established by W. E. B. Du Bois and others.
Gifford Pinchot appointed head of U.S. Forest Service.

1906 Upton Sinclair, *The Jungle*.

1907 William James, *Pragmatism*.

1908 William Howard Taft elected president.
Model T Ford introduced.

1909 Ballinger-Pinchot controversy.
National Association for the Advancement of Colored People (NAACP) founded.
Herbert Croly, *The Promise of American Life*.
Daniel Burnham, *Plan of Chicago*.

1910 Jane Addams, *Twenty Years at Hull House*.
Insurgents curb power of House Speaker Joseph Cannon.

1911 Triangle Shirtwaist Company fire.
Frederick W. Taylor, *Scientific Management*.

1912 Republican party split; Progressive (Bull Moose) party founded.
Woodrow Wilson elected president.
International Opium Treaty.
Theodore Dreiser, *The Financier*.

1913 Thirty thousand march for woman suffrage in New York.

1914 American Social Hygiene Association founded.

1915 D. W. Griffith, *The Birth of a Nation*.
Mary Ware Dennett founds National Birth Control League.

1916 Wilson reelected.
John Dewey, *Democracy and Education*.
Margaret Sanger opens nation's first birth-control clinic in Brooklyn, New York.
National Park Service created.
Louis Brandeis appointed to Supreme Court.
Madison Grant, *The Passing of the Great Race*.

22

Global Involvements and World War I, 1902–1920

It was April 6, 1917, and Jane Addams was troubled. By overwhelming margins, Congress had just supported President Woodrow Wilson's call for a declaration of war on Germany. Addams belonged to the Daughters of the American Revolution (DAR); her father had served in the Illinois legislature with future President Abraham Lincoln. But she believed in peace and deplored her nation's decision to go to war. As the founder of Hull House, a Chicago settlement house, Addams had worked to overcome tensions among different ethnic groups. In *Newer Ideals of Peace* (1907), she had insisted that the multiethnic "internationalism" of America's immigrant neighborhoods proved that national and ethnic hostilities could be overcome. Addams had also observed how war spirit can inflame a people. During the Spanish-American War, she had watched Chicago street urchins playing at killing "Spaniards."

When war broke out in Europe in 1914, Addams worked to end the conflict and to keep America out of the fray. A founder of the Woman's Peace party in January 1915, she attended an International Congress of Women in April that called on the warring nations to submit their differences to arbitration. Addams personally met with President Wilson to enlist his support for arbitration, but with no success.

Now America had entered the war, and Addams had to take a stand. Deepening her dilemma, many of her friends, including philosopher and educator John Dewey, were lining up behind Wilson. Theodore Roosevelt, whose 1912 Progressive party presidential campaign Addams had enthusiastically supported, was beating the drums for war.

Despite the pressures, Addams concluded that she must remain faithful to her conscience and oppose the war. The reaction was swift. Editorial writers who had earlier praised her settlement house work now criticized her. The DAR expelled her. For years after, the DAR, the American Legion, and other patriotic organizations attacked Addams for her "disloyalty" in 1917.

Addams did not sit out the war on the sidelines. She traveled across America, giving speeches urging increased food production to aid refugees and other war victims. Once the war ended, she resumed her work for peace. In 1919 she was elected first president of the Women's International League for Peace and Freedom.

She described her wartime isolation in a moving book, *Peace and Bread in Time of War* (1922). In 1931 she won the Nobel Peace Prize. During the 1960s, some opponents of the Vietnam War found inspiration in her earlier example.

Addams's experience underscores how deeply World War I affected American life. Whether they donned uniforms, worked on farms or in factories, or simply experienced U.S. life in wartime, all Americans were touched by the war. Beyond its immediate effects, the war had long-lasting social, economic, and political ramifications.

Well before 1917, however, events abroad gripped the attention of government officials, the media, and ordinary Americans. From this perspective, World War I was one episode in a larger process of deepening U.S. involvement overseas. In the late nineteenth century, America had become an industrial and economic powerhouse seeking markets and raw materials worldwide. In the early twentieth century, these broadening economic interests helped give rise to a new international role for the nation. This expanded role profoundly influenced developments at home as well as U.S. actions abroad, and has continued to shape American history to the present. These broader global realities, culminating in World War I, are the focus of this chapter.

This chapter will focus on five major questions:

What general motivations or objectives underlay America's involvement in Asia and Latin America in the early twentieth century?

Considering both immediate provocations and broader factors, why did the United States enter the European war in April 1917?

How did America's participation in the war affect the home front and the reform spirit of the prewar Progressive Era?

How did the role of the federal government in the U.S. economy, and in American life generally, change in 1917–1918?

What was President Woodrow Wilson's role in the creation of the League of Nations and in the Senate's rejection of U.S. membership in the League?

DEFINING AMERICA'S WORLD ROLE, 1902–1914

As we saw in Chapter 20, the annexation of Hawaii, the Spanish-American War, the occupation of the Philippines, and other developments in the 1890s signaled an era of intensified U.S. involvement abroad, especially in Asia and Latin America. These foreign engagements reflected a growing determination to assert American might in an age of imperial expansion by European powers, to protect and extend U.S. business investments abroad, and to impose American standards of good government beyond the nation's borders. This process of foreign engagement continued under Presidents Theodore Roosevelt, William Howard Taft, and Woodrow Wilson. The strongly moralistic tone of the progressive movement, whose domestic manifestations we examined in Chapter 21, emerged in America's dealings with other nations as well.

The "Open Door": Competing for the China Market As the campaign to suppress the Philippines insurrection dragged on (see Chapter 20), American policy makers turned their attention farther west, to China. Their aim was not territorial expansion but rather protection of U.S. commercial opportunities. Proclaimed Indiana Senator Albert J. Beveridge in 1898, "American factories are making more than the American people can use; American soil is producing more than they can consume. . . . [T]he trade of the world must and shall be ours."

The China market beckoned. Textile producers dreamed of clothing China's millions of people; investors envisioned Chinese railroad construction. As China's 250-year-old Manchu Ch'ing empire grew weaker, U.S. businesspeople watched carefully. In 1896 a consortium of New York capitalists formed a company to promote trade and railroad investment in China.

But other nations were also eyeing the China market. Some pressured the weak Manchu rulers to designate certain ports and regions as "spheres of influence" where they would enjoy exclusive trading and development rights. In 1896 Russia won both the right to build a railway across Manchuria and a twenty-five-year lease on much of the region. In 1897 Germany forcibly secured a ninety-nine-year lease on a Chinese port as well as mining and railroad rights in the adjacent province. The British won various concessions, too.

In September 1899 U.S. Secretary of State John Hay asked the major European powers with economic interests in China not to interfere with American trading rights in China. Specifically, he requested them to open the ports in their spheres of influence to all countries. The six nations gave noncommittal answers, but Hay blithely announced that they had accepted the principle of an "Open Door" to American business in China.

Hay's Open Door note showed how commercial considerations were increasingly influencing American foreign policy. It reflected a form of economic expansionism that has been called "informal empire." The U.S. government had no desire to occupy Chinese territory, but it did want to keep Chinese markets open to American businesses.

As Hay pursued this effort, a more urgent threat emerged in China. For years, antiforeign feeling had simmered in China, fanned by the aged Ch'ing empress who was disgusted by the growth of Western influence. In 1899 a fanatical antiforeign secret society known as the Harmonious Righteous Fists (called "Boxers" by Western journalists) killed thousands of foreigners and Chinese Christians. In June 1900 the Boxers occupied Beijing (Peking), the Chinese capital, and besieged the district housing the foreign legations. The United States contributed twenty-five hundred soldiers to an international army that marched on Beijing, drove back the Boxers, and rescued the occupants of the threatened legations.

The defeat of the Boxer uprising further weakened China's government. Fearing that the regime's collapse would allow European powers to carve up China, John Hay issued a second, more important, series of Open Door notes in 1900. He reaffirmed the principle of open trade in China for all nations and announced America's determination to preserve China's territorial and administrative integrity. In general, China remained open to U.S. business interests as well as to Christian missionary effort. In the 1930s, when Japanese expansionism menaced China's survival, Hay's policy helped shape the American response.

The Panama Canal: Hardball Diplomacy

Traders had long dreamed of a canal across the forty-mile-wide ribbon of land joining North and South America to eliminate the hazardous voyage around South America. In 1879 a French company secured permission from Colombia to build a canal across Panama, then part of Colombia. But mismanagement and yellow fever doomed the project, and ten years and $400 million later, with the canal half completed, it went bankrupt. Seeking to recoup its losses, the French company offered its assets, including the still-valid concession from Colombia, to the United States for $109 million.

America was in an expansionist mood. In 1902, after the French lowered their price to $40 million, Congress authorized President Theodore Roosevelt to accept the offer. The following year, Secretary of State Hay signed an agreement with the Colombian representative, Tomás Herrán, granting the United States a ninety-nine-year lease on the proposed canal for a down payment of $10 million and an annual fee of $250,000. But the Colombian senate, seeking a better deal, rejected the agreement. An outraged Roosevelt, using the racist language of the day, privately denounced the Colombians as "greedy little anthropoids."

Determined to have his canal, Roosevelt found a willing collaborator in Philippe Bunau-Varilla, an official of the bankrupt French company. Dismayed that his company might lose its $40 million, Bunau-Varilla organized a "revolution" in Panama from a New York hotel room. While his wife stitched a flag, he wrote a declaration of independence and a constitution for the new nation. When the "revolution" occurred as scheduled on November 3, 1903, a U.S. warship hovered offshore. Proclaiming Panama's independence, Bunau-Varilla appointed himself its first ambassador to the United States. John Hay quickly recognized the newly hatched nation and signed a treaty with Bunau-Varilla granting the United States a ten-mile-wide strip of land across Panama "in perpetuity" (that is, forever) on the same terms earlier rejected by Colombia. Theodore Roosevelt later summed up the episode: "I took the Canal Zone, and let Congress debate, and while the debate goes on, the canal does also."

The U.S. canal builders' first challenge was to overcome the yellow fever that had haunted the French. Leading this effort was Dr. Walter Reed of the Army Medical Corps. Earlier, in a brilliant research project in Cuba, Reed and his associates had used themselves and army volunteers as experimental subjects to prove that the yellow-fever virus was spread by female mosquitoes that bred in stagnant water. In Panama Reed organized a large-scale drainage project that eradicated the disease-bearing mosquito—a remarkable public-health achievement. Construction began in 1906, and in August 1914 the first ship sailed through the canal. In 1921, implicitly conceding the dubious methods used to acquire the Canal Zone, the

U.S. Senate voted a payment of $25 million to Colombia. But the ill feeling generated by Theodore Roosevelt's high-handed actions, combined with other instances of U.S. interventionism, would long shadow U.S.–Latin American relations.

Roosevelt and Taft Assert U.S. Power in Latin America and Asia

While the Panama Canal remains the best-known foreign-policy achievement of these years, other actions by Presidents Theodore Roosevelt and William Howard Taft underscored their belief that Washington had to assert U.S. power and protect U.S. business interests in Latin America and Asia. Two crises early in Roosevelt's presidency arose as a result of European powers' intervention in Latin America. In 1902 German, British, and Italian warships blockaded and bombarded the ports of Venezuela, which had defaulted on its debts to European investors. The standoff ended when all sides agreed to Roosevelt's proposal of arbitration.

The second crisis flared in 1904 when several European nations threatened to invade the Dominican Republic, a Caribbean island nation that had also defaulted on its debts to them. Roosevelt reacted swiftly. If anyone were to intervene, he believed, it should be the United States. While denying any territorial ambitions in Latin America, Roosevelt in December 1904 declared that "chronic wrongdoing" by any Latin American nation would justify U.S. intervention.

This pronouncement has been called "the Roosevelt Corollary" to the Monroe Doctrine of 1823, which had warned European powers against intervening in Latin America. Now Roosevelt asserted that in cases of "wrongdoing" (a word he left undefined), the United States had the right to precisely such intervention. Suiting actions to words, the Roosevelt administration ended the threat of European intervention by taking over the Dominican Republic's customs service for two years and managing its foreign debt. Roosevelt summed up his foreign-policy approach in a 1901 speech quoting what he said was an old African proverb, "Speak softly and carry a big stick." (He followed the second part of this rule more consistently than the first.)

The foreign policy of the Taft administration (1909–1913) focused on advancing American commercial interests abroad, a policy some called "dollar diplomacy." A U.S.-backed revolution in Nicaragua in 1911 brought to power Adolfo Díaz, an officer of an American-owned mine. Washington feared growing British influence in Nicaragua's affairs, and also that a foreign power might build a canal across Nicaragua to rival the Panama Canal. In exchange for control of Nicaragua's national bank, customs service, and railroad, American bankers lent Díaz's government $1.5 million. When a revolt against Díaz broke out in 1912, Taft ordered in the marines to protect the bankers' investment. Except for one brief interval, marines occupied Nicaragua until 1933.

In Asia, too, both Roosevelt and Taft sought to project U.S. power and advance the interests of American business. In 1900, exploiting the turmoil caused by the Boxer uprising, Russian troops occupied the Chinese province of Manchuria, and Russia promoted its commercial interests by building railroads. This alarmed the

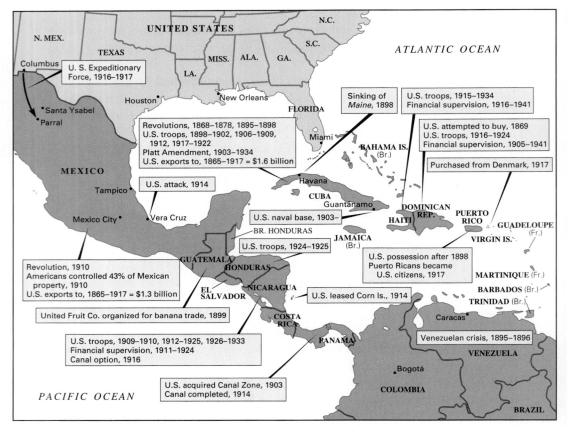

U.S. Hegemony in the Caribbean and Latin America

Through many interventions, territorial acquisitions, and robust economic expansion, the United States became the predominant power in Latin America in the early twentieth century. Acting on Theodore Roosevelt's assertion of a U.S. right to combat "wrongdoing" in Latin America and the Caribbean, the United States dispatched troops to the region where they met nationalist opposition.

Japanese, who also had designs on Manchuria and nearby Korea. In February 1904 a surprise Japanese attack destroyed Russian ships anchored at Port Arthur, Manchuria. Japan completely dominated in the Russo-Japanese War that followed. For the first time, European imperialist expansion had been checked by an Asian power.

Roosevelt, while pleased to see Russian expansionism challenged, believed that a Japanese victory would disrupt the Asian balance of power and threaten America's position in the Philippines. Accordingly, he invited Japan and Russia to a peace conference at Portsmouth, New Hampshire. In September 1905 the two rivals signed a peace treaty. Russia recognized Japan's rule in Korea and made other territorial concessions. After this outcome, curbing Japanese expansionism—

TR and the Great White Fleet, 1909 *President Theodore Roosevelt greets the crew of the* U.S.S. Constitution *as the fleet returns from a world cruise designed to impress other nations with America's emergence as a world power.*

peacefully, if possible—became America's major objective in Asia. For his role in ending the war, Roosevelt, in the unaccustomed role of peacemaker, received the Nobel Peace Prize.

Meanwhile, U.S.-Japanese relations soured when the San Francisco school board, reflecting West Coast hostility to Asian immigrants, assigned all Asian children to segregated schools in 1906. Japan angrily protested this insult. Summoning the school board to Washington, Roosevelt persuaded them to reverse this discriminatory policy. In return, in 1908 the administration negotiated a "gentlemen's agreement" with Japan by which Tokyo pledged to halt Japanese emigration to America. Racist attitudes continued to poison U.S.-Japanese relations, however. In 1913, the California legislature prohibited Japanese aliens from owning land.

While Californians warned of the "yellow peril," Japanese journalists, eyeing America's military strength and involvement in Asia, spoke of a "white peril." In 1907 Roosevelt ordered sixteen gleaming U.S. battleships on a "training operation" to Japan. Although officially treated as friendly, this "Great White Fleet" underscored America's growing naval might.

Under President Taft, U.S. foreign policy in Asia continued to focus on dollar diplomacy, which in this case meant promoting U.S. commercial interests in China—the same goal Secretary of State John Hay had sought with his Open Door notes. As it happened, however, a plan for a U.S.-financed railroad in Manchuria did not work out. Not only did U.S. bankers find the project too risky, but Russia and Japan signed a treaty carving up Manchuria for commercial purposes, freezing out the Americans.

Wilson and
Latin America

Upon entering the White House in 1913 as the first Democratic president in sixteen years, Woodrow Wilson criticized his Republican predecessors' expansionist policies. The United States, he pledged, would "never again seek one additional foot of territory by conquest." But he, too, soon intervened in Latin America. In 1915, after upheavals in Haiti and the Dominican Republic (two nations sharing the Caribbean island of Santo Domingo), Wilson sent in the marines. A Haitian constitution favorable to U.S. commercial interests was overwhelmingly ratified in 1918 in a vote supervised by the marines. Under Major General Smedley ("Old Gimlet Eye") Butler, marines brutally suppressed Haitian resistance to U.S. rule. The marines remained in the Dominican Republic until 1924 and in Haiti until 1934.

The most serious crisis Wilson faced in Latin America was the Mexican Revolution. Mexico had won independence from Spain in 1820, but the nation remained divided between a small landowning elite and an impoverished peasantry. In 1911 rebels led by the democratic reformer Francisco Madero had ended the thirty-year rule of President Porfirio Díaz, who had defended the interests of the wealthy elite. Early in 1913, just as Wilson took office, Mexican troops loyal to General Victoriano Huerta, a full-blooded Indian, overthrew and murdered Madero.

In this turbulent era, Wilson tried to promote good government, protect U.S. investments, and safeguard U.S. citizens living in Mexico or along its border. Forty thousand Americans had settled in Mexico under Díaz's regime, and U.S. investors had poured some $2 billion into Mexican oil wells and other ventures. Reversing the long-standing U.S. policy of recognizing all governments, Wilson refused to recognize Huerta's regime, which he called "a government of butchers." Authorizing arms sales to General Venustiano Carranza, Huerta's rival, Wilson also ordered the port of Veracruz blockaded to prevent a shipment of German arms from reaching Huerta. Announced Wilson, "I am going to teach the South American republics to elect good men." In April 1914 seven thousand U.S. troops occupied Veracruz and engaged Huerta's forces. Sixty-five Americans and approximately five hundred Mexicans were killed or wounded. Bowing to U.S. might, Huerta abdicated; Carranza took power; and the U.S. troops withdrew.

But the turmoil continued. In January 1916 a bandit chieftain in northern Mexico, Pancho Villa, murdered sixteen U.S. mining engineers. Soon after, Villa's gang burned the town of Columbus, New Mexico, and killed nineteen inhabitants. Enraged Americans demanded action. Wilson dispatched a punitive expedition into Mexico under General John J. Pershing. When Pancho Villa not only eluded Pershing but also brazenly staged another cross-border raid into Texas, Wilson ordered 150,000 National Guardsmen to the Mexican border—a heavy-handed response that embittered U.S.-Mexican relations for years after.

Although soon overshadowed by World War I, these involvements in Asia and Latin America illuminate the U.S. foreign-policy goal, which was, essentially, to achieve an international system based on democratic values and capitalist enterprise. Washington planners envisioned a harmonious, stable global order that would welcome both American political values and American business. President Wilson summed up this view in a speech to corporate leaders: "[Y]ou are Americans and are meant to carry liberty and justice and the principles of humanity wherever you go. . . . [G]o out and sell goods that will make the world more comfortable and more happy, and convert them to the principles of America." Wilson's vision of an American-based world order shaped his response to a crisis unfolding in Europe.

WAR IN EUROPE, 1914–1917

When war engulfed Europe in 1914, most Americans wished only to remain aloof. For nearly three years, the United States stayed neutral. But by April 1917 cultural ties to England and France, economic considerations, visions of a world remade in America's image, and German violations of Wilson's definition of neutral rights all combined to draw the United States into the maelstrom.

The Coming of War Europe was at peace through much of the nineteenth century, and some people concluded that war was a thing of the past. Beneath the surface, however, ominous developments, including a complex web of alliances, belied such hopes. Germany, Austria, and Italy signed a mutual-defense treaty in 1882. In turn, France concluded military treaties with Russia and Great Britain.

Beyond the treaties imperial ambitions and nationalistic passions stirred. The once-powerful Ottoman Empire, centered in Turkey, grew weaker in the 1870s, leaving in its wake such newly independent nations as Romania, Bulgaria, and Serbia.

Serbian patriots dreamed of creating a greater Serbia that would include Serbs living in Bosnia-Herzegovina, Serbia's neighbor to the west. Russia, home to millions of Slavs, the same ethnic group as the Serbian population, supported Serbia's expansionist ambitions. Meanwhile, the Austro-Hungarian Empire, with its capital in Vienna, also saw opportunities for expansion as the Ottoman Empire faded. In 1908 Austria-Hungary annexed (took over) Bosnia-Herzegovina, alarming Russia and Serbia.

Germany, ruled by Kaiser Wilhelm II, also displayed expansionist impulses. Many Germans believed that their nation had lagged in the race for empire. Expansion, modernization, and military power became the goal in Berlin.

Such was the context when Archduke Franz Ferdinand of Austria made a state visit to Bosnia in June 1914. As he and his wife rode in an open car through Sarajevo, the Bosnian capital, a young Bosnian Serb nationalist gunned them down. In response, Austria declared war on Serbia on July 28. Russia, which had a secret treaty with Serbia, mobilized for war. Germany declared war on Russia and Russia's ally France. Great Britain, linked by treaty to France, declared war on Germany. An assassin's bullet had plunged Europe into war.

This was the start of the conflict that we today know as World War I. Until the outbreak of World War II in 1939, however, it was simply called The Great War. On one side were Great Britain, Russia, and France, called the Allies. On the other side were the Central Powers: Germany and Austria-Hungary. Italy, although bound by treaty to the Central Powers, switched sides and joined the Allies in 1915.

The Perils of Neutrality

Proclaiming U.S. neutrality, President Wilson urged the nation to be neutral "in thought as well as in action." Most Americans, grateful that an ocean lay between them and the war, fervently agreed. A popular song summed up the mood: "I Didn't Raise My Boy to Be a Soldier."

Neutrality proved difficult, however. Wilson privately dreaded a victory by militaristic Germany. Strong economic interests bound the United States and Britain. Many Americans, including Wilson himself, had ancestral ties to England. Well-to-do Americans routinely traveled in England. Schoolbooks stressed the English origins of American institutions. The English language itself—the language of Shakespeare, Dickens, and the King James Bible—deepened the bond. British propaganda subtly stressed the British-American link.

But not all Americans felt emotional ties to England. Many German-Americans sympathized with Germany's cause. Irish-Americans speculated that a German victory might free Ireland from British rule. Some Scandinavian immigrants identified more with Germany than with England. But these cultural and ethnic cross-currents did not at first override Wilson's commitment to neutrality. For most Americans, staying out of the conflict became the chief goal.

Neutral in 1914, America went to war in 1917. What caused this turnabout? Fundamentally, Wilson's vision of a world order in America's image conflicted with his neutrality. An international system based on democracy and capitalism would be impossible, he believed, in a world dominated by imperial Germany. Even an Allied victory would not ensure a transformed world order, Wilson gradually became convinced, without a U.S. role in the postwar settlement. To shape the peace, America would have to fight the war.

These underlying ideas influenced Wilson's handling of the immediate issue that dragged the United States into the conflict: neutral nations' rights on the high seas. When the war began, Britain started intercepting U.S. merchant ships bound for Germany, insisting that their cargo could aid Germany's war effort. Wilson's protests intensified in late 1914 and early 1915 when Britain declared the North Sea a war zone; planted it with explosive mines; and blockaded all German ports, choking off Germany's imports, including food. Britain was determined to exploit its naval advantage, even if it meant alienating American public opinion.

But Germany, not England, ultimately pushed the United States into war. If Britannia ruled the waves, Germany controlled the ocean depths with its torpedo-equipped submarines, or U-boats. In February 1915 Berlin proclaimed the waters around Great Britain a war zone and warned off all ships. Wilson quickly responded: Germany would be held to "strict accountability" for any loss of U.S. ships or lives.

On May 1, 1915, in a small ad in U.S. newspapers, the German embassy cautioned Americans against travel on British or French vessels. Six days later, a U-boat sank the British liner *Lusitania* off the Irish coast, with the loss of 1,198 lives, including 128 Americans. As headlines screamed the news, U.S. public opinion turned sharply anti-German. (The *Lusitania,* historians later discovered, had carried munitions destined for England.)

Wilson demanded that Germany stop unrestricted submarine warfare. He insisted that America could persuade the belligerents to recognize the principle of neutral rights without going to war. "There is such a thing as a man being too proud to fight," he said.

The *Lusitania* disaster exposed deep divisions in U.S. public opinion. Many Americans, now ready for war, ridiculed Wilson's "too proud to fight" speech. Theodore Roosevelt denounced the president's "abject cowardice." The National Security League, a lobby of bankers and industrialists, promoted a U.S. arms buildup and universal military training and organized "preparedness" parades in major cities. By late 1915 Wilson himself called for a military buildup.

Other citizens had taken Wilson's neutrality speeches seriously and deplored the drift toward war. Some feminists and reformers warned that war fever was eroding support for progressive reforms. Jane Addams lamented that the international movements to reduce infant mortality and improve care for the aged had been "scattered to the winds by the war."

As early as August 1914, fifteen hundred women marched down New York's Fifth Avenue protesting the war. Carrie Chapman Catt and other feminists joined Jane Addams in forming the Woman's Peace party. Late in 1915 automaker Henry Ford chartered a vessel to take a group of pacifists to Scandinavia to persuade the belligerents to accept neutral mediation and fulfill his dream of ending the war by Christmas.

Divisions surfaced even within the Wilson administration. Secretary of State William Jennings Bryan, believing that Wilson's *Lusitania* notes were too hostile to Germany, resigned in June 1915. His successor, Robert Lansing, let Wilson act as his own secretary of state.

Some neutrality advocates concluded that incidents like the *Lusitania* crisis were inevitable if Americans persisted in sailing on belligerent ships. Early in 1916, Congress considered a bill to ban such travel, but President Wilson successfully opposed it, insisting that the principle of neutral rights must be upheld.

For a time, Wilson's approach seemed to work. Germany ordered U-boat captains to spare passenger ships, and agreed to pay compensation for the American lives lost in the *Lusitania* sinking. In March 1916, however, a German submarine sank a French passenger ship, the *Sussex,* in the English Channel, injuring several Americans. Wilson threatened to break diplomatic relations—a step toward war. In response, Berlin pledged not to attack merchant vessels without warning, provided that Great Britain, too, observe "the rules of international law." Ignoring this qualification, Wilson announced Germany's acceptance of American demands. For the rest of 1916, the crisis over neutral rights eased.

U.S. bankers' financial support to the warring nations also undermined the principle of neutrality. Early in the war, Secretary of State Bryan had rejected banker J. P. Morgan's request to extend loans to France. Such loans, said Bryan, would be "inconsistent with the true spirit of neutrality." But economic considerations, combined with outrage over the *Lusitania* sinking, undermined this policy. In August 1915 Treasury Secretary William G. McAdoo warned Wilson of dire economic consequences if U.S. neutrality policy forced cuts in Allied purchases of American munitions and farm products. "To maintain our prosperity, we must finance it," McAdoo insisted. Only substantial loans to England, agreed Secretary of State Lansing, could prevent serious financial problems in the United States, including "unrest and suffering among the laboring classes." The neutrality principle must not "stand in the way of our national interests," warned Lansing.

Swayed by such arguments and personally sympathetic to the Allies, Wilson permitted Morgan's bank to lend $500 million to the British and French governments. By April 1917 U.S. banks had lent $2.3 billion to the Allies, in contrast to $27 million to Germany.

While Americans concentrated on neutral rights, the land war settled into a grim stalemate. An autumn 1914 German drive into France bogged down along the Marne River. The two sides then dug in, in trenches across France from the English Channel to the Swiss border. For more than three years, this line scarcely changed. Occasional offensives took a terrible toll. A German attack in February 1916 began with the capture of two forts near the town of Verdun and ended that June with the French recapture of the same two forts, now nothing but rubble, at a horrendous cost in human life. Trench warfare was a nightmare of mud, lice, rats, artillery bursts, poison gas, and random death.

British propaganda focused on the atrocities committed by "the Huns" (a derogatory term for the Germans), such as impaling babies on bayonets. After the war, much of this propaganda was exposed as false. Documents seized in 1915 revealing German espionage in U.S. war plants, however, further discredited the German cause.

The war dominated the 1916 presidential election. Woodrow Wilson faced Republican Charles Evans Hughes, a former governor of New York (and future chief justice of the U.S. Supreme Court). The Democrats' campaign theme emerged when a convention speaker, praising Wilson's foreign policy, aroused wild applause as he ended each episode with the refrain "We didn't go to war."

Hughes criticized Wilson's lack of aggressiveness while rebuking him for policies that risked war. Theodore Roosevelt, still influential in public life, campaigned more for war than for the Republican ticket. The only difference between Wilson and the bearded Hughes, he jeered, was a shave. While Hughes did well among Irish-Americans and German-Americans who considered Wilson too pro-British, Wilson held the Democratic base and won support from women voters in western states that had adopted woman suffrage. Wilson's victory, although extremely close, revealed the strength of the popular longing for peace as late as November 1916.

The United States Enters the War   In January 1917, facing stalemate on the ground, Germany resumed unrestricted submarine warfare. Germany's military leaders believed that even if the United States declared war as a result, full-scale U-boat warfare could bring victory before American troops reached the front.

Events now rushed forward with grave inevitability. Wilson broke diplomatic relations on February 3. During February and March, U-boats sank five American ships. A coded telegram from the German foreign secretary, Arthur Zimmermann, to Germany's ambassador to Mexico promised that if Mexico would declare war on the United States, Germany would help restore Mexico's "lost territories" of Texas, Arizona, and New Mexico. Intercepted and decoded by the British and passed along to Washington, the "Zimmermann telegram" further inflamed the war spirit in America.

Events in distant Russia also helped create favorable conditions for America's entry into the war. In March 1917 Russian peasants, industrial workers, intellectuals inspired by Western liberal values, and revolutionaries who embraced the communist ideology of Karl Marx all joined in a revolutionary uprising that overthrew the repressive government of Tsar Nicholas II. A provisional government under the liberal Alexander Kerensky briefly seemed to promise that Russia would take a democratic path, making it easier for President Wilson to portray the war as a battle for democracy.

On April 2 Wilson appeared before a joint session of Congress and solemnly called for a declaration of war. Applause and shouts rang out as Wilson eloquently described his vision of America's role in creating a postwar international order to make the world "safe for democracy." As the speech ended amid a final burst of cheers, Republican Senator Henry Cabot Lodge of Massachusetts, one of Wilson's staunchest political foes, rushed forward to shake his hand.

After a short but bitter debate, the Senate voted 82 to 6 for war. The House agreed, 373 to 50. Three key factors—German attacks on American shipping, U.S. economic investment in the Allied cause, and American cultural links to the Allies, especially England—had propelled the United States into the war.

MOBILIZING AT HOME, FIGHTING IN FRANCE, 1917–1918

America's entry into World War I underscored a deepening international involvement that had been underway for several decades. Yet compared to its effects on Europe, the war only grazed the United States. Russia, ill-prepared for war and geographically isolated from its allies, suffered very heavily. France, Great Britain, and Germany fought for more than four years; the United States, for nineteen months. Their armies suffered casualties of 70 percent or more; the U.S. casualty rate was 8 percent. The fighting left parts of France and Belgium brutally scarred; North America was physically untouched. Nevertheless, the war profoundly affected America. It changed not only those who participated directly in it, but also the American home front and the nation's government and economy.

Raising, Training, and Testing an Army

April 1917 found America's military woefully unprepared. The regular army consisted of 120,000 men, few with combat experience, plus 80,000 National Guard members. An aging officer corps dozed away the years until retirement. Ammunition reserves were paltry. The War Department was a snake pit of jealous bureaucrats, one of whom hoarded thousands of typewriters as the war approached.

While army chief-of-staff Peyton C. Marsh brought order to the military bureaucracy, Wilson's secretary of war, Newton D. Baker, concentrated on raising an army. Formerly the reform mayor of Cleveland, Baker lacked administrative talent but was a public-relations genius. The Selective Service Act of May 1917 required all men between twenty-one and thirty (later expanded to eighteen through forty-five) to register with local draft boards. Mindful of the Civil War draft riots, Baker planned the first official draft-registration day, June 5, 1917, as a "festival and patriotic occasion."

By the time the war ended in November 1918, more than 24 million men had registered, of whom nearly 3 million were drafted. Volunteers and National Guardsmen swelled the total to 4.3 million. Recruits got their first taste of army life in home-front training camps. Along with military discipline and combat instruction, the camps built morale through shows, games, and recreation provided by volunteer organizations. The American Library Association contributed books. YMCA volunteers staffed base clubs and offered classes in literacy, French slang, and Bible study. In Plattsburgh, New York, local women opened a "Hostess House" to provide a touch of domesticity for homesick recruits at the nearby training camp. The idea soon spread to other communities near military camps.

The War Department monitored the off-duty behavior of young men cut off from the watchful eye of family and community. The Commission on Training Camp Activities presented films, lectures, and posters on the dangers of alcohol and prostitution. Any soldier disabled by venereal (that is, sexually transmitted) disease, one poster warned, "is a Traitor!" Camp commanders confined trainees to the base until nearby towns closed all brothels and saloons. The army's antiliquor, antiprostitution policies strengthened the moral-reform campaigns of the Progressive Era (see Chapter 21).

Beginning in December 1917, all recruits also underwent intelligence testing. Psychologists were eager to demonstrate the usefulness of their new field of expertise and claimed that tests measuring recruits' "intelligence quotient" (IQ) could help in assigning their duties and showing who had officer potential. Intelligence testing, declared Robert M. Yerkes, president of the American Psychological Association, would "help win the war."

When the psychologists announced that a high percentage of recruits were "morons," editorial writers bemoaned the wave of imbecility supposedly sweeping the nation. In fact, the tests mostly revealed that many recruits lacked formal education and cultural sophistication. One question asked whether *mauve* was a drink, a color, a fabric, or a food. Another—at a time when automobiles were rare in rural America—asked in which city a particular car, the Overland, was built. The testing also confirmed racial and ethnic stereotypes: native-born recruits of northern European origins scored highest; African-Americans and recent immigrants lowest.

In short, the World War I training camps not only turned civilians into soldiers, they also reinforced the prewar moral-control reforms, and signaled changes ahead, including the national infatuation with standardized testing.

Some twelve thousand Native Americans served in the American Expeditionary Force (AEF). While some reformers eager to preserve Indian culture argued for all-Indian units, the army took a different view and integrated Native Americans into the general army. Some observers predicted that the wartime experience would hasten the assimilation of Indians into mainstream American life, considered by many a desirable goal at the time.

In April 1917 the African-American leader W. E. B. Du Bois urged African-Americans to "close ranks" and support the war. While some blacks resisted the draft, especially in the South (discussed later in "Wartime Intolerance and Dissent"), others followed Du Bois's advice. More than 260,000 blacks volunteered or were drafted, and 50,000 went to France. Racism pervaded the military, as it did American society. The navy assigned blacks only to menial positions, and the marines excluded them altogether.

One racist senator from Mississippi warned that the sight of "arrogant, strutting" black soldiers would trigger race riots. Blacks in training camps experienced crude racial abuse. Tensions exploded in Houston in August 1917 when some black soldiers, endlessly goaded by local whites, seized weapons from the armory and killed seventeen white civilians. After a hasty trial with no appeal process, thirteen black soldiers were hanged and forty-one imprisoned for life. Not since the 1906 Brownsville incident (see Chapter 21) had black confidence in military justice been so shaken.

Organizing the Economy for War

The war years of 1917–1918 helped shape modern America. As historian Ellis Hawley has shown, the war's administrative innovations sped up longer-term processes of social reorganization. Many key developments of the 1920s and beyond—including the spread of mass production; the collaboration between government, business, and labor; and the continued growth of new professional and managerial elites—were furthered by the war.

The war led to unprecedented government oversight of the economy. Populists and progressives had long urged more public control of corporations. Wartime brought an elaborate supervisory apparatus. In 1916 Congress had created an advisory body, the Council of National Defense, to oversee the government's preparedness program. After war was declared, this council set up the War Industries Board (WIB) to coordinate military purchasing; ensure production efficiency; and provide weapons, equipment, and supplies to the military. Wilson reorganized the WIB in March 1918 and put Bernard Baruch in charge. A South Carolinian of German-Jewish origin, Baruch had made a fortune on Wall Street. Awed by his range of knowledge, Wilson called him Dr. Facts. Under Baruch, the WIB controlled the industrial sector. It allocated raw materials, established production priorities, and induced competing companies to standardize and coordinate their products and processes to save scarce commodities. The standardization of bicycle manufacturing, for example, saved tons of steel.

Acting under the authority of a law passed in August 1917, Wilson set up two more new agencies, the Fuel Administration and the Food Administration. The Fuel Administration controlled coal output, regulated fuel prices and consumption, and introduced daylight-saving time—an idea first proposed by Benjamin Franklin in the 1770s. The Food Administration, headed by Herbert Hoover, oversaw the production and allocation of wheat, meat, and sugar to ensure adequate supplies for the army as well as for the desperately food-short Allies. Born in poverty in Iowa, Hoover had prospered as a mining engineer in Asia. He was organizing food relief in Belgium when Wilson brought him back to Washington.

These regulatory agencies relied on voluntary cooperation reinforced by official pressure. For example, a barrage of Food Administration posters and magazine ads urged Americans to conserve food. Housewives signed pledges to observe "meatless" and "wheatless" days. President Wilson pitched in by pasturing a flock of sheep on the White House lawn. Slogans such as "Serve Beans by All Means" promoted substitutes for scarce commodities.

Harriot Stanton Blatch, daughter of woman's-rights pioneer Elizabeth Cady Stanton, headed the Food Administration's Speakers' Bureau, which spread the administration's conservation message. Blatch also organized the Woman's Land Army, which recruited women to replace male farm workers.

These agencies were the tip of the regulatory iceberg. Nearly five thousand government boards supervised home-front activities. These included the Shipping Board, which oversaw the transport of goods by water; the National War Labor Board, which resolved labor-management disputes that jeopardized production; and the Railroad Administration, headed by Treasury Secretary William McAdoo. When a railroad tie-up during the winter of 1917–1918 threatened the flow of supplies to Europe, the Railroad Administration stepped in and soon transformed the thousands of miles of track owned by many competing companies into an efficient national rail system.

American business, much criticized by progressive reformers, utilized the war emergency to improve its image. Corporate executives ran regulatory agencies. Factory owners distributed prowar propaganda to workers. Trade associations coordinated war production.

The war sped up the ongoing process of corporate consolidation and economic integration. In place of trustbusting, the government now encouraged cooperation among businesses, and corporate mergers jumped sharply. Commenting on the epidemic of "mergeritis," one magazine observed, "The war has accelerated . . . a tendency that was already irresistible. . . . Instead of punishing companies for acting in concert, the government is now in some cases forcing them to unite."

Overall, the war was good for business. Despite added business taxes imposed by Congress, wartime profits soared. After-tax profits in the copper industry, for example, jumped from 12 percent in 1913 to 24 percent in 1917.

This colossal regulatory apparatus was quickly dismantled after the war, but its influence lingered. The wartime mergers, coordination, and business-government cooperation affected the evolution of American business. The old laissez-faire suspicion of government, already weakened, eroded further in 1917–1918. In the 1930s, when the nation faced a different crisis, the government activism of World War I would be remembered (see Chapter 24).

With the American Expeditionary Force in France
When the United States entered the conflict, Allied prospects looked bleak. Germany's resumption of unrestricted U-boat warfare was taking a horrendous toll on Allied shipping: 1.5 million tons in March and April 1917. A failed French offensive on the Marne that spring caused such losses that French troops mutinied. A British offensive along the French-Belgian border in November 1917 gained four miles at a cost of more than four hundred thousand killed and wounded. That same month, the Italian army suffered a disastrous defeat at Caporetto near the Austrian border.

Worsening the Allies' situation, Russia left the war late in 1917, after the communist faction of the revolutionary movement, the Bolsheviks (Russian for "majority"), won control. The Bolsheviks had gained the initiative in April when its top leaders, including Vladimir Lenin, returned from exile in Switzerland. On November 6, 1917 (October 24 by the Russian calendar), a Bolshevik coup led by Lenin and Leon Trotsky, another exile recently arrived from New York City, overthrew Alexander Kerensky and seized power. Early in 1918 the Bolsheviks signed an armistice with Germany, the Treaty of Brest-Litovsk, freeing thousands of German troops on the Russian front for fighting in France.

The stalemate in the trenches continued, broken by periodic battles. In November 1917, in an important breakthrough in the technology of war, the British mobilized three hundred tanks along a six-mile section of the front near Cambrai, France, shattering the German defenses.

Initially, U.S. assistance to the Allies consisted of supplying munitions and organizing a convoy system that safeguarded Allied ships crossing the dangerous Atlantic. The first U.S. troops arrived in France in October 1917. Eventually about 2 million American soldiers served in France as members of the AEF under General John J. Pershing. Ironically, Pershing was of German origin; his family name had been Pfoersching. A West Point graduate and commander of the 1916 expedition against Pancho Villa in Mexico, Pershing was an iron-willed officer with a ramrod bearing, steely eyes, and trim mustache. The death of his wife and three of their children in a fire in 1915 had further hardened him.

Most men of the AEF at first found the war a great adventure. Plucked from towns and farms, they sailed for Europe on crowded freighters; a lucky few traveled on captured German passenger liners. Once in France, railroad freight cars marked "HOMMES 40, CHEVAUX 8" (forty men, eight horses) took them to the front. Then began the routine of marching, training—and waiting.

The African-Americans in the AEF who reached France worked mainly as mess-boys (mealtime aides), laborers, and stevedores (ship-cargo handlers). Although discriminatory, the latter assignments vitally aided the war effort. Sometimes working twenty-four hours nonstop, black stevedores unloaded supply ships with impressive efficiency. Some whites of the AEF pressed the French to treat African-Americans as inferiors, but most ignored this advice and related to blacks without prejudice. This eye-opening experience would remain with blacks in the AEF after the war.

For the troops at the front, aerial dogfights between German and Allied reconnaissance planes offered spectacular sideshows. Germany's legendary "Red Baron," Manfred von Richthofen, shot down eighty British and French planes before his luck ran out in April 1918. In 1916 a group of American volunteers had joined the French air corps as the Lafayette Escadrille. Secretary of War Baker, grasping the military importance of air power, pushed a plane-construction program. Few planes were actually built, however—a rare failure of the U.S. war-production program.

France offered other diversions as well, and the U.S. military mobilized to warn young male recruits of the danger of venereal disease. One poster declared, "A German bullet is cleaner than a whore." When the French premier, Georges Clemenceau, offered to provide prostitutes for the American troops (as was the custom for French soldiers), Secretary of War Baker exclaimed, "For God's sake, don't show this to the President, or he'll stop the war."

The YMCA, Red Cross, and Salvation Army, including many young American women volunteers, provided a touch of home. Some 16,500 U.S. women served directly in the AEF in the United States and in France as nurses, telephone operators, canteen workers, and secretaries.

President Wilson, eager to underscore the distinctiveness of the U.S. role in the war, and to ensure a strong voice for America at the peace table, insisted that the United States be described as an "Associate Power" of the Allies. The French and British generals, however, facing desperate circumstances, wanted to absorb the Americans into existing units. But for both military and political reasons, Pershing and his superiors in Washington insisted that the AEF be "distinct and separate." A believer in aggressive combat, Pershing abhorred the defensive mentality ingrained by three years of trench warfare.

In March 1918, however, when Germany launched a major offensive along the Somme, the Allies created a unified command under Marshal Ferdinand Foch, chief of the French general staff. Some Americans participated in the fighting around Amiens and Armentières that stemmed the German advance.

The second phase of the Germans' spring 1918 offensive came in May along the Aisne River, where they broke through to the Marne and faced a nearly open route to Paris, fifty miles away. On June 4, as the French government prepared for evacuation, American forces arrived in strength. Parts of three U.S. divisions and a marine brigade helped stop the Germans at the town of Château-Thierry and nearby Belleau Wood, a huge German machine-gun nest. (An AEF division at full strength consisted of twenty-seven thousand men and one thousand officers, plus twelve thousand support troops.)

These two German offensives had punched deep holes (or salients) in the Allied line. A German drive aimed at the cathedral city of Rheims between these two salients was stopped with the help of some eighty-five thousand American troops. This was the war's turning point. At enormous cost, the German offensive had been defeated. Contributing to this defeat was the fact that many German soldiers,

The United States on the Western Front, 1918

American troops first saw action in the campaign to throw back Germany's spring 1918 offensive in the Somme and Aisne-Marne sectors. The next heavy American engagement came that autumn as part of the Allies' Meuse-Argonne offensive that ended the war.

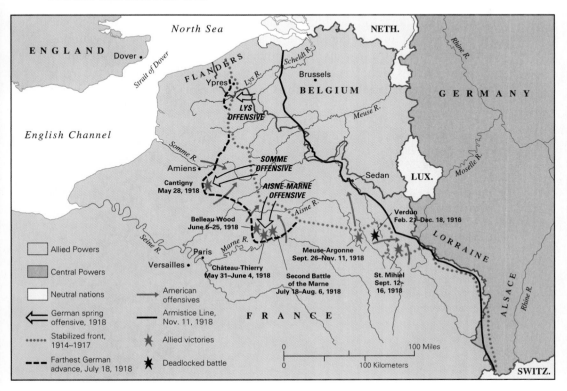

already weakened by battle fatigue and poor diet, fell victim to influenza, an infectious disease that would soon emerge as a deadly worldwide epidemic (see the section "Public Health Crisis: The 1918 Influenza Epidemic").

Turning the Tide   The final Allied offensive began on July 18, 1918. Some 270,000 American soldiers fought in the Allied drive to push the Germans back from the Marne. Rain pelted down as the Americans moved into position on the night of July 17. One wrote in his diary, "Trucks, artillery, infantry columns, cavalry, wagons, caissons, mud, MUD, utter confusion." Meanwhile, another 100,000 AEF troops joined a parallel British offensive north of the Somme to expel the Germans from that area.

Pershing's first fully independent command came in September, when Foch authorized an AEF campaign to close a German salient around the town of St. Mihiel on the Meuse River, about 150 miles east of Paris. Eager to test his offensive strategy, Pershing assembled nearly five hundred thousand American and one hundred thousand French soldiers. Shelling of German positions began at 1:00 A.M. on September 11. Recorded an American in his diary, "[I]n one instant the entire front . . . was a sheet of flame, while the heavy artillery made the earth quake." Within four days the salient was closed, in part because some German units had already withdrawn. Even so, St. Mihiel cost seven thousand U.S. casualties.

The war's last battle began on September 26 as some 1.2 million Americans joined the struggle to drive the Germans from the Meuse River and the dense Argonne Forest north of Verdun. The stench of poison gas (first used by the Germans in 1915) hung in the air, and bloated rats scurried in the mud, gorging on human remains. Americans now endured the filth, vermin, and dysentery familiar to veterans of the trenches. Frontline troops would never forget the terror of combat. As shells streaked overhead at night, one recalled, "We simply lay and

African-Americans at the Front *Black troops of the 369th Infantry Regiment in the trenches near Maffrecourt, France, in 1918. Most African-American soldiers were assigned to non-combat duty, such as unloading supplies and equipment.*

trembled from sheer nervous tension." Some welcomed injuries as a ticket out of the battle zone. Others collapsed emotionally and were hospitalized for "shell shock."

One all-black division, the ninety-second, saw combat in the Meuse-Argonne campaign. In addition, four black infantry regiments served under French command. One entire regiment received the French Croix de Guerre, and several hundred black soldiers were awarded French decorations for bravery. The Germans showered the ninety-second division with leaflets describing American racism and urging blacks to defect, but none did.

The AEF's assignment was to cut the Sedan-Mezières Railroad, a major German supply route. In the way lay three long, heavily fortified German trenches, called Stellungen. "We are not men anymore, just savage beasts," wrote a young American. Death came in many forms, and without ceremony. Bodies, packs, rifles, photos of loved ones, and letters from home sank indiscriminately into the all-consuming mud. Influenza struck on both sides of the line, killing thousands of AEF members at the front and in training camps back home. One day as General Pershing rode in his staff car, he buried his head in his hands and moaned his dead wife's name: "Frankie, Frankie, my God, sometimes I don't know how I can go on."

Religious and ethical principles faded as men struggled to survive. "Love of thy neighbor is forgotten," recalled one, with "all the falsities of a sheltered civilization." The war's brutality would shape the literature of the 1920s as writers such as Ernest Hemingway stripped away the illusions obscuring the reality of mass slaughter.

But the AEF at last overran the dreaded German trenches, and the survivors slogged northward. In early November the Sedan-Mezières Railroad was cut. The AEF had fulfilled its assignment, at a cost of 26,277 dead.

PROMOTING THE WAR AND SUPPRESSING DISSENT

In their own way, the war's domestic effects were as important as its battles. Patriotic fervor gripped America, in part because of the government's propaganda efforts. The war fever, in turn, encouraged intellectual conformity and intolerance of radical or dissenting ideas. Fueling the repressive spirit, government authorities and private vigilante groups hounded socialists, pacifists, and other dissidents, trampling citizens' constitutional rights.

Advertising
the War

To President Wilson, selling the war at home was crucial to success in France. "It is not an army we must shape and train for war, it is a nation," he declared. The administration drew on the new professions of advertising and public relations to pursue this goal. Treasury Secretary McAdoo (who had married Wilson's daughter Eleanor in 1914) orchestrated a series of five government bond drives, called Liberty Loans, that financed about two-thirds of the $35.5 billion (including loans to the Allies) that the war cost the United States. These bonds were essentially loans to the government to cover war expenses.

Posters exhorted citizens to "Fight or Buy Bonds." Liberty Loan parades featured flags, banners, and marching bands. Movie stars like Mary Pickford and Charlie Chaplin worked for the cause. Schoolchildren purchased "thrift stamps" convertible into war bonds. Patriotic war songs reached a large public through phonograph recordings. Beneath the ballyhoo ran a note of coercion. Only "a friend of Germany," McAdoo warned, would refuse to buy bonds.

The balance of the government's war costs came from taxes. Using the power granted it by the Sixteenth Amendment, Congress imposed wartime income taxes that reached 70 percent at the top levels. War-profits taxes, excise taxes on liquor and luxuries, and increased estate taxes also helped finance the war.

Journalist George Creel headed the key wartime propaganda agency, the Committee on Public Information (CPI). While claiming merely to combat rumors with facts, the Creel committee in reality publicized the government's version of events and discredited all who questioned that version. One of CPI's twenty-one divisions distributed posters drawn by leading illustrators. Another wrote propaganda releases that appeared in the press as "news" with no indication of their source. The *Saturday Evening Post* and other popular magazines published CPI ads that warned against spies, saboteurs, and anyone who "spreads pessimistic stories" or "cries for peace." Theaters screened CPI films bearing such titles as *The Kaiser: The Beast of Berlin*.

The CPI poured foreign-language pamphlets into immigrant neighborhoods and supplied prowar editorials to the foreign-language press. At a CPI media event at George Washington's Mount Vernon home on July 4, 1918, an Irish-born tenor sang "The Battle Hymn of the Republic" while immigrants from thirty-three nations filed reverently past Washington's tomb. The CPI also targeted workers. Factory posters attacked the charge by some socialists that this was a capitalists' war. Samuel Gompers of the American Federation of Labor headed a prowar "American Alliance for Labor and Democracy" funded by the CPI. An army of seventy-five thousand CPI volunteers gave short prowar talks to movie audiences and other gatherings. Creel later calculated that these "Four-Minute Men" delivered 7.5 million speeches.

Teachers, writers, religious leaders, and magazine editors overwhelmingly supported the war. These custodians of culture saw the conflict as a struggle to defend threatened values. Historians wrote essays contrasting German brutality with the Allies' lofty ideals. In *The Marne* (1918), expatriate American writer Edith Wharton expressed her love for France. The war poems of Alan Seeger enjoyed great popularity. A Harvard graduate who volunteered to fight for France and died in action in 1916, Seeger held a romantic vision of the conflict as a noble crusade. An artillery barrage was for him "the magnificent orchestra of war."

Many progressive reformers who had applauded Wilson's domestic program now cheered his war. Herbert Croly, Walter Lippmann, and other progressive intellectuals associated with the *New Republic* magazine zealously backed the war.

In gratitude, Wilson administration officials regularly briefed the editors on the government's policies.

The progressive educator John Dewey supported the war and condemned its opponents in a series of *New Republic* essays. Socially engaged intellectuals must accept reality and shape it toward positive social goals, he wrote, not stand aside in self-righteous isolation. The war, he went on, presented exciting "social possibilities." Domestically, government activism stimulated by the war could be channeled to reform purposes when peace returned. Internationally, America's entry into the war could transform an imperialistic struggle into a global democratic crusade.

Wartime Intolerance and Dissent Responding to the propaganda, some Americans became almost hysterical in their strident patriotism, their hatred of all things German, and their hostility to aliens and dissenters. Isolated acts of sabotage by German sympathizers, including the blowing up of a New Jersey munitions dump, fanned the flames. Persons believed to harbor pro-German sentiments were forced to kiss the flag or recite the Pledge of Allegiance. An Ohio woman suspected of disloyalty was wrapped in a flag, marched to a bank, and ordered to buy a war bond. In Collinsville, Illinois, a mob lynched German-born Robert Prager in April 1918. When a jury freed the mob leaders, a jury member shouted, "Nobody can say we aren't loyal now." The *Washington Post,* although deploring the lynching, saw it as evidence of "a healthful and wholesome awakening in the interior of the country."

An Iowa politician charged that "90 percent of all the men and women who teach the German language are traitors." German books vanished from libraries, towns with German names changed them, and on some restaurant menus "liberty sandwich" and "liberty cabbage" replaced "hamburger" and "sauerkraut." A popular evangelist, Billy Sunday, proclaimed, "If you turn hell upside down you will find 'Made in Germany' stamped on the bottom."

Even the music world suffered. The Boston Symphony Orchestra dismissed its conductor, Karl Muck, for having accepted a decoration from Kaiser Wilhelm. Except for Bach, Beethoven, Mozart, and Brahms, the Philadelphia Orchestra banned all German music.

The zealots also targeted war critics and radicals. A Cincinnati mob horse-whipped a pacifist minister. Theodore Roosevelt branded antiwar Senator Robert La Follette "an unhung traitor." Columbia University fired two antiwar professors. In Bisbee, Arizona, vigilantes forced twelve hundred miners who belonged to the Industrial Workers of the World onto a freight train and shipped them into the New Mexico desert without food or water. The IWW opposed the war, and its members were accused of aiding the German cause.

Despite the climate of intolerance, many Americans persisted in opposing the war. Some were immigrants with ancestral ties to Germany. Others were religious pacifists, including Quakers, Mennonites, and Jehovah's Witnesses. Congresswoman Jeannette Rankin of Montana, a pacifist and the first woman elected to Congress, voted against the declaration of war. "I want to stand by my country," she told the House of Representatives, "but I cannot vote for war."

Of some sixty-five thousand men who registered as conscientious objectors (COs), twenty-one thousand were drafted. Assigned to noncombat duty on military bases, such as cleaning latrines, these COs sometimes experienced considerable abuse. When two Hutterite brothers who had refused to wear military uniforms died in prison, their bodies were dressed in uniforms before they were shipped home.

Woodrow Wilson heaped scorn on the pacifists. "What I am opposed to is not [their] feeling . . . , but their stupidity," he declared in November 1917; "my heart is with them, but my mind has contempt for them. I want peace, but I know how to get it, and they do not."

Socialist leaders such as Eugene Debs and Victor Berger viewed the war as a capitalist contest for markets, with the soldiers as cannon fodder. The U.S. declaration of war, they insisted, mainly reflected Wall Street's desire to protect its loans to England and France. Other socialists supported the war, however, dividing the party.

The war split the women's movement as well. While some leaders joined Jane Addams in opposition, others endorsed the war while keeping their own goals in view. In *Mobilizing Woman-Power* (1918), Harriot Stanton Blatch offered a variant of Woodrow Wilson's theme: women who wished to help shape the peace, she said, must support the war. Anna Howard Shaw, a former president of the National American Woman Suffrage Association (NAWSA), accepted an appointment to chair the Woman's Committee of the Council of National Defense, a largely symbolic post.

Carrie Chapman Catt, Shaw's successor as president of NAWSA, had helped start the Woman's Peace party in 1915. But she supported U.S. entry into the war in 1917, sharing to some extent Wilson's vision of a more liberal postwar world order. Catt continued to focus mainly on woman suffrage, however, insisting that this was NAWSA's "number one war job." For this, some superpatriots accused her of disloyalty.

Draft resistance extended beyond the ranks of conscientious objectors. An estimated 2.4 to 3.6 million young men failed to register at all, and of those who did, about 12 percent either did not appear when drafted or deserted from training camp. Historian Jeanette Keith has documented high levels of draft resistance in the rural South. The urban elites who ran the draft boards were more inclined to defer young men of their own class than poor farmers, white or black, fueling class resentment. In June 1918 a truck loaded with U.S. soldiers seeking draft evaders in rural Georgia crashed when a wooden bridge collapsed, killing three soldiers and injuring others. Investigators found that the bridge timbers has been deliberately sawed nearly through.

Southern critics of the war included the one-time populist Tom Watson of Georgia. (Watson was also notoriously racist and anti-Semitic.) The war was a rich-man's plot, Watson charged in his paper *The Jeffersonian*, adding that draft boards discriminated against the poor.

Blacks had added reasons to oppose the draft. Of southern blacks who registered, one-third were drafted, in contrast to only one-quarter of whites. White draft boards justified this by arguing that low-income black families could more easily spare a male breadwinner. As an Alabama board observed: "[I]t is a matter of common knowledge that it requires more for a white man and his wife to live than it does a negro man and his wife, due to their respective stations in life." But the dynamics of race worked in complex ways: some southern whites, fearful of arming black men even for military service, favored drafting only whites.

The war's most incisive critic was Randolph Bourne, a young journalist. Although Bourne admired John Dewey, he rejected Dewey's prowar position and dissected his arguments in several penetrating essays. He dismissed the belief that reformers could direct the war to their own purposes. "If the war is too strong for you to prevent," he asked, "how is it going to be weak enough for you to control and mould to your liberal purposes?"

Eventually, many prowar intellectuals came to agree. By 1919 Dewey conceded that the war, far from promoting reform, had encouraged reaction and intolerance. Bourne did not live to see his vindication, however. He died in 1918, at the age of thirty-two, of influenza.

Suppressing
Dissent by Law

Wartime intolerance also surfaced in federal laws and official actions. The Espionage Act of June 1917 set stiff fines and prison sentences for a variety of loosely defined antiwar activities. The Sedition Amendment (May 1918) imposed heavy penalties on anyone convicted of using "disloyal, profane . . . or abusive language" about the government, the Constitution, the flag, or the military.

Wilson's attorney general, Thomas W. Gregory, used these laws to stamp out dissent. Opponents of the war, proclaimed Gregory, should expect no mercy "from an outraged people and an avenging government." Under the federal legislation and similar state laws, some fifteen hundred pacifists, socialists, IWW leaders, and other war critics were arrested. One socialist, Rose Pastor Stokes, received a ten-year prison sentence (later commuted) for telling an audience, "I am for the people, and the government is for the profiteers." Kate Richards O'Hare, a midwestern socialist organizer, spent over a year in jail for declaring, "The women of the United States are nothing more than brood sows, to raise children to get into the army and be made into fertilizer." Eugene Debs was imprisoned in 1918 for a speech discussing the economic causes of the war, and served for three years until his sentence was commuted by President Warren Harding.

Under the authority of the Espionage Act, Postmaster General Albert S. Burleson, a reactionary superpatriot, suppressed socialist periodicals, including *The Masses*, published by radicals in New York City's Greenwich Village, and Tom Watson's *Jeffersonian*. Burleson "didn't know socialism from rheumatism," according to socialist Norman Thomas, but he pursued his repressive crusade. In January 1919 Congressman-elect Victor Berger was convicted under the Espionage Act for publishing antiwar articles in his socialist newspaper, the *Milwaukee Leader*. (The Supreme Court reversed Berger's conviction in 1921.) Upton Sinclair protested to President Wilson that a man of Burleson's "childish ignorance" should wield such power; but Wilson did little to restrain Burleson's excesses.

A patriotic group called the American Protective League and local "Councils of Defense" operating with vague governmental authority further enforced ideological conformity. The 1917 Bolshevik takeover in Russia sharpened the wartime attacks on domestic radicals. As communists, the Bolsheviks believed in a one-party state and anticipated the violent overthrow of the capitalist system. Some Americans feared that the United States could fall to communism as well.

In three 1919 decisions, the U.S. Supreme Court upheld the Espionage Act convictions of war critics. In *Schenck* v. *United States,* Justice Oliver Wendell Holmes, Jr., writing for a unanimous court, justified such repression in cases where a person's exercise of the First Amendment right of free speech posed a "clear and present danger" to the nation.

The early wartime mood of idealism had degenerated into suspicion, narrow conformity, and persecution of all who failed to meet the zealots' notions of "100 percent Americanism." The effects of this wartime climate would linger long after the armistice was signed.

ECONOMIC AND SOCIAL TRENDS IN WARTIME AMERICA

The war affected the lives of millions of ordinary Americans, including industrial workers, farmers, women, and blacks. The moral-control aspects of progressivism gained momentum in 1917–1918, but for the most part progressive reform energies faded amid the distractions of war. Amid these social changes, a deadly influenza epidemic in 1918 took a grievous toll.

Boom Times in Industry and Agriculture

World War I benefited the U.S. economy. From 1914 to 1918 factory output grew by more than one-third. Even with several million men in the military, the civilian work force expanded by 1.3 million between 1916 and 1918, thanks largely to new jobs in war-related industries such as shipbuilding, munitions, steel, and textiles. Prices rose, but so did wages. Even unskilled workers enjoyed wartime wage increases averaging nearly 20 percent. Samuel Gompers urged workers not to strike during the war. Some IWW workers and maverick AFL locals went on strike anyway, but with the economy booming, most workers observed the no-strike request.

The war's social impact took many forms. The stream of job seekers pouring into industrial centers strained housing, schools, and municipal services. The consumption of cigarettes, which soldiers and workers could carry in their shirt pockets more conveniently than pipes or cigars, soared from 14 billion in 1914 to 48 billion in 1918. Reflecting wartime prosperity, automobile production quadru-pled, from 460,000 in 1914 to 1.8 million in 1917, then dipped briefly in 1918 as steel went for military production.

Farmers profited, too. With European farm production disrupted, U.S. agri-cultural prices more than doubled between 1913 and 1918, and farmers' real income rose significantly. Cotton prices rose from twelve cents a pound in 1913 to twenty-nine cents a pound by 1918, and corn prices surged upward as well.

This agricultural boom proved a mixed blessing. Farmers who borrowed heav-ily to expand production faced a credit squeeze when farm prices fell after the war. In the 1920s and 1930s, hard-pressed farmers would look back to the war years as a golden age of prosperity.

Blacks Migrate Northward   The war speeded up the exodus of southern blacks. An estimated half-million African-Americans moved north during the war, and most settled in cities. Each day fresh arrivals trudged through the railroad stations of Philadelphia, New York, Detroit, and Pittsburgh. Chicago's black population grew from 44,000 in 1910 to 110,000 in 1920, Cleveland's from 8,000 to 34,000.

Economic opportunity beckoned. The war nearly halted immigration from Europe, so booming industries hired black workers to help take up the slack. African-American newspapers like the *Chicago Defender* spread the word of job opportunities. Some companies sent labor agents south to recruit black workers. Letters and word-of-mouth reports swelled the ranks of blacks heading north. One southern black, newly settled near Chicago, wrote home, "Nothing here but money, and it is not hard to get." A Pittsburgh newcomer presented a more bal-anced picture: "They give you big money for what you do, but they charge you big things for what you get."

To the southern black sharecropper, the prospect of earning three dollars a day or more in a region where racism seemed less intense appeared a heaven-sent opportunity. By 1920, 1.5 million African-Americans were working in northern factories and other urban-based jobs.

These newcomers brought with them their social institutions—above all, the church. Large churches and storefront missions met the spiritual and social needs of deeply religious migrants from the South. The concentration of blacks in New York City laid the groundwork for the Harlem Renaissance, a cultural flowering of the 1920s (see "A Place in Time: Harlem in the Twenties" in Chapter 23). This migration also strengthened black organizations. The National Association for the Advancement of Colored People (NAACP) doubled its membership during the war.

Once the initial elation faded, newly arrived African-Americans often found that they had exchanged one set of problems for another. White workers resented the labor competition, and white homeowners lashed out as jammed black neigh-borhoods spilled over into surrounding areas. A bloody outbreak occurred on July 2, 1917, in East St. Louis, Illinois, home to thousands of recently arrived southern blacks. In a coordinated attack, a white mob torched black homes and shot the residents as they fled for their lives. At least thirty-nine blacks died, including a two-year-old who was shot and then thrown into a burning house.

A few weeks later, a silent march down New York's Fifth Avenue organized by the NAACP protested racist violence. One banner bore a slogan that echoed Wilson's phrase justifying U.S. involvement in the war: "Mr. President, Why Not Make AMERICA Safe for Democracy?" Like other wartime social trends, growing racial tensions did not end with the return of peace.

Women in Wartime　From one perspective, World War I seems a uniquely male experience. Male politicians and statesmen led their nations into war. Male generals sent other men into battle. Yet war touches all of society, not just half of it. The war affected women differently, but it affected them profoundly.

Feminist leaders like Carrie Chapman Catt and Anna Howard Shaw hoped that the war would lead to full equality and greater opportunity for women. For a time, these goals seemed attainable. In addition to the women who served with the AEF and in wartime volunteer agencies, about 1 million women worked in industry. Thousands more held other jobs, from streetcar conductors to bricklayers. "Out of . . . repression into opportunity is the meaning of the war to thousands of women," wrote Florence Thorne of the American Federation of Labor in 1917.

Hope glowed brightly as the woman-suffrage movement sped toward victory on a tide of wartime enthusiasm. Through their war service, President Wilson wrote Catt, women had earned the right to vote. As we saw in Chapter 21, New York passed a state woman-suffrage referendum in 1917. In 1919, barraged by prosuffrage petitions, the House and Senate overwhelmingly passed the Nineteenth Amendment granting women the vote. Ratification followed in 1920.

Beyond this victory, hopes that the war would permanently better women's status proved unfounded. Relatively few women actually entered the work force for the first time in 1917–1918; most simply moved to more highly paid jobs. Despite women's protests and War Labor Board rulings, even in these better-paying jobs most earned less than the men they replaced. As for the women in the AEF, the War Department refused their requests for military rank and benefits.

At the end of the war, many women lost their jobs to returning veterans. The New York labor federation advised, "The same patriotism which induced women to enter industry during the war should induce them to vacate their positions after the war." Male streetcar workers in Cleveland went on strike to force women conductors off the job. By 1920 the percentage of all U.S. women who were in the work force was actually slightly lower than it had been in 1910. As industrial researcher Mary Van Kleeck wrote in 1921, when the war emergency ended, traditional male attitudes toward women "came to life once more."

Public Health Crisis: The 1918 Influenza Epidemic　Amid battlefield casualties and home-front social changes, the nation also coped with influenza, a highly contagious viral infection often complicated by pneumonia. The 1918 epidemic, spread by a particularly deadly strain of the virus, killed as many as 30 million people worldwide. Despite medical and public-health advances, doctors had few weapons against the flu in 1918.

Moving northward from its origins in southern Africa, the epidemic spread from the war zone in France to U.S. military camps, striking Fort Riley, Kansas, in March and quickly advancing to other bases and the urban population. In September an army health official visiting Camp Devens in Massachusetts wrote, "I saw hundreds of young stalwart men in uniform coming into . . . the hospital. . . . The faces wore a bluish cast, a cough brought up blood-stained sputum. In the morning, the dead bodies are stacked about the morgue like cordwood."

The flu hit the cities hard. In Philadelphia on September 19, the day after 200,000 people had turned out for a Liberty Loan rally, 635 new influenza cases were reported. Many cities forbade all public gatherings. The worst came in October, when the flu killed 195,000 Americans. The total U.S. death toll was about 550,000, over six times the total of AEF battle deaths in France. The epidemic stimulated research, partially funded by a $1 million congressional appropriation to the U.S. Public Health Service, that eventually isolated the virus and produced vaccines and antibiotics that made future flu outbreaks less lethal.

The War and Progressivism

In assessing the war's effects on Progressive Era reform movements, historians paint a mixed picture.

The war strengthened the coercive, moral-control aspect of progressivism, including the drive for the prohibition of alcohol. Exploiting anti-German sentiment, prohibitionists pointed out that the nation's biggest breweries bore such German names as Pabst, Schlitz, and Anheuser-Busch. Beer, they hinted, was part of a German plot to undermine Americans' fitness for combat. With Herbert Hoover preaching food conservation, they stressed the wastefulness of using grain to make liquor. When the Eighteenth Amendment establishing national prohibition passed Congress in December 1917, it was widely seen as a war measure. Ratified in 1919, it went into effect on January 1, 1920.

As we have seen, the War Department reinforced the Progressive Era antiprostitution campaign by closing brothels near military bases, including New Orleans's famed Storyville. (As Storyville's jazz musicians moved north to Memphis, St. Louis, Kansas City, and Chicago, jazz reached a national audience.) The Commission on Training Camp Activities hired sixty female lecturers to tour the nation urging women to uphold standards of sexual morality. "Do Your Bit to Keep Him Fit" one wartime pamphlet advised women.

Congress contributed to the antiprostitution campaign by appropriating $4 million to combat venereal disease, especially among war workers. In San Antonio, a major military hub, an antiprostitution leader reflected the war mood when he declared, "We propose to fight vice . . . with the cold steel of the law, and to drive in the steel from the point to the hilt until the law's supremacy is acknowledged."

The surge of wartime moral-reform activity convinced some that traditional codes of behavior, weakening before the war, had been restored. One antiprostitution crusader exulted, "Young men of today . . . are nearer perfection in conduct, morals, and ideals than any similar generation of young men in the history of the world. Their minds have been raised to ideals that would never have been attained save by the heroism of . . . the World War."

Other reform causes gained momentum as well. The woman-suffrage movement finally achieved success. And the proworker side of progressivism made some gains. The War Labor Board (WLB), spurred by progressives interested in the cause of labor, encouraged workers to join unions and guaranteed unions' right to bargain collectively with management. The WLB also pressured factory owners to introduce the eight-hour workday, end child labor, provide worker-compensation benefits, and open their plants to safety and sanitation inspectors. William McAdoo's Railroad Administration also recognized railway workers' right to unionize. Under these favorable conditions, union membership rose from 2.7 million in 1916 to more than 5 million by 1920.

Another wartime agency, the United States Housing Corporation, built housing projects for workers, including some that encompassed schools, playgrounds, and recreational centers. Several state legislatures, concluding that worker-protection laws would help the war effort, passed wage-and-hour laws and other measures benefiting factory laborers.

The Bureau of War Risk Insurance (BWRI), created by Congress in October 1917 to aid soldiers' families, established an important precedent of government help for families at risk. As Julia Lathrop, head of the Federal Children's Bureau, observed, "The least a democratic nation can do, which sends men into war, is to give a solemn assurance that the families will be cared for." By the war's end, the BWRI was sending regular checks to 2.1 million families.

Despite some gains, however, the war's long-term effect was to weaken the progressive social-justice impulse. While the years 1917–1918 brought increased corporate regulation—a major progressive goal—the regulatory agencies were often dominated by the very business interests supposedly being supervised, and they were quickly dismantled when the war ended.

The government's repression of radicals and antiwar dissenters fractured the fragile coalition of left-leaning progressives, women's groups, trade unionists, and some socialists that had provided the momentum for prewar worker-protection laws, and ushered in a decade of reaction. The 1918 midterm election signaled the shift: the Democrats lost both houses of Congress to a deeply conservative Republican party.

Nevertheless, taking a still longer view, the Progressive Era reform coalition would reemerge in the depression decade of the 1930s. And as Franklin D. Roosevelt's New Deal took shape in 1933 (see Chapter 24), ideas and inspiration came from World War I precedents such as the War Labor Board, the United States Housing Corporation, and the Bureau of War Risk Insurance.

JOYOUS ARMISTICE, BITTER AFTERMATH, 1918–1920

In November 1918 the war finally ended. The peace conference that followed stands as a high point of America's growing internationalist involvement, but it also triggered a sharp domestic reaction against that involvement. Woodrow

Wilson dominated the peace conference but failed in his most cherished objective—American membership in the League of Nations. At home, as racism and intolerance worsened, the electorate repudiated Wilsonianism and in 1920 sent a conservative Republican to the White House.

Wilson's Fourteen Points; The Armistice From the moment the United States entered the war, President Wilson planned to put a "Made in America" stamp on the peace. U.S. involvement, he and his reform-minded supporters believed, could transform a sordid power conflict into a crusade for a more democratic world order. As the nation mobilized in 1917, Wilson recruited a group of advisers called The Inquiry to translate his vision into specific war aims. The need for a clear statement of U.S. war objectives grew urgent after the Bolsheviks, having seized power in Russia, published many of the self-serving secret treaties signed by European powers prior to 1914.

In a speech to Congress in January 1918, Wilson summed up U.S. war aims in fourteen points. Eight of these goals dealt with territorial settlements in postwar Europe; Wilson stated that the subject peoples of the Austro-Hungarian and Ottoman empires should have the right to determine their own political futures (self-determination). A ninth point insisted that colonial disputes take into account the interests of the colonized peoples. The remaining five points offered Wilson's larger postwar vision: a world of free navigation, free trade, reduced armaments, openly negotiated treaties, and "a general association of nations" to resolve conflicts peacefully. The Fourteen Points helped solidify American support for the war, especially among liberals. The high-minded objectives seemed proof that the United States had entered the war not for selfish reasons but out of noble motives.

In early October 1918, with the Allies advancing on several fronts, the German high command proposed an armistice based on Wilson's Fourteen Points. The British and French hesitated, but when Wilson threatened to negotiate a separate peace with Germany, they agreed. Meanwhile, in Berlin, Kaiser Wilhelm II had abdicated and a German republic had been proclaimed.

As dawn broke over the forest of Compiègne some fifty miles north of Paris on November 11, 1918, Marshal Foch and his German counterparts, seated in Foch's private railway car, signed an armistice ending hostilities at 11:00 A.M. An American air ace, Captain Edward Rickenbacker, flew over the lines and watched as the booming guns fell silent. Rockets burst over the front that night not in anger but in relief and celebration. Back home, cheering throngs (some wearing face masks against the influenza epidemic) filled the streets. "Everything for which America has fought has been accomplished," Wilson proclaimed.

Troop transports soon ferried the soldiers home. One returnee, artillery captain Harry Truman of Missouri, described his feelings in a letter to his fiancée, Bess Wallace:

> I've never seen anything that looks so good as the Liberty Lady in New York Harbor. . . . [T]he men have seen so much and have been in so many hard

places that it takes something real to give them a thrill, but when the band . . . played "Home Sweet Home" there were not many dry eyes. The hardest of hard-boiled cookies even had to blow his nose a time or two.

The Versailles Peace Conference, 1919

Eager to play a central role in forging the peace, Wilson made a crucial decision to lead the U.S. delegation to the peace conference. This was probably a mistake. The strain of long bargaining sessions soon took its toll on his frail nerves and slim reserve of energy.

Wilson compounded his mistake by his choices of his fellow negotiators. All but one were Democrats, and the sole Republican was an elderly diplomat with little influence in the party. Selecting one or two prominent Republicans might have spared Wilson future grief. The Democrats' loss of Congress in the 1918 midterm election was a further ill-omen.

Nevertheless, spirits soared on December 4, 1918, as the *George Washington,* a converted German liner, steamed out of New York bearing Wilson—the first president to cross the Atlantic while in office—to Europe. Ships' whistles blared as Wilson waved to the crowd on the docks. The giddy mood continued when Wilson reached France. In Paris, shouts of "Voodrow Veelson" rang out as he rode up the Champs-Élysées, the city's ceremonial boulevard. When Wilson visited England, children at the dock in Dover spread flowers in his path. In Italy an exuberant local official compared him to Jesus Christ.

The euphoria faded once the peace conference began at the palace of Versailles near Paris, where the treaty ending the Revolutionary War and granting American independence had been signed 136 years before. Joining Wilson were the other Allied heads of state: Italy's Vittorio Orlando; the aged and cynical Georges Clemenceau of France; and England's David Lloyd George, of whom Wilson said, "He is slippery as an eel, and I never know when to count on him." Japan participated in the conference as well.

The European statesmen at Versailles represented nations that had suffered greatly and were determined to avenge their losses. Their goals bore little relation to Wilson's liberal vision. As Clemenceau remarked, "God gave us the Ten Commandments and we broke them. Mr. Wilson has given us the Fourteen Points. We shall see."

Differences surfaced quickly. Orlando demanded a port for Italy on the eastern Adriatic Sea. Japan insisted on keeping the trading rights that it had seized from Germany in the Chinese province of Shandong (Shantung). Clemenceau was obsessed with revenge. At one point, an appalled Wilson threatened to leave the conference.

Reflecting this poisonous climate, the peace treaty forced upon a sullen German delegation on June 28, 1919, was harshly punitive. Germany was disarmed, stripped of its colonies, forced to admit sole blame for the war, and saddled with whopping reparation payments of $56 billion. France regained the provinces of Alsace and Lorraine lost to Germany in 1871 and took control for fifteen years of

Germany's coal-rich Saar Basin. The treaty demilitarized a zone of Germany thirty miles east of the Rhine and transferred a slice of eastern Germany to Poland. All told, Germany lost one-tenth of its population and one-eighth of its territory. The treaty granted Japan's Shandong claims and gave Italy a slice of Austria where two hundred thousand German-speaking inhabitants were then living. These harsh terms stirred bitter resentment in Germany, planting the seeds of a future, even more devastating, world war.

Wilson's theme of self-determination and democracy did influence some of the treaty's provisions. Germany's former colonies went to the various Allies under a "mandate" or trusteeship system that in theory would lead to eventual independence. The treaty also recognized the independence of Poland and the Baltic states of Estonia, Latvia, and Lithuania (territories that Germany had seized in its peace treaty with Bolshevik Russia in 1918). Separate treaties provided for the independence of two new nations carved from the old Austro-Hungarian and Ottoman empires: Czechoslovakia and Yugoslavia.

Palestine, a part of Turkey's collapsed Ottoman empire, went to Great Britain under a mandate arrangement. In 1917, after gaining military control of Palestine, the British had issued the Balfour Declaration supporting a Jewish "national home" in the region and also acknowledging the rights of the non-Jewish Palestinians.

But the treaty makers rejected the efforts of colonized peoples in Asia and Africa to throw off European rule. For example, Ho Chi Minh, a young Vietnamese nationalist who would later become head of his nation, visited Versailles in an unsuccessful effort to secure Vietnamese independence from France.

The framers of the Versailles Treaty and the other treaties shaping the postwar world made little effort to come to terms with revolutionary Russia. Indeed, in August 1918 a fourteen-nation Allied army, including some seven thousand U.S. troops, had landed at various Russian ports, ostensibly to protect Allied war materiel and secure the ports from German attack, but in fact to assist in efforts to overthrow the new Bolshevik regime, whose communist ideology and practice stirred deep fear in the capitals of Europe and America. Wilson, having welcomed the liberal Russian revolution of March 1917, viewed Lenin's coup that autumn and Russia's withdrawal from the war as a betrayal of the Allied cause and of his hopes for a democratic Russian future. The Versailles Treaty reflected this hostility. Its territorial settlements in eastern Europe were designed to weaken Russia. Before leaving Versailles, Wilson and the other Allied leaders agreed to support a Russian military leader who was still fighting the Bolsheviks. Not until 1933 did the United States recognize the Soviet Union.

The Fight over the League of Nations Dismayed by the treaty's vindictive features, Wilson focused on his one shining achievement at Versailles—the creation of a new international organization, the League of Nations. The agreement or "covenant" to establish the League, written into the peace treaty itself, embodied Wilson's vision of a liberal, harmonious, and peaceful world order.

But Wilson's dream would soon lie in ruins. A warning sign had come in February 1919 when thirty-nine Republican senators and senators-elect, including Henry Cabot Lodge, signed a letter rejecting the League in its present form. Wilson had retorted defiantly, "You cannot dissect the Covenant from the treaty without destroying the whole vital structure."

When Wilson sent the treaty to the Senate for ratification in July 1919, Lodge bottled it up in the Foreign Relations Committee. Furious at Lodge's tactics and convinced that he could rally popular opinion to his cause, Wilson left Washington on September 3 for a western speaking tour. Covering more than nine thousand miles by train, Wilson defended the League in thirty-seven speeches in twenty-two days. Crowds were large and friendly. People wept as Wilson described his visits to American war cemeteries in France and cheered his vision of a new world order.

But the grueling trip left Wilson exhausted. On September 25, he collapsed in Colorado. The train sped back to Washington, where Wilson suffered a devastating stroke on October 2. For a time, he lay near death. Despite a partial recovery, Wilson spent the rest of his term mostly in bed or in a wheelchair, a reclusive invalid, his mind clouded, his fragile emotions betraying him into vindictive actions and tearful outbursts. He broke with close advisers, refused to see the British ambassador, and dismissed Secretary of State Lansing, accusing him of disloyalty. In January 1920 his physician advised him to resign, but Wilson refused.

Wilson's first wife, Ellen, had died in 1914. His strong-willed second wife, Edith Galt, played a crucial behind-the-scenes role during these months. Fiercely guarding her incapacitated husband, she hid his condition from the public, controlled his access to information, and decided who could see him. Cabinet members, diplomats, and congressional leaders, even Vice President Thomas R. Marshall, were barred from the White House. When one political leader seeking a meeting urged Mrs. Wilson to consider "the welfare of the country," she snapped, "I am not thinking of the country now, I am thinking of my husband." Since Wilson remained alive and the Twenty-Fifth Amendment, dealing with issues of presidential disability, was not adopted until 1967, the impasse continued.

Under these trying circumstances, the League drama unfolded. On September 10, 1919, the Foreign Relations Committee at last sent the treaty to the Senate, but with a series of amendments. The Senate split into three groups: Democrats who supported the League covenant without changes; Republican "Irreconcilables," led by Hiram Johnson of California, Wisconsin's Robert La Follette, and Idaho's William Borah, who opposed the League absolutely; and Republican "Reservationists" led by Lodge, who demanded amendments to the League covenant as a condition of their support. The Reservationists especially objected to Article 10 of the covenant, which pledged each member nation to preserve the political independence and territorial integrity of all other members. This blank-check provision, the Reservationists believed, limited America's freedom of action in foreign affairs and infringed on Congress's constitutional right to declare war.

"Seein' Things"
(*Brooklyn Eagle,*
1919) *Supporters
of the League of
Nations believed that
the opponents exag-
gerated the threat to
U.S. sovereignty that
League membership
represented.*

Had Wilson accepted compromise, the Senate would probably have ratified the Versailles Treaty, bringing the United States into the League of Nations. But Wilson's illness aggravated his tendency toward rigidity. From his isolation in the White House, he instructed Senate Democrats to vote against the treaty with Lodge's reservations. Although international-law specialists believed that these reservations would not significantly weaken U.S. participation in the League, Wilson rejected them as "a knife thrust at the heart of the treaty."

Despite the positive responses to Wilson's speaking tour, the American people did not rally behind the League. The reactionary political mood that Wilson's own administration had helped create was not conducive to a grand gesture of political idealism. As the editor of *The Nation* magazine observed, "If [Wilson] loses his great fight for humanity, it will be because he was deliberately silent when freedom of speech and the right of conscience were struck down in America."

On November 19, 1919, pro-League Democrats obeying Wilson's instructions and anti-League Irreconcilables joined forces to defeat the Versailles Treaty with Lodge's reservations. A second vote the following March produced the same result. The United States would not join the League. A president elected amid high hopes in 1912, applauded when he called for war in 1917, and adulated when he arrived in Europe in 1918 lay isolated and sick, his leadership repudiated. What might have been Wilson's crowning triumph had turned to ashes.

**Racism and Red
Scare, 1919–1920**
The wartime spirit of "100 percent Americanism" left a bitter aftertaste. The years 1919–1920 saw new racial violence and fresh antiradical hysteria. Mobs in various parts

of the country lynched seventy-six blacks in 1919, the worst toll in fifteen years. The victims included ten veterans, several still in uniform. Some lynchings involved incredible brutality. In Omaha, Nebraska, a mob shot a black prisoner more than a thousand times, mutilated him, and hung his body in a busy intersection.

The bloodiest violence exploded in 1919 in Chicago, where the influx of southern blacks had pushed racial tension to a high level. On a hot July afternoon, whites at a Lake Michigan beach threw stones at a black youth swimming offshore. When he sank and drowned, black neighborhoods erupted in fury. A thirteen-day reign of terror followed as white and black marauders engaged in random attacks and arson. Black gangs stabbed an Italian peddler; white gangs pulled blacks from streetcars and shot or whipped them. Before an uneasy calm returned, the outbreak left fifteen whites and twenty-three blacks dead, over five hundred injured, and more than a thousand families, mostly black, homeless.

The wartime antiradical panic crested in a postwar Red Scare. (Communists were called "reds" because of the red flag favored by radical and revolutionary organizations, including the new Bolshevik regime in Russia.) Fears of "bolshevism" deepened when a rash of strikes broke out in 1919. When the IWW and other Seattle labor unions organized a general strike early that year, the mayor accused the strikers of seeking to "duplicate the anarchy of Russia" and called for federal troops to maintain public order. Anxiety crackled again in April, when various public officials received packages containing bombs. One blew off the hands of a senator's maid; another damaged the home of Attorney General A. Mitchell Palmer. When 350,000 steelworkers went on strike in September, mill owners broke the strike in part through newspaper ads describing the walkout as a Bolshevik plot engineered by "Red agitators."

The antiradical paranoia soon took political form. In November 1919 the House of Representatives refused to seat Milwaukee socialist Victor Berger because of his indictment under the Espionage Act. Milwaukee voters promptly reelected him, but the House stood firm. The New York legislature expelled several socialist members. The Justice Department set up a countersubversion division under young J. Edgar Hoover, future head of the Federal Bureau of Investigation, who ordered the arrest of hundreds of suspected communists and radicals. In December 1919 the government deported 249 Russian-born aliens, including radical Emma Goldman, a leader of the birth-control movement. The government's antiradical crusade won applause from the American Legion, a newly founded veterans' association, as well as the National Association of Manufacturers.

On January 2, 1920, in a dragnet coordinated by the Justice Department, federal marshals and local police raided the homes of suspected radicals and the headquarters of radical organizations in thirty-two cities. Without search warrants or arrest warrants, they took more than 4,000 persons into custody (some 550 were eventually deported) and seized papers and records. In Lynn, Massachusetts, police arrested a group of men and women meeting to plan a cooperative bakery. In Boston, police paraded arrested persons through the streets in handcuffs and chains and then confined them in crowded and unsanitary cells without formal charges or the right to post bail.

Attorney General Palmer, ambitious for higher office, coordinated these "Red raids." A Quaker who had compiled a reform record as a congressman, Palmer succumbed to the anticommunist hysteria. Defending his actions, Palmer later described the menace he believed the nation faced in 1919:

> The blaze of revolution was sweeping over every American institution of law and order . . . eating its way into the homes of the American workman, its sharp tongues of revolutionary heat . . . licking at the altars of the churches, leaping into the belfry of the school bell, crawling into the sacred corners of American homes, . . . burning up the foundations of society.

The Red Scare subsided as Palmer's lurid predictions failed to materialize. When a bomb exploded in New York City's financial district in September 1920, killing thirty-eight people, most Americans saw the deed as the work of an isolated fanatic, not evidence of approaching revolution.

The Election of 1920 In this unsettled climate, the election of 1920 approached. Wilson, out of touch with political reality, considered seeking a third term, but was persuaded otherwise. Treasury Secretary McAdoo and Attorney General Palmer harbored presidential hopes. But when the Democrats convened in San Francisco, the delegates sang "How Dry I Am" (prohibition had just taken effect), tepidly backed Wilson's League position, and nominated James M. Cox, the mildly progressive governor of Ohio. As Cox's running mate they chose the young assistant secretary of the navy, Franklin D. Roosevelt, who possessed a potent political name.

The confident Republicans, meeting in Chicago, nominated Senator Warren G. Harding of Ohio, an amiable politician whose principal qualification was his availability. As one Republican leader observed, "There ain't any first raters this year. . . . We got a lot of second raters, and Harding is the best of the second raters." For vice president, they chose Massachusetts governor Calvin Coolidge, who had won attention in 1919 with his denunciation of a Boston policemen's strike.

Wilson proclaimed the election a "solemn referendum" on the League, but a nation psychologically drained by the war and the emotional roller-coaster ride of the Wilson presidency ignored him. "The bitterness toward Wilson is everywhere . . .," wrote a Democratic campaign worker; "he hasn't a friend."

Harding, promising a return to "normalcy," delivered campaign speeches empty of content but vaguely reassuring. One critic described them as "an army of pompous phrases moving over the landscape in search of an idea." Whatever the shortcomings of his campaign, Harding piled up a landslide victory—16 million votes against 9 million for Cox. Nearly a million citizens defiantly voted for socialist Eugene Debs, who was behind bars in an Atlanta penitentiary.

"Convict No. 9653 for President"
Although socialist Eugene V. Debs was in prison in 1920, he still received over 900,000 votes for president.

The election dashed all hope for American entry into the League of Nations. During the campaign Harding had spoken vaguely of some form of "international organization," but once elected he bluntly declared the League question "dead." Senator Lodge, who had praised Wilson's idealistic war message so highly in 1917, now expressed grim pleasure that the voters had ripped "Wilsonism" up by the roots. The sense of national destiny and high purpose that Woodrow Wilson had evoked so eloquently in April 1917 survived only as an ironic memory as Americans impatiently turned to a new president and a new era.

IMPORTANT EVENTS, 1902–1920

1899 First U.S. Open Door note seeking access to China market.
Boxer Rebellion erupts in China.

1900 Second U.S. Open Door note.

1904 President Theodore Roosevelt proclaims "Roosevelt Corollary" to Monroe Doctrine.

1905 Roosevelt mediates the end of the Russo-Japanese War.

1906 At the request of Roosevelt, San Francisco ends segregation of Asian schoolchildren.
Panama Canal construction begins.

1911 U.S.-backed revolution in Nicaragua.

1912 U.S. Marines occupy Nicaragua.

1914 U.S. troops occupy Veracruz, Mexico.
Panama Canal opens.
World War I begins; President Wilson proclaims American
neutrality.

1915 U.S. Marines occupy Haiti and the Dominican Republic.
Woman's Peace party organized.
British liner *Lusitania* sunk by German U-boat.
Wilson permits U.S. bank loans to Allies.

1916 U.S. punitive expedition invades Mexico, seeking Pancho Villa.
Germany pledges not to attack merchant ships without warning.
Wilson reelected.

1917 U.S. troops withdraw from Mexico.
Germany resumes unrestricted U-boat warfare; United States declares war.
Selective Service Act sets up national draft.
War Industries Board, Committee on Public Information, and Food
Administration created.
Espionage Act passed.
War Risk Insurance Act authorizes payments to servicemen's dependents.
NAACP march in New York City protests upsurge in lynchings.
Bolsheviks seize power in Russia; Russia leaves the war.
New York State passes woman-suffrage referendum.
U.S. government operates the nation's railroads.

1918 Wilson outlines Fourteen Points.
Sedition Amendment passed.
Influenza epidemic sweeps nation.
National War Labor Board created.
American forces see action at Château-Thierry, Belleau Wood,
St. Mihiel, and Meuse-Argonne campaign.
Republicans win control of both houses of Congress (November 5).
Armistice signed (November 11).

1919 Eighteenth Amendment added to the Constitution (prohibition).
Peace treaty, including League of Nations covenant, signed at
Versailles.
Supreme Court upholds silencing of war critics in *Schenck* v. *U.S.*
Racial violence in Chicago.
Wilson suffers paralyzing stroke.
Versailles Treaty, with League covenant, rejected by Senate.

1920 "Red raids" organized by Justice Department.
Nineteenth Amendment added to the Constitution (woman suffrage).
Warren G. Harding elected president.

23

The 1920s: Coping with Change, 1920–1929

Sam Groipen of Medford, Massachusetts, was washing the windows of his grocery store, the Cooperative Cash Market, in June 1928 when a meat truck pulled up in front of the A&P supermarket next door. Sam knew the meaning of this seemingly ordinary event: his days as an independent grocer were numbered. A Russian-Jewish immigrant, Sam had opened his market in 1923, the year that he married. At first Sam and his wife did well. Sam served the customers; his wife kept the books. They knew their patrons by name and extended credit to neighbors short on cash.

In 1925, however, the chain stores came. A&P moved in next door, then First National and Stop & Shop across the street. Small by today's standards, the chain stores at first carried only brand-name groceries, not meat or fish. But the A&P added meat and fish in 1928. Sam watched as former customers who still owed him money walked past his door on their way to a supermarket. "I felt like I was being strangled," he later recalled; "those bastard chains were destroying me."

In 1935 Sam Groipen sold out. Abandoning his dream of prospering as an independent businessman, he joined the giant Prudential Life Insurance Company. Eventually, Sam's bitterness toward the chains softened. "I have been mellowed by the system," he reflected.

Groipen's experience paralleled that of many independent entrepreneurs in the 1920s, as corporate consolidation, new techniques of mass marketing, and rising consumer expectations transformed American society. In the 1920s, too, the nation's vast industrial capacity produced a tidal wave of automobiles, radios, electrical appliances, and other consumer goods. This stimulated the economy and transformed the lives of ordinary Americans. Ingrained patterns of diet, dress, travel, entertainment, and even thought changed rapidly as the economic order evolved.

These technological changes, following decades of immigration and urban growth, spawned social tensions. While Republican presidents espoused conservative political and cultural values, conflicts ripped at the social fabric. But this same ferment also stimulated creativity in literature and the arts.

In the 1920s many features of contemporary American life first became clearly evident. Indeed, in some ways the decade marks the dawn of the modern era. This chapter explores how different groups of Americans responded to technological, social, and cultural changes that could be both intensely exciting and deeply threatening.

This chapter focuses on five major questions:

What economic developments underlay American prosperity of the 1920s, and how did those developments affect different social groups?

What political values shaped public life in this era of Republican ascendancy? How did Herbert Hoover's social and political thought differ from that of Presidents Harding and Coolidge?

How did the Republican administrations of the 1920s promote U.S. economic interests abroad?

What is meant by "mass culture"? What forces helped create a mass culture in the 1920s, and how thoroughly did it penetrate U.S. society?

The 1920s saw both cultural creativity and social tensions. What developments in American society in these years contributed to both the creativity and the tensions?

A NEW ECONOMIC ORDER

Fueled by new consumer products, innovative corporate structures, and new methods of producing and selling goods, the economy surged in the 1920s. Not everyone benefited, and farmers in particular suffered chronic economic woes. Still, the overall picture seemed rosy. As we shall see in later sections, these economic changes influenced the political, social, and cultural climate of the decade, as Americans struggled to cope with a society that was changing with breathtaking rapidity.

Booming Business, Ailing Agriculture A sharp recession struck in 1920 after the government canceled wartime defense contracts and returning veterans reentered the job market. Recovery came in 1922, however, and for the next few years the industrial sector of the economy hummed. Unemployment fell to as low as 3 percent, prices held steady, and the gross national product (GNP) grew by 43 percent from 1922 to 1929.

New consumer goods, including home electrical products, contributed to the prosperity. Many factories were already electrified, but now the age of electricity dawned for urban households as well. By the mid-1920s, with more than 60 percent of the nation's homes electrified, a parade of appliances, from refrigerators, washing machines, and vacuum cleaners to fans, razors, and mixers, crowded the stores. The manufacture of such appliances, as well as of hydroelectric generating plants and equipment for the electrical industry itself, provided a massive economic stimulus.

The 1920s business boom rested, too, on the automobile. Already well established before World War I (see Chapter 21), the automobile in the 1920s fully came

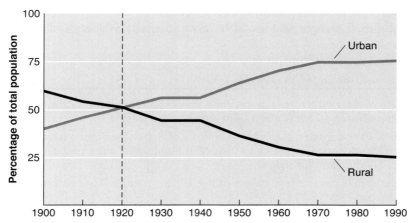

The Urban and Rural Population of the United States, 1900–2000

The urbanization of America in the twentieth century had profound political, economic, and social consequences.

Source: Theodore Caplow, Louis Hicks, Ben J. Wattenburg, *The First Measured Century: An Illustrated Guide to Trends in America, 1900–2000.* Reprinted with permission of the American Enterprise Institute for Public Policy Research, Washington, D.C.

into its own. Registrations jumped from about 8 million in 1920 to more than 23 million in 1930, by which time some 60 percent of U.S. families owned cars. The Ford Motor Company led the market until mid-decade, when General Motors (GM) spurted ahead by touting a range of colors (Ford's Model T came only in black) and greater comfort. GM's lowest-priced car, named for French automotive designer Louis Chevrolet, proved especially popular. Meeting the challenge, in 1927 Ford introduced the stylish Model A in various colors. By the end of the decade, the automobile industry accounted for about 9 percent of all wages in manufacturing and had stimulated such related industries as rubber, gasoline and motor oil, advertising, and highway construction.

Rising stock-market prices reflected the prevailing prosperity. As the stock market surged ever higher, a speculative frenzy gripped Wall Street. By 1929 the market had reached wholly unrealistic levels, creating conditions for a catastrophic collapse (see Chapter 24).

The business boom also stimulated capitalist expansion abroad. To supply overseas markets, Ford, GM, and other big corporations built production facilities abroad. Other U.S. firms acquired foreign factories or sources of raw materials. U.S. meatpackers built plants in Argentina; Anaconda Copper acquired Chile's biggest copper mine; and the mammoth United Fruit Company established processing plants across Latin America. Capital also flowed to Europe, especially Germany, as U.S. investors loaned European nations money to repay war debts and modernize their economies. U.S. private investment abroad increased nearly five-fold between 1914 and 1930.

But the era of a truly global economy still lay far in the future. Economic nationalism prevailed in the 1920s, as the industrialized nations, including the United States, erected high tariff barriers. The Fordney-McCumber Tariff (1922) and Smoot-Hawley Tariff (1930) pushed U.S. import duties to all-time highs, benefiting domestic manufacturers but stifling foreign trade. As a percentage of the GNP, U.S. exports actually fell between 1913 and 1929. Yet change was underway as U.S. industry retooled for mass production. Manufactured goods, less than half the value of total U.S. exports in 1913, rose to 61 percent of the total by the end of the 1920s.

While overall wage rates rose amid the general prosperity of the 1920s, workers benefited unequally, reflecting regional variations as well as discriminatory patterns rooted in stereotypes and prejudices. Of the regional variations, the one between North and South loomed largest. In 1928 the average unskilled laborer in New England earned forty-seven cents an hour, in contrast to twenty-eight cents in the South. Many textile corporations moved south in search of lower wage rates, devastating New England mill towns. Women workers, blacks, Mexican-Americans, and recent immigrants clustered at the bottom of the wage scale. African-American workers, many of them recent migrants from the rural South, faced special difficulties. "Last hired and first fired," they generally performed the most menial unskilled jobs.

Farmers did not share in the boom; for them, wartime prosperity gave way to hard times. Grain prices plummeted when government purchases for the army dwindled, European agriculture revived, and America's high protective tariff depressed agricultural exports. From 1919 to 1921, farm income fell by some 60 percent, and, unlike the industrial sector, it did not bounce back. When farmers compensated by increasing production, the result was large surpluses and still weaker prices. Farmers who had borrowed heavily to buy land and equipment during the war now felt the squeeze as payments came due.

New Modes of Producing, Managing, and Selling

Building on the industrial feats of the war years, the 1920s saw striking increases in productivity. New assembly-line techniques boosted the per capita output of industrial workers by some 40 percent during this decade. At the sprawling Ford plants near Detroit, workers stood in one place and performed repetitive tasks as chains conveyed the partly assembled vehicles past them.

Assembly-line production influenced industrial employees' view of their work and themselves. Managers discouraged expressions of individuality; even talking or laughter could divert workers from their repetitive task. Ford employees learned to speak without moving their lips and adopted an expressionless mask that some called "Fordization of the face." As work became more routine, its psychic rewards diminished. The assembly line did not foster pride in the skills that came from years of farming or mastering a craft. Nor did assembly-line labor offer much prospect of advancement. In Muncie, Indiana, factories employing over four thousand workers announced only ten openings for foremen in 1924 and 1925.

Nevertheless, the new mass-production methods had a revolutionary impact. *Fordism* became a synonym worldwide for American industrial might and assembly-line methods. In the Soviet Union, which purchased twenty-five thousand Ford tractors in the 1920s, the people "ascribed a magical quality to the name of Ford," a 1927 visitor reported.

Business consolidation, spurred by the war, continued. By the late 1920s, over a thousand companies a year vanished through merger. Corporate giants dominated the major industries: Ford, GM, and Chrysler in automobiles; General Electric and Westinghouse in electricity; and so forth. Among public-utilities companies, consolidation became epidemic. Samuel Insull of the Chicago Edison Company, for example, built a multi-billion-dollar empire of local power companies. By 1930 one hundred corporations controlled nearly half the nation's business. Without actually merging, companies that made the same product often cooperated through trade associations on such matters as pricing, product specifications, and division of markets.

As U.S. capitalism matured, more elaborate management structures arose. Giant corporations set up separate divisions for product development, market research, economic forecasting, employee relations, and so forth. Day-to-day oversight of these highly complex corporate operations increasingly fell to professional managers.

The modernization of business affected wage policies. Rejecting the old view that employers should pay the lowest wages possible, business leaders now concluded that higher wages would improve productivity and increase consumer buying power. Henry Ford had led the way in 1914 by paying his workers five dollars a day, well above the average for factory workers. Other companies soon followed his lead.

New systems for distributing goods emerged as well. Automobiles reached consumers through vast dealer networks. By 1926 the number of Ford dealerships approached ten thousand. Chain stores accounted for about a quarter of all retail sales by 1930. The A&P grocery chain, which caused Sam Groipen such grief in Medford, Massachusetts, boasted 17,500 stores by 1928. Department stores grew more inviting, with attractive display windows, remodeled interiors, and a larger array of goods. Air conditioning, an invention of the early twentieth century, made department stores (as well as movie theaters and restaurants) welcome havens on hot summer days.

Above all, the 1920s business boom bobbed along on a frothy sea of advertising. In 1929 corporations spent nearly $2 billion promoting their wares via radio, billboards, newspapers, and magazines, and the advertising business employed some six hundred thousand people. Advertising barons ranked among the corporate elite. Chicago ad man Albert Lasker owned the Chicago Cubs baseball team and his own golf course. As they still do, the advertisers in the twenties used celebrity endorsements ("Nine out of ten screen stars care for their skin with Lux toilet soap"), promises of social success, and threats of social embarrassment. Beneath a picture of a sad young woman, for example, a Listerine mouthwash ad proclaimed: "She was a beautiful girl and talented too. . . . Yet in the one pursuit that stands foremost in the mind of every girl and woman—marriage—she was a failure." The young woman's problem was "halitosis," or bad breath. The remedy, of course, was Listerine, and lots of it.

Advertisers offered a seductive vision of the new era of abundance. Portraying a fantasy world of elegance, grace, and boundless pleasure, ads aroused desires that the new consumer-oriented capitalist system happily fulfilled. As one critic wrote in 1925,

> [W]hen all is said and done, advertising . . . creates a dream world: smiling faces, shining teeth, schoolgirl complexions, cornless feet, perfect fitting [underwear], distinguished collars, wrinkleless pants, odorless breath, regularized bowels, . . . charging motors, punctureless tires, perfect busts, shimmering shanks, self-washing dishes, backs behind which the moon was meant to rise.

Americans of the 1920s increasingly bought major purchases on credit. In earlier days credit had typically involved pawnbrokers, personal loans, or informal arrangements between buyers and sellers. Now consumer credit was rationalized as retailers offered installment plans with fixed payment schedules. But while today's consumers use credit cards for all kinds of purchases, from restaurant meals to video rentals, credit buying in the 1920s involved mostly big-ticket items such as automobiles, furniture, and refrigerators. By 1929 credit purchases accounted for 75 percent of automobile sales.

Business values saturated the culture. As the *Independent* magazine put it in 1921: "America stands for one idea: Business. . . . Thru business, properly conceived, managed, and conducted, the human race is finally to be redeemed." Presidents Harding and Coolidge praised American business and hobnobbed with businessmen. Magazines profiled corporate leaders. A 1923 opinion poll ranked Henry Ford as a leading presidential prospect. In *The Man Nobody Knows* (1925), ad man Bruce Barton described Jesus Christ as a managerial genius who "picked up twelve men from the bottom ranks of business and forged them into an organization that conquered the world." In *Middletown* (1929), a study of Muncie, Indiana, sociologists Robert and Helen Lynd observed, "More and more of the activities of life are coming to be strained through the bars of the dollar sign."

Women in the New Economic Era
In the decade's advertising, glamorous women smiled behind the steering wheel, operated their new appliances, and smoked cigarettes in romantic settings. (One ad man promoted cigarettes for women as "torches of freedom.") The cosmetics industry flourished, offering women (in the words of historian Kathy Peiss) "hope in a jar." In the advertisers' dream world, housework became an exciting challenge. As one ad put it, "Men are judged . . . according to their power to delegate work. Similarly the wise woman delegates to electricity all that electricity can do."

As for women in the workplace, the assembly line, involving physically less-demanding work, theoretically should have increased job opportunities. In fact, however, male workers dominated the auto plants and other assembly-line factories. Although the ranks of working women increased by more than 2 million in the 1920s, their number as a proportion of the total female population hardly changed, hovering at about 24 percent.

Women workers faced wage discrimination. In 1929, for example, a male trimmer in the meatpacking industry received fifty-two cents an hour, a female trimmer, thirty-seven cents. The weakening of the union movement in the 1920s hit women workers hard. By 1929 the proportion of women workers belonging to unions fell to a minuscule 3 percent.

Many women found work in corporate offices. By 1930 some 2 million women were working as secretaries, typists, or filing clerks. Few women entered the managerial ranks, however. Indeed, office space was arranged to draw clear gender distinctions between male managers and female clerks. Nor did the professions welcome women. With medical schools imposing a 5 percent quota on female admissions, the number of women physicians actually declined from 1910 to 1930.

The proportion of female high-school graduates going on to college edged upward, however, reaching 12 percent by 1930. Nearly fifty thousand women received college degrees that year, almost triple the 1920 figure. Despite the hurdles, more college women combined marriage and career. Most took clerical jobs or entered traditional "women's professions" such as nursing, library work, social work, and teaching. A handful, however, followed the lead of Progressive Era feminist trailblazers to become faculty members in colleges and universities.

Struggling Labor Unions in a Business Age Organized labor faced tough sledding in the 1920s. Union membership fell from 5 million in 1920 to 3.4 million in 1929. Several factors underlay this decline. For one thing, despite various inequities and regional variations, overall wage rates climbed steadily in the decade, reducing the incentive to join a union. Industrial changes played a role as well. The trade unions' strength lay in established industries like printing, railroading, coal mining, and construction. These older craft-based unions were ill suited to the new mass-production factories.

Management hostility further weakened organized labor. Henry Ford hired thugs to intimidate union organizers. In Marion, North Carolina, deputy sheriffs shot and killed six striking textile workers. Violence also marked a 1929 strike in Gastonia, North Carolina, by the communist-led National Textile Workers Union. When armed thugs in league with the mill owners invaded union headquarters, the police chief was shot. Strike leader Ella May Wiggins was killed by a bullet fired at a truck on the way to a union rally.

The anti-union campaign took subtler forms as well. Manufacturers' associations renamed the nonunion shop the "open shop" and dubbed it the "American Plan" of labor relations. Some firms set up employee associations and provided cafeterias and recreational facilities for workers. A few big corporations such as U.S. Steel sold company stock to their workers at bargain prices. Some publicists praised "welfare capitalism" (the term for this new approach to labor relations) as

Gastonia, North Carolina, 1929 *Two women textile workers confront an armed guard in a bitter strike that took several lives.*

evidence of corporations' heightened ethical awareness. In reality, it mainly reflected management's desire to kill off independent unions.

By 1929 black membership in labor unions stood at only about eighty-two thousand, most of whom were longshoremen, miners, and railroad porters. The American Federation of Labor officially prohibited racial discrimination, but most AFL unions in fact barred African-Americans. Corporations often hired blacks as strikebreakers, increasing organized labor's hostility toward them. Black strikebreakers, denounced as "scabs," took such work only because they had to. As a jobless black character says in Claude McKay's 1929 novel *Home to Harlem,* "I got to live, and I'll scab through hell to live."

THE HARDING AND COOLIDGE ADMINISTRATIONS

With Republicans in control of Congress and the White House, politics in the 1920s reflected the decade's business orientation. Reacting to the unsettling pace of social change, many voters turned to conservative candidates who seemed to represent stability and traditional values. In this climate, former progressives, would-be reformers, and groups excluded from the prevailing prosperity had few political options.

Stand Pat Politics in a Decade of Change   In the 1920s the Republican party continued to attract northern farmers, corporate leaders, businesspeople, native-born white-collar workers and professionals, and some skilled blue-collar workers. The Democrats' base remained the white South and the immigrant cities.

With Republican progressives having bolted to Theodore Roosevelt in 1912, GOP conservatives controlled the 1920 convention and nominated Senator Warren G. Harding of Marion, Ohio, for president. A struggling newspaper editor, Harding had married the local banker's daughter, who helped manage his election to the Senate in 1915. A genial backslapper, he enjoyed good liquor, a good poker game, and occasional trysts with his mistress, Nan Britton. This amiable mediocrity overwhelmed his Democratic opponent James M. Cox. After the stresses of war and Wilson's lofty moralizing, Harding's blandness and empty oratory had a soothing appeal.

Harding made some notable cabinet selections: Henry C. Wallace, the editor of an Iowa farm periodical, as secretary of agriculture; Charles Evans Hughes, former New York governor and 1916 presidential candidate, secretary of state; and Andrew W. Mellon, a Pittsburgh financier, treasury secretary. Herbert Hoover, the wartime food czar, dominated the cabinet as secretary of commerce.

Harding also made some disastrous appointments: his political manager, Harry Daugherty, as attorney general; a Senate pal, Albert Fall of New Mexico, as secretary of the interior; a wartime draft dodger, Charles Forbes, as Veterans' Bureau head. These men set the sleazy and corrupt tone of the Harding presidency. By 1922 Washington rumor hinted at criminal activity in high places, and Harding confessed to a friend, "I have no trouble with my enemies. . . . But . . . my goddamn friends . . . keep me walking the floor nights." In July 1923, vacationing in the West, Harding suffered a heart attack; on August 2 he died in a San Francisco hotel.

In 1924 a Senate investigation pushed by Democratic Senator Thomas J. Walsh of Montana exposed the full scope of the scandals. Charles Forbes, convicted of stealing Veterans' Bureau funds, evaded prison by fleeing abroad. The bureau's general counsel committed suicide, as did an aide to Attorney General Daugherty accused of influence peddling. Daugherty himself narrowly escaped conviction in two criminal trials. Interior Secretary Fall went to jail for leasing government oil reserves, one in Teapot Dome, Wyoming, to two oilmen in return for a $400,000 bribe. Like "Watergate" in the 1970s, "Teapot Dome" became a shorthand label for a tangle of presidential scandals.

With Harding's death, Vice President Calvin Coolidge, on a family visit in Vermont, took the presidential oath by lantern light from his father, a local magistrate. A painfully shy youth, Coolidge had attended Amherst College in Massachusetts, where he struggled to eliminate all rural traces from his speech. Whereas Harding was outgoing and talkative, Coolidge's taciturnity became legendary. As he left California after a visit, a radio reporter asked for a parting message to the state. "Good-bye," Coolidge responded. Coolidge's appeal for old-stock

Americans in an era of rapid social change has been summed up by historian John D. Hicks: "They understood his small-town cracker-barrel philosophy, they believed in his honesty, and they tended to have the same respect he had for the big business leaders who had known how to get on in the world."

Republican Policy Making in a Probusiness Era The moral tone of the White House improved under Coolidge, but the probusiness climate, symbolized by the high tariffs of these years, persisted. Prodded by Treasury Secretary Andrew Mellon, Congress lowered income taxes and inheritance taxes for the wealthy. Mellon embraced what later came to be called the "trickle down" theory, which held that tax cuts for the wealthy would promote business investment, stimulate the economy, and thus benefit everyone. (Mellon did, however, resist pressure from rich Americans eager to abolish the income tax altogether. Such a step, he warned, would build support for socialists and other left-wing radicals.) In the same probusiness spirit, the Supreme Court under Chief Justice William Howard Taft, who was appointed by Harding in 1921, overturned several reform measures opposed by business, including a federal anti-child-labor law passed in 1919.

While eager to promote corporate interests, Coolidge opposed government assistance for other groups. His position faced a severe test in 1927 when torrential spring rains throughout the Mississippi River watershed sent a massive wall of water crashing downstream. Soil erosion caused by decades of poor farming practices worsened the flood conditions, as did ill-planned engineering projects aimed at holding the river within bounds and reclaiming its natural floodplain for development purposes. One official described the river as "writh[ing] like an imprisoned snake" within its artificial confines. From Cairo, Illinois, to the Gulf, the water poured over towns and farms, inundating twenty-seven thousand square miles in Illinois, Tennessee, Arkansas, Mississippi, and Louisiana. It is estimated that more than a thousand people died, and the refugee toll, including many African-Americans, reached several hundred thousand. Disease spread in makeshift refugee camps.

Despite the scope of the catastrophe, Coolidge rejected calls for government aid to the flood victims, and even ignored pleas from local officials to visit the flooded regions. The government had no duty to protect citizens "against the hazards of the elements," he declared primly. (Coolidge did, however, reluctantly sign the Flood Control Act of 1928 and appropriate $325 million for a ten-year program to construct levees along the Mississippi.)

Further evidence of Coolidge's views came when hard-pressed farmers rallied behind the McNary-Haugen bill, a price-support plan under which the government would annually purchase the surplus of six basic farm commodities—cotton, corn, rice, hogs, tobacco, and wheat—at their average price in 1909–1914 (when farm prices were high). The government would then sell these surpluses abroad at prevailing prices and make up any resulting losses through a tax on domestic sales of these commodities. Congress passed the McNary-Haugen bill in

1927 and 1928, but Coolidge vetoed it both times, warning of "the tyranny of bureaucratic regulation and control." The measure would help farmers at the expense of the general public, he went on, ignoring the fact that business had long benefited from high tariffs and other special-interest measures. These vetoes led many angry farmers to abandon their traditional Republican ties and vote Democratic in 1928.

Independent Internationalism
Although U.S. officials participated informally in some League of Nations activities in the 1920s, the United States refused to join the League or its International Court of Justice (the World Court) in the Netherlands. Despite isolationist tendencies, however, the United States remained a world power, and the Republican administrations of these years pursued global policies that they believed to be in America's national interest—an approach historians have called independent internationalism.

President Harding's most notable achievement was the Washington Naval Arms Conference. After the war ended in 1918, the United States, Great Britain, and Japan edged toward a dangerous (and costly) naval-arms race. In 1921 Harding called for a conference to address the problem. When the delegates gathered in Washington, Secretary of State Hughes startled them by proposing a specific ratio of ships among the world's naval powers. In February 1922 the three nations, together with Italy and France, pledged to reduce their battleship tonnage by specified amounts and to halt all battleship construction for ten years. The United States and Japan also agreed to respect each other's territorial holdings in the Pacific. Although this treaty ultimately failed to prevent war, it did represent an early arms-control effort.

Another U.S. peace initiative was mainly symbolic and accomplished little. In 1928 the United States and France, eventually joined by sixty other nations, signed the Kellogg-Briand Pact renouncing aggression and calling for the outlawing of war. Lacking any enforcement mechanism, this high-sounding document did nothing to prevent World War II.

The Republican administrations of these years actively used international diplomacy to promote U.S. economic interests. The government, for example, vigorously sought repayment of the $22 billion it claimed the Allies owed in war debts and Germany owed in reparation payments. A joint study commission in 1924 sharply reduced these claims, but high U.S. tariffs and economic problems in Europe, including runaway inflation in Germany, made repayment of even the reduced claims unrealistic. When Adolf Hitler rose to power in Germany in 1933 (see Chapter 25), he repudiated all reparations payments.

With U.S. foreign investments expanding, the government worked to advance American business interests abroad. For example, the Harding and Coolidge administrations opposed the Mexican government's efforts to reclaim title to oilfields earlier granted to U.S. companies. In 1927 Coolidge appointed Dwight Morrow, a New York banker, to negotiate the issue with Mexico, but the talks collapsed in 1928 when Mexico's president was assassinated. Complicating U.S.-

Mexican relations was Washington's fear that Mexico, gripped by revolutionary upheaval, might go communist. These fears deepened in 1924 when Mexico recognized the Soviet Union, nine years before the United States took the same step.

Progressive
Stirrings,
Democratic
Party Divisions

The reform spirit survived feebly in the legislative branch. Congress staved off Andrew Mellon's proposals for even deeper tax cuts for the rich. Senator George Norris of Nebraska prevented the Coolidge administration from selling a federal hydroelectric facility at Muscle Shoals, Alabama, to automaker Henry Ford at bargain prices. And in 1927 Congress created the Federal Radio Commission, extending the regulatory principle to this new industry.

In 1922, a midterm election year, labor and farm groups formed the Conference for Progressive Political Action (CPPA), which helped defeat some conservative Republicans. In 1924 CPPA delegates revived the Progressive party and nominated Senator Robert La Follette for president. The Socialist party and the American Federation of Labor endorsed La Follette.

The Democrats, split between urban and rural wings, met in New York City for their 1924 convention. By one vote, the delegates defeated a resolution condemning the Ku Klux Klan (see below). While the party's rural, Protestant, southern wing favored former Treasury Secretary William G. McAdoo for president, the big-city delegates rallied behind Governor Alfred E. Smith of New York, a Roman Catholic of Irish, German, and Italian immigrant origins. The split in the Democratic party mirrored deep divisions in the nation. After 102 ballots, the exhausted delegates gave up and nominated an obscure New York corporation lawyer, John W. Davis.

Calvin Coolidge easily won the Republican nomination. The Republican platform praised the high Fordney-McCumber Tariff and urged tax and spending cuts. With the economy humming, Coolidge polled nearly 16 million votes, about twice Davis's total. La Follette's 4.8 million votes on the Progressive party ticket cut into the Democratic total, contributing to the Coolidge landslide.

Women and
Politics in the
1920s: A Dream
Deferred

Suffragists' hope that votes for women would transform politics survived briefly after the war. The 1920 major-party platforms endorsed several measures proposed by the League of Women Voters. Polling places shifted from saloons to schools and churches as politics ceased to be an exclusively male pursuit. A coalition of women's groups called the Women's Joint Congressional Committee lobbied for child-labor laws, protection of women workers, and federal support for education. It also backed the Sheppard-Towner Act (1921), which funded rural prenatal and baby-care centers staffed by public-health nurses. Overall, however, the Nineteenth Amendment had little political effect. Women who had joined forces to work for suffrage now scattered across the political spectrum or withdrew from politics altogether.

As the women's movement splintered, it lost focus. The League of Women Voters, drawing middle-class and professional women, abandoned activism for "nonpartisan" studies of civic issues. Alice Paul's National Woman's party proposed an equal-rights amendment to the Constitution, but other reformers argued that such an amendment could jeopardize gender-based laws protecting women workers. The reactionary and materialistic climate of the 1920s underlay this disarray. Jane Addams and other women's-rights leaders faced accusations of communist sympathies. Women of the younger generation, bombarded by ads that defined liberation in terms of consumption, rejected the prewar feminists' civic idealism. One young woman in 1927 ridiculed "the old school of fighting feminists" for their lack of "feminine charm" and their "constant clamor about equal rights."

The few reforms achieved by women's groups often proved short-lived. The Supreme Court struck down child-labor laws in 1922 and women's protective laws in 1923. A 1924 child-labor constitutional amendment passed Congress after heavy lobbying by women's organizations, but few states ratified it. The Sheppard-Towner rural-health-care act, denounced by the American Medical Association as a threat to physicians' monopoly of the health business, expired in 1929.

Mass Society, Mass Culture

The torrent of new consumer products, together with the growth of advertising, innovations in corporate organization, assembly-line manufacturing, and new modes of mass entertainment, signaled profound changes in American life. Taken together, these changes infused the decade with an aura of modernity that some found tremendously exciting and others deeply disorienting.

Cities, Cars, Consumer Goods   In the 1920 census, for the first time, the urban population (defined as persons living in communities of twenty-five hundred or more) surpassed the rural. The United States had become an urban nation.

Urbanization affected different groups of Americans in different ways. African-Americans, for example, migrated cityward in massive numbers, especially after the terrible 1927 Mississippi River floods. By 1930 more than 40 percent of the nation's 12 million blacks lived in cities, 2 million of them in Chicago, Detroit, New York, and other metropolitan centers of the North and West. The first black congressman since Reconstruction, Oscar De Priest, won election in 1928 from Chicago's South Side.

For women, city life meant electric and gas appliances that reduced household labor. When the Lynds interviewed working-class women in Muncie in 1925, nearly 75 percent reported spending less time on housework than had their mothers. Vacuum cleaners supplanted brooms and dustpans. Wood-burning kitchen stoves became a memory. Store-bought clothes replaced homemade apparel. Electric refrigerators replaced labor-intensive iceboxes. The electric washing machine and electric iron lightened wash-day labor.

The African-American Urban Population, 1880–1960 (in millions)

The increase in America's urban black population from under one million in 1880 to nearly fourteen million by 1960 represents one of the great rural-urban migrations of modern history.

Source: Historical Statistics of the United States, Colonial Times to 1970 (Washington, D.C.: Bureau of the Census, 1975), vol. I, p. 12.

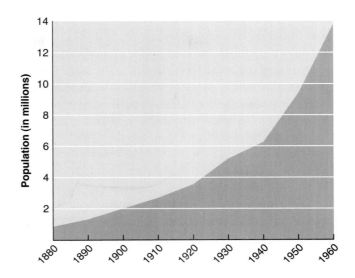

Food preparation and diet shifted in response to urbanization and technological changes. The availability of canned fruit and vegetables undermined the annual ritual of canning. Home baking declined with the rise of commercial bakeries. With refrigeration, supermarkets, and motor transport, fresh fruits, vegetables, and salads became available year-round.

For social impact, however, nothing matched the automobile. A Muncie resident challenged the Lynds, "Why . . . do you need to study what's changing this country? I can tell you . . . in just four letters: A-U-T-O."

Any effort to assess the A-U-T-O's social impact produces a decidedly mixed balance sheet. With increased mobility came new headaches. Traffic jams, parking problems, and highway fatalities (more than twenty-six thousand in 1924) attracted worried comment. In some ways, the automobile brought families together. Family vacations, rare a generation earlier, became more common. Tourist cabins and roadside restaurants served vacationing families. But in other respects, the automobile eroded family cohesion and parental authority. Young people could borrow the car to go to the movies, attend a dance miles from home, or simply park in a secluded "lover's lane."

Women of the middle and upper classes welcomed the automobile enthusiastically. They used the car to drive to work; run errands; attend meetings; visit friends; and, in the words of historian Virginia Scharff, simply to get out of the house and explore "new possibilities for excitement, for leisure and for sociability." Stereotypes of feminine delicacy and timidity faded as women demonstrated confident mastery of this new technology. As the editor of an automotive magazine wrote in 1927, "[E]very time a woman learns to drive—and thousands do every year—it is a threat at yesterday's order of things."

For farm families, the automobile offered easier access to neighbors and to the city, lessening the isolation of rural life. The automobile's country cousin, the tractor, proved instantly popular, with nearly a million in use in America by 1930, increasing productivity and reducing the heavy physical demands of farm labor. As farmers bought automobiles, tractors, and other mechanized equipment on credit, however, the rural debt crisis worsened.

Automobile ads celebrated the freedom of the open road, and indeed car owners, unlike train or streetcar passengers, could travel when and where they wished. Yet the automobile and other forms of motor transport in many ways further standardized American life. One-room schoolhouses stood empty as buses carried children to consolidated schools. Neighborhood grocery stores declined as people drove to supermarkets. With the automobile came the first suburban department stores, the first shopping center (in Kansas City), and the first fast-food chain (A & W Root Beer).

Even at $300 or $400, however, and despite a thriving used-car market, the automobile remained too expensive for many. The "automobile suburbs" that sprang up beyond the streetcar lines attracted mainly the prosperous. The urban poor remained behind, widening class divisions in American society. However one

Three Young Mexican-American Women of Tucson, Arizona *The spread of automobile culture in the early twentieth century gave a new freedom and mobility to many women, particularly the young and urban.*

assessed the automobile's social effects, one thing was certain: American life would never be the same.

Soaring Energy Consumption and a Threatened Environment

Electrification and the spread of motorized vehicles had implications for the nation's natural resources and for the environment. As electrical use more than tripled in the 1920s, generating plants consumed growing quantities of coal, oil, and natural gas. In 1929, with 20 million cars on the road, U.S. refineries used over a billion barrels of crude oil to meet the demand for gasoline.

Rising gasoline consumption underlay Washington's efforts to ensure U.S. access to Mexican oil; played a role in the Teapot Dome scandal; and triggered fevered activity in the oilfields of Texas and Oklahoma. As wildcatters made and lost fortunes, corporate giants like Standard, Texaco, and Gulf solidified their dominance of the industry. The natural gas found with petroleum seemed so abundant that much of it was simply burned off. In short, the profligate consumption of fossil fuels, though small by later standards and not yet recognized as a problem, already characterized American society by the 1920s.

The wilderness that had inspired nineteenth-century Americans became more accessible as the automobile, improved roads, and tourist facilities opened the national parks and once-pristine regions to easy access. Vacationing city dwellers—along with thousands of other motorized tourists—rediscovered the land. For the first time, millions of Americans came to view natural settings as places of recreation and leisure rather than of labor.

As with other technological and social changes of the time, this development had mixed effects. On the one hand, easier access to the wilderness democratized the environmental movement, creating a broad constituency for the cause of preservation. On the other hand, it subjected the areas to heavy pressures as more tourists arrived, expecting good highways, service stations, restaurants, and hotels. The problem of heavy auto tourism in the nation's parks and wilderness areas would grow more urgent in future decades.

These developments worried Secretary of Commerce Herbert Hoover. Hoover believed that urban dwellers benefited from periodically escaping the city, but the effects of tourism on parks and wilderness areas concerned him. Hoover created a National Conference on Outdoor Recreation to set national recreation policies and try to balance the Progressive Era conservationist ethic and the vacation-minded leisure culture of the 1920s.

The Sierra Club, the Audubon Society, and other groups worked to protect wilderness and wildlife. In 1923 the Izaak Walton League, devoted to recreational fishing, persuaded Congress to halt a private-development scheme to drain a vast stretch of wetlands on the upper Mississippi and instead declare the beautiful expanse of river a wildlife preserve. Aldo Leopold of the U.S. Forest Service warned of the dangers of unchecked technology. For too long, he wrote in 1925, "a stump was our symbol of progress." Few listened, however. The expansive, confident generation of the 1920s had little time for the environmental issues that would occupy future generations.

Mass-Produced Entertainment The routinization of work and the increase in disposable income contributed to the rising interest in leisure-time activities in the 1920s. In their free hours workers sought the fulfillment many found missing in the workplace.

For some, light reading provided diversion. Mass-circulation magazines flourished. By 1922 ten American magazines boasted circulation of more than 2.5 million. The venerable *Saturday Evening Post,* with its Norman Rockwell covers and fiction featuring small-town life, specialized in prepackaged nostalgia. *Reader's Digest,* founded in 1921 by DeWitt and Lila Wallace, offered condensed versions of articles originally published elsewhere. A kind of journalistic equivalent of the Model T or the A&P, the *Digest* offered familiar fare for mass consumption. Book publishers sold popular novels and other works not only through traditional bookstores, but also through department stores or directly to the public via the Book-of-the-Month Club and the Literary Guild, both launched in 1926. While these mass-market ventures were often accused of debasing literary taste, they did help sustain a common national culture in an increasingly diverse society.

Just as corporations standardized the production and marketing of consumer goods, the two fastest-growing media of the 1920s, radio and the movies, offered standardized cultural fare. Mass-produced culture was hardly new, but the process accelerated in the 1920s.

The radio era began on November 2, 1920, when Pittsburgh station KDKA reported Warren Harding's election. The following year New York's WEAF began a regular news program, and a Newark station broadcast the World Series (the New York Giants beat the New York Yankees). In 1922 five hundred new stations began operations, and radio quickly became a national obsession.

At first these new stations were independent ventures, but in 1926 three big corporations—General Electric, Westinghouse, and the Radio Corporation of America—formed the first radio network, the National Broadcasting Company (NBC). The Columbia Broadcasting System (CBS) followed in 1927. Testing popular taste through market research, the networks soon ruled radio broadcasting. Americans everywhere laughed at the same jokes, hummed the same tunes, and absorbed the same commercials.

WEAF broadcast the first sponsored program in 1922, and commercial sponsorship soon became the rule. The first network comedy show, the popular *Amos 'n' Andy* (1928), brought prosperity to its sponsor, Pepsodent toothpaste. White actors played the black characters on *Amos 'n' Andy,* which offered stereotyped caricatures of African-American life, softening the realities of a racist society.

The movies reached all social classes as they expanded from the rowdy nickelodeons of the immigrant wards into elegant uptown theaters with names like Majestic, Ritz, and Palace. Charlie Chaplin, who had played anarchic, anti-authority figures in his prewar comedies, now started his own production studio and softened his character in such feature-length films as *The Gold Rush* (1925). Rudolph Valentino, an uneducated Italian immigrant, offered female moviegoers fantasies of romance in exotic settings in *The Sheik* (1921) and other films. At a time when many young women were transgressing traditional behavior codes, "America's sweetheart" Mary Pickford, with her golden curls and look of frail vulnerability, played innocent girls in need of protection, reinforcing traditional gender stereotypes. (In fact, Pickford was a shrewd businesswoman who became enormously wealthy.) Director Cecil B. De Mille, the son of an Episcopal clergyman, pioneered lavish biblical spectacles with *The Ten Commandments* (1923). In this decade of rapid cultural change, De Mille's epic sternly warned of the consequences of breaking the moral law.

After Al Jolson's *The Jazz Singer* (1927) introduced sound to the movies, a new generation of screen idols arose, including the western hero Gary Cooper and the aloof Scandinavian beauty Greta Garbo. Walt Disney's Mickey Mouse debuted in a 1928 animated cartoon, *Steamboat Willy*.

Like radio, movies became more standardized. By 1930, with weekly attendance approaching 80 million, the corporate giants Metro-Goldwyn-Mayer, Warner Brothers, and Columbia, relying on predictable plots and typecast stars, produced most movies. In a cultural parallel to the overseas expansion of U.S. business, Hollywood increasingly sought foreign as well as domestic markets for its films.

Moviegoers entered a world far removed from reality. One ad promised "all the adventure, all the romance, all the excitement you lack in your daily life." These mass-produced fantasies shaped behavior and values, especially of the young. Hollywood, observed novelist John Dos Passos, offered a "great bargain sale of five-and-ten-cent lusts and dreams." The film industry also stimulated consumption with alluring images of the good life. Romantic comedies such as De Mille's lavish *Road to Yesterday* (1925) joined department stores, mass magazines, and advertisers in opening new vistas of consumer abundance.

This spread of mass culture was a by-product of urbanization, a social process that involves not only the physical movement of people, but also changing patterns of culture. Even when the radio networks, the movie industry, the advertisers, and the popular magazines nostalgically evoked rural or small-town life, they did so from big-city offices and studios.

For all its influence, however, the new mass culture penetrated society unevenly. It had less impact in rural America, and met strong resistance among evangelical Christians suspicious of modernity. Mexican-Americans preserved traditional festivals and leisure activities despite the "Americanization" efforts of non-Hispanic priests and well-intentioned outsiders. In big-city black neighborhoods, uninhibited rent parties featured dancing to local musicians or to blues and jazz phonograph records targeted to this market. Along with the network radio shows, local stations also broadcast farm reports, ethnic music, local news, and community announcements. Country music enlivened radio programming in the South. Despite a craze for professional sports, local athletic leagues flourished as well.

Similarly, along with the great downtown movie palaces, small neighborhood theaters provided opportunities for conversation, socializing, and sometimes jeering catcalls at the film being shown. The *Chicago Defender,* the voice of the city's black middle class, deplored the raucousness of movie theaters in poor black neighborhoods, where "during a death scene . . . you are likely to hear the orchestra jazzing away." In short, despite the power of the new mass media, the American cultural scene still had room for diversity in the 1920s.

Celebrity Culture   Professional sports and media-promoted spectacles provided entertainment as well. In 1921 Atlantic City business promoters launched a bathing-beauty competition they grandly called the Miss America Pageant. Larger-than-life celebrities dominated professional sports: Babe Ruth of the New York Yankees, who hit sixty home runs in 1927; Ty Cobb, the Detroit Tigers' manager, whose earlier record of 4,191 hits still inspired awe; prizefighters Jack Dempsey and Gene Tunney, whose two heavyweight fights drew thousands of fans and massive radio audiences. Ruth was a coarse, heavy-drinking womanizer; Cobb, an ill-tempered racist. Yet the alchemy of publicity transformed them into heroes with contrived nicknames: "the Sultan of Swat" (Ruth) and "the Georgia Peach" (Cobb).

This celebrity culture illuminates the anxieties and aspirations of ordinary Americans in these years of social change. For young women uncertain about society's shifting expectations, the beauty pageants offered one ideal to which they could aspire. For men whose sense of mastery had been shaken by unsettling developments from feminism to Fordism, the exploits of sports heroes like Dempsey or Ruth could momentarily restore confidence and self-esteem.

The psychological meaning of celebrity worship emerged most clearly in the response to Charles Lindbergh, a young pilot who flew solo across the Atlantic in his small biplane, *The Spirit of St. Louis,* on May 20–21, 1927. A Minnesotan of Swedish ancestry, Lindbergh was a daredevil stunt pilot who decided on impulse to enter a $25,000 prize competition offered by a New York hotel for the first nonstop New York to Paris flight. The flight captured the public's imagination. In New York, thousands turned out for a ticker-tape parade. Radio, newspapers, magazines, and movie newsreels provided saturation coverage.

Caught up in the celebrity culture, Lindbergh became a kind of blank screen onto which people projected their own hopes, fears, and ideologies. President Coolidge, who had no time for Mississippi flood victims, received him at the White House, praising the flight as a triumph of American business and corporate technology. Many editorial writers, on the other hand, saw Lindbergh as proof that even in an era of standardization and mechanization, the individual still counted. Others praised this native-born midwesterner of northern European origins as a more authentic American than the more recent immigrants crowding the cities.

Overall, the new mass media had mixed social effects. Certainly they promoted cultural standardization and uniformity of thought. But radio, movies, and mass-circulation magazines also helped forge a national culture and introduced new viewpoints and ways of behaving. Implicitly they conveyed a potent message: a person's horizons need not be limited by his or her immediate surroundings. They opened a larger world for ordinary Americans. If that world was often superficial and tawdry, it could also be exciting and liberating.

CULTURAL FERMENT AND CREATIVITY

American life in the 1920s involved more than political scandals, assembly lines, and media-created celebrities. College-age youth explored the possibilities of a postwar moment when familiar pieties and traditional ways came under challenge. A new generation of writers, artists, musicians, and scientists contributed to the modernist spirit of cultural innovation and intellectual achievement. African-Americans asserted a new pride and self-confidence through a cultural flowering known as the Harlem Renaissance.

The Jazz Age and the Postwar Crisis of Values The war and its aftermath of disillusionment sharpened the cultural restlessness already evident in the prewar years. The year 1918, wrote Randolph Bourne, marked "a sudden, short stop at the end of an intellectual era." Poet Ezra Pound made the same point more brutally in 1920. America had gone to war, he wrote, to save "a botched civilization; . . . an old bitch gone in the teeth."

The bubbling postwar cultural ferment took many forms. Some young people—especially affluent college students—boisterously assailed their elders' notion of proper behavior. Taking advantage of the era's prosperity and the freedom offered by the automobile, they threw parties, drank bootleg liquor, flocked to jazz clubs, and danced the Charleston. When asked about her favorite activity, a California college student replied, "I adore dancing; who doesn't?"

Young people also discussed—and sometimes indulged in—sex more freely than their parents. Wrote novelist F. Scott Fitzgerald, "None of the Victorian mothers had any idea how casually their daughters were accustomed to be kissed." Sigmund Freud, the Viennese founder of psychoanalysis who explored the role of sexuality in human psychological development, enjoyed a popular vogue in America in the 1920s.

For all the talk about sex, the 1920s' "sexual revolution" is known largely from anecdotes and journalistic accounts. Premarital intercourse may have increased, but it remained exceptional and widely disapproved. What *can* be documented are changing courtship patterns. "Courting" had once been a prelude to marriage. The 1920s brought the more informal ritual of "dating." Through casual dating, young people gained social confidence without necessarily contemplating marriage. The twenties brought greater erotic freedom, but within bounds. Despite moralists' charges of immorality, most 1920s youth drew a clear line between permissible and taboo behavior.

The double standard, which held women to a stricter code of conduct, remained in force. Young men could boast of their sexual adventures, but young women reputed to be "fast" risked a smirched reputation. Still, the postwar changes in behavior had a liberating effect on women. Female sexuality was more openly acknowledged. Skirt lengths crept up; wearing makeup became more acceptable; and the elaborate armor of petticoats and corsets fell away. The awesome matronly bosom mysteriously deflated as a more boyish figure became the fashion ideal. Unaware of the medical risks of tobacco, many young women took up cigarettes, especially college students and urban workers. For some, smoking became a feminist issue. As one woman college student put it, "[W]hy [should] men . . . be permitted to smoke while girls are expelled for doing it?"

Moral guardians protested the behavior of the young. A Methodist bishop denounced new dances that brought "the bodies of men and women in unusual relation to each other." When Bryn Mawr, a Pennsylvania women's college, permitted students to smoke in 1925, denunciations erupted.

Around 1922, according to F. Scott Fitzgerald, adults embraced the rebelliousness of the young. Middle-aged Americans "discovered that young liquor will take the place of young blood," he wrote, "and with a whoop the orgy began." But sweeping cultural generalizations can be misleading. During the years of Fitzgerald's alleged national orgy, the U.S. divorce rate remained constant, and millions of Americans firmly rejected alcohol and wild parties.

The most enduring twenties stereotype is the flapper, the sophisticated, pleasure-mad young woman. The term originated with a drawing by a magazine illustrator

The New Woman, 1920s Model *This 1928 novelty song, arranged for the newly popular Hawaiian ukulele, included the lyrics: "Has she the lips the boys adore? Does she know what she's got'm for? Oh! you have no idea."*

depicting a fashionable young woman whose rubber boots were open and flapping. Although the flapper stereotype was created by journalists, fashion designers, and advertisers, it played a significant cultural role. In the nineteenth century, the ideal-ized woman on her moral pedestal had symbolized an elaborate complex of cultural ideals. The flapper, with her bobbed hair, defiant cigarette, lipstick, and short skirt, similarly epitomized youthful rejection of the older stereotype of womanhood.

The entire Jazz Age was partially a media and novelistic creation. Fitzgerald's romanticized novel about the affluent postwar young, *This Side of Paradise* (1920), spawned many imitators. With his movie-idol good looks, the youthful Fitzgerald not only wrote about the Jazz Age but lived it. He and his wife Zelda partied away the early twenties in New York, Paris, and the French Riviera. A moralist at heart, Fitzgerald both admired and deplored the behavior he chronicled. His *The Great Gatsby* (1925) captured not only the glamorous, party-filled lives of the moneyed class of the 1920s, but also their materialism, self-absorption, and casual disregard of those below them on the social scale.

Old values persisted, of course. Millions of Americans adhered to traditional ways and standards. Most farmers, blacks, industrial workers, and recent immi-grants found economic survival more pressing than the latest fads and fashions. But like the flapper, the Jazz Age stereotype captured a part of the postwar scene, especially the brassy, urban mass culture and the hedonism so different from the high-minded reformism of the Progressive Era.

F. Scott Fitzgerald and His Wife Zelda *While Fitzgerald chronicled the 1920s in his fiction, he and Zelda lived the high life in New York and in Europe.*

Harlem in the Twenties

Braving chilly breezes, New Yorkers cheered warmly on February 17, 1919, as the all-black fifteenth infantry regiment, back from France, paraded up Fifth Avenue. Led by Lieutenant James Europe's band, thousands of black troops marched in formation. Banners blazed: "our heroes—welcome home." When the parade reached Harlem north of Central Park, discipline collapsed amid joyous reunions. A new day seemed at hand for black America, and Harlem stood at its center.

The part of Manhattan Island that the early Dutch settlers had called Nieuw Haarlem was in transition by 1920. An elite suburb in the late nineteenth century, Harlem evolved rapidly during the First World War as its black population swelled. Some 400,000 southern blacks in search of wartime work migrated northward from 1914 to 1918, and the influx continued in the 1920s. Blacks also poured in from Jamaica and other Caribbean islands. New York City's black community surged from 152,000 to 327,000. Most of the newcomers settled in Harlem, where handsome old brownstone apartments were subdivided to house them.

Racism and lack of education took their toll. Black Harlem had a small middle class of entrepreneurs, ministers, real-estate agents, and funeral directors, but most Harlemites held low-paying, unskilled jobs. Many found no work at all. Overcrowding and the population spurt gave rise to social problems and high rates of tuberculosis, infant mortality, and venereal disease.

Harlem also became a vibrant center of black culture in the twenties. The Mississippi-born classical composer William Grant Still moved to Harlem in 1922, pursuing his composition studies and completing his best-known work, *Afro American Symphony* (1931). On the musical-comedy stage, the 1921 hit *Shuffle Along* launched a series of popular all-black reviews. The 1923 show *Runnin' Wild* sparked the Charleston dance craze. The Cotton Club and other Harlem cabarets featured such jazz geniuses as Duke Ellington, Fletcher Henderson, and Jelly Roll Morton. Muralist Aaron Douglas, concert tenor Roland Hayes, and singer-actor Paul Robeson contributed to the cultural ferment.

Above all, the Harlem Renaissance was a literary movement. Poet Langston Hughes drew upon the oral traditions of transplanted southern blacks in *The Weary Blues* (1926). The Jamaican writer Claude McKay evoked Harlem's throbbing, sometimes sinister nightlife in *Home to Harlem* (1928). In his avant-garde work *Cane* (1923), Jean Toomer used poems, drama, and short stories to convey the thwarted efforts of a young northern mulatto to penetrate the mysterious, sensual world of the black South. In her novel *Quicksand* (1928), Nella Larsen, a native of the Danish West Indies, told of a mulatto woman's struggle with her own sexuality and her mixed ethnic background.

In essays and conversations at late-night parties, talented young blacks explored the challenge of finding a distinct cultural voice in white America. The gentle philosopher Alain Locke, a former Rhodes scholar who taught at Howard University in Washington, D.C., assembled essays, poems, and short stories in *The New Negro* (1925), a landmark work that hailed the Harlem Renaissance as black America's "spiritual coming of age." Wrote Locke, "Harlem, I grant you, isn't typical, but it is significant. It is prophetic."

White America quickly took notice. Book publishers courted black authors. Charlotte Mason, a wealthy Park Avenue matron, funded the aspiring writers Langston Hughes and Zora Neale Hurston. Novelist and photographer Carl Van Vechten introduced black artists and writers to editors, publishers, and producers. White writers discovered and sometimes distorted black life. Eugene O'Neill's play *The Emperor Jones,* produced in 1921, starred Charles Gilpin as a fear-crazed West Indian tyrant. King Vidor's 1929 movie *Hallelujah,* featuring an all-black cast, romanticized plantation life and warned of the city's dangers. The 1925 novel *Porgy,* by DuBose and Dorothy Heyward,

offered a sympathetic but sentimentalized picture of Charleston's black community. George Gershwin's musical adaptation, *Porgy and Bess,* appeared in 1935.

In a decade of prohibition and shifting sexual mores, Harlem seemed to offer sensuality, eroticism, and escape from taboos. Prostitutes, speakeasies, and cocaine were readily available. The whites who packed the late-night jazz clubs and the pulsating dance reviews and who patronized black writers and artists widely praised black culture for its "spontaneous," "primitive," or "spiritual" qualities. Few whites bothered to examine the more prosaic realities of Harlem life. The Cotton Club, controlled by gangsters, featured black performers but barred most blacks from the audience.

And with patronage came subtle attempts at control. When Langston Hughes began to write about urban

Poet and Novelist Langston Hughes, by Winold Reiss

poverty rather than Africa or black spirituality in the 1930s, Charlotte Mason angrily withdrew her support. Wrote Hughes later, "Concerning Negroes, she felt that they were America's great link with the primitive. . . . But unfortunately I did not feel the rhythms of the primitive surging through me. . . . I was only an American Negro. I was not Africa. I was Chicago and Kansas City and Broadway and Harlem."

The Harlem Renaissance lacked a political framework or organic ties to the larger African-American experience. Indeed, in *The New Negro* Alain Locke urged talented blacks to shift from "the arid fields of controversy and debate to the productive fields of creative expression." The writers and artists of the Renaissance mostly ignored the racism, discrimination, and economic troubles faced by African-Americans in the 1920s. They reacted with hostility to Marcus Garvey and his efforts to mobilize the urban black masses.

With the stock market crash in 1929 and the onset of the Great Depression, the Harlem Renaissance ended. In the 1930s a new generation of writers led by Richard Wright would launch a more politically engaged black cultural movement. Looking back in 1935, Alain Locke wrote sadly, "The rosy enthusiasm and hopes of 1925 were cruelly deceptive mirages. [The depression] revealed a Harlem that the social worker knew all along, but had not been able to dramatize. There is no cure or saving magic in poetry and art for precarious marginal employment, high mortality rates, and civic neglect." Langston Hughes tersely assessed the movement in his 1940 autobiography: "The ordinary Negroes hadn't heard of the Negro Renaissance. And if they had, it hadn't raised their wages any."

But for all its naïveté, the Harlem Renaissance left an important legacy. The post–World War II literary flowering that began with Ralph Ellison's *Invisible Man* (1952) and continued with the works of James Baldwin, Toni Morrison, Alice Walker, and others owed a substantial debt to the Harlem Renaissance. For black writers in the West Indies and in French West Africa, "Harlem" would become a symbol of racial achievement. A fragile flower battered by the cold winds of the depression, the Harlem Renaissance nevertheless stands as a monument to African-American cultural creativity even under difficult circumstances.

Alienated Writers Like Fitzgerald, many young writers found the cultural turbulence of the 1920s a creative stimulus. The decade's most talented writers equally disliked the moralistic pieties of the old order and the business pieties of the new. Novelist Sinclair Lewis took a sharply critical view of postwar America. In *Main Street* (1920) Lewis satirized the smugness and cultural barrenness of a fictional midwestern farm town, Gopher Prairie, based on his native Sauk Centre, Minnesota. In *Babbitt* (1922) he skewered a mythic larger city, Zenith, in the character of George F. Babbitt, a real estate agent trapped in middle-class conformity.

Lewis's journalistic counterpart was Henry L. Mencken, a Baltimore newspaperman who in 1924 launched *The American Mercury* magazine, the bible of the decade's alienated intellectuals. Mencken championed writers like Lewis and Theodore Dreiser while ridiculing small-town America, Protestant fundamentalism, the middle-class "Booboisie," and all politicians. His devastating essays on Wilson, Harding, Coolidge, and Bryan are classics of political satire. Asked why he remained in America, Mencken replied, "Why do people visit zoos?"

For this generation of writers, World War I was a watershed experience. This was particularly true of Ernest Hemingway, who was seriously wounded in July 1918 while serving in northern Italy as a youthful Red Cross volunteer. In 1921, at twenty-two, he became an expatriate in Paris. In *The Sun Also Rises* (1926) Hemingway portrayed a group of American and English young people, variously damaged by the war, as they drift around Spain. His *A Farewell to Arms* (1929), loosely based on his own experiences, depicts the war's futility and politicians' empty rhetoric. In one passage, the narrator says,

> I was always embarrassed by the words sacred, glorious, and sacrifice and the expression in vain. We . . . had read them, on proclamations that were slapped up . . . over other proclamations, now for a long time, and I had seen nothing sacred, and the things that were glorious had no glory and the sacrifices were like the stockyards at Chicago if nothing was done with the meat except to bury it.

Although writers like Lewis and Hemingway felt contempt for the inflated rhetoric of the war years and the materialistic culture of the postwar years, and even though some became expatriates, they remained American at heart. The desire to create a vital national culture inspired their literary efforts, as it had inspired the likes of Nathaniel Hawthorne, Herman Melville, and Walt Whitman in the nineteenth century.

The social changes of these years energized African-American cultural life as well. The growth of New York City's black population underlay the Harlem Renaissance. The artistic creativity of the Renaissance took many forms, from all-black Broadway musical reviews to poems and novels (see A Place in Time: Harlem in the Twenties). The Harlem Renaissance was important to different groups for different reasons. Black women writers and performers gained a welcome career boost. Young whites in rebellion against Victorian propriety romanticized black life, as expressed in the Harlem Renaissance, as freer and less inhibited. Cultural nationalists both black and white welcomed the Renaissance as a promising step toward an authentically American modernist culture.

Architects, Painters, and Musicians Celebrate Modern America

A burst of architectural activity transformed the urban skyline in the 1920s. By 1930 the United States boasted 377 buildings over seventy stories tall. The skyscraper, proclaimed one writer, "epitomizes American life and American civilization." Not everyone was thrilled. Cultural critic Lewis Mumford denounced crowded, impersonal cities, with their "audacious towers, [and] . . . endless miles of asphalted pavements." Mumford preferred a network of regional cultures and smaller communities on a more human scale.

For inspiration, artists turned to America—either the real nation around them or an imagined one. While muralist Thomas Hart Benton evoked a half-mythic past of cowboys, pioneers, and riverboat gamblers, Edward Hopper portrayed faded towns and lonely cities of the present. Hopper's painting *Sunday* (1926), picturing a man slumped on the curb of an empty street of abandoned stores, conveyed both the bleakness and the potential beauty of urban America.

Other 1920s artists offered more upbeat images. Charles Sheeler painted and photographed giant factory complexes, including Henry Ford's plant near Detroit. The Italian immigrant Joseph Stella captured the excitement and energy of New York in such paintings as *The Bridge* (1926), an abstract representation of the Brooklyn Bridge. Wisconsin's Georgia O'Keeffe moved to New York City in 1918 when the photographer Alfred Stieglitz (whom she later married) mounted a show of her work. O'Keeffe's 1920s paintings evoked both the congestion and the allure of the city.

The ferment of the 1920s reached the musical world as well. The composer Aaron Copland later recalled, "The conviction grew inside me that the two things that seemed always to have been so separate in America—music and the life about me—must be made to touch." While Copland drew upon folk traditions, others evoked the new urban-industrial America. Composer Frederick Converse's 1927 tone poem about the automobile, "Flivver Ten Million," for example, featured such episodes as "May Night by the Roadside" and "The Collision."

Of all the musical innovations, jazz best captured the modernist spirit. The Original Dixieland Jazz Band—white musicians imitating the black jazz bands of New Orleans—had debuted in New York City in 1917, launching a jazz vogue that spread by live performances, radio, and phonograph records. Popular white bandleader Paul Whiteman offered watered-down "jazz" versions of standard tunes. Of the white composers who embraced jazz, George Gershwin, with his *Rhapsody in Blue* (1924) and *An American in Paris* (1928), was the most gifted.

Meanwhile, black musicians preserved authentic jazz and explored its potential. Guitar picker Hudie Ledbetter (nicknamed Leadbelly) performed his blues and work songs before appreciative black audiences. Bessie Smith and Gertrude ("Ma") Rainey packed auditoriums on Chicago's South Side and recorded on black-oriented labels. Trumpeter and singer Louis Armstrong did his most creative work in the 1920s. The recordings by Armstrong's "Hot Five" and "Hot Seven" groups in the late 1920s decisively influenced the future of jazz. While the composer and bandleader Duke Ellington performed to sell-out audiences at Harlem's Cotton Club, Fats Waller and Ferdinand (Jelly Roll) Morton demonstrated the piano's jazz potential. Although much of 1920s popular culture faded quickly, jazz survived and flourished.

Advances in
Science and
Medicine

The creativity of the 1920s also found expression in science and medicine. Nuclear physicist Arthur H. Compton of the University of Chicago won the Nobel Prize in 1927 for his work on x-rays. In this decade, too, Ernest O. Lawrence of the University of California did the basic research that led to the cyclotron, or particle accelerator, an apparatus that enables scientists to study the atomic nucleus. These research findings would have profound implications for the future.

In medicine, Harvey Cushing of Harvard Medical School made dramatic advances in neurosurgery, while University of Wisconsin chemist Harry Steenbock created vitamin D in milk using ultraviolet rays. Other researches made key discoveries that helped conquer such killers as diphtheria, whooping cough, measles, and influenza, which had struck with devastating impact in 1918 (see Chapter 22).

In 1919 Robert Goddard, a physicist at Clark University in Massachusetts, published a little-noticed article entitled "A Method of Reaching Extreme Altitudes." In 1926 Goddard launched a small liquid-fuel rocket. Although Goddard was ridiculed at the time, his predictions of lunar landings and space exploration proved prophetic.

Of the many changes affecting American life in the 1920s, the achievements and rising cultural prestige of science loom large. In *Science and the Modern World* (1925), philosopher Alfred North Whitehead underscored science's growing role. Although "individually powerless," Whitehead concluded, scientists were "ultimately the rulers of the world." While some welcomed this prospect, others saw it as another of the decade's deeply disturbing developments.

A SOCIETY IN CONFLICT

Rapid social change often produces a backlash, and this proved especially true in 1920s' America as a series of highly charged episodes and social movements highlighted the era's tensions. While Congress restricted immigration from southern and eastern Europe and Asia, highly publicized court cases in Massachusetts and Tennessee spotlighted other sources of fear and uneasiness. Millions of whites embraced the racist bigotry and moralistic rhetoric of a revived Ku Klux Klan, and many newly urbanized African-Americans rallied to a magnetic black leader with a riveting message of racial pride. Prohibition, widely supported in the Progressive Era, proved another source of controversy in this conflict-ridden decade.

Immigration
Restriction

Fed by the effort in 1917–1918 to enforce unquestioning support for the war, the old impulse to remake America into a nation of like-minded, culturally homogenous people revived in the 1920s. In a study of the decade's immigration legislation and court decisions, historian Mae M. Ngai has shown how thoroughly they were shaped by eugenicist and racist thinking, and how systematically they sought to preserve America as a "white" nation.

The National Origins Act of 1924, a revision of the immigration law, restricted annual immigration from any foreign country to 2 percent of the total number of persons of that "national origin" in the United States in 1890. Since the great influx of southern and eastern Europeans had come after 1890, the intent of this provision was clear: to reduce the immigration of these nationalities. As Calvin Coolidge observed on signing the law, "America must be kept American."

In 1929 Congress changed the base year for determining "national origins" to 1920, but even under this formula, the annual quota for Poland stood at a mere 6,524; for Italy, 5,802; for Russia, 2,784; and for Hungary, 869. This quota system, which survived to 1965, represented a strong counterattack by native-born Protestant America against the immigrant cities. Total immigration fell from 1.2 million in 1914 to 280,000 in 1929. The law excluded Asians and South Asians entirely as "persons ineligible to citizenship."

Court rulings underscored the nativist message. In *Ozawa* v. *U.S.* (1922), the U.S. Supreme Court rejected a citizenship request by a Japanese-born student at the University of California–Berkeley. In 1923 the Supreme Court upheld a California law limiting the right of Japanese immigrants to own or lease farmland. That same year, the Supreme Court rejected an immigration application by a man from India who claimed that he was "Caucasian" and thus eligible for entry under the Nationality Act of 1790, which had limited naturalized citizenship to "free white persons." In framing this law, the court ruled, the founders had intended "to include only the type of man whom they knew as white . . . [those] from the British Isles and northwestern Europe."

Needed Workers/ Unwelcome Aliens: Hispanic Newcomers While the 1924 law excluded Asians and restricted immigration from southern and eastern Europe, it placed no restraints on immigrants from the Western Hemisphere. Accordingly, immigration from Latin America (as well as from French Canada) soared in the 1920s. Poverty and domestic political turmoil propelled thousands of Mexicans northward. By 1930 at least 2 million Mexican-born people lived in the United States, mostly in the Southwest. California's Mexican-American population mushroomed from 90,000 in 1920 to nearly 360,000 in 1930.

Many of the immigrants were low-paid migratory workers in the region's large-scale agribusinesses. Mexican labor sustained California's citrus industry. Cooperatives such as the Southern California Fruit Growers Exchange (Sunkist) hired itinerant workers on a seasonal basis, provided substandard housing in isolated settlements the workers called *colonias,* and fought the migrants' attempts to form labor unions.

Not all Mexican immigrants were migratory workers; many settled into U.S. communities. Mexican-Americans in the Midwest worked not only in agriculture, for example, but also in the automobile, steel, and railroad industries. While still emotionally linked to "México Lindo" (Beautiful Mexico), they formed local support networks and cultural institutions. Mexican-Americans were split, however, between recent arrivals and earlier immigrants who had become U.S. citizens. The strongest Mexican-American organization in the 1920s, the Texas-based League of United Latin-American Citizens, ignored the migrant laborers of the Southwest.

Though deeply religious, Mexican-Americans found little support from the U.S. Catholic church. Earlier, European Catholic immigrants had attended ethnic parishes and worshiped in their own languages, but church policy had changed by the 1920s. In "Anglo" parishes with non-Hispanic priests, Spanish-speaking Mexican newcomers faced discrimination and pressure to abandon their language, traditions, and folk beliefs.

Attitudes toward Mexican immigrants were deeply ambivalent. Their labor was needed, but their presence disturbed nativists eager to preserve a "white" and Protestant nation. While not formally excluded, would-be Mexican immigrants faced strict literacy and means tests. The Border Patrol was created in 1925; deportations increased; and in 1929 Congress made illegal entry a criminal offense. While these measures sharply reduced legal immigration from Mexico, the flow of illegal migration continued, as an estimated one hundred thousand Mexican newcomers arrived annually to fill pressing demands in the U.S. labor market.

Nativism, Anti-Radicalism, and the Sacco-Vanzetti Case
 The xenophobic, antiradical sentiments underlying the postwar Red Scare (see Chapter 22) and the immigration-restriction movement emerged starkly in a Massachusetts murder case that became a cause célèbre. On April 15, 1920, robbers shot and killed the paymaster and guard of a shoe factory in South Braintree, Massachusetts, and stole two cash boxes. The police charged two Italian immigrants, Nicola Sacco and Bartolomeo Vanzetti, and a jury found them guilty in 1921. After many appeals and a review of the case by a commission of notable citizens, they were electrocuted on August 23, 1927.

These bare facts hardly convey the passions the case aroused, mirroring fault lines in the larger society. Sacco and Vanzetti were anarchists, and the prosecution harped on their radicalism. The judge barely concealed his hostility to the defendants, whom he privately called "those anarchist bastards." While many conservatives insisted that these alien anarchists must die, liberals and socialists rallied to their defense. As the two went to the chair, the writer John Dos Passos summed up his bitterness in a poem that ended:

> All right you have won you will kill the brave men our friends tonight
> . . . all right we are two nations.

While the case against Sacco and Vanzetti was circumstantial and far from airtight, later research on Boston's anarchist community and ballistics tests on Sacco's gun pointed to their guilt. But the prejudices that tainted the trial remain indisputable, as does the case's symbolic importance in exposing the deep divisions in American society of the 1920s.

Fundamentalism and the Scopes Trial

Meanwhile, in Tennessee, an equally celebrated case cast a spotlight on another front in the cultural wars of the decade. Post–Civil War American Protestantism faced not only an expanding Catholic and Jewish population, but also the growing prestige of science, challenging religion's cultural standing. Scholars subjected the Bible to critical scrutiny, psychologists and sociologists studied supernatural belief systems as human social constructs and expressions of emotional needs, and biologists generally accepted the naturalistic explanation for the variety of life forms on Earth advanced in Charles Darwin's *Origin of Species* (1859).

Liberal Protestants accepted the findings of science and espoused the reform-minded Social Gospel. But a reaction was building, and it came to be called fundamentalism, after *The Fundamentals*, a series of essays published in 1909–1914. Fundamentalists insisted on the literal truth of the Bible, including the Genesis account of Creation. Religious "modernists," they charged, had abandoned the truths revealed in God's Word.

In the early 1920s fundamentalists especially targeted Darwin's theory of evolution as a threat to their faith. Legislators in many states introduced bills to bar the teaching of evolution in public schools, and several southern states enacted such laws. Texas governor Miriam ("Ma") Ferguson personally censored textbooks that discussed evolution. "I am a Christian mother," she declared, "and I am not going to let that kind of rot go into Texas textbooks." Fundamentalism's best-known champion, the former Democratic presidential candidate and secretary of state William Jennings Bryan, endorsed the anti-evolution cause.

When the Tennessee legislature barred the theory of evolution from the state's public schools in 1925, the American Civil Liberties Union (ACLU) offered to defend any teacher willing to challenge this law. A high-school teacher in Dayton, Tennessee, John T. Scopes, accepted the offer. He was encouraged by local businessmen who saw an opportunity to promote their town. Scopes summarized Darwin's theory to a science class and was arrested. Famed criminal lawyer Clarence Darrow headed the defense team, and Bryan assisted the prosecution. Journalists poured into Dayton; a Chicago radio station broadcast the proceedings live; and the Scopes trial became a media sensation.

Cross-examined by Darrow, Bryan insisted on the literal veracity of every Bible story and dismissed evolutionary theory. Although the jury found Scopes guilty, the Dayton trial exposed fundamentalism to ridicule. When Bryan died of a heart attack soon after, H. L. Mencken wrote a column mercilessly deriding him and the "gaping primates" who idolized him.

In fact, the Scopes trial was only one skirmish in a long battle. Numerous southern and western states passed anti-evolution laws after 1925, and textbook publishers deleted or modified their treatment of evolution to avoid offending local school boards. Fundamentalism weakened in mainstream Protestantism, but many local congregations, radio preachers, and newly formed conservative denominations upheld the traditional faith. So, too, did the flamboyant evangelist Billy Sunday, who denounced the loose living and modernism of the 1920s.

In Los Angeles, the charismatic Aimee Semple McPherson, anticipating later TV evangelists, regularly filled her cavernous Angelus Temple and reached thousands more by radio. The beautiful, white-gowned McPherson entranced audiences with theatrical sermons. She once used a gigantic electric scoreboard to illustrate the triumph of good over evil. Her followers, mainly transplanted midwesterners, embraced her fundamentalist theology while reveling in her mass-entertainment techniques. When she died in 1944, her International Church of the Foursquare Gospel had more than six hundred branches in the United States and abroad.

The Ku Klux Klan and the Garvey Movement The tensions and hostilities tearing at the American social fabric also emerged in a resurrected Ku Klux Klan (KKK) movement. The original Klan of the Reconstruction era had faded by the 1870s, but in November 1915 it was revived by hooded men gathered at Stone Mountain, Georgia. D. W. Griffith's glorification of the Klan in *The Birth of a Nation* (1915) provided further inspiration.

The movement remained obscure until 1920, when two Atlanta entrepreneurs organized a national membership drive. Sensing the appeal of the Klan's ritual and its nativist, white-supremacist ideology, they devised a recruitment scheme involving a ten-dollar membership fee divided among the salesman (called the Kleagle), the local sales manager (King Kleagle), the district sales manager (Grand Goblin), the state leader (Grand Dragon), and the national leader (Imperial Wizard)—with a rake-off to themselves. They also sold Klan robes and masks, the horse robe that every member had to buy, and the Chattahoochee River water used in initiation rites (ten dollars a bottle). This elaborate scam succeeded beyond their wildest dreams.

The Klan demonized a variety of targets, and won a vast following. Under the umbrella term "100 percent Americanism," it attacked not only African-Americans but also Catholics, Jews, and aliens. Some Klan groups carried out vigilante attacks on whites suspected of sexual immorality or prohibition-law violations. Estimates of membership in the KKK and its women's auxiliary in the early 1920s range as high as 5 million. From its southern base, the Klan spread through the Midwest and across the country from Long Island to the West Coast, especially among the working class and lower middle class in cities with native-born Protestant majorities. In 1922 Imperial Wizard Hiram Wesley Evans admitted the Klan's image as a haven of "hicks" and "rubes" and urged college graduates to support the great cause.

The Klan filled emotional needs for its members. Although corrupt at the top, it was not a haven for criminals or fanatics; observers commented on members' ordinariness. (Evans, a Texas dentist, called himself "the most average man in America.") The Klan's promise to restore the nation's lost purity—racial, ethnic, religious, and moral—appealed to many old-stock Protestants disoriented by social change. For some small businessmen caught between organized labor and the new corporate order, the Klan's litany of menace offered a vocabulary for articulating economic anxieties. Some citizens upset by changing sexual mores welcomed the Klan's defense of "the purity of white womanhood." Klan membership, in short, gave a sense of empowerment and group cohesion to people who felt marginalized by the new social order of immigrants, big cities, great corporations, mass culture, and racial and religious diversity. The rituals, parades, and cross burnings added drama to unfulfilling lives.

But if individual Klan members seemed more needy than sinister, the Klan's menacing potential as a mass movement was real. Some KKK groups resorted to intimidation, threats, beatings, and lynching in their quest for a purified America. In several states, the Klan won political power. Oklahoma's Klan-controlled legislature impeached and removed an anti-Klan governor. In Oregon the Klan elected a governor and pushed through legislation requiring all children to attend public school, a slap at the state's Catholic schools.

The Klan collapsed with shocking suddenness. In March 1925 Indiana's politically powerful Grand Dragon, David Stephenson, raped his young secretary. When she swallowed poison the next day, Stephenson panicked and refused to call a physician. The woman died several weeks later, and Stephenson went to jail. From prison he revealed details of political corruption in Indiana. Its moral pretensions in shreds, the KKK faded.

Among African-Americans who had escaped southern rural poverty and racism only to find continued poverty and more racism in the urban North, the decade's social strains produced a different kind of mass movement led by the spellbinding Marcus Garvey and his Universal Negro Improvement Association (UNIA). Born in Jamaica in 1887, Garvey founded UNIA in 1914 and two years later moved to New York City's Harlem, which became the movement's headquarters. In a white-dominated society, Garvey glorified all things black. Urging black economic solidarity, he founded a chain of UNIA grocery stores and other businesses. He summoned blacks to return to "Motherland Africa" and establish there a great nation.

An estimated eighty thousand blacks joined the UNIA, and thousands more felt the lure of Garvey's oratory; the uplift of UNIA parades, uniforms, and flags; and the seduction of Garvey's dream of a glorious future in Africa. Garvey's popularity unsettled not only white America but also the middle-class leaders of the NAACP and the black churches. W. E. B. Du Bois was one of Garvey's sharpest critics. The movement also highlighted social tensions in Harlem, where two long-separated streams of the African diaspora, one from the Caribbean, the other from the American South, came together in the 1920s. This convergence provoked rivalry for limited economic opportunities and political power. Garvey himself was Jamaican, and critics charged that Caribbean immigrants controlled UNIA.

In 1923 a federal court convicted Garvey of fraud in one of his business ventures, the Black Star Steamship Line. In 1927, after two years' imprisonment, he was deported to Jamaica, and the UNIA collapsed. But as the first mass movement in black America, it revealed both the seething discontent and the activist potential among African-Americans in the urban North. "In a world where black is despised," commented an African-American newspaper after Garvey's fall, "he taught his followers that black is beautiful."

Prohibition: Cultures in Conflict

The deep fissures in American society also surfaced in the controversy over alcohol. As we discussed in Chapter 21, many Progressive Era reformers supported prohibition as a legitimate response to the social problems associated with alcohol abuse. But the issue also had symbolic overtones, as native-born Americans struggled to maintain cultural and political dominance over the immigrant cities. When the Eighteenth Amendment took effect in January 1920, prohibitionists rejoiced. Billy Sunday proclaimed,

> The reign of tears is over. The slums will soon be only a memory. We will turn our prisons into factories and our jails into storehouses and corncribs. Men will walk upright now. Women will smile and children will laugh.

Sunday's dream seemed attainable as saloons closed, liquor advertising vanished, and arrests for drunkenness declined. In 1921 alcohol consumption stood at about one-third the prewar level. Yet prohibition gradually lost support, and in 1933 it ended.

What went wrong? Essentially, prohibition's failure illustrates the virtual impossibility of enforcing a widely opposed law in a democracy. From the beginning, the Volstead Act, the 1919 prohibition law, was underfunded and weakly enforced, especially in antiprohibition areas. New York, for example, repealed its prohibition-enforcement law as early as 1923. Would-be drinkers grew bolder as enforcement faltered. For rebellious young people, alcohol's illegality increased its appeal. "[P]rohibition has been an incentive for young folks to learn to drink," declared one college student. "It is the natural reaction of youth to rules and regulations."

Every city boasted speakeasies where customers could buy drinks, and rum-runners routinely smuggled liquor from Canada and the West Indies. Shady entrepreneurs sold flavored industrial-grade alcohol. People concocted their own home brew, and the demand for sacramental wine soared. By 1929 alcohol consumption was about 70 percent of the prewar level.

Organized crime helped circumvent the law. In Chicago rival gangs battled to control the liquor business. The city witnessed 550 gangland killings in the 1920s. Chicago gangster Al Capone controlled a network of speakeasies that generated annual profits of $60 million. Although not typical, Chicago's crime wave underscored prohibition's failure. A reform designed to produce a more orderly and virtuous America was turning citizens into lawbreakers and mobsters into celebrities.

Thus prohibition, too, became a battleground in the decade's cultural wars. The "drys"—usually native-born Protestants—praised it as a necessary social reform. The "wets"—liberals, alienated intellectuals, Jazz Age rebels, big-city immigrants—condemned it as moralistic meddling. At one college, the student newspaper suggested a campus distillery as the senior class gift, "with the proceeds going to the college."

Prohibition influenced the 1928 presidential campaign. While Democratic candidate Al Smith advocated repeal of the Eighteenth Amendment, Republican

Herbert Hoover praised it as "a great social and economic experiment, noble in motive and far-reaching in purpose." Once elected, Hoover appointed a commission to study the matter. In a confusing 1931 report, the commission conceded prohibition's failure, but urged its retention. A New York journalist parodied the findings:

> Prohibition is an awful flop.
> We like it.
> It can't stop what it's meant to stop.
> We like it.
> It's left a trail of graft and slime,
> It's filled our land with vice and crime,
> It don't prohibit worth a dime,
> Nevertheless we're for it.

By the time the Eighteenth Amendment was finally repealed in 1933, prohibition was thoroughly discredited and seemed little more than a relic of another age.

HOOVER AT THE HELM

Herbert Hoover, elected president in 1928, appeared well fitted to sustain the nation's prosperity. No standpat conservative like Harding and Coolidge, Hoover espoused a distinctive social and political philosophy that reflected his engineering background. In some ways, he seemed the ideal president for the new technological age.

The Election of 1928

A Hollywood casting agent could not have chosen two individuals who better personified the nation's social and cultural schisms than the 1928 presidential candidates. Al Smith, the governor of New York, easily won the Democratic nomination. The party's urban-immigrant wing had gained strength since the deadlocked 1924 convention. A Catholic and a wet, Smith exuded the flavor of immigrant New York City. Originally a machine politician and basically conservative, he had won the support of progressive reformers by backing social-welfare measures. His inner circle included several reform-minded women, notably Frances Perkins, the head of the state industrial board, and Belle Moskowitz, a key adviser.

Secretary of Commerce Herbert Hoover won the Republican nomination after Calvin Coolidge chose not to run. Some conservative party leaders, however, mistrusted the brilliant but aloof Hoover, who had never held elective office and indeed had spent much of his adult life abroad. Born in Iowa and orphaned at an early age, Hoover had put himself through Stanford University and made a fortune as a mining engineer in China and Australia. His service as wartime food administrator had won him a place in the Harding and Coolidge cabinets.

Hoover disdained handshaking and baby kissing. Instead, he issued "tons of reports on dull subjects" (in Mencken's jaundiced view) and read radio speeches in a droning monotone. His boring campaign style obscured the originality of his ideas. Smith, by contrast, campaigned spiritedly across the nation. This may actually

The Election of 1928

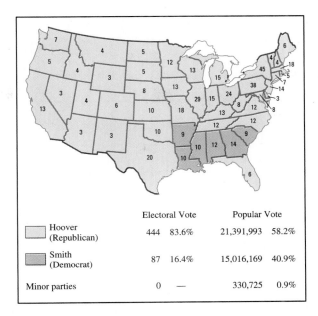

	Electoral Vote		Popular Vote	
Hoover (Republican)	444	83.6%	21,391,993	58.2%
Smith (Democrat)	87	16.4%	15,016,169	40.9%
Minor parties	0	—	330,725	0.9%

have hurt him, however, because his big-city wisecracking and New York accent grated on many voters in the heartland.

Whether Smith's Catholicism helped or hurt his candidacy remains debatable. Hoover urged tolerance, and Smith denied any conflict between his faith and the duties of the presidency, but anti-Catholic prejudice unquestionably played a role. Rumors circulated that the Vatican would relocate to the United States if Smith won. (A postelection joke had Smith sending the pope a one-word telegram, "Unpack.") The decisive campaign issue was probably not popery but prosperity. Republican orators pointed to the booming economy and warned that a Smith victory would mean "soup kitchens instead of busy factories." In his nomination-acceptance speech, Hoover foresaw "the final triumph over poverty."

Hoover won in a landslide, grabbing 58 percent of the vote and even making deep inroads in the Democratic "solid South." Socialist Norman Thomas received only 267,000 votes, less than a third of Eugene V. Debs's 1920 total. However, the election also offered evidence of an emerging political realignment. Smith did well in the rural Midwest, where hard-pressed farmers, angered by Coolidge's insensitivity to their plight, abandoned their normal Republican allegiance. In northern cities, Catholic and Jewish immigrant wards voted heavily Democratic. In 1924 the nation's twelve largest cities had all gone Republican; in 1928 Smith carried all twelve. Should prosperity end, these portents suggested, the Republican party faced trouble.

Herbert Hoover's Social Thought   Americans looked hopefully to their new president, whom admirers dubbed the Great Engineer. Hoover had described his social creed in a 1922 book *American Individualism*.

Presidential Voting by Selected Ethnic Groups in Chicago, 1924, 1928, and 1932

	Percent Democratic		
	1924	1928	1932
Blacks	10	23	21
Czechoslovaks	40	73	83
Germans	14	58	69
Italians	31	63	64
Jews	19	60	77
Lithuanians	48	77	84
Poles	35	71	80
Swedes	15	34	51
Yugoslavs	20	54	67

Source: John M. Allswang, *A House for All Peoples: Ethnic Politics in Chicago, 1890–1936* (Lexington: University Press of Kentucky, 1971).

Although a self-made man himself, he did not uncritically praise big business. His Quakerism, humanitarian activities, engineering experience, and Republican loyalties combined to produce a unique social outlook.

Like Theodore Roosevelt (whom he had supported in 1912), Hoover disapproved of cutthroat capitalist competition. Rational economic development, he insisted, demanded corporate cooperation in marketing, wage policy, raw-material allocation, and product standardization. The economy, in short, should operate like an efficient machine. Believing that business had social obligations, Hoover welcomed the growth of welfare capitalism. But above all, he believed in voluntarism. The cooperative, socially responsible economic order that he envisioned must arise from the voluntary action of capitalist leaders, not government coercion or labor-management power struggles.

Hoover had put his philosophy into practice as secretary of commerce. To encourage corporate consolidation and cooperation, he had convened more than 250 conferences in which business leaders discussed such issues as unemployment, pricing policies, and labor-management relations. He urged higher wages to increase consumer purchasing power, and in 1923 he persuaded the steel industry to adopt an eight-hour workday as an efficiency measure. During the disastrous 1927 Mississippi River floods, as President Coolidge remained in Washington, Hoover had rushed to the stricken area and helped mobilize relief efforts.

Hoover's ideology had its limitations. He showed more interest in cooperation among capitalists than among consumers or workers. His belief that capitalists would voluntarily embrace enlightened labor policies and an ethic of social responsibility overestimated the role of altruism in business decision making. And his opposition to government economic intervention brought him grief when such intervention became urgently necessary.

Hoover's early months as president seemed promising. He set up a President's Council on Recent Social Trends and other commissions to study public issues and gather data to guide policy makers. Responding to the farm problem, he secured passage of legislation creating a Federal Farm Board (1929) to promote cooperative commodity marketing. This, he hoped, would raise farm prices while preserving the voluntarist principle.

By late summer 1929, the Hoover administration appeared to be off to a good start. But while Hoover applied his engineering skills to the machinery of government, a crisis was approaching that would overwhelm and ultimately destroy his presidency.

IMPORTANT EVENTS, 1920–1929

1915	Modern Ku Klux Klan founded.
1916	Marcus Garvey moves to New York City.
1919	Volstead Act (Prohibition).
1920–1921	Sharp postwar recession.
1920	Warren G. Harding elected president. Radio station KDKA, Pittsburgh, broadcasts election returns. Sinclair Lewis, *Main Street*.
1921	Economic boom begins; agriculture remains depressed. Sheppard-Towner Act. *Shuffle Along*, all-black musical review.
1921–1922	Washington Naval Arms Conference.
1922	Supreme Court declares child-labor law unconstitutional. Fordney-McCumber Tariff restores high rates. Herbert Hoover, *American Individualism*. Sinclair Lewis, *Babbitt*.
1923	Harding dies; Calvin Coolidge becomes president. Supreme Court strikes down minimum-wage law for women.
1924	Teapot Dome scandals investigated. National Origins Act. Calvin Coolidge elected president. McNary-Haugen farm bill introduced.
1925	Scopes trial. Ku Klux Klan scandal in Indiana. Alain Locke, *The New Negro*. Dorothy and DuBose Heyward, *Porgy*. F. Scott Fitzgerald, *The Great Gatsby*.

1926   Book-of-the-Month Club founded.
             National Broadcasting Company founded.
             Langston Hughes, *The Weary Blues.*

1927   *The Jazz Singer,* first sound movie.
             Coolidge vetoes the McNary-Haugen bill.
             Henry Ford introduces the Model A.
             Execution of Sacco and Vanzetti.
             Charles A. Lindbergh's transatlantic flight.
             Marcus Garvey deported.
             Mississippi River flood.

1928   Herbert Hoover elected president.

1929   Federal Farm Board created.
             Sheppard-Towner program terminated.
             Hallelujah, first all-black movie.
             Ernest Hemingway, *A Farewell to Arms.*
             Stock market speculative frenzy.

24

The Great Depression and the New Deal, 1929–1939

Rugged Campobello Island lying off Eastport, Maine, was sunlit that August afternoon in 1921. A small sailboat bobbed in the waters off the island. At the helm, with several of his children, was thirty-nine-year-old Franklin D. Roosevelt. Assistant secretary of the navy during World War I, Roosevelt had been the Democratic party's vice-presidential candidate in 1920. But all this was far from his mind now. He loved sailing, and he loved Campobello Island.

The idyllic afternoon suddenly took an ominous turn when Roosevelt spotted a fire. Beaching the boat, he and the children frantically beat back the spreading flames. The exertion left Roosevelt unusually fatigued. The next morning his left leg dragged when he tried to walk. Soon all sensation disappeared in both legs. He had suffered an attack of poliomyelitis (infantile paralysis), a viral infection that most often struck children but sometimes struck adults as well. Except for a cumbersome shuffle with crutches and heavy metal braces, he would never walk again.

This illness changed the lives of both Franklin Roosevelt and his wife Eleanor. To Franklin, it seemed the end of his career. But he endured endless therapy and gradually reentered politics. In 1928, laboriously mounting the podium at the Democratic National Convention, he nominated his friend Al Smith for president. That fall, he himself was elected governor of New York.

Somewhat superficial and even arrogant before 1921, this privileged only child became, through his ordeal, more understanding of the disadvantaged and far more determined. "If you had spent two years in bed trying to wiggle your big toe," he once said, "after that everything else would seem easy!"

Eleanor Roosevelt at first devoted herself to her husband's care and to the child-rearing duties that now fell to her. But she also encouraged his return to politics, resisting his domineering mother's efforts to turn him into an invalid at the family home at Hyde Park, New York. Eleanor became her husband's eyes and ears. Already involved with social issues, she now became active in the New York Democratic party and edited its newsletter for women. Painfully shy, she forced herself to make public speeches.

The Roosevelts would soon need the qualities of character they had acquired. Elected president in 1932 amidst the worst depression in American history,

Franklin Roosevelt dominated U.S. politics until his death in 1945. Roosevelt's presidency, the so-called New Deal, spawned an array of laws, agencies, and programs that historians ever since have tried to whip into coherent form. And, indeed, certain patterns do emerge. In what some label the First New Deal (1933–1935), the dual themes were relief and recovery through a united national effort. In 1935, facing political challenges on the left and right, Roosevelt charted a more radical course. In the so-called Second New Deal (1935–1936), the administration placed less emphasis on unity and more on business regulation and on policies benefiting workers, small farmers, sharecroppers, migrant laborers, and others at the lower end of the scale.

The New Deal involved myriad programs, political infighting, and countless officials and bureaucrats. But in the public mind, it meant Roosevelt. Loved by some almost like a family member and reviled by others as a demagogue or would-be dictator, Roosevelt was a consummate politician whose administration set the national political agenda for a generation.

This chapter develops two interconnected themes. The first is the New Deal's profound effect on ideas about government, as it defined a more expansive view of the role of the state in promoting economic and social welfare. The second theme is the response of the American people to the Great Depression. From assembly-line workers, urban blacks, and migrant laborers to moviemakers, artists, writers, and photographers, diverse groups met the crisis with resourcefulness, social activism, and creative expression.

The chapter focuses on five major questions:

What were the main causes of the Great Depression?

What depression-fighting strategy underlay the so-called First New Deal, and why did the Roosevelt administration change course in 1935, giving rise to the so-called Second New Deal?

Which New Deal programs have had the greatest long-term effect, and how did ideas about the role of government change as a result of the New Deal?

How did the depression and the New Deal affect specific groups in the United States? (Consider, for example, small farmers and sharecroppers, Native Americans, industrial workers, women, African-Americans, and Mexican-Americans.)

How did American culture—including both the mass-entertainment industries and the efforts of novelists, artists, photographers, and composers—respond to the events of the 1930s?

CRASH AND DEPRESSION, 1929–1932

The prosperity of the 1920s came to a jolting end in October 1929 with the collapse of the stock market. The Wall Street crash, and the deeper economic problems that underlay it, launched a depression that reached every household. President Hoover struggled with the crisis, but his ideological commitment to private initiative and his horror of governmental coercion limited his effectiveness. In November 1932 voters turned to the Democratic party and its new leader, Franklin Roosevelt. This pivotal election set the stage for a vast expansion in the role of the federal government in addressing social and economic issues.

Black Thursday and the Onset of the Depression   Stock prices had risen steadily through much of the 1920s, but 1928–1929 brought a frenzied upsurge as speculators plunged into the market. In 1925 the market value of all stocks had stood at about $27 billion; by October 1929, with some 9 million Americans playing the market, it hit $87 billion. With stockbrokers lending speculators up to 75 percent of a stock's cost, credit or "margin" buying spread. The income-tax cuts promoted by Treasury Secretary Andrew Mellon had increased the volume of money available for speculation. Optimistic pronouncements also fed the speculative boom. In March 1929 former president Calvin Coolidge declared stocks "cheap at current prices." "Investment trusts," akin to today's mutual funds, but totally unregulated, lured novices into the market. The construction industry declined sharply in 1928–1929—an omen few heeded.

In 1928, and again in September 1929, the Federal Reserve Board tried to dampen speculation by raising the interest rate on federal reserve notes. Early in 1929 the Fed warned member banks to tighten their lending policies. But with speculators willing to pay up to 20 percent interest for money to buy more stock, lending institutions continued to loan money freely—an act akin to dumping gasoline on a raging fire. Stock prices zoomed ever higher.

The collapse came on October 24, 1929—"Black Thursday." As prices fell, some stocks found no buyers at all: they had literally become worthless. On Tuesday, October 29, a record 16 million stocks changed hands in frantic trading. In the ensuing weeks, feeble upswings alternated with further plunges.

President Hoover, in the first of many optimistic statements, pronounced the economy "sound and prosperous." But few listened. By mid-November the loss in the value of stocks stood at $30 billion. A weak upswing early in 1930 suggested that the worst might be over. However, instead of recovering, as many analysts predicted, the economy went into a long tailspin, producing a full-scale depression.

What were the underlying causes of this depression? Many economists focus on structural problems that made 1920s' prosperity so unstable. The agricultural sector remained depressed throughout the decade. In the industrial sector, increased productivity did not generate fully equivalent wage increases, but rather took the form of higher corporate profits. In 1929 the 40 percent of Americans who were lowest on the economic scale received only about 12 percent of the total national income. This reduced consumer purchasing power. At the same time, assembly-line methods encouraged overproduction. By summer 1929 the automobile, housing, textile, tire, and other durable-goods industries were seriously overextended. Further, important sectors of industry—including railroads, steel, textiles, and mining—lagged technologically in the 1930s and could not attract the investment needed to stimulate recovery.

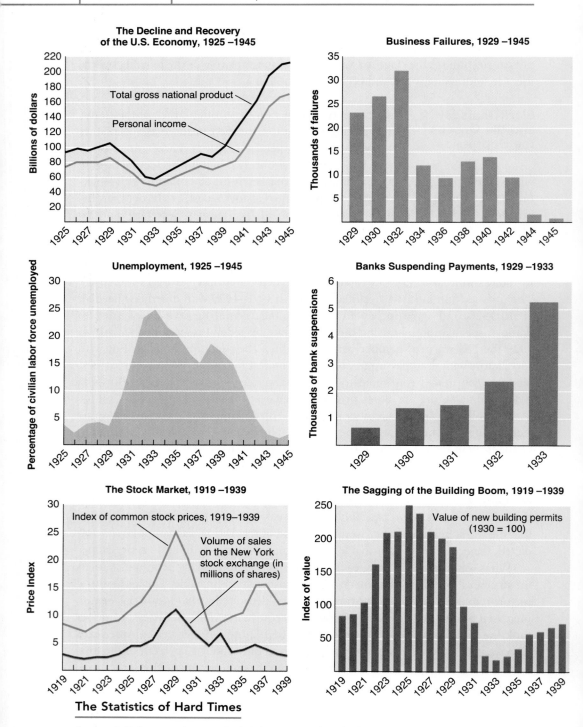

The Decline and Recovery of the U.S. Economy, 1925–1945

Billions of dollars

Total gross national product

Personal income

Business Failures, 1929–1945

Thousands of failures

Unemployment, 1925–1945

Percentage of civilian labor force unemployed

Banks Suspending Payments, 1929–1933

Thousands of bank suspensions

The Stock Market, 1919–1939

Price Index

Index of common stock prices, 1919–1939

Volume of sales on the New York stock exchange (in millions of shares)

The Sagging of the Building Boom, 1919–1939

Index of value

Value of new building permits (1930 = 100)

The Statistics of Hard Times

Sources: C. D. Bremmer, *American Bank Failures* (New York: Columbia University Press, 1935), 42; Thomas C. Cochran, *The Great Depression and World War II: 1929–1945* (Glenview, Illinois: Scott, Foresman, 1968); *Historical Statistics of the United States, Colonial Times to 1970* (Washington, D.C.: U.S. Government Printing Office, 1975).

Some economists, the so-called monetarist school, also focus on the banking system's collapse in the early 1930s, which they blame on Federal Reserve System's tight-money policies. These policies, they charge, strangled any hope of economic recovery by reducing the amount of money available to businesses for investment and growth.

All analysts link the U.S. depression to a global economic crisis. European economies, already enfeebled by war debt payments and a severe trade imbalance with the United States, collapsed in 1931. This larger crisis depressed U.S. exports and fed the fear gripping the nation.

Whatever the causes, the depression had a chilling impact on the U.S. economy. From 1929 to 1932, the gross national product dropped from $104 billion to $59 billion. Farm prices, already low, fell by nearly 60 percent. By early 1933 more than fifty-five hundred banks had closed, and unemployment stood at 25 percent, or nearly 13 million workers. In some cities the jobless rate far exceeded the national average. In Toledo in 1932, for example, it stood at 80 percent. Many who still had jobs faced cuts in pay and hours.

Hoover's Response

Historically, Americans had viewed depressions as acts of nature: little could be done other than ride out the storm. President Hoover, an intelligent moderate with activist impulses, disagreed. Drawing upon the legacy of progressive reform and his service as U.S. food administrator in World War I, Hoover initially confronted the crisis boldly. But his approach also reflected his belief in localism and private initiative.

Acting on his convictions, Hoover urged business leaders to maintain wages and employment. Viewing unemployment as a local issue, he advised municipal and state governments to create public-works projects. In October 1930 he set up an Emergency Committee for Employment to coordinate voluntary relief efforts. In 1931 he persuaded the nation's largest banks to set up a private lending agency, the National Credit Corporation, to help hard-pressed smaller banks make business loans.

These antidepression measures did little good. As the crisis worsened and joblessness increased, public opinion turned against Hoover. In the 1930 midterm election, the Republicans lost the House of Representatives and gave up eight Senate seats. In 1931, dreading a budget deficit, Hoover called for a tax increase, further angering hard-pressed Americans. That same year, despite their pledges to Hoover, U.S. Steel, General Motors, and other big corporations announced major wage cuts. The crisis quickly swamped private charities and local welfare agencies. Philadelphia, with more than three hundred thousand jobless by 1932, cut weekly relief payments to $4.23 per family and then suspended them entirely.

In 1932, a presidential election year, Hoover swallowed his principles and launched a bold federal response to the crisis. In January, at Hoover's recommendation, Congress set up a new agency, the Reconstruction Finance Corporation (RFC), to make loans to major economic institutions such as banks and insurance companies. By July the RFC had pumped $1.2 billion into the economy. Congress also authorized the RFC to grant $2 billion to state and local governments for job-creating public-works programs, and allocated $750 million for loans to businesses struggling to survive.

Hoover approved all these measures, but he reaped little political benefit from them. He supported them reluctantly, warning that they could open the door to "socialism and collectivism." Blaming global forces for the depression, he argued that only international measures would help. Some of his proposals, such as a moratorium on war-debt and reparations payments by European nations, made sense, but seemed irrelevant to the plight of ordinary Americans.

As Hoover issued press releases urging self-help and local initiative and endlessly saw prosperity "just around the corner," his relations with the news media soured. When he appointed a new press secretary disliked by the White House journalists, one reporter called it the first instance of a rat boarding a sinking ship. An administration launched so hopefully in 1929 by a widely admired president was ending in bitterness and failure.

Mounting
Discontent and
Protest

An ominous mood spread over the nation as hordes of the jobless waited in breadlines, slept on park benches, trudged the streets, and rode freight trains from city to city seeking work. Americans reared on the ethic of hard work and self-support experienced chronic unemployment as a shattering psychic blow. Because most of the jobless had families, the unemployment figures must be multiplied several times over to reflect the full impact of the crisis. Family savings vanished as banks failed.

Newspapers humanized the crisis. The *New York Times* described "Hoover Valley"—a section of Central Park where jobless men lived in boxes and packing crates. In winter they wrapped themselves in layers of newspapers they called Hoover blankets. The suicide rate climbed nearly 30 percent between 1928 and 1932. In Youngstown, Ohio, a fifty-seven-year-old jobless father of ten whose family faced eviction jumped to his death from a bridge. Violence threatened in some cities when people unable to pay their rent were evicted from homes and apartments.

Hard times battered the nation's farms. Many underwent mortgage foreclosures or forced sales because of tax delinquency, with Iowa and the Dakotas especially hard hit. Driving through the midwestern farm belt early in 1931, writer Malcolm Cowley found much of it untended and empty. "I wondered," Cowley wrote in the *New Republic*, "how much more of it will be abandoned next spring, after the milch cows have been sold for beef, the tractors and combine harvesters seized by finance corporations, the notes and mortgages allowed to go unpaid." At some forced farm auctions, neighbors bought the foreclosed farm for a trivial sum, and returned it to the evicted family.

In 1931 midwestern farmers organized a boycott movement called the Farmers' Holiday Association to force prices up by withholding grain and livestock from the market. Dairy farmers angered by low prices dumped milk in Iowa and Wisconsin.

The most alarming protest came from World War I veterans. In 1924 Congress had voted veterans a bonus stretched over a twenty-year period. In June 1932 some ten thousand veterans, many jobless, descended on Washington to lobby for immediate payment of these bonuses. When Congress refused, most of the "bonus marchers" went home, but about two thousand stayed on, building makeshift shelters on the outskirts of Washington. President Hoover called in the army.

On July 28 a thousand troops commanded by General Douglas MacArthur armed with tear gas, tanks, and machine guns drove the veterans from their encampment and burned their shelters. A journalist described the scene:

> [The veterans and their families] wandered from street to street or sat in ragged groups, the men exhausted, the women with wet handkerchiefs laid over their smarting eyes, the children waking from sleep to cough and whimper from the tear gas in their lungs. The flames behind them were climbing into the night sky. . . . Their shanties and tents had been burned, their personal property destroyed, except for the few belongings they could carry on their backs.

To many Americans, this action symbolized the administration's utter bankruptcy.

Matching the mood of discontent, American fiction of the early depression exuded disillusionment and despair. In *The 42nd Parallel* (1930), the first volume of a trilogy, John Dos Passos drew a dark panorama of twentieth-century America as money-mad, exploitive, and lacking spiritual meaning. As one character says, "Everything you've wanted crumbles in your fingers as you grasp it." In *Young Lonigan* (1932), which also launched a trilogy, James T. Farrell portrayed the empty existence of Studs Lonigan, a working-class Irish-immigrant youth in Chicago. Unable to find work and feeling betrayed by the American dream, Studs wanders the streets, trying to piece together a coherent worldview from the bits of mass culture that drift his way.

Some radical novelists of the early thirties attacked the capitalist system even more explicitly. The Communist party encouraged such fiction through writers' clubs and contests for working-class writers. Jack Conroy's *The Disinherited* (1933), dealing with life in the Missouri coal fields, gained force from the fact that Conroy's father and brother had died in a mine disaster.

The Election
of 1932
Gloom pervaded the 1932 Republican convention that renominated Hoover. The Democrats who gathered in Chicago, by contrast, scented victory. Their platform, crafted to erase the party divisions of the 1920s, appealed to urban voters with a call for repeal of prohibition, to farmers with support for aid programs, and to fiscal conservatives with demands for a balanced budget and cuts in federal spending. Rejecting Al Smith, the party's 1928 standard-bearer, the delegates nominated Franklin D. Roosevelt, governor of New York, for president.

Breaking precedent, FDR flew to Chicago to accept the nomination in person with a rousing speech pledging "a new deal for the American people." Despite this

The Election of 1932

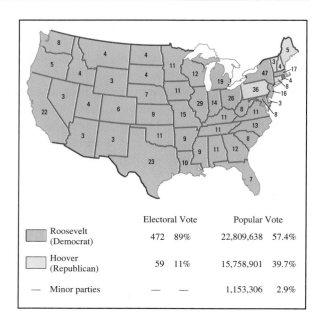

		Electoral Vote		Popular Vote	
Roosevelt (Democrat)		472	89%	22,809,638	57.4%
Hoover (Republican)		59	11%	15,758,901	39.7%
— Minor parties		—	—	1,153,306	2.9%

ringing phrase, Roosevelt's campaign offered no clear program. He called for "bold persistent experimentation" and compassion for "the forgotten man at the bottom of the economic pyramid," yet he also attacked Hoover's "reckless" spending and insisted that "only as a last resort" should the federal government play a larger depression-fighting role.

But Roosevelt exuded confidence, and above all he was not Hoover. On November 8, FDR and his running mate, Texas congressman John Nance Garner, received nearly 23 million votes, compared to fewer than 16 million for Hoover. Both houses of Congress went heavily Democratic. What did this landslide mean in terms of public policies? The nation waited.

THE NEW DEAL TAKES SHAPE, 1933–1935

The Roosevelt years began on a note of feverish activity. Enjoying strong majorities in Congress, FDR proposed an array of emergency measures that passed by large margins. These measures reflected differing and sometimes contradictory approaches, but they involved three basic goals: industrial recovery through business-government cooperation and pump-priming federal spending; agricultural recovery through crop reduction; and short-term emergency relief funneled through state and local agencies when possible, but directly by the federal government if necessary. Taken together, these programs expressed the vision of an activist government addressing urgent national problems. Hovering over the bustle loomed a confident Franklin Roosevelt, cigarette holder jauntily tilted upward, a symbol of hope. By 1935, however, some early New Deal programs were in trouble, and opposition was building.

Roosevelt and His Circle

FDR's inaugural address dedicated his administration to helping a people in crisis. "The only thing we have to fear," he intoned, "is fear itself." In an outpouring of support, half a million approving letters deluged the White House.

Roosevelt seemed an unlikely figure to become a popular hero. Like his distant cousin Theodore, FDR was of the social elite, with merchants and landowners among his Dutch-immigrant ancestors. He attended Harvard College and Columbia Law School. But as a state senator and governor of New York, he had allied with the Democratic party's urban-immigrant wing. When the depression struck, he had introduced innovative measures in New York, including unemployment insurance and a public-works program. Intent on reviving the economy while preserving capitalism and democracy, Roosevelt had no detailed agenda. He encouraged competing proposals, compromised (or papered over) differences, and then backed the measures he sensed could be sold to Congress and the public.

Eleanor Roosevelt Visits a West Virginia Coal Mine, 1933 *A New Yorker cartoon of 1933 portrayed one coal miner exclaiming to another: "Oh migosh, here comes Mrs. Roosevelt." But reality soon caught up with humor, as the First Lady immersed herself in the plight of the poor and the exploited.*

Roosevelt brought to Washington a circle of advisers nicknamed the brain trust. It included Columbia University professor Rexford G. Tugwell and lawyer Adolph A. Berle. Shaped by the progressive reform tradition, Tugwell and Berle rejected laissez-faire ideas and advocated federal economic planning and corporate regulation. But no single ideology or set of advisers controlled the New Deal, for FDR sought a broad range of opinions.

Eleanor Roosevelt played a key role. A niece of Theodore Roosevelt, she had a keen social conscience expressed in settlement house work and Florence Kelley's National Consumers' League. Through her, FDR met reformers, social workers, and advocates of minority rights. Recalled Rexford Tugwell: "No one who ever saw Eleanor Roosevelt sit down facing her husband, and holding his eyes firmly, say to him 'Franklin, I think you should . . . ,' or 'Franklin, surely you will not . . .' will ever forget the experience." Mrs. Roosevelt traveled ceaselessly and served as an astute observer for her wheelchair-bound husband. (A Washington newspaper once headlined "MRS. ROOSEVELT SPENDS NIGHT AT WHITE HOUSE.") In 1935 she began writing a syndicated newspaper column, "My Day."

Roosevelt's cabinet reflected the New Deal's diversity. Postmaster General James Farley, FDR's top political adviser, distributed patronage jobs, managed the 1932 and 1936 campaigns, and dealt with state and local Democratic leaders. Secretary of Labor Frances Perkins, the first woman cabinet member, had served as industrial commissioner of New York. Interior Secretary Harold Ickes had organized liberal Republicans for Roosevelt in 1932. Secretary of Agriculture Henry A. Wallace of Iowa held the same post his father had occupied in the 1920s. Treasury Secretary Henry Morgenthau, Jr., FDR's Hudson valley neighbor and political ally, though a fiscal conservative, tolerated the unbalanced budgets necessary to finance New Deal antidepression programs.

A host of newcomers poured into Washington in 1933—former progressives, liberal-minded professors, bright young lawyers. Joining the administration, they drafted bills, competed for influence, and debated recovery strategies. From this pressure-cooker environment emerged the laws, programs, and agencies gathered under a catch-all label: the New Deal.

The Hundred Days   Between March 9 and its adjournment on June 16, 1933, a period labeled the "Hundred Days," Congress enacted more than a dozen important measures. Rooted in the experience of the Progressive Era, World War I, and the Hoover presidency, these measures expanded the federal government's involvement in the nation's economic life.

FDR first addressed the banking crisis. As borrowers defaulted, panicky depositors withdrew savings, and homeowners missed mortgage payments, thousands of banks had failed, undermining confidence in the entire system. On March 5 Roosevelt ordered all banks to close for four days. At the end of this so-called bank holiday, he proposed an Emergency Banking Act. This law, supplemented by a later one, permitted healthy banks to reopen, set up procedures for managing failed banks, increased government oversight of banking, and required banks to separate

Major Measures Enacted During the "Hundred Days" (March 9–June 16, 1933)

March 9	Emergency Banking Act
20	Economy Act
31	Unemployment Relief Act (Civilian Conservation Corps)
May 12	Agricultural Adjustment Act
12	Federal Emergency Relief Act
18	Tennessee Valley Authority
27	Federal Securities Act
June 13	Home Owners' Refinancing Act
16	Farm Credit Act
16	Banking Act of 1933 (Federal Deposit Insurance Corporation)
16	National Industrial Recovery Act (National Recovery Administration; Public Works Administration)

their savings deposits from their investment funds. Congress also created the Federal Deposit Insurance Corporation (FDIC) to insure all bank deposits up to five thousand dollars. In the first of a series of radio talks dubbed "fireside chats," the president assured Americans that they could again trust their banks.

Other measures of the Hundred Days addressed the problem of relief—the urgent plight of Americans struggling to survive. Two new agencies assisted those who were losing their homes. The Home Owners Loan Corporation (HOLC) helped city dwellers refinance their mortgages. The Farm Credit Administration provided loans to rural Americans to meet their farm payments.

Another early New Deal relief program, the Civilian Conservation Corps (CCC), employed jobless youths in such government projects as reforestation, park maintenance, and erosion control. The CCC thus combined work relief with environmental programs. By 1935 half a million young men were earning thirty-five dollars a month in CCC camps—a godsend to families with no income at all.

The principal relief measure of the Hundred Days, the Federal Emergency Relief Act, appropriated $500 million for state and local relief agencies that had exhausted their funds. To head this program, FDR chose Harry Hopkins, the relief administrator in New York State. A gaunt chain smoker who enjoyed parties and the racetrack, Hopkins soon emerged as a powerful New Deal figure.

While supplying money for immediate relief of the needy, the early New Deal also faced the longer-term challenge of promoting recovery in the agricultural and industrial sectors of the economy. In confronting the chronic problem of low farm prices, New Dealers held different opinions. Some favored the approach of the 1920s McNary-Haugen bill (see Chapter 23) by which the government would buy agricultural surpluses and sell them abroad. Others, however, advocated reduced production as a means of raising farm income, and this approach won the day.

As a first step to cutting production, the government paid southern cotton planters to plow under much of their crop and midwestern farmers to slaughter some 6 million piglets and pregnant sows. This proved a public-relations nightmare, as Americans criticized the killing of pigs amid widespread hunger. Pursuing the same goal more systematically, Congress passed the Agricultural Adjustment Act in May 1933. This law set up a program by which producers of the major agricultural commodities—including hogs, wheat, corn, cotton, and dairy products—received payments, called subsidies, in return for cutting production. A tax on grain mills and other food processors (a tax ultimately passed along to consumers) financed these subsidies. A new agency, the Agricultural Adjustment Administration (AAA), supervised the program.

The other key recovery measure of the Hundred Days, the National Industrial Recovery Act, appropriated $3.3 billion for heavy-duty government public-works programs to provide jobs and stimulate the economy. Interior Secretary Harold Ickes headed the agency that ran this program, the Public Works Administration (PWA).

This law also set up another new agency, the National Recovery Administration (NRA). The NRA brought together business leaders to draft codes of "fair competition" for their industries. These codes set production limits, prescribed wages and working conditions, and forbade price cutting and unfair competitive practices. The aim was to promote recovery by breaking the cycle of wage cuts, falling prices, and layoffs. This approach revived the trade associations that Washington had encouraged during World War I (see Chapter 22). Indeed, the NRA's head, Hugh Johnson, had served with the War Industries Board of 1917–1918. The NRA also echoed the theme of business-government cooperation that Herbert Hoover had promoted as secretary of commerce in the 1920s.

The NRA's success depended on voluntary support by both business and the public. Johnson, a flamboyant showman, used parades, billboards, magazine ads, and celebrity events to persuade people to buy only from companies that subscribed to an NRA code and that displayed the NRA symbol, a blue eagle, and its slogan, "We Do Our Part."

While the NRA's purpose was to promote economic recovery, some New Dealers saw its reform potential as well. Under pressure from Labor Secretary Frances Perkins, the NRA's textile-industry code banned child labor. And thanks to Senator Robert Wagner of New York, Section 7a of the National Industrial Recovery Act affirmed workers' right to organize unions and to bargain collectively.

The Reconstruction Finance Corporation, dating from the Hoover years, remained active in the New Deal era. Under its chairman Jesse H. Jones, a Houston banker, the RFC lent billions of dollars to banks, insurance companies, and even new business ventures, making the RFC a potent financial resource for corporate America. The early New Deal thus had a strong probusiness flavor. In his speeches of 1933–1935, FDR always included business as a key player in the "all-American team" fighting the depression.

A few measures adopted during the Hundred Days, however, took a more regulatory approach to business. The stock-market crash had produced a strong antibusiness reaction and led to a Senate investigation of Wall Street. This probe revealed that not one of the twenty partners of the Morgan Bank had paid any income tax in 1931 or 1932. People jeered when the president of the New York Stock Exchange told a Senate committee considering regulatory legislation, "You gentlemen are making a big mistake. The Exchange is a perfect institution."

Reflecting the antibusiness mood, the early New Deal legislation also included a key regulatory measure, the Federal Securities Act. This law required corporations to inform the Federal Trade Commission fully on all stock offerings, and made executives personally liable for any misrepresentation of securities their companies issued. (In 1934 Congress curbed the purchase of stock on credit—a practice that had contributed to the crash of 1929—and created the Securities and Exchange Commission [SEC], to enforce the new regulations.)

The most innovative long-range recovery program of the Hundred Days was the Tennessee Valley Authority (TVA). This program had its origins in World War I, when the government had built a hydroelectric station on the Tennessee River in Alabama to power a nearby nitrate plant run by the War Department. In the 1920s Senator George Norris of Nebraska had urged the use of this facility to supply electricity to nearby farmers. Expanding Norris's idea, TVA advanced the economic and social development of the entire Tennessee River valley, one of the nation's most poverty-stricken regions.

A European visitor in the 1930s described the region's farms:

[A] very large percentage of them had kitchens with ovens burning wood. . . . They were lighted by dim, smoking, smelly oil lamps. . . . [T]he washing of clothes was done by hand in antiquated tubs. . . . [T]he water was brought into the house by women and children, from wells invariably situated at inconvenient and tiring distances. . . . Ordinarily there is no icebox, so many products that might be grown to vary the horribly monotonous diet are out of the question; they could not be stored.

Such conditions stunted the lives of the region's inhabitants. Wrote a Tennessee school administrator of the children in her schools, "Due to insufficient clothing and food, many are unable to attend school. . . . It is not uncommon for a child to have but one dress or one shirt. They have to stay at home the day the mother launders them."

TVA's ambitious goal was to remedy such conditions. A series of TVA dams supplied cheap hydroelectric power, bringing electricity to the region. TVA also promoted flood control, water recreation, and erosion prevention. Under director David Lilienthal, TVA proved one of the New Deal's most popular and enduring achievements.

For many Americans, the mind-boggling burst of laws and the "alphabet-soup" of new agencies during the Hundred Days symbolized both the dynamism and the confusion of the New Deal. How these new programs and agencies would work in practice remained to be seen.

Failures and Controversies Plague the Early New Deal

As the depression persisted, several early New Deal programs, including the NRA, the AAA, and the various relief agencies, faced difficulties. The NRA's problems related partly to the personality of the hard-driving, hard-drinking Hugh Johnson. But the trouble went deeper. As the unity spirit of the Hundred Days faded, corporate America chafed under NRA regulation. Code violations increased. Small businesses complained that the codes favored big corporations. The agency itself, meanwhile, became bogged down in drafting trivial codes. The shoulder-pad industry, for example, had its own code. Corporate trade associations used the codes to restrict competition and maintain prices, not to stimulate recovery.

Gradually, the NRA sank of its own weight. Johnson left in 1934, and in May 1935 the Supreme Court unanimously ruled the NRA unconstitutional. The Court cited two reasons: first, the law gave the president regulatory powers that constitutionally belonged to Congress; second, the NRA regulated commerce within states, violating the constitutional provision limiting federal regulation to interstate commerce. Few mourned the NRA. As a recovery measure, it had failed.

The AAA fared better, but it too proved controversial. Farm prices did rise as production declined, fulfilling the planners' hopes. In 1933–1937, overall farm income increased by 50 percent. But the AAA did not help farm laborers or migrant workers; indeed, its crop-reduction payments actually hurt southern tenants and sharecroppers when cotton growers removed acreage from production, banked the subsidy checks, and evicted the sharecroppers. One Georgia sharecropper wrote Harry Hopkins, "I have Bin farming all my life But the man I live with Has Turned me loose . . . I can't get a Job."

Some victims of this process resisted. In 1934 the interracial Southern Tenant Farmers' Union, led by the Socialist party, emerged in Arkansas. Declared one black sharecropper at the organizing meeting, "The same chain that holds my people holds your people too. . . . [We should] get together and stay together." The landowners struck back, harassing union organizers.

Debate raged between New Dealers intent on raising total agricultural income and others who urged special attention to the poorest farmers. FDR at first backed the former group, but the advocates of a more class-based farm policy soon gained influence. Their cause was strengthened as a parching drought turned the Great Plains into a dust bowl. The rains failed in 1930, devastating wheat and livestock on the southern plains. In 1934 dust clouds spread across the nation, darkening cities from Chicago to Boston and Savannah before blowing out to sea. Through 1939, each summer brought a new scourge of dust. The worst year was 1937, with the dust storms centered in Kansas, Oklahoma, Texas, Colorado, and New Mexico.

Survivors never forgot the experience. Even night brought no relief. Recalled a Kansas woman, "A trip for water to rinse the grit from our lips, and then back to

The Dust Bowl

From the Dakotas southward to the Mexican border, farmers in the Great Plains suffered from a lack of rainfall and severe soil erosion in the 1930s, worsening the hardships of the Great Depression.

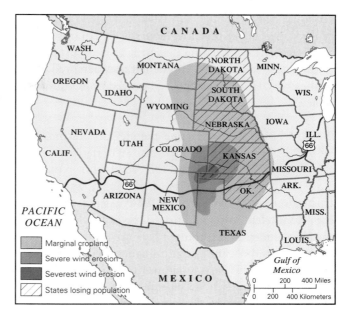

Marginal cropland

Severe wind erosion

Severest wind erosion

States losing population

---

bed with washcloths over our noses. We try to lie still, because every turn stirs the dust on the blankets." Folk singer Woody Guthrie recalled his 1930s' boyhood in Oklahoma and Texas in his song "The Great Dust Storm." It began:

> It fell across our city like a curtain of black rolled down. We thought it was our judgment, we thought it was our doom.

Battered by debt and drought alike, many families gave up, leaving behind abandoned houses and farms. Nearly 3.5 million people left the Great Plains in the 1930s; the population of Cimarron County, Oklahoma, fell by 40 percent. Some migrated to nearby cities, further swamping relief rolls. Others packed their meager belongings into old cars and headed west. Though coming from various states, they all bore a derisive nickname, Okies. The plight of dust-bowl migrants further complicated New Deal agricultural planning.

Rivalries and policy differences also plagued the New Deal relief program. As unemployment continued, Harry Hopkins convinced Roosevelt to support direct federal relief programs, rather than channeling funds through state and local agencies. Late in 1933 FDR named Hopkins to head a temporary public-works agency, the Civil Works Administration (CWA). Through the winter the CWA expended nearly a billion dollars on short-term work projects for the jobless. When warm weather returned, FDR abolished the CWA. Like his conservative critics, FDR feared creating a permanent underclass living on welfare payments. But persistent unemployment swamping local relief agencies made further federal programs inevitable.

Hopkins and Harold Ickes, head of the Public Works Administration, competed to control federal relief policy. The cautious Ickes examined every PWA proposal with a fine-tooth comb. Large-scale PWA public-works projects did promote economic recovery, but "Honest Harold's" deliberate approach left billions in relief funds stalled in the pipeline. Hopkins, by contrast, wanted to put people to work and get money circulating. Even make-work projects like raking leaves and collecting litter had merit, he argued, if they achieved these goals. Given the urgency of the crisis, Hopkins's approach proved more influential in shaping federal relief policy.

1934–1935: Challenges from Right and Left

Despite the New Deal's brave beginnings, the depression persisted. In 1934 national income rose about 25 percent above 1933 levels, but remained far below that of 1929. Millions had been jobless for three or four years. The rising frustration found expression in 1934 in nearly two thousand strikes, some of them communist-led, from New York taxi drivers to San Francisco dockworkers. With the NRA under attack, conflict flaring over farm policy, and relief spending growing rather than declining, criticism mounted. Conservatives attacked the New Deal as socialistic. In 1934 several business leaders, joined by an embittered Al Smith, formed the anti–New Deal American Liberty League. The U.S. Chamber of Commerce blasted the New Deal. Anti-Roosevelt jokes circulated among the rich, many of whom denounced him as a traitor to his class.

But the New Deal remained popular, reflecting both its achievements and FDR's political skills. Assisted by speechwriters and publicists, Roosevelt commanded the political stage. Pursuing his "national unity" theme, Roosevelt exhorted everyone to join the battle for economic recovery just as Americans had united in 1917 against a foreign foe. Although Republican newspaper publishers remained hostile, FDR enjoyed good relations with the working press. He loved bantering with reporters, and they responded by portraying his administration favorably.

In contrast to Hoover, Roosevelt loved public appearances and took naturally to radio. Frances Perkins described his radio talks: "His head would nod and his hands would move in simple, natural, comfortable gestures. His face would smile and light up as though he were actually sitting on the front porch or in the parlor with [his listeners]." Roosevelt's mastery of radio provided a model for his successors in the era of television.

The 1934 midterm election ratified the New Deal's popularity. Reversing the usual pattern, the Democrats increased their congressional majorities. As for FDR, Kansas journalist William Allen White observed, "He's been all but crowned by the people." As the returns rolled in, Harry Hopkins exulted to a group of New Deal friends, "Boys, this is our hour!"

Despite this seeming vote of confidence, the political scene was highly unstable in 1934–1935. While conservatives criticized the New Deal for going too far, critics on the left attacked it for not going far enough. Socialists and communists ridiculed Roosevelt's efforts to include big business in his "all-American team." Clifford Odets's 1935 play *Waiting for Lefty* portrayed noble workers battling evil bosses and ended by inciting the audience to chant "Strike! Strike! Strike!"

Pushing the New Deal's experimental spirit still further, demagogues peddled more radical social and economic programs. The Detroit Catholic priest and radio spellbinder Charles Coughlin attacked FDR as a "great betrayer and liar," made anti-Semitic allusions, and called for nationalization of the banks. For a time, Coughlin's followers, organized as the National Union of Social Justice and drawn mainly from the lower middle class, seemed a potent force.

Meanwhile, California physician Francis Townsend proposed that the government pay two hundred dollars a month to all retired citizens, requiring them to spend the money within thirty days. This plan, Townsend insisted, would help the elderly, stimulate the economy, and open up jobs by encouraging retirement. The scheme would have bankrupted the nation, but many older citizens, especially in California, rallied to Townsend's banner.

FDR's wiliest rival was flamboyant Huey Long of Louisiana. A country lawyer elected governor of Louisiana in 1928, Long built highways, schools, and public housing. He roared into Washington as a senator in 1933, preaching his "Share Our Wealth" program: a 100 percent tax on all incomes over $1 million and appropriation of all fortunes in excess of $5 million. With this money, Long promised, every family could enjoy a comfortable income, a house, a car, old-age benefits, and free college education. "Every man a king," Long proclaimed, and millions responded. By 1935 he boasted 7.5 million supporters. The title of his 1935 book, *My First Days in the White House,* made clear his ultimate goal. An assassin's bullet killed Long that September, but his organization survived.

Responding vigorously to these challenges, Roosevelt regained the political high ground in 1935 with a bold series of legislative initiatives. The result was a fresh surge of social legislation that rivaled that of the Hundred Days.

THE NEW DEAL CHANGES COURSE, 1935–1936

As the spirit of national unity faded and Roosevelt faced criticism from the left and right, he abandoned the unity theme and veered leftward. In 1935–1936, Roosevelt pushed through a bundle of reform measures so impressive that some call this phase the Second New Deal. His commitment to fighting the depression and to an activist role for government continued. But while he had initially tried to win the support of all Americans including big business, from 1935 on FDR increasingly criticized the wealthy and the business class, and focused on aiding the most disadvantaged Americans.

In his January 1935 State of the Union address, Roosevelt offered six initiatives reflecting his new priorities: an expanded public-works program, assistance to the rural poor, support for organized labor, benefits for retired workers and other needy groups, tougher business regulation, and heavier taxes on the well-to-do. These goals shaped his program thereafter.

Expanding
Federal Relief

With unemployment still high, Congress passed the $5 billion Emergency Relief Appropriation Act in April 1935. Roosevelt swiftly set up the Works Progress Administration (WPA) and put Harry Hopkins in charge. Like the Civil Works Administration of 1933–1934, the WPA funneled assistance directly to individuals. Roosevelt insisted

Major Later New Deal Legislation (November 1933–1938)

Nov. 1933	Civilian Works Administration
1934	Civil Works Emergency Relief Act
	Home Owners' Loan Act
	Securities Exchange Act (Securities and Exchange Commission)
	Communications Act (Federal Communications Commission)
	Federal Farm Bankruptcy Act
	National Housing Act (Federal Housing Administration)
	Taylor Grazing Act
1935	Emergency Relief Appropriations Act (Works Progress Administration)
	National Youth Administration
	National Labor Relations Act (Wagner Act)
	Revenue Act of 1935
	Social Security Act
	Public Utilities Holding Company Act
	Banking Act of 1935
	Resettlement Administration
	Rural Electrification Act
1936	Soil Conservation and Domestic Allotment Act
1937	National Housing Act
	Bankhead-Jones Farm Tenancy Act (Farm Security Administration)
1938	Fair Labor Standards Act
	Agricultural Adjustment Act of 1938

that the WPA provide work, not handouts, for the jobless. Over its eight-year life, the WPA employed more than 8 million Americans; pumped $11 billion into the economy; constructed or improved 650,000 miles of roads; built or repaired 124,000 bridges; and erected 125,000 schools, hospitals, post offices, and other public buildings.

The WPA also assisted writers, performers, and artists. In the South, WPA workers collected the reminiscences of former slaves. The Federal Writers' Project employed jobless authors to produce state guides and histories of ethnic and immigrant groups. Under the Federal Music Project, unemployed musicians gave free concerts, often featuring American composers. By 1938 more than 30 million Americans had attended an FMP concert.

The Federal Theatre Project (FTP) employed actors. One FTP project, the Living Newspaper, which dramatized contemporary social issues, was criticized as

Construction of a Dam, by William Gropper (1897–1977) *The New Deal's Federal Arts Project commissioned murals for post offices and other public buildings. Gropper, whose work often exposed social injustice and class inequalities, painted this upbeat mural for the Department of the Interior building in Washington, D.C.*

New Deal propaganda. Marc Blitzstein's radical musical *The Cradle Will Rock* (1937), which had FTP funding, was cancelled by nervous WPA officials before the opening-night performance. The cast and audience defiantly walked to another theater, and the show went on. FTP drama companies touring small-town America gave many their first taste of theater. Artists working for the Federal Arts Project designed posters, offered school courses, and decorated post offices and courthouses with murals.

Harold Ickes's Public Works Administration, after a slow start, now picked up steam, expending more than $4 billion over its life span. PWA workers completed some thirty-four thousand construction projects, including dams, bridges, and public buildings. Among the PWA's undertakings were New York City's Triborough Bridge and Lincoln Tunnel, and the awesome Grand Coulee Dam on the Columbia River.

With heavy relief spending came large federal budget deficits, cresting at $4.4 billion in 1936. These deficits were covered by government borrowing. According to British economist John Maynard Keynes, governments should deliberately use deficit spending during depressions to fund public-works programs, thereby increasing purchasing power and stimulating recovery. The New Deal approach, however, was not Keynesian. Because all the dollars spent on relief and recovery programs were withdrawn from the economy through taxation or government borrowing, the stimulus effect was nil. FDR saw deficits as an unwelcome necessity, not a positive good.

Aiding Migrants, Supporting Unions, Regulating Business, Taxing the Wealthy The second phase of the New Deal was more frankly geared to the interests of workers, the poor, and the disadvantaged. Social-justice advocates like Frances Perkins and Eleanor Roosevelt helped shape this program, but so did hard-headed politics. Looking to 1936, FDR's political advisers feared that the followers of Coughlin, Townsend, and Long could siphon off enough votes to cost him the election. This worry underlay FDR's 1935 political agenda.

The Second New Deal's agricultural policy addressed the plight of sharecroppers (a plight the AAA had helped create) and other poor farmers. The Resettlement Administration (1935), directed by Rexford Tugwell, made loans to help tenant farmers buy their own farms and to enable displaced sharecroppers, tenants, and dust-bowl migrants move to more productive areas. The Rural Electrification Administration, also started in 1935, made low-interest loans to utility companies and farmers' cooperatives to extend electricity to the 90 percent of rural America that still lacked it. By 1941, 40 percent of U.S. farms enjoyed electric power.

The agricultural-recovery program suffered a setback in January 1936 when the Supreme Court declared the Agricultural Adjustment Act unconstitutional. The processing tax that funded the AAA's subsidies, the Court held, was an illegal use of the government's tax power. To replace the AAA, Congress passed a soil-conservation act that paid farmers to plant grasses and legumes instead of soil-depleting crops such as wheat and cotton (which also happened to be the major surplus commodities).

Organized labor won a key victory in 1935, again thanks to Senator Robert Wagner. During the New Deal's national-unity phase, FDR had criticized Wagner's campaign for a prolabor law as "special interest" legislation. But Wagner persisted, and in 1935, when the Supreme Court ruled the NIRA, including Section 7a protecting union members' rights, unconstitutional, FDR called for a labor law that would survive constitutional scrutiny. The National Labor Relations Act of July 1935 guaranteed collective-bargaining rights, permitted closed shops (in which all employees must join a union), and outlawed such management tactics as black-listing union organizers. The law created the National Labor Relations Board (NLRB) to supervise shop elections and deal with labor-law violations. The Wagner Act, as it was called, stimulated a wave of unionization (see below).

The Second New Deal's more class-conscious thrust shaped other 1935 measures as well. The Banking Act strengthened the Federal Reserve Board's control over the nation's financial system. The Public Utilities Holding Company Act, targeting the sprawling public-utility empires of the 1920s, restricted gas and electric companies to one geographic region.

In 1935, too, Roosevelt called for steeper taxes on the rich to combat the "unjust concentration of wealth and economic power." Congress responded with a revenue act, also called the Wealth Tax Act, that raised taxes on corporations and on the well-to-do to a maximum of 75 percent on incomes above $5 million. Though this law had many loopholes and was not quite the "soak the rich" measure some believed, it did express the Second New Deal's more radical spirit.

The Social Security Act of 1935; End of the Second New Deal

The Social Security Act of 1935, perhaps the most important of all New Deal laws, stands out for its long-range significance. Drafted by a committee chaired by Frances Perkins, this measure had complex sources, including Progressive Era ideas and the social-welfare programs of England and Germany. It established a mixed federal-state system of workers' pensions; unemployment insurance; survivors' benefits for victims of industrial accidents; and aid for disabled persons and dependent mothers with children.

Taxes paid partly by employers and partly by workers (in the form of amounts withheld from their paychecks) funded the pension and survivors' benefit features. This payroll-withholding provision helped bring on a recession in 1937. But it made sense politically because workers would fight any effort to end a pension plan they had contributed to. As Roosevelt put it, "With those taxes in there, no damned politician can ever scrap my social security program."

The initial Social Security Act paid low benefits and bypassed farmers, domestic workers, and the self-employed. But it established the principle of federal responsibility for social welfare and laid the foundation for a vastly expanded welfare system in the future.

By September 1935, when Congress adjourned, the Second New Deal, with its historic record of legislative accomplishment, was complete. Without embracing the panaceas preached by Coughlin, Townsend, or Long, FDR had addressed the grievances they had exploited. Although conservatives called this phase of the New Deal "antibusiness," FDR always insisted that he had saved capitalism by addressing the social problems it spawned. During much of the post–Civil War era the business class had dominated government, marginalizing other groups. Business remained influential in the 1930s, but as the New Deal evolved, it increasingly acted as a broker for all organized interest groups, including organized labor, not just corporate America. And in 1935, with an election looming, New Deal strategists reached farther still, to address the situation of sharecroppers and migrant workers, the disabled, the elderly, needy mothers with dependent children, and others whose plight had rarely concerned politicians of the past.

In the process, the New Deal vastly expanded the role of the federal government in American life, as well as the power of the presidency. Building on precedents set by Theodore Roosevelt a generation earlier, FDR so dominated the politics of the 1930s that Americans began to expect presidents to offer "programs," address national issues, and shape the terms of public debate. This decisively altered the balance of power between the White House and Congress. The New Deal's importance thus lies not only in specific laws, but also in the way it redefined the scope of the executive branch and, more broadly still, the social role of the state.

The 1936 Roosevelt Landslide and the New Democratic Coalition
With the Second New Deal in place, FDR faced the 1936 campaign with confidence. "There's one issue . . . ," he told an aide; "it's myself, and people must be either for me or against me."

The Republican candidate, Governor Alfred Landon of Kansas, was a fiscal conservative who nevertheless believed that government must address social issues. Landon proved to be an earnest if inept campaigner. ("Wherever I have gone in this country, I have found Americans," he revealed in one speech.) When Republicans lambasted FDR's alleged dictatorial ambitions and charged that the social security law would require all workers to wear metal dog tags, he struck back with his usual zest. Only the forces of "selfishness and greed" opposed him, he declared at an enthusiastic election-eve rally in New York City, adding, "They are united in their hatred for me—and I welcome their hatred."

In the most crushing electoral victory since 1820, FDR carried every state but Maine and Vermont. Landon even lost Kansas. Pennsylvania went Democratic for the first time since 1856. The Democrats increased their already top-heavy majorities in Congress. Roosevelt buried his minor-party opponents as well. Socialist Norman Thomas received under 200,000 votes, the Communist party's presidential candidate only about 80,000. The Union party, a coalition of the Coughlinites, Townsendites, and Huey Long supporters who had appeared so formidable in 1935, polled only 892,000 votes.

FDR's 1936 landslide victory announced the emergence of a potent new Democratic coalition. Since Reconstruction, the Democrats had counted on three bases of support: the white South, parts of the West, and urban white ethnic voters mobilized by big-city Democratic machines. FDR retained and solidified these centers of strength. He rarely challenged state or local party leaders who produced the votes, whether they supported the New Deal or not. In Virginia he even withdrew support from a pro–New Deal governor who clashed with the state's conservative but powerful Democratic senators. When the Democratic boss of Jersey City, Frank Hague, faced mail tampering charges, FDR said to Jim Farley, "Tell Frank to knock it off . . . , but keep this thing quiet because we need Hague's support if we want New Jersey."

Building on Al Smith's urban breakthrough in 1928, FDR carried the nation's twelve largest cities. Not only did New Deal relief programs aid city dwellers, but Roosevelt wooed them persuasively. When the presidential entourage swept through cities like New York and Boston, cheering crowds lined the route. FDR also appointed many representatives of the newer urban-immigrant groups, including Catholics and Jews, to New Deal positions.

Expanding the Democratic base, FDR reached out to four partially overlapping groups: farmers, union members, northern blacks, and women. Midwestern farmers, long rock-ribbed Republicans, liked the New Deal's agricultural program and switched to Roosevelt. In Iowa, where Democrats had garnered scarcely 20 percent of the vote in the 1920s, FDR won decisively in 1936. Organized labor also joined the New Deal coalition. The unions pumped money into Roosevelt's campaigns (although far less than business gave the Republicans), and union members voted overwhelmingly for Roosevelt. Despite his early foot dragging on the Wagner bill, FDR's reputation as a "friend of labor" proved unassailable.

Although most southern blacks remained disfranchised, northern blacks voted in growing numbers, and as late as 1932 two-thirds of them went for Hoover, leading one exasperated African-American editor to advise: "[T]urn Lincoln's picture to the wall. That debt has been paid in full." The New Deal era saw a historic shift. In 1934 Chicago's black voters replaced Republican Congressman Oscar DePriest with a Democrat. In 1936, 76 percent of black voters supported FDR.

In economic terms, this shift made sense. Owing mainly to racial discrimination, blacks' unemployment rates in the 1930s surpassed those of the work force as a whole. Thus, jobless blacks benefited heavily from New Deal relief programs.

On issues of racial justice, however, the New Deal's record was mixed at best. Some NRA codes contained racially discriminatory clauses, leading black activists to dismiss the agency as "Negroes Ruined Again." TVA and other New Deal agencies tolerated racial bias. Lynchings increased in the 1930s as some whites translated economic worries into racial aggression, but Roosevelt kept aloof from the NAACP's campaign to make lynching a federal crime. An antilynching bill passed the House of Representatives in 1935, but southern Democratic senators killed it with a filibuster. To protect his legislative program and retain southern white voters,

FDR did little. Blacks must realize, the NAACP concluded bitterly, "that . . . the Roosevelt administration [has] nothing for them."

In limited ways, however, FDR did address racial issues. Assuring an audience at Howard University, a black institution in Washington, D.C., that there would be "no . . . forgotten races" in his administration, Roosevelt cautiously worked to rid New Deal agencies of blatant racism. He appointed more than a hundred blacks to policy-level and judicial positions, including Mary McLeod Bethune as director of minority affairs in the National Youth Administration. Bethune, a Florida educator, head of the National Council of Negro Women, and a friend of Eleanor Roosevelt, led the so-called black cabinet that linked the administration and black organizations. The "Roosevelt Supreme Court" that took shape after 1936 issued antidiscrimination rulings in cases involving housing, voting rights, wage inequity, and jury selection.

The New Deal also supported racial justice in symbolic ways. In 1938, when a meeting of the interracial Southern Conference for Human Welfare in Birmingham, Alabama, was segregated in compliance with local statutes, Mrs. Roosevelt pointedly placed her chair halfway between the white and black delegates. In 1939, when the Daughters of the American Revolution barred black contralto Marian Anderson from performing in Washington's Constitution Hall, Mrs. Roosevelt resigned from the organization, and Harold Ickes arranged an Easter concert by Anderson at the Lincoln Memorial. Even symbolic gestures outraged many southern whites. When a black minister delivered the invocation at the 1936 Democratic convention, Senator Ed Smith of South Carolina noisily stalked out.

The Roosevelt administration courted women voters. The head of the Democratic party's women's division, Molly Dewson, a friend of the Roosevelts, led this effort. In the 1936 campaign Dewson mobilized fifteen thousand women who went door to door distributing flyers describing New Deal programs. "[W]e did not make the old-fashioned plea that our nominee was charming," she later recalled; " . . . we appealed to [women's] intelligence."

Unlike earlier feminists, Dewson did not promote a specifically feminist agenda. New Deal efforts for economic recovery and social welfare, she argued, served the best interests of both sexes. She did, however, push for more women in federal policy-level positions. FDR appointed not only the first woman cabinet member but also the first woman ambassador and unprecedented numbers of female federal judges. Through Dewson's efforts, the 1936 Democratic platform committee reflected a fifty-fifty gender balance.

Symbolic gestures and the appointment of a few blacks and women ought not be overemphasized. Racism and sexism pervaded American society in the 1930s, and Roosevelt, preoccupied with the economic crisis, did relatively little to change things. That challenge would await a later generation.

The Environment, the West, and Indian Policy

Environmental issues loomed large in the 1930s, reflecting FDR's own priorities. As early as 1910, in the New York Senate, he had sought to regulate logging that threatened wildlife. As president, he prodded the Civilian Conservation Corps to plant trees, thin forests, and build hiking trails.

Soil conservation emerged as a major priority. The Great Plains dust storms of the 1930s resulted not only from drought but also from years of overgrazing and unwise farming practices. Throughout history, periodic drought had struck the Great Plains beyond the hundredth meridian, which bisects central Kansas. But the dust storms were not inevitable. For decades settlers had used ever more powerful tractors and combines to cultivate more land. In the process they had plowed up the grama-buffalo grass and other native grasses that anchored the soil, leaving the topsoil exposed to parching winds when the rains failed. By the 1930s, 9 million acres of farmland had been lost to erosion in the Great Plains, the South, and elsewhere, with more in jeopardy.

The Department of Agriculture's Soil Conservation Service set up projects to demonstrate the value of contour plowing, crop rotation, and soil-strengthening grasses. The Taylor Grazing Act of 1934—enacted as dust clouds darkened the skies over Washington, D.C.—restricted the grazing on public lands that had contributed to the problem. The TVA helped control the floods that worsened erosion in the Tennessee valley.

New Deal planners avidly promoted the national-park movement. Olympic National Park in Washington, Virginia's Shenandoah National Park, and Kings Canyon National Park in California all date from the 1930s. The administration also established some 160 new national wildlife refuges. Roosevelt even closed a Utah artillery range that threatened a nesting site of the endangered trumpeter swan.

The wilderness movement won powerful new adherents. In 1935 Robert Marshall of the U.S. Forest Service and environmentalist Aldo Leopold helped found the Wilderness Society to lobby for the cause. Under pressure from wilderness advocates, Congress set aside a large portion of Kings Canyon National Park as a wilderness area. These movements sometimes created unusual alliances. For example, the National Wildlife Federation (1936) was funded by the firearms industry, which had an economic interest in preserving wilderness areas and wild game for hunters.

To be sure, today's environmental issues—pollution, pesticides, dwindling fossil fuels, and so forth—received little attention in the 1930s. Most New Dealers welcomed ever-rising levels of energy consumption. The decade's hydroelectric projects, while necessary at a time when most farmers still lacked electricity, nevertheless fed an ideology of boundless consumption that in retrospect seems heedless and wasteful. Nor did the ecological effects of these projects attract much attention. The Grand Coulee Dam, for example, destroyed salmon spawning on much of the Columbia River's tributary system. As Joseph E. Taylor shows in *Making Salmon: An Environmental History of the Northwest Fisheries* (1999), not only Grand Coulee but also other New Deal dams disrupted fragile ecosystems and adversely affected local residents, particularly Native American communities, that depended on them for their livelihood.

Still, when viewed in context, the New Deal's environmental record remains impressive. While coping with a grave economic crisis, the Roosevelt administration focused a level of attention on environmental issues that had not been seen since the Progressive Era, and would not be seen again for a generation.

The depression profoundly affected the American West, particularly as hordes of hard-hit citizens, including dust-bowl refugees, sought a fresh start in the region, especially in California. Continuing a long-term demographic trend, the West Coast's share of the population spiked upward in the 1930s, and Los Angeles jumped from tenth to fifth among U.S. cities.

The New Deal had a big impact on the West as well, especially because the federal government owned a third or more of the land in eleven western states. New Deal agencies and laws such as the AAA, the Soil Conservation Service, the Taylor Grazing Act, and the Farm Security Administration (see below) set new rules for western agriculture from the grain and cattle of the Great Plains to the Pacific Coast citrus groves and truck farms dependent on migrant labor.

Some of the largest PWA and WPA projects were built in the West, including thousands of public buildings (246 in Washington State alone) from courthouses and post offices to tourist facilities such as Timberline Lodge on Oregon's Mount Hood. The highways linking the West to the rest of America, such as the Lincoln Highway from Philadelphia to San Francisco, Yellowstone Trail from Chicago to Seattle, and Route 66 from Chicago to Los Angeles, were upgraded in the 1930s with federal assistance.

Above all, the PWA in the West built dams—not only Grand Coulee, but also Shasta on the Sacramento River, Bonneville on the Columbia, Glen Canyon on the Colorado, and others. Boulder (later Hoover) Dam on the Colorado, authorized by Congress in 1928, was completed by the PWA. Despite their ecological effect, these great undertakings—among the largest engineering projects in human history—supplied hydroelectric power to vast regions while also contributing to flood control, irrigation, and soil conservation.

A New Deal initiative with special importance for the West was Harold Ickes's National Planning Board of 1934, later renamed the National Resources Planning Board. This agency facilitated state and regional management of natural resources, including water, soil, timber, and minerals. Despite the West's celebrated "rugged individualism," the New Deal's emphasis on planning, in tandem with the PWA's dams and infrastructure development, reshaped the public life of the region.

The 1930s also revived attention to the nation's 330,000 Native Americans, most of whom endured poverty, scant education, poor health care, and bleak prospects. The Dawes Severalty Act of 1887 (see Chapter 17) had dissolved the tribes as legal entities, allocated some tribal lands to individual Indians, and offered the rest for sale. By the 1930s whites held about two-thirds of the land that Indians had possessed in 1887, including much of the most valuable acreage. Indians had been granted full citizenship and voting rights in 1924, but this did little to improve their lot.

In the 1920s a reform movement arose to reverse the Dawes Act approach. One reformer, John Collier, who had lived among the Pueblo Indians of New Mexico, founded the American Indian Defense Association in 1923 to preserve what he saw as the spiritual beauty and harmony of traditional Indian life. Gertrude Bonnin, a Yankton Dakota Sioux and president of the National Council of American Indians, while not sharing all of Collier's goals, also pressed for reform.

Appointed commissioner of Indian affairs in 1933, Collier cadged funds from New Deal agencies to construct schools, hospitals, and irrigation systems on reservations, and to preserve sites of cultural importance. The Civilian Conservation Corps employed twelve thousand Indian youths to work on projects on Indian lands.

Pursuing his vision of renewed tribal life, Collier drafted a bill to halt the sale of tribal land, restore the remaining unallocated lands to tribal control, create new reservations, and expand existing ones. It also envisioned tribal councils with broad governing powers and required Indian schools to teach Native American history and handicrafts. Collier's bill sparked opposition in western states. Some Indian leaders criticized it as a plan to transform the reservations into living museums and to treat Native Americans as an exotic people cut off from modern life. Indians who had succeeded as individual property owners or entrepreneurs rejected the bill's tribalist assumptions. The bill did, indeed, reflect the idealism of well-meaning outsiders rather than the views of the nation's diverse Native American groups.

The Indian Reorganization Act of 1934, a compromise measure, halted the sale of tribal lands and enabled tribes to regain title to unallocated lands. But Congress scaled back Collier's proposals for tribal self-government and dropped his calls for renewal of traditional tribal culture.

A majority of tribes approved the law (a requirement for it to go into effect), but opinion was divided. Of the tribes that voted, 181, representing 130,000 Indians, approved, while 77, comprising 86,000 persons, did not. America's largest tribal group, the 40,000-strong Navajo, voted no, largely because the law, to promote soil conservation, restricted grazing rights.

Indian policy clearly remained contentious. But the law did reflect greater recognition of Indian interests and a greater acceptance of cultural diversity. The restoration of tribes as legal entities laid the groundwork for later tribal business ventures as well as tribal lawsuits seeking to enforce long-violated treaty rights (see Chapters 30 and 31).

THE NEW DEAL'S END STAGE, 1937–1939

Buoyed by his landslide victory in 1936, Roosevelt launched an abortive attack on the Supreme Court. Bloodied by this divisive fight, an embattled FDR confronted both a stubborn recession and newly energized conservative opposition. With a few final measures in 1937–1938, the New Deal came to a close.

FDR and the Supreme Court   In 1937 the Supreme Court was made up of nine elderly justices, four of whom were arch-conservatives who abhorred the New Deal. Joined by others of more moderate views, these conservatives had invalidated the NRA, the AAA, and progressive state laws. With good reason, Roosevelt feared that key measures of the Second New Deal, including the Social Security Act and the Wagner Act, would meet a similar fate. Indeed, some corporate lawyers were so sure that the Social Security Act would be found unconstitutional that they advised their clients to ignore it.

In February 1937 FDR proposed a court-reform bill that would have allowed him to appoint an additional Supreme Court member for each justice over age seventy, up to a total of six. Roosevelt blandly insisted that he was concerned about the heavy workload of aging justices, but his political motivation was obvious.

FDR hoped that his personal popularity would assure support for his Court plan, but in fact the congressional and public reaction was sharply hostile. The Supreme Court's size (unspecified in the Constitution) had fluctuated several times in the early Republic, but the membership of nine, dating to 1869, had become almost sacrosanct. Conservatives blasted the "court-packing" scheme. Some feared a power grab by FDR in the wake of his electoral triumph; others resented the devious way FDR presented the plan. Even some New Dealers disapproved. When the Senate voted down the scheme in July, FDR quietly gave up the fight.

But was it a defeat? One conservative justice retired in May 1937; others announced retirement plans. In April and May the Court upheld several key New Deal measures, including the Wagner Act, as well as a state minimum-wage law. This outcome may have been Roosevelt's objective all along. His challenge to the Court, plus his 1936 victory, sent powerful political signals that the justices heeded. From 1937 to 1939 FDR appointed four new members to the Supreme Court, laying the groundwork for a liberal majority that would long outlive Roosevelt and his New Deal.

The Roosevelt Recession

After improving in 1936 and early 1937, the economy again plunged ominously in August 1937. Industrial production slumped. Steel output sank to 19 percent of capacity. Jobless rates of more than 20 percent again dominated the headlines. This short but severe "Roosevelt recession" resulted in part from federal policies that reduced consumer income. Social-security payroll taxes withdrew some $2 billion from circulation. A drastic contraction of the money supply undertaken by the Federal Reserve Board to forestall inflation contributed to the recession. Furthermore, concerned about mounting deficits, FDR had seized on the signs of recovery to end or cut back the various New Deal relief programs.

Echoing Hoover, FDR assured his cabinet, "Everything will work out all right if we just sit tight and keep quiet." Meanwhile, however, some New Dealers had been persuaded by the Keynesian view that deficit spending was the key to recovery. Aware that FDR would have to be persuaded by political rather than economic arguments, they warned the president of a political backlash if breadlines and soup kitchens returned. Convinced, in April 1938 FDR authorized new relief spending. WPA work-relief checks soon rained down on the parched economy, and the PWA received a new lease on life. By late 1938 unemployment declined and industrial output increased.

Final Measures; Growing Opposition

Preoccupied by the Supreme Court fight, the 1937–1938 recession, and a menacing world situation (see Chapter 25), FDR offered few domestic initiatives in his second term. Congress, however, enacted several significant measures.

The Farm Tenancy Act of 1937 created the Farm Security Administration (FSA), replacing Rexford Tugwell's Resettlement Administration. The FSA made low-interest loans enabling tenant farmers and sharecroppers to buy family-size farms. Although the FSA generally bypassed the poorest farmers, considering them a bad credit risk, it did lend more than $1 billion through 1941, easing the plight of many rural folk battered by hard times.

The FSA operated camps offering clean, sanitary shelter and medical services to migrant farm workers living in wretched conditions. The FSA also commissioned some of the nation's most gifted photographers to record the lives of tenants, migrants, and uprooted dust-bowl families. These FSA photographs helped shape a starkly realistic documentary style that pervaded 1930s' popular culture, including Hollywood movies and Henry Luce's photo magazine *Life*, launched in 1936. Today they comprise a haunting album of depression-era images.

Other late New Deal measures set important precedents for the future. The Housing Act of 1937 appropriated $500 million for urban slum clearance and public housing, projects that would loom large in the 1950s. The Fair Labor Standards Act of 1938 banned child labor and set a national minimum wage (initially forty cents an hour) and a maximum workweek of forty hours. This measure reflected not only humanitarianism but also some northern legislators' desire to undermine the competitive edge of the South, with its low wage scales. Despite many loopholes, the law improved conditions for some of the nation's most

A Camera's-Eye View of Depression-Era America *This 1937 image by Dorothea Lange, a photographer with the Farm Security Administration, pictures migrants from the Texas dust bowl gathered at a roadside camp near Calipatria in southern California.*

exploited workers, and underscored the government's role in regulating abuses by employers.

In a final stab at dealing with farm surpluses and low farm prices, the Agricultural Adjustment Act of 1938 set up new procedures for limiting production of basic commodities. It also created a mechanism by which the government, in years of big harvests and low prices, would make loans to farmers and warehouse their surplus crops. When prices rose, farmers could repay their loans and market their commodities. This complicated system of price supports set the basic framework of federal agricultural policy for decades to come.

Overall, however, the New Deal's pace clearly slowed after 1935. This reflected in part the rise of an anti–New Deal congressional coalition of Republicans and conservative southern Democrats. In 1937 this coalition teamed up to torpedo FDR's proposal for a major reorganization of the executive branch. The plan made administrative sense, but critics warned darkly of a White House dictatorship.

The conservative coalition also slashed relief appropriations; cut corporate taxes in 1938; and in 1939 killed the WPA's Federal Theatre Project, long a conservative target for its alleged radicalism. The 1939 Hatch Act, forbidding federal employees from participating in electoral campaigns, reflected conservatives' suspicions that FDR was using WPA staff for campaign purposes. The Fair Labor Standards Act became law only after intense White House lobbying and watering down by conservatives. Congress and the public, lamented Harry Hopkins, had become "bored with the poor, the unemployed, the insecure."

Although FDR campaigned actively in the midterm election of 1938, the Republicans gained heavily in the House and Senate and won a net of thirteen governorships. Roosevelt also tried to purge several prominent anti–New Deal Democratic senators, but his major targets all won reelection. Focusing on foreign affairs in his January 1939 State of the Union message, FDR proposed no new domestic measures and merely noted the need to "preserve our reforms." The New Deal was over.

SOCIAL CHANGE AND SOCIAL ACTION IN THE 1930s

For a fuller picture of American life in the 1930s, we must look beyond the New Deal and take a broader view of society and culture. The depression's effects were psychological and social as well as economic and political. The crisis was traumatic for the jobless and their families; it had significant implications for working women; and it affected all age groups. For industrial workers, African-Americans, and migrant laborers, the activist climate of the New Deal stimulated movements to resist exploitation and discrimination.

The Depression's Psychological and Social Impact   This decade of hard times brought untold human suffering and marked all who lived through it. Despite the New Deal, unemployment never fell below about 14 percent in the 1930s, and for much of the decade it was considerably higher. Even those who remained employed were often forced to take jobs below their level of training: college alumni pumped gas; business-school graduates sold furniture; a retired navy captain became an usher in a movie theater. With rural America the scene of bankruptcies, foreclosures, and abandoned farms, a quarter of all farm families had to accept public or private assistance during the 1930s.

Psychologists described "unemployment shock": jobless persons who walked the streets seeking work and then lay awake at night worrying. When shoe soles wore out, cardboard or folded newspapers had to serve. Tacks pierced worn shoe heels, cutting the skin. "You pass . . . shoe-shops where a tack might be bent down," one young man recalled, "but you can't pull off a shoe and ask to have that done—for nothing."

In the face of adversity, some people went to great lengths to maintain appearances. Advertisements for mouthwashes, deodorants, and correspondence courses exploited feelings of shame and failure. Women's magazines described low-cost meals and other budget-trimming strategies. Habits of scrimping and saving acquired in the 1930s often survived into more affluent times. As Caroline Bird wrote in *The Invisible Scar*, a social history of the 1930s, the depression for many boiled down to "a dull misery in the bones."

New York Senator Robert Wagner called the working woman in the depression "the first orphan in the storm." Indeed, for the 25 percent of American women employed in 1930, the depression brought difficult times. The female jobless rate stood at more than 20 percent through much of the decade. Women desperate to continue working often did so only by taking lower-paying jobs. A laid-off factory worker might become a waitress. Many young women new to the job market had to settle for temporary or part-time work. Competition from displaced male workers reduced the proportion of women even in such traditional "women's professions" as library work, social work, and school teaching.

Married women workers faced harsh criticism. Although most worked because of economic necessity, they were accused of stealing jobs from unemployed men. Even Secretary of Labor Frances Perkins joined in the criticism, urging married women to stay out of the labor market so more jobless men could be hired. Many cities refused to employ married women as teachers and even fired women teachers who married.

Women workers also faced wage discrimination. In 1939, for example, the average woman teacher earned nearly 20 percent less than the average male with comparable experience. Female office workers generally earned far less than male factory workers. A number of the NRA codes authorized lower pay for women workers. The minimum-wage clause of the Fair Labor Standards Act helped some women workers, but did not cover many, including the more than 2 million women who worked for wages in private households.

A unionization campaign of the later 1930s (see below) had mixed effect on women workers. Some who were employed in the mass-production industries benefited, but the most heavily female sectors of the labor force—textile, clerical, service, and sales work—proved resistant to unionization. A 1937 campaign to unionize mostly female clerical workers was opposed by male bosses and many male union leaders, and made little progress.

Despite the roadblocks, the proportion of women working for wages crept up in the 1930s. In the face of criticism, the percentage of wage-earning married women increased from under 12 percent to nearly 16 percent. The crisis may actually have accelerated the long-term movement of women into the workplace as married women took jobs to augment the family income. One working wife explained, "One day in '32 [my husband] just went fishing . . . and he fished for the rest of the bad times. . . . So at twenty-eight, with two little girls, . . . I took a job as a salesclerk in the J.C. Penney, and worked through the Depression."

As this woman's account suggests, the depression had a profound effect on families, old and young alike. Bank failures wiped out the savings of many older Americans. By 1935 a million Americans over sixty-five were on relief. The birthrates fell in the early thirties as married couples postponed a family or limited its size. Family planning became easier with the spread of birth-control devices such as condoms and diaphragms. A declining birthrate plus reduced immigration held population growth in the 1930s to a scant 7 percent, in contrast to an average of 20 percent per decade between 1900 and 1930.

For parents, running a household in the 1930s often meant a struggle to make ends meet and hold the family together. They patched clothes, stretched food resources, and turned to public assistance when necessary. In homes with a tradition of strong male authority, the husband's loss of a job and consequent erosion of self-esteem often had a devastating psychological impact. "I would rather turn on the gas and put an end to the whole family than let my wife support me," one man told a social investigator. Desertions increased, and the divorce rate, after a dip in the early and mid-1930s, edged upward, hitting a then all-time high by 1940.

As for young people, one observer compared them to a team of runners waiting for a starting gun that never sounded. High-school enrollment increased sharply, since many youths, seeing no jobs in view, simply stayed in school. The marriage rate declined as young people facing bleak prospects postponed this step. Commented Eleanor Roosevelt in 1934, "I have moments of real terror when I think we might be losing this generation. We have got to bring these young people into the active life of the community and make them feel that they are necessary."

Children found vacation plans canceled, birthdays with few presents, and mealtimes tense with anxious discussions. Maria Tighe of Long Island, who was seven years old when the stock market crashed, recalled sneaking to 6 A.M. mass so her friends would not see her shoes, which were provided by the welfare bureau. Many children of the depression wrote sad letters to Eleanor Roosevelt. A Michigan high-school senior described her shame at not having a graduation dress. "I give all I earn for food for the family," she explained. A thirteen-year-old Arkansas girl wrote, "I have to stay out of school because I have no books or clothes to ware."

Out of necessity, many depression-era families also rediscovered traditional skills. They painted their own houses and repaired their own cars. Domestic skills such as baking and canning revived. Many who lived through the 1930s would later recall it as a time when adversity encouraged cooperation, savoring simple pleasures, and sharing scant resources.

For the neediest families, among them blacks, Hispanics, and southern share-croppers, the depression imposed added misery on poverty-blighted lives. In his novel *Native Son* (1940), Richard Wright vividly portrayed the desperate conditions of depression-era family life in Chicago's black slums. Yet not all was bleak. Emotional resilience, long-standing patterns of mutual aid, and survival skills developed through years of oppression helped many black families cope with the depression. In New York's Harlem a charismatic black religious leader calling himself Father Divine institutionalized this cooperative spirit by organizing kitchens that distributed thousands of free meals daily.

Industrial Workers Unionize Between 1900 and 1930, the ranks of factory workers had soared from 3.7 million to 7.7 million. Yet most of these workers remained unorganized. Major industries such as steel, automobiles, and textiles had resisted attempts to unionize their workers. The prosperity and probusiness mood of the 1920s had further weakened the labor movement.

But in the 1930s hard times and a favorable government climate bred a new labor militancy. When the Wagner Act of 1935 guaranteed labor's right to bargain collectively, tremors of activism shook the American Federation of Labor. In November 1935 John L. Lewis of the United Mine Workers (UMW) and Sidney Hillman of the Amalgamated Clothing Workers, frustrated by the AFL's slowness in organizing factory workers, started the Committee for Industrial Organization (CIO) within the AFL. Young CIO activists preached unionization in Pittsburgh steel mills, Detroit auto plants, Akron rubber factories, and southern textile mills. Unlike the craft-based and racially exclusive AFL unions, CIO unions welcomed all workers in a particular industry, regardless of race, gender, or degree of skill.

The Growth of Labor Union Membership, 1933–1946

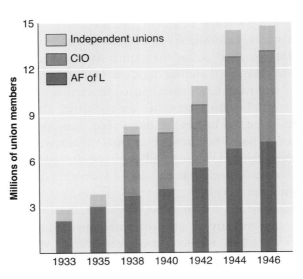

In 1936 a CIO-sponsored organizing committee geared up for a major strike to win union recognition by the steel industry. (In fact, John L. Lewis had already secretly worked out a settlement with the head of U.S. Steel.) In March 1937 U.S. Steel recognized the steelworkers' union, granted a wage increase, and accepted a forty-hour workweek. Other big steel companies followed suit, and soon four hundred thousand steelworkers had signed union cards.

Meanwhile, organizers had mapped a campaign to unionize General Motors, an antiunion stronghold. Their leader was a redheaded young autoworker and labor activist, Walter Reuther. Reuther's father, of German-immigrant stock, was a socialist who idolized Eugene V. Debs. When the depression hit, Reuther and his brother Victor rediscovered their socialist roots. In December 1936 employees at GM's two body plants in Flint stopped work and peacefully occupied the factories, carefully protecting the equipment and the cars on the assembly lines. This "sit-down strike" paralyzed GM's production.

Although women workers did not participate in the plant occupation (to avoid gossip that might discredit the strike), they picketed on the outside. A Women's Auxiliary organized by strikers' wives, sisters, and daughters fed the striking workers, set up a speakers' bureau, and marched through downtown Flint.

GM's management responded by calling in local police to harass the sit-down strikers, sending spies to union meetings, and threatening to fire strikers. A January 1937 showdown with the police at one of the body plants led to the formation of the Women's Emergency Brigade, on twenty-four-hour alert for picket duty. With red berets and armbands, Emergency Brigade members played a key role during the rest of the strike.

Perhaps recalling the army's eviction of protesting veterans from Washington in 1932, GM asked the Roosevelt administration and the governor of Michigan to send troops to expel the strikers by force. Both officials declined, however. Although FDR disapproved of the sit-down tactic, he refused to intervene with troops.

On February 11 GM signed a contract recognizing the United Automobile Workers (UAW). Bearded workers who had vowed not to shave until victory was won streamed out of the plants. As Chrysler fell into line also, the UAW soon boasted more than four hundred thousand members. Unionization of the electrical and rubber industries moved forward as well.

In 1938 the Committee for Industrial Organization broke with the AFL to become the Congress of Industrial Organizations, a 2-million-member association of industrial unions including the autoworkers. In response to the CIO challenge, the AFL began to adapt to the changed nature of the labor force. Overall, union membership in the United States shot from under 3 million in 1933 to over 8 million in 1941.

Some big corporations fought on. Henry Ford hated unions, and his tough lieutenant Harry Bennett organized a squad of union-busting thugs to fight the UAW. In 1937 Bennett's men viciously beat Walter Reuther and other UAW officials outside Ford's plant near Detroit. Not until 1941 did Ford yield to the union's pressure.

The Republic Steel Company, headed by a union hater named Tom Girdler, dug in as well. Even after U.S. Steel and other major steelmakers signed with the CIO, Republic and a group of smaller companies known collectively as "Little Steel" resisted. In May 1937 workers in twenty-seven Little Steel plants, including Republic's factory in South Chicago, walked off the job. Anticipating the strike, Girdler had assembled an arsenal of riot guns and tear gas. On May 30, Memorial Day, a mass of strikers approached over 250 police guarding the factory. When someone threw a large stick at the police, they responded with a hail of gunfire that left four strikers dead and scores wounded. A blue-ribbon investigative committee found that the killings had been "clearly avoidable by the police." In 1941, under growing pressure, the Little Steel companies, including Republic, finally accepted the CIO union.

Another holdout was the textile industry, with over six hundred thousand workers, mostly in the South and 40 percent female. Most textile workers earned very low wages and had no recourse against autocratic bosses. The AFL's United Textile Workers had made little headway in the 1920s owing to a series of failed strikes, a lack of support from AFL officials, and a policy of admitting only skilled workers. In 1934 the CIO launched its own drive to organize textile workers. Some four hundred thousand workers went on strike, but the mill owners viciously fought back. Southern governors mobilized the National Guard to fight the strike. Several strikers were killed, many wounded, and thousands arrested. The strike failed, and the 1930s ended with most textile workers still unorganized.

Also left behind by this unionizing wave was a large pool of low-paid workers—domestics, agricultural laborers, department-store clerks, and restaurant and laundry workers, for example—who tended to be women, blacks, or recent immigrants. Overall, more than three-quarters of nonfarm workers remained unorganized in 1940. Nevertheless, the unionization of key sectors of America's industrial work force ranks as one of the decade's most memorable developments.

Why did powerful corporations finally yield to unionization after resisting for so long? Certainly workers' militancy and the tactical skill of labor leaders like Reuther were crucial. But labor's successes also reflected a changed government climate. Historically, corporations had routinely called on the government to help break strikes. Although this still occasionally happened in the 1930s, as in the failed textile-industry strike, in general the Roosevelt administration and key state officials refused to intervene on the side of management. The Wagner Act, the Fair Labor Standards Act, and the oversight role of the National Labor Relations Board made clear that Washington would no longer automatically back management in labor disputes. Once corporate managers realized this, unionization soon followed.

Organized labor's apparent unity by the end of the 1930s concealed some complex tensions. A hard core of activists, many of them advocates of radical social change, had led the unionizing drive. But most rank-and-file factory workers had no desire to overthrow the capitalist system. Indeed, many initially held back from striking, fearful for their jobs. But once the CIO's militant minority showed that picket lines and sit-down strikes could win union contracts and tangible gains, workers signed up by the thousands. As they did, the radical organizers lost influence, and the unions became more conservative.

Reuther himself, despite his socialist roots, reflected the shift and tried to rein in the more radical spirits in the CIO unions. After World War II, in a different political climate, Reuther purged from the CIO some of the same leftists and communists who had led the organizational battles of the 1930s.

Blacks and Hispanic-Americans Resist Racism and Exploitation

The depression also brought social changes to and stirred activism within the African-American and Hispanic communities. Black migration to northern cities continued in the 1930s, though at a slower rate than in the 1920s. Four hundred thousand southern blacks moved to northern cities in the 1930s, and by 1940 23 percent of the nation's 12 million blacks lived in the urban North.

Rural or urban, life was hard. Black tenant farmers and sharecroppers often faced eviction. Among black industrial workers, the depression-era jobless rate far outran the rate for whites, largely because of racism and discriminatory hiring policies. Although black workers in some industries benefited from the CIO's nondiscriminatory policy, workplace racism remained a fact of life.

Lynching and miscarriage of justice continued, especially in the South. Twenty-four blacks died by lynching in 1933. In 1931 an all-white jury in Scottsboro, Alabama, sentenced eight black youths to death on highly suspect charges of rape. In 1935, after heavy publicity and an aggressive defense, the Supreme Court ordered a new trial for the "Scottsboro Boys" because they had been denied legal counsel and blacks had been excluded from the jury. Five of the group were again convicted, however, and served long prison terms.

But a rising tempo of activism signaled changes ahead. The NAACP battled in courts and legislatures against lynching, segregation, and the denial of voting rights. The Urban League campaigned against businesses in black neighborhoods that employed only whites. Under the banner "don't shop where you can't work," black protesters picketed and boycotted businesses that refused to hire blacks. In March 1935 hostility toward white-owned businesses in Harlem, fueled by more diffuse anger over racism and joblessness, ignited a riot that caused an estimated $200 million in damage and left three blacks dead.

The Communist party publicized lynchings and racial discrimination as part of a depression-era recruitment effort in the black community. A defense committee formed by the Communist party supplied lawyers for the "Scottsboro Boys." But despite a few notable recruits (including the young novelist Richard Wright), few blacks joined the party.

Other minority groups also faced discrimination. California continued its efforts to prevent Japanese-Americans from owning land. In 1934 Congress set an annual quota of fifty for immigrants from the newly created Commonwealth of the Philippines, still a U.S. colony—lower than that for any other nation. Congress also offered free travel "home" for Filipinos long settled in the United States.

The more than 2 million Hispanic-Americans faced trying times as well. Some were citizens with ancestral roots in the Southwest, but most were recent arrivals from Mexico or Caribbean islands such as Cuba and Puerto Rico (a U.S. holding whose residents were and are American citizens). While the Caribbean immigrants (including those from Jamaica, a British colony) settled in East Coast cities, most Mexican newcomers worked as migratory agricultural laborers in the Southwest and elsewhere, or in midwestern steel or meatpacking plants.

As the depression deepened, Mexican-born residents endured rising hostility. The western trek of thousands of "Okies" fleeing the dust bowl worsened the job crisis for local Hispanic farm workers. By 1937 more than half of Arizona's cotton workers were out-of-staters who had supplanted Mexican-born laborers. With their traditional patterns of migratory work disrupted, Mexican-Americans poured into the barrios (Hispanic neighborhoods) of southwestern cities. Some later recalled signs warning "NO NIGGERS, MEXICANS, OR DOGS ALLOWED."

Young Mexican Cotton Picker in the 1930s
Whether in agricultural labor or urban barrios, Mexican-Americans endured harsh conditions during the depression.

Lacking work, half a million Mexicans returned to their native land in the 1930s. Many did so voluntarily; others were repatriated by immigration officials and local authorities. Los Angeles welfare officials announced free one-way transportation to Mexico. The annual savings in relief payments, they calculated, would more than offset the cost of sending a full trainload of *repatriados* to Mexico. Though the plan was "voluntary," those who remained were denied relief payments or jobs with the various New Deal work programs. Under combined federal and local pressure, an estimated seventy thousand Mexicans left Los Angeles in 1931 alone.

Mexican-American farm workers who remained endured appalling conditions and near-starvation wages. A wave of protests and strikes (some led by Communist party organizers) swept California. A labor organization called the Confederación de Uniones de Campesinos y Obreros Mexicanos (Confederation of Unions of Mexican Workers and Farm Laborers) emerged from a 1933 strike of grape workers in El Monte, California. More strikes erupted in 1935–1936 from the celery fields and citrus groves around Los Angeles to the lettuce fields of the Salinas Valley.

Organizations like the Associated Farmers of California and the California Fruit Growers Exchange (which marketed its citrus under the brand name Sunkist) fought the unions, sometimes with violence. In October 1933 bullets presumably fired by someone hostile to the strikers ripped into a cotton pickers' union hall in Pixley, California, killing two men and wounding others. Undeterred, the strikers won a 20 percent increase in pay. Other Mexican-American farm workers gained a few hard-fought victories. Striking cotton pickers, for example, increased the rate for a hundred pounds of cotton from sixty cents to seventy-five cents. These strikes awakened at least some Americans to the plight of one of the nation's most exploited groups.

THE AMERICAN CULTURAL SCENE IN THE 1930S

Hard times and the New Deal shaped American cultural life in the 1930s. While radio and the movies offered escapist fare, novelists, artists, playwrights, and photographers responded to the crisis as well. When the depression first struck, as we have seen, their view of U.S. society and of the capitalist system tended to be highly critical. As the decade wore on, however, a more positive and affirmative view emerged, reflecting both the renewed hope stimulated by the New Deal and apprehensions stirred by a deepening threat of war.

Avenues of Escape: Radio and the Movies
The standardization of mass culture continued in the 1930s. Each evening, millions of Americans gathered around their radios to listen to network news, musical programs, and comedy shows. Radio humor flourished as hard times battered the real world. Comedians like Jack Benny and the husband-and-wife team George Burns and Gracie Allen attracted millions.

So, too, did the fifteen-minute afternoon domestic dramas known as soap operas (for the soap companies that sponsored them). Despite their assembly-line quality, these daily dollops of romance and melodrama won a devoted audience, consisting mostly of housewives. Some wrote letters advising the characters how to handle their problems. Identifying with the ordeals of the radio heroines, female listeners gained at least temporary escape from their own difficulties. As one put it, "I can get through the day better when I hear they have sorrows, too."

The movies were also extremely popular in depression America, when most people could still afford the twenty-five-cent admission. In 1939, 65 percent of Americans went to the movies at least once a week. The motion picture, declared one Hollywood executive, had become "as necessary as any other daily commodity."

A few movies dealt realistically with such social issues as labor unrest and the sharecroppers' plight. Two New Deal documentaries, *The Plow That Broke the Plains,* on the origins of the dust bowl, and *The River,* dealing with soil erosion and floods in the Mississippi valley, evoked the human and environmental toll of westward expansion.

Warner Brothers studio (which had close ties with the Roosevelt administration) made a series of movies in 1934–1936 celebrating the New Deal. And in *Mr. Deeds Goes to Town* (1936) and *Mr. Smith Goes to Washington* (1939), director Frank Capra, the son of Italian immigrants, offered the idealistic message that "the people" would ultimately triumph over entrenched interests.

The gangster movies of the early thirties, drawing inspiration from real-life criminals like Al Capone and John Dillinger, served up a different style of film realism. Films like *Little Caesar* (1930) and *The Public Enemy* (1931) offered gritty images of urban America: looming skyscrapers; menacing, rain-swept streets; lonely bus depots and all-night diners; the rat-tat-tat of machine guns as rival gangs battled. When civic groups protested the glorification of crime, Hollywood simply made the police and "G-men" (FBI agents) the heroes, while retaining the violence. The movie gangsters played by Edward G. Robinson and James Cagney represented variants of the Horatio Alger hero struggling upward against adversity. Their portrayals appealed to depression-era moviegoers facing equally heavy odds.

Above all, Hollywood offered escape—the chance briefly to forget the depression. The publicist who claimed that the movies "literally laughed the big bad wolf of the depression out of the public mind" exaggerated, but cinema's escapist function in the 1930s is clear. Musicals such as *Gold Diggers of 1933* (with its theme song, "We're in the Money") offered dancing, music, and cheerful plots involving the triumph of pluck over all obstacles. When color movies arrived in the late 1930s, they seemed an omen of better times ahead.

The Marx Brothers provided the depression decade's zaniest movie moments. In comedies like *Animal Crackers* and *Duck Soup,* these vaudeville troupers of German-Jewish immigrant origins created an anarchic world that satirized authority, fractured the English language, and defied logic. Amid widespread cynicism about the economic and social order that had collapsed so spectacularly in 1929, the Marx Brothers' mockery matched the American mood.

Thirties' movies dealt with African-Americans, if at all, largely in stereotypes. Hollywood confined black performers to such roles as the scatterbrained maid played by Butterfly McQueen in *Gone with the Wind* and the indulgent house servant played by tap dancer Bill Robinson and patronized by child star Shirley Temple in *The Little Colonel* (1935). Under the denigrating screen name Stepin Fetchit, black actor Lincoln Perry played the slow-witted butt of humor in many movies.

In representing women, Hollywood offered mixed messages. While many 1930s' movie heroines found fulfillment in traditional marriage and subordination to a man, a few films chipped away at the stereotype. Joan Bennett played a strong-willed professional in *The Wedding Present* (1936) and Carol Lombard emerged as a brilliant comedienne in *My Man Godfrey* (1936). Mae West, brassy, openly sexual, and fiercely independent, mocked conventional stereotypes in *I'm No Angel* and other 1930s hits. Toying with would-be lovers and tossing off double entendres, West made clear that she was her own woman.

The Later 1930s: Opposing Fascism; Reaffirming Traditional Values As the 1930s drew to a close, many Americans viewed the nation with a newly appreciative eye. It had survived the economic crisis. The social fabric remained whole; revolution had not come. As other societies collapsed into dictatorships, American democracy endured. Writers, composers, and other cultural creators reflected the changed climate, as despair and pessimism gave way to a more upbeat and patriotic outlook.

International developments and a domestic political movement known as the Popular Front influenced this shift. In the early 1930s, as we have seen, the U.S. Communist party attacked Roosevelt and the New Deal. But in 1935 Russian dictator Joseph Stalin, fearing attack by Nazi Germany, called for a worldwide alliance, or Popular Front, against Adolf Hitler and his Italian fascist counterpart, Benito Mussolini. (Fascism is a form of government involving one-party rule, extreme nationalism, hostility to minority groups, and the forcible suppression of dissent.) Parroting the new Soviet line, U.S. communists now praised Roosevelt and summoned writers and intellectuals to the antifascist cause. Many noncommunists, alarmed by developments in Europe, responded to the call.

The high-water mark of the Popular Front came during the Spanish Civil War of 1936–1939. In July 1936 Spanish fascist general Francisco Franco launched a revolt against Spain's legally elected government, a coalition of left-wing parties. With military aid from Hitler and Mussolini, Franco won backing from Spanish monarchists, landowners, industrialists, and the Roman Catholic hierarchy.

In America, the cause of the anti-Franco Spanish Loyalists (that is, those loyal to the elected government) rallied support from writers, artists, and intellectuals who backed the Popular Front. The novelist Ernest Hemingway, who visited Spain in 1936–1937, was among the writers who supported the Loyalists. In contrast to his disillusioned novels of the 1920s (see Chapter 23), Hemingway's *For Whom the Bell Tolls* (1940) told of a young American volunteer who dies while fighting with a Loyalist guerrilla band. Looking back on these years, Hemingway recalled, "The

Spanish Civil War offered something which you could believe in wholly and completely, and in which you felt an absolute brotherhood with the others who were engaged in it."

The Popular Front collapsed in August 1939 when the Soviet Union and Nazi Germany signed a nonaggression pact and divided Poland between them. Overnight, enthusiasm for working with the communists under the banner of "antifascism" faded. But while it lasted, the Popular Front helped shape U.S. culture and alerted Americans to threatening developments abroad.

The New Deal's programs for writers, artists, and musicians, as well as its turn leftward in 1935–1936, contributed mightily to the cultural shift of the later 1930s as well. The satirical and cynical tone of the 1920s and early 1930s now gave way to a more hopeful view of grass-roots America. In John Steinbeck's best-selling novel *The Grapes of Wrath* (1939), an uprooted dust-bowl family, the Joads, make their difficult way from Oklahoma to California along Route 66. Steinbeck stressed not only the strength and endurance of ordinary Americans in depression America, but also their social cooperation and mutual support. As Ma Joad tells her son Tom, "They ain't gonna wipe us out. Why, we're the people—we go on." Made into a movie by John Ford, and starring Henry Fonda, *The Grapes of Wrath* stands as one of the most memorable cultural products of the 1930s.

In 1936 journalist James Agee and photographer Walker Evans spent several weeks living with Alabama sharecropper families while researching a magazine article. From this experience came Agee's masterpiece, *Let Us Now Praise Famous Men* (1941). Enhanced by Walker Evans's unforgettable photographs, Agee's intensely personal work evoked the strength and decency of Americans living on society's margins.

The new cultural mood also found expression on the stage. Thornton Wilder's play *Our Town* (1938) portrayed a New England town in which everyday events become, in memory, infinitely precious. William Saroyan's *The Time of Your Life* (1939) affectionately celebrated the foibles and virtues of a colorful collection of American "types" gathered in a San Francisco waterfront bar.

Composers, too, caught the spirit of cultural nationalism. In such works as *Billy the Kid* (1938), Aaron Copland drew upon American legends and folk melodies. George Gershwin's 1935 opera *Porgy and Bess,* adapted from a play by DuBose and Dorothy Heyward, portrayed black street life in Charleston, South Carolina.

Jazz surged in popularity thanks to swing, a flowing, danceable style originated by the pianist Fletcher Henderson and popularized by the big bands of Count Basie, Benny Goodman, Duke Ellington, and others. The Basie band started at Kansas City's Reno Club, where, as Basie later recalled, "We played from nine o'clock in the evening to five or six the next morning, . . . and the boys in the band got eighteen dollars a week and I got twenty one." Moving to New York in 1936, Basie helped launch the swing era.

Benny Goodman, of a Chicago immigrant family, had played the clarinet as a boy at Jane Addams's Hull House. Challenging the color line in jazz, Goodman included black musicians like pianist Teddy Wilson and vibraphonist Lionel

Hampton along with white performers in his orchestra. A turning point in the acceptance of jazz as a serious musical form came in 1938, when Goodman's band performed at New York's Carnegie Hall, a citadel of high culture.

In *Swingin' the Dream: Big Band Jazz and the Rebirth of American Culture* (1998), historian Lewis Erenberg links swing to the politics of the later 1930s. In its optimism, innovativeness, and "democratic ethos," he argues, swing "expressed in cultural form many of the themes of . . . the New Deal."

The later 1930s also saw a heightened interest in regional literature, painting, and folk art. Zora Neale Hurston's novel *Their Eyes Were Watching God* (1937), exploring a black woman's search for fulfillment, was set in rural Florida. In *Absalom, Absalom!* (1936) William Faulkner continued the saga of his mythic Yoknapatawpha County in Mississippi. Painters Thomas Hart Benton of Missouri (a descendant of the nineteenth-century senator of the same name), John Steuart Curry of Kansas, and Grant Wood of Iowa struck strongly regional notes in their work.

Galleries displayed Amish quilts, New England weather vanes, and paintings by colonial folk artists. A 1938 show at New York's Museum of Modern Art introduced Horace Pippin, a black Philadelphia laborer whose right arm had been shattered in World War I. In such paintings as *John Brown Going to His Hanging*, Pippin revealed a genuine, if untutored, talent. In 1939 the same museum featured seventy-nine-year-old Anna "Grandma" Moses of Hoosick Falls, New York, whose memory paintings of her farm girlhood enjoyed great popularity.

The surge of cultural nationalism heightened interest in the nation's past. Americans flocked to historical re-creations such as Henry Ford's Greenfield Village near Detroit and Colonial Williamsburg in Virginia, restored by the Rockefeller Foundation. In 1936–1939 Texans restored the Alamo in San Antonio, the "Cradle of Texas Liberty." Historical novels like Margaret Mitchell's epic of the Old South, *Gone with the Wind* (1936), became best-sellers. These re-creations and fictions often presented a distorted view of history. Slavery was blurred or sentimentalized at Colonial Williamsburg and in Mitchell's novel. "Texas Liberty" had a different meaning for the state's African-American, Indian, and Hispanic populations than it did for the patriotic organizations that turned the Alamo into a tourist shrine.

Streamlining and a World's Fair: Corporate America's Utopian Vision

The visual culture of late 1930s' America was also shaped by a design style called streamlining. This innovation originated in the 1920s when a group of industrial designers, inspired by the romance of flight, introduced rounded edges and smoothly flowing curves into the design of commercial products. Streamlining appealed to American business in the 1930s. It made products more attractive to consumers—a vital consideration during the depression. When Raymond Loewy streamlined Sears Roebuck's Coldspot refrigerators, sales surged. Streamlined products also helped corporate America rebuild its tarnished image and present itself as the benevolent shaper of a better future. Products ranging from house trailers to cigarette lighters emerged in sleek new forms. Pencil sharpeners evolved into gleaming, aerodynamic works of art poised for takeoff. The streamlined service stations that Norman Bel Geddes designed for Texaco, he boasted, would make oil changes "a stimulating experience" rather than a boring necessity.

Under the theme "The World of Tomorrow," the 1939 New York World's Fair represented the high point of the streamlining vogue and of corporate America's public-relations blitz. The fair's instantly famous logo was the Trylon and Perisphere: a seven-hundred-foot needle and a globe that seemed to float on a circular pool of water. Inside the Perisphere, visitors found "Democracity," a revolving diorama portraying a thriving, harmonious city of the future.

The hit of the fair was Futurama, the General Motors exhibit designed by Norman Bel Geddes. Visitors entered a darkened circular auditorium where, amid piped-in music and a resonant recorded narration, a vision of America in the distant year of 1960 majestically unfolded. A multilane highway network complete with cloverleaf exits and stacked interchanges dominated the imagined landscape. A brilliant public-relations investment by GM, Futurama built support for the interstate highway system that would soon become a reality.

Also featuring such wonders as television and automatic dishwashers, the World's Fair did, indeed, offer a glimpse of "The World of Tomorrow" as a smoothly functioning technological utopia made possible by the nation's great corporations. A business magazine editorialized, "If there are any doubters left, a visit to the New York World's Fair should convince them that American business has been the vehicle which carried the discoveries of science and the benefits of machine production to the doorstep of American consumers." The fair epitomized corporate capitalism's version of the patriotism and hopefulness that pervaded American culture as the 1930s ended.

The hopefulness was mixed with muted fear. The nation had survived the worst of the depression, but danger loomed beyond the seas. The anxiety triggered by the menacing world situation surfaced on October 31, 1938, when CBS radio aired an adaptation of H. G. Wells's science-fiction story *War of the Worlds* directed by Orson Welles. In realistic detail, the broadcast reported the landing of a spaceship in New Jersey, the emergence of aliens with ray guns, and their advance toward New York City. The show sparked a panic as horrified listeners concluded that the end was at hand. Some jumped in their cars and sped off into the night. Others prayed. A few attempted suicide. Beneath the terror lay a more well-founded fear: of approaching war. For a decade, as Americans had coped with the depression, the international situation had steadily worsened. By October 1938 radio news bulletins warned of impending war between Germany and England.

The panic triggered by Orson Welles's Halloween prank quickly changed to sheepish embarrassment, but the fear aroused by the real dangers looming on the horizon only escalated. By the time the New York World's Fair offered its vision of "The World of Tomorrow," the actual world of 1939 had become very scary indeed.

IMPORTANT EVENTS, 1929–1939

1929	Stock-market crash; onset of depression.
1932	Reconstruction Finance Corporation. Veterans' bonus march. Franklin D. Roosevelt elected president.
1933	Repeal of Eighteenth Amendment. Civilian Conservation Corps (CCC). Federal Emergency Relief Act (FERA). Tennessee Valley Authority (TVA). Agricultural Adjustment Administration (AAA). National Recovery Administration (NRA). Public Works Administration (PWA).
1934	Securities and Exchange Commission (SEC). Taylor Grazing Act. Indian Reorganization Act.
1934–1936	Strikes by Mexican-American agricultural workers in the West.
1935	Supreme Court declares NRA unconstitutional. Works Progress Administration (WPA). Resettlement Administration. National Labor Relations Act (Wagner Act). Social Security Act. NAACP campaign for federal antilynching law. Huey Long assassinated. Revenue Act raises taxes on corporations and the wealthy. Supreme Court reverses conviction of the "Scottsboro Boys." Harlem riot.
1935–1939	Era of the Popular Front.
1936	Supreme Court declares AAA unconstitutional. Roosevelt wins landslide reelection victory. Autoworkers' sit-down strike against General Motors begins (December).
1937	Roosevelt's "court-packing" plan defeated. Farm Security Administration. GM, U.S. Steel, and Chrysler sign union contracts.
1937–1938	The "Roosevelt Recession."
1938	Fair Labor Standards Act. Republicans gain heavily in midterm elections. Congress of Industrial Organizations (CIO) formed. Carnegie Hall concert by Benny Goodman orchestra.
1939	Hatch Act. Marian Anderson concert at the Lincoln Memorial. John Steinbeck, *The Grapes of Wrath*.
1940	Ernest Hemingway, *For Whom the Bell Tolls*.

25

Americans and a World in Crisis, 1933–1945

ost Americans have agreed that the United States fought a just war to meet the crisis of military aggression by Nazi Germany and Japan. As the years passed, particularly after the traumas of the Vietnam War and the economic setbacks of the 1970s, that necessary war—a complex, uncertain, chaotic event—became remembered as a golden age, as the "Good War" fought by the "Greatest Generation." Nostalgic myths abounded of a nation fully united and sure of its cause, of Americans of every race, religion, and ethnicity working together in the foxhole as well as the factory, of courageous U.S. soldiers—who never committed atrocities—quickly and easily returning to civilian life after clear-cut victories.

Such myths have little to do with the war experienced by E. B. Sledge. Born in 1923, Sledge enjoyed a carefree boyhood of fishing, hunting, and riding in Mobile, Alabama, until the United States entered the Second World War. Filled with idealism and patriotism, he dropped out of school to join the marines and defend his country. His harrowing experiences drove him to write a wartime memoir, *With the Old Breed,* of unrelenting horror. Describing the battles of Peleliu and Okinawa, Sledge depicts a brutal landscape of war without mercy, of kill or be killed, of prisoners tortured and the dead mutilated, of the most savage violence coupled with the most lethal technology of modern warfare.

On Peleliu, where Sledge's Company K reported 64 percent casualties in an island campaign later deemed unnecessary, he witnessed helpless comrades being slaughtered. Because the closeness of the enemy made it too dangerous to try to reclaim the dead, he watched as buddies oozed into a wasteland of mud and excreta, land crabs feeding on them. He saw a fellow marine use a knife to try to extract the gold teeth of a wounded Japanese soldier. Frustrated in the attempt, the marine sliced open the prisoner's cheeks and continued to gouge and pry, unfazed by the man's thrashing and gurgling. On Okinawa's Half Moon Hill he dreamed that the decomposed bodies of marines sprawled about him slowly rose, unblinkingly stared at him, and said, "It is over for us who are dead, but you must struggle, and will carry the memories all your life. People back home will wonder why you can't forget."

The wartime experiences of few Americans matched those of Sledge. Yet World War II fundamentally changed national institutions and behavior, immensely affecting most Americans. History's greatest armed conflict proved as much a turning point in personal lives as in world affairs. Amidst strikes and overcrowding, profiteering and black markets, the war lifted the nation out of the depression, redistributed income, and transformed the United States into a middle-class society. Despite continuing discrimination and prejudice, it gave millions of women and minorities an opportunity to savor independence and prosperity. As it destroyed certain traditional American ways and communities, it created a new world order that left the United States at the pinnacle of its power and sowed the seeds of a postwar crisis. It was indeed, in Eleanor Roosevelt's words, "no ordinary time."

This chapter focuses on five major questions:

How did the Roosevelt administration and the American people respond to the international crises of the 1930s?

How did war mobilization transform the American economy and government?

What were the major aspects of Allied military strategy in Europe and Asia?

What were the major effects of World War II on American society, including minorities and women?

What were the arguments for and against the use of the atomic bomb to end the war with Japan?

THE UNITED STATES IN A MENACING WORLD, 1933–1939

Apart from improving relations with Latin America, the early administration of President Franklin D. Roosevelt (FDR) remained largely aloof from the crises in the world. Americans reacted ambivalently as Italy, Germany, and Japan grew more aggressive. Millions of Americans, determined not to stumble into war again, supported neutrality. Others insisted that the United States help embattled democracies abroad. All the while, the world slid toward the precipice.

Nationalism and the Good Neighbor

During the Great Depression, Roosevelt put U.S. economic interests above all else. He showed little interest in pursuing his secretary of state's hopes for free trade and international economic cooperation.

He did, however, adopt an internationalist approach in Latin America, where bitterness over decades of "Yankee imperialism" ran high. He announced a "Good Neighbor" policy, and in late 1933 the United States signed a formal convention that "No state has the right to intervene in the internal or external affairs of another." To support this policy, FDR withdrew the last U.S. troops from Haiti and the Dominican Republic, persuaded American bankers to loosen their grip on

Haiti's central banking system, renounced the Platt Amendment that had given the United States control over the Cuban government since 1901, and reduced the U.S. role in Panamanian affairs.

The key tests of the Good Neighbor policy came in Cuba and Mexico. In Cuba, an economic crisis in 1933 brought to power a leftist regime that the United States opposed. Instead of sending in the marines, as earlier administrations might have done, the United States provided indirect aid to a conservative revolt led by Fulgencio Batista in 1934 that overthrew the radical government. To shore up the Batista regime, Washington lowered the tariff on Cuban sugar cane. American economic assistance allowed Batista to retain power, for the most part, until he was overthrown by Fidel Castro in 1959.

In Mexico, a reform government came to power in 1936 and promptly nationalized several oil companies owned by U.S. and British corporations. While insisting on fair compensation, the United States refrained from military intervention and conceded Mexico's right to nationalize the companies. After lengthy negotiations, Mexico and the oil companies reached a compromise compensation agreement.

The Good Neighbor policy thus neither ended U.S. interference in Latin American affairs nor stemmed the increasing envy of "rich Uncle Sam" by his southern neighbors. But it did substitute economic leverage for heavy-handed intervention, particularly military occupation. The better relations fostered by FDR would become important when the United States sought hemispheric solidarity in World War II, and later in the Cold War.

The Rise of Aggressive States in Europe and Asia

As early as 1922, economic and social unrest in Italy enabled Benito Mussolini and his Fascist party to seize power. The regime suppressed dissent, imposed one-party rule, and, hoping to recreate a Roman empire, invaded Ethiopia in October 1935.

The rise of Adolf Hitler in Germany proved more menacing. Hitler's National Socialist (Nazi) party, capitalizing on Germany's hard times and resentment of the harsh Versailles Treaty, gained strength. In January 1933, five weeks before the inauguration of Franklin Roosevelt, Hitler became Germany's chancellor. (The two men's lives would fatefully intertwine for the next twelve years until they died within two weeks of each other in April 1945.) Crushing opponents and potential rivals, Hitler imposed a brutal dictatorship on Germany and began a program to purify it of Jews—whom he considered an "inferior race" responsible for Germany's defeat in World War I.

Violating the Versailles Treaty, Hitler began a military buildup in 1935. A year later German troops reoccupied the Rhineland, the demilitarized region west of the Rhine River that had been controlled by France since the end of World War I. In 1938, as German tanks rolled into Vienna, Hitler proclaimed an *Anschluss* (union) between Austria and Germany. London, Paris, and Washington murmured their disapproval but took no action.

An emboldened Hitler then turned to the Sudetenland, a part of neighboring Czechoslovakia containing 3 million ethnic Germans. Insisting that the area must be part of Germany, Hitler thundered his determination to take it. British prime minister Neville Chamberlain and his French counterpart, eager to avoid hostilities, appeased Hitler and at a conference in Munich in September 1938 agreed to turn the Sudetenland over to Germany. Believing in Chamberlain's claim to have achieved "peace in our time," FDR and most Americans applauded the Munich Pact for having avoided war.

In Japan, meanwhile, militarists had gained control of the government. To gain the raw materials needed for heavy industry, especially coal, metals, petroleum, and timber, they launched a fateful course of expansion. In 1931 Japan sent troops into the northern Chinese province of Manchuria, and within two years took total control of the province. Then, having signed treaties of political alliance and mutual defense with Germany and Italy, Japan began a full-scale war against China in July 1937; within a year Japan controlled most of that vast nation. Weak protests by Washington did little to deter Japan's plans for further aggression in Asia and the Pacific.

The American Mood: No More War

The feeble responses to aggression by the Roosevelt administration reflected the American people's belief that the decision to go to war in April 1917 had been a mistake. This conviction was rooted in the nation's isolationist tradition— its wish to avoid military and political entanglements in Old World quarrels—as well as in its desire to have the government focus on economic matters, not foreign affairs, in the midst of the Great Depression. A series of books and films stressing American disillusionment with World War I's failure to make the world safe for democracy strengthened isolationist sentiment. So did a 1934–1936 Senate investigation headed by Republican Gerald P. Nye of North Dakota, which concluded that banking and munitions interests, whom it called "merchants of death," had tricked the United States into war to protect loans and weapon sales to England and France.

By the mid-1930s an overwhelming majority of Americans thought that the United States should have stayed out of World War I and that the "mistake" of intervention should never be repeated. Congress responded by passing a series of Neutrality Acts in 1935–1937. To prevent a repetition of 1917, these measures outlawed arms sales and loans to nations at war and barred Americans from traveling on the ships of belligerent powers. Considering even these laws an insufficient safeguard against war, in 1938 Indiana congressman Louis Ludlow proposed a constitutional amendment requiring a national referendum on any U.S. declaration of war except in cases of direct attack. Only a direct appeal from FDR steeled Congress to reject the Ludlow Amendment by the narrowest of margins.

With American companies like IBM heavily invested in Nazi Germany, the sole confrontation with the fascist onslaught in the thirties came in the sports arena. At the 1936 Olympics in Berlin, African-American track star Jesse Owens made a mockery of Nazi theories of racial superiority by winning four gold medals and breaking or tying three world records. In 1938, in a boxing match laden with symbolism, the black American Joe Louis knocked out German fighter Max Schmeling in the first round of their world heavyweight championship fight. Although Americans cheered Louis, they still opposed any policies that might involve them in war.

The Gathering Storm: 1938–1939 The reduced tension that followed the Munich Pact proved tragically brief. "Peace in our time" lasted a mere 5 1/2 months. On March 15, 1939, Nazi troops occupied what remained of Czechoslovakia, violating the Munich accords. Five months later, Hitler reached an agreement with Stalin in the German-Soviet Nonaggression Pact that their nations would not fight one another and that they would divide Poland after Germany invaded it. No longer worried about a Soviet reaction, Hitler took aim on Poland despite claims by Britain and France that they would come to an invaded Poland's assistance.

Such actions intensified the debate over America's role abroad. Some warned that American involvement in war would destroy the reform impulse and spawn reaction, as it had a generation earlier. "The place to save democracy is at home," argued historian Carl Becker. But pacifist and neutralist opinion was weakening. Warning of the "cancerous spread" of fascism, critic Lewis Mumford issued "A Call to Arms" in the *New Republic,* exhorting Americans to mobilize against fascism.

President Roosevelt began to do so. After the fall of Czechoslovakia, he called for actions "short of war" to demonstrate America's will to check fascism, and he asked Hitler and Mussolini to pledge not to invade thirty-one listed nations. A jeering Hitler read FDR's message to an amused German Reichstag (legislative assembly), while in Rome Mussolini mocked Roosevelt's physical disability, joking that the president's paralysis must have reached his brain.

Roosevelt, however, did more than send messages. In October 1938 he asked Congress for a $300 million military appropriation; in November he instructed the Army Air Corps to plan for an annual production of twenty thousand planes; and in January 1939 he submitted a $1.3 billion defense budget. Hitler and Mussolini, the now-aroused president proclaimed, were "two madmen" who "respect force and force alone."

America and the Jewish Refugees Hitler and the Nazis had used the power of the state and their own paramilitary organizations to assault German Jews, confiscate their property, and force them to emigrate. The Nuremberg Laws of 1935 outlawed marriage and sexual intercourse between Jews and non-Jews, stripped Jews of the rights of German citizenship, and increased restrictions on Jews in all spheres of German educational, social, and economic life. This campaign of hatred reached a violent crescendo on November 9–10, 1938, when the Nazis unleashed *Kristallnacht* (Night of the Broken Glass), a frenzy of arson, destruction, and looting against Jews throughout Germany.

Isolationism vs. Interventionism *In front of the White House in 1941, an American soldier grabs a sign from an isolationist picketing against the United States entering the war in Europe. A diverse group, isolationists ran the gamut from pacifists who opposed all wars, to progressives who feared the growth of business and centralized power that a war would bring, to ultra-rightists who sympathized with fascism and/or shared Hitler's anti-Semitism.*

No longer could anyone mistake the perilous situation of German Jews or misunderstand Hitler's evil intent. Jews left Germany by the tens of thousands. Among those coming to the United States were hundreds of distinguished scholars, artists, and scientists including pianist Rudolph Serkin, architect Walter Gropius, political theorist Hannah Arendt, and future secretary of state Henry Kissinger. Among the many gifted physicists were Leo Szilard, James Franck, and Enrico Fermi, who would play key roles in building the atomic bomb. It is hard to imagine what the cultural, intellectual, and scientific achievements of the United States in the second half of the twentieth century would have been without the contributions of these refugees.

But the United States of the 1930s, in the grip of the depression and imbued with its own anti-Semitism, proved reluctant to grant sanctuary to the mass of Nazism's Jewish victims. Roosevelt did little other than deplore Hitler's persecution of the Jews, and Congress consistently rejected efforts to liberalize the immigration law or abolish its discriminatory quotas (see Chapter 23). Few Americans seemed bothered that the sixty thousand Jews admitted to the United States by the end of 1938 constituted just a tiny ripple of the refugee tide. When asked by pollsters that year whether the immigration law should be changed to admit "a larger number of Jewish refugees from Germany," 75 percent said no.

The consequences of such attitudes became clear in June 1939 when the *St. Louis*, a vessel jammed with nine hundred Jewish refugees, asked permission to put its passengers ashore at Fort Lauderdale, Florida. Immigration officials refused the request and, according to the *New York Times*, had a Coast Guard ship deployed "to prevent possible attempts by refugees to jump off and swim ashore." The *St. Louis* turned slowly away from the lights of America and sailed back to Germany, where the majority of its passengers would die at the hands of the Nazis.

INTO THE STORM, 1939–1941

After a decade of crises—worldwide depression and regional conflicts—war erupted in Europe in 1939. While initially relying on neutrality to keep America out of the war, President Roosevelt switched to economic intervention following the lightning German victories in western Europe in spring 1940. He knew that extending increasing amounts of aid to those resisting aggression by the so-called Rome-Berlin-Tokyo Axis, as well as his toughening conduct toward Germany and Japan, could, as he said, "push" the U.S. into the crisis of worldwide war. Japan's attack on the U.S. fleet at Pearl Harbor would provide the push.

The European War
Hitler began the war by demanding that Poland return the city of Danzig (Gdansk), taken from Germany after World War I. When Poland refused, Nazi troops poured into Poland on September 1, 1939. Two days later, Britain and France, honoring commitments to Poland, declared war on Germany. Although FDR invoked the Neutrality Acts, he would not ask Americans to be impartial in thought and deed (as had President Wilson in 1914).

Tailoring his actions to the public mood, which favored both preventing a Nazi victory and staying out of war, FDR persuaded Congress in November to amend the Neutrality Acts to allow the belligerents to purchase weapons from the United States if they paid cash and carried the arms away in their own ships. He assumed that "cash-and-carry" would mainly aid the Allies, given their control of the seas.

"Cash-and-carry" did not stop the Nazis. In spring 1940, after a winter lull that followed the defeat of Poland, Hitler's armies taught the world the meaning of *Blitzkrieg* (lightning war) as they quickly overwhelmed Denmark, Norway, Belgium, Holland, Luxembourg, and France and pinned the British army against the sea at Dunkirk. Narrowly escaping disaster, the British used every possible craft to evacuate their army and some French troops across the English Channel. By then, however, Hitler virtually controlled western Europe, and on June 22 he dictated France's surrender in the same spot and the same railway car in which Germany had surrendered in 1918.

Hitler now took aim at Great Britain. The *Luftwaffe* (German air force) intended to terror-bomb Britain into submission, or at least prepare the ground for a

German invasion. Round-the-clock aerial assaults killed or wounded thousands of civilians, destroyed the city of Coventry, and reduced parts of London to rubble. Britain's new Prime Minister Winston Churchill, who replaced Chamberlain in May 1940, pleaded for more U.S. aid. Most Americans, shocked at the use of German air power against British civilians, wanted to give it to him. But a large and vocal minority opposed it as wasteful of materials needed for U.S. defenses or as a ruse to draw Americans into a war not vital to their interests.

From Isolation to Intervention
In the United States in 1940, news of the "battle of Britain" competed with speculation about whether FDR would break with tradition and run for an unprecedented third term. Not until the eve of the Democrats' July convention did he reveal that, given the world crisis, he would consent to being drafted by his party. The sense of being at a critical moment in world affairs clinched his renomination and forced conservative Democrats to accept the very liberal Henry Wallace, FDR's former secretary of agriculture, as his running mate. Republicans bowed to the public mood by nominating an all-out internationalist who championed greater aid to Britain, Wendell Willkie of Indiana.

With the GOP uncertain how to oppose Roosevelt effectively, FDR played the role of the crisis leader too busy to engage in politics. He appointed Republicans Henry Stimson and Frank Knox as secretaries of war and the navy. He signed the Selective Service and Training Act, the first peacetime draft in U.S. history, and approved an enormous increase in spending for rearmament. With Willkie's support, FDR engineered a "destroyers-for-bases" swap with England, sending fifty vintage ships to Britain in exchange for leases on British naval and air bases in the Western Hemisphere. Although FDR pictured the agreement as a way to keep the country out of war, it infuriated isolationists.

In the 1930s the isolationist camp had included prominent figures from both major parties and both the Right and Left. But in 1940 the arch-conservative America First Committee was isolationism's dominant voice. Largely financed by Henry Ford, the committee featured pacifist Charles Lindbergh as its most popular speaker. It insisted that "Fortress America" could stand alone. But a majority of Americans supported Roosevelt's effort to assist Great Britain while staying out of war. Reassured by the president's promise never to "send an American boy to fight in a European war," 55 percent of the voters chose to give Roosevelt a third term.

Calling on the United States to be the "great arsenal of democracy," Roosevelt now proposed a "lend-lease" program to supply war materiel to cash-strapped Britain. While Roosevelt likened the plan to loaning a garden hose to a neighbor whose house was on fire, isolationist Senator Robert Taft compared it to chewing gum: after a neighbor uses it, "you don't want it back." A large majority of Americans supported lend-lease, however, and Congress approved the bill in March 1941, abolishing the "cash" provision of the Neutrality Acts and allowing the president to lend or lease supplies to any nation deemed "vital to the defense of the United States." Shipments to England began at once, and after Hitler invaded the U.S.S.R.

in June, U.S. war supplies flowed to the Soviet Union as well, despite American hostility toward communism. To defeat Hitler, FDR confided, "I would hold hands with the Devil."

In April 1941, to counter the menace of German submarines to the transatlantic supply line, Roosevelt authorized the U.S. navy to help the British track U-boats. In mid-summer the navy began convoying British ships carrying lend-lease supplies, with orders to destroy enemy vessels if necessary to protect the shipments. U.S. forces also occupied Greenland and Iceland to keep those strategic Danish islands out of Nazi hands.

In August Roosevelt met with Churchill aboard a warship off the coast of Newfoundland to map strategy. They issued a document, the Atlantic Charter, that condemned international aggression, affirmed the right of national self-determination, and endorsed the principles of free trade, disarmament, and collective security. Providing the ideological foundation of the anti-Axis cause, the Charter envisioned a postwar world in which the peoples of "all the lands may live out their lives in freedom from fear and want."

After a U-boat torpedoed and sank the *Reuben James*, killing 115 American sailors, Roosevelt persuaded Congress in November to permit the arming of merchant ships and their entry into belligerent ports in war zones. Virtually nothing now remained of the Neutrality Acts. Unprepared for a major war, America was already fighting a limited one, and full-scale war seemed imminent.

Pearl Harbor and the Coming of War

Hitler's triumphs in western Europe encouraged Japan to expand farther into Asia. Seeing Germany as its primary danger, the Roosevelt administration tried to apply just enough pressure to frighten off the Japanese without provoking Tokyo to war before the United States had built the "two-ocean navy" authorized by Congress in 1940. "It is terribly important for the control of the Atlantic for us to keep peace in the Pacific," Roosevelt told Harold Ickes in mid-1941. "I simply have not got enough navy to go around—and every episode in the Pacific means fewer ships in the Atlantic."

Both Japan and the United States hoped to avoid war, but neither would compromise. Japan's desire to create a Greater East Asia Co-Prosperity Sphere (an empire embracing much of China, Southeast Asia, and the western Pacific) matched America's insistence on the Open Door in China and status quo in the rest of Asia. Japan saw the U.S. stand as a ploy to block its rise to world power; and the United States viewed Japan's talk of legitimate national aspirations as a smoke screen to hide aggression. Decades of "yellow peril" propaganda had hardened American attitudes toward Japan. Widely depicted in American media as bow-legged little people with buck teeth and thick spectacles, the Japanese appeared pushovers for the American navy. With isolationists as virulently anti-Japanese as internationalists, no significant groups organized to prevent a war with Japan.

The two nations became locked in a deadly dance. In 1940, believing that economic coercion would force the Japanese out of China, the United States ended a long-standing trade treaty with Japan and banned the sale of aviation fuel and scrap metal to it. Tokyo responded by occupying northern Indochina, a French colony, and signing the Tripartite Pact with Germany and Italy in September, creating a military alliance, the Berlin-Rome-Tokyo Axis, that required each government to help the others in the event of a U.S. attack.

With the French and Dutch defeated by Germany, and Britain with its back to the wall, Japan gambled on a war for hegemony in the western Pacific. It chose to conquer new lands to obtain the resources it needed rather than retreat from China to gain a resumption of trade with the United States. Fatefully, Japan overran the rest of Indochina in July 1941. In turn, expecting that firmness would more likely deter Japan than provoke her to war, FDR froze all Japanese assets in the United States, imposed a new fuel embargo, and clamped a total ban on trade with Japan. But as Japan's fuel meters dropped toward empty, the expansionist General Hideki Tojo replaced a more conciliatory prime minister in October. Tojo set the first week in December as a deadline for a preemptive attack if the United States did not yield.

By late November U.S. intelligence's deciphering of Japan's top diplomatic code alerted the Roosevelt administration that war was imminent. Negotiators made no concessions, however, during the eleventh-hour talks under way in Washington. "I have washed my hands of it," Secretary of State Hull told Secretary of War Stimson on November 27, "and it is now in the hands of you and Knox—the Army and the Navy." War warnings went out to all commanders in the Pacific, advising that negotiations were deadlocked and that a Japanese attack was expected. But where? U.S. officials assumed that the Japanese offensive would continue southward, striking Malaya or the Philippines. The Japanese banked on a knockout punch; they believed that a surprise raid on Pearl Harbor would destroy America's Pacific fleet and compel a Roosevelt preoccupied with Germany to seek accommodation with Japan.

On Sunday morning, December 7, 1941, Japanese dive-bombers and torpedo planes attacked the U.S. fleet at anchor in Pearl Harbor on the Hawaiian island of Oahu. Pounding the harbor and nearby airfields, the Japanese sank or crippled nearly a score of warships, destroyed or damaged some 350 aircraft, killed more than 2,400 Americans, and wounded another 1,200. American forces suffered their most devastating loss in history, and simultaneous attacks by Japan on the Philippines, Malaya, and Hong Kong opened the way for Japan's advance on Australia.

Some critics later charged that Roosevelt knew the attack on Pearl Harbor was coming and deliberately left the fleet exposed in order to bring the United States into the war against Germany. There is no conclusive evidence to support this accusation. Roosevelt and his advisers knew that war was close but did not expect an assault on Pearl Harbor. Neither did the U.S. military officials at Pearl Harbor, who took precautions only against possible sabotage by the Japanese in Hawaii. In part because of their own prejudices, Americans underestimated the resourcefulness, skill, and daring of the Japanese. They simply did not believe that Japan would attack an American stronghold nearly five thousand miles from its home base. At the same time, Japanese leaders counted on a paralyzing blow to compel the soft, weak-willed Americans, unready for a two-ocean war, to compromise rather than fight. That miscalculation ensured Roosevelt an aroused and united nation determined to avenge the attack that, he said, "will live in infamy."

On December 8 Congress approved a declaration of war against Japan. (The only dissenter was Montana's Jeannette Rankin, who had also cast a nay vote against U.S. entry into World War I.) Three days later, honoring Germany's treaty obligation to Japan, Hitler declared war on the "half Judaized and the other half Negrified" American people; Mussolini followed suit. Congress immediately reciprocated without a dissenting vote. The United States faced a global war that it was not ready to fight.

After Pearl Harbor, U-boats wreaked havoc in the North Atlantic and prowled the Caribbean and the East Coast of the United States. Every twenty-four hours, five more Allied vessels went to the bottom. German submarines even bottled up the Chesapeake Bay for nearly six weeks. By the end of 1942, U-boat "wolf packs" had sunk more than a thousand Allied ships, offsetting the pace of American ship production. The United States was losing the Battle of the Atlantic.

The war news from Europe and Africa, as Roosevelt admitted, was also "all bad." Hitler had painted the swastika across an enormous swath of territory, from the outskirts of Moscow and Leningrad—a thousand miles deep into Russia—to the Pyrenees on the Spanish-French border, and from northern Norway to the Libyan desert. In North Africa the German Afrika Korps swept toward Cairo and the Suez Canal, the British oil lifeline. It seemed as if the Mediterranean would become an Axis sea and that Hitler would be in India to greet Tojo marching across Asia before the United States was ready to fight.

Japan followed its attack on Pearl Harbor by seizing Guam, Wake Island, Singapore, Burma, and the Dutch East Indies. Having pushed the U.S. garrison on the Philippines first onto the Bataan peninsula and then onto the tiny island of Corregidor, Japan took more than eleven thousand American soldiers prisoner early in May 1942. Japan's Rising Sun blazed over hundreds of islands in the Pacific and over the entire eastern perimeter of the Asian mainland from the border of Siberia to the border of India.

AMERICA MOBILIZES FOR WAR

In December 1941 American armed forces numbered just 1.6 million, and only 15 percent of industrial output was going to war production. Finally committed to full involvement in the world crisis, the United States now had to harness all the strengths and resources of the nation and the American people. Congress passed a War Powers Act granting the president unprecedented authority over all aspects of the conduct of the war. Volunteers and draftees swelled the armed forces; by war's end more than 15 million men and nearly 350,000 women would serve. More would work in defense industries. Mobilization required unprecedented coordination of the American government, economy, and military. In 1942 those responsible for managing America's growing war machine moved into the world's largest building, the newly constructed Pentagon. Like the Pentagon, which was intended to house civilian agencies after the war, American attitudes, behavior, and institutions would also be significantly altered by far-reaching wartime domestic changes.

Organizing for Victory
To direct the military engine, Roosevelt formed the Joint Chiefs of Staff, made up of representatives of the army, navy, and army air force. (Only a minor "corps" within the army as late as June 1941, the air force would grow more dramatically than any other branch of the service, achieve virtual autonomy, and play a vital role in combat strategy.) The changing nature of modern warfare also led to the creation of the Office of Strategic Services (OSS), forerunner of the Central Intelligence Agency, to conduct the espionage required for strategic planning.

To organize the conversion of American industry to war production, Roosevelt established a host of new government agencies. The War Production Board (WPB) allocated materials, limited the production of civilian goods, and distributed contracts among manufacturers. The War Manpower Commission (WMC) supervised the mobilization of men and women for the military, agriculture, and industry, while the National War Labor Board (NWLB) mediated disputes between management and labor. Finally, the Office of Price Administration (OPA) rationed scarce products and imposed price controls to check inflation. Late in 1942 FDR persuaded Justice James F. Byrnes to leave the Supreme Court to become his "assistant president" in charge of the domestic war effort, and in May 1943 he formally appointed him to head the new Office of War Mobilization (OWM), which coordinated the production, procurement, transportation, and distribution of civilian and military supplies. "If you want something done, go see Jimmie Byrnes," understood those in the know.

"The Americans can't build planes," a Nazi commander had jeered, "only electric iceboxes and razor blades." But soon after February 1942, when the last civilian car came off an assembly line, the United States achieved a miracle of war production. Automakers retooled to produce planes and tanks; a merry-go-round factory switched to fashioning gun mounts; a pinball-machine maker converted to armor-piercing shells. By late 1942 a third of the economy was committed to war production, equaling the military output of Germany, Italy, and Japan combined. Whole new industries appeared virtually overnight. With almost all of the nation's crude-rubber supply now in Japanese-controlled territory, the government built some fifty new synthetic-rubber plants. By the end of the war, the United States, once the world's largest importer of crude rubber, had become the world's largest exporter of synthetic rubber.

America also became the world's greatest weapons' manufacturer, producing twice as much war material than all its Axis enemies by 1944. "To American production," Stalin would toast FDR and Churchill, "without which the war would have been lost." Indeed, the three hundred thousand military aircraft, 2.6 million machine guns, 6 million tons of bombs, and more than five thousand cargo ships and eighty-six thousand warships assembled by Americans did essentially win the war for the United States and its allies. Henry J. Kaiser, who had supervised the construction of Boulder Dam, introduced prefabrication to cut the time needed to produce a Liberty-class merchant ship from six months in 1941 to less than two weeks in 1943, and then just ten days. In 1945 Kaiser, dubbed "Sir Launchalot," and other shipbuilders were completing a cargo ship a day.

Such breakneck production had its costs. The size and powers of the government swelled as defense spending zoomed from 9 percent of the GNP in 1940 to 46 percent in 1945 and the budget soared from $9 billion to $98 billion. The number of federal civilian employees mushroomed from 1.1 million to 3.8 million. The executive branch, directing the war effort, grew the most; and an alliance formed between the defense industry and the military. (A generation later, Americans would call these concentrations of power the "imperial presidency" and the "military-industrial complex.") Because the government sought the greatest volume of war production in the shortest possible time, it encouraged corporate profits. "If you are going to try to go to war in a capitalist country," Secretary of War Stimson pointed out, "you have to let business make money out of the process or business won't work."

"Dr. New Deal," in FDR's words, gave way to "Dr. Win the War." To encourage business to convert to war production and expand its capacity, the government guaranteed profits, provided generous tax write-offs and subsidies, and suspended antitrust prosecutions. America's ten biggest corporations got a third of the war contracts, and two-thirds of all war-production spending went to the hundred largest firms, greatly accelerating trends toward economic concentration.

The War Economy The United States spent more than $320 billion ($250 million a day) to defeat the Axis—ten times more than the cost of World War I in real dollars and nearly twice the amount that had been spent by the government since its founding. This massive expenditure ended the depression and stimulated an industrial boom that brought prosperity to most American workers. It doubled U.S. industrial output and the per capita GNP, created 17 million new jobs, increased corporate after-tax profits by 70 percent, and raised the real wages or purchasing power of industrial workers by 50 percent.

The government poured nearly $40 billion into the West, more than any other region, and four times as much as it had in the preceding decade, making the West an economic powerhouse. California alone secured more than 10 percent of all federal funds, and by 1945 nearly half the personal income in the state came from expenditures by the federal government.

A newly prospering South also contributed to the emergence of a dynamic Sunbelt. In an arc stretching from the Southeast to the Southwest, the billions spent by Uncle Sam meant millions of jobs in the textile, oil and natural gas, chemical, and aluminum industries, as well as in the shipyards of Norfolk, Mobile, and New Orleans, and the aircraft plants in Dallas–Fort Worth and Marietta, Georgia.

Gross National Product

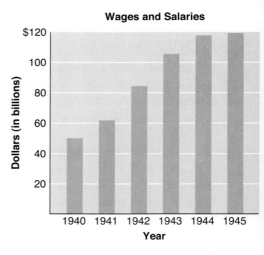

Wages and Salaries

Female Employment

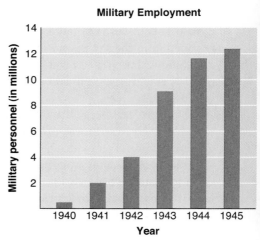

Military Employment

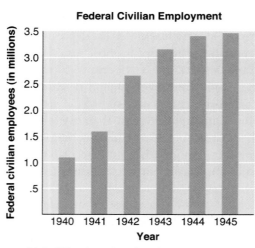

Federal Civilian Employment

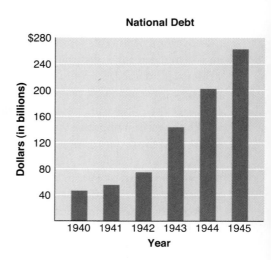

National Debt

U.S. Wartime Production

Between 1941 and 1945, the economy grew at a remarkable pace.

The South's industrial capacity increased by 40 percent, and per capita income tripled. Boom times enabled hundreds of thousands of sharecroppers and farm tenants to leave the land for better-paying industrial jobs. While the South's farm population decreased by 20 percent in the 1940s, its urban population grew 36 percent.

Full employment, longer workweeks, larger paychecks, and the increased hiring of minorities, women, the elderly, and teenagers made the United States a truly middle-class nation. In California the demand for workers in the shipyards and aircraft factories opened opportunities for thousands of Chinese-Americans previously confined to menial jobs in their own communities. In San Diego 40 percent of retirees returned to work. Deafening factories hired the hearing-impaired, and aircraft plants employed dwarfs as inspectors because of their ability to crawl inside small spaces. The war years produced the only significant twentieth-century shift in the distribution of income toward greater equality. The earnings of the bottom fifth of all workers rose 68 percent, and those of the middle class doubled. The richest 5 percent, conversely, saw their share of total disposable income drop from 23 to 17 percent.

Large-scale commercial farmers prospered as a result of higher consumer prices and increased productivity, thanks to improved fertilizers and more mechanization. As the consolidation of small farms into fewer large ones proceeded, commercial farming became dominated by corporations. Organized agriculture (later called agribusiness) took its seat in the council of power, alongside big government, big business, and organized labor.

Labor-union membership leaped from 9 million in 1940 to 14.8 million in 1945 (35 percent of nonagricultural employment). This growth resulted from the huge increase in the work force and the NWLB's "maintenance-of-membership" rule, which automatically enrolled new workers in unions and required workers to retain their union membership through the life of a contract. In return, unions agreed not to strike and to limit wage increases to 15 percent. In lieu of higher pay, they negotiated unprecedented fringe benefits for their members, including paid vacation time, health insurance, and pension plans.

Only a tiny minority of unionists broke the no-strike pledge. Most were "wildcat strikes," not authorized by union officials, and of brief duration. All told, strikes amounted to less than one-tenth of 1 percent of wartime working hours, barely affecting war production. In the most glaring exception, John L. Lewis, the iron-willed head of the United Mine Workers (UMW), led more than half a million coal-field workers out of the pits three times in 1943. Although the miners won wage concessions, their victory cost the union movement dearly. Many states passed laws to limit union power and, over Roosevelt's veto, Congress passed the Smith-Connally War Labor Disputes Act of 1943, which empowered the president to take over any facility where strikes interrupted war production.

Far more than strikes, inflation threatened the wartime economy. Throughout 1942 prices climbed by 2 percent a month as a result of the combination of increased spending power and a scarcity of consumer goods. At the end of the year, Congress gave the president authority to control wages, prices, and rents, and as the OPA clamped down, inflation slowed dramatically. Consumer prices rose just 8 percent during the last two years of war.

The OPA also instituted rationing to combat inflation and conserve scarce materials. Under the slogan "Use it up, wear it out, make it do or do without," the OPA rationed gasoline, coffee, sugar, butter, cheese, and meat. Americans endured "meatless Tuesdays" and cuffless trousers, ate sherbet instead of ice cream, and put up with imitation chocolate that tasted like soap and imitation soap that did not lather. American men and women planted 20 million victory gardens, served as air-raid wardens, and organized collection drives to recycle cooking grease and used paper and tires, while their children, known as "Uncle Sam's Scrappers" and "Tin-Can Colonels," scoured their neighborhoods for scrap metal and other valuable trash.

Buying war bonds further curtailed inflation by decreasing consumer purchasing power, while giving civilians a sense of involvement in the distant war. The sale of bonds—"bullets in the bellies of Hitler's hordes!" claimed the Treasury department—to schoolchildren, small investors, and corporations raised almost half the money needed to finance the war. Roosevelt sought to raise the rest by drastically increasing taxes. Congress refused the president much of what he sought. Still, the Revenue Act of 1942 raised the top income-tax rate from 60 percent to 94 percent and imposed income taxes on middle- and lower-income Americans for the first time, quadrupling the number of people who paid taxes. Beginning in 1943, the payroll-deduction system automatically withheld income taxes from wages and salaries. By 1945 the federal government was taking in nearly twenty times the tax revenue that it had in 1940.

"A Wizard War"   Winston Churchill labeled the conflict "a wizard war" in tribute to the importance of wartime scientific and technological developments. As never before, the major combatants mobilized scientists into virtually armies of invention. Their labors brought forth both miracles in healing and advances in the technology of killing, as well as a new faith that the minds of engineers and scientists, plus enough money, could overcome any obstacles.

In early 1941 Roosevelt had formed a committee to organize scientists for a weapons race against the Axis, and created the Office of Scientific Research and Development (OSRD) for the development of new ordnance. OSRD spent more than $1 billion to generate radar and sonar devices, rocket weapons, and bomb fuses. It advanced the development of jet aircraft and high-altitude bombsights, and its employment of scientists to devise methods for utilizing new weapons resulted in a brand-new field called operational analysis. The need to improve military radar spurred the development of the laser, while research in quantum physics to build atomic bombs later became the basis for transistors and semiconductors. The need to supply rapidly advancing troops with unspoiled food resulted in the instant mashed potatoes we eat today.

The quest for greater accuracy in ordnance, moreover, required the kind of rapid, detailed calculations that only computing machines could supply. So a half-dozen teams of scientists went to work in 1942 to develop what would become the earliest computers. By mid-1944 navy personnel in the basement of Harvard's physics laboratory were operating IBM's Automatic Sequence Controlled Calculator, known as Mark I—a cumbersome device 51 feet long and 8 feet high that weighed five tons, used 530 miles of wire, and contained 760,000 parts. ENIAC, developed to improve artillery accuracy for the army, reduced the time required to multiply two tenth-place numbers from Mark I's three seconds to less than three-thousandths of a second.

Military needs also hastened improvements in blood-transfusion and blood-banking techniques, heart and lung surgery, and the use of synthetic drugs to substitute for scarce quinine and toxoid vaccine to prevent tetanus. So-called miracle drugs, antibiotics to combat infections, a rarity on the eve of war, would be copiously produced. The military, which had only enough penicillin for about a hundred patients at the Battle of Midway in June 1942, had enough for all major casualties by D-Day in June 1944, and far more than it could use by V-J Day in August 1945, allowing the beginning of the sale of penicillin for civilian use.

Insecticides initially seemed as much a miracle. The use of DDT cleared many islands of malaria-carrying mosquitoes, like those that in 1942 had infected more than half the men of the First Marine Division, forcing it to be withdrawn from the Pacific war. DDT also stopped an incipient typhus epidemic in Naples in January 1944. Along with innovations like the Mobile Auxiliary Surgical Hospital (MASH), science helped save tens of thousands of lives, halving the World War I death rate of wounded soldiers who reached medical installations. It improved the health of the nation as well. Life expectancy rose by three years during the war, and infant mortality fell by more than a third.

No scientific endeavor had a higher priority than the Manhattan Project to develop the atomic bomb. In August 1939 physicist Albert Einstein, a Jewish refugee, warned Roosevelt that German scientists were seeking to construct a weapon of extraordinary destructiveness. The president promptly established an advisory committee and in late 1941 launched an Anglo-American secret program—the Soviets were excluded—to produce atomic bombs. In 1942 the participating physicists, both Americans and Europeans, achieved a controlled atomic reaction under the University of Chicago football stadium, the first step toward developing the bomb. In 1943–1944 the Manhattan Engineer District—the code name for the atomic project—stockpiled uranium-235 at Oak Ridge, Tennessee, and plutonium at Hanford, Washington. In 1945 engineers and scientists headquartered in Los Alamos, New Mexico, assembled two bombs utilizing those fissionable materials. By then the Manhattan Project had employed more than 120,000 people and spent nearly $2 billion.

Just before dawn on July 16, 1945, a blinding fireball with "the brightness of several suns at midday" rose over the Alamogordo, New Mexico, desert at a test site

All Have a Role to Play
This poster by the famous artist Thomas Hart Benton emphasized the need for all Americans to do their part in winning the war—by buying war bonds and laboring in factories and fields, as well as by fighting in the armed forces and, not incidentally, contributing their artistic talents.

named Trinity. A huge, billowing mushroom cloud soon towered 40,000 feet above the ground. With a force of twenty thousand tons of TNT, the blast shattered windows more than 120 miles away. "A few people laughed, a few people cried," recalled J. Robert Oppenheimer, the Manhattan Project's scientific director. "Most people were silent. I remembered the line from the Hindu scripture, the Bhagavad-Gita: 'Now I am become Death, the destroyer of worlds.'" A new era had dawned.

Propaganda and Politics   People as well as science and machinery had to be mobilized for the global conflict. To sustain a spirit of unity and fan the fires of patriotism, the Roosevelt administration managed public opinion. The Office of Censorship examined letters going overseas and worked with publishers and broadcasters to suppress information that might hinder the war effort. A year passed before casualty and damage figures from Pearl Harbor were disclosed. Fearful of demoralizing the public, the government banned the publication of photographs of American war dead until 1943. Then, concerned that the public had become overconfident, the media was prompted to display pictures of American servicemen killed by the enemy and to emphasize accounts of Japan's atrocities against American prisoners.

To shape public opinion and sell the faraway war to the American people, Roosevelt created the Office of War Information (OWI) in June 1942. The OWI employed more than four thousand artists, writers, and advertising specialists to explain the war and counter enemy propaganda. The OWI depicted the war as a mortal struggle between good and evil and harped on the necessity of totally destroying, not merely defeating, the enemy.

Hollywood answered the OWI directive—"Will this help win the war?"—by highlighting the heroism and unity of the American forces, while inciting hatred of the enemy. Films about the war portrayed the Japanese, in particular, as treacherous and cruel, as beasts in the jungle, as "slant-eyed rats." Jukeboxes blared songs like "We're Gonna Have to Slap the Dirty Little Jap." U.S. propaganda also presented the war as a struggle to preserve the "American way of life," usually depicted in images of small-town, middle-class, white Americans enjoying a bountiful consumer society.

While the Roosevelt administration concentrated on the war, Republican critics seized the initiative in domestic politics. Full employment and higher wages undercut the appeal of the New Deal, and resentment over wartime shortages and dismay over Axis victories further weakened the Democrats. With voter turnout low because many soldiers and defense workers were far from the hometowns where they had registered and were thus unable to vote, the Republicans gained forty-four seats in the House and nine in the Senate in 1942.

Politics shifted to the Right. The conservative coalition of Republicans and southern Democrats abolished some New Deal agencies, such as the WPA and CCC, drastically curtailed others, and rebuffed the adoption of new liberal programs. But the dynamics of the war enormously expanded governmental power, especially the power of the executive branch. As never before, the federal government managed the economy, molded public opinion, funded scientific research, and influenced people's daily lives.

THE BATTLEFRONT, 1942–1944

Following the Japanese attack on Pearl Harbor, the outlook for the Allies appeared critical. Then America's industrial might and Soviet manpower turned the tides of war. Diplomacy followed the tides of war in its wake. Allied unity dwindled as Germany and Japan weakened. As the United States, Soviet Union, and Great Britain each sought wartime strategies and postwar arrangements best suited to its own interests, the Allies sowed the seeds of a postwar crisis.

Liberating Europe Although British and American officials agreed to concentrate on defeating Germany first and then smashing Japan, they differed on where to attack. While German U-boats sank Allied ships at an appalling rate in early 1942, Hitler's forces advanced toward the Suez Canal in Egypt and penetrated deeper into the Soviet Union. Roosevelt sought to placate Stalin, who demanded a second front in western Europe to relieve the pressure on the Soviet Union, which faced the full fury of two hundred German divisions. But Churchill, fearing a repeat of the World War I slaughter in the trenches of France and wanting American assistance in maintaining British control of the vital Suez Canal, persuaded FDR to postpone the "second front" in Europe and invade North Africa instead. In Operation Torch, begun in November 1942, American forces under U.S. General Dwight D. Eisenhower pressed eastward from Morocco and Algeria. General Bernard Montgomery's British troops, which had stopped the Germans at El Alamein in Egypt and then advanced westward toward Tunisia, caught the retreating army of Field Marshall Erwin Rommel in a vise and forced some 260,000 German and Italian troops to surrender, despite Hitler's orders to fight to the death.

The Soviet Union proved to be the graveyard of the Wehrmacht (German army). In the turning point of the European war, the Russians defeated the Germans in the protracted Battle of Stalingrad (August 1942–January 1943). As the Russian snow turned red with blood (costing each side more battle deaths in half a year than the United States suffered in the entire war), and its hills strewn with human bones became "white fields," Soviet forces saved Stalingrad, defended Moscow, and relieved besieged Leningrad.

Stalin pleaded again for a second front; Churchill objected again; and again Roosevelt gave in to Churchill, agreeing to invade Sicily. In summer 1943, after a month of fighting, the Allies seized Sicily and landed in southern Italy. Italian

"Full Victory—Nothing Else!" *Supreme Commander of the Allied Expeditionary Force General Dwight D. ("Ike") Eisenhower gives the order of the day to U.S. paratroopers in England on the eve of D-Day.*

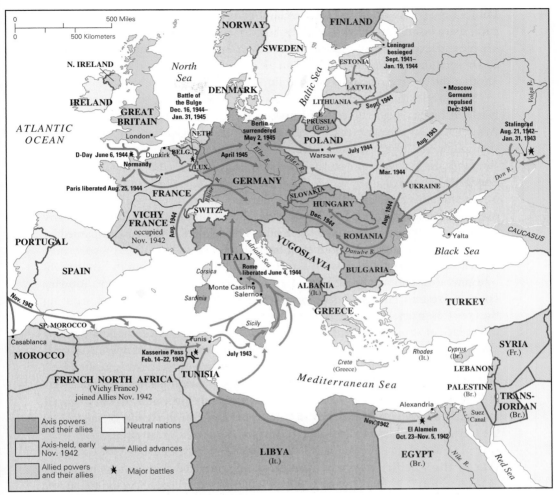

World War II in Europe and Africa

The momentous German defeats at Stalingrad and in Tunisia early in 1943 marked the turning point in the war against the Axis. By 1945 Allied conquest of Hitler's "thousand-year" Reich was imminent.

military officials deposed Mussolini and surrendered to the Allies in early September. But as Allied forces moved up the Italian peninsula, German troops poured into Italy. Facing elite Nazi divisions in strong defensive positions, the Allies spent eight months inching their way 150 miles to Rome. They were still battling through the mud and snow of northern Italy when the war in Europe ended in 1945.

In 1943–1944 the Allies turned the tide in the Atlantic and instituted round-the-clock bombardment of Germany. American science and industry developed sophisticated radar and sonar systems and better torpedoes and depth charges, and produced ever-increasing quantities of destroyers and aircraft. Britain's Royal Air Force by night and the U.S. army air force by day rained thousands of tons of bombs on German cities. In raids on Hamburg in July 1943 Allied planes dropped incendiary bombs mixed with high explosives, killing nearly a hundred thousand people and leveling the city, much as they had earlier done to Cologne and would do to Dresden in February 1945, where an estimated sixty thousand people died and another thirty-seven thousand were injured.

Meanwhile, in July 1943 German and Soviet divisions fought the largest tank battle in history near the city of Kursk in the Ukraine, and the victorious Red Army began an offensive that rid the Soviet Union of Germans by mid-1944. It then plunged into Poland and established a puppet government, took control of Romania and Bulgaria, and assisted communist guerrillas led by Josip Broz Tito in liberating Yugoslavia.

As the Soviets swept across eastern Europe, Allied forces finally opened the long-delayed second front. Early on the morning of June 6, 1944—D-Day—nearly two hundred thousand American, British, and Canadian troops, accompanied by six hundred warships and more than ten thousand planes, stormed a sixty-mile stretch of the Normandy coast in the largest amphibious invasion in history. Led by General Eisenhower, now Supreme Commander of the Allied Expeditionary Force in Western Europe, Operation Overlord gradually pushed inland, securing the Low Countries, liberating Paris, and approaching the border of Germany. There, in the face of supply problems and stiffened German resistance, the Allied offensive ground to a halt. In mid-December, as the Allies prepared for a full-scale assault on Germany, Hitler threw his last reserves against Americans in the forest of Ardennes. The Battle of the Bulge—named for the eighty-mile-long and fifty-mile-wide "bulge" that the German troops drove inside the American lines—raged for nearly a month, and ended with American forces on the banks of the Rhine, the German army depleted, and the end of the European war in sight.

War in the Pacific   The day after the Philippines fell to Japan in mid-May 1942, the U.S. and Japanese fleets clashed in the Coral Sea off northeastern Australia in the first battle in history fought entirely by planes from aircraft carriers. Each lost a carrier, but the battle stymied the Japanese advance on Australia.

Less than a month later, a Japanese armada, eager to knock the Americans out of the war, headed toward Midway Island, a crucial American outpost between Hawaii and Japan. The U.S. Signal Corps, however, had broken the Japanese naval code. Knowing the plans and locations of Japan's ships, the U.S. carriers and planes won a decisive victory, sinking four Japanese carriers and destroying hundreds of planes. Suddenly on the defensive, the stunned Japanese could now only try to hold what they had already won.

On the offensive, U.S. marines waded ashore at Guadalcanal in the Solomon Islands in August 1942. Facing fierce resistance as well as such tropical diseases as malaria, the Americans needed six months to take the island, a bitter preview of the battles to come. As the British moved from India to retake Burma, the United States began a two-pronged advance toward Japan in 1943. The army, under

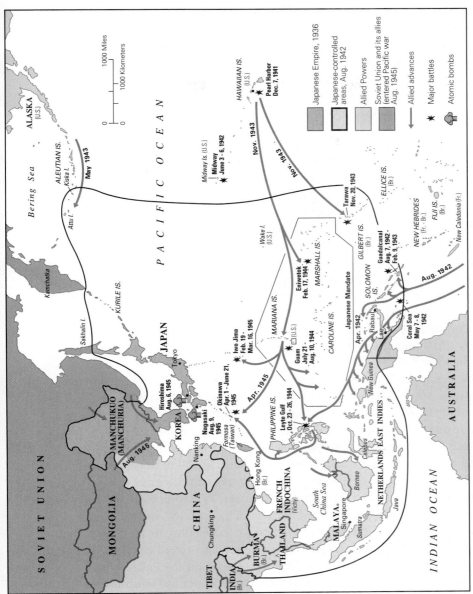

World War II in the Pacific

American ships and planes stemmed the Japanese offensive at the Battles of the Coral Sea and Midway Island. Thereafter, the Japanese were on the defensive against American amphibious assaults and air strikes.

The following text labels appear on the map:

Japanese Empire, 1936
Japanese-controlled areas, Aug. 1942
Allied Powers
Soviet Union and its allies (entered Pacific war Aug. 1945)
Allied advances
Major battles
Atomic bombs

SOVIET UNION
MONGOLIA
MANCHUKUO (MANCHURIA)
Aug. 1945
TIBET
INDIA (Br.)
BURMA (Br.)
THAILAND
CHINA
Chungking
Nanking
KOREA
JAPAN
Tokyo
Hiroshima Aug. 6, 1945
Nagasaki Aug. 9, 1945
Formosa (Taiwan)
Hong Kong (Br.)
FRENCH INDOCHINA (Vichy)
MALAYA
Singapore
Sumatra
Java
Borneo
Celebes
NETHERLANDS EAST INDIES
South China Sea
INDIAN OCEAN
AUSTRALIA
New Guinea
PHILIPPINE IS.
Leyte Gulf Oct. 23–26, 1944
Okinawa Apr. 1 – June 21, 1945
Apr. 1945
Iwo Jima Feb. 19 – Mar. 16, 1945
MARIANA IS.
Guam July 21 – Aug. 10, 1944 (U.S.)
CAROLINE IS.
Japanese Mandate
Eniwetok Feb. 17, 1944
MARSHALL IS.
Wake I. (U.S.)
Tarawa Nov. 20, 1943
GILBERT IS. (Br.)
ELLICE IS. (Br.)
SOLOMON IS.
Rabaul
Lae
Apr. 1942
Coral Sea May 7–8, 1942
Guadalcanal Aug. 7, 1942 – Feb. 9, 1943
Aug. 1942
NEW HEBRIDES (Fr.–Br.)
FIJI IS. (Br.)
New Caledonia (Fr.)
PACIFIC OCEAN
Midway Is. (U.S.)
Midway June 3–6, 1942
Nov. 1943
HAWAIIAN IS. (U.S.)
Pearl Harbor Dec. 7, 1941
ALASKA (U.S.)
ALEUTIAN IS.
Kiska I.
Attu I.
May 1943
Bering Sea
Kamchatka
KURILE IS.
Sakhalin I.

1000 Miles
1000 Kilometers
0

General Douglas MacArthur, advanced north on the islands between Australia and the Philippines, and the navy and marines, under Admiral Chester Nimitz, "island-hopped" across the central Pacific to seize strategic bases and put Tokyo in range of American bombers. In fall 1944 the navy annihilated what remained of the Japanese fleet at the battles of the Philippine Sea and Leyte Gulf, giving the United States control of Japan's air and shipping lanes and leaving the Japanese home islands open to invasion.

The Grand Alliance

President Roosevelt had two main goals for the war: the total defeat of the Axis at the least possible cost in American lives, and the establishment of a world order strong enough to preserve peace, open trade, and ensure national self-determination in the postwar era. Aware that only a common enemy fused the Grand Alliance together, Roosevelt tried to promote harmony by concentrating on military victory and postponing divisive postwar matters.

Churchill and Stalin had other goals. Britain wanted to create a balance of power in Europe and retain its imperial possessions. As Churchill said, he had "not become the King's First Minister to preside over the liquidation of the British Empire." The Soviet Union wanted a permanently weakened Germany and a sphere of influence in eastern Europe to protect itself against future attacks from the West. To hold together this fragile alliance, FDR relied on personal diplomacy to mediate conflicts.

The first president to travel by plane while in office, Roosevelt arrived in Casablanca, Morocco's main port, in January 1943 to confer with Churchill. They resolved to attack Italy before invading France and proclaimed that the war would continue until the "unconditional surrender" of the Axis. By so doing, they sought to reduce Soviet mistrust of the West, which had deepened because of the postponement of the second front. Ten months later, in Cairo, Roosevelt met with Churchill and Jiang Jieshi (Chiang Kai-shek), the anticommunist head of the Chinese government. To keep China in the war, FDR promised the return of Manchuria and Taiwan to China and a "free and independent Korea." From Cairo, FDR and Churchill continued on to Tehran, Iran's capital, to meet with Stalin. Here they set the invasion of France for June 1944, and agreed to divide Germany into zones of occupation and to impose reparations on the Reich. Most importantly to Roosevelt, Stalin pledged to enter the war against Japan after Hitler's defeat.

Roosevelt then turned his attention to domestic politics. Increasing conservative sentiment in the nation led him to drop the liberal Henry A. Wallace from the ticket and accept Harry S. Truman as his vice-presidential candidate. A moderate senator from Missouri now dubbed "the new Missouri Compromise," Truman restored a semblance of unity to the Democrats for the 1944 campaign. To compete, the Republicans nominated moderate and noncontroversial New York governor Thomas E. Dewey. The campaign focused more on personalities than on issues, and the still-popular FDR defeated his dull GOP opponent, but with the narrowest margin since 1916—winning just 53 percent of the popular vote. A weary Roosevelt, secretly suffering from hypertension and heart disease, now directed his waning energies toward defeating the Axis and constructing an international peacekeeping system.

WAR AND AMERICAN SOCIETY

The crisis of war altered the most basic patterns of American life, powerfully affecting those on the home front as well as those who served in the armed forces. Few families were untouched: more than 15 million Americans went to the war, an equal number were on the move, and unprecedented numbers of women went to work outside the home. As well, the war opened some doors of opportunity for African-Americans and other minorities, although most remained closed. It heightened minority aspirations and widened cracks in the wall of white racist attitudes and policy, while maintaining much of America's racial caste system, thereby tilling the ground for future crises.

The GIs' War   Most Americans in the armed forces griped about regimentation and were more interested in dry socks than in ideology. They knew little of the big strategies, and cared less. They fought because they were told to and wanted to stay alive. Reluctant recruits rather than heroic warriors, most had few aims beyond returning to a safe, familiar United States.

But the GIs' war dragged on for almost four years, transforming them in the process. Millions who had never been far from home traveled to unfamiliar cities and remote lands, shedding their parochialism. Sharing tents and foxholes with Americans of different religions, ethnicities, and classes, their military service acted as a "melting pot" experience that freed them from some prewar prejudices.

In countless ways, the war modified how GIs saw themselves and others. Besides serving with people they had never previously encountered, over a million married overseas, broadening personal horizons and sowing the seeds of a more tolerant and diverse national culture that placed far less emphasis on divisions of class, national origin, region, and religion. At the same time many GIs became evermore distrustful of foreigners and outsiders, and returned home obsessed with the flag as a symbol of patriotism.

Physical misery, chronic exhaustion, and, especially, intense combat took a heavy toll, leaving lasting psychological as well as physical wounds. Both American and Japanese troops saw the other in racist images, as animals to be exterminated, and brutality became as much the rule as the exception in "a war without mercy." Both sides machine-gunned hostile flyers in parachutes; both tortured and killed prisoners in cold blood; both mutilated enemy dead for souvenirs. In the fight against Germany, cruelties and atrocities also occurred, although on a lesser scale. A battalion of the second armored division calling itself "Roosevelt's Butchers" boasted that it shot all the German soldiers it captured. Some U.S. pilots laughed at the lifeboats they strafed and the bodies they exploded out of trucks.

Some became cynical about human life. Some still languish in veterans' hospitals, having nightmares about the war.

The Home Front Nothing transformed the social topography more than the vast internal migration of an already mobile people. About 15 million men moved because of military service, often accompanied by family members. Many other Americans moved to secure new economic opportunities, especially in the Pacific Coast states. Nearly a quarter of a million found jobs in the shipyards of the Bay area and at least as many in the aircraft industry that arose in the orange groves of southern California. More than one hundred thousand worked in the Puget Sound shipyards of Washington State and half as many in the nearby Boeing airplane plants. Others flocked to the world's largest magnesium plant in Henderson, Nevada, to the huge Geneva Steel Works near Provo, Utah, and to the Rocky Mountain Arsenal and Remington Rand arms plant outside Denver.

At least 6 million people left farms to work in urban areas, including several million southern blacks and whites. They doubled Albuquerque's population and increased San Diego's some 90 percent. This mass uprooting of people from familiar settings made Americans both more cosmopolitan and more lonely, alienated, and frustrated. Lifestyles became freewheeling as Americans left their hometowns and ignored traditional values. Housing shortages left millions living in converted garages and trailer camps, and even in their own cars. Some workers in Seattle lived in chicken coops. The swarms of migrants to Mobile, Alabama, attracted by a new aluminum plant, two massive shipyards, an air base, and an army supply depot, transformed a sleepy fishing village into a symbol of urban disorder.

There and elsewhere, overcrowding along with wartime separations strained family and community life. High rates of divorce, mental illness, family violence, and juvenile delinquency reflected the disruptions caused in part by the lack of privacy, the sense of impermanence, the absence of familiar settings, and the competition for scarce facilities. Few boom communities had the resources to supply their suddenly swollen populations with transportation, recreation, and social services. Urban blight and conflicts between newcomers and old-timers accelerated.

While military culture fostered a sexist mentality toward women, emphasizing the differences between "femininity" and "masculinity," millions of American women donned pants, put their hair in bandannas, and went to work in defense plants. Reversing a decade of efforts to exclude women from the labor force, the federal government urged women into war production in 1942. Songs like "We're the Janes Who Make the Planes" appealed to women to take up war work, and propaganda called upon them to "help save lives" and "release able-bodied men for fighting." More than 6 million women entered the labor force during the war, increasing the number of employed women to 19 million. Less than a quarter of the labor force in 1940, women constituted well over a third of all workers in 1945.

Before the war most female wage earners had been young and single. By contrast, 75 percent of the new women workers were married, 60 percent were over

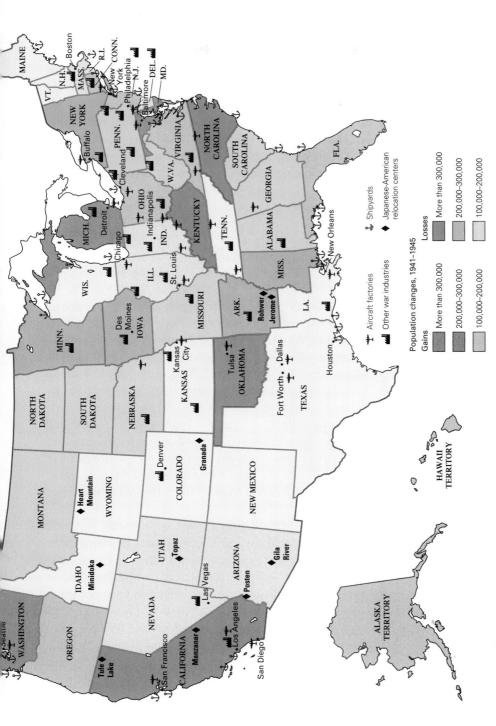

The Home Front

War-related production finally ended the Great Depression, but it also required many Americans to move, especially to western states where the jobs were. This map shows major war-related industries and the states that gained and lost populations. For Japanese-Americans, relocation did not mean new jobs, but a loss of freedom as they were assigned to one of ten relocation centers across the country.

Aircraft factories

Other war industries

Shipyards

Japanese-American relocation centers

Population changes, 1941–1945

Gains
- More than 300,000
- 200,000–300,000
- 100,000–200,000

Losses
- More than 300,000
- 200,000–300,000
- 100,000–200,000

MAINE
VT.
N.H.
MASS. — Boston
R.I.
CONN.
New York
N.J.
Philadelphia — DEL.
Baltimore — MD.
NEW YORK
Buffalo
PENN.
Cleveland
W.VA.
VIRGINIA
NORTH CAROLINA
SOUTH CAROLINA
OHIO
Indianapolis
IND.
KENTUCKY
TENN.
GEORGIA
ALABAMA
FLA.
MICH.
Detroit
Chicago
ILL.
St. Louis
MISS.
LA.
New Orleans
WIS.
MINN.
Des Moines
IOWA
MISSOURI
ARK.
Rohwer
Jerome
Kansas City
KANSAS
OKLAHOMA
Tulsa
Dallas
Fort Worth
TEXAS
Houston
NORTH DAKOTA
SOUTH DAKOTA
NEBRASKA
Denver
COLORADO
Granada
NEW MEXICO
Heart Mountain
WYOMING
MONTANA
UTAH
Topaz
ARIZONA
Gila River
Posten
IDAHO
Minidoka
NEVADA
Las Vegas
OREGON
WASHINGTON
Seattle
San Francisco
CALIFORNIA
Tule Lake
Manzanar
Los Angeles
San Diego
HAWAII TERRITORY
ALASKA TERRITORY

953

thirty-five, and more than 33 percent had children under the age of fourteen. They tended blast furnaces, operated cranes, greased locomotives, drove taxis, welded hulls, loaded shells, and worked in coke plants and rolling mills. On the Pacific Coast, more than one-third of all workers in aircraft and shipbuilding were women. "Rosie the Riveter," holding a pneumatic gun in arms bulging with muscles, became the symbol of the woman war worker; she was, in the words of a popular song, "making history working for victory."

Yet wartime also strengthened traditional convictions, and gender discrimination flourished throughout the war. Women earned only about 65 percent of what men earned for the same work. Government propaganda portrayed women's war work as a temporary response to an emergency. "A woman is a substitute," claimed a War Department brochure, "like plastic instead of metal." Work was pictured as an extension of women's roles as wives and mothers. A newspaperwoman wrote of the "deep satisfaction which a woman of today knows who has made a rubber boat which may save the life of her aviator husband, or helped fashion a bullet which may avenge her son!" As a result, the public attitude about women's employment changed little in World War II. In 1945 only 18 percent of the respondents in a poll approved of married women working.

Traditional notions of a woman's place and the stigma attached to working mothers also shaped government resistance to establishing child-care centers for women employed in defense. "A mother's primary duty is to her home and children," the Labor Department's Children's Bureau stated. "This duty is one she cannot lay aside, no matter what the emergency." New York Mayor Fiorello LaGuardia proclaimed that the worst mother was better than the best nursery. Funds for federal child-care centers covered fewer than 10 percent of defense workers' children, and the young suffered. Terms like "eight-hour orphans" and "latch-key children" were coined to describe unsupervised children forced to fend for themselves. Fueling the fears of those who believed that the employment of women outside the home would cause the family to disintegrate, juvenile delinquency increased fivefold and the divorce rate zoomed from 16 per 100 marriages in 1940 to 27 per 100 in 1944.

The impact of war on women and the family proved multifaceted and even contradictory. As the divorce rate soared, so did marriage rates and birthrates. Although some women remained content to roll bandages for the Red Cross, more than three hundred thousand joined the armed forces and, for the first time in American history, were given regular military status and served in positions other than that of nurse. As members of the Women's Army Corps (WACs) and the Navy's Women Appointed for Volunteer Emergency Service (WAVES) they replaced men in such noncombat jobs as mechanics and radio operators. About a thousand women served as civilian pilots with the WASPs (Women's Airforce Service Pilots). When they left the service, moreover, they had the same rights and privileges as the male veterans.

Despite lingering notions of separate spheres, female workers gained unprecedented employment opportunities and public recognition. Although some eagerly gave up their jobs at the end of the war, others did not relish losing the income and self-esteem they had gained in contributing to the war effort. As Inez Sauer, who went to work for Boeing in Seattle, recalled,

> My mother warned me when I took the job that I would never be the same. She said, "You will never want to go back to being a housewife." She was right, it definitely did. At Boeing I found a freedom and an independence I had never known. After the war I could never go back to playing bridge again, being a clubwoman and listening to a lot of inanities when I knew there were things you could use your mind for. The war changed my life completely.

Overall, women gained a new sense of their potential. The war proved their capabilities and widened their world. Recalled one war wife whose returning husband did not like her independence, "He had left a shrinking violet and come home to a very strong oak tree." Wartime experiences markedly affected a generation of women and the sons and daughters they later raised.

Some of these women were among the 350,000 teachers who took better-paying war work or joined the armed services, leaving schools badly understaffed. Students, too, abandoned school in record numbers. High-school enrollments sank as the full-time employment of teenagers rose from 900,000 in 1940 to 3 million in 1944.

The loss of students to war production and the armed services forced colleges to admit large numbers of women and to contract themselves out to the armed forces. Nearly a million servicemen took college classes in science, engineering, and foreign languages. The military presence was all-pervasive. Harvard University awarded four military-training certificates for every academic degree it conferred. The chancellor of one branch of the University of California announced that his school was "no longer an academic tent with military sideshows. It is a military tent with academic sideshows." Higher education became more dependent on the federal government, and most universities sought increased federal contracts and subsidies, despite their having to submit to greater government interference and regulation. The universities in the West received some $100 billion from the Office of Scientific Research and Development, more money than had been spent on scientific research by all the western universities since their founding.

The war profoundly affected American popular culture as well. The media, emphasizing mass production and targeting mass audiences as never before, emerged from the war more highly organized and with greater concentrations of power. Expenditures on books and theater entertainment doubled between 1941 and 1945. Between 60 million and 100 million Americans a week (in a population of 135 million) went to the movies, and the film industry reached its zenith in 1945–1946. But as the war dragged on, people tired of patriotic war films, and Hollywood reemphasized romance and nostalgia with such stars as Katharine Hepburn and Judy Garland.

Similarly, popular music early in the war featured patriotic themes. "Goodbye, Mama, I'm Off to Yokohama" became the first hit of 1942. As the war continued, themes of lost love and loneliness dominated lyrics. Numbers like "They're Either Too Young or Too Old" expressed the laments of women separated from the men they loved. So, too, did the dozens of "dream songs" in which love denied by the real world could be achieved only in a dream. By 1945 bitterness rather than melancholy pervaded the lyrics of best-selling records, and songs like "Saturday Night Is the Loneliest Night of the Week" revealed impatience for the war's end.

In bookstores, nonfiction ruled the roost and every newsmagazine increased its circulation. Wendell Willkie's *One World* (1943) became the fastest-selling title in publishing history to that time, with 1 million copies snapped up in two months. A euphoric vision of a world without military alliances and spheres of influence, this brief volume expressed hope that an international organization would extend peace and democracy through the postwar world. The Government Printing Office published Armed Services Editions, paperback reprints of classics and new releases; and the nearly 350 million copies distributed free to soldiers sped up the American acceptance of quality paperbacks, which were introduced in 1939 by the Pocket Book Company.

An avid interest in wartime news also spurred the major radio networks to increase their news programs from 4 percent to nearly 30 percent of broadcasting time, and enticed Americans to listen to the radio an average of 4 1/2 hours a day. Daytime radio serials, like those featuring Dick Tracy tracking down Axis spies, reached the height of their popularity, as did juvenile comic books in which a platoon of new superheroes, including Captain America and Captain Marvel, saw action on the battlefield. Even Bugs Bunny donned a uniform to combat America's foes.

Racism and New Opportunities Recognizing that the government needed the loyalty and labor of a united people, black leaders entered World War II determined to secure equal rights. In 1942 civil-rights spokesmen insisted that African-American support of the war hinged on America's commitment to racial justice. They called for a "Double V" campaign— victory over racial discrimination as well as over the Axis.

Membership in the NAACP multiplied nearly ten times, reaching half a million in 1945. The association pressed for legislation outlawing the poll tax and lynching, decried discrimination in defense industries and the armed services, and sought to end black disfranchisement. The campaign for voting rights gained momentum when the Supreme Court, in *Smith* v. *Allwright* (1944), ruled the Texas all-white primary unconstitutional. The decision eliminated a bar that had existed in eight southern states, although these states promptly resorted to other devices to minimize voting by blacks.

A new civil-rights organization, the Congress of Racial Equality (CORE), was founded in 1942. Employing the same forms of nonviolent direct action that Mohandas Gandhi used in his campaign for India's independence, CORE sought to desegregate public facilities in northern cities.

Also proposing nonviolent direct action, A. Philip Randolph, president of the Brotherhood of Sleeping Car Porters, in 1941 called for a "thundering march" of one hundred thousand blacks on Washington "to wake up and shock white America as it has never been shocked before." He warned Roosevelt that if the president did not end discrimination in the armed services and the defense industry, African-Americans would besiege Washington. FDR agreed to compromise.

In June 1941 Roosevelt issued Executive Order 8802, the first presidential directive on race since Reconstruction. It prohibited discriminatory employment practices by federal agencies and all unions and companies engaged in war-related work, and established the Fair Employment Practices Commission (FEPC) to enforce this policy. Although the FEPC lacked effective enforcement powers, booming war production and a labor supply depleted by military service resulted in the employment of some 2 million African-Americans in industry and two hundred thousand in the federal civil service. Between 1942 and 1945 the proportion of blacks in war-production work rose from 3 to 9 percent. Black membership in labor unions doubled to 1.25 million, and the number of skilled and semiskilled black workers tripled. Formerly mired in low-paying domestic and farm jobs, some three hundred thousand black women found work in factories and the civil service. "Hitler was the one that got us out of the white folks' kitchen," recalled one black woman who went to work for Boeing in Seattle, a city whose black population rose from four thousand to forty thousand during the war. Overall, the average wage for African-Americans increased from $457 to $1,976 a year, compared with a gain from $1,064 to $2,600 for whites.

About 1 million African-Americans served in the armed forces. Wartime needs forced the military to end policies of excluding blacks from the marines and coast guard, restricting them to jobs as mess boys in the navy, and confining them to noncombatant units in the army. From just five in 1940, the number of black officers grew to over seven thousand in 1945. The all-black 761st tank battalion gained distinction fighting in Germany, and the 99th pursuit squadron won eighty Distinguished Flying Crosses for its combat against the *Luftwaffe* in Europe. In 1944 both the army and navy began token integration in some training facilities, ships, and battlefield platoons.

The great majority of blacks, however, served throughout the war in segregated service units commanded by white officers. This indignity, made worse by the failure of military authorities to protect black servicemen off the post and by the use of white military police to keep blacks "in their place," sparked rioting on army bases. At least fifty black soldiers died in racial conflicts during the war. "I used to sing gospel songs until I joined the Army," recalled blues-guitar great B. B. King; "then I sang the blues."

Violence within the military mirrored growing racial tensions on the home front. As blacks protested against discrimination, many whites stiffened their resistance to racial equality. Numerous clashes occurred. Scores of cities reported pitched battles between blacks and whites. Race riots erupted in 1943 in Harlem,

Mobile, and Beaumont, Texas. The bloodiest melee exploded in Detroit that year when white mobs assaulted blacks caught riding on trolleys or sitting in movie theaters and blacks smashed and looted white-owned stores and shops. After thirty hours of racial beatings, shootings, and burning, twenty-five African-Americans and nine whites lay dead, more than seven hundred had been injured, and over $2 million of property had been destroyed. The fear of continued violence led to a greater emphasis on racial tolerance by liberal whites and to a reduction in the militancy of African-American leaders.

Yet the war brought significant changes that would eventually result in a successful drive for black civil rights. The migration of over seven hundred thousand blacks from the South turned a southern problem into a national concern. It created a new attitude of independence in African-Americans freed from the stifling constraints of caste. Despite the continuation of racial prejudice and discrimination, most who left the rural South found a more abundant and hopeful life than the one they had left behind. As the growing numbers of blacks in the industrial cities of the North began to vote, moreover, the bloc of African-American voters could tip the victory to either Democrats or Republicans in close elections. This prompted politicians in both major parties to extend greater recognition to blacks and to pay more attention to civil-rights issues.

African-American expectations of greater government concern for their rights also resulted from the new prominence of the United States as a major power in a predominantly nonwhite world. As Japanese propaganda appeals to the peoples of Asia and Latin America emphasized lynchings and race riots in the United States, Americans had to confront the peril that white racism posed to their national security. In addition, the horrors of Nazi racism made Americans more sensitive to the harm caused by their own white-supremacist attitudes and practices. As a former governor of Alabama complained, Nazism has "wrecked the theories of the master race with which we were so contented so long." Swedish economist Gunnar Myrdal, in his massive study of race problems, *An American Dilemma* (1944), concluded that "not since Reconstruction had there been more reason to anticipate fundamental changes in American race relations."

Black veterans, with a new sense of self-esteem gained from participating in the war effort, returned to civilian life with high expectations. Like the athlete Jackie Robinson, who as a young lieutenant had refused to take a seat at the rear of a segregated bus and had fought and won his subsequent court martial, African-Americans faced the postwar era resolved to gain all the rights enjoyed by whites.

War and Diversity   Wartime winds of change also brought new opportunities and difficulties to other minorities. More than twenty-five thousand Native Americans served in the armed forces during the war. Navajo "code talkers" confounded the Japanese by using the Navajo language to relay messages between U.S. command centers. "Were it not for the Navajos, the Marines would never have taken Iwo Jima," one Signal Corps officer declared.

Another fifty thousand Indians left the reservation to work in defense industries, mainly on the West Coast. The Rosebud Reservation in South Dakota lost more than a quarter of its population to migration during the war. It was the first time most had lived in a non-Indian world, and the average income of Native American households tripled during the war. Such economic improvement encouraged many Indians to remain outside the reservation and to try to assimilate into mainstream life. But anti-Indian discrimination, particularly in smaller towns near reservations such as Gallup, New Mexico, and Billings, Montana, forced many Native Americans back to their reservations, which had suffered severely from budget cuts during the war. Prodded by those who coveted Indian lands, lawmakers demanded that Indians be taken off the backs of the taxpayers and "freed from the reservations" to fend for themselves. To mobilize against the campaign to end all reservations and trust protections, Native Americans organized the National Congress of American Indians in 1944.

To relieve labor shortages in agriculture, caused by conscription and the movement of rural workers to city factories, the U.S. government negotiated an agreement with Mexico in July 1942 to import *braceros,* or temporary workers. Classified as foreign laborers rather than as immigrants, an estimated two hundred thousand *braceros,* half of them in California, received short-term contracts guaranteeing adequate wages, medical care, and decent living conditions. But farm owners frequently violated the terms of these contracts and also encouraged an influx of illegal migrants from Mexico desperate for employment. Unable to complain about their working conditions without risking arrest and deportation, hundreds of thousands of Mexicans were exploited by agribusinesses in Arizona, California, and Texas. At the same time, tens of thousands of Chicanos left agricultural work for jobs in factories, shipbuilding yards, and steel mills. By 1943 about half a million Chicanos were living in Los Angeles County, 10 percent of the total population. In New Mexico nearly 20 percent of Mexican-American farm laborers escaped from rural poverty to urban jobs. Even as their occupational status and material conditions improved, most Mexican-Americans remained in communities called *colonias,* segregated from the larger society and frequently harassed by the police.

Much of the hostility toward Mexican-Americans focused on young gang members who wore "zoot suits"—a fashion that originated in Harlem and emphasized long, broad-shouldered jackets and pleated trousers tightly pegged at the ankles. Known as *pachucos,* zoot-suited Mexican-Americans aroused the ire of servicemen stationed or on leave in Los Angeles who saw them as delinquents and draft dodgers. After a series of minor clashes, bands of sailors from nearby bases and soldiers on leave in Los Angeles rampaged through the city in early June 1943, stripping *pachucos,* cutting their long hair, and beating them. Military authorities looked the other way. City police intervened only to arrest Mexican-Americans. *Time* magazine described the violence as "the ugliest brand of mob action since the coolie race riots of the 1870s"; yet Los Angeles officials praised the servicemen's actions, and the city council made the wearing of a zoot suit a misdemeanor. Nothing was done about the substandard housing, disease, and racism Hispanics had to endure.

Unlike African-Americans, however, more than 350,000 Mexican-Americans served in the armed forces without segregation, and in all combat units. They volunteered in much higher numbers than warranted by their percentage of the population and earned a disproportionate number of citations for distinguished service as well as seventeen Medals of Honor. Air corps hero Jose Holguin from Los Angeles won the Distinguished Flying Cross, the Air Medal, and the Silver Star. Returning Mexican-American GIs joined long-standing antidiscrimination groups, like the League of United Latin American Citizens (LULAC) and organized their own associations, like the American GI Forum, to press for veterans' interests and equal rights.

Thousands of gay men and lesbians who served in the armed forces also found new wartime opportunities. Although the military officially barred those they defined as "sexual perverts," the urgency of building a massive armed forces led to just four to five thousand men out of eighteen million examined for induction to be excluded because of homosexuality. For the vast majority of gays not excluded, being emancipated from traditional expectations and the close scrutiny of family and neighbors, and living in overwhelmingly all-male or all-female environments, brought freedom to meet like-minded gay men and women and to express their sexual orientation. Like other minorities, many gays saw the war as a chance to prove their worth under fire. Some were ideologically committed because the Nazis had targeted European homosexuals for liquidation. On one American warship, the most highly regarded officer was "a notorious Queen" who wore a hair net. Yet others suspected of being gay were dishonorably discharged, sent to psychiatric hospitals, or imprisoned in so-called queer stockades, where some were mentally and physically abused by military police. The anger of gays at having fought against oppression while remaining oppressed themselves led them to think far more than ever before about their right to equal treatment and opportunity. In 1945 gay veterans established the Veteran's Benevolent Association, the first major gay organization in the United States to combat discrimination.

The Internment of Japanese-Americans   Far more than any other minority in the United States, Japanese-Americans suffered grievously during the war. The internment of about thirty-seven thousand first-generation Japanese immigrants (Issei) and nearly seventy-five thousand native-born Japanese-American citizens of the United States (Nisei) in "relocation centers" guarded by military police was a tragic reminder of the fragility of civil liberties in wartime.

The internment reflected forty years of anti-Japanese sentiment on the West Coast, rooted in racial prejudice and economic rivalry. Nativist politicians and farmers who wanted Japanese-American land had long decried the "yellow peril." Following the attack on Pearl Harbor they whipped up the rage of white

Californians, aided by a government report falsely blaming Japanese Americans in Hawaii for aiding the Japanese naval force. One barber advertised "free shave for Japs," but "not responsible for accidents." Patriotic associations and many newspapers clamored for evacuating the Japanese Americans, as did local politicians, West Coast congressional delegations, and the army general in charge of the Western Defense Command, who proclaimed, "A Jap is a Jap. It makes no difference whether he is an American citizen or not. . . . I don't want any of them."

In February 1942 President Roosevelt gave in to the pressure and issued Executive Order 9066, authorizing the removal from military areas of anyone deemed a threat. Although not a single Japanese-American was apprehended for espionage or sedition and neither the FBI nor military intelligence uncovered any evidence of disloyal behavior by Japanese-Americans, the military ordered the eviction of all Nisei and Issei from the West Coast. Only Hawaii was excepted. Despite the far larger number of Hawaiians of Japanese ancestry, as well as of Japanese living in Hawaii, no internment policy was implemented there, and no sabotage occurred (see A Place in Time: Honolulu, Hawaii, 1941–1945).

Forced to sell their lands and homes quickly at whatever prices they could obtain, Japanese-Americans lost an estimated $2 billion in property and possessions. Tagged with numbers rather than names, they were herded into barbed-wire-encircled detention camps in the most remote and desolate parts of the West and Great Plains—places, wrote one historian, "where nobody had lived before

A Japanese-American child being evacuated from Los Angeles in April 1942. It did not matter that she, along with some 80,000 other Nisei, were American citizens. "A Jap's a Jap," said General John De Witt, commander of West Coast defenses.

and no one has lived since." Few other Americans protested the incarceration. Stating that it would not question government claims of military necessity during time of war, the Supreme Court upheld the constitutionality of the evacuation in the *Korematsu* case (1944). By then the hysteria had subsided, and the government had begun a program of gradual release, allowing some Nisei to attend college or take factory jobs (but not on the West Coast); about eighteen thousand served in the military. The 442nd regimental combat team, entirely Japanese-American, became the most decorated unit in the military.

In 1982 a special government commission concluded in its report, *Personal Justice Denied,* that internment "was not justified by military necessity." It blamed the Roosevelt administration's action on "race prejudice, war hysteria, and a failure of political leadership" and apologized to Japanese-Americans for "a grave injustice." In 1988 Congress voted to pay twenty thousand dollars in compensation to each of the nearly sixty-two thousand surviving internees; and in 1998 President Bill Clinton further apologized for the injustice by giving the nation's highest civilian honor, the Presidential Medal of Freedom, to Fred Korematsu, who had protested the evacuation decree all the way to the Supreme Court.

TRIUMPH AND TRAGEDY, 1945

Spring and summer 1945 brought stunning changes and new crises. In Europe a new balance of power emerged after the collapse of the Third Reich. In Asia continued Japanese reluctance to surrender led to the use of atomic bombs. And in the United States a new president, Harry Truman, presided over both the end of World War II and the beginning of the Cold War and the nuclear age.

The Yalta Conference   By the time Roosevelt, Churchill, and Stalin met in the Soviet city of Yalta in February 1945, the military situation favored the Soviet Union. The Red Army had overrun Poland, Romania, and Bulgaria; driven the Nazis out of Yugoslavia; penetrated Austria, Hungary, and Czechoslovakia; and was massed just fifty miles from Berlin. American forces, in contrast, were still recovering from the Battle of the Bulge and facing stiff resistance on the route to Japan. The Joint Chiefs of Staff, contemplating the awesome cost in American casualties of an invasion of Japan, insisted that Stalin's help was worth almost any price. And Stalin was in a position to make demands. The Soviet Union had suffered most in the war against Germany, it already dominated eastern Europe, and, knowing that the United States did not want to fight a prolonged war against Japan, Stalin had the luxury of deciding whether and when to enter the Pacific war.

The Yalta accords reflected these realities. Stalin again vowed to declare war on Japan "two or three months" after Germany's surrender, and in return Churchill and Roosevelt reneged on their arrangement with Jiang Jieshi (made in Cairo) and promised the Soviet Union concessions in Manchuria and the territories it had lost in the Russo-Japanese War (1904). Unable to reach agreement about the future of

Germany, the Big Three delegated a final settlement of the reparations issue to a postwar commission, and left vague the matter of partitioning Germany and its eventual reunification. Similarly without specific provisions or timetables, the conference called for interim governments in eastern Europe "broadly representative of all democratic elements" and, ultimately, for freely elected permanent governments. On the matter dearest to FDR's heart, the negotiators accepted a plan for a new international organization and agreed to convene a founding conference of the new United Nations in San Francisco in April 1945.

Stalin proved adamant about the nature of the postwar Polish government. Twice in the twentieth century German troops had used Poland as a springboard for invading Russia. Stalin would not expose his land again, and after the Red Army had captured Warsaw in January 1945 he installed a procommunist regime and brutally subdued the anticommunist Poles. Refusing to recognize the communist government, Roosevelt and Churchill called for free, democratic elections. But at Yalta they sidestepped this crucial issue by accepting Stalin's vague pledge to include some prowesterners in the new Polish government and to allow elections "as soon as possible." Conservative critics would later charge that FDR "gave away" eastern Europe. Actually, the Soviet Union gained little it did not already control, and short of going to war against the Soviet Union while still battling Germany and Japan, FDR could only hope that Stalin would keep his word.

Victory in Europe As the Soviets prepared for their assault on Berlin, American troops crossed the Rhine at Remagen in March 1945 and encircled the Ruhr Valley, Germany's industrial heartland. Churchill now proposed a rapid thrust to Berlin. But Eisenhower, with Roosevelt's backing, overruled Churchill. They saw no point in risking high casualties to rush to an area of Germany that had already been designated as the Soviet occupation zone. So Eisenhower advanced methodically along a broad front until the Americans met the Russians at the Elbe River on April 25. By then the Red Army had taken Vienna and reached the suburbs of Berlin. On April 30, as Soviet troops approached his headquarters, Hitler committed suicide. Berlin fell to the Soviets on May 2, and on May 8 a new German government surrendered unconditionally.

Jubilant Americans celebrated Victory in Europe (V-E) Day less than a month after they had mourned the death of their president. On April 12 an exhausted President Roosevelt had abruptly clutched his head, moaned that he had a "terrific headache," and fell unconscious. A cerebral hemorrhage ended his life. As the nation grieved, Roosevelt's unprepared successor assumed the burden of ending the war and dealing with the Soviet Union.

"I don't know whether you fellows ever had a load of hay or a bull fall on you," Harry S. Truman told reporters on his first full day in office, "but last night the moon, the stars, and all the planets fell on me." An unpretentious politician awed by his new responsibilities, Truman struggled to continue FDR's policies. But Roosevelt had made no effort to familiarize his vice president with world affairs. Perhaps sensing his own inadequacies, Truman adopted a tough pose toward adversaries. In office less than two weeks, he lashed out at Soviet ambassador V. M. Molotov that the United States was tired of waiting for the Russians to allow free elections in Poland, and he threatened to cut off lend-lease aid if the Soviet Union did not cooperate. The Truman administration then reduced U.S. economic assistance to the Soviets and stalled on their request for a $1 billion reconstruction loan. Simultaneously, Stalin strengthened his grip on eastern Europe, ignoring the promises he had made at Yalta.

The United States would neither concede the Soviet sphere of influence in eastern Europe nor take steps to terminate it. Although Truman still sought Stalin's cooperation in establishing the United Nations and in defeating Japan, Soviet-American relations deteriorated. By June 1945, when the Allied countries succeeded in framing the United Nations Charter, hopes for a new international order had dimmed, and the United Nations emerged as a diplomatic battleground. Truman, Churchill, and Stalin met at Potsdam, Germany, from July 16 to August 2 to complete the postwar arrangements begun at Yalta. But the Allied leaders could barely agree to demilitarize Germany and to punish Nazi war criminals. All the major divisive issues were postponed and left to the Council of Foreign Ministers to resolve later. Given the diplomatic impasse, only military power remained to determine the contours of the postwar world.

Yalta Conference, 1945 *The palaces where Roosevelt, Churchill, Stalin, and their advisers gathered were still standing, but the rest of Yalta had been reduced to ruin during the German occupation.*

The Holocaust   When news of the Holocaust—the term later given to the Nazis' extermination of European Jewry—first leaked out in early 1942, many Americans discounted the reports. Not until November did the State Department admit knowledge of the massacres. A month later the American broadcaster Edward R. Murrow, listened to nationwide, reported on the systematic killing of millions of Jews: "It is a picture of mass murder and moral depravity unequalled in the history of the world. It is a horror beyond what imagination can grasp. . . . There are no longer 'concentration camps'—we must speak now only of 'extermination camps.' "

Most Americans considered the annihilation of Europe's 6 million Jews beyond belief. There were no photographs to prove it, and, some argued, the atrocities attributed to the Germans in World War I had turned out to be false. So few took issue with the military's view that the way to liberate those enslaved by Hitler was by speedily winning the war. Pleas by American Jews for the Allies to bomb the death camps and the railroad tracks leading to them fell on deaf ears. In fall 1944 U.S. planes flying over Auschwitz in southern Poland bombed nearby factories but left the gas chambers and crematoria intact, in order, American officials explained, not to divert air power from more vital raids elsewhere. "How could it be," historian David Wyman has asked, "that Government officials knew that a place existed where 2,000 helpless human beings could be killed in less than an hour, knew that this occurred over and over again, and yet did not feel driven to search for some way to wipe such a scourge from the earth?"

How much could have been done remains uncertain. Still, the U.S. government never seriously considered rescue schemes or searched for a way to curtail the Nazis' "final solution" to the "Jewish question." Its feeble response was due to its overwhelming focus on winning the war as quickly as possible, congressional and public fears of an influx of destitute Jews into the United States, Britain's wish to placate the Arabs by keeping Jewish settlers out of Palestine, and the fear of some Jewish-American leaders that pressing the issue would increase anti-Semitism at home. The War Refugee Board managed to save the lives of just two hundred thousand Jews and twenty thousand non-Jews. Six million other Jews, about 75 percent of the European Jewish population, were gassed, shot, and incinerated, as were several million gypsies, communists, homosexuals, Polish Catholics, and others deemed unfit to live in the Third Reich.

"The things I saw beggar description," wrote General Eisenhower after visiting the first death camp liberated by the U.S. army. He sent immediately for a delegation of congressional leaders and newspaper editors to make sure Americans would never forget the gas chambers and human ovens. Only after viewing the photographs and newsreels of corpses stacked like cordwood, boxcars heaped with the bones of dead prisoners, bulldozers shoving emaciated bodies into hastily dug ditches, and liberated, barely-alive living skeletons lying in their own filth, their vacant, sunken eyes staring through barbed wire, did most Americans see that the Holocaust was no myth.

Honolulu, Hawaii, 1941–1945

Much as the war came to the United States initially and most dramatically at Pearl Harbor, the outlines of an increasingly multicultural United States emerging from the Second World War could be seen first and most clearly in Hawaii. The nearly one million soldiers, sailors, and marines stopping in Hawaii on their way to the battlefront, as well as the more than one hundred thousand men and women who left the mainland to find war work on the islands, expected the Hollywood image of a simple Pacific paradise: blue sky, green sea, white sand, palm trees, tropical sunsets, and exotic women with flowers in their hair. They found instead a complex multiracial and multiethnic society. The experience would change them, as they in turn would change the islands.

Before December 7, 1941, few Americans knew where Hawaii was or that it was part of their country, a colonial possession annexed by the U.S. government in 1898. Few realized that Honolulu, a tiny fishing village when Captain James Cook sailed by its harbor in 1778, had become a gritty port city that would serve as the major staging ground for the war to be waged in the Pacific. And few knew that, as a result of successive waves of immigration by Chinese, Portuguese, Japanese, and Filipinos, this American outpost had a population in which native Hawaiians and white Americans (called *haoles,* which in Hawaiian means "strangers") each constituted only 15 percent of the islands' inhabitants.

The approximately 160,000 Hawaiians of Japanese ancestry— including some 100,000 second-generation Japanese, or Nisei, who had been born in Hawaii and were therefore U.S. citizens—made up Hawaii's largest ethnic group, more than a third of the population. Japan's attack on Pearl Harbor immediately raised fears of sabotage or espionage by them. Rumors flew of arrow-shaped signs cut in the sugarcane fields to direct Japanese planes to military targets and of Nisei women waving kimonos to signal Japanese pilots. But in stark contrast to the internment of Japanese-Americans in the Pacific coast states, military policy in the islands was to maintain traditional interracial harmony throughout the war, and to treat all law-abiding inhabitants of Japanese ancestry justly and humanely. "This is America and we must do things the American way," announced Hawaii's military governor. "We must distinguish between loyalty and disloyalty among our people." There was no mass internment of the Nisei and Issei (those who emigrated from Japan) and there were no acts of sabotage.

For many Issei, loyalty to the United States had become an obligation, a matter of honor. To eliminate potential associations with the enemy, they destroyed old books, photographs of relatives, and brocaded *obi* (kimono sashes) and replaced portraits of the Japanese emperor with pictures of President Roosevelt. A burning desire to prove that they were true Americans prompted many of their Hawaiian-born children, often referred to as AJAs (Americans of Japanese ancestry), to become superpatriots. AJAs contributed heavily to war-bond drives and sponsored their own "Bombs on Tokyo" campaign. They converted the halls of Buddhist temples, Shinto shrines, and Japanese-language schools (all closed for the duration and reopened after the war) into manufactories of bandages and hospital gowns. Their newly expanded contact with other Hawaiians, including *haoles,* hastened their assimilation into the larger Hawaiian society. In addition, AJAs served in the military campaigns in the Pacific as interpreters—translating, interrogating, intercepting transmissions, and cracking enemy codes—and they fought in Europe with the all-Nisei 442d regimental combat team, the most highly decorated organization in the U.S. army.

These contributions gave the Japanese in Hawaii, as it did other ethnic groups in the United States, a new sense of their worth and dignity. The war experience aroused expectations of equal opportunity and equal treatment, of full participation in island politics, of no longer accepting a subordinate status to *haoles.*

The attitudes of many Hawaiians toward *haoles* changed as native islanders witnessed large numbers of whites doing manual labor for the first time. Their view that whites would always hold superior positions in society—as bosses, plantation owners, and politicians—was turned topsy-turvy by the flood of Caucasian mainland war workers, mostly from the fringes of respectability, and easily stereotyped as drunks and troublemakers. The hordes of white servicemen crowding into Honolulu's Hotel Street vice district for liquor, for posed pictures with hula girls in grass skirts, for three-dollar sex at the many brothels, and then for treatment at prophylaxis stations to ward off venereal diseases also tarnished traditional notions of white superiority. White prostitutes who brazenly operated in Honolulu further mocked the belief that those with white skin had a "natural" right to rule those of a darker hue.

The Hawaiian experience, in turn, changed the outlooks of many of the servicemen and war workers stationed there. In Honolulu they grew accustomed to women holding full-time jobs, as a far higher percentage of women worked outside the home than was the case on the mainland. Given the scarcity of "available" white women, the men gradually became less uneasy about interracial dating, joking that "the longer you were on the island, the lighter [skinned] the girls became." Not a few GIs ultimately married women of Chinese, Filipino, or Hawaiian ancestry.

Most of the whites who had come to Hawaii had never lived where whites did not constitute a majority and where they were the ones who were different. Most had never before encountered or conversed with people of African or Asian ancestry. Suddenly, they were in the midst of a mixture of ethnic and racial groups unmatched anywhere in the United States, in a diverse society where people of different backgrounds worked together for a common cause. This example of multicultural harmony was especially an eye-opener for the nearly thirty thousand African-American servicemen and workers who came to Honolulu before the war's end. In the fluid and relaxed racial relations of Hawaiian society, blacks discovered an alternative to the racist America they knew. "I thank God often," wrote a black shipyard worker, "for letting me experience the occasion to spend a part of my life in a part of the world where one can be respected and live as a free man should." Some chose never to go back to the mainland. Others returned home to press for the rights and freedoms they had first tasted in Hawaii. In so many ways, wartime Hawaii, termed "the first strange place" by historians Beth Bailey and David Farber, would anticipate the "strangeness" of U.S. society today.

The Atomic Bombs

Meanwhile, the war with Japan ground on. Early in 1945 an assault force of marines invaded Iwo Jima, 700 miles from Japan. In places termed the "Meat Grinder" and "Bloody Gorge," the marines savagely battled thousands of Japanese soldiers hidden in tunnels and behind concrete bunkers and pillboxes. Securing the five-square-mile island would cost the marines nearly twenty-seven thousand casualties, and one-third of all the marines killed in the Pacific. In June American troops waded ashore on Okinawa, 350 miles from Japan and a key staging area for the planned U.S. invasion of the Japanese home islands. Death and destruction engulfed Okinawa as waves of Americans attacked nearly impregnable Japanese defenses head-on, repeating the bloody strategy of World War I. After eighty-three days of fighting on land and sea, twelve thousand Americans lay dead and three times as many wounded, a 35 percent casualty rate, higher than at Normandy.

The appalling rate of loss on Iwo Jima and Okinawa weighed on the minds of American strategists as they thought about an invasion of the Japanese home islands. The Japanese Cabinet showed no willingness to give up the war despite Japan's being blockaded and bombed daily (on March 9–10 a fleet of B-29s dropped napalm-and-magnesium-bombs on Tokyo, burning sixteen square miles of the city to the ground and killing some eighty-four thousand). Its military leaders insisted on fighting to the bitter end; surrender was unthinkable. Japan possessed an army of over 2 million, plus up to 4 million reservists and five thousand kamikaze aircraft, and the U.S. Joint Chiefs estimated that American casualties in invasions of Kyushu and Honshu (the main island of Japan) might exceed 1 million.

The successful detonation of history's first nuclear explosion at Alamagordo in mid-July gave Truman an alternative. On July 25, while meeting with Stalin and Churchill in Potsdam, Truman ordered the use of an atomic bomb if Japan did not surrender before August 3. The next day he warned Japan to surrender unconditionally or face "prompt and utter destruction." Japan rejected the Potsdam Declaration on July 28. On August 6 a B-29 bomber named *Enola Gay* took off from the Marianas island of Tinian and dropped a uranium bomb on Hiroshima, plunging the city into what Japanese novelist Masuji Ibuse termed "a hell of unspeakable torments." The 300,000 degree centigrade fireball incinerated houses and pulverized people. More than sixty thousand died in the initial searing blast of heat, and many of the seventy thousand injured died later from burns and radiation poisoning. On August 8 Stalin declared war on Japan, and U.S. planes dropped leaflets on Japan warning that another bomb would be dropped if it did not surrender. The next day, at high noon, the *Bock's Car* flattened Nagasaki with a plutonium bomb, killing thirty-five thousand and injuring more than sixty thousand. On August 14 Japan accepted the American terms of surrender, which implicitly permitted the emperor to retain his throne but subordinated him to the U.S. commander of the occupation forces. General MacArthur received Japan's surrender on the battleship *Missouri* on September 2, 1945. The war was over.

Some historians have subsequently questioned whether the United States needed to resort to atomic weapons to end the war promptly. They believe that racist American attitudes toward the Japanese motivated the decision to drop the bombs. As war correspondent Ernie Pyle wrote, "The Japanese are looked upon as something inhuman and squirmy—like some people feel about cockroaches or mice." While racial hatred undoubtedly stirred exterminationist sentiment, those involved in the Manhattan Project had regarded Germany as the target; and considering the ferocity of the Allied bombings of Hamburg and Dresden, there is little reason to assume that the Allies would not have dropped atomic bombs on Germany had they been available. By 1945 the Allies as well as the Axis had abandoned restraints on attacking civilians.

Other historians contend that demonstrating the bomb's terrible destructiveness on an uninhabited island would have moved Japan to surrender. We will never know for sure. American policy makers had rejected a demonstration bombing because the United States had an atomic arsenal of only two bombs, and they did not know whether the mechanism for detonating them in the air would work. Still others argue that Japan was ready to surrender and that an invasion of the home islands was unnecessary. Again, we cannot know for sure. All that is certain is that as late as July 28, 1945, Japan refused a demand for surrender, and not until after the bombs were used did Japan capitulate.

The largest number of historians critical of Truman's decision believe that the president, aware of worsening relations between the United States and the U.S.S.R., ordered the atomic attack primarily to end the Pacific war before Stalin could enter it and also to intimidate Stalin into making concessions in eastern Europe. Referring to the Soviets, President Truman noted just before the atomic test at Alamogordo, "If it explodes, as I think it will, I'll certainly have a hammer on those boys." Truman's new secretary of state, James Byrnes, thought that the bomb would "make Russia more manageable" and would "put us in a position to dictate our own terms at the end of the war."

Although the president and his advisers believed that the atomic bombs would strengthen their hand against the Soviets, that was not the foremost reason the bombs were dropped. As throughout the war, American leaders in August 1945 relied on production and technology to win the war with the minimum loss of American life. Every new weapon was put to use; the concept of "total war" easily accommodated the bombing of civilians; and the atomic bomb was one more item in an arsenal that had already wreaked enormous destruction on the Axis. The rules of war that had once stayed the use of weapons of mass destruction against enemy civilians no longer prevailed. No responsible official counseled that the United States should sacrifice American servicemen to lessen death and destruction in Japan, or not use a weapon developed with 2 billion taxpayer dollars. To the vast majority of Americans, the atomic bomb was, in Churchill's words, "a miracle of deliverance" that saved Allied lives. So E. B. Sledge and his comrades in the First Marine Division, slated to take part in the first wave of the invasion of Japan's home islands, breathed "an indescribable sense of relief." Hearing the news of the atomic bombs and Japan's surrender, Sledge wrote, they sat in stunned silence:

> We remembered our dead. So many dead. So many maimed. So many bright futures consigned to the ashes of the past. So many dreams lost in the madness that engulfed us. Except for a few widely scattered shouts of joy, the survivors of the abyss sat hollow-eyed and silent, trying to comprehend a world without war.

IMPORTANT EVENTS, 1933–1945

1931–1932	Japan invades Manchuria and creates a puppet government.
1933	Adolf Hitler becomes chancellor of Germany and assumes dictatorial powers.
1934–1936	Nye Committee investigations.
1935–1937	Neutrality Acts.
1937	Japan invades China.
1938	Germany annexes Austria; Munich Pact gives Sudetenland to Germany.
	Kristallnacht, night of Nazi terror against German and Austrian Jews.
1939	Nazi-Soviet Pact.
	Germany invades Poland; World War II begins.
1940	Germany conquers the Netherlands, Belgium, France, Denmark, Norway, and Luxembourg.
	Germany, Italy, and Japan sign the Tripartite Pact.
	Selective Service Act.
	Franklin Roosevelt elected to an unprecedented third term.
1941	Lend-Lease Act.
	Roosevelt establishes the Fair Employment Practices Commission (FEPC).
	Germany invades the Soviet Union.
	Japan attacks Pearl Harbor; the United States enters World War II.
	War Powers Act.
1942	Battles of Coral Sea and Midway halt Japanese offensive.
	Internment of Japanese-Americans.
	Revenue Act expands graduated income-tax system.
	Allies invade North Africa (Operation Torch).
	First successful atomic chain reaction.
	CORE founded.
1943	Soviet victory in Battle of Stalingrad.
	Coal miners strike; Smith-Connally War Labor Disputes Act.
	Detroit and Los Angeles race riots.
	Allied invasion of Italy.
	Big Three meet in Tehran.
1944	Allied invasion of France (Operation Overlord).
	U.S. forces invade the Philippines.
	Roosevelt wins fourth term.
	Battle of the Bulge.
1945	Big Three meet in Yalta.
	Battles of Iwo Jima and Okinawa.
	Roosevelt dies; Harry S. Truman becomes president.
	Germany surrenders.
	Truman, Churchill, and Stalin meet in Potsdam.
	United States drops atomic bombs on Hiroshima and Nagasaki; Japan surrenders.

26

The Cold War Abroad and at Home, 1945–1952

Dan Collins grew up in Boston's South End community. Like most other Irish-American Catholic teenagers from families that had a hard time during the Great Depression, Dan could not wait to enlist once the Second World War began. He served with the U.S. First Army in North Africa and the Tenth Army in Okinawa, witnessing, as he put it, "more than I care to talk about." His body intact, although he suffered recurring nightmares, Dan returned to Boston in 1946 and stashed his uniform in the attic, "hoping to relax, get rich, and enjoy a bit of the good life."

Qualifying under the GI Bill of Rights for a small business loan, Collins started a Massachusetts construction company. He married, had a family, and, like many veterans, fretted about his wife's working outside the home, consulted Dr. Benjamin Spock's child-care manual, took his children's pictures with the first Polaroid camera, bought a Ford with automatic transmission, and moved to a split-level house in the suburbs. Dan earned more money in construction during the postwar housing boom than he had ever dreamed possible, and gained reassurance by attending church regularly and unfurling his flag on holidays. But he couldn't shake the nightmares, and peace of mind seemed as elusive as peace in the world. The decisive changes at home and abroad brought about by the Second World War intruded on and disturbed Dan Collins and most other Americans.

Disagreement over the postwar fate of Eastern Europe had sparked a confrontation in which the Soviet Union and the United States each sought to reshape the postwar world to serve its own national interests. An uncompromising Truman squared off against an obsessive Stalin, each intensifying the insecurities of the other. A new form of international conflict emerged—a Cold War, or state of mutual hostility short of direct armed confrontation—in which the two powers did all they could to thwart the other's objectives.

Abandoning its historic aloofness from events outside the Western Hemisphere, the United States plunged into a global struggle to contain the Soviet Union and stop communism. In 1940 the United States had no military alliances, a small defense budget, and limited troops. By 1952 it had built a massive military establishment, signed mutual-defense pacts with some forty countries, directly intervened in the affairs of allies and enemies alike, erected military bases on every continent, and embarked on a seemingly unending nuclear-arms race.

Containing communism abroad also profoundly affected American thoughts and actions at home. It directly affected the economy, minority rights, and domestic politics. The anxieties provoked by fears of communist aggression and domestic subversion, moreover, spawned a second "Red Scare" reminiscent of the first one in 1919, with witch hunts undermining civil liberties. The reckless hurling of unfounded charges of disloyalty added "McCarthyism" to the American vocabulary. McCarthyism destroyed careers, silenced criticism, fueled intolerance, and discredited both the American Left and the Truman administration.

Dan Collins and many Americans thought McCarthyism made sense. The presence of communist spies at home and American setbacks abroad convinced him that "McCarthy must be on target in attacking those liberals in Washington." In 1952, believing the Truman administration to be "riddled with Reds and corruption," Collins, whose family had been staunch Democrats, decided that "it was time to give the other guys a chance." He turned to his hero, Dwight D. Eisenhower, the favorite general of most of his GI buddies, as the man needed in dangerous times.

This chapter focuses on five major questions:

How did the postwar policies of the United States and the Soviet Union contribute to the beginnings of the Cold War?

What was the doctrine of containment, and how was it implemented from 1947 to 1952?

What accounts for the decline of the New Deal spirit after World War II, and what effect did this have on Truman's domestic program?

How did the Cold War affect the rights of African-Americans?

What were the main domestic and international factors leading to the postwar Red Scare, and why did Americans react to it as they did?

THE POSTWAR POLITICAL SETTING, 1945–1946

After going without during the Great Depression and World War II, Americans like Dan Collins looked forward to the postwar era. The emerging Cold War, however, profoundly changed the United States for better and for worse. It spurred a quarter of a century of economic growth and prosperity, the longest such period in American history. It propelled research in medicine and science that, for the most part, made lives longer and better. And it contributed to a vast expansion of higher education that enabled many Americans to become middle class.

Demobilization
and Reconversion

As soon as the war ended, GIs and civilians alike wanted those who had served in the military "home alive in '45." Troops demanding transport ships barraged Congress with threats of "no boats, no votes." On a single day in December 1945, sixty thousand postcards arrived at the White House with the message "Bring the Boys Home by Christmas." Truman bowed to popular demand. American military strength dropped from 12 million men at war's end to just 1.5 million by 1948.

The psychological problems of readjustment faced by veterans were intensified by a drastic housing shortage and soaring divorce rate. By 1950 more than a million couples who had married during the war had gotten divorced. Some veterans could not reestablish prewar ties with family and friends or adjust to the greater independence of once-submissive wives. Some experienced profound loneliness, missing the companionship and community of their wartime buddies. Others worried that automation—machines performing industrial operations faster and more accurately than human workers—would displace them, or that the stalled unionization drive, especially in the South and West, would depress wages. As war plants closed, reviving memories of the hard times immediately after World War I (see Chapter 22), many feared unemployment and economic depression. Defense spending dropped from $76 billion in 1945 to under $20 billion in 1946, and more than a million defense jobs vanished.

"What's Become of Rosie the Riveter?" asked the *New York Times Magazine* in May 1946. She had probably lost her job in war industry, married that year, and had a child and/or had gone back to work. By the end of the decade more women were working outside the home than during World War II. Most women did not enter heavy industry, as they had during the war, or surge into the professions. Rather, they took jobs in traditional women's fields, especially office work and sales, to pay for family needs. Although the postwar economy created new openings for women in the labor market, many public figures urged women to seek fulfillment at home. With feminist ideology and organizations at low ebb, popular culture romanticized married bliss and demonized career women as a threat to social stability. Having endured depression and war, many women looked forward to traditional roles in a secure, prosperous America, and few answered negatively when popular magazines asked, "Isn't a Woman's Place in the Home?"

The GI Bill of Rights   In 1944 Congress had enacted the Servicemen's Readjustment Act. Commonly called the GI Bill of Rights or GI Bill, it was designed to forestall the expected recession by easing veterans back into the work force, as well as to reward the "soldier boys" and reduce their fears of female competition. The GI Bill gave veterans priority for many jobs, occupational guidance, and, if need be, fifty-two weeks of unemployment benefits. It also established veterans' hospitals and provided low-interest loans to returning GIs who were starting businesses or buying homes or farms. Almost 4 million veterans bought homes with government loans, fueling a baby boom, suburbanization, and a record demand for new goods and services.

Most vitally in the long run, the government promised to pay Dan Collins and millions of others who had served in the armed forces for up to four years of further education or job training. Not all Americans approved. Some opposed it as opening the door to socialism or to demands by minorities to special entitlements. Many university administrators, fearing that riffraff would sully their bastions of privilege, echoed the complaint of the University of Chicago president that their hallowed halls of learning would become "educational hobo jungles."

In 1946, flush with stipends of sixty-five dollars a month—ninety dollars for those with dependents—and up to five hundred dollars a year for tuition and books, 1.5 million veterans were attending college, spurring a huge increase in higher education and the creation of many new state and community colleges. Almost immediately, California State University established additional campuses in Fullerton, Hayward, Long Beach, Los Angeles, Northridge, Sacramento, and San Bernardino. Various "normal schools" for the training of teachers were upgraded into full-fledged colleges to create the State University of New York in 1948. Veterans made up over half of all college students in 1947. Often married and the fathers of young children, they were less interested in knowledge (frequently asking "what good will it do me?") than in a degree and a higher-paying job.

Veterans Go to College *So many World War II veterans wanted to use their GI benefits for higher education that colleges were overwhelmed; many had to turn away students. In 1946, registration of new students was done at temporary desks set up in Wildermuth Field House at Indiana University.*

To accommodate them, colleges converted old military barracks and Quonset huts into so-called Veterans' Village housing units and featured accelerated programs and more vocational or career-oriented courses. Campus life, at least for a time, became less social and less fun, as the survivors of Normandy spurned fraternity high-jinks in favor of "learning and earning," getting on with life.

To make room for the millions of GIs pursuing higher education after the war, many colleges limited the percentage of women admitted or barred students from out of state. The percentage of college graduates who were women dropped from 40 percent in 1949 to 25 percent in 1950. By then most women students were the working wives of the 8 million veterans who were taking advantage of the GI Bill to go college.

The GI Bill democratized higher education. It allowed many more Americans (most the first in their families to attend) to go to college. Later they expected their children to follow suit, and higher education became an accepted part of the American Dream. Speaking for many other veterans, the president of a Midwest publishing firm would later say that "the GI Bill made all the difference in the world" to him; otherwise he "could never have afforded college." No longer a citadel of privilege, universities awarded almost a half-million degrees in 1950, more than twice as many as in 1940.

The cost was huge. Between 1945 and 1956, when the education benefits ended, the government spent $14.5 billion to send 2.2 million veterans to colleges,

Gross National Product, 1929–1990

Following World War II, the United States achieved the highest living standard in world history. Between 1950 and 1970, the real GNP, which factors out inflation and reveals the actual amount of goods and services produced, steadily increased. However, in 1972, 1974–1975, 1980, and 1982 the real GNP declined.

Source: Economic Report of the President, 1991.

Note: Data shown in 1982 dollars.

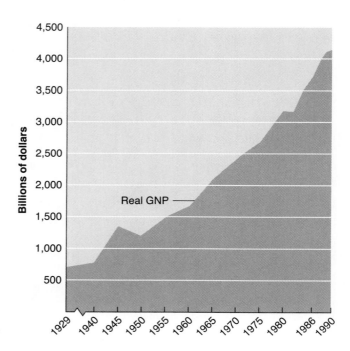

3.5 million to technical schools, and seven hundred thousand to agricultural instruction on farms. The money was well spent. The GI Bill fueled the upward mobility of veterans, enabling them to return in income taxes the money advanced to them by the government. It propelled millions of veterans into middle-class status in employment, education, and residence—the dream of Dan Collins and his buddies in the trenches—accelerating the postwar demand for goods and services.

The Economic Boom Begins In addition to the assistance given returning servicemen, a 1945 tax cut of $6 billion spurred corporate investment in new factories and equipment and helped produce an economic boom that began in late 1946. Boosting postwar growth and prosperity, Americans spent much of the $135 billion they had saved from wartime work and service pay to satisfy their desire for consumer goods formerly beyond their means or not produced during the war. As advertisements promising "a Ford in your future" and an "all-electric kitchen of the future" furthered the rage to consume, sales of homes, cars, and appliances skyrocketed. Scores of new products—televisions, high-fidelity phonographs, filter cigarettes, automatic transmissions, freezers, and air conditioners—soon defined the middle-class lifestyle.

In 1944 representatives of the wartime Allies had met in Bretton Woods, New Hampshire, to hammer out a framework for the global economy in the postwar world. The Bretton Woods Agreement created the International Monetary Fund (IMF) to stabilize exchange rates by valuing ("pegging") other currencies in relation to the U.S. dollar. The agreement established the International Bank for Reconstruction and Development (World Bank) to help rebuild war-battered Asia and Europe. It also laid the groundwork for the 1947 General Agreement on Tariffs and Trade (GATT) to break up closed trading blocs and expand international trade. Since the United States largely controlled and funded these powerful economic institutions, they further aided the speedy reconversion of the American economy and gave the United States an especially favorable position in international trade and finance.

With many nations temporarily in ruins, American firms could import raw materials cheaply; with little competition from other industrial countries, they could increase exports to record levels. U.S. economic dominance also resulted from the 35 percent increase in the productivity of American workers in the decade following the war. Wartime advances in science and technology, which led to revolutionary developments in such industries as electronics and plastics, further bolstered the notion of the postwar years as the dawn of "the American century."

Truman's Domestic Program The hunger to enjoy the fruits of affluence left Americans with little appetite for more New Deal reforms, and Truman agreed. "I don't want any experiments," he confided to an aide. "The American people have been through a lot of experiments and they want a rest." Accordingly, the only major domestic accomplishment of the Seventy-ninth Congress was the Employment Act of 1946. The act committed the federal government to ensuring economic growth and established the Council of Economic Advisers to confer with the president and formulate policies for maintaining employment, production, and purchasing power. Congress gutted both the goal of full employment and the enhanced executive powers to achieve that objective, blocking Truman's main effort to advance beyond the New Deal.

Congressional eagerness to dismantle wartime controls worsened the nation's chief economic problem: inflation. Consumer demand outran the supply of goods, intensifying the pressure on prices. The Office of Price Administration (OPA) sought to hold the line by enforcing price controls, but food producers, manufacturers, and retailers opposed continuing wartime controls. While some consumers favored the OPA, others deplored it as an irksome relic of the war. In June 1946 Truman vetoed a bill that would have extended the OPA's life, but deprived it of power, effectively ending all price controls. Within a week food costs rose 16 percent and the price of beef doubled. "PRICES SOAR, BUYERS SORE, STEERS JUMP OVER THE MOON," headlined the *New York Daily News*.

Congress then passed, and Truman signed, a second bill extending price controls in weakened form. Protesting any price controls, farmers and meat producers threatened to withhold food from the market. Knowing that "meatless voters are opposition voters," "Horsemeat Harry," as some now referred to Truman, lifted controls on food prices just before the 1946 midterm elections. When Democrats fared poorly anyway, Truman ended all price controls. By then the consumer price index had jumped nearly 25 percent since the end of the war.

This staggering increase in the cost of living, coming on top of the end of wartime bonuses and overtime, intensified organized labor's demand for the higher wages that had been disallowed during the war. More than 4.5 million workers went on strike in 1946. When a United Mine Workers walkout paralyzed the economy for forty days, Truman ordered the army to seize the mines. A week later, after Truman had pressured owners to grant most of the union's demands, the miners returned to work, only to walk out again six months later. Meanwhile, on the heels of the first mine workers settlement, railway engineers and trainmen announced that they would shut down the nation's railroad system for the first time in history. "If you think I'm going to sit here and let you tie up this whole country," Truman shouted at the heads of the two unions, "you're crazy as hell." In May he asked Congress for authority to draft workers who struck vital industries. Before he could finish his speech, the unions gave in. Still, Truman's threat alienated most labor leaders.

By fall 1946, Truman had angered virtually every major interest group. Less than a third of the Americans polled approved of his performance. "To err is Truman," some gibed. One commentator suggested that the Democrats nominate Hollywood humorist W. C. Fields for president: "If we're going to have a comedian in the White House, let's have a good one." Summing up the public discontent Republicans asked, "Had enough?" In the 1946 elections they captured twenty-five governorships and, for the first time since 1928, won control of both houses of Congress.

The public mood reflected more than just economic discontent. Under the surface laughter at stores advertising atomic sales or bartenders mixing atomic cocktails ran a new, deep current of fear, symbolized by the rash of "flying saucer" sightings that had begun after the war. An NBC radio program depicted a nuclear attack on Chicago in which most people died instantly. "Those few who escaped the blast, but not the gamma rays, died slowly after they had left the ruined city," intoned the narrator. "No attempt at identification of the bodies or burial ever took place. Chicago was simply closed." There was much talk of urban dispersal—resettling people in small communities in the country's vast open spaces—and of how to protect oneself in a nuclear attack. Some schoolchildren wore dog tags in order to be identified after an atomic attack, while also practicing crawling under their desks and putting their hands over their heads—"Duck and Cover"—to protect themselves from the bomb. The end of World War II had brought an uneasy peace.

ANTICOMMUNISM AND CONTAINMENT, 1946–1952

By late 1946 the simmering antagonisms between Moscow and Washington had come to a boil. With the Nazis defeated, the "shotgun wedding" between the United States and the U.S.S.R. dissolved into a struggle to fill the power vacuums left by the defeat of Germany and Japan, the exhaustion of Western Europe, and the crumbling of colonial empires in Asia and Africa. Misperception and misunderstanding mounted as the two powers sought greater security, each feeding the other's fears. The Cold War was the result.

Polarization and Cold War   The destiny of Eastern Europe, especially Poland, stood at the heart of the strife between the United States and the U.S.S.R. Wanting to end the Soviet Union's vulnerability to invasions from the West, Stalin insisted on a buffer zone of nations friendly to Russia along its western flank, and sought a demilitarized and deindustrialized Germany. He considered a Soviet sphere of influence in Eastern Europe essential to Russian security, a just reward for bearing the brunt of the war against Germany, and no different than the American spheres of influence in Western Europe, Japan, and Latin America. Stalin also believed that Roosevelt and Churchill had implicitly accepted a Soviet zone in Eastern Europe at the Yalta Conference (see Chapter 25).

With the 10-million-strong Red Army occupying most of Eastern Europe at war's end, Stalin had installed pro-Soviet puppet governments in Bulgaria and Romania by the time of the Potsdam Conference in July 1945, and supported the establishment of communist regimes in nominally independent Albania and Yugoslavia. Ignoring the Yalta Declaration of Liberated Europe, Stalin barred free elections in Poland and brutally suppressed Polish democratic parties. Poland, he said, was "not only a question of honor for Russia, but one of life and death."

Stalin's insistence on dominance in Eastern Europe collided with Truman's unwillingness to concede Soviet supremacy beyond Russia's borders. What Stalin saw as critical to Russian security, Truman viewed as a violation of national self-determination, a betrayal of democracy, and a cover for communist aggression. Truman and his advisers believed that the appeasement of dictators fed their appetites for expansion. They thought that traditional balance-of-power politics and spheres of influence had precipitated both world wars, and that only a new world order maintained by the United Nations could guarantee peace.

Truman also thought that accepting the "enforced sovietization" of Eastern Europe would betray American war aims and condemn nations rescued from Hitler's tyranny to another totalitarian dictatorship. He worried, too, that a Soviet stranglehold on Eastern Europe would hurt American businesses dependent on exports and on access to raw materials. Truman understood that the Democratic party would invite political disaster if he reneged on the Yalta agreements. The Democrats counted on winning most of the votes of the 6 million Polish-Americans and millions of other Americans of Eastern European origin, who remained keenly interested in the fates of their homelands. Not appearing "soft on communism" was a political necessity.

Combativeness fit the temperament of the feisty Truman. Eager to prove he was in command, the president matched Stalin's intransigence on Polish elections with his own demands for Polish democracy. Encouraged by America's monopoly of atomic weapons and its position as the world's economic superpower, the new president hoped that the United States could, in the words of a November 1945 State Department document, "establish the kind of world we want to live in."

The Iron Curtain Descends

As Stalin's and Truman's mistrust of one another grew, Stalin tightened his grip on Eastern Europe, stepping up his confiscation of materials and factories from occupied territories and forcing his satellite nations (countries under Soviet control) to close their doors to American trade and influence. In a February 1946 speech that the White House considered a "declaration of World War III," Stalin asserted that there could be no lasting peace with capitalism and vowed to overcome the American lead in weaponry no matter what the cost.

Two weeks later, George F. Kennan, an American diplomat in Moscow, wired a long telegram to his superiors at the State Department. A leading student of Russian affairs, Kennan described Soviet expansionism as moving "inexorably along a prescribed path, like a toy automobile wound up and headed in a given direction, stopping only when it meets some unanswerable force." Therefore, he concluded, U.S. policy must be the "long-term, patient but firm and vigilant containment of Russian expansive tendencies." The idea that only strong, sustained U.S. resistance could "contain" Soviet expansionism suited the mood of Truman, who a month earlier had insisted that the time had come "to stop babying the Soviets" and "to get tough with Russia." If they did not like it, the president added, they could "go to hell." "Containment"—a doctrine uniting military, economic, and diplomatic strategies to prevent communism from spreading and to enhance America's security and influence abroad—became Washington gospel.

In early March 1946 Truman accompanied former British Prime Minister Winston Churchill to Fulton, Missouri. In an address at Westminister College, Churchill warned of a new threat to Western democracies, this time from Moscow. Stalin, he said, had drawn an iron curtain across the eastern half of Europe. The threat of further Soviet aggression required an alliance of the English-speaking peoples and an Anglo-American monopoly of atomic weapons: "There is nothing the Communists admire so much as strength and nothing for which they have less respect than for military weakness."

Truman agreed. In spring 1946 he threatened to send in American combat troops unless the Soviets withdrew from oil-rich Iran. In June he submitted an atomic-energy control plan to the United Nations requiring the Soviet Union to stop all work on nuclear weapons and to submit to U.N. inspections before the United States would destroy its own atomic arsenal. As expected, the Soviets rejected the proposal and offered an alternative plan equally unacceptable to the United States. With mutual hostility escalating, the Soviets and Americans rushed to develop their own doomsday weapons. In 1946 Congress established the Atomic Energy Commission (AEC) to develop nuclear energy and nuclear weaponry. The AEC devoted more than 90 percent of its effort to atomic weapon development. By 1950, one AEC adviser reckoned, the United States "had a stockpile capable of somewhat more than reproducing World War II in a single day."

Thus, less than a year after American and Soviet soldiers had jubilantly met at the Elbe River to celebrate Hitler's defeat, the Cold War had begun. It would be waged by economic pressure, nuclear intimidation, propaganda, proxy wars, and subversion rather than by direct U.S.-Soviet military confrontation. It would be viewed by many Americans as an ideological conflict pitting democracy against dictatorship, freedom against totalitarianism, religion against atheism, and capitalism against socialism. It would affect American life as decisively as any military engagement that the nation had fought.

Containing Communism   On February 21, 1947, the British informed the United States that they could no longer afford to assist Greece and Turkey in their struggles against communist-supported insurgents and Soviet pressure for access to the Mediterranean. A stricken Britain asked the United States to bear the costs of thwarting communism in the eastern Mediterranean. The harsh European winter, the most severe in memory, intensified the sense of urgency in Washington. The economies of Western Europe had come to a near-halt. Famine and tuberculosis plagued the Continent. European colonies in Africa and Asia had risen in revolt. Cigarettes and candy bars circulated as currency in Germany, and the communist parties in France and Italy appeared ready to topple democratic coalition governments. Truman resolved to meet the challenge.

Truman first had to mobilize support for a radical departure from the American tradition of avoiding entangling alliances. In a tense White House on February 27, the new secretary of state, former army chief of staff George C. Marshall, presented the case for aid to Greece and Turkey to key congressional leaders. They balked, more concerned about inflation at home than civil war in Greece. But Dean Acheson, the newly appointed undersecretary of state, seized the moment. The issue, he said, was not one of assisting the Greek oligarchy and Turkey's military dictatorship, but rather a universal struggle of freedom against tyranny. "Like apples in a barrel infected by the corruption of one rotten one," he warned, the fall of Greece or Turkey would open Asia, Western Europe, and the oil fields of the Middle East to the Red menace. "The Soviet Union [is] playing one of the greatest gambles in history," Acheson concluded. "We and we alone are in a position to break up this play." Shaken, the congressional leaders agreed to support the administration's request if Truman could "scare hell out of the country."

Truman did. On March 12, 1947, addressing a joint session of Congress, he asked for $400 million in military assistance to Greece and Turkey. In a world endangered by communism, Truman said, the United States must support free peoples everywhere "resisting attempted subjugation by armed minorities or by outside pressures." If we fail to act now, the president concluded, "we may endanger the peace of the world—and we shall surely endanger the welfare of our own nation." His rhetoric worked. Congress appropriated funds that helped the Greek monarchy defeat the rebel movement and helped Turkey stay out of the Soviet orbit.

Truman's statement of a new policy of active U.S. engagement to contain communism, soon known as the Truman Doctrine, persisted long after the crisis in the Mediterranean. It became as comprehensive as the Monroe Doctrine's "Keep Out" sign posted on the Western Hemisphere. It laid the foundation for American Cold War policy for much of the next four decades.

To back up the new international initiative, Congress passed the National Security Act of 1947. It created the National Security Council (NSC) to advise the president on strategic matters. It established the Central Intelligence Agency (CIA) to gather information abroad and to engage in covert activities in support of the nation's security. And it began the processes of transforming the old War and Navy Departments into a new Department of Defense and combining the leadership of the army, navy, and air force (now a separate and equal military service) under the Joint Chiefs of Staff.

Congress also approved the administration's proposal for massive U.S. assistance for European recovery in 1947. Advocated by the secretary of state, and thus called the Marshall Plan, it was to be another weapon in the arsenal against the spread of communism. With Europe, in Churchill's words, "a rubble heap . . . a breeding ground of pestilence and hate," Truman wanted to end the economic devastation believed to spawn communism. Truman correctly guessed that the Soviet Union and its satellites would refuse to take part in the plan, because of the controls linked to it, and accurately foresaw that Western European economic

The Berlin Airlift, 1948 *German children watch an American plane in "Operation Vittles" bring food and supplies to their beleaguered city. The airlift kept a city of 2 million people alive for nearly a year and made West Berlin a symbol of the West's resolve to contain the spread of Soviet communism.*

recovery would expand sales of American goods abroad and promote prosperity in the United States.

Although denounced by the Left as a "Martial Plan" and by isolationist voices on the Right as a "Share-the-American-Wealth Plan," the Marshall Plan more than fulfilled its sponsors' hopes. By 1952 the economic and social chaos that communists had exploited had been overcome in the sixteen nations that shared the $17 billion in aid provided by the plan. Industrial production had risen 200 percent in Western Europe between 1947 and 1952, and that region had became a major center of American trade and investment.

Confrontation in Germany Reacting to the Truman Doctrine and the Marshall Plan, the Soviet Union tightened its grip on Eastern Europe. Communist takeovers added Hungary and Czechoslovakia to the Soviet sphere in 1947 and 1948. Stalin then turned his sights on Germany. The 1945 Potsdam Agreement had divided Germany into four separate zones (administered by France, Great Britain, the Soviet Union, and the United States) and created a joint four-power administration for Germany's capital, Berlin, lying 110 miles within the Soviet-occupied eastern zone. As the Cold War intensified, the Western powers moved toward uniting their zones into an anti-Soviet West German state to help contain communism. Stalin viewed that with alarm. Demanding a powerless Germany that could never attack the Soviet Union again, he responded in June 1948 by blocking all rail and highway routes through the Soviet zone into Berlin. He calculated that the Western powers would be unable to provision the 2 million Berliners under their control and would either have to abandon plans to create a West German nation or accept a communist Berlin.

Truman resolved neither to abandon Berlin nor to shoot his way into the city and possibly trigger World War III. Instead he ordered a massive airlift to provide Berliners with the food and fuel necessary for survival. American cargo planes landed at West Berlin's Tempelhof Airport every three minutes around the clock, bringing a mountain of supplies. To prevent the Soviets from shooting down the U.S. planes, Truman ordered a fleet of B-29s, the only planes capable of delivering atomic bombs, to bases in England in July 1948. Truman hinted that he would use "the bomb" if necessary. Tensions rose. The president confided to his diary that "we are very close to war." Meanwhile, for nearly a year, "Operation Vittles" provided the blockaded city with a precarious lifeline.

In May 1949 the Soviets ended the blockade. Stalin's gambit had failed. The airlift highlighted American determination and technological prowess, revealed Stalin's readiness to starve innocent people to achieve his ends, and dramatically heightened anti-Soviet feeling in the West. U.S. public opinion polls in late 1948 revealed an overwhelming demand for "firmness and increased 'toughness' in relations with Russia."

Continuing fears of a Soviet attack on Western Europe fostered support for a rearmed West German state and for an Atlantic collective security alliance. In May 1949 the United States, Britain, and France ended their occupation of Germany and approved the creation of the Federal Republic of Germany (West Germany). A month earlier, ten nations of Western Europe had adopted the North Atlantic Treaty, establishing a mutual defense pact with the United States and Canada in which "an armed attack against one or more of them . . . shall be considered an attack against them all." For the first time in its history, the United States entered into a peacetime military alliance. In effect, Western Europe now lay under the American "nuclear umbrella," protected from Soviet invasion by the U.S. threat of nuclear retaliation. Senator Robert Taft of Ohio, speaking for a small band of Republican senators, warned that this agreement would provoke the Soviets to respond in kind, stimulate a massive arms race, and open the floodgates of American military aid to Europe. But the Senate overwhelmingly approved the treaty, and in July the United States officially joined the North Atlantic Treaty Organization (NATO), marking the formal end of U.S. isolationism.

Truman ranked the Marshall Plan and NATO as his proudest achievements, convinced that if the latter had been in existence in 1914 and 1939 the world would have been spared two disastrous wars. Accordingly, he spurred Congress to authorize $1.3 billion for military assistance to NATO nations, persuaded General Dwight D. Eisenhower to become supreme commander of NATO forces, and authorized the stationing of four American army divisions in Europe as the nucleus of the NATO armed force. As Taft had predicted, the Soviet Union responded in kind to what it saw as a series of anti-Soviet provocations. It created the German

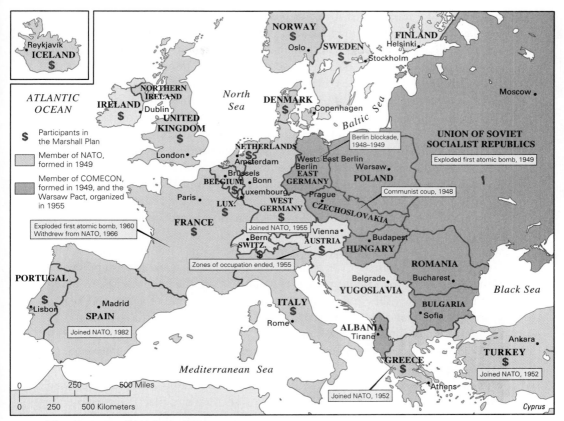

The Postwar Division of Europe

The wartime dispute between the Soviet Union and the Western Allies over Poland's future hardened after World War II into a Cold War that split Europe into competing American and Russian spheres of influence.

Democratic Republic (East Germany) in 1949, and exploded its own atomic bomb that same year. Finally, in 1955, it set up a rival Eastern bloc military alliance, the Warsaw Pact. The United States and Soviet Union had divided Europe into two armed camps.

The Cold War in Asia

Moscow-Washington hostility also carved Asia into contending camps. The Russians created a sphere of influence in Manchuria; the Americans occupied and imposed a U.S.-written democratic constitution on Japan; and both partitioned a helpless Korea.

As head of the U.S. occupation forces in Japan, General Douglas MacArthur oversaw that nation's transformation from an empire in ruins into a prosperous democracy. By 1948 the Cold War had caused American policy to shift from keeping Japan's economy and government weak, thereby preventing it from threatening peace again, to making it as strong as possible an ally in a vital part of the world. The Japanese economy flourished, and, although the official occupation ended in 1952, a military security treaty allowed the U.S. to retain its Japanese bases and brought Japan under the American "nuclear umbrella." In further pursuit of containment, the United States helped crush procommunist insurgency in the Philippines and aided the efforts of France to reestablish its colonial rule in Indochina (Vietnam, Laos, and Cambodia), despite American declarations in favor of national self-determination and against imperialism.

In China, however, U.S. efforts to block communism failed. The Truman administration first tried to mediate the civil war between the Nationalist government of Jiang Jieshi (Chiang Kai-shek) and the communist forces of Mao Zedong (Mao Tse-tung). It also sent nearly $3 billion in aid to the Nationalists between 1945 and 1949. American dollars, however, could not force Jiang's corrupt government to reform itself and win the support of the Chinese people, whom it had widely alienated. As Mao's well-disciplined and motivated troops marched south, Jiang's soldiers mutinied or surrendered without fighting. Unable to stem revolutionary sentiment or to hold the countryside—where the communists, in Mao's words, "swam like fishes in the peasant sea"—Jiang's regime collapsed, and he fled to exile on the island of Taiwan (Formosa), off the coast of southeast China.

Mao's establishment of the communist People's Republic of China (PRC) shocked Americans. The most populous nation in the world, imagined by Washington as a counterforce to Asian communism and a market for American exports, had become "Red China." Although the Truman administration explained that it could have done nothing to alter the outcome and placed the blame for Jiang's defeat on his failure to reform China, most Americans were unconvinced. China's "fall" especially embittered conservatives who believed that America's power in the world rested on Asia, not Europe. The pressure from the China lobby, which included congressional Republicans, conservative business leaders, and religious groups, influenced the administration's refusal to recognize the PRC, block its admission to the United Nations, and proclaim Jiang's Nationalist government in Taiwan as the legitimate government of China.

In September 1949, as the "Who lost China" debate raged, the president announced that the Soviet Union had exploded an atomic bomb, ending the American monopoly on nuclear weapons. Suddenly the world had changed, shattering illusions of American invincibility. While military leaders and politicians pressed Truman to develop an even more powerful weapon, ordinary Americans sought safety in civil defense. Public schools held air-raid drills. "We took the drills seriously," recalled novelist Annie Dillard; "surely Pittsburgh, which had the nation's steel, coke, and aluminum, would be the enemy's first target." Four million Americans volunteered to be Sky Watchers, looking for Soviet planes. More than a million purchased or constructed their own family bomb shelters. Those who could not afford a bomb shelter were advised by the Federal Civil Defense Administration to "jump in any handy ditch or gutter . . . bury your face in your arms . . . never lose your head."

National Defense Spending, 1941–1960

In 1950 the defense budget was $13 billion, less than a third of the total federal outlay. In 1961 defense spending reached $47 billion, fully half of the federal budget and almost 10 percent of the gross national product.

Source: Economic Report of the President, 1991. *Note:* Data shown in 1982 dollars.

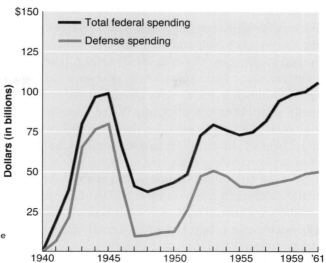

On January 31, 1950, stung by charges that he was "soft on communism," Truman ordered the development of a fusion-based hydrogen bomb (H-bomb). In November 1952 the United States exploded its first thermonuclear bomb, nicknamed Mike, containing ten times more power than the Hiroshima atomic bomb. The blast, equal to more than 10 million tons of TNT, completely vaporized one of the Marshall Islands in the Pacific, carved a mile-long crater in the ocean floor, and spilled radioactive dust over thousands of square miles. Nine months later the Soviets detonated their own H-bomb. The danger of thermonuclear terror escalated.

Truman also called for a top-secret review of defense policy by the National Security Council in early 1950. Completed in April, its secret report, NSC-68, emphasized the Soviet Union's military strength and aggressive intentions. To counter what the NSC saw as the U.S.S.R.'s "design for world domination"—the mortal challenge posed by the Soviet Union "not only to this Republic but to civilization itself"—NSC-68 urged a militarized anticommunist offensive, not merely containment. It endorsed massive increases in America's nuclear arsenal, a large standing army, vigorous covert actions by the CIA, and a quadrupling of the defense budget. Truman hesitated. An aide to Secretary of State Acheson recalled, "We were sweating over it, and then, with regard to NSC-68, thank God Korea came along." By the end of 1950 NSC-68 had become official U.S. policy.

The Korean War, 1950–1953   After World War II the United States and Soviet Union temporarily divided Korea, which had been controlled by Japan since the Russo-Japanese War of 1904, at the thirty-eighth parallel for purposes of military occupation. This line then solidified into a political frontier between the American-supported Republic of Korea, or South Korea, and the Soviet-backed Democratic People's Republic of Korea in the north, each claiming the sole right to rule all of Korea.

On June 24, 1950, North Korean troops swept across the thirty-eighth parallel to attack South Korea. Truman decided to fight back, viewing the assault as a Soviet test of U.S. will and containment. "Korea is the Greece of the Far East," Truman maintained. "If we are tough enough now, if we stand up to them like we did in Greece . . . they won't take any next steps." Mindful of the failure of appeasement at Munich in 1938, he believed that the communists were doing in Korea exactly what Hitler and the Japanese had done in the 1930s: "Nobody had stood up to them. And that is what led to the Second World War." Having been accused of "selling out" Eastern Europe and "losing" China, Truman needed to prove he could stand up to "the Reds."

Without consulting Congress, Truman ordered air and naval forces to Korea from their bases in Japan on June 27. That same day he asked the United Nations to authorize action to repel the North Korean attack. Fortunately for Truman, the Soviet delegate was boycotting the Security Council to protest the U.N.'s unwillingness to seat a representative from Mao's China, and Truman gained approval for a U.N. "police action" to restore South Korea's border. He appointed General Douglas MacArthur to command the U.N. effort and ordered American ground troops into the fray. The Cold War had turned hot.

U.S. Marines Battling for Seoul, September 1950 *From the start Truman believed that the Soviet Union had orchestrated the North Korean invasion of South Korea. He steadfastly maintained that "if the Russian totalitarian state was intending to follow in the path of the dictatorship of Hitler and Mussolini, they [had to] be met head on in Korea."*

The Korean War, 1950–1953

The experience of fighting an undeclared and limited war for the limited objective of containing communism confused the generation of Americans who had just fought an all-out war for the total defeat of the Axis. General MacArthur spoke for the many who were frustrated by the Korean conflict's mounting costs in blood and dollars: "There is no substitute for victory."

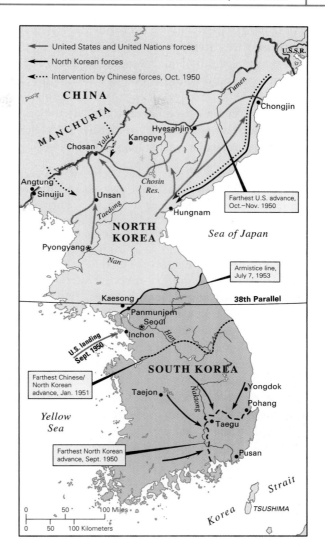

North Korean forces initially routed the disorganized American and South Korean troops. "All day and night we ran like antelopes," recalled Sergeant Raymond Remp. "We didn't know our officers. They didn't know us. We lost everything we had." Then, in mid-September, with U.N. forces cornered on the tip of the peninsula around Pusan, struggling to avoid being pushed into the sea, MacArthur's troops landed at Inchon in a brilliant amphibious maneuver. Within two weeks, U.S. and South Korean forces drove the North Koreans back across the thirty-eighth parallel. Seeking an all-out victory, MacArthur persuaded Truman to let him cross the border to liberate all of Korea from communism.

As U.N. troops swept across the thirty-eighth parallel and neared the Yalu River—the boundary between Korea and China—the Chinese warned that they would not "sit back with folded hands and let the Americans come to the border." Dismissing the threat as "hot air," an overconfident MacArthur deployed his forces in a thin line south of the river. On November 25 thirty-three Chinese divisions (about three hundred thousand men) counterattacked. Within two weeks they had driven the U.N. forces south of the thirty-eighth parallel. By winter's end the contending forces were deadlocked at roughly the original dividing line between the two Koreas. "We were eyeball to eyeball," recalled Bev Scott, one of the first black lieutenants to head a racially integrated infantry squad.

> Just 20 meters of no man's land between us. We couldn't move at all in the daytime without getting shot at. . . . It was like World War I. We lived in a maze of bunkers and deep trenches. . . . There were bodies strewn all over the place. Hundreds of bodies frozen in the snow. We could see the arms and legs sticking up. Nobody could get their dead out of there.

Stalemated, Truman reversed course. In spring 1951 he sought a negotiated peace based on the original objective of restoring the integrity of South Korea. MacArthur rocked the boat, however, pressing for authority to blockade and bomb Mao's China and to "unleash" Jiang Jieshi's forces to invade the mainland. "In war," MacArthur insisted, "there is no substitute for victory." But Truman, fearing such actions would bring the Soviet Union into the conflict, shot back, "We are trying to prevent a world war—not start one."

When MacArthur continued to criticize Truman's limited war—publicly blasting his decision to keep the fight confined to one area and not use nuclear weapons—the president fired the general on April 10, 1951. The Joint Chiefs endorsed Truman's decision, but public opinion backed the general. The very idea of limited war, of containing rather than defeating the enemy, baffled many Americans; and the mounting toll of American casualties in pursuit of a stalemate angered them. It seemed senseless. Despite the warning by General Omar Bradley, Chairman of the Joint Chiefs of Staff, that MacArthur's proposals "would involve us in the wrong war at the wrong place in the wrong time and with the wrong enemy," a growing number of Americans listened sympathetically to Republican charges that communist agents were in control of American policy.

After two more years of fighting, the two sides reached an armistice in July 1953 that left Korea as divided as it had been at the start of the war. The "limited" conflict cost the United States 54,246 lives, another 103,284 wounded, and some $54 billion. The Chinese lost about 900,000 men, and both Korean armies lost about 800,000. Following the pattern of World War II, massive U.S. "carpet bombing" killed over 2 million civilians, and left North Korea looking like a moonscape.

The so-called forgotten war also had significant consequences. It accelerated implementation of NSC-68 and the expansion of containment into a global policy. From 1950 to 1953 defense spending zoomed from $13 billion to $60 billion— from one-third to two-thirds of the entire federal budget—and the American atomic stockpile mushroomed from 150 to 750 nuclear warheads. The United States acquired new bases around the world, committed itself to rearm West

Germany, and joined a mutual-defense pact with Australia and New Zealand. Increased military aid flowed to Jiang Jieshi on Taiwan, and American dollars supported the French army fighting the communist Ho Chi Minh in Indochina (Vietnam, Laos, and Cambodia). By 1954 the United States would be paying three-quarters of the cost of France's war in Indochina.

Truman's intervention in Korea preserved a precarious balance of power. It stepped up the administration's commitment to the anticommunist struggle as well as the shift of that struggle's focus from Europe to Asia. Containment, originally advanced to justify U.S. aid to Greece and Turkey, had become the ideological foundation for a major war in Korea and, ominously, for a deepening U.S. involvement in Vietnam. Truman's actions enhanced the powers of an already powerful presidency and set the precedent for later undeclared wars. It helped spark an economic boom and added fuel to a second Red Scare.

THE TRUMAN ADMINISTRATION AT HOME, 1945–1952

Since 1929 most Americans had known little but the sufferings and shortages of depression and war. They wanted to enjoy life. The Cold War both hindered that and helped create a postwar affluence that changed dreams into reality. Americans flocked to the suburbs, launched a huge baby boom, and rushed to buy refrigerators and new cars. Sales of TV sets soared from fewer than seven thousand in 1946 to more than 7 million by 1949, and by 1953 half of all U.S. homes had at least one television. Not all Americans shared these good times. Poverty remained a stark fact of life for millions. Minorities experienced the grim reality of racism. Yet a major movement by African-Americans for equality emerged from these Cold War years.

Family and career, not public issues, interested most Americans. The New Deal's reform energies subsided into complacency. Although Truman occasionally sought liberal measures, the mood of the times was against him. An increasingly conservative political order wanted to reduce taxes, not raise them, and to contract, not expand, the power of government and organized labor. Anticommunism bred repression, stifled dissent, and rewarded conformity, further undercutting efforts for progressive change.

The Eightieth Congress, 1947–1948
The Republicans of the Eightieth Congress interpreted the 1946 elections as a mandate to reverse the New Deal. As "Mr. Republican," Senator Robert A. Taft of Ohio, declared, "We have got to break with the corrupting idea that we can legislate prosperity, legislate equality, legislate opportunity." Congress defeated Democratic bills to raise the minimum wage and to provide federal funds for education and housing.

Truman and the GOP waged their major battle over the pro-union Wagner Act of 1935 (see Chapter 24). The massive postwar strikes by miners and railway workers had created a consensus for curbing union power. In 1947 more than twenty states passed laws to restrict union activities. Most important, Congress passed the

Taft-Hartley Act (officially the Labor-Management Relations Act), which barred the closed shop, outlawed secondary boycotts, required union officials to sign loyalty oaths, and permitted the president to call a cooling-off period to delay any strike that might endanger national safety or health. Although hardly the "slave labor bill" that unions characterized it, the Taft-Hartley Act weakened organizing drives in the nonunion South and West, hastening the relocation of labor-intensive industries, such as textiles, from the Northeast and Midwest to the Sunbelt. It also helped drive communists and other leftists out of CIO leadership positions, making organized labor less of a social justice movement and more of a special-interest group.

Eager for labor's support in the upcoming presidential election, Truman vetoed the bill. Congress overrode the veto. But Truman had taken a major step toward reforging FDR's majority coalition. He played the role of a staunch New Dealer to the hilt, urging Congress to repeal Taft-Hartley; raise the minimum wage, social-security benefits, and price supports for farmers; enact federal aid to education and housing; and adopt a federal health insurance program. To woo ethnic voters of Eastern European descent, Truman stressed his opposition to the Iron Curtain. To court Jewish-American voters as well as express his deep sympathy toward Holocaust survivors, he overrode the objections of the State Department, which feared alienating the oil-rich Arab world, and extended diplomatic recognition to the new state of Israel immediately after it proclaimed independence on May 14, 1948.

The Politics of Civil Rights and the Election of 1948

In 1947 Jackie Robinson, the grandson of a slave, joined the Brooklyn Dodgers, breaking major-league baseball's color barrier. It would not be an easy trip around the bases to interracial harmony. Unhappy fans insulted Robinson and mailed death threats. Opposition pitchers tried to bean him and runners to spike him. The humiliations and stress injured him physically and psychologically. But Robinson endured and triumphed, winning Rookie of the Year and then going on to win Most Valuable Player in the National League, be inducted into the Baseball Hall of Fame, and see every major-league team integrated by the late 1950s. Robinson's example also led to the start of integration by the Cleveland and Los Angeles franchises of the All-American Football Conference and the Boston Celtics of the National Basketball Association. African-Americans took heart and pressed assertively for an end to racial discrimination.

In 1945 Walter White, the head of the NAACP, had noted, "World War II has immeasurably magnified the Negro's awareness of the disparity between the American profession and practice of democracy." The war had heightened African-American expectations for racial equality, and numerous blacks, especially veterans, were actively demanding a permanent Fair Employment Practices Commission (FEPC), the outlawing of lynching, and the end of the poll tax. Voter-registration drives raised the percentage of southern blacks registered to vote from 2 percent in 1940 to 12 percent in 1947.

Jackie Robinson, 1947 *Before he became the first African-American to play major-league baseball, Robinson had excelled at track as well as baseball at UCLA and had been an army officer in World War II. Even his brilliant play for the Brooklyn Dodgers did not save him from racial taunts of fans and players or exclusion from restaurants and hotels that catered to his white teammates.*

Fearful of further gains as well as of a bold new spirit among African-Americans, some southern whites turned to violence. In 1946 whites killed several black war veterans who had voted that year in rural Georgia, flogged to death an "uppity" black tenant farmer in Mississippi, blowtorched a young black in Louisiana for daring to enter a white woman's house, and blinded a black soldier for failing to sit in the rear of a bus in South Carolina. In Columbia, Tennessee, in 1946 whites rioted against blacks who insisted on their rights. The police then arrested seventy blacks and did nothing as a white mob broke into the jail to murder two black prisoners.

In September 1946 Truman met with a delegation of civil-rights leaders. Believing that every American should enjoy the full rights of citizenship and knowing the political importance of the growing black vote, particularly in northern cities, he promised action. Truman realized, too, that white racism damaged U.S. relations with much of the world. The U.S.S.R. highlighted the mistreatment of African-Americans, both to undercut U.S. appeals to the nonwhites of Africa, Asia, and Latin America, and to counter criticism of its own repression behind the Iron Curtain. Accordingly, Truman established the first President's Committee on

Civil Rights. Its 1947 report, *To Secure These Rights,* dramatized the inequities of life in Jim Crow America and emphasized all the compelling moral, economic, and international reasons for the government to enact federal legislation outlawing lynching and the poll tax, establish a permanent FEPC, desegregate the armed forces, and support a legal assault on segregation in education, housing, and interstate transportation.

Southern segregationists reacted immediately, accusing Truman of "stabbing the South in the back" and warning of a Dixie boycott of the national Democratic ticket. Truman backtracked. Cowed by the prospect of losing the Solid South, he dropped plans to submit civil-rights bills to Congress and endorsed a weak civil-rights plank for the Democratic platform. But liberals and urban politicians who needed the votes of African-Americans rejected the president's feeble civil-rights plank at the Democratic convention in July 1948 and committed the party to act on Truman's original proposals. Thirty-five delegates from Alabama and Mississippi stalked out, joining other southern segregationists to form the States' Rights Democratic party, which nominated Governor Strom Thurmond of South Carolina for the presidency. The "Dixiecrats" hoped to win enough electoral votes to deny Truman reelection, restore their dominance in the Democratic party, and preserve the segregationist "southern way of life." They placed their electors on the ballot as the regular Democratic ticket in several states, posing a major roadblock to Truman's chances of victory.

Truman's electoral hopes faded further when left-wing Democrats joined with communists to launch a new Progressive party, which nominated former Vice President Henry A. Wallace for president and called for friendly relations with the Soviet Union. The Wallace candidacy threatened Truman's chances in key northern states, where many urban Democrats saw Wallace as the true heir of New Deal liberalism. The divisions in the Democratic party heartened Republicans. To play it safe they bypassed conservative, controversial senator Robert A. Taft and nominated moderate, bland governor Thomas E. Dewey of New York. Confident of victory, Dewey ran a complacent campaign designed to offend the fewest people. Truman, in contrast, campaigned tirelessly, blasting the "no-good, do-nothing" Republican-controlled Eightieth Congress. To shouts of "Give 'em hell, Harry," the president crisscrossed the country hammering away at the GOP as the party of "privilege, pride, and plunder." Political pundits applauded Truman's spunk, but all fifty of the experts polled by *Newsweek* predicted a sure Dewey victory.

A surprised nation awoke the day after the election to learn that the president had won the biggest upset in electoral history and that his party had regained control of both houses of Congress. Ironically, the Progressives and Dixiecrats had helped Truman. Their radicalism had kept moderate Democrats safely in the fold. The Berlin crisis, a coup in Czechoslovakia, and Wallace's failure to repudiate communist support forced most liberals away from the Progressives. Although the support for Thurmond signaled the first cracks in the Solid South, few southern

Democrats felt sufficiently threatened by Truman's civil-rights stand to desert the party in 1948. "The only sane and constructive course to follow is to remain in the house of our fathers—even though the roof leaks, and there be bats in the belfry, rats in the pantry, a cockroach in the kitchen and skunks in the parlor," explained a southern officeholder. Moreover, Dixiecrat defections had freed Truman to campaign as a champion of civil rights. In July 1948 he had issued executive orders barring discrimination in federal employment and requiring "equality of treatment and opportunity for all persons in the armed services without regard to race, color, religion or national origin." Truman had also benefited from Supreme Court decisions declaring segregation in interstate bus transportation unconstitutional (*Morgan* v. *Virginia*) and outlawing restrictive housing covenants that forbade the sale or rental of property to minorities (*Shelley* v. *Kraemer*).

Truman's unexpected victory proved his skills as a campaigner and, even more, the political power of the New Deal coalition of workers, farmers, and ethnic and racial minorities. "In a sense," wrote one journalist, "Roosevelt won his greatest victory after his death."

The Fair Deal

Proclaiming in his inaugural address of 1949 that "every segment of our population . . . has a right to expect from our government a fair deal," Truman proposed a domestic agenda that included civil rights, national health care legislation, and federal aid to education, among many other measures. Unlike the New Deal, the Fair Deal was based on the belief in continual economic growth: the constantly expanding economic pie would mean a progressively bigger piece for most Americans (so they would not resent helping those left behind) and for the government (so it would have the revenue to pay for social welfare programs).

The Eighty-first Congress complied with Truman's requests to extend existing programs but rejected new Fair Deal measures. It raised the minimum wage; increased social-security benefits and coverage; expanded appropriations for public power, conservation, and slum clearance; and authorized the construction of nearly a million low-income housing units. It also enacted the Displaced Persons Act, which allowed entry to 205,000 survivors of the Nazi forced-labor and death camps. But Congress rejected federal aid to education, national health insurance, civil-rights legislation, larger farm subsidies, and repeal of the Taft-Hartley Act.

Congress's rejection of most Fair Deal proposals stemmed from Truman's own lessening commitment to domestic reform in favor of foreign and military affairs, as well as from the power of the coalition of Republicans and conservative Democrats that held sway in Congress. Widening prosperity sapped public enthusiasm for reform. In 1949, according to the Hickock Manufacturing Company, the belt size of the average American man had expanded to thirty-four inches, up from the depression years' average of thirty-one inches. The full-belly sense of well-being and popular fears of communism doomed hopes for expanded liberal reform.

THE POLITICS OF ANTICOMMUNISM

As the Cold War worsened, many Americans came to believe that communist spies and traitors at home were the cause of setbacks for the United States abroad. How else could the communists have defeated Jiang in China and built an atomic bomb? Millions of fearful Americans enlisted in a crusade that equated dissent with disloyalty and sought scapegoats to blame for the nation's problems.

Similar intolerance had prevailed in the Red Scare of 1919–1920 (see Chapter 22). Since its establishment in 1938, the House Committee on Un-American Activities (later called the House Un-American Activities Committee, or HUAC) had served as a platform for right-wing denunciations of the New Deal as a communist plot. Only the extreme Right initially took such charges seriously. But after World War II mounting numbers of Democrats as well as Republicans climbed aboard the anti-Red bandwagon.

The Great Fear affected both governmental and personal actions. Millions of Americans were subjected to security investigations and loyalty oaths. Anticommunist extremism destroyed the Left, undermined labor militancy, spawned a "silent generation" of college students, and ensured foreign-policy rigidity and the defeat of liberal reforms.

Loyalty and
Security

American fear of a war with the Soviet Union and of other countries' going communist raised legitimate concerns about security in the United States. The Communist party had claimed eighty thousand members in the United States during the Second World War, and far more sympathizers. No one knew how many party members occupied sensitive government and military positions. In mid-1945 a raid on the offices of a procommunist magazine, *Amerasia*, revealed that classified documents had been given to the periodical by two State Department employees and a naval intelligence officer. Then the Canadian government exposed a major spy network that had passed American atomic secrets to the Soviets during the war. Republicans accused the Democratic administration of being "soft on communism."

A week after his Truman Doctrine speech of March 1947, the president issued Executive Order 9835, establishing the Federal Employee Loyalty Program to root out subversives in the government. The first such peacetime program, it barred members of the Communist party and anyone guilty of "sympathetic association" with it from federal employment. "Reasonable grounds for belief that the person is disloyal," such as being homosexual, led to dismissal. Those suspected were allowed neither to face their accusers nor to require investigators to reveal sources. Instead of focusing on potential subversives in high-risk areas, review boards extended the probe to the associations and beliefs of every government worker.

Mere criticism of American foreign policy could result in an accusation of disloyalty. Clouds of suspicion hovered over those who liked foreign films and favored the unionization of federal workers or civil rights for blacks. "Of course the fact that a person believes in racial equality doesn't prove he's a communist," mused an Interior Department Loyalty Board chairman, "but it certainly makes you look twice, doesn't it?" Some people lost jobs because they had friends who were radicals or had once belonged to organizations now declared disloyal. People's reading became fair game. An employee was asked if he read the *New Republic*. Another was asked, "What do you think of female chastity?" Tastes in music might trigger concern.

Of the 4.7 million jobholders and applicants who underwent loyalty checks by 1952, 560 were fired or denied jobs on security grounds, several thousand resigned or withdrew their applications, and countless were intimidated. Although Loyalty Board probes uncovered no proof of espionage or subversion, they heightened people's fears of what Truman called "the enemy within," adding credibility to the Red Scare. "Why lead with your chin?" became a dominant reflex. "If communists like apple pie and I do," claimed one federal worker, "I see no reason why I should stop eating it. But I would."

The Anticom-
munist Crusade
The fear of disloyalty generated by Truman's inquest fed mounting anticommunist hysteria. It promoted fears of communist infiltrators and legitimated a witch hunt for subversives. FBI chief J. Edgar Hoover claimed that colleges were centers of "red propaganda," and a senator, decrying "communist-line textbooks" and professors, accused colleges of admitting "good Americans" and returning them "four years later as wild-eyed radicals." At Yale the FBI, with the consent of the college administration, spied on students and faculty, screening candidates for jobs and fellowships. Many universities banned controversial speakers, and Truman's Office of Education introduced a "Zeal for Democracy" campaign, providing local school boards with curriculum materials to combat "communist subversion." New York State's Department of Education added a new unit on "How Can We Fight Communism?" to its *Teaching American History* curriculum. Popular magazines featured articles like "Reds Are After Your Child." Comics joined the fray: "Beware, commies, spies, traitors, and foreign agents! Captain America, with all loyal, free men behind him, is looking for you, ready to fight until the last one of you is exposed for the yellow scum you are." The Ford Motor Company put FBI agents on its payroll to look for communists on the assembly line.

By the end of Truman's term, thirty-nine states had created loyalty programs, most with virtually no procedural safeguards. Schoolteachers, college professors, and state and city employees throughout the nation had to sign loyalty oaths or lose their jobs. No one knows for sure how many were dismissed, denied tenure, or quietly drifted away, leaving behind colleagues too frightened to speak out.

In 1947 the House Un-American Activities Committee began hearings to expose communist influence in American life. HUAC's probes blurred distinctions between dissent and disloyalty, between radicalism and subversion. Those called to testify were in a bind. When asked whether they had ever been members of the Communist party, witnesses could say yes and be forced to reveal the names of others; say no and be vulnerable to charges of perjury; or refuse to answer, pleading the

First or Fifth Amendments, and risk being viewed by the public as a communist. In Washington, D.C., a man who invoked the Fifth Amendment lost his license to sell secondhand furniture, and his livelihood. A woman who did the same suffered a boycott that destroyed her once-thriving drugstore. A Stanford University biochemist poisoned himself rather than respond to HUAC's questions. In a suicide note he blasted the committee for wrecking careers and lives: "The scientific mind cannot flourish in an atmosphere of fear, timidity, and imposed conformity."

To gain publicity for itself and to influence the content of movies, HUAC also probed Hollywood. In its hearings on "Communist infiltration of the motion picture industry," HUAC listened to testimony by "friendly witnesses," such as conservative novelist Ayn Rand, film producer Walt Disney, and Screen Actors Guild president Ronald Reagan. They saw as proof of communist activity wartime films about the Soviet Union showing Russians smiling, or movies featuring the line "share and share alike, that's democracy." In 1947, HUAC cited for contempt of Congress a group of prominent film directors and screenwriters who, claiming the freedom of speech and assembly guaranteed by the First Amendment, refused to say whether they had been members of the Communist party. The so-called Hollywood Ten—some of them Communists, all of them leftists—were convicted of contempt and sent to prison. The threat of further investigations prompted the movie colony, financially dependent on favorable press and public opinion, to deny work to them as well as to other "unfriendly witnesses," such as directors Orson Welles and Charlie Chaplin. Soon the studios established a blacklist barring the employment of anyone suspected of communism.

Between 1947 and 1952 Hollywood brought out almost fifty anticommunist movies. One studio canceled a film on Longfellow, explaining that Hiawatha had tried to stop wars between Indian tribes and that some might see the effort as communist propaganda for peace. Another withdrew plans to film the story of Robin Hood because he took from the rich and gave to the poor.

HUAC also frightened the labor movement into expelling communists and avoiding progressive causes. Fearful of appearing "red," or even "pink," most unions focused on securing better pay and benefits for their members.

The 1948 presidential election campaign also fed national anxieties. Truman lambasted Henry Wallace as a Stalinist dupe and accused the Republicans of being "unwittingly the ally of the communists." In turn, the GOP dubbed the Democrats "the party of treason." Republican Congressman Richard Nixon of California charged that Democrats bore responsibility for "the unimpeded growth of the communist conspiracy in the United States."

To blunt such accusations, Truman's Justice Department prosecuted eleven top leaders of the American Communist party under the Smith Act of 1940, which outlawed any conspiracy advocating the overthrow of the government. In 1951, in *Dennis* v. *United States,* the Supreme Court affirmed the conviction and jailing of the communists, despite the absence of any acts of violence or espionage, declaring that Congress could curtail freedom of speech if national security required such restriction.

Ironically, the Communist party was fading into obscurity at the very time when politicians magnified its threat. By 1950 its membership had shrunk to fewer than thirty thousand. Yet Truman's attorney general warned that American Reds "are everywhere—in factories, offices, butcher stores, on street corners, in private businesses—and each carries in himself the germ of death for society."

Alger Hiss and the Rosenbergs Nothing set off more alarms of a Red conspiracy in Washington than the case of Alger Hiss. Amid the 1948 political campaign, HUAC conducted a hearing in which Whittaker Chambers, a *Time* editor and former Soviet agent who had broken with the communists in 1938, identified Hiss as belonging to a secret communist cell in the 1930s.

A rumpled, repentant, former communist and college dropout, Chambers appeared to be a tortured soul crusading to save the West from the Red peril. The elegant Hiss, in contrast, seemed the very symbol of the liberal establishment. He was a Harvard-trained lawyer who had clerked for Supreme Court Justice Oliver Wendell Holmes, served FDR in the New Deal and later as a State Department official, and presided over the inaugural meeting of the United Nations. For conservative Republicans, a better villain could not have been invented. Hiss denied any communist affiliation or even knowing Chambers, and most liberals believed him. They saw him as a victim of conservatives bent on tarnishing New Deal liberalism. Truman denounced Chambers's allegation as a "red herring" being used to deflect attention from the failures of the Eightieth Congress.

To those suspicious of the Roosevelt liberal tradition, Chambers's persistence and Hiss's bizarre notions—"Until the day I die, I shall wonder how Whittaker Chambers got into my house to use my typewriter"—intensified fears that the Democratic administration teemed with communists. Under relentless questioning by Congressman Richard Nixon, Hiss finally admitted that he had known Chambers and had even let Chambers have his car and live in his apartment. But he still denied ever having been a communist. Chambers then broadened his accusation, claiming that Hiss had committed espionage in the 1930s by giving him secret State Department documents to be sent to the Soviet Union. To prove his charge, Chambers led federal agents to his farm in Maryland where, in a hollowed-out pumpkin, he had microfilm copies of confidential government papers that had been copied on a typewriter traced to Hiss. A grand jury then indicted Hiss for perjury. (The statute of limitations for espionage prevented a charge of treason.) After one trial ended in a hung jury, a second resulted in a conviction and a five-year prison sentence for Hiss. While prominent Democrats continued to defend Hiss, Republican conservatives were emboldened. Who knew how many other bright young New Dealers had betrayed the country?

Hard on the heels of the Hiss conviction, another spy case shocked Americans. In February 1950 the British arrested Klaus Fuchs, a German-born scientist involved in the Manhattan Project, for passing atomic secrets to the Soviets during the Second World War. Fuchs's confession led to the arrest of his American accomplice, Harry Gold, who then implicated David Greenglass, a machinist who had worked at Los Alamos. Greenglass named his sister and brother-in-law, Ethel and Julius Rosenberg, as co-conspirators in the wartime spy network. The children of Jewish immigrants, the Rosenbergs insisted that they were victims of anti-Semitism and were being persecuted for their leftist beliefs. In March 1951 a jury found both of them guilty of conspiring to commit espionage. The trial judge, declaring their crime "worse than murder," sentenced them to die in the electric chair. Offered clemency if they named other spies, neither Rosenberg would confess. On June 19, 1953, they were executed—the first American civilians to lose their lives for espionage.

Both the Rosenbergs and Alger Hiss protested their innocence to their end, and their defenders continued to do so for decades. Soviet secret documents released by the National Security Agency in the 1990s—called the Venona Intercepts—lent weight to Chambers's charges against Hiss and confirmed Julius Rosenberg's guilt. (Ethel's role in her husband's spying remained uncertain.)

McCarthyism   At the time, when few Americans could separate fact from fantasy, the Hiss and Rosenberg cases tarnished liberalism and fueled other loyalty investigations. Only a conspiracy, it seemed, could explain U.S. weakness and Soviet might. Frustrated by their unexpected failure to win the

McCarthyism *A term invented by cartoonist Herblock, McCarthyism to most liberals and Democrats meant the use of lies, slander, and innuendo to attack and discredit the Democratic party for "twenty years of treason."*

White House in 1948, Republicans eagerly exploited the fearful mood and abandoned restraint in accusing the "Commiecrats" of selling out America.

No individual would inflict as many wounds on the Democrats as Republican Senator Joseph R. McCarthy of Wisconsin. Falsely claiming to be a wounded war hero, "Tail-Gunner Joe" won a Senate seat in the 1946 Republican landslide, and promptly gained a reputation for lying and heavy drinking. His political future in jeopardy, McCarthy decided to imitate Republicans like Richard Nixon who had gained popularity by accusing Democrats of being "soft on communism." In February 1950 McCarthy told an audience in Wheeling, West Virginia, that the United States found itself in a "position of impotency" because of "the traitorous actions" of high officials in the Truman administration. "I have here in my hands a list of 205," McCarthy claimed as he waved a laundry ticket, "a list of names known to the Secretary of State as being members of the Communist party and who nevertheless are still working and shaping policy." Although McCarthy offered no evidence, the newspapers printed his charges, giving him a national forum. McCarthy soon repeated his accusations, reducing his numbers to 81, to 57, and to "a lot," and toning down his rhetoric from "card-carrying communists" to "subversives" to "bad risks." A Senate committee found McCarthy's charges "a fraud and a hoax," but he persisted.

Buoyed by the partisan usefulness of Senator McCarthy's onslaught, Republicans encouraged even more accusations. "Joe, you're a dirty s.o.b.," declared Ohio Senator John Bricker, "but there are times when you've got to have an s.o.b. around, and this is one of them." Even the normally fair-minded Robert Taft, who privately dismissed McCarthy's charges as "nonsense," urged him "to keep talking, and if one case doesn't work, try another." He did just that, and "McCarthyism" became a synonym for personal attacks on individuals by means of indiscriminate allegations, especially unsubstantiated charges.

As the Korean War dragged on, McCarthy's efforts to "root out the skunks" escalated. He ridiculed Secretary of State Dean Acheson as the "Red Dean," termed Truman's dismissal of MacArthur "the greatest victory the communists have ever won," and charged George Marshall with having "aided and abetted a communist conspiracy so immense as to dwarf any previous such venture in the history of man."

Such attacks appealed most to Republicans indignant about the Europe-first emphasis of Truman's foreign policy and eager to turn the public's fears into votes for the GOP. For many in the American Legion and the Chambers of Commerce, anticommunism was a weapon of revenge against liberals and internationalists, as well as a means to regain the controlling position that conservative forces had once held. McCarthy also won a devoted following among blue-collar workers who identified with his charge that a person was either a true American who detested "communists and queers" or an "egg sucking phony liberal." Laborers praised his demand that the war against communism be fought with brass knuckles, not kid gloves, while both small and big businessmen sniffed an opportunity to destroy the power of organized labor. McCarthy's flag-waving appeals held a special attraction for traditionally Democratic Catholic ethnics, who sought to gain acceptance as "100 percent Americans" by their anticommunist zeal, especially after such tactics had won the blessings of New York's Cardinal Francis Spellman and television personality Bishop Fulton J. Sheen. Countless Americans also shared McCarthy's scorn for privilege and gentility, for the "bright young men who are born with silver spoons in their mouths," for the "striped-pants boys in the State Department."

While McCarthy's conspiratorial explanation offered the public an appealingly simple answer to the perplexing questions of the Cold War, his political power rested on the support of the Republican establishment and on Democrats' fears of antagonizing him. McCarthy appeared invincible after he helped GOP candidates in the 1950 congressional elections unseat Democrats who had denounced him. "Look out for McCarthy" became the Senate watchword. "Joe will go that extra mile to destroy you," warned the new majority leader, Democrat Lyndon B. Johnson of Texas. Few dared incur McCarthy's wrath.

In 1950, over Truman's veto, federal lawmakers adopted the McCarran Internal Security Act, which required organizations deemed communist by the attorney general to register with the Department of Justice. It also authorized the arrest and detention during a national emergency of "any person as to whom there is reason to believe might engage in acts of espionage or sabotage." As part of this effort, a Senate committee sought to root out homosexuals holding government jobs. The linking of disloyalty with homosexuality in turn legitimated the armed forces' effort to dismiss "queers" and the raiding of gay bars by city police. The McCarran-Walter Immigration and Nationality Act of 1952, also enacted over Truman's veto, maintained the quota system that severely restricted immigration from southern and eastern Europe, increased the attorney general's authority to prevent homosexuals from entering the country, and gave the Justice Department the power to exclude or deport aliens suspected of sympathy for communism.

The Election of 1952

In 1952 public apprehension about the loyalty of government employees combined with frustration over the Korean stalemate to sink Democratic electoral prospects to their lowest level since the 1920s. Both business and labor also resented Truman's decision to freeze wages and prices during the Korean conflict. Revelations of bribery and influence peddling by some of Truman's old political associates gave Republicans ammunition for charging the Democrats with "plunder at home, and blunder abroad."

With Truman too unpopular to run for reelection, dispirited Democrats drafted Governor Adlai Stevenson of Illinois. But Stevenson could not separate himself politically from Truman, and his lofty speeches failed to stir most voters. An intellectual out of touch with the common people, he was jokingly referred to as an "egghead," someone with more brains than hair. Above all, Stevenson could not overcome the widespread sentiment that twenty years of Democratic rule was enough.

Compounding Democratic woes, the GOP nominated popular war hero Dwight D. Eisenhower. In 1948 Eisenhower had rejected Democratic pleas that he head their ticket, insisting that "lifelong professional soldiers should abstain from seeking higher political office." But in 1952 he answered the call of the moderate wing of the Republican party and accepted the nomination. As a concession to the hard-line anticommunists in the party, "Ike" chose as his running mate Richard Nixon, who had won a seat in the Senate in 1950 by red-baiting his opponent, Helen Gahagan Douglas, as "pink right down to her underwear."

Eisenhower and Nixon proved unbeatable. With his captivating grin and unimpeachable record of public service, Eisenhower projected both personal warmth and the vigorous authority associated with military command. His smile, wrote one commentator, was one "of infinite reassurance." At the same time, Nixon kept public apprehensions at the boiling point. Accusing the Democrats of treason, he charged that the election of "Adlai the appeaser . . . who got a Ph.D. from Dean Acheson's College of Cowardly Communist Containment" would bring "more Alger Hisses, more atomic spies."

The GOP ticket stumbled when newspapers revealed the existence of a "slush fund" that California businessmen created to keep Nixon in "financial comfort." But Nixon saved himself with a heart-tugging speech on the new medium of television. Less than two weeks before the election, Eisenhower dramatically pledged to "go to Korea" to end the stalemated war. It worked, and 62.7 percent of those eligible to vote (compared to just 51.5 percent in 1948) turned out in 1952 and gave the Republican ticket 55 percent of the ballots. Ike cracked the Solid South, carrying thirty-nine states. Enough Republicans rode his coattails to give the GOP narrow control of both houses of Congress.

IMPORTANT EVENTS, 1945–1952

1944 Servicemen's Readjustment Act (GI Bill).

1945 Postwar strike wave begins.

1946 Employment Act.
George Kennan's "long telegram."
Winston Churchill's "iron curtain" speech.
Coal miners' strike.
More than a million GIs attend college.
Inflation soars to more than 18 percent.
Republicans win control of Congress.

1947 Truman Doctrine.
Federal Employee Loyalty Program.
Jackie Robinson breaks major-league baseball's color line.
Taft-Hartley Act.
National Security Act.
Marshall Plan to aid Europe proposed.
President's Committee on Civil Rights issues *To Secure These Rights*.
HUAC holds hearings on Hollywood.

1948 Communist coup in Czechoslovakia.
State of Israel founded.
Soviet Union begins blockade of Berlin; United States begins airlift.
Congress approves Marshall Plan.
Truman orders an end to segregation in the armed forces.
Communist leaders put on trial under the Smith Act.
Truman elected president.

1949 North Atlantic Treaty Organization (NATO) established.
East and West Germany founded as separate nations.
Communist victory in China; People's Republic of China established.
Soviet Union detonates an atomic bomb.

1950 Truman authorizes building a hydrogen bomb.
Soviet spy ring at Los Alamos uncovered.
Alger Hiss convicted of perjury.
Joseph McCarthy launches anticommunist crusade.
Korean War begins.
Julius and Ethel Rosenberg arrested as atomic spies.
McCarran Internal Security Act.
Truman accepts NSC-68.
China enters the Korean War.

1951 Douglas MacArthur dismissed from his Korean command.
Supreme Court upholds Smith Act.
Rosenbergs convicted of espionage.

1952 First hydrogen bomb exploded.
Dwight D. Eisenhower elected president; Republicans win control of Congress.

27

America at Midcentury, 1952–1960

66 It starts with these giant ants that crawl out of the ground from that place in New Mexico where they tested the atomic bomb—Alamogordo. They're desperate for sugar, and they rip apart anybody who gets in their way. It ends in the sewers of Los Angeles—and it's really scary!"

The year was 1954, and moviegoers shivered in terror at *Them!* the giant-ant film that was part of a wave of mutant movies pouring out of Hollywood. In *The Incredible Shrinking Man,* the unlucky hero is accidentally exposed to "atomic dust" and begins to shrink. In *The Attack of the Fifty-Foot Women,* the process is reversed. Nuclear radiation spawned a giant octopus in *It Came from Beneath the Sea,* unleashed *The Attack of the Crab Monsters,* and was responsible for the *Invasion of the Body Snatchers* by pods from outer space.

The popularity of science fiction movies reflected both the amusing and fearful aspects of the 1950s. It was a happy, confident decade for some, a troubled time for others, and a mix of both for the majority of Americans. The Cold War and expanding economic prosperity dominated the 1950s, deeply and widely shaping life in the United States. Despite President Eisenhower's calm assurances, and beneath the placid surface of a supposedly complacent people, many Americans worried about the spread of communism, juvenile delinquency, and homosexuality (usually depicted as an "alien" lifestyle, and associated with blackmail by Soviet agents). Parents particularly worried about the arms race. *Them!* and other films highlighted the fears of atmospheric nuclear testing that pumped strontium 90, a cancer-causing chemical that accumulates in the teeth and bone marrow of children, into the world's environment.

As such fears dimmed, later decades plagued by turmoil looked back with nostalgia at the seemingly tranquil "nifty fifties." In the distorting lens of memory, the decade came to seem a time of pervasive affluence and consumerism, of cheap gasoline and big cars, of new suburban homes and family togetherness, of conservatism and conformity. The mass media portrayed the 1950s as a sunny time when almost everybody liked Ike and loved Lucy, except teenagers who idolized Elvis Presley.

Like many historical generalizations, "the Fifties," now a singular noun, substituted sweeping, simplistic images for analysis. Many Americans did enjoy the fruits of the decade's consumer culture. Having endured the hard times of the depression and war years, they reveled in prosperity guided by a popular president. They trusted Dwight Eisenhower and welcomed the thaw in the Cold War that came after the Korean War. Some high-school students did lead the carefree, fun-filled existence captured in later media images.

Widespread poverty also existed in the 1950s, as did racial discrimination and Americans who railed against mainstream values. A complex era, the decade saw scientists end the scourge of polio, unravel the structure of DNA, invent the maser that then became the laser, and send satellites into space. It was a time of hydrogen bombs as well as of Women Strike for Peace, an organization of mostly middle-class housewives concerned about radioactivity in the atmosphere and the possibility of nuclear war. It was a period of intense political passions, kindled by Senator Joseph McCarthy, the Warren Court, and civil-rights leader Martin Luther King, Jr. A time of fundamental changes and of portents of yet greater change, the 1950s brought the advent of an automated and computerized postindustrial society, television's growing power, and the baby boom, as well as mass suburbanization and a remarkable internal migration. Midcentury America encompassed peace and a widening Cold War, prosperity and persistent poverty, civil-rights triumphs and rampant racism, consensus and alienation. Although the 1950s were good years for many Americans, they were hardly placid, and they sowed the seeds of future crises.

This chapter focuses on five major questions:

What domestic policies support the notion of Eisenhower as a centrist or moderate politician?

In what ways did Eisenhower continue Truman's foreign policy, and in what ways did he change it? How successfully did Eisenhower accomplish his foreign-policy goals?

What were the main sources, and consequences, of economic prosperity in the 1950s?

How accurate is the image of the 1950s as a period of conservatism and conformity?

What strategies did minorities adopt in order to gain greater equality in the 1950s, and how successful were they?

THE EISENHOWER PRESIDENCY

Rarely in U.S. history has a president better fit the national mood than did Dwight David Eisenhower. Exhausted by a quarter-century of upheaval—the depression, World War II, the Cold War—Americans craved peace and stability. Eisenhower delivered. He gave a nation weary of partisanship a sense of unity; he inspired confidence; and his moderate politics pleased most Americans.

President Eisenhower steered a middle course between Democratic liberalism and traditional Republican conservatism. In the main, he neither expanded nor dismantled New Deal and Fair Deal policies and programs. He did little publicly to challenge Joseph McCarthy or to support the desegregation of public education, until events forced his hand.

"Dynamic Conservatism"

The most distinguished general of the Second World War, Eisenhower projected the image of a plain but good man. He expressed complicated issues in simple terms, yet governed a complex, urban, technological society. The hero who had vanquished Hitler, a grandfatherly figure with twinkling blue eyes, Ike comforted an anxious people.

Born in Denison, Texas, on October 14, 1890, Dwight Eisenhower grew up in Abilene, Kansas, in a poor, strongly religious family. More athletic than studious, he graduated from the U.S. Military Academy at West Point in 1915. In directing the Allied invasion of North Africa in 1943 and of Western Europe in 1944, he proved himself a brilliant war planner and organizer, widely lauded for his managerial ability and skill at conciliation.

Eisenhower's approach to the presidency reflected his wartime leadership style. He concentrated on "the big picture," delegating authority while reconciling contending factions. His restrained view of presidential powers stemmed from his respect for the constitutional balance of power as well as his sense of the dignity of the Oval Office. He rarely intervened publicly in the legislative process. He shunned using his office as a "bully pulpit." He promised his cabinet that he would "stay out of its hair." This low-key style led Democrats to scoff at Eisenhower as a bumbler who preferred golf to government, who "reigned but did not rule."

The image of passivity actually masked an active and occasionally ruthless politician. Determined to govern the nation on business principles, Eisenhower staffed his administration with corporate executives. "Eight millionaires and a plumber," jested one journalist about the cabinet. (The "plumber" was union leader Martin Durkin, who headed the Labor Department, and soon resigned.) The president initially worked with the Republican-controlled Congress to reduce the size of government and to slash the federal budget. He promoted the private development of hydroelectric and nuclear power, and persuaded Congress to turn over to coastal states the oil-rich "tidelands" that the Supreme Court had previously awarded to the federal government.

For the most part, however, the Eisenhower administration followed a centrist course. More pragmatic than ideological, he wished to reduce taxes, contain inflation, and govern efficiently. Summing up the president's views, his brother and adviser Milton Eisenhower declared, "We should keep what we have, catch our breath for a while, and improve administration; it does not mean moving backward."

Eager to avoid a depression, Eisenhower relied heavily on the Council of Economic Advisers (CEA) despite conservative calls for its abolition. He followed

The Interstate Highway System

As a young lieutenant after World War I, Dwight Eisenhower had been given the task of accompanying a convoy of army trucks across the country. The woefully inadequate state of the roads for military transport dismayed him then as much as he would later be impressed by the German autobahns that allowed Hitler to deploy troops around Germany with incredible speed. Not surprisingly, when he became president he sought a transportation system that would facilitate the rapid movement of the military, as well as increase road safety and aid commerce. The arms race with the Soviet Union, moreover, necessitated a network of highways for evacuating cities in case of a nuclear attack—a change, according to the *Bulletin of the Atomic Scientists,* from "Duck and Cover" to "Run Like Hell."

In 1954 Eisenhower set up a high-powered commission to recommend a highway program that would cost as much as a war. He appointed an army general to head it to emphasize the connection between highways, national defense, and the concerns Americans had about their security. The next year, with the entire federal budget at $71 billion, Eisenhower asked Congress for a $40 billion, forty-one-thousand-mile construction project, to be financed by government bonds. Conservative Republicans, fearful of increasing the federal debt, balked. So Ike switched to a financing plan based on new gasoline, tire, bus, and trucking taxes. The federal government would use the taxes to pay 90 percent of the construction costs in any state willing to come up with the other 10 percent.

Millions of suburbanites commuting to central cities loved the idea of new multilane highways. So did motorists dreaming of summer travel; the powerful coalition of automobile manufacturers, oil companies, asphalt firms, and truckers, who stood to benefit financially the most; and the many special interests in virtually every congressional district, including real-estate developers, shopping mall entrepreneurs, engineers, and construction industries. Indeed, the interstate highway bill promised something to almost everybody except the inner-city poor. It sailed through Congress in 1956, winning by voice vote in the House and by an 89 to 1 margin in the Senate.

The largest and most expensive public works scheme in American history, the interstate highway system was designed and built as a single project for the entire country, unlike the haphazard development of the canal and railroad networks. It required taking more land by eminent domain than had been taken in the entire history of road building in the United States. Expected increases in highway use, speed of travel, and weight of loads necessitated drastic changes in road engineering and materials. Utilizing the technological advances that had produced high-quality concrete and asphalt, diesel-powered roadbed graders, reinforced steel, and safely controlled explosives, construction crews built superhighways with standardized twelve-foot-wide lanes, ten-foot shoulders, and median strips of at least thirty-six feet in rural areas. Terrain in which a dirt trail was difficult to blaze was laced with cloverleaf intersections and some sixteen thousand exits and entrances. More than fifty thousand bridges, tunnels, and overpasses traversed swamps, rivers, and mountains. Road curves were banked for speeds of seventy miles per hour, with grades no greater than 3 percent and minimum sight distances of six hundred feet. The massive amounts of concrete poured, Ike later boasted, could have made "six sidewalks to the moon" or sixty Panama Canals.

The network of four-to-eight-lane roads linking cities and suburbs made it possible to drive from New York to San Francisco without encountering a stoplight. It more than fulfilled the initial hopes of most of its backers, enormously speeding the movement of goods and people across the country, invigorating the tourist industry, providing steady work for construction firms, enriching those who lived near the interstates and sold their lands to developers, and hastening suburban development.

The freeways that helped unify Americans by increasing the accessibility of once-distant regions also helped homogenize the nation with interchangeable shopping malls, motels, and fast-food chains. In 1955 Ray Kroc, who supplied the Multimixers for milk shakes to the original McDonald's drive-in in San Bernardino, California, began to franchise similar family restaurants beside highways, each serving the same standardized foods under the instantly recognizable logo of the golden arches. By century's end McDonald's would be the world's largest private real-estate enterprise, as well as the largest food provider, serving more than 40 million meals daily in some hundred countries.

Moreover, the expressways boosting the interstate trucking business hastened the decline of the nation's railroad lines and urban mass-transportation systems. The highways built to speed commuters into the central cities—"white men's roads through black men's bedrooms" said the National Urban League—often bulldozed minority neighborhoods out of existence or served as barriers between black and white neighborhoods. The beltways that lured increasingly more residents and businesses to suburbia eroded city tax bases, which, in turn, accelerated urban decay, triggering the urban crisis that then furthered suburban sprawl. The interstates had locked the United States into an ever-increasing reliance on cars and trucks, drastically increasing air pollution and American dependence on a constant supply of cheap and plentiful gasoline.

FOCUS QUESTIONS

- Why did Congress authorize the construction of an interstate highway system?
- Describe some of the unintended consequences of the new highway system.

the advice of CEA head Arthur Burns (the only government official other than the secretary of state who had a weekly appointment with Ike) to act positively to fine-tune the economy. When recessions struck in 1953 and 1957, Eisenhower abandoned his balanced budgets and increased government spending in order to restore prosperity.

The president labeled his ideas "dynamic conservatism" and "modern Republicanism." Whatever the slogan, Eisenhower went along with Congress when it extended social-security benefits to more than 10 million Americans. He approved raising the minimum wage from seventy-five cents to a dollar an hour, making 4 million more workers eligible for unemployment benefits, and increasing federally financed public housing for low-income families. He also approved establishing a Department of Health, Education and Welfare. He supported constructing the St. Lawrence Seaway, linking the Great Lakes and the Atlantic Ocean, and he proposed that the federal government take the lead in building forty thousand miles of freeways to replace old, unsafe roads (see Technology and Culture: The Interstate Highway System).

Republicans renominated Ike by acclamation in 1956, and voters gave him a landslide victory over Democrat Adlai Stevenson. With the GOP crowing "Everything's booming but the guns," Eisenhower won by the greatest popular majority since FDR's in 1936 and carried all but seven states.

The Downfall of Joseph McCarthy Although he despised McCarthy—and called him a "pimple on the path to progress"—Eisenhower considered it beneath his dignity to "get into the gutter with that guy." Fearing a direct confrontation with the senator, he tried to steal McCarthy's thunder by tightening security requirements for government employees. When that failed, he allowed McCarthy to grab plenty of rope in the hope that the demagogue would hang himself. McCarthy did so in 1954. Angry that one of his aides had not received a draft deferment, the senator accused the army of harboring communist spies. The army then charged McCarthy with using his influence to gain preferential treatment for the aide who had been drafted.

The resulting nationally televised Senate investigation, begun in April 1954, brought McCarthy down. A national audience witnessed McCarthy's boorish behavior firsthand on television. His dark scowl, raspy voice, endless interruptions ("point of order, Mr. Chairman, point of order"), and disregard for the rights of others repelled many viewers. He behaved like the bad guy in a TV western, observed novelist John Steinbeck: "He had a stubble of a beard, he leered, he sneered, he had a nasty laugh. He bullied and shouted. He looked evil." In June McCarthy slurred the reputation of a young lawyer assisting Joseph Welch, the army counsel. Suddenly the mild-mannered Welch turned his wrath on McCarthy, "Until this moment, Senator, I think I really never gauged your cruelty or your recklessness. . . . Have you no sense of decency?" The gallery burst into applause.

McCarthy's popularity ratings plummeted. The GOP no longer needed him to drive the "Commiecrats" from power. The Democrats eagerly sought to be rid of their scourge. The Senate, with Eisenhower applying pressure behind the scenes, voted in December 1954 to censure McCarthy for contemptuous behavior. This powerful rebuke—only the third in the Senate's history—demolished McCarthy as a political force. McCarthyism, Ike gloated, had become "McCarthywasism."

In 1957 McCarthy died a broken man, suffering from the effects of alcoholism. But the fears he exploited lingered. Congress established Loyalty Day in 1955 and annually funded the House Un-American Activities Committee's search for suspected radicals. State and local governments continued to require teachers to take loyalty oaths.

McCarthyism also remained a rallying call of conservatives disenchanted with the postwar consensus. Young conservatives like William F. Buckley, Jr. (a recent Yale graduate who founded the *National Review* in 1955), and the Christian Anti-Communist Crusade continued to claim that domestic communism was a major subversive threat. None did so more than the John Birch Society, which denounced Eisenhower as a conscious agent of the communist conspiracy, and equated liberalism with treason. Its grass-roots network of as many as a hundred thousand activists promoted like-minded political candidates, while waging local struggles against taxes, gun control, and sex education in the schools. Although few saw all the dangers lurking in every shadow that the John Birch Society did, Barry Goldwater, George Wallace, and Ronald Reagan, among others, used its anticommunist, antigovernment rhetoric to advantage. Stressing victory over communism, rather than its containment, the self-proclaimed "new conservatives" (or radical right, as their opponents called them) criticized the "creeping socialism" of Eisenhower, advocated a return to traditional moral standards, and condemned the liberal rulings of the Supreme Court.

Jim Crow in Court Led by a new chief justice, Earl Warren (1953), the Supreme Court incurred conservatives' wrath for defending the rights of persons accused of subversive beliefs. In *Jencks* v. *United States* (1957) the Court held that the accused had the right to inspect government files used by the prosecution. In *Yates* v. *United States* (1957) the justices overturned the convictions of Communist party officials under the Smith Act (see Chapter 26), emphasizing the distinction between unlawful concrete acts and the teaching of revolutionary ideology. *Yates* essentially ended further prosecutions of communists, and right-wing opponents of the decision demanded limitations on the Court's powers and plastered "Impeach Earl Warren" posters on highway billboards.

These condemnations paled beside those of segregationists following *Brown* v. *Board of Education of Topeka* (May 17, 1954). Argued by the NAACP's Thurgood Marshall, *Brown* combined lawsuits from four states and the District of Columbia in which black plaintiffs claimed that segregated public education was unconstitutional. It built on an earlier federal court ruling that had prohibited the segregation of Mexican-American children in California schools, as well as on cases in 1950 in which the Supreme Court had significantly narrowed the possibility of separate education being in fact equal education, and thus constitutional.

Chief Justice Warren, speaking for a unanimous Court, reversed *Plessy* v. *Ferguson* (see Chapter 20). The high court held that separating schoolchildren "solely because of their race generates a feeling of inferiority as to their status in the community that may affect their hearts and minds in a way unlikely ever to be undone," thereby violating the equal protection clause of the Fourteenth Amendment. "In the field of public education," the Court concluded, "the doctrine of 'separate but equal' has no place. Separate educational facilities are inherently unequal." A year later, the Court ordered federal district judges to monitor compliance with *Brown,* requiring only that desegregation proceed "with all deliberate speed"—an oxymoron that implied the necessity for gradualism—the price Warren paid to gain a unanimous decision.

The border states complied, and in such cities as Baltimore, St. Louis, and Washington, D.C., African-American and white students sat side by side for the first time in history. But in the South, where segregation was deeply entrenched in law and social custom, politicians vowed resistance, and Eisenhower refused to press them to comply. "The fellow who tries to tell me that you can do these things by force is just plain nuts," he stated. "I don't believe you can change the hearts of men with laws or decisions." Although not personally a racist, Ike never publicly endorsed the *Brown* decision and privately called his appointment of Earl Warren "the biggest damn fool mistake I ever made."

Public-opinion polls in 1954 indicated that some 80 percent of white southerners opposed the *Brown* decision. Encouraged by the president's silence, white resistance stiffened. White Citizens Councils sprang up, and the Ku Klux Klan revived. Declaring *Brown* "null, void, and of no effect," southern legislatures claimed the right to "interpose" themselves against the federal government and adopted a strategy of "massive resistance" to thwart compliance with the law. They denied state aid to local school systems that desegregated and even closed public schools ordered to desegregate. Most effectively, the states enacted pupil-placement laws that permitted school boards to assign black and white children to different schools.

In 1956 more than a hundred members of Congress signed the Southern Manifesto, denouncing *Brown* as "a clear abuse of judicial power." White southern politicians competed to "outnigger" each other in opposition to desegregation. When a gubernatorial candidate in Alabama promised to go to jail to defend segregation, his opponent swore that he would die for it. Segregationists also resorted to violence and economic reprisals against blacks to maintain all-white schools. At the end of 1956, not a single African-American attended school with whites in the Deep South, and few did so in the Upper South.

The Laws of the Land   Southern resistance reached a climax in September 1957. Although the Little Rock school board had accepted a federal court order to desegregate Central High School, Arkansas Governor Orval E. Faubus mobilized the state's National Guard to bar nine African-American students from entering the school. After another court order

Little Rock, 1957 *Elizabeth Eckford, age fifteen, one of the nine black students to desegregate Central High School, endures abuse on her way to school, September 4, 1957. Forty years later, the young white woman shouting insults asked for forgiveness.*

forced Faubus to withdraw the guardsmen, an angry mob of whites blocked the black students' entry.

Although Eisenhower sought to avoid the divisive issue of civil rights, he believed he had to uphold federal law. He also worried that the Soviets were "gloating over this incident and using it everywhere to misrepresent our whole nation." The Cold War had made segregation in the United States a national security liability. Understanding that racism at home hampered American efforts to gain the support of nonwhite Third World nations, the president federalized the Arkansas National Guard and, for the first time since Reconstruction, dispatched federal troops to protect blacks' rights. To ensure the safety of the black students, soldiers patrolled Central High for the rest of the year. Rather than accept integration, however, Faubus shut down Little Rock's public high schools for two years. At the end of the decade, fewer than 1 percent of African-American students in the Deep South attended desegregated schools.

Nevertheless, Little Rock strengthened the determination of African-Americans for desegregation. The crisis also foreshadowed television's vital role in the demise of Jim Crow. The contrast between the images of howling white racists and those of resolute black students projected on the TV screen immensely aided the civil-rights cause. According to a 1957 public-opinion poll, fully 90 percent of whites outside the South approved the use of federal troops in Little Rock.

Most northern whites also favored legislation to enfranchise southern blacks, and during the 1956 campaign Eisenhower proposed a voting rights bill. The Civil Rights Act of 1957, the first since Reconstruction, established a permanent commission on civil rights with broad investigatory powers, but did little to guarantee the ballot to blacks. The Civil Rights Act of 1960 only slightly strengthened the first measure's enforcement provisions. Neither act empowered federal officials to register African-Americans to vote. Like the *Brown* decision, however, these laws implied a changing view of race relations by the federal government, and that further encouraged blacks to fight for their rights.

THE COLD WAR CONTINUES

Eisenhower continued Truman's containment policy. Stalin's death in 1953 and Eisenhower's resolve to reduce the risk of nuclear war did bring a thaw in the Cold War, but the United States and the U.S.S.R. remained deadlocked. Neither the Cold War nor American determination to check communism ceased. Fears at home and abroad of a nuclear holocaust mounted as both the United States and Soviet Union stockpiled increasingly destructive weapons.

Honoring his campaign pledge, Eisenhower visited Korea in December 1952, but did not bring home a settlement. The fate of thousands of prisoners of war (POWs) who did not want to return to communist rule remained the sticking point. The uncertainty in the communist world after Stalin's death and Eisenhower's veiled threat to use nuclear weapons broke the stalemate. The armistice signed in July 1953 established a panel of representatives from neutral nations to oversee the return of POWs and set the boundary between North and South Korea once again at the thirty-eighth parallel. Some Americans claimed that communist aggression had been thwarted and containment vindicated; others condemned the truce as peace without honor.

Ike and Dulles   Eager to ease Cold War tensions, Eisenhower first sought to quiet the GOP right-wing clamoring to roll back the Red tide. To do so he chose as his secretary of state, John Foster Dulles. A rigid Presbyterian whose humorlessness led some to dub him "Dull, Duller, Dulles," the secretary of state talked of a holy war against "atheistic communism," "liberating" the captive peoples of Eastern Europe, and unleashing Jiang Jieshi against Communist China. Believing that the Soviet Union understood only force, Dulles threatened "instant, massive retaliation" with nuclear weapons in response to Soviet aggression. He insisted on the necessity of "brinksmanship," the art of never backing down in a crisis, even if it meant risking war.

Such saber-rattling pleased the Right, but Eisenhower preferred conciliation. Partly because he feared a nuclear war with the Soviet Union, which had tested its own H-bomb in 1953, Eisenhower refused to translate Dulles's rhetoric into action. Aware of the limits of American power, the United States did nothing to check the Soviet interventions that crushed uprisings in East Germany (1953) and Hungary (1956).

As Hiroshima-size atomic bombs gave way to multimegaton thermonuclear weapons in the American and Soviet arsenals, Eisenhower tried to reduce the probability of mutual annihilation. He proposed an "atoms for peace" plan, whereby both superpowers would contribute fissionable materials to a new U.N. agency for use in industrial projects. In the absence of a positive Soviet response, the government began construction of the Distant Early Warning Line across the Aleutians and arctic Alaska, providing a twenty-four-hour-a-day electronic air defense system that would alert the United States to an invasion by the "over-the-pole" route. The government then built the Cheyenne Mountain Operations Center, a Rocky Mountain fortress where, behind twenty-five-ton blast doors, military crews scanned radar and satellite signals for signs of a Soviet attack.

Work also began on commercial nuclear plants in the mid-1950s, promising electricity "too cheap to meter." However, the lion's share of the money for nuclear research continued to be military-related, like that going to naval captain Hyman Rickover's development of nuclear-powered submarines. Mounting fears over radioactive fallout from atmospheric atomic tests, especially the 1954 U.S. test series in the Pacific that spread strontium 90 over a wide area, heightened world concern about the nuclear-arms race.

In 1955 Eisenhower and the Soviet leaders met in Geneva for the first East-West summit conference since World War II. Mutual talk of "peaceful coexistence" led reporters to hail the "spirit of Geneva." The two nations could not agree on a specific plan for nuclear-arms control, but Moscow suspended further atmospheric tests of nuclear weapons in March 1958, and the United States followed suit.

Still, the Cold War continued. Dulles negotiated mutual-defense pacts with any nation that would join the United States in opposing communism. His "pactomania" committed the United States to the defense of forty-three nations. The administration relied primarily on the U.S. nuclear arsenal to deter the Soviets. Tailored to suit fiscally conservative Republicans, the "New Look" defense program promised "more bang for the buck" by emphasizing nuclear weapons and reducing conventional forces. It spurred the Soviets to seek "more rubble for the ruble" by expanding their nuclear stockpile. In anticipation of nuclear war, Congress built a 112,000-square-foot bunker for itself 700 feet below the grounds of the elegant Greenbrier resort in West Virginia. It featured dormitories, a restaurant, an operating clinic, decontamination showers, and chambers in which the legislators would meet.

Meanwhile, the focus of the Cold War shifted from Europe to the Third World, the largely nonwhite developing nations. There the two superpowers waged war by proxy, using local guerrillas and military juntas to battle in isolated deserts and steamy jungles. There, too, the Central Intelligence Agency (CIA) fought covert wars against those deemed to imperil American interests.

CIA Covert
Actions

To command the CIA, Eisenhower chose Allen Dulles, a veteran of wartime OSS cloak-and-dagger operations and the brother of the secretary of state. Established in 1947 to conduct foreign intelligence gathering, the CIA became increasingly involved in secret operations to topple regimes friendly to communism. By 1957 half its personnel and 80 percent of its budget were devoted to "covert action"—subverting governments, putting foreign leaders (like King Hussein of Jordan) on its payroll, supporting foreign political parties (such as the Liberal Democratic Party of Japan), and subsidizing foreign newspapers and labor unions that hewed to a pro-American line.

To woo influential foreign thinkers away from communism, the CIA also sponsored intellectual conferences and jazz concerts. It bankrolled exhibitions of abstract expressionist paintings to counter Soviet socialist realism art. It purchased the film rights to George Orwell's *Animal Farm* and *1984* to make their messages more overtly anticommunist. It subsidized magazines like *Encounter* to publish articles supporting Washington's foreign policy. College students and businessmen traveling abroad were recruited as "fronts" in clandestine CIA activities.

Led by a grandson of Teddy Roosevelt, the CIA's "Operation Ajax" orchestrated a coup to overthrow the government of Iran in 1953. Fearing that the prime minister who had nationalized oil fields might open oil-rich Iran to the Soviet Union, the CIA replaced him with the pro-American Shah Reza Pahlavi. The United States thus gained a loyal ally on the Soviet border, and American oil companies prospered when the shah made low-priced oil available to them. But the seeds of Iranian hatred of America had been sown—an enmity that would haunt the United States a quarter-century later.

To ensure another pro-American government in 1953, the CIA helped the anticommunist Ramon Magaysay become president of the Philippines. The next year, in "Operation Success," a CIA-trained and financed band of mercenaries overthrew Jacobo Arbenz Guzman's elected government in Guatemala. Strongly influenced by the Guatemalan Communist party, Guzman had nationalized and redistributed tracts of land owned by the United Fruit Company. The new pro-American regime restored United Fruit's lands and trampled all political opposition.

The Vietnam
Domino

The most extensive CIA covert operations during the 1950s took place in Indochina. As a result of Mao Zedong's victory in China and the outbreak of war in Korea, the United States viewed Indochina as a key battleground in the Cold War. The Truman administration had provided France with large-scale military assistance to fight the Vietminh, a broad-based Vietnamese nationalist coalition led by the communist Ho Chi Minh (see Chapter 26). By 1954 American aid accounted for three-quarters of French expenditures. Nevertheless, France tottered near defeat. In early 1954 the Vietminh trapped twelve thousand French troops in the northern valley of Dienbienphu, near the border with Laos.

The Great Debate, July 24, 1959 *At the opening of the American National Exhibit in Moscow, Vice President Richard Nixon and Soviet Premier Nikita Khrushchev engaged in a "kitchen debate," arguing not about the strength of their rockets or bombs but about the relative merits of American and Soviet washing machines and television sets.*

France appealed for U.S. intervention, and some American officials toyed with the idea of launching a ground invasion or nuclear strike. "You boys must be crazy," the president replied. "We can't use those awful things against Asians for the second time in ten years. My God." When the Democratic majority leader, Senator Lyndon Johnson of Texas, opposed "sending American GIs into the mud and muck of Indochina on a blood-letting spree to perpetuate colonialism and white man's exploitation in Asia," Ike refused to commit U.S. troops. In May the French surrendered at Dienbienphu and gave up the effort to retake Vietnam. An international conference in Geneva arranged a cease-fire and temporarily divided Vietnam at the seventeenth parallel, pending elections in 1956 to choose the government of a unified nation.

Although Eisenhower would not take the United States into an Asian land war, he also would not permit a communist takeover of all of Vietnam. In what became known as the "domino theory," Eisenhower warned that if Vietnam fell to the communists, then Thailand, Burma, Indonesia, and ultimately all of Asia would fall like dominos. Accordingly, the United States refused to sign the Geneva Peace Accords, and in late 1954 created the Southeast Asia Treaty Organization (SEATO), a military alliance patterned on NATO.

The CIA installed Ngo Dinh Diem, a fiercely anticommunist Catholic, as premier and then president of an independent South Vietnam. It helped Diem train his armed forces and secret police, eliminate political opposition, and block the 1956 election to reunify Vietnam specified by the Geneva agreement. As Eisenhower admitted, "possibly 80 percent of the population would have voted for the communist Ho Chi Minh as their leader." "Because we know of no one better," said John Foster Dulles, Washington pinned its hopes on Diem, and Vietnam became a test of its ability to defeat communism in Asia with American dollars rather than American lives.

The autocratic Diem, who saw himself as "the mediator between the people and heaven," never rallied public support. His Catholicism alienated the predominantly Buddhist population, and his refusal to institute land reform and to end corruption spurred opposition. In 1957 former Vietminh guerrillas began sporadic antigovernment attacks, and in December 1960 opposition to Diem coalesced in the National Front for the Liberation of Vietnam (NLF). Backed by North Vietnam, the insurgency attracted broad support and soon controlled half of South Vietnam. Although few Americans were aware of what was happening, the administration's commitment to "sink or swim with Ngo Dinh Diem" had cost over $1 billion, and Diem was sinking.

Troubles in the Third World

Eisenhower faced his greatest crisis in the Middle East. In 1954 Gamal Abdel Nasser came to power in Egypt, determined to modernize his nation. To woo him, the United States offered to finance a dam at Aswan to harness the Nile River. When Nasser purchased arms from Czechoslovakia and officially recognized the People's Republic of China, Dulles cancelled the loan. Nasser then nationalized the British-owned Suez Canal.

Viewing the canal as the lifeline of its empire, Britain planned to take it back by force. The British were supported by France, which feared Arab nationalism in their Algerian colony, and by Israel, which feared the Egyptian arms buildup. The three countries, America's closest allies, coordinated an attack on Egypt in October 1956 without consulting Eisenhower. Ike fumed that the military action would drive the Arab world and its precious oil to the Russians. When Moscow threatened to intervene, Eisenhower forced his allies to withdraw their troops.

The Suez crisis had major consequences. It swelled antiwestern sentiment in the Third World; and the United States replaced Britain and France as the protector of western interests in the Middle East. Determined to keep Arab oil flowing to the West, the president announced the Eisenhower Doctrine, a proclamation that the United States would send military aid and, if necessary, troops to any Middle Eastern nation threatened by "Communist aggression." To back up his words, Eisenhower ordered fourteen thousand marines into Lebanon in July 1958 to quell a threatened Muslim revolt against the Christian-dominated, prowestern regime.

Such interventions intensified anti-American feelings in the Third World. Shouting "yanqui imperialism," angry crowds in Peru and Venezuela spat at Vice

President Nixon and stoned his car in 1958. The next year Fidel Castro overturned a dictatorial regime in Cuba, confiscating American properties without compensation. In 1960 anti-American riots forced Eisenhower to cancel his visit to Japan.

An even tougher blow came on May 1, 1960. Two weeks before a scheduled summit conference with Soviet premier Nikita Khrushchev, the Soviets shot down a U.S. spy plane far inside their border. Khrushchev displayed to the world the captured CIA pilot and the photos he had taken of Soviet missile sites. Eisenhower refused to apologize to the Soviet Union. The summit to limit nuclear testing collapsed, and both sides resumed atmospheric tests in 1961.

The Eisenhower Legacy   Just before leaving office, Eisenhower offered Americans a farewell and warning. The demands of national security, he stated, had produced the "conjunction of an immense military establishment and a large arms industry that is new in the American experience." Swollen defense budgets had yoked American economic well-being to military expenditures. Military contracts had become the staff of life for research scholars, politicians, and the nation's largest corporations. This combination of interests, Eisenhower believed, exerted enormous leverage and threatened the traditional subordination of the military in American life. "We must guard against the acquisition of unwarranted influence . . . by the military-industrial complex. The potential for the disastrous rise of misplaced power exists and will persist."

The president concluded that he had avoided war but that lasting peace was not in sight. Most scholars agreed. Eisenhower had ended the Korean War, avoided direct intervention in Vietnam, begun relaxing tensions with the Soviet Union, and suspended atmospheric nuclear testing. He had also presided over an accelerating nuclear-arms race and a widening Cold War, and had given the CIA a green light to intervene in local conflicts around the globe.

The moderate, centrist Eisenhower had pleased neither the Left nor the Right. His acceptance of New Deal social-welfare measures angered conservative Republicans, and liberal Democrats grumbled about his passivity in the face of McCarthyism and racism. Yet Ike had given most Americans what they most wanted—prosperity, reassurance, and a breathing spell in which to relish the comforts of life.

THE AFFLUENT SOCIETY

In 1958 economist John Kenneth Galbraith published *The Affluent Society,* a study of postwar America whose title reflected the broad-based prosperity that made the 1950s seem the fulfillment of the American dream. By the end of the decade, about 60 percent of American families owned homes; 75 percent, cars; and 87 percent, at least one TV. The gross national product (GNP) increased 50 percent in the 1950s as a consequence of heavy government spending, a huge upsurge in productivity, and a steadily increasing demand for consumer goods and services.

Three brief recessions and a rising national debt, almost $290 billion by 1961, evoked concern but did little to halt economic growth or stifle optimism. The United States had achieved the world's highest living standard ever. Historian David Potter labeled Americans a "people of plenty" in 1954; and by 1960 the average worker's income, adjusted for inflation, was 35 percent higher than in 1945. With just 6 percent of the world's population, the United States produced and consumed nearly half of everything made and sold on Earth.

The New Industrial Society   Federal spending constituted a major source of economic growth. It nearly doubled in the 1950s to $180 billion, as did the outlays of state and local governments. Federal expenditures (accounting for 17 percent of the GNP in the mid-1950s, compared to just 1 percent in 1929) built roads and airports, financed home mortgages, supported farm prices, and provided stipends for education. More than half the federal budget—about 10 percent of the GNP—went to defense industries, a development highlighted by Eisenhower's choice of Charles Wilson of General Motors and then Neil McElroy of Procter and Gamble to head the Department of Defense. Continued superpower rivalry in atomic munitions, missile-delivery systems, and the space race kept the federal government the nation's main financier of scientific and technological research and development (R&D).

For the West, especially, it was as if World War II never ended, as the new Air Force Academy in Colorado Springs signified. Politicians from both parties labored to keep defense spending flowing westward. Liberal and conservative members of Congress from California sought contracts for Lockheed. So did those from Texas for General Dynamics and those from Washington State for Boeing. In the late 1950s California alone received half the space budget and a quarter of all major military contracts. By then, as well, Denver had the largest number of federal employees outside Washington, D.C.; Albuquerque boasted more Ph.D. degrees per capita than any other U.S. city; and over a third of those employed in Los Angeles depended on defense industries. The Mormon dream of an agricultural utopia gave way to a Utah that led the nation in receiving expenditures per capita on space and defense research. Government spending transformed the mythic West of individualistic cowboys, miners, and farmers into a West of bureaucrats, manufacturers, and scientists dependent on federal funds.

Science became a ward of the state, with government funding and control transforming both the U.S. military and industry. Financed by the Atomic Energy Commission (AEC) and utilizing navy scientists, the Duquesne Light Company began construction in Shippingport, Pennsylvania, of the nation's first nuclear-power plant in 1954. Chemicals surged from the fiftieth-largest industry before the war to the nation's fourth-largest in the 1960s. As chemical fertilizers and pesticides contaminated groundwater supplies, and as the use of plastics for consumer products reduced landfill space, Americans—unaware of the hidden perils—marveled at fruits and vegetables covered with Saran Wrap and delighted in their Dacron suits, Orlon shirts, Acrilan socks, and Teflon-coated pots and pans.

Electronics became the fifth-largest American industry, providing industrial equipment and consumer appliances. Electricity consumption tripled in the 1950s as industry automated and consumers, "to live better electrically," as commercials urged, purchased electric washers and dryers, freezers, blenders, television sets, and stereos. Essential to the expansion of both the chemical and the electronics industries was inexpensive petroleum. With domestic crude-oil production increasing close to 50 percent and petroleum imports rising from 74 million to 371 million barrels between 1945 and 1960, oil replaced coal as the nation's main energy source. Hardly anyone paid attention when a physicist warned in 1953 that "adding 6 billion tons of carbon dioxide to the atmosphere each year is warming up the Earth."

Plentiful, cheap gasoline fed the growth of the automobile and aircraft industries. The nation's third-largest industry in the 1950s, aerospace depended heavily on defense spending and on federally funded research. In Washington State, the manufacturers of jet aircraft, ballistic missiles, and space equipment employed more people than did logging and timbering firms. The four metropolitan areas of Seattle, Dallas–Fort Worth, San Diego, and Los Angeles accounted for nearly all of the nation's aircraft production. The automobile industry, still the titan of the American economy, also utilized technological R&D. Where it had once partially replaced human labor with machinery, it now used automation to control the machines. Between 1945 and 1960 the industry halved the number of hours and of workers required to produce a car. Other manufacturers followed suit, investing $10 billion a year throughout the fifties on labor-saving machinery.

The Age of Computers

The computer was a major key to the technological revolution. In 1944 International Business Machines (IBM), cooperating with Harvard scientists, had produced the Mark I calculator to decipher secret Axis codes. It was a slow, cumbersome device of five hundred miles of wiring and three thousand electromechanical relays. Two years later, to improve artillery accuracy, the U.S. army developed ENIAC, the first electronic computer. Still unwieldy, and having to be "debugged" of the insects attracted to its heat and light (giving rise to the term still used for solving computer glitches), ENIAC reduced the time required to multiply two tenth-place numbers from Mark I's three seconds to less than three-thousandths of a second. Then came the development of operating instructions, or programs, that could be stored inside the computer's memory; the substitution of printed circuits for wired ones; and in 1948, at Bell Labs, the invention of tiny solid-state transistors that ended reliance on radio tubes.

The computer changed the American economy and society as fundamentally as the steam engine in the First Industrial Revolution and the electric motor and internal combustion engine in the Second. Sales of electronic computers to industry rose from twenty in 1954 to more than a thousand in 1957 and more than two thousand in 1960. Major manufacturers used them to monitor production lines, track inventory, and ensure quality control. The government, which used three machines in computing the 1950 census returns, employed several hundred on the 1960 census. They became as indispensable to Pentagon strategists playing war games as to the Internal Revenue Service, as integral to meteorologists as to scientists "flying" rockets on the drawing board. By the mid-1960s more than thirty thousand mainframe computers were used by banks, hospitals, and universities. Further developments led to the first integrated circuits and to what would ultimately become the Internet, fundamentally changing the nature of work as well as its landscape.

The development of the high-technology complex known as Silicon Valley began with the opening of the Stanford Industrial Park in 1951. Seeking to develop its landholdings around Palo Alto and to attract financial aid from business and the military, Stanford University utilized its science and engineering faculties to design and produce products for the Fairchild Semiconductor and Hewlett-Packard companies. This relationship became a model followed by other high-tech firms. Soon apricot and cherry orchards throughout the Santa Clara valley gave way to industrial parks filled with computer firms and pharmaceutical laboratories. Initially a far cry from dirty eastern factories, these campus-like facilities would eventually choke the valley with traffic congestion, housing developments, and smog. Similar developments would follow the military-fueled research complexes along Boston's Route 128, near Austin, Texas, and in North Carolina's Research Triangle.

The Costs of Bigness

Rapid technological advances accelerated the growth and power of big business. In 1950 twenty-two U.S. firms had assets of more than $1 billion; ten years later more than fifty did. By 1960 one-half of 1 percent of all companies earned more than half the total corporate income in the United States. The wealthiest, which could afford huge R&D outlays, became oligopolies, swallowing up weak competitors. Three television networks monopolized the nation's airwaves; three automobile and three aluminum companies produced more than 90 percent of America's cars and aluminum; and a handful of firms controlled the lion's share of assets and sales in steel, petroleum, chemicals, and electrical machinery. Corporations also acquired overseas facilities to become "multinational" enterprises, and formed "conglomerates" by merging companies in unrelated industries: International Telephone and Telegraph (ITT) owned hotel chains, insurance businesses, and car-rental companies. Despite talk of "people's capitalism," the oil-rich Rockefeller family alone owned more corporate stock than all the nation's wage earners combined.

Growth and consolidation brought further bureaucratization. "Executives" replaced "capitalists." Rewarded in their own careers for "fitting in" rather than sticking out, they knew not to rock the corporate boat. Success required conformity not creativity, teamwork not individuality. According to sociologist David Riesman's *The Lonely Crowd* (1950), the new "company people" were "other directed," eager to follow the cues from their peers and not think innovatively or act independently. In the old nursery rhyme "This Little Pig Went to Market," Riesman noted, each pig went his own way. "Today, however, all little pigs go to market; none stay home; all have roast beef, if any do; and all say 'we-we.' "

Changes in American agriculture paralleled those in industry. Farming grew increasingly scientific and mechanized. Technology cut the work hours necessary to grow crops by half between 1945 and 1960. In 1956 alone, one-eleventh of the farm population left the land. Meanwhile, well-capitalized farm businesses, running "factories in the field," prospered by using more and more machines and chemicals.

Until the publication of Rachel Carson's *Silent Spring* in 1962, few Americans understood the extent to which fertilizers, herbicides, and pesticides poisoned the environment. Carson, a former researcher for the Fish and Wildlife Service, dramatized the problems caused by the use of the insecticide DDT and its spread through the food chain. Her depiction of a "silent spring" caused by the death of songbirds from DDT toxicity led many states to ban its use. The federal government followed suit. But the incentives for cultivating more land, and more marginal land, led to further ravages. The Army Corps of Engineers and the Bureau of Reclamation dammed the waters of the West, turning the Columbia and Missouri Rivers into rows of slack-water reservoirs, killing fish and wildlife as well as immersing hundreds of square miles of Indian tribal lands.

Rachel Carson *The mother of modern ecology, Carson exposed the dangers of pesticides to animal and human life in her 1962 bestseller* Silent Spring, *an enormously influential work that helped redefine the way humans look at their place in nature.*

Blue-Collar Blues Consolidation also transformed the labor movement. In 1955 the merger of the AFL and CIO brought 85 percent of union members into a single federation. AFL-CIO leadership promised aggressive unionism, but organized labor fell victim to its own success. The benefits earned at the bargaining table bred complacency. Higher wages, shorter workweeks, paid vacations, health-care coverage, and automatic wage hikes tied to the cost of living led union leaders to view themselves as middle class rather than as a militant proletariat. The 1950s saw far fewer strikes than the 1930s.

A decrease in the number of blue-collar workers further sapped organized labor. Automation reduced membership in the once-mighty coal, auto, and steelworkers' unions by more than half. Most of the new jobs in the 1950s were in the service sector and in public employment, which banned collective bargaining by labor unions.

In 1956, for the first time in U.S. history, white-collar workers outnumbered blue-collar workers, leading some to believe that the United States had become a "postindustrial" society. This notion minimized the fact that more service jobs involved manual labor than intellect. Most office work was as routinized as any factory job. Yet few unions sought to woo white-collar workers. The percentage of the unionized labor force dropped from a high of 36 percent in 1953 to 31 percent in 1960.

Prosperity and the Suburbs As real income (adjusted for inflation) rose, Americans spent a smaller percentage of their income on necessities and more on powered lawnmowers and air conditioners. After the deprivations of the 1930s and the scarcities of the war years, they heaped their shopping carts with frozen, dehydrated, and fortified foods. When they lacked cash, they signed installment contracts at the appliance store and charged the new furniture on department-store credit cards. In 1950 Diner's Club issued the first credit card; American Express followed in 1958. Installment buying, home mortgages, and auto loans tripled Americans' total private indebtedness in the 1950s. Advertising expenditures also tripled. Business spent more on advertising each year than the nation spent on public education. Virtually everywhere one looked, advertisements appealed to people's desire for status and glamor to convince them to buy what they did not need.

Responding to the slogan "You auto buy now," Americans purchased 58 million new cars during the 1950s. Manufacturers enticed people to trade up by offering flashier models. One could now purchase two-tone colors, extra-powerful engines—like Pontiac's 1955 "Sensational Strato-Streak V-8," which could propel riders more than twice as fast as any speed limit—and tail fins inspired by the silhouette of the Lockheed P-38 fighter plane. Seat belts remained an unadvertised extra-cost option. The consequences were increases in highway deaths, air pollution, oil consumption, and "autosclerosis"—clogged urban arteries.

Government policy as well as "auto mania" spurred white Americans' exodus to the suburbs. Federal spending on highways skyrocketed from $79 million in

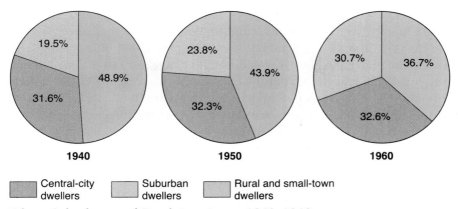

Central-city dwellers

Suburban dwellers

Rural and small-town dwellers

Urban, Suburban, and Rural Americans, 1940–1960

In the fifteen years following World War II, more than 40 million Americans migrated to the suburbs, where, as one father put it, "a kid could grow up with grass stains on his pants." Over the same period, fourteen of the fifteen largest U.S. cities lost population.

Source: Adapted from U.S. Bureau of the Census, *Current Censuses,* 1930–1970 (Washington, D.C.: U.S. Government Printing Office).

1946 to $2.6 billion in 1960, putting once-remote areas within "commuting distance" for city workers (see Technology and Culture: The Interstate Highway System). The income tax code stimulated home sales by allowing deductions for home-mortgage interest payments and for property taxes. Both the Federal Housing Administration (FHA) and Veterans Administration (VA) offered low-interest loans; and neither promoted housing desegregation, despite the Supreme Court's 1948 ruling that state courts could not enforce restrictive covenants (see Chapter 23). In 1960 suburbia was 98 percent white.

Eighty-five percent of the 13 million new homes built in the 1950s were in the suburbs. While social critics lampooned the "ticky-tacky" houses in "disturbia," many families considered them the embodiment of the American Dream. They longed for single-family homes of their own, good schools, a safe environment for the children, fresh air, and friendly neighbors just like themselves.

Park Forest, Illinois, was carefully planned to be a "complete community for middle-income families with children." While wives stayed home to raise the kids and shop at the Plaza, husbands commuted the thirty miles to Chicago on the Illinois Central Railroad or drove into the city on Western Avenue. On Long Island, some thirty miles from midtown Manhattan, Alfred and William Levitt used the mass-production construction techniques they perfected building housing for wartime navy workers in Norfolk, Virginia, to construct thousands of standardized 720-square-foot houses as quickly as possible. All looked alike. Deeds to the property required door chimes, not buzzers, prohibited picket fences, mandated regular lawn mowing, and even specified when the wash could be hung to dry in the backyard. All the town streets curved at the same angle. A tree was planted every twenty-eight feet. The Levitts then built a second, larger Levittown in Bucks County, Pennsylvania, and a third in Willingboro, New Jersey.

In the greatest internal migration in its history, some 20 million Americans moved to the suburbs in the 1950s—doubling the numbers and making the suburban population equal to that of the central cities. Contractors built 2 million new homes a year, 85 percent of them in the suburbs. By 1960 over 60 percent of American families owned their homes—the symbol of the affluent society.

Many former servicemen who had first glimpsed the Sunbelt in military camps returned to take up residence, as did others lured by job opportunities, the climate, and the pace of life. California's population went from 9 to 19 million between 1945 and 1964, supplanting New York as the most populous state. Los Angeles epitomized the enormous expansion of the suburbs as well as the rapid growth of the Sunbelt. It boasted the highest per capita ownership of private homes and automobiles of any city, as well as 250 miles of freeways by 1960. Bulldozers ripped out three thousand acres of orange groves a day in Los Angeles County to make way for new housing developments. Orange County, bordering Los Angeles, doubled its population in the 1940s and then tripled it in the 1950s.

Industry also headed South and West. Drawn by low taxes, low energy costs, and anti-union right-to-work laws, industrialists transferred their conservative politics along with their plants and corporate headquarters. Senior citizens, attracted to places like Sun City, Arizona, "a complete community geared to older Americans," brought a more conservative outlook to the Sunbelt as well. By 1980 the population of the Sunbelt, which stretched from the Old Confederacy across Texas to southern California, exceeded that of the North and East. The political power of the Republican party rose accordingly.

CONSENSUS AND CONSERVATISM

Not everyone embraced the conformity of 1950s consumer culture. Intellectuals found a wide audience for their attack on "an America of mass housing, mass markets, massive corporations, massive government, mass media, and massive boredom." These critics targeted "organization men" bent on getting ahead by going along and "status seekers" pursuing external rewards to compensate for inner insecurities. Others took aim at the consumerist middle class: "all items in a national supermarket—categorized, processed, labeled, priced, and readied for merchandising."

This social criticism oversimplified reality. It ignored ethnic and class diversity. It overlooked the acquisitiveness and conformity of earlier generations—the peer-group pressures in small-town America. It failed to gauge the currents of dissent swirling beneath the surface. It caricatured rather than characterized American society. But the critique rightly spotlighted the elevation of comfort over challenge, and of private pleasures over public affairs. It was, in the main, a time of political passivity and preoccupation with personal gain. Americans, indeed, sought refuge in "the good life." Voices of protest were muted, and a large majority shared aspirations and agreed on values, rejecting radicalism at home and opposing the spread of communism abroad.

Togetherness and the Baby Boom In 1954 *McCall's* magazine coined the term "togetherness" to celebrate the "ideal" couple: the man and woman who married young and centered their lives around home and children. Americans in the 1950s wed at an earlier age than had their parents (one woman in three married by age nineteen). Confident in continued economic prosperity and influenced by the popular culture, they had more babies sooner. The fertility rate (the number of births per thousand women), 80 in 1940, peaked at 123 in 1957, when an American baby was born every seven seconds.

New antibiotics subdued such diseases as diphtheria and whooping cough, and the Salk and Sabin vaccines ended the dread of poliomyelitis (polio). Prior to the April 1955 announcement by Dr. Jonas Salk of an effective vaccine, fear of a child being paralyzed or killed by polio haunted American families. Most knew of a stricken child wearing metal leg braces or confined to an iron lung. Millions contributed to the March of Dimes to fund research; and the number of American children afflicted dropped from fifty-eight thousand in 1952 to fifty-seven hundred in 1958. The decline in childhood mortality helped raise American life expectancy from 65.9 years in 1945 to 70.9 years in 1970. Coupled with the "baby boom," it brought a 19 percent increase in the U.S. population during the 1950s— a larger jump than in any previous decade. By 1960 children under fourteen made up one-third of the population.

The immense size of the baby-boom generation (the 76 million Americans born between 1946 and 1964) guaranteed its historical importance. Its movement through each stage of life would be as contorting as the digestion of a pig by a boa constrictor. First came the bulge in baby carriages in the late 1940s. In the 1950s school construction boomed, as did college enrollments in the 1960s. Then in the 1970s—as the baby boomers had families—home construction and sales peaked. The 1980s and 1990s brought a surge in retirement investments that sent the stock market soaring. In the 1950s the baby boom also made child rearing a huge concern, reinforcing the idea that women's place was in the home. With Americans convinced of the psychological importance of early childhood experiences, motherhood became an increasingly vital, time-consuming calling.

No one did more to emphasize children's need for the love and care of full-time mothers than Dr. Benjamin Spock. Only the Bible outsold his *Common Sense Book of Baby and Child Care* (1946) in the 1950s. Spock urged mothers not to work outside the home, in order to create the atmosphere of warmth and intimacy necessary for their children to mature into well-adjusted adults. Crying babies were to be comforted so that they would not feel rejected. Breast-feeding came back into vogue. Spock's advice also led to less scolding and spanking and to more "democratic" family discussions. In some homes his "permissive" approach produced a "filiarchy" in which kids ruled the roost; in many it unduly burdened mothers.

Domesticity   Popular culture in the 1950s glorified marriage and par-
                   enthood more than ever before. Bolstered by "experts,"
often cloaked in psychological garb, and drawing support from such developments
as prosperity, suburban growth, and the baby boom, domesticity emphasized
women's role as a helpmate to her husband and a full-time mother to her children.
Smiling movie stars like Doris Day showed how to win a man, the assumed goal of
every woman; and as actress Debbie Reynolds declared in *The Tender Trap* (1955),
"A woman isn't a woman until she's been married and had children."

Television invariably pictured women as at-home mothers. Women's magazines featured articles with titles like "Cooking to Me Is Poetry." While *Esquire*
magazine called working wives a "menace," *Life* lauded Marjorie Sutton for marrying at sixteen, cooking and sewing for the family, raising four children, being a
pillar of the PTA and Campfire Girls, and working out on a trampoline "to keep
her size 12 figure." Millions of teenage girls swooned when Paul Anka sang "You're
Having My Baby" and read *Seventeen* magazine's advice to them in 1957:

> In dealing with a male, the art of saving face is essential. Traditionally he is the
> head of the family, the dominant partner, the man in the situation. Even on
> those occasions when you both know his decision is wrong, more often than
> not you will be wise to go along with his decision.

According to a Gallup public-opinion poll in 1962, 96 percent of the women
surveyed declared themselves extremely, or very, happy. "Being subordinate to
men is part of being feminine," an Arizona mother told the pollster. "Women who
ask for equality fight nature," added one from New Jersey.

Education reinforced these notions. While girls learned typing and cooking,
boys were channeled into carpentry and courses leading to professional careers.
Guidance counselors cautioned young women not to "miss the boat" of marriage
by pursuing higher education. "Men are not interested in college degrees but in the
warmth and humanness of the girls they marry," stressed a textbook on the family. While a higher percentage of women than men graduated from high school in
the 1950s, more men than women went to college. Almost two-thirds of college
women failed to complete a degree. They dropped out, people joked, to get their
M.R.S. degree and a Ph.T.—"Putting Hubbie Through." The laughter sometimes
hid dissatisfaction: cooking the perfect dinner could still leave a woman starved for
fulfillment in her own life.

From 1947 on, despite domesticity's holding sway, increasing numbers of
women entered the work force. By 1952, 2 million more women worked outside
the home than had during the war; and by 1960, twice as many did as in 1940. In
1960 one-third of the labor force was female, and one out of three married women
worked outside the home. Of all women workers that year, 60 percent were married, while 40 percent had school-age children.

Forced back into low-paying, gender-segregated jobs, most women worked to
add to the family income, not to fulfill personal aspirations or challenge stereotypes. White women mostly filled clerical positions, while African-Americans held

service jobs in private households and restaurants. Some, as during World War II, developed a heightened sense of expectations and empowerment as a result of employment. Transmitted to their daughters, their experience would lead to a feminist resurgence in the late 1960s.

Religion and Education

"Today in the U.S.," *Time* claimed in 1954, "the Christian faith is back in the center of things." Domestic anxieties and Cold War fears catalyzed a surge of religious activity. Evangelist Billy Graham, Roman Catholic Bishop Fulton J. Sheen, and Protestant minister Norman Vincent Peale all had syndicated newspaper columns, best-selling books, and radio and television programs. None was more influential than Graham. Backed to the hilt by the Hearst press and Luce publications, Graham peddled a potent mixture of religious salvation and aggressive anticommunism. In what he pictured as a duel to the death against the atheistic Kremlin, Graham supported McCarthyism and backed GOP demands to "unleash" Jiang's troops against mainland China. He termed communism "a great sinister anti-Christian movement masterminded by Satan" and echoed Billy Sunday's emphasis on the traditional morality of the nineteenth-century American village, lashing out at homosexuals and working wives.

The turn to religion found expression in Hollywood religious extravaganzas, such as *Ben Hur* and *The Ten Commandments,* and in popular songs like "I Believe" and "The Man Upstairs." Sales of Bibles reached an all-time high. Television proclaimed that "the family that prays together stays together." Dial-a-Prayer offered telephone solutions for spiritual problems. Congress added "under God" to the Pledge of Allegiance and required "IN GOD WE TRUST" to be put on all U.S. currency.

"Everybody should have a religious faith," President Eisenhower declared, "and I don't care what it is." Most Americans agreed. Church attendance swelled, and the percentage of people who said they belonged to a church or synagogue increased from 49 percent in 1940 to 55 percent in 1950, and to a record-high 69 percent in 1959. It had become "un-American to be unreligious" noted *The Christian Century* in 1954. Professions of faith became a way to affirm "the American way of life" and to relieve anxieties.

While increasing numbers of Americans identified with some denomination, the intensity of religious faith diminished for many. Religious belief was intermixed with patriotism, family togetherness, and Thursday night bingo. Mainstream Protestant churches downplayed sin and evil and emphasized fellowship, offering a sense of belonging in a rapidly changing society. Many Jews spurned the orthodoxy of their parents for the easier-to-follow practices of Reform or Conservative Judaism. Catholicism broadened its appeal as a new pope, John XXIII, charmed the world with ecumenical reforms.

Similarly, education flourished in the 1950s yet seemed shallower than in earlier decades. Swelled by the baby boom, primary school enrollment rose by 10 million in the 1950s (compared with 1 million in the 1940s). California opened a new school every week throughout the decade and still faced a classroom shortage.

The proportion of college-age Americans in higher education climbed from 15 percent in 1940 to more than 40 percent by the early 1960s. "Progressive" educators promoted sociability and self-expression over science, math, and history. The "well-rounded" student became more prized than one who was highly skilled or knowledgeable. Surveys of college students found them conservative, conformist, and careerist, a "silent generation" seeking security above all.

While administrators ran universities like businesses, faculty focused on the cultural and psychological aspects of American society. Few challenged the economic structure or ideology of the United States, or addressed the problems of minorities and the poor. Many historians downplayed past class conflicts. Instead, they highlighted the pragmatic ideas and values shared by most Americans, differentiating the American experience from that of Europe. It became commonplace to assert that America's unique national character had been shaped primarily by economic abundance.

The Culture of the Fifties   American culture reflected the expansive spirit of prosperity as well as Cold War anxieties. With increasing leisure and fatter paychecks, Americans spent one-seventh of the 1950s GNP on entertainment. Yellowstone National Park lured four times as many people through its gates each summer as lived in Wyoming; Glacier National Park attracted more visitors than lived in Montana. Spectator sports boomed; new symphony halls opened; and book sales doubled.

With the opening of a major exhibit of abstract expressionists by the Museum of Modern Art in 1951, New York replaced Paris as the capital of the art world. Like the immense canvases of Jackson Pollock and the cool jazz of trumpeter Miles Davis, introspection and improvisation characterized the major novels of the era. Their personal yearnings sharply contrasted with the political engagement and social realism of literature in the 1930s. Novels such as John Cheever's *The Wapshot Chronicles* (1957) and John Updike's *Rabbit Run* (1960) presented characters dissatisfied with jobs and home, longing for a more vital and authentic existence, yet incapable of decisive action.

Southern, African-American, and Jewish-American writers turned out the decade's most vital fiction. William Faulkner continued his dense saga of Yoknapatawpha County, Mississippi, in *The Town* (1957) and *The Mansion* (1960), while Eudora Welty evoked southern small-town life in *The Ponder Heart* (1954). The black experience found memorable expression in James Baldwin's *Go Tell It on the Mountain* (1953) and Ralph Ellison's *Invisible Man* (1951). Bernard Malamud's *The Assistant* (1957) explored the Jewish immigrant world of New York's Lower East Side, and Philip Roth's *Goodbye Columbus* (1959) dissected the very different world of upwardly mobile Jews.

The many westerns, musicals, and costume spectacles churned out by Hollywood further reflected the diminished interest in political issues. Most films about contemporary life portrayed Americans as one happy white, middle-class family. Minorities and the poor remained invisible, and the independent career women of films of the 1940s were replaced by "dumb blondes" and cute help-mates. Movie attendance dropped 50 percent as TV viewing soared, and a fifth of the nation's theaters became bowling alleys and supermarkets by 1960. Hollywood tried to recoup by developing three-dimensionality and wide-screen processes that accentuated the difference from television's small black-and-white image. No technological wizardry, however—not even Smell-O-Vision and its rival Aroma-Rama—could stem TV's astounding growth.

The Message
of the Medium
No cultural medium ever became as popular and as powerful as quickly, or so reinforced the public mood, as television. Ownership of a TV set soared from one of every eighteen thousand households in 1946 to nine of ten American homes by 1960. By then, more Americans had televisions than had bathrooms.

Business capitalized on the phenomenon. The three main radio networks—ABC, CBS, and NBC—gobbled up virtually every TV station in the country, and, just as in radio, they profited by selling time to advertisers who wanted to reach the largest possible audiences. By the mid-fifties, the three networks each had larger advertising revenues than any other communications medium in the world. Whereas advertisers had spent some $50 million on TV in 1949, they would be spending more than $1.5 billion a decade later.

Introduced in 1952, *TV Guide* outsold every other periodical and was being published in fifty-three separate regional editions by 1960. The TV dinner, first

The Television Revolution, 1950–1994

As televisions became commonplace in the 1950s, TV viewing altered the nature of American culture and politics.

Source: Statistical Abstracts of the United States.

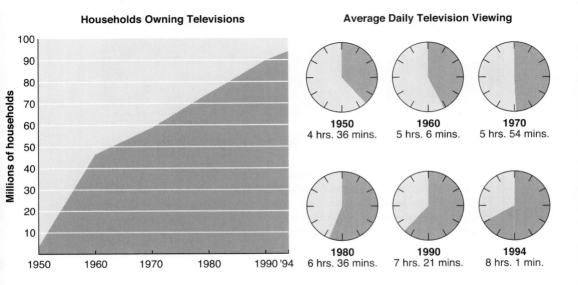

Households Owning Televisions

Millions of households

1950 1960 1970 1980 1990 '94

Average Daily Television Viewing

1950
4 hrs. 36 mins.

1960
5 hrs. 6 mins.

1970
5 hrs. 54 mins.

1980
6 hrs. 36 mins.

1990
7 hrs. 21 mins.

1994
8 hrs. 1 min.

marketed in 1954, altered the nation's eating habits. Television, it seemed, could sell almost anything. When Walt Disney produced a show on Davy Crockett in 1955, stores could not keep up with the massive demand for "King of the Wild Frontier" coonskin caps. Television quickly became the vital center of the consumer culture. Corporations spent fortunes on TV ads creating needs and wants for the consumer. "The message of the media," a critic noted, "is the commercial."

The TV Culture Geared to its initial small audiences, TV showcased talent and creativity. Opera performances appeared in prime time, as did sophisticated comedies and political dramas, and documentaries like Edward R. Murrow's *See It Now*. Early situation comedies such as *The Life of Riley* and *The Goldbergs* featured ethnic working-class families. As the price of TV sets came down and program producers felt the chill of McCarthyism, the networks' appetite for a mass audience transformed TV into a cautious celebration of conformity and consumerism. Controversy went off the air, and conflict disappeared from the screen. Only a few situation comedies, like Jackie Gleason's *The Honeymooners,* set in Brooklyn, did not feature suburban, consumer-oriented, upper-middle-class families. Most, like *Leave It to Beaver* and *The Adventures of Ozzie and Harriet,* portrayed perfectly coiffed moms who loved to vacuum in high

Model 17K7—Big 17 in. screen...Mahogany or Limed Oak Cabinet

TV adds so much to family happiness

Motorola TV and Family Happiness *The television set, so grandly advertised and displayed, itself was a symbol of postwar affluence, and both advertising and programming, which featured largely middle-class, consumption-oriented suburban families, stimulated the consumer culture. Overall, TV powerfully reinforced the conservative, celebratory values of everyday American life in the 1950s.*

heels, frisky yet ultimately obedient kids, and all-knowing dads who never lost their tempers. Even Lucille Ball and Desi Arnaz in *I Love Lucy*—which no network initially wanted because an all-American redhead was married to a Cuban—had a baby and left New York for suburbia.

Decrying TV's mediocrity in 1961, the head of the Federal Communications Commission dared broadcasters to watch their own shows for a day: "I can assure you that you will observe a vast wasteland." A steady parade of soaps, unsophisticated comedies, and violent westerns led others to call TV the "idiot box."

Measuring television's impact is difficult. Depending on the many factors that differentiate individuals, people read the "texts" of TV (or of movies or books) their own way and so receive their own messages or signals from the media. While TV bound some to the status quo, it brought others glimpses of unaccustomed possibilities that raised expectations. It functioned simultaneously as conservator and spur to change. In the main, television reflected existing values and institutions. It stimulated the desire to be included in American society, not to transform it. It spawned mass fads for Barbie dolls and hula hoops, spread the message of consumerism, and made Americans ever more name-brand conscious. It reinforced gender and racial stereotypes. TV rarely showed African-Americans and Latinos—except in servile roles or prison scenes. It extolled male violence in fighting evil; and it portrayed women as either zany madcaps (*My Friend Irma*) or self-effacing moms (*The Donna Reed Show*). It virtually ended network radio, returning local stations to a music-based format, especially "Top-40" programs geared to youth. While promoting professional baseball and football into truly national phenomena, TV decreased the audience of motion picture theaters and of general interest magazines such as *Look* and *Life*.

Television also changed the political life of the nation. Politicians could effectively appeal to the voters over the heads of party leaders, and appearance mattered more than content. Millions watched Senator Estes Kefauver grill mobsters about their ties to city governments, instantly transforming the Tennessean into a serious contender for the presidency. At least 20 million observed the combative Senator Joseph McCarthy bully and slander witnesses during the hearings on disloyalty in the army. The 58 million who witnessed Richard Nixon's appeal for support in the "Checkers" speech helped save his place on the GOP ticket. And Eisenhower's pioneering use of brief "spot advertisements" combined with Stevenson's avoidance of televised appearances clinched Ike's smashing presidential victories. In 1960 John F. Kennedy's "telegenic" image would play a significant role in his winning the presidency.

Television vastly increased the cost of political campaigning while decreasing the content level of political discussion. It helped produce a more-national culture, diminishing provincialism and regional differences. Its overwhelming portrayal of a contented citizenry reinforced complacency and hid the reality of "the other America."

THE OTHER AMERICA

"I am an invisible man," declared the African-American narrator of Ralph Ellison's *Invisible Man;* "I am invisible, understand, simply because people refuse to see me." Indeed, few middle-class white Americans perceived the extent of social injustice in the United States. "White flight" from cities to suburbs produced physical separation of the races and classes. New expressways walled off ghettos and rural poverty from middle-class motorists speeding by. Popular culture focused on affluent Americans enjoying the "good life." In the consensus of the Eisenhower era, deprivation had supposedly disappeared. In reality, poverty and racial discrimination were rife and dire, and the struggles for social justice intensified.

Poverty and Urban Blight Although the percentage of poor families (defined as a family of four with a yearly income of less than three thousand dollars) declined from 34 percent in 1947 to 22 percent in 1960, 35 million Americans remained below the "poverty line." Eight million senior citizens existed on annual incomes below one thousand dollars. A third of the poor lived in depressed rural areas, where 2 million migrant farm workers experienced the most abject poverty. Observing a Texas migratory-labor camp in 1955, a journalist reported that 96 percent of the children had consumed no milk in the previous six months; eight out of ten adults had eaten no meat; and most slept "on the ground, in a cave, under a tree, or in a chicken house." In California's Imperial Valley, the infant death rate among migrant workers was more than seven times the statewide average.

The bulk of the poor huddled in decaying inner-city slums. Displaced southern blacks and Appalachian whites, Native Americans forced off reservations, and newly arrived Hispanics strained cities' inadequate facilities. Nearly two hundred thousand Mexican-Americans were herded into San Antonio's Westside barrio. A local newspaper described them as living like cattle in a stockyard, "with roofed-over corrals for homes and chutes for streets." A visitor to New York City's slums in 1950 found "25 human beings living in a dark and airless coal cellar ten feet below the street level. . . . No animal could live there long, yet here were 17 children, the youngest having been born here two weeks before." The " 'promised land' that Mammy had been singing about in the cotton fields for many years," observed Claude Brown, had become a slum, "a dirty, stinky, uncared-for closet-size section of a great city."

As described by Michael Harrington in *The Other America: Poverty in the United States* (1962), the poor were trapped in a vicious cycle of want and a culture of deprivation. Because they could not afford good housing, a nutritious diet, and doctors, the poor got sick more often and for longer than more affluent Americans. Losing wages and finding it hard to hold steady jobs, they could not pay for decent housing, good food, or doctors—that would keep them from getting and staying sick. The children of the poor started school disadvantaged, quickly fell behind, and, lacking encouragement and expectation of success, dropped out. Living with neither hope nor the necessary skills to enter the mainstream of American life, the poor bequeathed a similar legacy to their children.

The pressing need for low-cost housing went unanswered. In 1955 fewer than 200,000 of the 810,000 public-housing units called for in the Housing Act of 1949 had been built. A decade later only 320,000 had been constructed. "Slum clearance" generally meant "Negro clearance," and "urban renewal" meant "poor removal," as developers razed low-income neighborhoods to put up parking garages and expensive housing. The Los Angeles barrio of Chavez Ravine was bulldozed to construct Dodger Stadium.

At the same time, landlords, realtors, and bankers deliberately excluded nonwhites from decent housing. Half of the housing in New York's Harlem predated 1900. A dozen people might share a tiny apartment with broken windows, faulty plumbing, and gaping holes in the walls. Harlem's rates of illegitimate births, infant deaths, narcotics use, and crime soared above the averages for the city and the nation. "Where flies and maggots breed, where the plumbing is stopped up and not repaired, where rats bite helpless infants," black social psychologist Kenneth Clark observed, "the conditions of life are brutal and inhuman."

Blacks' Struggle for Justice   The collision between the hopes raised by the 1954 *Brown* decision and the indignities of persistent discrimination and segregation sparked a new phase in the civil-rights movement. To sweep away the separate but rarely equal Jim Crow facilities in the South, African-Americans turned to new tactics, organizations, and leaders. They utilized nonviolent direct-action protest to engage large numbers of blacks in their own freedom struggle and to arouse white America's conscience.

In the 1950s racism still touched even the smallest details of daily life. In Montgomery, Alabama, black bus riders had to surrender their seats so that no white rider would stand. Although they were more than three-quarters of all passengers, the African-Americans had to pay their fares at the front of the bus, leave, and reenter through the back door, sit only in the rear, and then give up their seats to any standing white passengers.

On December 1, 1955, Rosa Parks refused to get up so that a white man could sit. Parks, an officer of the Montgomery NAACP who would not drink from fountains labeled "Colored Only" and who climbed stairs rather than use a segregated elevator, was arrested. Montgomery's black leaders organized a boycott of the buses to protest. "There comes a time when people get tired," declared Martin Luther King, Jr., a twenty-seven-year-old African-American minister who articulated the anger of Montgomery blacks, "tired of being segregated and humiliated; tired of being kicked about by the brutal feet of oppression." The time had come, King continued, to cease being patient "with anything less than freedom and justice." This speech marked the beginning of what would become a year-long bus boycott by fifty thousand black citizens of Montgomery. "My soul has been tired for a long time," an old woman told a minister who had stopped his car to offer her a ride; "now my feet are tired, and my soul is resting." When the city leaders would not budge, the blacks challenged the constitutionality of bus segregation. In November 1956 the U.S. Supreme Court affirmed a lower-court decision outlawing segregation on the buses.

The Montgomery bus boycott demonstrated African-American strength and determination. It shattered the myth that blacks favored segregation and that only outside agitators fought Jim Crow. It affirmed the possibility of social change. It vaulted Dr. King, whose oratory simultaneously inspired black activism and touched white consciences, into the national spotlight.

King's philosophy of civil disobedience fused the spirit of Christianity with the strategy of nonviolent resistance. His emphasis on direct action gave every African-American an opportunity to demonstrate the moral evil of racial discrimination; and his insistence on nonviolence diminished the likelihood of bloodshed. Preaching that blacks must lay their bodies on the line to provoke crises that would force whites to confront their racism, King urged his followers to love their enemies. By so doing, he believed, blacks would convert their oppressors and bring "redemption and reconciliation." In 1957 King and a group of black ministers formed the Southern Christian Leadership Conference (SCLC) "to carry on nonviolent crusades against the evils of second-class citizenship." Yet more than on leaders, the movement's triumphs would depend on the domestic servants who walked instead of riding the buses, the children on the front lines of the battle for school desegregation, and the tens of thousands of ordinary people who marched, rallied, and demonstrated.

Latinos and Latinas

Hispanic-Americans initially made less headway in ending discrimination. High unemployment on the Caribbean island and cheap airfares to New York City brought a steady stream of Puerto Ricans, who as U.S. citizens could enter the mainland without restriction. From seventy thousand in 1940 to a quarter of a million in 1950 and then nearly a million in 1960, El Barrio in New York City's East Harlem had a larger Puerto Rican population and more bodegas than San Juan by the late 1960s.

In New York they suffered from inadequate schools and police harassment, and were denied decent jobs and political recognition. More than half lived in inadequate housing. Like countless earlier immigrants, Puerto Ricans gained greater personal freedom in the United States while losing the security of a strong cultural tradition. Family frictions flared in the transition to unaccustomed ways. Parents felt upstaged by children who learned English and obtained jobs that were closed to them. The relationship between husbands and wives changed as women found readier access to jobs than did men. One migrant explained, "Whether I have a husband or not I work . . . and if my husband dare to complain, I throw him out. That is the difference; in Puerto Rico I should have to stand for anything a man asks me to do because he pays the rent. Here I belong to myself." Others hoped to earn money in the United States and then return home. Most stayed. Yet however much they tried to embrace American ways, many could not enjoy the promise of the American Dream because of their skin color and Spanish language.

A Periodic Roundup *Los Angeles police remove a group of undocumented Mexican immigrants from a freight train and prepare to send them back across the border.*

Mexican-Americans suffered the same indignities. Most were underpaid, overcharged, and segregated from mainstream American life. The presence of countless "undocumented aliens" compounded their woes.

After World War II, new irrigation systems added 7.5 million acres to the agricultural lands of the Southwest, stimulating farm owners' desire for cheap Mexican labor. In 1951, to stem the resulting tide of illegal Mexican immigrants, Congress reintroduced the wartime "temporary worker" program that brought in seasonal farm laborers called *braceros*. The workers were supposed to return to Mexico at the end of their labor contract, but many stayed without authorization, joining a growing number of Latinos who entered the country illegally.

During the 1953–1955 recession, the Eisenhower administration's "Operation Wetback" (*wetback* was a term of derision for illegal Mexican immigrants who supposedly swam across the Rio Grande to enter the United States) deported some 3 million allegedly undocumented entrants. Periodic roundups, however, did not substitute for a sound labor policy or an effective enforcement strategy, and millions of Mexicans continued to cross the poorly guarded two-thousand-mile border. The *bracero* program itself peaked in 1959, admitting 450,000 workers. Neither the *Asociación Nacional México-Americana* (founded in 1950) nor the

League of United Latin American Citizens (LULAC) could stop their exploitation or the widespread violations of the rights of Mexican-American citizens.

The Mexican-American population of Los Angeles County doubled to more than six hundred thousand, and the *colonias* of Denver, El Paso, Phoenix, and San Antonio grew proportionately as large. The most rural of all major ethnic groups in 1940, the percentage of Mexican-Americans living in urban areas rose to 65 percent in 1950 and to 85 percent by 1970. As service in World War II gave Hispanics an increased sense of their own American identity and a claim on the rights supposedly available to all American citizens, urbanization gave them better educational and employment opportunities. Unions like the United Cannery, Agricultural, Packing and Allied Workers of America sought higher wages and better working conditions for their Mexican-American members, and such middle-class organizations as LULAC, the GI Forum, and the Unity League campaigned to desegregate schools and public facilities.

In 1954 the Supreme Court banned the exclusion of Mexican-Americans from Texas jury lists. The mobilization of Hispanic voters led to the election of the first Mexican-American mayor, in El Paso in 1958. Latinos also took pride in baseball star Roberto Clemente and their growing numbers in the major leagues, in Nobel Prize winners like biologist Severo Ochoa, and in such Hollywood stars as Ricardo Montalban and Anthony Quinn. But the existence of millions of undocumented aliens and the continuation of the *bracero* program stigmatized all people of Spanish descent and depressed their wages. The median income of Hispanics was less than two-thirds that of Anglos. At least a third lived in poverty.

Native Americans Native Americans remained the poorest minority, with a death rate three times the national average. Unemployment rates on reservations during the 1950s reached 70 percent for the Blackfeet of Montana and the Hopi of New Mexico, and a staggering 86 percent for the Choctaw of Mississippi. After World War II Congress veered away from John Collier's efforts to reassert Indian sovereignty and cultural autonomy and had moved toward the goal of assimilation. This meant terminating treaty relationships with tribes, ending the federal trusteeship of Indians. Some favored it as a move toward Indian self-sufficiency; others desired an end to the communal culture of Indians; and still others wanted access to Indian lands and mineral resources. Between 1954 and 1962 Congress passed a dozen termination bills, withdrawing financial support from sixty-one reservations.

First applied to Menominees of Wisconsin and Klamaths of Oregon, who owned valuable timberlands, the termination policy proved disastrous. Further impoverishing the Indians whom it affected, the law transferred more than five hundred thousand acres of Native American lands to non-Indians. To lure Indians off the reservations and into urban areas, and to speed the sale of Indian lands to developers, the government established the Voluntary Relocation Program. It provided Native Americans with moving costs, assistance in finding housing and jobs, and living expenses until they obtained work. "We're like wheat," said one Hopi woman who went to the city. "The wind blows, we bend over. . . . You can't stand up when there's wind."

By the end of the decade about sixty thousand reservation Indians had been relocated to cities. Some became assimilated into middle-class America. Most could not find work and ended up on state welfare rolls living in rundown shantytowns. A third returned to the reservations. Not surprisingly, the National Congress of American Indians vigorously opposed termination, and most tribal politicians advocated Indian sovereignty, treaty rights, federal trusteeship, and the special status of Indians.

SEEDS OF DISQUIET

Late in the 1950s apprehension ruffled the calm surface of American life. Academics spotlighted shortcomings and questioned the nation's values. Periodic recessions, rising unemployment, and the growing national debt made Khrushchev's 1959 threat to bury the United States economically, and his boast that "your grandchildren will live under communism," ring in American ears. Third World anticolonialism, especially in Cuba, diminished Americans' sense of national pride, adding to their discontent. So did the growing alienation of American youth and a technological breakthrough by the Soviet Union.

Sputnik   On October 4, 1957, the Soviet Union launched the first artificial satellite, *Sputnik* ("Little Traveler"). Weighing 184 pounds and a mere twenty-two inches in diameter, it circled Earth at eighteen thousand miles per hour. *Sputnik* dashed the American myth of unquestioned technological superiority; and when *Sputnik II,* carrying a dog, went into a more distant orbit on November 3, critics charged that Eisenhower had allowed a "technological Pearl Harbor." Democrats warned of a "missile gap" between the United States and the Soviet Union.

The Eisenhower administration publicly disparaged the Soviet achievement. Behind the scenes it hurried to have the American Vanguard missile launch a satellite. On December 6, with millions watching on TV, the Vanguard rose six feet in the air and exploded. Newspapers rechristened the missile "Flopnik."

Eisenhower did not find it a laughing matter. He doubled the funds for missile development to $4.3 billion in 1958 and raised the amount to $5.3 billion in 1959. He also established the Science Advisory Committee, whose recommendations led to the creation of the National Aeronautics and Space Administration (NASA) in July 1958. By the end of the decade, the United States had launched several space probes and successfully tested the Atlas intercontinental ballistic missile (ICBM).

Critics had long complained that Americans honored football stars more than brainy students. To no avail they warned that the Soviet Union was producing twice as many scientists and engineers as the United States. *Sputnik* suddenly provided the impetus for a crash program to improve American education. Political barriers to federal aid for education crumbled. Funds from Washington built new classrooms and laboratories, raised teachers' salaries, and installed instructional television systems in schools. In 1958 Congress passed the National Defense Education Act, providing loans to students, funds for teacher training, and money to develop instructional materials in the sciences, mathematics, and foreign languages.

Americans now banked on higher education to ensure national security. The number of college students, 1.5 million in 1940 and 2.5 million in 1955, skyrocketed to 3.6 million in 1960. That year the U.S. government funneled $1.5 billion to universities, a hundred-fold increase over 1940. Linked directly to the Cold War, federal aid to education raised unsettling questions. By 1960 nearly a third of scientists and engineers on university faculties worked full-time on government research, primarily defense projects. Some would dub it the "military-industrial-educational complex."

A Different Beat   Few adults considered the social implications of their affluence on the young, or the consequences of having a generation of teenagers who could stay in school instead of working. Few thought about the effects of growing up in an age when traditional values like thrift and self-denial had declining relevance, or of maturing at a time when young people had the leisure and money to shape their own subculture. Little attention was paid to the decline in the age of menarche (first menstruation), or the ways that the relatively new institution of the junior high school affected the behavior of youth. Despite talk of family togetherness, fathers were often too busy to pay much attention to their children, and mothers sometimes spent more time chauffeuring their young than listening to them. Indeed, much of what adults knew about teenagers (a noun that first appeared in the 1940s and was not commonly used until the 1950s) they learned from the mass media, which focused on the sensational and the superficial.

Accounts of juvenile delinquency abounded. News stories portrayed high schools as war zones, city streets as jungles, and teenagers as zip-gun-armed hoodlums. Highly publicized hearings by a Senate subcommittee on juvenile delinquency stoked the fears. Teenage crime, in fact, had barely increased. Male teenagers aroused alarm by sporting black leather motorcycle jackets and slicking their hair back in a "ducktail."

As dismaying to parents, young Americans embraced rock-and-roll. In 1951 Alan Freed, the host of a classical music program on Cleveland radio, had observed white teenagers dancing to rhythm-and-blues records by such black performers as Chuck Berry, Bo Diddley, and Little Richard. In 1952 Freed started a new radio program, "Moondog's Rock and Roll Party," to play "race music." It was popular, and in 1954 Freed took the program to New York, creating a national craze for rock-and-roll.

Just as white musicians in the 1920s and 1930s had adapted black jazz for white audiences, white performers in the 1950s transformed rhythm-and-blues into "Top Ten" rock-and-roll. In 1954 Bill Haley and the Comets dropped the sexual allusions from Joe Turner's "Shake, Rattle, and Roll," added country-and-western guitar riffs, and had the first major white rock-and-roll hit. When Haley performed "Rock Around the Clock" in *The Blackboard Jungle,* a 1955 film about juvenile delinquency, many parents linked rock-and-roll with disobedience and crime. Red-hunters saw it as a communist plot to corrupt youth. Segregationists claimed it was a ploy "to mix the races." Psychiatrists feared it was "a communicable disease." Some churches condemned it as the "devil's music."

Nothing confirmed their dismay as much as swaggering Elvis Presley. Born in Tupelo, Mississippi, Elvis was a nineteen-year-old truck driver in 1954 when he paid four dollars to record two songs at a Memphis studio. He melded the Pentecostal music of his boyhood with the powerful beat and sexual energy of the rhythm-and-blues music he heard on Memphis's Beale Street, and his songs like "Hound Dog" and "All Shook Up" transformed the cloying pop music that youth found wanting into a proclamation of teenage "separateness." Presley's smirking lips and bucking hips shocked white middle-class adults. The more adults condemned rock-and-roll, the more teenagers loved it. Record sales tripled between 1954 and 1960, and Dick Clark's *American Bandstand* became the decade's biggest TV hit. As teens listened to 45-rpm records in their own rooms and to radios in their own cars, the music directed to them by such "outsiders" as Buddy Holly from West Texas, Richie Valens (Valenzuela) from East Los Angeles, and Frankie Lymon from Spanish Harlem nourished the roots of the coming youth revolt.

Portents of Change Teens cherished rock-and-roll for its frankness and exuberance. They elevated the characters played by Marlon Brando in *The Wild One* (1954) and James Dean in *Rebel Without a Cause* (1955) to cult status for their overturning of respectable society's mores. They delighted in *Mad* magazine's ridiculing of the phony and pretentious in middle-class America. They customized their cars to reject Detroit's standards. All were signs of their variance from the adult world, of their distinct community.

Nonconformist writers known as the Beats expressed a more fundamental revolt against middle-class society. In Allen Ginsberg's *Howl* (1956) and Jack Kerouac's *On the Road* (1957), the Beats scorned conformity and materialism as much as they did conventional punctuation. They scoffed at the "square" America described by Kerouac as "rows of well-to-do houses with lawns and television sets in each living room with everybody looking at the same thing and thinking the same thing at the same time." They romanticized society's outcasts—the mad ones, wrote Kerouac, "the ones who never yawn or say a commonplace thing, but burn, burn, burn like fabulous yellow roman candles exploding like spiders across the stars." Outraging respectability, they glorified uninhibited sexuality and spontaneity in the search for "It," the ultimate authentic experience, foreshadowing the counterculture to come.

The mass media scorned the Beats, as they did all dissenters. *Look* magazine derided them as Americans "turned inside out. The goals of the Beats are *not* watching TV, *not* wearing gray flannel, *not* owning a home in the suburbs, and especially—*not* working." But some college youth admired their rejection of conformity and complacency. Students protested capital punishment and demonstrated against the continuing investigations of the House Un-American Activities Committee. Others decried the nuclear-arms race. In 1958 and 1959 thousands participated in Youth Marches for Integrated Schools in Washington. Together with the Beats and rock music, this vocal minority of the "silent generation" heralded a youth movement that would explode in the 1960s.

IMPORTANT EVENTS, 1952–1960

1946 ENIAC, the first electronic computer, begins operation.

1947 Levittown, New York, development started.

1948 Bell Labs develops the transistor.

1950 *Asociación Nacional México-Americana* established.

1952 Dwight D. Eisenhower elected president.

1953 Korean War truce signed.
Earl Warren appointed chief justice.
Operation Wetback begins.

1954 Army-McCarthy hearings.
Brown v. *Board of Education of Topeka*.
Fall of Dienbienphu; Geneva Conference.
Father Knows Best begins on TV.

1955 Salk polio vaccine developed.
AFL-CIO merger.
First postwar U.S.-Soviet summit meeting.
James Dean stars in *Rebel Without a Cause*.
Montgomery bus boycott begins.

1956 Interstate Highway Act.
Suez crisis.
Soviet intervention in Poland and Hungary.

1957 Eisenhower Doctrine announced.
Civil Rights Act (first since Reconstruction).
Little Rock school-desegregation crisis.
Soviet Union launches *Sputnik*.
Peak of baby boom (4.3 million births).
Southern Christian Leadership Conference founded.

1958 National Defense Education Act.
United States and Soviet Union halt atomic tests.
National Aeronautics and Space Administration (NASA) founded.

1959 Fidel Castro comes to power in Cuba.
Khrushchev and Eisenhower meet at Camp David.

1960 U-2 incident.
Second Civil Rights Act.
Suburban population almost equals that of central city.

28

The Liberal Era, 1960–1968

On the afternoon of February 1, 1960, four students at North Carolina Agricultural and Technical (A&T) College in Greensboro—Ezell Blair, Jr., Franklin McCain, Joseph McNeil, and David Richmond—entered the local Woolworth's and sat down at the whites-only lunch counter. "We don't serve colored here," the waitress replied when the freshmen asked for coffee and doughnuts. The black students remained seated. They would not be moved. Middle class in aspirations, the children of urban civil servants and industrial workers, they believed that the Supreme Court's *Brown* decision of 1954 should have ended the indignities of racial discrimination and segregation. But the promise of change had outrun reality. Massive resistance to racial equality still proved the rule throughout Dixie. In 1960 most southern blacks could neither vote nor attend integrated schools. They could not enjoy a cup of coffee alongside whites in a public restaurant.

Impatient yet hopeful, the A&T students could not accept the inequality their parents had endured. They had been inspired by the Montgomery bus boycott led by Martin Luther King, Jr., as well as by successful African independence movements in the late 1950s. They vowed to sit in until the store closed and to repeat their request the next day and beyond, until they were served.

On February 2 more than twenty A&T students joined them in their protest. The following day, over sixty sat in. By the end of the week, the students overflowed Woolworth's and sat in at the lunch counter in the nearby S. H. Kress store. Six months later, after prolonged sit-ins, boycotts, and demonstrations, and violent white resistance, Greensboro's white civic leaders grudgingly allowed blacks to sit down at restaurants and be served.

Meanwhile, the example of the Greensboro "coffee party" had inspired similar sit-ins throughout North Carolina and in neighboring states. By April 1960 sit-ins had disrupted seventy-eight southern communities. The black students endured beatings, tear-gassing, and jailing. Yet by September 1961 some seventy thousand students had sat in to desegregate eating facilities, as well as "kneeled in" in churches, "slept in" in motel lobbies, "waded in" on restricted beaches, "read in" at public libraries, "played in" at city parks, and "watched in" at segregated movie theaters.

The determination of the students transformed the struggle for racial equality. Their activism emboldened black adults to voice their dissatisfaction; their courage inspired other youths to act. Stokely Carmichael, a student at Howard University initially indifferent to the civil-rights movement, saw "those young kids on TV, getting back up on the lunch counter stools after being knocked off them, sugar in their eyes, ketchup in their hair—well, something happened to me. Suddenly I was burning." Their assertiveness both desegregated facilities and generated a new sense of self-esteem and strength. "I possibly felt better on that day than I've ever felt in my life," remembered Franklin McCain. "I myself desegregated a lunch counter, not somebody else, not some big man, some powerful man, but little me," claimed another student. "I walked the picket line and I sat-in and the walls of segregation toppled." Each new victory convinced thousands more that "nothing can stop us now."

As well as beginning the 1960s stage of the freedom movement, the sit-ins helped redefine liberalism. In the liberal's management of the economy, greater emphasis was now placed on equalizing the possibilities of opportunity and targeting benefits to those who had earlier been ignored. In their concern for civil liberties and civil rights, liberals sought to expand individual freedoms and to free African-Americans from the shackles of racial discrimination and segregation. Liberalism was also redefined by others, including Ralph Nader sounding the consumer alarm that many automobiles were "unsafe at any speed," Betty Friedan writing *The Feminine Mystique* to denounce "the housewife trap" that caused educated women to subordinate their own aspirations to the needs of men, and students protesting against what they saw as an immoral war in Vietnam.

These endeavors symbolized a spirit of new beginnings. The impatience and idealism of the young would lead many to embrace John Kennedy's New Frontier and to rally behind Lyndon Johnson's Great Society. Both liberal administrations advocated an active federal government, particularly an activist presidency, to attack domestic and international problems and to achieve economic and social justice. Both relied on expanding economic growth to increase the social-welfare responsibilities of the government and give greater government benefits to the disadvantaged. Both also pursued an assertive foreign policy, boldly intervening abroad in Cuba and Vietnam. The new era of liberal activism thus generated fervent hopes and lofty expectations for diverse Americans, and an intensification of Cold War conflicts that triggered a militant antiwar movement. Assassinations of cherished leaders, increasing racial strife, and a frustrating war in Vietnam would dampen optimism, and a reaction by the majority who opposed radical change would curtail reform. The liberal era that began with bright promise would end in discord and disillusionment.

This chapter focuses on five major questions:

How liberal was the New Frontier in civil rights and economic matters?

What was the new liberalism of the 1960s, and how did Lyndon Johnson's Great Society exemplify it?

What were the major successes and failures of the black movements for civil rights and socioeconomic progress from 1964 to 1968?

In what ways did 1960s liberalism affect other minorities and women, and how did minorities and women affect liberalism?

How did the United States get involved in Vietnam, and to what extent was President Johnson responsible for the tragedy of Vietnam?

THE KENNEDY PRESIDENCY, 1960–1963

Projecting an image of vigor and proposing new approaches to old problems, John F. Kennedy personified the self-confident liberal who believed that an activist state could improve life at home and confront the Communist challenge abroad. His wealthy father, Joseph P. Kennedy, had held appointive office under Franklin D. Roosevelt until his outspoken isolationism ended his public career. Seething with ambition, he raised his sons to attain the political power that had eluded him. He instilled in each a passion to excel and to rule. Despite a severe back injury, John Kennedy served in the navy in World War II, and the elder Kennedy persuaded a popular novelist to write articles lauding John's heroism in rescuing his crew after their PT boat had been sunk in the South Pacific.

Esteemed as a war hero, John Kennedy used his charm and his father's connections to win election to the House of Representatives in 1946 from a Boston district in which he had never lived. Kennedy earned little distinction in Congress, but the voters of Massachusetts, captivated by his personality, sent him to the Senate in 1952 and overwhelmingly reelected him in 1958. By then he had a beautiful wife, Jacqueline, and a Pulitzer Prize for *Profiles in Courage* (1956), written largely by a staff member.

Despite the obstacle of his Roman Catholic faith, the popular Kennedy won a first-ballot victory at the 1960 Democratic convention. Just forty-two years old, he sounded the theme of a "New Frontier" to "get America moving again" by liberal activism at home and abroad.

A New Beginning "All at once you had something exciting," recalled Don Ferguson, a University of Nebraska student. "You had a guy who had little kids and who liked to play football on his front lawn. Kennedy was talking about pumping new life into the nation and steering it in new directions." But most voters, middle aged and middle class, wanted the stability and continuation of Eisenhower's "middle way" promised by the Republican candidate, Vice President Richard M. Nixon. Although scorned by liberals for his McCarthyism,

The Sit-Ins *The sit-ins of 1960 initiated the student phase of the civil-rights movement. Across the South, young black activists challenged segregation by staging nonviolent demonstrations to demand access to public facilities. Their courage and commitment reinvigorated the movement, leading to still greater grass-roots activism.*

Nixon was better known and more experienced than Kennedy, a Protestant, and identified with the still-popular Ike.

Nixon fumbled his opportunity, agreeing to meet his challenger in televised debates. More than 70 million tuned in to the first televised debate between presidential candidates, a broadcast that secured the dominance of television in American politics. The tanned, dynamic Kennedy contrasted strikingly with his pale, haggard opponent. The telegenic Democrat radiated confidence; Nixon, sweating visibly, appeared insecure. Radio listeners judged the debate a draw, but the far more numerous television viewers declared Kennedy the victor. He shot up in the polls, and Nixon never regained the lead.

Kennedy also benefited from an economic recession in 1960, as well as from his choice of a southern Protestant, Senate Majority Leader Lyndon B. Johnson, as his running mate. Still, the election was the closest since 1884. Only 120,000 votes separated the two candidates. Kennedy's religion cost him millions of popular votes, but his capture of 80 percent of the Catholic vote in the closely contested midwestern and northeastern states delivered crucial electoral college votes, enabling him to squeak to victory.

The Election of 1960

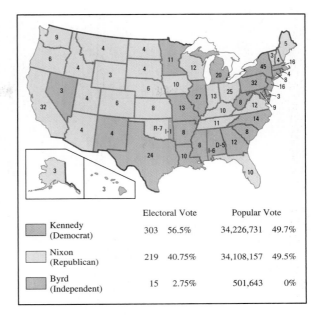

	Electoral Vote		Popular Vote	
Kennedy (Democrat)	303	56.5%	34,226,731	49.7%
Nixon (Republican)	219	40.75%	34,108,157	49.5%
Byrd (Independent)	15	2.75%	501,643	0%

Kennedy's inauguration set the tone of a new era: "the torch has been passed to a new generation of Americans." In sharp contrast to Eisenhower's "eight millionaires and a plumber" (see Chapter 27), Kennedy surrounded himself with liberal intellectuals—the "best and brightest," in author David Halberstam's wry phrase. For attorney general he selected his brother Robert Kennedy. "I see nothing wrong with giving Robert some legal experience before he goes out to practice law," JFK joked.

"America's leading man," novelist Norman Mailer called him. Kennedy seemed more a celebrity than a politician, and his dash played well on TV, highlighting his charisma and determination "to get America moving again." Aided by his wife, he adorned his presidency with the trappings of culture and excellence, inviting distinguished artists to perform at the White House and studding his speeches with quotations from Emerson. Awed by his grace and taste, as well as by his wit and wealth, the media extolled him as a vibrant leader and adoring husband. The public knew nothing of his fragile health, frequent use of mood-altering drugs to alleviate pain, and extramarital affairs.

Kennedy's Domestic Record
Media images obscured Kennedy's lackluster domestic record. The Kennedy years saw little significant social legislation. His narrow victory, and the conservative coalition of Republicans and southern Democrats that had stifled Truman's Fair Deal, doomed the New Frontier. Lacking the necessary votes, JFK rarely pressed Congress, maintaining that "there is no sense in raising hell, and then not being successful."

JFK made economic growth the key to his liberal agenda. To stimulate the economy, he combined higher defense expenditures with investment incentives

Inspiring Idealism *An excited Bill Clinton, almost 17, meets President John Kennedy at the White House. Many young Americans, like the future 42nd president of the United States, were captivated by the Kennedy aura and responed to his call to action: "Ask not what your country can do for you—ask what you can do for your country."*

for private enterprise. In 1961 he persuaded Congress to boost the defense budget by 20 percent. He vastly increased America's nuclear stockpile, strengthened the military's conventional forces, and established the Special Forces ("Green Berets") to engage in guerrilla warfare. By 1963 the defense budget reached its highest level as a percentage of total federal expenditures in the entire Cold War era. To further boost the economy as well as avoid "another *Sputnik*," Kennedy also persuaded Congress to finance a "race to the moon." The effort to land astronauts Neil Armstrong and Buzz Aldrin on the lunar surface in 1969 would cost more than $25 billion. Most importantly, to pay for the federal aid to education, medical care for the elderly, and urban renewal that he proposed, Kennedy accepted his liberal advisers' Keynesian approach to economic growth. He called for a huge cut in corporate taxes that would greatly increase the deficit but would presumably provide capital for business to invest in ways that would stimulate the economy and thus increase tax revenues. Economic growth, accordingly, was the way for the government to create a better life for all Americans.

When the Kennedy presidency ended suddenly in November 1963, the proposed tax cut was bottled up in Congress (symbolic of JFK's overall failure in domestic legislation). Military spending, continued technological innovation, heightened productivity, and low-cost energy, however, had already doubled the 1960 rate of economic growth, decreased unemployment, and held increases in inflation to 1.3 percent a year. The United States was in the midst of its longest uninterrupted boom ever. The boom would both cause further ecological damage and provide the affluence that enabled Americans to care about the environment.

Environmentalism had its roots in both the older conservation movement, emphasizing the efficient use of resources, and the preservation movement, focusing on preserving "wilderness." The fallout scare of the 1950s raised questions about the biological well-being of the planet. The publication in 1962 of Rachel Carson's *Silent Spring* (see Chapter 27), which described the devastating effects of pesticides on the environment, particularly birds, intensified concern. Additionally, postwar prosperity made large numbers of Americans less concerned with increased production and more concerned with the quality of life. Responding to the furor set off by Carson's documentation of the hazards of DDT, Kennedy appointed an advisory committee that warned against widespread pesticide use. In 1963 Congress passed a Clean Air Act, regulating automotive and industrial emissions. After decades of heedless pollution, hardly helped by the introduction of aluminum pop-top cans in 1963, Washington hesitatingly began to deal with environmental problems.

Cold War Activism   In his inaugural address Kennedy proclaimed, "we shall pay any price, bear any burden, meet any hardship, support any friend, oppose any foe to assure the survival and success of liberty." To back up that pledge he launched a major buildup of the military arsenal, made foreign policy his top priority, and surrounded himself with Cold Warriors who shared his belief that American security depended on superior force and the willingness to use it. At the same time, he gained congressional backing for liberal programs of economic assistance to Third World countries to counter the appeal of communism. The Peace Corps, created in 1961, exemplified the New Frontier's liberal anticommunism. By 1963 five thousand Peace Corps volunteers were serving two-year stints as teachers, sanitation engineers, crop specialists, and health workers in more than forty Third World nations. They were, according to liberal historian and Kennedy aide Arthur Schlesinger, Jr., "reform-minded missionaries of democracy who mixed with the people, spoke the native dialects, ate the food, and involved themselves in local struggles against ignorance and want."

In early 1961 a crisis flared in Laos, a tiny, landlocked nation created by the Geneva agreement in 1954 (see Chapter 27). There a civil war between American-supported forces and Pathet Lao rebels seemed headed toward a communist triumph. Considering Laos strategically insignificant, in July 1962 Kennedy agreed to a face-saving compromise that restored a neutralist government but left communist forces dominant in the countryside. The accord stiffened Kennedy's resolve not to allow further communist gains.

Spring 1961 brought Kennedy's first major foreign-policy crisis. To eliminate a communist outpost on America's doorstep, he approved a CIA plan, drawn up in the Eisenhower administration, for anti-Castro exiles, "La Brigada," to invade Cuba. In mid-April fifteen hundred exiles stormed Cuba's Bay of Pigs, assuming that their arrival would trigger a general uprising to overthrow Fidel Castro. It was a fiasco. Deprived of air cover by Kennedy's desire to conceal U.S. involvement, the invaders had no chance against Castro's superior forces. Although Kennedy accepted blame for the failure, he neither apologized nor ceased attempting to topple Castro.

In July 1961, on the heels of the Bay of Pigs failure, Kennedy met Soviet premier Nikita Khrushchev in Vienna to try to resolve a peace treaty with Germany (see Chapter 26). Comparing the American troops in the divided city of Berlin to "a bone stuck in the throat," Khrushchev threatened war unless the West retreated. A shaken Kennedy returned to the United States and declared the defense of West Berlin essential to the Free World. He doubled draft calls, mobilized 150,000 reservists, and requested an additional $3 billion defense appropriation. The threat of nuclear war escalated until mid-August, when the Soviets constructed a wall to seal off East Berlin and end the exodus of brains and talent to the West. The Berlin Wall became a concrete symbol of communism's denial of personal freedom until it fell in 1989.

To the Brink of Nuclear War In mid-October 1962 aerial photographs revealed that the Soviet Union had built bases for intermediate-range ballistic missiles (IRBMs) in Cuba, which could reach U.S. targets as far as twenty-two hundred miles away. Kennedy responded forcefully, fearing unchecked Soviet interference in the Western Hemisphere, still smarting from the Bay of Pigs disaster, and believing that his credibility was at stake. In a somber televised address he denounced the Soviet "provocative threat to world peace" and demanded that the missiles be removed. The United States, he asserted, would "quarantine" Cuba—impose a naval blockade—to prevent delivery of more missiles and would dismantle by force the missiles already in Cuba if the Soviets did not do so.

Kennedy's ultimatum, and Khrushchev's defiant response that the quarantine was "outright banditry," rocked the world. More than ever before, the two superpowers appeared on a collision course toward nuclear war. Apprehension mounted as the Soviet technicians worked feverishly to complete missile launch pads and as Soviet missile-carrying ships steamed toward the blockade. Americans stayed glued to their radios and television sets as 180 U.S. naval ships in the Caribbean prepared to confront the Soviet freighters; B-52s armed with nuclear bombs took to the air; and nearly a quarter-million troops assembled in Florida to invade Cuba. Secretary of State Dean Rusk reported, "We're eyeball to eyeball."

"I think the other fellow just blinked," a relieved Rusk announced on October 25. The Cuba-bound Soviet ships stopped dead in the water, and Kennedy received a message from Khrushchev promising to remove the missiles if the U.S. pledged never to invade Cuba. As Kennedy prepared to respond positively, a second, more belligerent, message arrived from Khrushchev insisting that American missiles be withdrawn from Turkey as part of the deal. Hours later an American U-2 reconnaissance plane was shot down over Cuba. It was "the blackest hour of the crisis," recalled a Kennedy aide. Various presidential advisers urged an immediate invasion, but the president, heeding Robert Kennedy's advice, decided to ignore the second Soviet message and accept the original offer. That night, October 27, the president's brother met secretly with the Soviet ambassador to inform him that this was the only way to avoid nuclear war. The next morning Khrushchev pledged to remove the missiles in return for Kennedy's noninvasion promise. Less publicly, Kennedy subsequently removed U.S. missiles from Turkey.

The full dimensions of the crisis became known only after the end of the Cold War, when the Russian military disclosed that Soviet forces in Cuba had possessed thirty-six nuclear warheads as well as nine tactical nuclear weapons for battlefield use. Soviet field commanders had independent authority to use these weapons. Worst of all, Kennedy had not known that the Soviets already had the capability to launch a nuclear strike from Cuba. "We do not need to speculate," said a shaken McNamara in 1992, "about what would have happened had the U.S. attack been launched, as many in the U.S. government—military and civilian alike—were recommending to the President on October 27th and 28th. We can predict the results with certainty. . . . No one should believe that U.S. troops could have been attacked by tactical nuclear warheads without the U.S.'s responding with nuclear warheads. . . . And where would it have ended? In utter disaster."

Staring over the brink of nuclear war chastened both Kennedy and Khrushchev. "Having come so close to the edge," JFK's national security adviser said, "the leaders of the two governments have since taken care to keep away from the cliff." They agreed to install a Kremlin–White House "hot line" so that the two sides could communicate instantly in future crises. In June 1963 JFK advocated a relaxation of superpower tensions, and two months later the two nations agreed to a treaty outlawing atmospheric and undersea nuclear testing. These efforts signaled a new phase of the Cold War, later called détente, in which the superpowers moved from confrontation to negotiation. Ironically, the Cuban missile crisis also had the unintended consequence of accelerating the arms race for another twenty-five years. It confirmed American belief in the need for nuclear superiority to prevent war while convincing Russian leaders that they must overtake the American lead in nuclear missiles to avoid future humiliation.

The Thousand-Day Presidency On November 22, 1963, during a trip to Texas to improve his chances for victory in the 1964 presidential election, John and Jackie Kennedy rode in an open car along Dallas streets, smiling at the cheering crowds. As the motorcade slowed to turn, shots rang out. The president slumped, his skull and throat shattered. While the driver sped the mortally wounded president to a nearby hospital, where the doctors pronounced Kennedy dead, Secret Service agents rushed Lyndon Johnson to Air Force One to be sworn in as president.

Grief and disbelief numbed the nation. Millions of Americans sat stunned in front of TV sets during the next four days, staring at the steady stream of mourners filing by the slain president's coffin in the Capitol rotunda; at the countless replays of the murder of Kennedy's accused assassin, Lee Harvey Oswald, in the Dallas city jail by a nightclub owner; at the somber state funeral, with the small boy saluting his father's casket; at the grieving family lighting an eternal flame at Arlington National Cemetery. Few who watched would ever forget. Kennedy had helped make television central to American politics, and now television, which made Kennedy a celebrity in life, made him, in death, the heroic king of Camelot.

The assassination made a martyr of JFK. More admired by the public in death than in life, he was now ranked with Washington, Lincoln, and Roosevelt as a "great" president. For decades after, despite revelations of character blemishes, JFK would loom large in the American imagination, his romantic aura a reminder of what seemed a better time. Emphasizing "might have beens," Kennedy loyalists have stressed his intelligence, his ability to change and grow. His detractors, however, point to the gap between rhetoric and substance, the discrepancy between his public image and his compulsive, even reckless, private sexual behavior. Some deplore his aggressive Cold War tactics; others condemn him for raising unrealistic expectations and expanding presidential powers.

Kennedy's rhetoric expressed the new liberalism, but he rarely made liberal ideas a reality. Economic expansion came from spending on missiles and the space race, not on social welfare and human needs. Constrained by the lack of a liberal majority, Kennedy frequently compromised with conservative and segregationist congressional leaders. Partly because his own personal behavior made him beholden to J. Edgar Hoover, JFK allowed the FBI unprecedented authority to infringe on civil liberties, even as the CIA was conniving with the Mafia to assassinate Fidel Castro. (The tangled web of plots and policies that enmeshed John and Robert Kennedy, FBI Director J. Edgar Hoover, organized crime, and the national security agencies remains to be sorted out by scholars.) The New Frontier barely existed for environmental protection, for slowing corporate consolidation, or for women. (JFK appointed fewer women to high-level federal posts than had his predecessors and was the first president since Herbert Hoover not to have a woman in the cabinet.)

Internationally, Kennedy left a mixed record. He signed the world's first nuclear-test-ban treaty, yet also initiated a massive nuclear-arms buildup. He compromised on Laos but deepened U.S. involvement in Vietnam. Despite gradually changing from a Cold Warrior to a leader who questioned the necessity of conflict with the Soviets, JFK nevertheless insisted on maintaining U.S. global superiority and halting the spread of international communism. He did so, moreover, by increasing the powers of the executive branch, particularly his own White House staff. As never before, a small group of aides, personally loyal to the president, secretly dominated policy making.

Yet JFK had fired the energies and imaginations of millions of Americans. He gave liberals new hope, aroused the poor and the powerless, and challenged the young, stimulating a flowering of social criticism and political activism. Like other heroes, Kennedy left the stage before his glory tarnished. He would leave his successor a liberal agenda as well as soaring expectations at home and a deteriorating entanglement in Vietnam. That legacy, as well as his assassination, would shatter illusions, leading an increasing number of Americans to lose confidence in their government and their future.

LIBERALISM ASCENDANT, 1963–1968

Distrusted by liberals as "a Machiavelli in a Stetson" and regarded as a usurper by Kennedy loyalists, Lyndon Baines Johnson had achieved his highest ambition as a result of the assassination of a popular president in Johnson's home state of Texas. Though just nine years older than JFK, he seemed a relic of the past, a back-room wheeler-dealer, as crude as Kennedy was smooth, as insecure as his predecessor was self-confident.

Yet Johnson had substantial political assets. He had served in Washington almost continuously since 1932. No modern president came to office with more national political experience. He excelled in wooing allies, neutralizing opponents, building coalitions, and achieving results. He loved the political maneuvering and legislative detail that Kennedy loathed. He confided to an aide the day after JFK's assassination, "Kennedy was a little too conservative to suit my taste."

Johnson's first three years as president demonstrated his determination to prove himself to liberals. He deftly handled the transition of power, won a landslide victory in 1964, and guided through Congress the greatest array of liberal legislation in U.S. history, fulfilling and surpassing the New Deal liberal agenda of the 1930s. But LBJ's swollen yet fragile ego could not abide the sniping of Kennedy loyalists, and he frequently complained that the media did not give him "a fair shake." Wondering aloud, "Why don't people like me?" Johnson pressed to outdo the liberal FDR, to ensure that everyone shared in the promise of the American Dream, to enhance the quality of life for all Americans, to vanquish all foes at home and abroad. Ironically, in seeking consensus and affection, Johnson would divide the nation and leave office repudiated.

Johnson Takes Over Calling for quick passage of the tax-cut and civil-rights bills as a memorial to his slain predecessor, Johnson used his skills to win passage of the Civil Rights Act of 1964 (discussed later) and a $10 billion tax-reduction bill, which produced a surge in capital investment and personal consumption that spurred economic growth and shrank the budget deficit. More boldly, Johnson declared "unconditional war on poverty in America."

Largely invisible in an affluent America, according to Michael Harrington's *The Other America* (1962), some 40 million people dwelled in substandard housing and subsisted on inadequate diets. Unaided or only minimally assisted by a social-welfare bureaucracy, they lived with little hope in a "culture of poverty." They lacked the education, medical care, and employment opportunities that most Americans took for granted. More than being deprived of material things,

The LBJ Treatment *Not content unless he could wholly dominate friend as well as foe, Lyndon Johnson used his body as well as his voice to bend others to his will and gain his objectives.*

Harrington asserted, to be poor "is to be an internal alien, to grow up in a culture that is radically different from the one that dominates the society."

LBJ proposed an array of training programs and support services to bring these "internal exiles" into the mainstream. Designed to promote greater opportunity, to offer a "hand up, not a handout," the Economic Opportunity Act (1964) established the Office of Economic Opportunity to wage "unconditional war on poverty." Its arsenal of antipoverty programs included: the Job Corps to train young people in marketable skills; a domestic peace corps, VISTA (Volunteers in Service to America); Project Head Start to provide free compensatory education for preschoolers from disadvantaged families; the Community Action Program to encourage the "maximum feasible participation" of the poor in decisions that affected them; and public-works and training programs.

Summing up his goals in 1964, Johnson offered a cheering crowd in Ann Arbor, Michigan, his vision of the Great Society. First must come "an end to poverty and racial injustice." That would be just the beginning. The Great Society would also be a place where all children could enrich their minds and enlarge their talents, where people could renew their contact with nature, and where all would be "more concerned with the quality of their goals than the quantity of their goods."

The 1964 Election Johnson's Great Society horrified the "new conservatism" of the 1960s expressed in William F. Buckley's *National Review* and by the college student members of Young Americans for Freedom (YAF). The most persuasive criticism came from Arizona Senator Barry Goldwater. A product of the twentieth-century West, Goldwater was an outsider fighting the power of Washington, a fervent anticommunist, a proponent of individual freedom. His opposition to big government, deficit spending, racial liberalism, and social-welfare programs found a receptive audience on Sunbelt golf courses and in working-class neighborhoods.

Johnson's racial liberalism frightened southern segregationists and blue-collar workers in northern cities who dreaded the integration of their communities, schools, and workplaces. Their support of Alabama's segregationist Governor George Wallace in the spring 1964 presidential primaries heralded a "white backlash" against the civil-rights movement.

Buoyed by the white backlash, conservatives took control of the GOP in 1964. They nominated Barry Goldwater and adopted a platform totally opposed to the new liberalism. Determined to offer the nation "a choice not an echo," Goldwater lauded his opposition to the Civil Rights Act and the censure of McCarthy. He denounced the War on Poverty in Appalachia, called for the sale of the TVA to private interests in Tennessee, opposed high price supports for farmers in the Midwest, and advocated scrapping social security in St. Petersburg, Florida, a major retirement community. "We have gotten where we are," he declared, "not because of government, but in spite of government." Goldwater also accused the Democrats of a "no-win" strategy in the Cold War, hinting that he might use nuclear weapons against Cuba and North Vietnam. His candidacy appealed most to those angered by the Cold War stalemate, the erosion of traditional moral values, and the increasing militancy of African-Americans. While his campaign slogan, "In your heart you know he's right," summed up the zeal of his followers, it allowed his liberal opponents to quip, "In your guts you know he's nuts."

Goldwater's conservative crusade let LBJ and his running mate, Senator Hubert Humphrey of Minnesota, run as liberal reformers and still be the moderates. They depicted Goldwater as an extremist not to be trusted with the nuclear trigger. When the Arizonan charged that the Democrats had not pursued total victory in Vietnam, Johnson appeared the apostle of restraint: "We are not going to send American boys nine or ten thousand miles from home to do what Asian boys ought to be doing for themselves."

LBJ won a landslide victory with 43 million votes to Goldwater's 27 million. The GOP carried only Arizona and five southern states. It lost thirty-eight seats in the House of Representatives, two in the Senate, and five hundred in state legislatures. Many proclaimed the death of conservatism. But Goldwater's coalition of antigovernment westerners, economic and religious conservatives, and whites opposed to racial integration presaged the Right's future triumph. More a beginning than an end, the Goldwater candidacy launched the modern conservative movement in politics. It transformed the Republicans from a moderate, Eastern-dominated party to one decidedly conservative, southern, and western. It built a national base of financial support for conservative candidates; mobilized future leaders of the party, like Ronald Reagan; and led to the Republican "southern strategy" that would bring the election of Republican presidents in subsequent campaigns. But in the short run, the liberals had a working majority.

Triumphant Liberalism

"Hurry, boys, hurry," an exhilarated LBJ urged his aides. "Get that legislation up to the hill and out. Eighteen months from now ol' Landslide Lyndon will be Lame-Duck Lyndon." Johnson flooded Congress with liberal proposals—sixty-three of them in 1965 alone. He got most of what he requested.

The Eighty-ninth Congress—"the Congress of Fulfillment" to LBJ, and Johnson's "hip-pocket Congress" to his opponents—enlarged the War on Poverty and passed another milestone civil-rights act. It enacted a Medicare program providing health insurance for the aged under social security, and a Medicaid health plan for the poor. By 1975 the two programs would be serving 47 million people at a cost of $28 billion, a quarter of the nation's total health-care expenditures. The legislators appropriated funds for public education and housing, for redevelopment aid to Appalachia, and for revitalizing inner-city neighborhoods. They also created new departments of transportation and of housing and urban development (the latter headed by Robert Weaver, the first African-American cabinet member) and the National Endowments for the Arts and the Humanities.

Of enormous future significance, Congress enacted a new immigration law, abolishing the national-origins quotas of the 1920s. It opened America's gates to the world and shook up its ethnic kaleidoscope. Legal immigration would increase from about a quarter of a million a year before the act to well over a million annually, and the vast majority of new immigrants would come from Asia and Latin America. Between 1965 and 1970 nearly four hundred thousand Cubans emigrated to the United States. In those five years the population of Chinese, Koreans, and Filipinos in the United States more than doubled, and twenty years after the act the number of Asian-Americans had risen from 1 million to 5 million. Less than 1 percent of the U.S. population in 1960, Asian-Americans would be more than 3 percent in 1990; and the Hispanic population would increase from 4.5 percent in 1970 to 9 percent in 1990. The so-called browning of America enormously expanded the nation's culinary, linguistic, musical, and religious spectrum.

The Great Society battled what LBJ described as the problem "of vanishing beauty, of increasing ugliness, of shrinking open space, and of an overall environment that is diminished daily by pollution and noise and blight." In 1964 Congress passed the National Wilderness Preservation Act, setting aside 9.1 million acres of wilderness. It then established the Redwood National Park and defeated efforts to dam the Colorado River and flood the lower Grand Canyon; strengthened the Clean Water and Clean Air Acts; protected endangered species; preserved scenic rivers; and lessened the number of junkyards and billboards. Responding to the

Major Great Society Programs

1964

Tax Reduction Act cuts by some $10 billion the taxes paid primarily by corporations and wealthy individuals.

Civil Rights Act bans discrimination in public accommodations, prohibits discrimination in any federally assisted program, outlaws discrimination in most employment, and enlarges federal powers to protect voting rights and to speed school desegregation.

Economic Opportunity Act authorizes $1 billion for a War on Poverty and establishes the Office of Economic Opportunity to coordinate Head Start, Upward Bound, VISTA, the Job Corps, and similar programs.

1965

Elementary and Secondary Education Act, the first general federal-aid-to-education law in American history, provides more than $1 billion to public and parochial schools for textbooks, library materials, and special-education programs.

Voting Rights Act suspends literacy tests and empowers "federal examiners" to register qualified voters in the South.

Medical Care Act creates a federally funded program of hospital and medical insurance for the elderly (Medicare) and authorizes federal funds to the states to provide free health care for welfare recipients (Medicaid).

Omnibus Housing Act appropriates nearly $8 billion for low- and middle-income housing and for rent supplements for low-income families.

Immigration Act ends the discriminatory system of national-origins quotas established in 1924.

Appalachian Regional Development Act targets $1 billion for highway construction, health centers, and resource development in the depressed areas of Appalachia.

Higher Education Act appropriates $650 million for scholarships and low-interest loans to needy college students and for funds for college libraries and research facilities.

National Endowments for the Arts and the Humanities are created to promote artistic and cultural development.

1966

Demonstration Cities and Metropolitan Development Act provides extensive subsidies for housing, recreational facilities, welfare, and mass transit to selected "model cities" and covers up to 80 percent of the costs of slum clearance and rehabilitation.

Motor Vehicle Safety Act sets federal safety standards for the auto industry and a uniform grading system for tire manufacturers.

Truth in Packaging Act broadens federal controls over the labeling and packaging of foods, drugs, cosmetics, and household supplies.

uproar caused by Ralph Nader's revelations about unsafe cars, Congress set the first federal safety standards for automobiles (National Traffic and Motor Vehicle Safety Act) and required states to establish highway safety programs (Highway Safety Act).

The Great Society increased opportunity and improved the lives of millions. The proportion of the poor in the population dropped from 22 percent in 1960 to 13 percent in 1969; infant mortality declined by a third; Head Start reached more than 2 million poor children; and African-American family income rose from 54 percent to 61 percent of white family income. The percentage of blacks living below the poverty line plummeted from 40 percent to 20 percent. But in part because Johnson oversold the Great Society and Congress underfunded it, liberal aspirations outdistanced results.

For many in need, the Great Society remained more a dream than a reality. The war against poverty was, in the words of Martin Luther King, Jr., "shot down on the battlefields of Vietnam." In 1966 Johnson spent twenty times more to wage war in Vietnam than to fight poverty in the United States. Yet the perceived liberality of federal programs and the "ungratefulness" of rioting blacks alienated many middle- and working-class whites. Others resented liberal regulation of business and federal involvement in public education. Increasing numbers of Americans feared the growing intrusiveness of the liberal state in managing their daily lives. The Democrats' loss of forty-seven House seats in 1966 sealed liberalism's fate.

The Warren Court in the Sixties No branch of the federal government did more to support and promote the liberal agenda than the Supreme Court. A liberal majority on the court, led by Chief Justice Earl Warren, acted to expand individual rights to a greater extent than ever before in American history. Kennedy's appointment of two liberals to the Court, and Johnson's selection of the even more liberal Abe Fortas and Thurgood Marshall, the Court's first black justice, would result in rulings that changed the lives of Americans for decades to come.

In a series of landmark cases, the Court prohibited Bible reading and prayer in public schools, limited local power to censor books and films, and overturned state bans on contraceptives. In *Baker* v. *Carr* and related decisions, the Court ruled that "one person, one vote" must prevail in both state and national elections. This ended rural overrepresentation and increased the political power of cities and suburbs. The Court's upholding of the rights of the accused in criminal cases, at a time of soaring crime rates, particularly incensed many Americans.

Criticism of the Supreme Court reached a climax in 1966 when it ruled in *Miranda* v. *Arizona* that police must warn all suspects that anything they say can be used against them in court and that they can choose to remain silent. In 1968 both Richard Nixon and George Wallace would win favor by promising to appoint judges who emphasized "law and order" over individual liberties.

Major Decisions of the Warren Court

1954

Brown v. *Board of Education of Topeka* rejects the separate-but-equal concept and outlaws segregation in public education.

1957

Watkins v. *U.S.* restricts Congress's investigatory power to matters directly pertinent to pending legislation.

Yates v. *U.S.* limits prosecutions under the Smith Act to the advocacy of concrete revolutionary action and disallows prosecutions for the preaching of revolutionary doctrine.

1962

Baker v. *Carr* holds that the federal courts possess jurisdiction over state apportionment systems to ensure that the votes of all citizens carry equal weight.

Engel v. *Vitale* prohibits prayer in the public schools.

1963

Abington v. *Schempp* bans Bible reading in the public schools.

Gideon v. *Wainwright* requires states to provide attorneys at public expense for indigent defendants in felony cases.

Jacobellis v. *Ohio* extends constitutional protection to all sexually explicit material that has any "literary or scientific or artistic value."

1964

New York Times Co. v. *Sullivan* expands the constitutional protection of the press against libel suits by public figures.

Wesberry v. *Sanders* and *Reynolds* v. *Sims* hold that the only standard of apportionment for state legislatures and congressional districts is "one man, one vote."

1966

Miranda v. *Arizona* requires police to advise a suspect of his or her constitutional right to remain silent and to have a counsel present during interrogation.

1967

Loving v. *Virginia* strikes down state antimiscegenation laws, which prohibit marriage between persons of different races.

1968

Katzenbach v. *Morgan* upholds federal legislation outlawing state requirements that a prospective voter must demonstrate literacy in English.

Green v. *County School Board of New Kent County* extends the *Brown* ruling to require the assignment of pupils on the basis of race, to end segregation.

THE STRUGGLE FOR BLACK EQUALITY, 1961–1968

Following the lunch-counter sit-ins, civil-rights activists tried to force President Kennedy to match his liberal rhetoric with action. Focusing mainly on foreign affairs and secondarily on the economy, JFK initially straddled the race issue, fearing it would divide the nation, split the Democratic party, immobilize Congress in filibusters, and jeopardize his reelection. He viewed civil rights as a thorny thicket to avoid, not a moral issue requiring decisive leadership. Thus he balanced his appointment of an unprecedented number of African-Americans to federal jobs with the nomination of white racists to judgeships. He stalled for two years before issuing the weakest possible executive order banning discrimination in federally financed housing. Steady pressure by those in the movement for black equality made "the responsibility of the federal government to advance the civil rights of African Americans" the top issue defining the new liberalism. Kennedy changed accordingly.

Nonviolence and Violence

In spring 1961 the Congress of Racial Equality (CORE), an interracial protest group founded in 1942, organized a "freedom ride" through the Deep South. It was designed to dramatize the widespread violation of a 1960 Supreme Court decision outlawing segregation in interstate transportation. It succeeded by arousing white wrath. When the freedom riders were savagely beaten in Anniston, Alabama, and their bus burned, and when they were mauled by a white mob in Birmingham, the freedom rides became front-page news. Yet only after further assaults on the freedom riders in Montgomery did Kennedy, fearful that the violence would undermine American prestige abroad, dispatch federal marshals to end the violence. Not until after scores more freedom rides and the arrest of over three hundred protesters did the president press the Interstate Commerce Commission to enforce the Supreme Court's ruling. Clearly, only crisis, not moral suasion, forced Kennedy to act.

Many of the freedom riders were members of the Student Nonviolent Coordinating Committee (SNCC), formed in April 1960 by participants in the sit-ins. SNCC stressed both the nonviolent civil disobedience strategy of Martin Luther King, Jr., and the need to stimulate local, grass-roots activism and leadership. In fall 1961 it chose Albany, Georgia, as the site of a campaign to desegregate public facilities. Despite King's involvement, wily local authorities avoided the overt violence that won the freedom riders national sympathy. Without the national indignation that would bring a White House response, the Albany movement collapsed. But the lesson had been learned by civil-rights leaders.

It had not been learned by Mississippi whites. An angry mob rioted in fall 1962 when a federal court ordered the University of Mississippi to enroll James Meredith, a black air force veteran. Rallying behind Confederate flags, troublemakers laid siege to the campus, attacking the federal marshals who escorted Meredith to "Ole Miss." The clash left two dead, hundreds injured, the campus shrouded in tear gas, and federal troops upholding the right of a black American to attend the university of his home state. Some five hundred soldiers and marshals would still be on guard at Meredith's graduation.

The African-American Revolution

As television coverage of the struggle for racial equality brought mounting numbers of African-Americans into the movement, civil-rights leaders applied increasing pressure on Kennedy to act decisively. They realized that it would take decades to dismantle segregation piecemeal; the only practical remedy would be comprehensive national legislation, backed by the power of the federal government, guaranteeing full citizenship for African-Americans. To get this they needed a crisis that would outrage the conscience of the white majority and force Kennedy's hand.

Determined to provoke a confrontation that would expose the violent extremism of southern white racism, King and his advisers selected Birmingham as the stage for the next act in the civil-rights drama. The most rigidly segregated big city in America, Birmingham's officials had even removed a book from the library that featured white and black rabbits. Past violence by whites against civil-rights protesters had earned the city the nickname "Bombingham," and the black neighborhood, "Dynamite Hill." Few doubted Police Commissioner Eugene "Bull" Connor's pledge that "blood would run in the streets of Birmingham before it would be integrated."

In early April 1963 Martin Luther King, Jr., initiated a series of marches, sit-ins, and pray-ins that violated local laws and filled the jails with protesters. Commissioner Connor scoffed that King would soon "run out of niggers," and various religious leaders criticized King, calling for an end to demonstrations. While imprisoned, King penned his eloquent "Letter from the Birmingham Jail," detailing the humiliations of racial discrimination and segregation and defending civil disobedience.

> We know through painful experience that freedom is never voluntarily given by the oppressor; it must be demanded by the oppressed. Frankly, I have yet to engage in a direct-action campaign that was "well-timed" in the view of those who have not suffered unduly from the disease of segregation. For years now I have heard the word "Wait!" It rings in the ear of every Negro with piercing familiarity. This "Wait" has almost always meant "Never." We must come to see, with one of our distinguished jurists, that "justice too long delayed is justice denied."

In May thousands of schoolchildren, some only six years old, joined King's crusade. The bigoted Connor grew impatient and tried to crush the black movement with overwhelming force. As the television cameras rolled, he unleashed his men—armed with electric cattle prods, high-pressure water hoses, and snarling attack dogs—on the nonviolent demonstrators. The ferocity of Connor's attacks horrified the world.

"The civil-rights movement should thank God for Bull Connor," JFK remarked. "He's helped it as much as Abraham Lincoln." Indeed, Connor's vicious tactics seared the nation's conscience. The combination of mounting white support for equal rights and African-American activism pushed Kennedy to arrange a settlement that ended the demonstrations in return for the desegregation of Birmingham's stores and the upgrading of black workers. By mid-1963 the rallying cry "Freedom Now!" reverberated through the land as all the civil-rights groups became more militant, competing with each other in organizing marches, demonstrations, and lawsuits. The number and magnitude of protests soared. Concerned about America's image abroad as well as the "fires of frustration and discord" raging at home, Kennedy acted. He believed that if the federal government did not lead the way toward "peaceful and constructive" changes in race relations, blacks would turn to violent leaders and methods. When Governor George Wallace refused to allow two black students to enter the University of Alabama in June 1963, Kennedy forced Wallace—who had pledged "Segregation now! Segregation tomorrow! Segregation forever!"—to capitulate to a court desegregation order.

On June 11 the president went on television to define civil rights as "a moral issue" and to declare that "race has no place in American life or law." Describing the plight of blacks in the Jim Crow America of 1963, he asked, "Who among us would be content to have the color of his skin changed and stand in his place? Who among us would then be content with the counsels of patience and delay?" A week later Kennedy proposed the most comprehensive civil-rights measure in American history, outlawing segregation in public facilities and authorizing the federal government to withhold funds from programs that discriminated. Although House liberals moved to toughen Kennedy's proposal, most members of Congress did not heed the president's plea. To compel Congress to act, African-Americans gathered in force in the Capitol.

The March on Washington, 1963 The idea for a March on Washington had originally been proposed by A. Philip Randolph in 1941 to protest discrimination against blacks in the defense mobilization (see Chapter 25). Twenty-two years later, Randolph revived the idea and convinced the major civil-rights leaders to support it.

A quarter of a million people, including some fifty thousand whites, converged on Washington, D.C., on August 28, 1963. It was the largest political assembly to date. After a long, sweltering day of speeches and songs, Martin Luther King, Jr., took the podium to remind Americans that blacks "can never be satisfied as long as our children are stripped of their selfhood and robbed of their dignity by signs stating: 'For Whites Only.' " He told of his dream "of a day when the sons of former slaves and the sons of former slaveowners will be able to sit down together at the table of brotherhood . . . when all of God's children . . . will be able to join hands and sing . . . 'Free at last, free at last; thank God Almighty, we are free at last.'"

King's eloquence that day did not speed the progress of the civil-rights bill through Congress. It did not end racism or erase poverty and despair. It did not prevent the ghetto riots that lay ahead, or the white backlash that would ultimately smother the civil-rights movement and destroy King himself. But King had turned a political rally into a historic event. In one of the great speeches of history, he recalled America to the ideals of justice and equality, proclaiming that the color of one's skin ought never be a burden or a liability in American life.

In 1963 King's oratory did not quell the rage of the bitterest opponents of civil rights. Medgar Evers, the head of the Mississippi branch of the NAACP, was murdered by a sniper in Jackson, Mississippi. In September the Ku Klux Klan bombing of a black church in Birmingham killed four girls attending Sunday School. (Not until 2002 was the last of the four main suspects brought to justice.) Still others would have to die before civil rights for all could be achieved.

The Civil Rights and Voting Rights Acts   Kennedy himself was the first to die. As a southerner who had initially opposed civil rights for blacks, Lyndon Johnson knew that he either had to prove himself on this issue or the liberals "would get me. They'd throw up my background against me. . . . I had to produce a civil rights bill," he later wrote, "that was even stronger than the one they'd have gotten if Kennedy had lived." Johnson succeeded in doing just that, employing all his skills to toughen the bill's provisions and to break a southern filibuster in the Senate.

The most significant civil-rights law in U.S. history, the 1964 act banned racial discrimination and segregation in public accommodations. It also outlawed bias in federally funded programs; granted the federal government new powers to fight school segregation; and forbade discrimination in employment, creating the Equal Employment Opportunity Commission (EEOC) to enforce the ban on job discrimination by race, religion, national origin, or sex.

The Civil Rights Act did not address the right to vote in state and local elections. So CORE and SNCC activists, believing that the ballot box was the key to power for African-Americans in the South, mounted a major campaign to register black voters. They organized the Mississippi Freedom Summer Project of 1964 to focus on the most racially divided state in the Union, where African-Americans constituted 42 percent of the population but only 5 percent of the registered voters. About a thousand white students, from nearly two hundred colleges and universities, volunteered to help register black voters and to teach the practices of democracy and black history in "Freedom Schools." Harassed by Mississippi law-enforcement officials and Ku Klux Klansmen, the activists endured the firebombing of black churches and civil-rights headquarters, as well as arrests.

Although they registered only twelve hundred blacks to vote, the civil-rights workers enrolled nearly sixty thousand disfranchised blacks in the Mississippi Freedom Democratic Party (MFDP). In August 1964 they took their case to the national Democratic convention. They insisted that since the MFDP was the only freely elected party in Mississippi, the convention should seat its delegates in place of the all-white delegation chosen by the segregationist Mississippi Democratic party. To head off a walkout by southern white delegates who threatened to bolt the convention if the party supported the MFDP, Johnson forged a compromise that offered two at-large seats to the MFDP and barred delegations from states that disfranchised blacks from all future conventions. The compromise angered southern segregationists and alienated the militants in the civil-rights movement. Within SNCC, the failure of the liberals to support seating the MFDP delegates proved to be a turning point in their disillusionment with the Democratic party and liberals.

Still, most blacks shared the optimism of Martin Luther King, Jr., and other mainstream civil-rights leaders, and over 90 percent of African-American voters cast their ballots for Democrats in 1964, leaving Johnson and the liberals in firm control. Both King and the liberal Democrats were eager to counter GOP gains in the South by opening the voting booths to increasing numbers of blacks. Determined to win a strong voting-rights law, the SCLC organized mass protests in Selma, Alabama, in March 1965. Blacks were half the population of Dallas County, where Selma was located, yet only 1 percent were registered to vote.

King knew he had to again create a crisis to arouse national indignation in order to pressure Congress to act. Selma's county sheriff, Jim Clark, every bit as violence-prone as Birmingham's "Bull" Connor, attacked the protesters brutally. Showcased on TV, the attacks increased support for a voting-rights bill. But not till SCLC and other activists sought to march from Selma to Montgomery, to petition Governor George Wallace, and were clubbed and tear-gassed by lawmen did they provoke national outrage. Many thousands marched in sympathy in northern cities. Johnson grasped the mood of the country and delivered a televised address urging Congress to pass a voting-rights bill, beseeching all Americans, "Their cause must be our cause, too." Because "it's not just Negroes, really, it's all of us who must overcome the crippling legacy of bigotry and injustice. And," invoking the movement's anthem, "we *shall* overcome."

Signed by the president in August 1965, the Voting Rights Act invalidated the use of any test or device to deny the vote and authorized federal examiners to register voters in states that had disfranchised blacks. The law dramatically expanded black suffrage, boosting the number of registered black voters in the South from 1 million in 1964 to 3.1 million in 1968, and transformed southern politics.

From fewer than two dozen in the South in 1964, the number of blacks holding elective office swelled to almost five hundred in 1970. It mushroomed to nearly twelve hundred in 1972. That brought jobs for African-Americans, contracts for black businesses, and improvements in the facilities and services in black neighborhoods. Most importantly, as Fannie Lou Hamer recalled, when African-Americans could not vote, "white folks would drive past your house in a pickup truck with guns hanging up on the back and give you hate stares. . . . Those same people now call me Mrs. Hamer."

Fire in the Streets The civil-rights movement profoundly changed, but did not revolutionize, race relations. It ended legal segregation

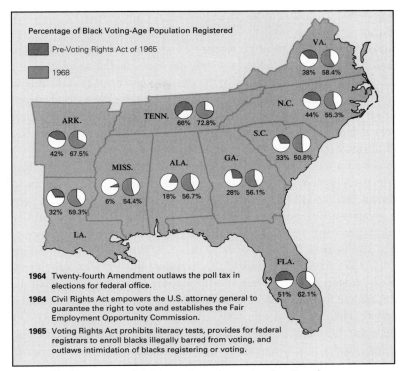

Percentage of Black Voting-Age Population Registered

◼ Pre-Voting Rights Act of 1965

◻ 1968

VA. 38% 58.4%

N.C. 44% 55.3%

TENN. 66% 72.8%

ARK. 42% 67.5%

S.C. 33% 50.8%

MISS. 6% 54.4%

ALA. 18% 56.7%

GA. 28% 56.1%

LA. 32% 59.3%

FLA. 51% 62.1%

1964 Twenty-fourth Amendment outlaws the poll tax in elections for federal office.

1964 Civil Rights Act empowers the U.S. attorney general to guarantee the right to vote and establishes the Fair Employment Opportunity Commission.

1965 Voting Rights Act prohibits literacy tests, provides for federal registrars to enroll blacks illegally barred from voting, and outlaws intimidation of blacks registering or voting.

Voter Registration of African-Americans in the South, 1964–1968

As blacks overwhelmingly registered to vote as Democrats, some former segregationist politicians, among them George Wallace, started to court the black vote, and many southern whites began to cast their ballots for Republicans, inaugurating an era of real two-party competition in the South.

by race, broke the monopoly on political power in the South held by whites, and galvanized a new black sense of self and of dignity. "Now if we do want to go to McDonald's we can go to McDonald's," mused a black woman in Atlanta. "It's just knowing! It's a good feeling." As much as any particular gain, the civil-rights movement had raised hopes for the possibility of change, legitimated protest, pointed the way Americans could redress grievances. But its inability to transform equality of opportunity into equality of results underscored the limitations of liberal change, especially in the urban ghetto. The anger bubbling below the surface soon boiled over.

On August 11, 1965, five days after the signing of the Voting Rights Act, a confrontation between white police and young blacks in Watts, the largest black district in Los Angeles, ignited the most destructive race riot in decades. For six days nearly fifty thousand blacks looted shops, firebombed white-owned businesses, and sniped at police officers and fire fighters. When the riot ended, thirty-four people were dead, nine hundred injured, and four thousand arrested. Blacks in

Chicago and Springfield, Massachusetts, then took to the streets, looting, burning, and battling police.

In the summer of 1966 more than a score of ghetto outbreaks erupted in northern cities. Blacks rioted to force whites to pay heed to the squalor of the slums and to the brutal behavior of police in the ghetto—problems that the liberal civil-rights movement had failed to solve. Frustrated by the allure of America's wealth portrayed on TV and by what seemed the empty promise of civil-rights laws, black mobs stoned passing motorists, ransacked stores, torched white-owned buildings, and hurled bricks at the troops sent to quell the disorder.

The following summer, black rage at oppressive conditions and impatience with liberal change erupted in 150 racial skirmishes and 40 riots—the most intense and destructive period of racial violence in U.S. history. In Newark, New Jersey, twenty-seven people died and more than eleven hundred were injured. The following week, Detroit went up in smoke. As the fires spread, so did the looting. Children joined adults in racing from store to store to fill their arms with liquor and jewelry; cars pulled up to businesses so they could be stocked with appliances. By the time the Michigan National Guard and U.S. army paratroopers quelled the riot, forty-three people had died, two thousand were injured, and seven thousand had been arrested. Then in 1968, following the assassination of Martin Luther King, Jr. (see Chapter 29), black uprisings flared in the ghettos of a hundred cities. Overall, the 1964–1968 riot toll would include some two hundred dead, seven thousand injured, forty thousand arrested, at least $500 million in property destroyed, and King's "beloved community" ashes in the fires.

A frightened, bewildered nation asked why such rioting was occurring just when blacks were beginning to achieve many of their goals. Militant blacks explained the riots as revolutionary violence to overthrow a racist, reactionary society. The Far Right saw them as evidence of a communist plot. Conservatives described the riots as senseless outbursts by troublemakers. The administration's National Advisory Commission on Civil Disorders (known as the Kerner Commission) indicted "white racism" for fostering an "explosive mixture" of poverty, slum housing, poor education, and police brutality in America's cities. Warning that "our nation is moving toward two societies, one black, one white—separate and unequal," the commission recommended increases in federal expenditures to assist urban blacks. Johnson, aware of the backlash against the War on Poverty as well as the cost of the war in Vietnam, ignored the advice. "Each war feeds on the other," observed Senator William Fulbright, "and, although the President assures us that we have the resources to win both wars, in fact we are not winning either of them."

"Black Power"   For some African-Americans, liberalism's response to racial inequality proved "too little, too late." The demand for Black Power sounded in 1966 expressed the eagerness of younger activists for confrontation and rapid social change. The slogan encapsulated both their bitterness

Black Power *Rejecting the faith long held by African-Americans in the United States and in the professed intentions of white America to remedy injustices, advocates of Black Power insisted on controlling their own movement and institutions, shaping their own agenda and programs, and defining their own demands and destiny.*

toward a white society that blocked their aspirations and their rejection of King's commitment to nonviolence, integration, and alliances with liberals.

Less an ideology than a cry of fury and frustration, Black Power owed much to the teachings of Malcolm X. Born in Omaha, Nebraska, in 1925, the son of a preacher active in the Garvey movement, Malcolm Little pimped and sold drugs before being arrested and jailed in 1946. In prison he converted to the Nation of Islam (NOI), the Black Muslim group founded by Wallace Fard and led by Elijah Muhammad (Elijah Poole). Released in 1952 and renamed Malcolm X, a symbolic repudiation of the "white man's name," he quickly became the Black Muslims' most dynamic street orator and recruiter.

Building on separatist and nationalist impulses long present in the black community—racial solidarity and uplift, self-sufficiency and self-help—Malcolm X insisted that blacks "wake up, clean up, and stand up" to achieve true independence. "I don't see any American dream," he often said. "I see an American nightmare." He urged blacks to be proud of their blackness and their African roots. He wanted them to see themselves with their "own eyes not the white man's," and to separate themselves from the "white devil." Critical of civil-rights leaders like King—"just a twentieth-century Uncle Tom"—for emphasizing desegregation instead of building black institutions, he insisted that blacks seize their freedom "by any means necessary": "If ballots won't work, bullets will," he said. "If someone puts a hand on you, send him to the cemetery." In February 1965, after he broke with the Nation of Islam, Malcolm X was assassinated by three gunmen affiliated with the NOI. He was not silenced. His account of his life and beliefs, *The Autobiography of Malcolm X* (1965) became the main text of the rising Black Power movement.

Two days after winning the world heavyweight championship in 1964, boxer Cassius Clay shocked the sports world by announcing his conversion to the NOI and his new name, Muhammad Ali. Refusing induction into the armed services on religious grounds, Ali was found guilty of draft evasion, stripped of his title, and exiled from boxing for three and a half years during his athletic prime. Inspired by the examples of Ali and Malcolm X, young African-Americans—more insistent than their parents on immediate change and less willing to endure discrimination—abandoned civil disobedience and reformist strategies. In 1966 CORE and SNCC changed from interracial organizations committed to achieving integration nonviolently to all-black groups advocating racial separatism and Black Power "by any means necessary."

The most notorious champion of self-determination for African-American communities was the Black Panther party. Founded in Oakland, California, in 1966 by Huey P. Newton and Bobby Seale, it urged black men to become "panthers—smiling, cunning, scientific, striking by night and sparing no one." Although the Panthers also founded schools and engaged in peaceful community activism, they were mostly known for their shootouts with the police. "The heirs of Malcolm X," claimed Newton, "have picked up the gun." Confrontations with police and the FBI left many of its members dead or in prison, effectively destroying the organization and, together with the riots, galvanizing white opposition.

Although the concept remained imprecise and contested and included people ranging from businesspeople who used it to push black capitalism to revolutionaries who sought an end to capitalism, Black Power exerted a significant influence. It helped organize scores of community self-help groups and institutions that did not depend on whites. It was used to establish black studies programs at colleges, to mobilize black voters to elect black candidates, and to encourage greater racial pride and self-esteem—"black is beautiful." James Brown sang, "Say it loud—I'm black and I'm proud," and as never before African-Americans rejected skin bleaches and hair straighteners, gave their children African names and Kwanzaa gifts instead of Christmas presents, and gloried in soul music. "I may have lost hope," SCLC leader Jesse Jackson had students repeating with him, "but I am . . . somebody. . . . I am . . . black . . . beautiful . . . proud. . . . I must be respected." This message reverberated with other marginalized groups as well, and helped shape their protest movements.

VOICES OF PROTEST

The aura of liberalism in the 1960s markedly affected Native Americans, Hispanic-Americans, and women. They, too, were inspired by Kennedy's rhetoric, by Johnson's actions, and by liberalism's emphasis on government intervention to solve social problems. Each followed the black lead in challenging the status quo, demanding full and equal citizenship rights, emphasizing group identity and pride, and seeing its younger members push for ever more radical action.

Native American Activism — In 1961 representatives of sixty-seven tribes drew up a Declaration of Purposes criticizing the termination policy of the 1950s. In 1964 hundreds of Indians lobbied in Washington for the inclusion of Native Americans in the War on Poverty. Indians suffered the worst poverty, the most inadequate housing, the highest disease and death rates, and the least access to education of any group in the United States. President Johnson responded by establishing the National Council on Indian Opportunity in 1965. It funneled more federal funds onto reservations than any previous program. Johnson also appointed the first Native American to head the Bureau of Indian Affairs (BIA) since 1870, and promised to erase "old attitudes of paternalism." He rejected the termination policy and advocated Indian self-determination, insisting in a special message to Congress in 1968 on "the right of the First Americans to remain Indians while exercising their rights as Americans."

By 1968 younger Indian activists, calling themselves "Native Americans," demanded "Red Power." They voiced dissatisfaction with the accommodationist approach of their elders, the lack of protection for Indian land and water rights, the desecration of Indian graves and sacred sites, and legal prohibitions against certain Indian religious practices. They mocked Columbus Day and staged sit-ins against museums that housed Indian bones. They established reservation cultural programs to reawaken spiritual beliefs and teach Native languages. The Puyallup held "fish-ins" to assert old treaty rights to fish in the Columbia River and Puget Sound. The Wampanoag in Massachusetts named Thanksgiving a National Day of Mourning. The Navajo and Hopi protested strip-mining in the Southwest, and the Taos Pueblo organized to reclaim the Blue Lake sacred site in northern New Mexico.

The most militant group, the American Indian Movement (AIM), was founded in 1968 by Chippewas, Sioux, and Ojibwa from the northern Plains. Its goals were to protect the traditional ways of Native Americans, prevent police harassment of Indians in urban "red ghettos," and establish "survival schools" to teach Indian history and values. In late 1969 AIM executed a sustained protest, occupying Alcatraz Island. Citing a Sioux Indian treaty that unused federal lands would revert to Indian control, an armed AIM contingent held the island for nineteen months before being dispersed.

AIM's militancy aroused other Native Americans to be proud of their heritage. Their members "had a new look about them, not that hangdog reservation look

I was used to," Mary Crow Dog remembered, and they "loosened a sort of earth-quake inside me." Many of the eight hundred thousand who identified themselves as Indians in the 1970 census did so for the first time.

Hispanic-Americans Organize

The fastest-growing minority, Latinos, or Hispanic-Americans, also grew impatient with their establishment organizations. The Mexican American Political Association and other organizations had been able to do little to ame-liorate the dismal existence of most of the 5 million Hispanic-Americans. With a median annual wage half the poverty level, with 40 percent of Mexican-American adults functionally illiterate, and with de facto segregation common throughout the Southwest, Latinos like César Chávez turned to the more militant tactics and strategies of the civil-rights movement.

Born on an Arizona farm first cultivated in the 1880s by his grandfather, Chávez grew up a migrant farm worker, joined the U.S. navy in World War II, and then devoted himself to gaining union recognition and improved working condi-tions for the mostly Mexican-American farm laborers in California. A charismatic leader who, like Martin Luther King, Jr., used religion and nonviolent resistance to fight for social change, Chávez led his followers in the Delano vineyards of the San Joaquin valley to strike in 1965. Similar efforts had been smashed in the past. But Chávez and United Farm Workers (UFW) cofounder Dolores Huerta organized consumer boycotts of table grapes to dramatize the farm workers' struggle. They made *La Causa* part of the common struggle of the entire Mexican-American community and part of the larger national movement for civil rights and social justice. For the first time, farm workers gained the right to unionize to secure bet-ter wages. Just as the UFW flag featured an Aztec eagle and the Virgin of Guadalupe, Chávez combined religion, labor militancy, and Mexican heritage to stimulate ethnic pride and politicization.

Also in the mid-1960s young Hispanic activists began using the formerly pejo-rative terms *Chicano* and *Chicana* to express a militant sense of collective identity and solidarity for all those of Mexican and Latin American descent. They insisted on a self-selected designation to highlight their insistence on self-determination: "Our main goal is to orient the Chicano to *think* Chicano so as to achieve equal status with other groups, not to emulate the Anglo."

Rejecting assimilation, Chicano student organizations came together in *El Movimiento Estudiantil Chicano de Aztlan (MEChA)* in 1967. They led Chicano high-school students in Los Angeles, Denver, and San Antonio in boycotts of classes (called "blowouts") in 1968 to demand bilingual education and more Latino teachers, and demonstrated at their own colleges to obtain Chicano Studies programs and Chicana-only organizations. At the inaugural Chicano Youth Liber-ation Conference in 1969 they adopted *El Plan Espiritual de Aztlan,* a manifesto of cultural and political nationalism, and, on September 16, Mexican Independence Day, they led high-school students in the First National Chicano Boycott of schools throughout the Southwest.

Similar zeal led poet Rodolfo "Corky" Gonzales to found the Crusade for Justice in Colorado to fight police brutality and improve job opportunities for Chicanos. It led Reies Lopez Tijerina to form the *Alianza Federal de Mercedes* in New Mexico to reclaim land usurped by whites in the 1848 Treaty of Guadalupe Hidalgo (see Chapter 13). It also led Jose Angel Gutierrez and others in Texas to create an alternative political party in 1967, *La Raza Unida,* to elect Latinos and instill cultural pride. As "brown is beautiful" came into vogue and young Chicanos grew *guerrillero* beards, David Sanchez organized the paramilitary Brown Berets in East Los Angeles.

Puerto Ricans in New York City founded the Young Lords, which they modeled on the Brown Berets. They published *Palante* ("forward in the struggle"), which, like the newspapers *La Raza* in Los Angeles and *El Papel* in Albuquerque, popularized movement strategies and aims. The Young Lords started drug treatment programs, and hijacked ambulances and occupied a hospital to demand better medical services in the South Bronx. They also blockaded the streets of East Harlem with trash to force the city to provide improved sanitation services for the six hundred thousand Puerto Ricans living there.

Like their counterparts, young activists rejected the term *Oriental* in favor of *Asian-American,* to signify a new ethnic consciousness among people with roots in the Far East. They too campaigned for special educational programs and for the election of Asian-Americans to office. Formed at the University of California in 1968, the Asian American Political Alliance encouraged Asian-American students to claim their own cultural identity and, in racial solidarity with their "Asian brothers and sisters," to protest against the U.S. war in Vietnam. As did other ethnic groups, Asian-American students marched, sat-in, and went on strike to promote causes emphasizing their unique identity.

None of these movements for ethnic pride and power could sustain the fervent activism and media attention that they attracted in the late sixties. But by elevating the consciousness and nurturing the confidence of the younger generation, each contributed to the cultural pride of its respective group, and to the politics of identity that would continue to grow in importance.

A Second Feminist Wave

The rising tempo of activism in the 1960s also stirred a new spirit of self-awareness and dissatisfaction among educated women. A revived feminist movement emerged, profoundly altering women's view of themselves and their role in American life.

Several events fanned the embers of discontent into flames. John Kennedy, who exploited women in fleeting sexual encounters before and after his marriage, established the Presidential Commission on the Status of Women. Its 1963 report documented occupational inequities suffered by women that were similar to those endured by minorities. Women received less pay than men for comparable work. They had less chance of moving into professional or managerial careers. Only 7 percent of doctors were women, and less than 4 percent of lawyers. The women who served on the presidential commission successfully urged that the

Civil Rights Act of 1964 prohibit gender-based as well as racial discrimination in employment.

Dismayed by the Equal Employment Opportunity Commission's reluctance to enforce the ban on sex discrimination in employment, which was mandated by Title VII of the Civil Rights Act, Betty Friedan, Bella Abzug, Aileen Hernandez, and others formed the National Organization for Women (NOW) in 1966. A civil-rights group for women, NOW sought liberal change through the political system. It lobbied for equal opportunity, filed lawsuits against gender discrimination, and mobilized public opinion against the sexism then pervasive in America.

NOW's prominence owed much to the publication of Betty Friedan's *The Feminine Mystique* (1963). Friedan deplored the narrow view that women should seek fulfillment solely as wives and mothers. Suburban domesticity—the "velvet ghetto"—left many women with feelings of emptiness, with no sense of accomplishment, afraid to ask "the silent question—'Is this all?'" Friedan wanted women to pursue careers and establish "goals that will permit them to find their own identity." Her message rang true to many middle-class women who found the creativity of homemaking and the joys of motherhood exaggerated. It informed unfulfilled women that they were not alone, and gave them a vocabulary with which to express their dissatisfaction.

Still another catalyst for feminism came from the involvement of younger women in the civil-rights and anti–Vietnam War movements. These activists had gained confidence in their own potential, an ideology to understand oppression, and experience in the strategy and tactics of organized protest. Their activism made them conscious of their own second-class status, as they were sexually exploited and relegated to menial jobs by male activists. In 1965 civil-rights activists Mary King and Casey Hayden drew a parallel "between treatment of Negroes and treatment of women in our society as a whole."

> Assumptions of male superiority are as widespread and deep-rooted and every much as crippling to the woman as the assumptions of white supremacy are to the Negro. . . . [We need to] stop the discrimination and start the slow process of changing values and ideas so that all of us gradually come to understand that this is no more a man's world than it is a white world.

The memo struck a responsive chord among female activists, and by 1967 they had created a women's liberation movement more critical of sexual inequality than was the liberal NOW.

Women's Liberation   Militant feminists in 1968 adopted the technique of "consciousness-raising" as a recruitment device and a means of transforming women's perceptions of themselves and society. Tens of thousands of women assembled in small groups to share experiences and air grievances. They soon realized that others felt dissatisfaction similar to their own. "When I saw that what I always felt were my own personal hangups was as true for every other woman in that room as it was for me! Well, that's when my consciousness was raised," a participant recalled. Women learned to regard their personal, individual problems as shared problems with social causes and political solutions—"the personal is political." They came to understand the power dynamics in marriage, the family, and the workplace. Consciousness-raising opened eyes and minds. "It wasn't just whining, it was trying to figure out why, why we felt things and what we could do to make our marriages more equal and our lives better." This new consciousness begot a commitment to end sexism and a sense that "sisterhood is powerful."

Women's liberation groups sprang up across the nation. They employed a variety of publicity-generating and confrontational tactics. In 1968 radical feminists crowned a sheep Miss America to dramatize that such contests degraded women, and set up "freedom trash cans" in which women could discard high-heeled shoes, girdles, and other symbols of their subjugation. They insisted on being included in the Boston Marathon, no longer accepting the excuse that "it is unhealthy for women to run long distances." They established health collectives and shelters for abused women, created day-care centers and rape crisis centers, founded abortion-counseling services and women's studies programs. They demanded equality in education and the workplace, and protested the negative portrayals of women in the media and advertising. Terms like *male chauvinist pig* entered the vocabulary and those like *chicks* exited. Some feminists claimed patriarchy, the power of men, to be the main cause of all oppressions and exploitations. Most rejected the notion that women were naturally passive and emotional, and that they suffered from "penis envy" if they sought to do things beyond their "female dispositions."

Despite a gulf between radicals and liberals, the quarreling factions set aside their differences in August 1970 to join in the largest women's rights demonstration ever. Commemorating the fiftieth anniversary of woman suffrage, the Women's Strike for Equality brought out tens of thousands of women nationwide to parade for the right to equal employment and safe, legal abortions. By then the women's movement had already pressured many financial institutions to issue credit to single women and to married women in their own names. It had filed suit against hundreds of colleges and universities to secure salary raises for women faculty members victimized by discrimination, and ended newspapers' practice of listing employment opportunities under separate "Male" and "Female" headings. Guidelines that required corporations receiving federal funds to adopt nondiscriminatory hiring practices and equal pay scales had been established. By 1970 more than 40 percent of all women held full-time jobs outside the home.

The right to control their own sexuality and decisions whether to have children also became a feminist rallying cry. In 1960 "the Pill" came on the market, giving women greater freedom to be sexually active without the risk of pregnancy. Many women, aware of the dangers of illegal abortions, pushed for their legalization. Some challenged demeaning obstetrical practices. Others explored alternatives to hospital births and popularized alternatives to radical mastectomy for breast cancer. Women had become aware, in historian Gerda Lerner's words, that they belong to a subordinate group; that they have suffered wrongs as a group; that their condition of subordination is not natural, but societally determined; that they must join with other women to remedy these wrongs; and finally, that they must and can provide an alternative vision of societal organization in which women as well as men will enjoy autonomy and self-determination.

THE LIBERAL CRUSADE IN VIETNAM, 1961–1968

The activist liberals who boldly tried to end poverty and uplift the downtrodden also went to war on the other side of the globe to contain communism and export liberty, democracy, and self-determination. Kennedy escalated Eisenhower's efforts in Vietnam in order to hold "the cornerstone of the Free World in Southeast Asia, the keystone in the arch, the finger in the dike." Johnson resolved, "I am not going to lose Vietnam, I am not going to be the president who saw Southeast Asia go the way China went." They would make a stand. The war in Vietnam pursued by liberals ended the era of liberalism. By the time the nation's longest war ended, the liberal consensus would be a distant memory and the United States more divided than at any time since the Civil War.

Kennedy and Vietnam

Following the compromise settlement in Laos, President Kennedy resolved not to give further ground in Southeast Asia. He ordered massive shipments of weaponry to South Vietnam and increased the number of American forces stationed there from less than seven hundred in 1960 to more than sixteen thousand by the end of 1963. JFK refused to stand by and let Vietnam go communist. He feared it would lead to a Republican-led, anticommunist backlash, damaging him politically. Like Eisenhower, he believed that letting "aggression" go unchecked would lead to wider wars (the Munich analogy) and that the communist takeover of one nation would mean that others in the region would soon fall as well (the domino theory). Kennedy viewed international communism as a monolithic force, a single global enemy controlled by Moscow and Beijing. Seeing Third World conflicts as tests of America's, and his own, will, he wanted to show the world that the United States was not the "paper tiger" that Mao Zedong (Mao Tse-tung) mocked.

To counter the success of the National Liberation Front (NLF), or Vietcong, in the countryside, the United States uprooted Vietnamese peasants and moved them into fortified villages, or "strategic hamlets." But South Vietnamese president Diem rejected American pressure to gain popular support through liberal reform measures, instead crushing demonstrations by students and Buddhists. By mid-1963 Buddhist monks were setting themselves on fire to protest Diem's repression, and Diem's own generals were plotting a coup.

Frustrated American policy makers concluded that only a new government could prevent a Vietcong victory. They secretly backed the efforts of Vietnamese army officers planning Diem's overthrow. On November 1 the military leaders staged their coup, captured Diem and his brother, and shot them. The United States promptly recognized the new government (the first of nine South Vietnamese regimes in the next five years), but it too made little headway against the Vietcong. JFK would either have to increase the combat involvement of American forces or withdraw and seek a negotiated settlement.

What Kennedy would have done remains unknown. Less than a month after Diem's death, President Kennedy himself fell to an assassin's bullet. His admirers contend that by late 1963 a disillusioned Kennedy was favoring the withdrawal of American forces after the 1964 election. "It is their war," he said publicly. "We can help them, we can send them equipment, we can send our men out there as advisers, but in the final analysis it is their people and their government who have to win or lose the struggle." Skeptics note that the president followed this comment with a ringing restatement of his belief in the domino theory and a promise that America would not withdraw from the conflict. Virtually all his liberal advisers, moreover, held that an American victory in Vietnam was essential to check the advance of communism in Asia. National Security Adviser McGeorge Bundy, Secretary of Defense Robert McNamara, and Secretary of State Dean Rusk would counsel Kennedy's successor accordingly.

Escalation
of the War

Now it was Johnson who had to choose between intervening decisively or withdrawing from Vietnam. Privately describing Vietnam as "a raggedy-ass fourth-rate country" undeserving of American blood and dollars, LBJ feared that an all-out American military effort might provoke Chinese or Soviet entry and lead to World War III. He foresaw that full-scale engagement in "that bitch of a war" would destroy "the woman I really loved—the Great Society." Yet Johnson did not want the United States to appear weak. Only American strength and resolve, he believed, would prevent a wider war. Like Kennedy, he worried that a pullout would leave him vulnerable to conservative attack. Johnson had no intention of allowing the charge that he was soft on communism to be used to destroy him or his liberal programs.

Trapped between unacceptable alternatives, Johnson widened America's limited war, hoping that U.S. firepower would force Ho Chi Minh to the bargaining table. But the North Vietnamese and NLF calculated that they could gain more by outlasting the United States than by negotiating. So the war ground on.

In 1964 Johnson took bold steps to impress North Vietnam with American resolve and to block his opponent, Barry Goldwater, from capitalizing on Vietnam in the presidential campaign. In February he ordered the Pentagon to prepare for air strikes against North Vietnam. In May his advisers drafted a congressional resolution authorizing an escalation of American military action. In July the president appointed General Maxwell Taylor, a proponent of greater American involvement in the war, as ambassador to Saigon.

In early August North Vietnamese patrol boats allegedly clashed with two American destroyers in the Gulf of Tonkin. Evidence of the attack was unclear, yet Johnson announced that Americans had been victims of "open aggression on the high seas." Johnson condemned the attacks as unprovoked, never admitting that the U.S. ships had been aiding the South Vietnamese in secret raids against North Vietnam. He ordered air strikes on North Vietnamese naval bases and asked Congress to pass the previously prepared resolution. It authorized him to "take all necessary measures to repel any armed attack against the forces of the United States and to prevent further aggression." The Senate passed the Gulf of Tonkin Resolution 88 to 2, and the House 416 to 0, assured by the president that this meant no "extension of the present conflict."

Privately, LBJ called the resolution "grandma's nightshirt—it covered everything." He considered it a mandate to commit U.S. forces as he saw fit. The blank check to determine the level of force made massive intervention more likely; and having once used force against North Vietnam made it easier to do so again. But the resolution created an eventual credibility problem for Johnson, allowing opponents of the war to charge that he had misled Congress and lied to the American people. Thus, at the height of LBJ's popularity and power, his political downfall began.

The Endless War Early in 1965 Johnson cashed his blank check, ordering "Operation Rolling Thunder," the sustained bombing of North Vietnam. It accomplished none of its purposes: to inflict enough damage to make Hanoi negotiate, to boost the morale of the Saigon government, and to stop the flow of soldiers and supplies coming from North Vietnam via the so-called Ho Chi Minh Trail. So LBJ escalated America's air war. Between 1965 and 1968 the U.S. dropped eight hundred tons of bombs a day on North Vietnam, three times the tonnage dropped by all the combatants in World War II.

Unable to turn the tide by bombing, Johnson committed U.S. combat troops to Vietnam. They pursued a "meat-grinder" or attrition strategy, trying to force the communists to the peace table by inflicting unacceptable losses on them. This required 185,000 Americans in Vietnam by the end of 1965; 385,000 a year later; and 485,000 (a greater military force than the U.S. had deployed in Korea) after another year. But superiority in numbers and weaponry did not defeat an enemy that could choose when and where to attack and then melt back into the jungle. Hanoi, determined to battle until the United States lost the will to fight, matched each American troop increase with its own. No end was in sight.

Doves Versus Hawks First on college campuses and then in the wider society, a growing number of Americans began to oppose the war. A week after marines splashed ashore at Danang, South Vietnam, in March 1965, students and faculty at the University of Michigan staged the first teach-in to raise questions about U.S. intervention. All-night discussions of the war followed at other universities. Some twenty-five thousand people, mainly students, attended a rally in Washington that spring to demonstrate against the escalation. In 1966 large-scale campus protests against the war erupted. Students angrily demonstrated against the draft and against university research for

The Vietnam War, to 1968

Wishing to guarantee an independent, noncommunist government in South Vietnam, Lyndon Johnson remarked in 1965, "We fight because we must fight if we are to live in a world where every country can shape its own destiny. To withdraw from one battlefield means only to prepare for the next."

the Pentagon. "Yesterday's ivory tower," observed the president of Hunter College, "has become today's foxhole."

Intellectuals and clergy joined the chorus of opposition to the war. Some decried the massive bombing of an underdeveloped nation; some doubted that the United States could win at any reasonable cost; some feared the demise of liberalism. In 1967 prominent critics of the war, including Democratic Senators William Fulbright, Robert Kennedy, and George McGovern, pediatrician Dr. Benjamin Spock, and

LBJ's Vietnam Nightmare *The Vietnam War spelled Johnson's undoing. Young peace demonstrators made known their feelings about the president's role in the war during a massive antiwar protest at the Pentagon in October 1967.*

Martin Luther King, Jr., spurred hundreds of thousands to participate in antiwar protests.

Critics also noted that the war's toll fell most heavily on the poor. Owing to college deferments, the use of influence, and a military-assignment system that shunted the better-educated to desk jobs, lower-class youths were twice as likely to be drafted and, when drafted, twice as likely to see combat duty as middle-class youths. About 80 percent of the enlisted men who fought in Vietnam came from poor and working-class families.

TV coverage of the war further eroded support. Scenes of children maimed by U.S. bombs and of dying Americans, replayed in living rooms night after night, laid bare the horror of the war and undercut the optimistic reports of government officials. Americans shuddered as they watched defoliants and napalm (a burning glue that adheres to skin and clothing) lay waste to Vietnam's countryside and leave tens of thousands of civilians dead or mutilated. They saw American troops, supposedly winning the hearts and minds of the Vietnamese, burn their villages and desecrate their burial grounds.

Yet most Americans still either supported the war or remained undecided. "I want to get out, but I don't want to give up" expressed a widespread view. They acknowledged that, in McNamara's words, "the picture of the world's greatest superpower killing or seriously injuring a thousand noncombatants a week, while trying to pound a tiny backward country into submission on an issue whose merits are hotly disputed, is not a pretty one." But they were not prepared to accept a communist victory over the United States.

Equally disturbing was how polarized the nation had grown. "Hawks" would accept little short of total victory, whereas "doves" insisted on negotiating, not fighting. Civility vanished. As Johnson lashed out at his critics as "nervous Nellies" and refused to de-escalate the conflict, demonstrators paraded past the White House chanting, "Hey, hey, LBJ, how many kids did you kill today?" A virtual prisoner in the White House, unable to speak in public without being shouted down, Johnson had become a casualty of the far-off war. So had an era of hope and liberalism. Few Americans still believed in Kennedy's confident assurance that the nation could "pay any price, bear any burden, meet any hardship, support any friend, oppose any foe."

IMPORTANT EVENTS, 1960–1968

1960	Sit-ins to protest segregation begin. John F. Kennedy elected president.
1961	Peace Corps and Alliance for Progress created. Bay of Pigs invasion. Freedom rides. Berlin Wall erected.
1962	Michael Harrington, *The Other America*. Cuban missile crisis.
1963	Civil-rights demonstrations in Birmingham. March on Washington. Test-Ban Treaty between the Soviet Union and the United States. Kennedy assassinated; Lyndon B. Johnson becomes president. Betty Friedan, *The Feminine Mystique*.
1964	Freedom Summer in Mississippi. California becomes most populous state. Civil Rights Act. Gulf of Tonkin incident and resolution. Economic Opportunity Act initiates War on Poverty. Johnson elected president.
1965	Bombing of North Vietnam and Americanization of the war begin. Assassination of Malcolm X. Civil-rights march from Selma to Montgomery. César Chávez's United Farm Workers strike in California. Teach-ins to question U.S. involvement in War in Vietnam begin. Voting Rights Act. Watts riot in Los Angeles.
1966	Stokely Carmichael calls for Black Power. Black Panthers formed. National Organization for Women (NOW) founded.
1967	Massive antiwar demonstrations. Race riots in Newark, Detroit, and other cities.

29

A Time of Upheaval, 1968–1974

Dorothy Burlage grew up in southeast Texas. She learned to be a proper southern belle as well as a self-reliant "frontier woman" who knew how to ride a horse, shoot a gun, and fix a flat tire. Her conservative Southern Baptist parents taught her to believe in the brotherhood of man and also to conform to the conservative values of her community, which was steeped in the lore of its slaveholding past. At the University of Texas she watched with awe as black students her age engaged in a civil-rights struggle she likened to a holy crusade.

Dorothy left the sorority that disapproved of her interest in the civil-rights movement and moved into the university's only desegregated dormitory. She joined the Christian Faith-and-Life Community, a residential religious study center, where she imbibed a heady brew of liberal Christian existentialism. Its commitment to nonviolence and radical change propelled Burlage into the civil-rights movement and its quest for the "beloved community." The young activists in SNCC became her political model, their ethos her moral beacon.

Dorothy Burlage attended the founding conference of SDS in 1962. She felt a part of history in the making. It exhilarated her to be together with like-minded idealists from different backgrounds, all eager to create a better world. "It was a rare moment in history and we were blessed to be given that opportunity," she later recalled. She gloried in being surrounded by peers who shared her values, who reaffirmed her view of the world, and who validated her activities. Burlage remained involved in the explosive activities of SDS for the rest of the decade, until disillusioned by the constant need to be "more radical and more willing to take risks to *prove* yourself." Turning away from political agitation, she initially thought the women's movement "frivolous, that there were people who were genuinely poor and people who were genuinely discriminated against because of color. And I didn't see women as such an oppressed class at that time." Later she would, and share their rage.

In 1970, feeling herself "a lost soul," Dorothy decided to go back to school to become a child psychologist. Dissatisfied with radical politics, she turned to providing better care for children and running a counseling center for women. Yet she still rejected the liberal consensus and longed to feel as committed to fundamental change, as engaged in unbridled protest, as she had in the 1960s.

Fiery commitment and engagement would be characteristic of many of Dorothy's peers, on the right as well as the left. American youth spawned a tumultuous student movement and convulsive counterculture that gave the decade its distinctive aura of upheaval. They exploded the well-kept world of the 1950s, when "nice" girls did not have sex or pursue careers, when African-Americans feared to vote or assert themselves. They revived both the left and right. Then, disillusioned with the slow pace of change, many became, and remained, preoccupied with themselves—which unexpectedly transformed the nation.

Richard Nixon was both an agent in and beneficiary of the era's upheavals and political realignment. He barely won the presidency in 1968, but continuing convulsive events ensured him an overwhelming reelection victory in 1972. Presiding over the most radical changes in American foreign policy since the start of the Cold War, Nixon eschewed ideology and morality in favor of practical, realistic goals. He ended U.S. involvement in Vietnam and inaugurated a period of détente with China and the Soviet Union. But he flouted the very laws he had pledged to uphold, and Nixon's abuse of power ignited new storms of protest and a constitutional crisis that did not end until he resigned in disgrace in 1974 to avoid impeachment. Nixon's legacy was the further disillusionment of many citizens and a public disrespect for politics seldom matched in U.S. history.

This chapter focuses on five major questions:

In what ways did the furor over the war in Vietnam affect the student movement?

What were the main causes and consequences of the politics of upheaval in 1968?

What fundamental changes in American foreign policy were made by President Nixon?

How did Richard Nixon's political strategy reflect the racial upheavals and radicalism of this era?

What were the main causes of the Watergate scandal?

THE YOUTH MOVEMENT

In the 1950s the number of American students pursuing higher education rose from 1 million to 4 million, and the number doubled to 8 million in the 1960s. By then, more than half the U.S. population was under thirty years of age. Their sheer numbers gave the young a collective identity and guaranteed that their actions would have force.

Most baby boomers followed conventional paths in the 1960s. They sought a secure place in the system, not its overthrow. They preferred beer to drugs, and football to political demonstrations. They joined fraternities and sororities and majored in subjects that would equip them for the job market. Whether or not they went to college—and fewer than half did—the vast majority had their eyes fixed on a good salary, a new car, and a traditional family. Many disdained the long-haired protesters and displayed the same bumper stickers as their elders: "My Country—Right or Wrong" and "America—Love It or Leave It."

Tens of thousands of young people mobilized on the right, joining organizations like Young Americans for Freedom (YAF). These youths idolized Barry Goldwater, not John Kennedy. They supported the war in Vietnam as a necessary part of the long struggle for victory over communism. While many adhered to traditional values, other young conservatives embraced libertarian notions. Yet all student activists, the New Right and the New Left, saw themselves as part of an upheaval that would fundamentally change America.

Toward a New Left

In the 1960s an insurgent minority of liberal arts majors and graduate students got the lion's share of attention. This liberal-minded minority welcomed the idealism of the civil-rights movement and the rousing call of President Kennedy for service to the nation. They admired the mavericks and outsiders of the fifties: Martin Luther King, Jr.; iconoclastic comedian Mort Sahl; Beat poet Allen Ginsberg; and pop-culture rebel James Dean.

Determined not to be a "silent generation," sixty students adopted the Port Huron Statement in June 1962. A broad critique of American society and a call for more genuine human relationships, it proclaimed "a new left" and gave birth to the Students for a Democratic Society (SDS). Inspired by the young black activists, SDS envisioned a nonviolent youth movement transforming the United States into a "participatory democracy" in which individuals would directly control the decisions that affected their lives. SDS assumed that such a system would value love and creativity and would end materialism, militarism, and racism.

The generation of activists who found their agenda in the Port Huron Statement had their eyes opened by the images of police dogs and fire hoses in Birmingham, the assassination of President Kennedy, and the destruction of Vietnam brought so graphically into their homes by television. Most never joined SDS, instead associating with what they vaguely called "the Movement" or "the New Left." Unlike the Leftists of the 1930s, they rejected Marxist ideology; emulated SNCC's rhetoric and style; and were radicalized by the rigidity of campus administrators and mainstream liberalism's inability to achieve swift, fundamental change. Only a radical rejection of compromise and consensus, they presumed, could restructure society along humane and democratic lines.

From Protest to Resistance

Returning from the Mississippi Freedom Summer to the Berkeley campus of the University of California in fall 1964, Mario Savio and other student activists ventured to solicit funds and recruit volunteers near the campus gate, a spot traditionally open to political activities. Prodded by local conservatives, the university suddenly banned such practices. That led Savio to found the Berkeley Free Speech Movement (FSM), a coalition of student groups insisting on the right to campus political activity. Savio claimed that the university served the interests of corporate

America and treated students as interchangeable machine parts. He called on students to resist: "There is a time when the operation of the machine becomes so odious, makes you so sick to heart, that you've got to put your bodies upon the gears and upon the wheels . . . and you've got to make it stop." More than a thousand students followed Savio into Sproul Hall to stage a sit-in. Their arrests led to more demonstrations and strikes by students holding signs that read "I Am a Student: Do Not Fold, Bend, or Mutilate" and "Shut This Factory Down."

By 1965 Mario Savio's call for students to throw their bodies upon "the machine" until it ground to a halt had reverberated on campuses nationwide. Students sat in to halt compulsory ROTC (Reserve Officers' Training Corps) programs, rallied to protest dress codes and parietal rules, and marched to demand changes in the grading system. They demanded fewer required courses, smaller classes, and teaching-oriented rather than research-oriented professors. They threatened to close down universities unless they admitted more minority students and stopped doing research for the military-industrial complex.

The escalation of the war in Vietnam, and the abolition of automatic student deferments from the draft in January 1966, turned the Movement into a mass movement. Popularizing the slogan "Make Love—Not War," SDS organized teach-ins, sponsored antiwar marches and rallies, and harassed campus recruiters for the military and for the Dow Chemical Company, the chief producer of napalm and Agent Orange, chemicals used in Vietnam to burn villages and defoliate forests. While the Vietnam Veterans Against the War (1967) did much to legitimize antiwar activism, SDS leaders encouraged even more provocative acts in 1967. With the rallying cry "From Protest to Resistance," they supported draft resistance and civil disobedience in selective service centers, and clashed with federal marshals during the "siege of the Pentagon" in October's "Stop the Draft Week." At the Spring Mobilization to End the War in Vietnam, which attracted a half-million antiwar protesters to New York's Central Park, SDS members led the chants of "Burn cards, not people" and "Hell, no, we won't go!" By 1968 SDS claimed one hundred thousand members on three hundred campus chapters.

That spring saw at least forty thousand students on a hundred campuses demonstrate against war and racism. Most, but not all, stayed peaceful. In April militant Columbia University students shouting "Gym Crow must go" took over the administration building and held a dean captive to denounce the university's proposed expansion into Harlem to construct a gymnasium for student use only. The protest then expanded into a demonstration against the war and the university's military research. A thousand students barricaded themselves inside campus buildings, declaring them "revolutionary communes." Outraged by the harshness of the police who retook the buildings by storm and sent more than a hundred demonstrators to the hospital, the moderate majority of Columbia students joined a boycott of classes that shut down the university and brought the academic year to a premature end. Elsewhere, students in France, Germany, Ireland, Italy, Japan, and Mexico rose up to demand reform that year. In Prague, Czechoslovakian students singing Beatles songs battled Soviet tanks.

The highpoint of Movement activism came in mid-1969 with the New Mobilization, a series of huge antiwar demonstrations culminating in mid-November with a March Against Death. Three hundred thousand protesters came to Washington, D.C., to march through a cold rain carrying candles and signs with the names of soldiers killed and villages destroyed in Vietnam. By then, antiwar sentiment pervaded many national institutions, including Congress; and by 1972 it would be dominant. In sharp contrast to the image of apolitical students of the 1950s, youth in the 1960s saw themselves as a political force, able to influence what affected their own lives.

Kent State— Jackson State

A storm of violence in the spring of 1970 marked the effective end of the student movement as a political force. On April 30, 1970, Richard M. Nixon, LBJ's successor, jolted a war-weary nation by announcing that he had ordered U.S. troops to invade Cambodia. Nominally neutral, Cambodia was being used by North Vietnam as a staging area for its troops. Nixon had previously decided to extricate the United States from Vietnam by "Vietnamizing" the ground fighting (that is, using South Vietnamese troops instead of Americans). Students, lulled by periodic announcements of troop withdrawals from Vietnam, now felt betrayed. They exploded in hatred for Nixon and the war.

At Kent State University in Ohio, as elsewhere, student frustrations unleashed new turmoil. Radicals broke windows and tried to firebomb the ROTC building. Nixon branded the protesters "bums," and his vice president compared them to Nazi storm troopers. Ohio governor James Rhodes slapped martial law on the university. Three thousand National Guardsmen in full battle gear rolled onto the campus in armored personnel carriers.

The day after the guard's arrival, six hundred Kent State students demonstrated against the Cambodian invasion. Suddenly a campus policeman boomed through a bullhorn, "This assembly is unlawful! This is an order—disperse immediately!" Students shouted back, "Pigs off campus!" Some threw stones. With bayonets fixed, the guardsmen moved toward the rally and laid down a blanket of tear gas. Hundreds of demonstrators and onlookers, choking and weeping, ran from the advancing troops. Guardsmen in Troop G, poorly trained in crowd control, raised their rifles and fired a volley into the retreating crowd. When the shooting stopped, four students lay dead, two of them women merely passing by on their way to lunch.

Ten days later, Mississippi state patrolmen fired into a women's dormitory at Jackson State College, killing two black students. Nationwide, students reeled from shock and exploded in protest. A wave of student strikes closed down four hundred colleges, many of which had seen no previous unrest. Hundreds of thousands of once-moderate students now identified themselves as "radical or far Left."

The upheaval polarized the United States. Although most students blamed Nixon for widening the war and applauded the demonstrators' goals, more Americans blamed the victims for the violence and criticized students for undermining U.S. foreign policy. Both class resentment of privileged college students and a fear of

"My God, They're Killing Us" *Following rioting downtown and the firebombing of the ROTC building, Ohio Governor James Rhodes called in the National Guard to stop the antiwar protests at Kent State University. On May 4, after retreating from rock-throwing students, nervous guardsmen turned and began to shoot. When the firing stopped, four students lay dead and eleven were wounded.*

social chaos animated working-class people's condemnation of protesters. Many Kent townspeople shared the view of a local merchant who asserted that the guard had "made only one mistake—they should have fired sooner and longer." A local ditty promised, "The score is four, and next time more."

Legacy of Student Frenzy   The campus disorders after the invasion of Cambodia were the final spasm of a tumultuous movement. When a bomb planted by three antiwar radicals destroyed a science building at the University of Wisconsin in summer 1970, killing a graduate student, most young people condemned the tactic. With the resumption of classes in the fall, the fad of "streaking"—racing across campus in the nude—more reminiscent of the 1920s than the 1960s, signaled a change in the student mood. Frustrated by their failure to end the war, much less to revolutionize American society, antiwar activists turned to other causes. Some became involved in the women's and ecology movements. Others sought refuge in mystic cults and rural communes. Many settled into careers and parenthood. A handful of radicals went underground, committing terrorist acts that resulted in government repression of what remained of the antiwar movement. The New Left was finished, a victim of government harassment, its own internal contradictions, and Nixon's winding down of the Vietnam War.

The consequences of campus upheavals outlived the New Left. Student radicalism spurred the resentment of millions of Americans, helping shatter the liberal consensus. Religious fundamentalists, southern segregationists, and blue-collar workers united in a conservative resurgence. This backlash propelled conservatives like Ronald Reagan to prominence. In 1966 he won California's governorship by denouncing Berkeley demonstrators and Watts rioters. The actor-turned-politician then won a resounding reelection victory by condemning young radicals. "If it takes a bloodbath, let's get it over with," he declared. "No more appeasement!" Conservatives gained office nationwide by sounding the same theme. Images of student radicalism, moreover, would be used to strengthen conservatism's appeal for the rest of the century.

The New Left had, however, helped mobilize public opposition to the Vietnam War. It energized campuses into a force that the government could not ignore, and it made continued U.S. involvement in Vietnam difficult. The Movement also liberalized many facets of campus life and made university governance less authoritarian. Dress codes and curfews virtually disappeared; ROTC went from a requirement to an elective; minority recruitment increased; and students assisted in shaping their education. History and literature courses began to include the contributions of minorities and women; what would later be called "multiculturalism" emerged.

Some New Left veterans continued their activism into the 1970s, joining the environmental, consumer rights, and antinuclear movements. Female students in the Movement formed the backbone of a women's liberation movement. These separate movements fell short of the New Left vision of remaking the social and political order. While masses of students could be mobilized in the short run for a particular cause, only a few made long-term commitments to radical politics. The generation that the New Left had hoped to organize as the vanguard of radical change preferred pot to politics, and rock to revolution.

THE COUNTERCULTURE

The alienation and hunger for change that drew some youths into radical politics led many more to cultural rebellion, to focusing on personal rather than political change, to rejecting the prevailing middle-class values, attitudes, and practices. Often called hippies, they disdained regular employment and consumerism, preferring to make what they needed, share it with others, and not want what they did not have. In the second half of the 1960s they joined communes and tribes that glorified liberation from traditional social rules. They rejected monogamy and reason as "hang-ups." In urban areas such as Seattle's University District and Atlanta's Fourteenth Street—"places where you could take a trip without a ticket"—they experimented with drugs and rejected the work ethic, materialism, and inhibited sexuality. In 1969 historian Theodore Roszack called them "a 'counter culture': meaning, a culture so radically disaffiliated from the mainstream assumptions of our society that it scarcely looks to many as a culture at all, but takes on the alarming appearance of a barbarian intrusion."

Hippies and Drugs

Illustrative of the gap between the two cultures, one saw marijuana as a "killer weed," a menace to health and life, and the other thought it a harmless social relaxant. In the absence of scientific evidence that the drug was dangerous, at least half the college students in the late sixties tried marijuana. A minority used hallucinogenic or mind-altering drugs, particularly LSD. The high priest of LSD was Timothy Leary, a former Harvard psychologist fired in 1963 for encouraging students to experiment with drugs—to "tune in, turn on, drop out." On the West Coast, writer Ken Kesey and his followers, the Merry Pranksters, promoted hallucinogens by conducting "acid tests" (distributing free tablets of LSD in orange juice). They created the "psychedelic" craze of Day-Glo-painted bodies gyrating to electrified rock music under flashing strobe lights to simulate the use of LSD. Musicals like *Hair* (1967) and such films as *Alice's Restaurant* (1969) depicted "tripping" on drugs as natural and safe.

Influenced by LSD's reality-bending effects, the counterculture sought a world in which magic and mysticism replaced science and reason, and where competitive individuals became caring and loving. Jim Morrison's rock group the Doors took inspiration and its name from Aldous Huxley's paean to hallucinogens, *The Doors of Perception*. Bands like the Jefferson Airplane launched the San Francisco sound of "acid rock," an electronically dazzling experience of sights and sounds—the perfect marriage of "sex, drugs, and rock-and-roll"—in the mid-1960s.

Distancing themselves from middle-class respectability, youths flaunted outrageous personal styles ("do your own thing"). They showed disdain for consumerism by wearing surplus military clothing, torn jeans, and tie-dyed T-shirts. Citing R. Buckminster Fuller—"There is no such thing as genius; some children are less damaged than others"—they started "free schools" that emphasized student autonomy and curricular experimentation. Young men sported shaggy beards and long hair. Young people saw doing as they pleased as a sign of freedom; their elders saw it as a contempt for social conventions. Typical of the generation that had been schooled in the deprivation and duty of the 1930s and 1940s, Ronald Reagan, then governor of California, defined a hippie as one "who looked like Tarzan, walked like Jane, and smelled like Cheetah."

Musical Revolution

Popular music both echoed and developed a separate generational identity, a distinct youth culture. Early in the 1960s folk music was the vogue on college campuses. Songs protesting war and racism, such as "Where Have All the Flowers Gone?" and "If I Had a Hammer," mirrored the early decade's idealism. Bob Dylan sang hopefully of changes "Blowin' in the Wind" that would transform society. His "The Times They Are a-Changing" proclaimed youth's impatience in 1964.

That year Beatlemania swept the country. The Beatles offered visions of pleasure and freedom. They embodied playful hedonism. Moving quickly beyond "I Want to Hold Your Hand," the English group soon gloried in the counterculture's drugs ("I'd love to turn you on"), sex ("why don't we do it in the road?"), and radicalism ("you say you want a revolution?"). They would be joined by the aggressively uninhibited Rolling Stones, the Motown rhythm-and-blues beat, and eardrum-shattering acid rockers. A phalanx of young musicians fought for social justice with guitars, their angry songs upbraiding the status quo, energizing the antiwar and racial struggles, and contributing to the upheavals of the 1960s.

In August 1969, four hundred thousand young people gathered for the Woodstock festival in New York's Catskill Mountains to celebrate their vision of freedom and harmony. For three days and nights they reveled in rock music and openly shared drugs, sexual partners, and contempt for the Establishment. Woodstock became a community. The counterculture heralded the festival as the dawning of an era of love and sharing, the Age of Aquarius.

In fact, the counterculture's luster had already dimmed. The pilgrimage of "flower children" to the Haight-Ashbury district of San Francisco (see A Place in Time: Haight-Ashbury) and to New York's East Village in 1967 brought in its wake a train of rapists and dope peddlers. In December 1969 Charles Manson and his "family" of runaways ritually murdered a pregnant movie actress and four of her friends. Then a Rolling Stones concert at the Altamont Raceway near San Francisco, in which the Hell's Angels motorcycle gang had been hired for five hundred dollars' worth of beer to maintain order, deteriorated into a violent melee in which several concertgoers died. In 1970 the Beatles disbanded. On his own, John Lennon sang, "The dream is over. What can I say?"

Advertisers awoke to the economic potential of the youth culture, using "rebellion" and "revolution" to sell cars, cigarettes, and jeans. Many if not most youths moved into conventional jobs and conventional lifestyles, recreational drug use notwithstanding. In films like *The Big Chill* (1983), cynics concluded that counterculture values were not deeply held. However, the optimistic view of humankind and skeptical view of authority continued to influence American education and society long after the 1960s. Self-fulfillment remained a popular goal, and Americans did not return to the puritanical, repressive sexual standards of the 1950s.

| The Sexual Revolution | The counterculture's "if it feels good, do it" approach to sex fit into the overall atmosphere of greater permissiveness in the 1960s. This shift in attitude and behavior constituted a |

sexual revolution. Although the AIDS epidemic and the graying of the baby boomers in the late 1980s chilled the ardor of heedless promiscuity, liberalized sexual mores were more publicly accepted than ever before.

Many commentators linked the increase in sexual permissiveness to waning fears of unwanted pregnancy. In 1960 oral contraceptives reached the market, and by 1970 10 million women were taking the Pill. Still other women used the intrauterine device (IUD, later banned as unsafe) or the diaphragm for birth control. Some states legalized abortion. In New York in 1970 one fetus was legally aborted for every two babies born. The Supreme Court's *Roe* v. *Wade* (1973) struck down all remaining state laws infringing on a woman's right to abortion during the first trimester (three months) of pregnancy.

By the end of the 1960s, the Supreme Court had ruled unconstitutional any laws restricting "sexually explicit" art with "redeeming social importance," and had upheld the right of individuals to own and use pornographic materials in their own homes. Mass culture exploited the new permissiveness. *Playboy* featured ever-more-explicit erotica, and women's periodicals encouraged their readers to enjoy recreational sex. The commercial success of films given "R" or "X" ratings led Broadway producers to present plays featuring full-frontal nudity (*Hair*) and simulated sexual orgies (*Oh, Calcutta!*). Even television taboos tumbled as network censors allowed blatantly sexual jokes and frank discussions of previously forbidden subjects.

Identifying pornography and obscenity as "a matter of national concern," in 1967 Congress established a special commission to suggest a plan of attack. Instead, in 1970 the commission recommended the repeal of all obscenity and pornography legislation. By then, most barriers to expressions of sexuality had fallen. A year before, the best-selling novels were Gore Vidal's *Myra Breckenridge* (transsexualism) and Philip Roth's *Portnoy's Complaint* (masturbation). The two most popular films were *Easy Rider,* which romanticized the drug and hippie culture, and *Midnight Cowboy,* an X-rated movie about homosexuality, male prostitution, and drug dealing that won the Academy Award.

Attitudinal changes brought behavioral changes, and vice versa. The song "D-I-V-O-R-C-E" topped the charts in 1968, and the practice became as acceptable as premarital sex. The divorce rate rose from 2.2 per thousand in 1960 to 3.5 in 1970, then nearly doubled in the 1970s. Cohabitation—living together without marriage—became thinkable to average middle-class Americans. Experts even touted "open marriage" (in which spouses are free to have sex with other partners) and "swinging" (sexual sharing with other couples) as cures for stale relationships. The use of contraceptives (and to some extent, even of abortion) spread to women of all religious backgrounds, including Roman Catholics, despite the Catholic church's stand against "artificial" birth control. The national birthrate plunged steadily throughout the 1960s and 1970s.

Gay Liberation   Stimulated by the other protest movements in the sixties, gay liberation emerged publicly in late June 1969. During a routine raid by New York City police, the homosexual patrons of the Stonewall Inn, a gay bar in Greenwich Village, unexpectedly fought back. The furor triggered a surge of "gay pride," a new sense of identity and self-acceptance, and widespread activism. The new Gay Liberation movement that emerged built on the reform-minded Mattachine Society and the Daughters of Bilitis, as well as other "homophile" groups interested in ending discrimination and legal oppression. But adherents went far beyond these groups in brazenly asserting their sexual orientation: "We are going to be who we are."

Supporters of the Gay Liberation Front came primarily from the gay subcultures found in the largest cities. By 1973 some eight hundred openly gay groups were fighting for equal rights for homosexuals, for incorporating lesbianism into the women's movement, and for removing the stigma of immorality and depravity attached to being gay. That year, they succeeded in getting the American Psychiatric Association to rescind its official view of homosexuality as a mental disorder, and to reclassify it as a normal sexual orientation.

Simultaneously, several cities and states began to broaden their civil-rights statutes to include "sexual orientation" as a protected status, and in 1975 the U.S. Civil Service Commission officially ended its ban on the employment of homosexuals. Millions of gays had "come out," demanding public acceptance of their sexual identity.

In a few years, the baby boomers had transformed sexual relations as well as gender and racial relations. The institutions of marriage and family were fundamentally altered. Women could have access to birth control, abortion, and an active sex life with or without a male partner. But what some hailed as liberation others bemoaned as moral decay. Offended by the sudden visibility of openly gay men and lesbians and by "topless" bars, X-rated theaters, and "adult" bookstores, many Americans applauded politicians who promised a war on smut. The public association of the counterculture and the sexual revolution with student demonstrations and ghetto riots swelled the tide of conservatism as the decade ended.

1968: THE POLITICS OF UPHEAVAL

The social and cultural upheavals of the late sixties unfolded against a backdrop of frustration with the war in Vietnam and an intensifying political crisis. The stormy events of 1968 would culminate in a tempest of a political campaign and a turbulent realignment in American politics, the first since the New Deal.

The Tet Offensive in Vietnam   In January 1968 liberal Democratic Senator Eugene McCarthy of Minnesota, a critic of the Vietnam War, announced that he would challenge LBJ for the presidential nomination. Experts scoffed that McCarthy had no chance of unseating Johnson, who had won the presidency in 1964 by the largest margin in U.S. history. The last time such an insurgency had been attempted, in 1912, even the charismatic Teddy Roosevelt had failed. Yet McCarthy persisted, determined that at least one Democrat would enter the primaries on an antiwar platform.

Suddenly, on January 31—the first day of Tet, the Vietnamese New Year—America's hopes for victory in Vietnam exploded, mortally wounding LBJ's reelection plans. National Liberation Front (NLF) and North Vietnamese forces mounted a huge Tet offensive, attacking more than a hundred South Vietnamese cities and towns and even the U.S. embassy in Saigon. U.S. troops repulsed the

A Picture Worth a Thousand Words *The widely published photo of a young burned girl fleeing from a U.S. napalm attack brought the war home to Americans. The shocking images of violence and of the horrifying consequences of war caused doubts as to the justness of America's cause.*

offensive after a month of ferocious fighting, killing thirty-seven thousand enemy forces and inflicting a major military defeat on the communists.

The media, however, emphasized the staggering number of American casualties and the daring scope of the Tet offensive. Americans at home reacted sharply to the realization that no area of South Vietnam was secure from the enemy, and that a foe that the president had claimed was beaten could initiate such bravado attacks. Many stopped believing reports of battlefield success coming from the White House and doubted that the United States could win the war at an acceptable cost.

After Tet, McCarthy's criticism of the war won new sympathizers. *Time, Newsweek,* and the most influential newspapers published editorials urging a negotiated settlement. NBC news anchorman Frank McGee concluded that "the grand objective—the building of a free nation—is not nearer, but further, from realization." The nation's premier newscaster, Walter Cronkite of CBS, observed, "it seems now more certain than ever that the bloody experience of Vietnam is to end in a stalemate." "If I've lost Walter," President Johnson sighed, "then it's over. I've lost Mr. Average Citizen." Johnson's approval rating dropped to 35 percent. The number of Americans who described themselves as prowar "hawks" slipped from 62 percent in January to 41 percent in March, while the proportion of anti-war "doves" climbed from 22 percent to 42 percent.

Haight-Ashbury

Bordering Golden Gate Park, the Haight-Ashbury district of San Francisco became a haven for young people seeking an alternative to the "straight" world in 1965. They were attracted to the two-square-mile area of ornate Victorian homes by the seemingly carefree lifestyle of the artists and "beatniks" who had moved there after being forced out of nearby North Beach. Fittingly, in a city once notorious for its opium dens and whose original name, Yerba Buena, meant "good herb," Haight-Ashbury emerged as the capital of hippiedom, mainly because of the easy availability of hallucinogenic drugs, which California did not outlaw until late 1966.

A distinctive counterculture developed in "Hashbury," as some called it.

"We used to think of ourselves as little clumps of weirdos," Janis Joplin blared. "But now we're a whole new minority group." The I/Thou Coffee Shop served organic or macrobiotic meals. The Psychedelic Shop sold drug paraphernalia; hippie clothing could be had at the Blushing Peony. The Free Medical Clinic dispensed aid for bad drug trips and venereal diseases. Disciples of the Radha Krishna Temple roamed the streets in flowing orange robes, preaching universal peace and chanting the Hare Krishna. Underground newspapers like *The Oracle* provided commentaries on drugs, politics, mysticism, and rock music.

Local music groups like the Grateful Dead lived there communally, gave free concerts in the park, played benefits to legalize marijuana and raise funds for the

Janis Joplin with Big Brother and the Holding Company *Joplin once summed up her approach to her career and life for a reporter, "If I miss, I'll never have a second chance. . . . I gotta risk it. I never hold back, man. I'm always on the outer limits of probability." Along with Jim Morrison and Jimi Hendrix, other musical stars of the counterculture, Joplin died from a drug overdose.*

Black Panthers, and invited their fans, dubbed Dead Heads, to tape concerts—notwithstanding the loss of record revenues. The Diggers—who took their name from seventeenth-century English radicals who defined property owning as theft—distributed free food and clothing. Many residents shared work, meals, and sex.

Early in 1967 the first Human Be-In at Golden Gate Park made Haight-Ashbury a focus of media attention. Seeking to titillate their audiences, reporters and television crews dwelled on the twenty thousand "flower children" who rang bells, danced ecstatically, and did drugs. Accounts of the festival played up Timothy Leary's preaching of the virtues of LSD, Beat poet Allen Ginsberg's chanting of Buddhist mantras, and the Jefferson Airplane's "acid rock" music. Soon everyone was talking about hippies. *Time* put them on its cover. About seventy-five thousand runaways, drug addicts, and bewildered children crowded into the Haight for the 1967 "summer of love."

"If you're going to San Francisco," the song went, "be sure to wear some flowers in your hair . . . you're going to meet some gentle people there." But close behind them came gawking tourists, "weekend hippies" looking for easy sex and exotic drugs, heroin addicts, and a legion of robbers and rapists. The Haight-Ashbury denizens' trust in strangers and faith in love and peace faded as crime soared, drugs took the lives of rock stars, and narcotics agents cracked down on abusers. "Love is the password in the Haight-Ashbury," observed one reporter, "but paranoia is the style. Nobody wants to go to jail."

"Hashbury" deteriorated into an overcrowded, overcommercialized slum. In October 1967 a Death of Hippie ceremony marked its unofficial end as mecca and haven. Those who could pursued their dream of living a life of sharing closer to nature on rural communes. Some were inspired by the Transcendentalists of Brook Farm or the Rappites of Harmony. Others were influenced by Robert Rimmer's novel, *The Harrad Experiment,* or B. F. Skinner's *Walden Two*. Most of the more than two thousand communes in existence by 1970 found, as a disillusioned hippie said, that "we were together at the level of peace and freedom and love. We fell apart over who would cook and wash the dishes and pay the bills." Yet the Haight-Ashbury ethos lingered, promoting recreational drug use, popularizing health foods and vegetarianism, influencing rock music, making fashion more colorful and comfortable, and creating greater tolerance for alternative lifestyles.

A Shaken President	Beleaguered, Johnson pondered a change in American policy. When the Joint Chiefs of Staff sought 206,000 more men for Vietnam, he turned to old friends for advice.

Former secretary of state and venerable Cold Warrior Dean Acheson told the president that "the Joint Chiefs of Staff don't know what they're talking about." Clark Clifford, once a hawk and now secretary of defense, said he was "convinced that the military course we were pursuing was not only endless but hopeless."

Meanwhile, nearly five thousand college students had dropped their studies to stuff envelopes and ring doorbells for Eugene McCarthy in the New Hampshire primary contest. To be "clean for Gene," they cut their long hair and dressed conservatively so as not to alienate potential supporters. McCarthy astonished the experts by winning nearly half the popular vote as well as twenty of the twenty-four nominating-convention delegates in a state usually regarded as conservative.

After this upset, twice as many students swarmed to Wisconsin to canvass its more liberal Democratic voters. They expected a resounding McCarthy triumph in the nation's second primary. Hurriedly, Senator Robert Kennedy, also promising to end the war, entered the Democratic contest on March 16. Projecting Kennedy glamor and magnetism, Robert Kennedy was the one candidate whom Johnson feared could deny him renomination. Indeed, millions viewed Kennedy as the rightful heir to the White House. Passionately supported by minorities, the poor, and working-class ethnic whites, Kennedy was described by a columnist as "our first politician for the pariahs, our great national outsider."

On March 31, exactly three years after the marines had splashed ashore at Danang, Johnson surprised a television audience by announcing a halt to the bombing in North Vietnam. Adding that he wanted to devote all his efforts to the search for peace, LBJ startled listeners when he concluded, "I shall not seek, and I will not accept, the nomination of my party for another term as your president." Reluctant to polarize the nation further, LBJ called it quits. "I tried to make it possible for every child of every color to grow up in a nice house, eat a solid breakfast, to attend a decent school and to get a good and lasting job," he grumbled privately. "But look at what I got instead. Riots in 175 cities. Looting. Burning. Shooting. . . . Young people by the thousands leaving the university, marching in the streets." He lamented, "The only difference between the [John F.] Kennedy assassination and mine is that I am alive and it has been more tortuous." Two days later, pounding the final nail into Johnson's political coffin, McCarthy trounced the president in the Wisconsin primary.

Ignored and often forgotten in retirement, LBJ would die of a heart attack on the same day in January 1973 that the United States signed the Paris Peace Accords that ended America's direct combat role in the Vietnam War. In many ways a tragic figure, Johnson largely carried out Vietnam policies initiated by his predecessors and received little acclaim for his enduring domestic achievements, especially in civil rights. Although he had often displayed high idealism and generosity of spirit, the enduring images of LBJ remained those of a crude, overbearing politician with an outsized ego that masked deep insecurities.

Assassinations and Turmoil   On April 4, three days after the Wisconsin primary, Martin Luther King, Jr., was killed in Memphis, Tennessee, where he had gone to support striking sanitation workers. The assassin was James Earl Ray, an escaped convict and white racist. Ray would confess, be found guilty, and then recant, leaving aspects of the killing unclear. Some believed that other conspirators were involved both before and after the assassination. As in the assassination of John Kennedy, it seemed too insignificant that one misfit was alone responsible for murdering such a great man. More people must be involved, many thought, fueling conspiracy theories. What was clear in 1968 was that the greatest national symbol of nonviolent protest and progressive social change was dead.

As the news spread, black ghettos in 125 cities burst into violence. Twenty blocks of Chicago's West Side went up in flames, and Mayor Richard Daley ordered police to shoot to kill arsonists. In Washington, D.C., under night skies illuminated by seven hundred fires, army units in combat gear set up machine-gun nests outside the Capitol and White House. The rioting left 46 dead, 3,000 injured, and nearly 27,000 in jail—an ironic contrast to King's dream of reconciliation.

Entering the race as the favorite of the party bosses and labor chieftains, LBJ's vice president, Hubert Humphrey, turned the Democratic contest for the presidential nomination into a three-cornered scramble. McCarthy remained the candidate of the "new politics," a moral crusade against the war directed mainly to affluent, educated liberals. Kennedy campaigned as the tribune of the less privileged, the sole candidate who appealed to white ethnics and the minority poor. He also matched McCarthy's moral outrage at the war. "Don't you understand," Kennedy lectured students, "that what we are doing to the Vietnamese is not very different than what Hitler did to the Jews." On June 5, 1968, after his victory in the California primary, the brother of the murdered president was himself assassinated by a Palestinian refugee, Sirhan Sirhan, who loathed Kennedy's pro-Israeli views.

The deaths of King and Kennedy further estranged activists, convinced many people that nonviolent strategies were futile, and made it yet more difficult for the Democrats to unite against the Republicans. No one of national stature could speak effectively across the abyss of race. The dream of peace and justice turned to despair. "I won't vote," a youth said. "Every good man we get they kill." "We shall not overcome," concluded a Kennedy speechwriter. "From this time forward things would get worse, not better. Our best political leaders were part of memory now, not hope."

Some Democrats turned to third-party candidate George Wallace's thinly-veiled appeal for white supremacy or to the GOP nominee Richard M. Nixon. The Republican appealed to those disgusted with inner-city riots and antiwar demonstrations. He promised to end the war in Vietnam honorably and to restore "law and order." Nixon also said he would heed "the voice of the great majority of Americans, the forgotten Americans, the non-shouters, the non-demonstrators, those who do not break the law, people who pay their taxes and go to work, who send their children to school, who go to their churches, . . . who love this country." Tapping the same wellsprings of anger and frustration, Wallace pitched a fiery message to those fed up with black militants and student protesters. If elected, Wallace vowed to crack down on rioters and "long-hair, pot-smoking, draft-card-burning youth."

In August 1968 violence outside the Democratic National Convention in Chicago reinforced the appeal of both Wallace and Nixon. Thousands descended on the city to protest the Vietnam War. Some radicals wanted to provoke a confrontation to discredit the Democrats. A handful of anarchistic "Yippies" (the Youth International Party led by counterculture guru Abbie Hoffman) sought to ridicule the political system by threatening to dump LSD in Chicago's water system and to release greased pigs in the city's crowded Loop area.

Determined to avoid the rioting that had wracked Chicago after King's assassination, Mayor Richard Daley gave police a green light to attack "the hippies, the Yippies, and the flippies." The savagery of the Chicago police fulfilled the radicals' desire for mass disorder. On August 28, as a huge national television audience looked on and protesters chanted "The whole world is watching," Daley's bluecoats randomly clubbed demonstrators, casual bystanders, and television crews filming the melee. The brutality on the streets overshadowed Humphrey's nomination and tore the Democrats farther apart, fixing Americans' image of them as the party of dissent and disorder.

Conservative Resurgence

Nixon capitalized on the televised turmoil to attract the support of socially conservative white voters. His TV commercials flashed images of campus and ghetto upheavals. He portrayed himself as the candidate of the Silent Majority, "the working Americans who have become forgotten Americans." He criticized the Supreme Court for safeguarding the rights of criminals and radicals, promised to appoint tough "law and order" judges, vowed to get people off welfare rolls and on payrolls, and asserted that "our schools are for education—not integration."

Capitalizing on similar resentments, George Wallace raged across the political landscape. He stoked the fury of the working class against welfare mothers, school integrationists, "bearded anarchists, smart-aleck editorial writers, and pointy-headed professors looking down their noses at us." Promising to keep peace in the streets if it took "thirty thousand troops armed with three-foot bayonets," he vowed that "if any demonstrator ever lays down in front of my car, it'll be the last car he'll ever lie down in front of."

By September Wallace had climbed to 21 percent in voter-preference polls. Although many shared his views, few believed he had any chance of winning, and either did not vote or switched to his opponents. Still, 14 percent of the electorate—primarily young, lower-middle-class, small-town workers—cast their votes for Wallace.

Nixon and Humphrey split the rest of the vote almost evenly. Nixon garnered just 43.4 percent of the popular vote and only 301 electoral votes, the narrowest triumph since Woodrow Wilson's in 1916. But, with Humphrey receiving just 38 percent of the white vote (12 million votes less than Johnson in 1964) and not even close to half the labor vote, the long-dominant New Deal coalition was shattered. The 1968 election brought both the inauguration of a new president and the end of the liberal era.

The 57 percent of the electorate who chose Nixon or Wallace would dominate American politics for the rest of the century. While the Democratic party fractured into a welter of contending groups, the Republicans attracted a new majority who lived in the suburbs, the West, and the Sunbelt. The GOP appealed to those most concerned with traditional values, most upset by high taxes, and most opposed to racial integration and special efforts to assist minorities and people on welfare. Of all the states in the South and West, the Democrats would carry only Texas and Washington in 1968, and not a single one four years later. The new conservative

The Election of 1968

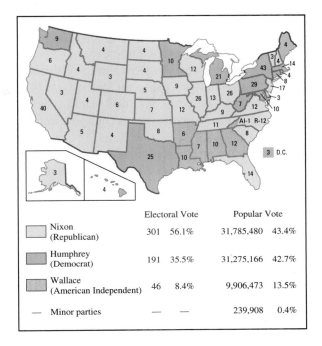

		Electoral Vote		Popular Vote	
Nixon (Republican)		301	56.1%	31,785,480	43.4%
Humphrey (Democrat)		191	35.5%	31,275,166	42.7%
Wallace (American Independent)		46	8.4%	9,906,473	13.5%
— Minor parties		—	—	239,908	0.4%

coalition looked hopefully to the Republican president to end the Vietnam War and restore social harmony.

NIXON AND WORLD POLITICS

A Californian of Quaker origins, Richard Milhous Nixon had worked with the wartime Office of Price Administration before joining the navy. Elected to Congress in 1946, he won prominence for his role in the House Un-American Activities Committee investigation of Alger Hiss (see Chapter 26) and advanced to the Senate in 1950 by accusing his Democratic opponent of disloyalty. After two terms as Eisenhower's vice president, Nixon lost to Kennedy in 1960 and made an unsuccessful 1962 bid for the California governorship, which seemingly ended his political career. But Nixon persevered, campaigned vigorously for GOP candidates in 1966, and won his party's nomination and the presidency in 1968 by promising to restore domestic tranquillity.

Nixon focused mainly on foreign affairs. Considering himself a master of realpolitik—a pragmatic approach stressing national interest rather than ethical goals—he sought to check Soviet expansionism and to reduce superpower conflict, to limit the nuclear-arms race and to enhance America's economic well-being. He planned to get the United States out of Vietnam and into a new era of détente—an easing of tensions—with the communist world. To manage diplomacy, Nixon chose Henry Kissinger, a refugee from Hitler's Germany and professor of international relations, who shared Nixon's penchant for secrecy and for the concentration of decision-making power in the White House.

Vietnamization   Nixon's grand design hinged on ending the Vietnam War. It was sapping American military strength, worsening inflation, and thwarting détente. Announcing the Nixon Doctrine in August 1969, the president redefined America's role in the Third World as that of a helpful partner rather than a military protector. Nations facing communist subversion could count on U.S. support, but they would have to defend themselves. Sales of American military supplies abroad jumped from $1.8 billion to $15.2 billion in the next six years.

The Nixon Doctrine reflected the president's understanding of the war weariness of both the electorate and the U.S. troops in Vietnam. Johnson's decision to negotiate rather than escalate had left American troops with the sense that little mattered except survival. Morale plummeted. Discipline collapsed. Army desertions rocketed from twenty-seven thousand in 1967 to seventy-six thousand in 1970, and absent-without-leave (AWOL) rates rose even higher. Racial conflict became commonplace. Drug use soared; the Pentagon estimated that two out of three soldiers in Vietnam were smoking marijuana and that one in three had tried heroin. The army reported hundreds of cases of "fragging," the assassination of officers and noncommissioned officers by their own troops.

The toll of atrocities against the Vietnamese also mounted. Increasing instances of Americans' dismembering enemy bodies, torturing captives, and murdering civilians came to light. In March 1968, in the hamlet of My Lai, an army unit led by Lieutenant William Calley massacred several hundred South Vietnamese. The soldiers gang-raped girls, lined up women and children in ditches and shot them, and burned the village. Revelations of such incidents, and the increasing number of returning soldiers who joined Vietnam Veterans Against the War, undercut the already-diminished support for the war.

Despite pressure to end the war, Nixon claimed that he would not sacrifice U.S. prestige. Seeking "peace with honor," he acted on three fronts. First was "Vietnamization," replacing American troops with South Vietnamese. It was hardly a new idea; the French had tried *jaunissement* or "yellowing" in 1951, and it had not worked. By 1972 the U.S. forces in Vietnam had been reduced to thirty thousand, down from more than half a million when Nixon took office in 1969, and the policy still had not worked. Second, bypassing South Vietnamese leaders who feared that any accord with the communists would doom them, Nixon sent Kissinger to secretly negotiate with North Vietnam's foreign minister, Le Duc Tho. Third, to force the communists to compromise despite the withdrawal of U.S. combat troops, Nixon escalated the bombing of North Vietnam and secretly ordered air strikes on their supply routes in Cambodia and Laos. He told an aide,

> I want the North Vietnamese to believe I've reached the point where I might do *anything* to stop the war. We'll just slip the word to them that "for God's sake, you know Nixon is obsessed about communism. We can't restrain him when he's angry—and he has his hand on the nuclear button"—and Ho Chi Minh himself will be in Paris in two days begging for peace.

LBJ's War Becomes Nixon's War   The secret B-52 raids against Cambodia neither made Hanoi beg for peace nor disrupted communist supply bases. They did, however, undermine the stability of that tiny republic and precipitated a civil war between pro-American and communist factions. In early 1970 North Vietnam increased its infiltration of troops into Cambodia both to aid the Khmer Rouge (Cambodian communists) and to escalate its war in South Vietnam. Nixon ordered a joint U.S.–South Vietnamese incursion into Cambodia at the end of April 1970. The invaders seized large caches of arms and bought time for Vietnamization. But the costs were high. The invasion ended Cambodia's neutrality, widened the war throughout Indochina, and provoked massive American protests against the war, culminating in the student deaths at Kent State and Jackson State Universities.

In 1971 Nixon combined Vietnamization with renewed blows against the enemy. In February he had South Vietnamese troops invade Laos to destroy communist bases there and to restrict the flow of supplies and men southward from North Vietnam. The South Vietnamese were routed. Emboldened by its success, North Vietnam mounted a major campaign in April 1972—the Easter Offensive—their largest since 1968. Nixon retaliated by mining North Vietnam's harbors and unleashing B-52s on its major cities. "The bastards have never been bombed like they are going to be bombed this time," he vowed.

America's Longest War Ends   The 1972 bombing helped break the impasse in the Paris peace talks, stalemated since 1968. In late October, just days before the 1972 presidential election, Kissinger announced that "peace is at hand." The cease-fire agreement he had secretly negotiated with Le Duc Tho required the withdrawal of all U.S. troops, provided for the return of American prisoners of war, and allowed North Vietnamese troops to remain in South Vietnam.

Kissinger's negotiation sealed Nixon's reelection, but South Vietnam's President Thieu refused to sign a cease-fire permitting North Vietnamese troops to remain in the South. An angry Le Duc Tho then pressed Kissinger for additional concessions. Nixon again resorted to massive B-52 raids. The 1972 Christmas bombing of Hanoi and Haiphong, the most destructive of the war, roused fierce opposition in Congress and the United Nations, but broke the deadlock. Nixon's secret reassurance to Thieu that the United States would "respond with full force should the settlement be violated by North Vietnam" ended Saigon's recalcitrance.

The Paris Accords, signed in late January 1973, essentially restated the terms of the October truce. Nixon and Kissinger knew well that it would not end the war or bring an honorable peace. At best they hoped that the war would remain stalemated until Nixon was safely out of office. The agreement ended hostilities between the United States and North Vietnam, but left unresolved the differences between North and South Vietnam, guaranteeing that Vietnam's future would yet be settled on the battlefield. Even before the ink on the treaty had dried, both North and South Vietnam, seeking military advantage, began to violate its terms.

The war in Vietnam would continue despite fifty-eight thousand American dead, three hundred thousand wounded, and an expenditure of at least $150 billion. Twenty percent of the Americans who served in Vietnam, nearly five hundred thousand, received less-than-honorable discharges—a measure of the desertion rate, drug usage, antiwar sentiment in the military, and immaturity of the troops (the average U.S. soldier in Vietnam was just nineteen years old, seven years younger than the average American GI in World War II).

Virtually all who survived, wrote one marine, returned "as immigrants to a new world. For the culture we had known dissolved while we were in Vietnam, and the culture of combat we lived in so intensely . . . made us aliens when we returned." Reminders of a war that Americans wished to forget, most veterans were ignored. Other than media attention to their psychological difficulties in readjusting to civilian life, which principally fostered an image of them as disturbed and dangerous, the nation paid little heed to its Vietnam veterans.

Relieved that the long nightmare had ended, most Americans wanted "to put Vietnam behind us" and just forget. The bitterness of many veterans, as of embattled hawks and doves, moderated with time. Few gave much thought to the 2 million casualties and the devastation in Vietnam, or to the suffering in Laos, or the price paid by Cambodia. After the war had spread there, the fanatical Khmer Rouge took power and killed 3 million Cambodians, 40 percent of the population.

"We've adjusted too well," complained Tim O'Brien, a veteran and novelist of the war, in 1980. "Too many of us have lost touch with the horror of war. . . . It would seem that the memories of soldiers should serve, at least in a modest way, as a restraint on national bellicosity. But time and distance erode memory. We adjust, we lose the intensity. I fear that we are back where we started. I wish we were more troubled."

Détente

Disengagement from Vietnam helped Nixon achieve a turnabout in Chinese-American relations and détente with the communist powers. These developments, the most significant shift in U.S. foreign policy since the start of the Cold War, created a new relationship among the United States, the Soviet Union, and China.

Presidents from Truman to Johnson had refused to recognize the People's Republic of China, allow its admission to the United Nations, or permit American allies to trade with it. But by 1969 a widening Sino-Soviet split made the prospect of improved relations attractive to both Mao Zedong and Nixon. China wanted to end its isolation; the United States wanted to play one communist power off against the other; and both wanted to thwart U.S.S.R. expansionism in Asia.

In fall 1970 Nixon opened what Kissinger called "the three-dimensional game" by calling China "the People's Republic" rather than "Red China." Kissinger began secret negotiations with Beijing, and in mid-1971 Nixon announced that he would go to the People's Republic "to seek the normalization of relations." In February 1972 Air Force One landed in China, the first visit ever by a sitting American president to the largest nation in the world. Although differences between the two powers delayed official diplomatic relations until 1979, Nixon's trip, the Chinese foreign minister said, bridged "the vastest ocean in the world, twenty-five years of no communication."

Equally significant, Nixon went to Moscow in May 1972 to sign agreements with the Soviets on trade, technological cooperation, and the limitation of nuclear weapons. The Strategic Arms Limitation Talks (SALT I), ratified by the Senate in October 1972, limited each nation to two antiballistic missile systems, froze each side's offensive nuclear missiles for five years, and committed both countries to strategic equality rather than nuclear superiority. SALT I reflected the belief that the fear of destruction offered the surest guarantee against nuclear war and that mutual fear could be maintained only if neither side built nationwide missile-defense systems. Although it did not end the arms race, SALT I reduced Soviet-American tensions and, in an election year, enhanced Nixon's stature.

Shuttle Diplomacy Not even rapprochement with China and détente with the Soviet Union could ensure global stability. The Middle East, in particular, remained an arena of conflict. After the Six-Day War of 1967 in which Israeli forces routed the forces of Egypt, Jordan, and Syria and seized strategic territories from the three nations, the Arab states continued to refuse to negotiate with Israel or to recognize its right to exist. Palestinians, many of them refugees since the creation of Israel in 1948, turned increasingly to the militant Palestinian Liberation Organization (PLO), which demanded Israel's destruction.

War exploded again in October 1973 when Egypt and Syria launched surprise attacks against Israel on Yom Kippur, the most sacred Jewish holy day. Only massive shipments of military supplies from the United States enabled a reeling Israel to stop the assault and counterattack. In retaliation, the Arab states launched their biggest weapon, cutting off oil shipments to the United States and its allies. The five-month embargo dramatized U.S. dependence on foreign energy sources. It spawned acute fuel shortages, which spurred coal production in Montana and Wyoming, triggered an oil boom on Alaska's North Slope, and provided the impetus for constructing more nuclear-power plants. Most immediately, the hike in the price of crude oil from three dollars to more than twelve dollars a barrel sharply intensified inflation.

The dual shocks of the energy crisis and rising Soviet influence in the Arab world spurred Kissinger to engage in "shuttle diplomacy." Flying from one Middle East capital to another for two years, he negotiated a cease-fire, pressed Israel to cede captured Arab territory, and persuaded the Arabs to end the oil embargo. Although Kissinger's diplomacy left the Palestinian issue festering, it successfully excluded the Soviets from a major role in Middle Eastern affairs.

To counter Soviet influence, the Nixon administration also supplied arms and assistance to the shah of Iran, the white supremacist regime of South Africa, and President Ferdinand Marcos in the Philippines. Nixon-Kissinger realpolitik based American aid on a nation's willingness to oppose the Soviet Union, not on the nature of its government. Thus, the administration gave aid to antidemocratic regimes in Argentina, Brazil, Nigeria, and South Korea, as well as to Portuguese colonial authorities in Angola.

When Chileans elected a Marxist, Salvador Allende, president in 1970, Nixon secretly funneled $10 million to the CIA to fund opponents of the leftist regime. The United States also cut off economic aid to Chile, blocked banks from granting loans, and pressed the World Bank to lower Chile's credit rating. In September 1973 a military junta overthrew the Chilean government and killed Allende. Nixon quickly recognized the dictatorship, and economic aid and investment again flowed to Chile.

The administration's active opposition to Allende reflected the extent to which American policy remained committed to containing communist influence. At the same time, Nixon understood the limits of U.S. power and the changed realities of world affairs. Discarding the model of a bipolar conflict that had shaped American foreign policy since 1945, Nixon took advantage of the Chinese-Soviet rift to improve American relations with both nations. His administration also improved the U.S. position in the Middle East and ended American involvement in Vietnam. The politician who had built his reputation as a hard-line Cold Warrior had initiated a new era of détente.

Domestic Problems and Divisions

Richard Nixon yearned to be remembered as an international statesman, but domestic affairs kept intruding. He displayed creativity in seeking to reform the welfare system and in grappling with complex economic problems. But the underside of Nixon's personality appealed to the darker recesses of national character and intensified the fears and divisions among Americans.

Richard Nixon: Man and Politician

Close observers of Nixon noted the multiple levels of his character. Beneath the calculated public persona hid a shadowy man who rarely revealed himself. Nixon the politician was highly intelligent, yet also displayed the rigid self-control of a man monitoring his own every move. Largely hidden was the insecure Nixon, suspicious and filled with anger. Seething with resentments, he saw life as a series of crises to be met and surmounted. His conviction that enemies lurked everywhere, waiting to destroy him, verged on paranoia. Accordingly, he sought to annihilate, not merely defeat, his partisan enemies, particularly the "eastern liberal establishment" that had long opposed him.

Probing the source of his furies, some viewed him as the classic outsider: reared in pinched surroundings, physically awkward, unable to relate easily to others. Even at the height of national power, Nixon remained fearful that he would never be accepted. At the beginning of his administration, his strengths stood out. He spoke of national reconciliation, took bold initiatives internationally, and dealt with domestic problems responsibly. But the darker side ultimately prevailed and drove him from office in disgrace.

The Nixon Presidency

Nixon began his presidency in a moderate manner reminiscent of Eisenhower. Symbolic of this harmonious start, a united nation joined the president in celebrating the first successful manned mission to the moon. On July 21, 1969, the Apollo 11 lunar module, named *Eagle,* descended to the Sea of Tranquillity. As millions watched on television, astronaut Neil Armstrong, the first human to set foot on another celestial body, walked on the moon's surface and proclaimed, "That's one small step for man, one giant leap for mankind." Americans were proud that the United States had come from behind to win the space race. They thrilled as Armstrong and Buzz Aldrin planted an American flag, collected rock and soil samples, and left a plaque reading, "Here men from planet earth first set foot on the moon, July 1969 A.D. We came in peace for all mankind." By 1973 five more American missions visited the lunar surface; and in 1975, when U.S. and Soviet spacecraft met in space, docked, and conducted joint research and shared information for nine days, the space race essentially ended, superseded by cooperative international efforts to explore the rest of the universe.

The first newly elected president since 1849 whose party controlled neither house of Congress, Nixon could not pursue a consistently conservative course. He instituted wage and price controls, inaugurated affirmative action policies, and approved the vote for eighteen-year-olds. More grudgingly, he responded to an energized environmental movement. It had been aroused by the horrible sights in 1969, televised throughout the nation, of the polluted Cuyahoga River near Cleveland bursting into flames and of two oil spills off the coast of California soiling both birds and beaches with globs of gooey, black oil. It had been informed by Barry Commoner's warnings on the hazards of nuclear wastes and chemical pollution in *Science and Survival* (1966) and by Paul Ehrlich's *The Population Bomb* (1968) on the dangers of overpopulation. Its fury would help bring new laws limiting pesticide use, further protecting endangered species and marine mammals, safeguarding coastal lands, and controlling strip-mining. Further legislation regulated consumer-product safety and the transportation of hazardous materials, established maximum levels for the emissions of pollutants into the air, created the Occupational Safety and Health Administration (OSHA) to enforce health and safety standards in the workplace, and required federal agencies to prepare an environmental-impact analysis of all proposed projects. Overseeing all these regulations and restrictions was the newly established Environmental Protection Agency (EPA).

Growing environmental awareness culminated in 20 million Americans celebrating the first Earth Day in April 1970. Speeches and demonstrations spotlighted such problems as thermal pollution, dying lakes, oil spills, and dwindling resources, introducing Americans to the idea of "living lightly on the earth." Organic gardening, vegetarianism, solar power, recycling, composting, and preventive health care came into vogue, as did zero population growth—the birthrate should not exceed the death rate.

Conservatives grumbled as government grew larger and more intrusive; under Nixon, the number of pages in the Federal Register detailing federal regulations tripled. Race-conscious employment regulations for all federal contractors (including quotas to increase minority access to skilled jobs) displeased them even more. Conservatives grew still angrier when Nixon unveiled the Family Assistance Plan (FAP) in 1969. A bold effort to overhaul the welfare system, FAP proposed a guaranteed minimum annual income for all Americans. Caught between liberals who thought the income inadequate and conservatives who disliked both the cost and the principle of the program, FAP died in the Senate.

A Troubled Economy   Nixon inherited the fiscal consequences of President Johnson's effort to wage the Vietnam War and finance the Great Society—to have both "guns and butter"—by deficit financing. He faced a "whopping" budget deficit of $25 billion in 1969 and an inflation rate of 5 percent. As mounting energy prices threatened worse inflation, Nixon cut government spending and encouraged the Federal Reserve Board to raise interest rates. The result was the first recession since Eisenhower plus inflation, a combination economists called "stagflation" and Democrats termed "Nixonomics."

Accelerating inflation wiped out some families' savings and lowered the standard of living of many more. It sparked a wave of strikes as workers sought wage hikes to keep up with the cost of living. It encouraged the wealthy to invest in art and real estate rather than technology and factories. That meant more plant shutdowns, fewer industrial jobs, and millions of displaced workers whose savings were depleted, mortgages foreclosed, and health and pension benefits lost.

Throughout 1971 Nixon lurched from policy to policy in an effort to curb inflation and cure the recession. Early in the year, declaring "I am now a Keynesian," Nixon increased deficit spending to stimulate the private sector. That resulted in the largest budget deficit since World War II, yet economic decline continued. Then, in mid-1971, Nixon changed course, devaluing the dollar to correct the balance-of-payment deficit and imposing a ninety-day freeze on wages, prices, and rents. This "Band-Aid" gave the economy a shot in the arm that worked until after the 1972 election.

In January 1973, safely reelected, Nixon again reversed course, replacing wage-and-price ceilings with "voluntary restraints" and "guidelines." Inflation zoomed to 9 percent, then to 12 percent in 1974 as the Organization of Petroleum Exporting Countries (OPEC) boycott quadrupled the price of crude oil. Inflation and sluggish growth would dog the U.S. economy throughout the decade.

Law and Order   Despite his public appeals for unity, Nixon hoped to divide the American people in ways that would make him unbeatable in the 1972 election. He understood the appeal of Merle Haggard's "Okie from Muskogee," ridiculing "the hippies up in San Francisco" and bragging of drinking "white lightning" instead of doing drugs. He knew that circulation of the *National Review* had more than doubled in the 1960s, and that editor William Buckley's

"Earth Day," May 4, 1970 *Designed to alert people about the threats to the air, land, and water, the first Earth Day signaled the emergence of the modern environmental movement. It would put pressure on the federal government to take major steps in cleaning up the nation's environment and educate a genera-tion of Americans to understand the ecol-ogy of the planet as a delicate, intercon-nected series of ele-ments, in which dam-age to any single ele-ment damages many others.*

once-fringe denunciations of the welfare state, campus unrest, black violence, and the radical Left had become mainstream. To outflank George Wallace and win the sup-port of blue-collar workers, southern segregationists, and northern ethnics—voters whom political strategist Kevin Phillips described as "in motion between a Democratic past and a Republican future"—Nixon opposed court-ordered busing and took a tough stand against criminals, drug users, and radicals.

The president used the full resources of the government against militants. The IRS audited their tax returns; the Small Business Administration denied them loans; and the National Security Agency illegally wiretapped them and intercepted their communications. While the FBI worked with local law officials to disrupt and immobilize the Black Panthers, the CIA illegally investigated and compiled dossiers on thousands of American citizens, and the Justice Department prose-cuted antiwar activists and black radicals in highly publicized trials. Nixon himself drew up an "enemies list" of adversaries to be harassed by the government. "Anyone who opposes us, we'll destroy," warned a top White House official. "As a matter of fact, anyone who doesn't support us, we'll destroy."

In 1970 Nixon widened his offensive against the antiwar movement by approv-ing the Huston Plan. It called for extensive wiretapping and infiltrating of radical organizations by White House operatives, as well as their breaking into the homes and offices of militants to gather or plant evidence. FBI chief J. Edgar Hoover

Inflation, 1946–1993

Inflation, which had been moderate during the two decades following the Second World War, began to soar with the escalation of the war in Vietnam in the mid-1960s. In 1979 and 1980 the nation experienced double-digit inflation in two consecutive years for the first time since World War I.

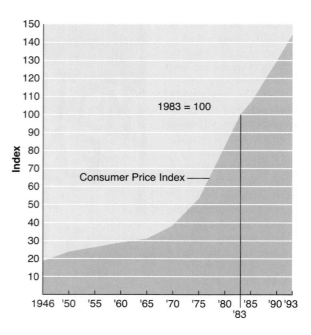

1983 = 100

Consumer Price Index ——

opposed the Huston Plan as a threat to the bureau's power. Blocked, Nixon secretly created his own operation to discredit his opposition and to ensure executive secrecy. Nicknamed "the plumbers" because of their assignment to plug government leaks, the team was head by former FBI agent G. Gordon Liddy and former CIA operative E. Howard Hunt.

The plumbers first targeted Daniel Ellsberg, a former Defense Department analyst who had given the press the Pentagon Papers, a secret documentary history of U.S. involvement in Vietnam. On June 13 the *New York Times* began publishing the Pentagon Papers, revealing a long history of White House lies to Congress, foreign leaders, and the American people. Although the papers contained nothing damaging about his administration, Nixon, fearing that they would undermine trust in government and establish a precedent for publishing classified material, sought to bar their publication. The Supreme Court, however, ruled that their publication was protected by the First Amendment. Livid, Nixon directed the Justice Department to indict Ellsberg for theft and ordered the plumbers to break into the office of Ellsberg's psychiatrist in search of information to discredit the man who had become a hero to the antiwar movement.

The Southern Strategy
Nixon especially courted whites who were upset by the drive for racial equality. The administration opposed extension of the Voting Rights Act of 1965, sought to cripple enforcement of the Fair Housing Act of 1968, pleaded for the postponement of desegregation in Mississippi's schools, and filed suits to prohibit busing schoolchildren in order to desegregate public schools. In 1971, when the Supreme Court upheld busing as a constitutional and necessary tactic in *Swann* v. *Charlotte-Mecklenburg Board of Education*, Nixon condemned the ruling and asked Congress

to enact a moratorium on busing. That pleased white parents who disliked the inconvenience of having their children transported to schools farther from home, feared for the children's safety in strange schools, and opposed the integration of black and white schoolchildren for racist reasons. Busing to desegregate education, combined with conflicts between whites and African-Americans over jobs and housing, had made working-class ethnic white voters in metropolitan areas an inviting target for the GOP.

The strategy of wooing white southerners also dictated Nixon's Supreme Court nominations. To reverse the Warren court's liberalism, he sought strict constructionists, judges who would not "meddle" in social issues or be "soft" on criminals. In 1969 he appointed Warren Burger as chief justice. Although the Senate then twice rejected southern conservatives nominated by Nixon, by 1973 the president had appointed three additional justices to the Supreme Court. Harry Blackmun of Minnesota, Lewis Powell of Virginia, and William Rehnquist of Arizona, along with Burger, steered the Court in a decidedly more moderate direction. Although ruling liberally in cases involving abortion, desegregation, and the death penalty, the Burger court shifted to the right on civil liberties, community censorship, and police power.

As the 1970 congressional elections neared, Nixon encouraged his vice president, Spiro T. Agnew, to step up attacks on "hooligans, hippies, and radical liberals." Agnew assailed the Democrats as "sniveling hand-wringers," intellectuals as "an effete corps of impudent snobs," and the news media as "nattering nabobs of negativism." Liberals deplored Agnew's alarming alliterative allegations, but conservatives found them on target. The 1970 elections ended in a draw, with the GOP losing nine House seats and winning two Senate seats.

THE CRISIS OF THE PRESIDENCY

President Nixon won a resounding reelection in 1972 and pledged, in his second inaugural, "to make these four years the best four years in America's history." Ironically, they would rank among its sorriest. His vice president would resign in disgrace; his closest aides would go to jail; and he would serve barely a year and a half of his second term before resigning to avoid impeachment.

The Election of 1972   Nixon's reelection appeared certain. He faced a deeply divided Democratic party. His diplomatic successes and the winding down of the Vietnam War appealed to moderate voters. The southern strategy and law-and-order posture attracted Democrats who had voted for George Wallace in 1968. Nixon's only possible worry, another third-party candidacy by Wallace, vanished on May 15, 1972. During a campaign stop in Maryland, Wallace was shot and paralyzed from the waist down. He withdrew from the race, leaving Nixon a monopoly on the white backlash.

Capitalizing on the support of antiwar activists, the Senate's most outspoken dove, George McGovern of South Dakota, blitzed the Democratic primaries. He gained additional support from new party rules requiring state delegations to include minority, female, and youthful delegates in approximate proportion to their numbers. Actress Shirley MacLaine approvingly described California's delegation as "looking like a couple of high schools, a grape boycott, a Black Panther rally, and four or five politicians who walked in the wrong door." A disapproving labor leader grumbled about "too much hair and not enough cigars at this convention." McGovern won the nomination on the first ballot.

Perceptions of McGovern as inept and radical drove away all but the most committed supporters. After pledging to stand behind his vice-presidential running mate Thomas Eagleton "1,000 percent" when it became known that Eagleton had received electric-shock therapy for depression, McGovern dumped him and suffered the embarrassment of having several prominent Democrats publicly decline to run with him. McGovern's endorsement of income redistribution, decriminalization of marijuana, immediate withdrawal from Vietnam, a $30 billion defense-budget cut, and pardons for those who had fled the United States to avoid the draft exposed him to GOP ridicule as the candidate of the radical fringe.

Remembering his narrow loss to Kennedy in 1960 and too-slim victory in 1968, Nixon left no stone unturned. To do whatever was necessary to win, he appointed his attorney general, John Mitchell, to head the Committee to Re-Elect the President (CREEP). Millions of dollars in campaign contributions financed "dirty tricks" to create dissension in Democratic ranks and an espionage unit to spy on the opposition. Led by Liddy and Hunt of the White House plumbers, the Republican undercover team received Mitchell's approval to wiretap telephones at the Democratic National Committee headquarters in the Watergate apartment and office complex in Washington. Early one morning in June 1972, a security guard foiled the break-in to install the bugs. Arrested were James McCord, the security coordinator of CREEP, and several other Liddy and Hunt associates.

A White House cover-up began immediately. Nixon claimed that "no one in the White House staff, no one in this administration, presently employed, was involved in this bizarre incident." He then ordered staff members to expunge Hunt's name from the White House telephone directory. To buy the silence of those arrested, he approved $400,000 in hush money and hints of a presidential pardon. On the pretext that an inquiry would damage national security, the president directed the CIA to halt the FBI's investigation of the Watergate break-in. With the McGovern campaign a shambles and Watergate seemingly contained, Nixon won overwhelmingly, amassing nearly 61 percent of the popular vote and 520 electoral votes. The southern strategy had worked to perfection. Strongly supported only by minorities and low-income voters, McGovern carried only Massachusetts and the District of Columbia. The election solidified the 1968 realignment.

The GOP, however, gained only twelve seats in the House and lost two in the Senate, demonstrating the growing difficulty of unseating incumbents, the rise in ticket-splitting, and the decline of both party loyalty and voter turnout. Only 55.7 percent of eligible voters went to the polls (down from 63.8 percent in 1960).

Whether indifferent to politics or disenchanted with the choices offered, a growing number of citizens no longer bothered to participate in the electoral process.

The Watergate Upheaval   The scheme to conceal links between the White House and the accused Watergate burglars had succeeded during the 1972 campaign. But after the election, federal judge "Maximum John" Sirica, known for his tough treatment of criminals, refused to accept the defendants' claim that they had acted on their own. Threatening severe prison sentences, Sirica coerced James McCord of CREEP into confessing that White House aides had known in advance of the break-in and that the defendants had committed perjury during the trial. Two *Washington Post* reporters, Carl Bernstein and Bob Woodward, following clues furnished by a secret informant named "Deep Throat" (the title of a notorious pornographic film of the time), wrote a succession of front-page stories tying the break-in to illegal contributions and "dirty tricks" by CREEP.

In February 1973 the Senate established the Special Committee on Presidential Campaign Activities to investigate. As the trail of revelations led closer to the Oval Office, Nixon fired his special counsel, John Dean, who refused to be a scapegoat, and announced the resignations of his two principal aides, H. R. Haldeman and John Ehrlichman. Pledging to get to the bottom of the scandal, the president appointed Secretary of Defense Elliot Richardson, a Boston patrician of unassailable integrity, as his new attorney general, and instructed Richardson to appoint a special Watergate prosecutor with broad powers of investigation and subpoena. Richardson selected Archibald Cox, a Harvard law professor and a Democrat.

In May the special Senate committee began a televised investigation. Chaired by Sam Ervin of North Carolina, the hearings revealed the existence of a White House "enemies list," the president's use of government agencies to harass opponents, and administration favoritism in return for illegal campaign donations. Most damaging to Nixon, the hearings exposed the White House's active involvement in the Watergate cover-up. But the Senate still lacked concrete evidence of the president's criminality, the "smoking gun" that would prove Nixon's guilt. Because it was his word against that of John Dean, who testified that the president directed the cover-up, Nixon expected to survive the crisis.

Then another presidential aide dropped a bombshell by revealing that Nixon had installed a secret taping system that recorded all conversations in the Oval Office. The Ervin committee and Cox insisted on access to the tapes, but Nixon refused, claiming executive privilege. In October, when Cox sought a court order to obtain the tapes, Nixon ordered Richardson to fire him. Richardson instead resigned in protest, as did the deputy attorney general, leaving it to the third-ranking official in the Department of Justice, Solicitor General Robert Bork, to dump Cox. The furor stirred by this "Saturday Night Massacre" sent Nixon's public-approval rating rapidly downward. Even as Nixon named a new special prosecutor, Leon Jaworski, the House Judiciary Committee began impeachment proceedings.

A President Disgraced

Adding to Nixon's woes that October, Vice President Agnew, charged with income-tax evasion and accepting bribes, pleaded no contest—"the full equivalent to a plea of guilty," according to the trial judge. Dishonored, Agnew left office with a three-year suspended sentence, a $10,000 fine, and a letter from Nixon expressing "a great sense of personal loss." Popular House Minority Leader Gerald R. Ford of Michigan replaced Agnew.

In March 1974 Jaworski and the House Judiciary Committee subpoenaed the president for the tape recordings of Oval Office conversations after the Watergate break-in. Nixon released edited transcripts of the tapes, filled with gaps and the phrase "expletive deleted." Despite the excisions, the president emerged as petty and vindictive. "We have seen the private man and we are appalled," declared the staunchly Republican *Chicago Tribune.*

Nixon's sanitized version of the tapes satisfied neither Jaworski nor the House Judiciary Committee. Both pressed for unedited tapes. In late July the Supreme Court rebuffed the president's claim to executive privilege. Citing the president's obligation to provide evidence necessary for the due process of law, Chief Justice Burger ordered Nixon to release the unexpurgated tapes.

In late July the House Judiciary Committee adopted three articles of impeachment, accusing President Nixon of obstruction of justice for impeding the

The Cover-up Unravels *James McCord's revelation of White House involvement in the Watergate burglary led President Nixon to dismiss White House counsel John Dean, announce the resignations of Ehrlichman and Haldeman, and promise "There can be no whitewash at the White House." Nevertheless, a special committee of the Senate, chaired by Sam Ervin of North Carolina, began its own investigation of Watergate in May 1973.*

Watergate investigation, abuse of power for his partisan use of the FBI and IRS, and contempt of Congress for refusing to obey a congressional subpoena for the tapes. Checkmated, Nixon conceded in a televised address on August 5 that he had withheld relevant evidence. He then surrendered the subpoenaed tapes, which contained the "smoking gun" proving that the president had ordered the cover-up, obstructed justice, subverted one government agency to prevent another from investigating a crime, and lied about his role for more than two years. Impeachment and conviction were now certain. On August 9, 1974, Richard Nixon became the first president to resign, and Gerald Ford took office as the nation's first chief executive who had not been elected either president or vice president.

IMPORTANT EVENTS, 1968–1974

1960 Birth-control pill marketed.

1963 Bob Dylan releases "Blowin' in the Wind."

1964 Berkeley Free Speech Movement (FSM).
The Beatles arrive in the United States, and "I Want to Hold Your Hand" tops the charts.

1965 Ken Kesey and Merry Pranksters stage first "acid test."

1966 Abolition of automatic student deferments from the draft.

1967 March on the Pentagon.
Israeli-Arab Six-Day War.

1968 Tet offensive.
President Lyndon Johnson announces that he will not seek reelection.
Martin Luther King, Jr., assassinated; race riots sweep nation.
Students take over buildings and strike at Columbia University.
Robert F. Kennedy assassinated.
Violence mars Democratic convention in Chicago.
Vietnam peace talks open in Paris.
Richard Nixon elected president.

1969 Apollo 11 lands first Americans on the moon.
Nixon begins withdrawal of U.S. troops.
Woodstock festival.
March Against Death in Washington, D.C.
Lieutenant William Calley charged with murder of civilians at My Lai.

1970 United States invades Cambodia.
Students killed at Kent State and Jackson State Universities.
Nixon proposes Huston Plan.
Environmental Protection Agency established.
OSHA created.
Earth Day first celebrated.
The Beatles disband; Janis Joplin and Jimi Hendrix die of drug overdoses.

1971 United States invades Laos.
Swann v. *Charlotte-Mecklenburg Board of Education.*
New York Times publishes Pentagon Papers.

Nixon institutes wage-and-price freeze.

South Vietnam invades Laos with the help of U.S. air support.

1972 Nixon visits China and the Soviet Union.

SALT I agreement approved.

Break-in at Democratic National Committee headquarters in Watergate complex.

Nixon reelected in landslide victory.

Christmas bombing of North Vietnam.

1973 Vietnam cease-fire agreement signed.

Trial of Watergate burglars.

Senate establishes Special Committee on Presidential Campaign Activities to investigate Watergate.

President Salvador Allende ousted and murdered in Chile.

Vice President Spiro Agnew resigns; Gerald Ford appointed vice president.

Row v. *Wade.*

Yom Kippur War; OPEC begins embargo of oil to the West.

Saturday Night Massacre.

1974 Supreme Court orders Nixon to release Watergate tapes.

House Judiciary Committee votes to impeach Nixon.

Nixon resigns; Ford becomes president.

30

Society, Politics, and World Events from Ford to Reagan, 1974–1989

In October 1985 *Forbes* business magazine hailed "the richest man in America," Sam Walton of Arkansas, founder of the Wal-Mart Corporation, one of the discount chains that transformed U.S. mass marketing after 1960. Estimating his wealth at "$20 or $25 billion," he lived modestly, sported a Wal-Mart baseball cap, and got his haircuts at the local barbershop.

Born in Oklahoma in 1918, Walton grew up in Missouri. While his father, a mortgage agent, repossessed farms during the Great Depression, young Sam sold magazine subscriptions door-to-door. In 1945, after serving in World War II and marrying Helen Robson, he became the manager of a Ben Franklin variety store in Newport, Arkansas. Sam and Helen opened their own Walton's Five and Dime in Bentonville, Arkansas, in 1950 and a second one in nearby Fayetteville two years later. Walton tirelessly searched out bargain-priced merchandise that he sold at a small markup. As the Fayetteville store manager recalled, "Sam used to come down . . . driving an old fifty-three Plymouth. He had that car so loaded up he barely had room to drive. And would you like to guess what he had in it? Ladies' panties. Three for $1.00 and four for $1.00 and nylon hose."

By the later 1960s Wal-Mart stores dotted Arkansas, Oklahoma, Missouri, and beyond. "We just started repeating what worked, stamping out stores cookie-cutter style," Walton recalled. Together with other chains, including Target, Woolco, and K-Mart, Walton pioneered discount selling. As inflation eroded consumer buying power in the 1970s, Wal-Mart with its rock-bottom prices prospered. Walton also created a unique corporate culture that included promotional gimmicks such as "shopping cart bingo" and employee rallies punctuated by cheers and company songs. Thanks to successive stock splits, one hundred shares of Wal-Mart stock purchased for $1,650 in 1970 were worth about $11.5 million by 2002.

Walton had critics. Labor organizers attacked his anti-union policies. Small-town merchants battered by Wal-Mart's price-slashing complained bitterly. Responded Walton, "[Their] customers were the ones who shut [them] down. They voted with their feet. . . . Wal-Mart has actually [saved] quite a number of

small towns . . . by offering low prices [and] . . . by creating hundreds of thousands of jobs."

On March 17, 1992, shortly before Walton's death of bone cancer, President
George Bush awarded him the Medal of Freedom. Said Bush, "Sam Walton
embodies the entrepreneurial spirit and epitomizes the American dream." By 2002,
with 1.3 million employees and nearly six thousand Wal-Marts, Sam's Clubs, and
Super Centers worldwide, Wal-Mart Corporation boasted annual sales of more
than $220 billion and was the world's largest retailer of general merchandise.

Wal-Mart extended trends that had long been underway: the rise of great corporations; marketing innovations from department stores to shopping malls; the
spread of a national consumer culture through the mass distribution of standardized goods. Wal-Mart also contributed to changes that transformed the U.S. economy in the 1970s and 1980s. The service sector grew rapidly as discount stores,
fast-food outlets, and high-tech industries expanded and prospered. Other sectors
of the economy, including family farms, the inner cities, and the factories of the
old industrial heartland, did not fare as well. Sam Walton may have lived the
American Dream, but that dream proved elusive for many Americans.

This chapter, covering the years from Nixon's resignation in 1974 to the end of
Ronald Reagan's presidency in 1989, is structured around two key themes. The
first is the sustained impact of the 1960s on U.S. culture and politics. On one hand,
the activist, radical spirit of the sixties continued to influence the environmental
movement, the women's movement, and changing sexual norms. On the other
hand, these years also saw a reaction against the 1960s, expressed both in a retreat
from public concerns to private pursuits and in a sharp conservative backlash.

These years also brought important social changes affecting middle-class
women, farmers, African-Americans, Native Americans, and the growing ranks of
Hispanic and Asian immigrants. All Americans coped with an unsettled economy
marked by inflation, recessions, boom times, and soaring budget deficits.

The second theme, which emerges as the chapter progresses, is the continuing
importance of events abroad. Although many citizens turned inward after
Vietnam, the outside world remained inescapable. As Americans of the 1970s
faced rising gasoline prices, long lines at gas stations, and soaring inflation—all
linked to economic decisions made in distant capitals—they realized that however
much they might wish otherwise, they could not turn their backs on the world.
Worsening Cold War tensions in the late 1970s and early 1980s, Middle East crises,
and deadly terrorist attacks underscored the fact that America's future could not
be separated from unfolding world events.

This chapter focuses on five major questions:

How were the cultural climate and social activism of 1974–1989 influenced by the
1960s?

What social developments most affected farmers, middle-class women, African-
Americans, and Native Americans in these years, and how did patterns of immigration change?

What core beliefs shaped Ronald Reagan's political ideology, and what steps did his administration take to translate this ideology into practice?

How did U.S.-Soviet relations evolve from the late 1970s through 1988?

In what respects did the international situation improve during these years, from the U.S. perspective, and in what ways did it grow more threatening?

THE LONG SHADOW OF THE 1960S: CULTURAL CHANGES AND CONTINUITIES

Social and cultural trends of the 1970s and 1980s reflected both the afterglow of 1960s activism and a reaction against that decade. While many young people turned away from public issues to pursue personal goals, some social trends and causes rooted in the 1960s survived and even gained momentum. A backlash against the sixties, as well as the sobering effects of the AIDS epidemic, also shaped the culture of these years. Radicals of the 1960s had celebrated sexual freedom and alternative lifestyles, and feminists had demanded reproductive choice, but the years after 1970 brought a conservative reaction and fierce debates over abortion, homosexuality, and other issues. The pace of change also led to a quest for moral certitude and a revival of religion.

The Post-1960s Mood: Personal Preoccupations; New Activist Energies

The Vietnam War shattered the liberal consensus, and the New Left coalition that protested the war soon fragmented as well, creating a vacuum of political leadership on the Left. The Watergate crisis, in turn, temporarily disoriented conservatives. With politics in disarray, personal preoccupations beckoned. To replace the long-haired, pot-smoking "campus radical" of the 1960s, journalists created a new stereotype, the "Yuppie" (young urban professional), preoccupied with physical fitness and consumer goods.

The stereotype had a basis in fact. Physical well-being became a middle-class obsession. Yuppies jogged and exercised, ate natural foods free of pesticides and additives, and stopped smoking when medical evidence linked cigarettes to lung cancer and heart disease. Meditation techniques won devoted followers. Reversing the middle-class flight to the suburbs, yuppies purchased and restored rundown inner-city apartments. This process, known as gentrification, often had the effect of pushing out poorer and elderly residents.

Self-improvement could easily turn selfish. Historian Christopher Lasch summed up his view of the era in the title of his 1978 book, *The Culture of Narcissism.* Novelist Tom Wolfe satirized the "Me Generation." *Newsweek* magazine, proclaiming "the Year of the Yuppie" in 1984, commented, "[T]hey're making lots of money, spending it conspicuously, and switching political candidates like they test cuisines."

TV viewing time increased. Prime-time soap operas like *Dallas,* chronicling the steamy affairs of a Texas oil family, captivated millions. *The Brady Bunch,* with its family of teenagers, recalled the insipid TV sit-coms of the 1950s. The Disney

Corporation launched its Florida theme park Disney World in 1982. Blockbuster movies like *Jaws* (1975), *Star Wars* (1977), and *E.T.* (1982) offered escapist fare. Baseball's World Series, football's Super Bowl, and the National Basketball Association playoffs attracted vast TV audiences.

The politically engaged songs of the 1960s gave way to bland disco tunes, suitable for dancing but carrying little cultural weight. In *Saturday Night Fever* (1977), with a soundtrack by a disco group called the Bee Gees, John Travolta plays a self-absorbed working-class Brooklyn youth whose life revolves around dance contests but who readily abandons his friends to pursue a career in Manhattan. A fitting symbol for this aspect of the 1970s, suggests historian Bruce Schulman, was the brief fad of pet rocks, "which just sat there doing nothing."

Innovations in consumer electronics shaped the era as well. By the early 1990s, 70 percent of U.S. households had VCRs (videocassette recorders), enabling users to tape TV shows for later viewing and to rent movies on cassette. As entertainment became privatized, families stayed home with the VCR instead of going to the movies. In the music field, the compact disc (CD), in which laser beams "read" millions of dots molded into concentric circles on the disk, offered remarkably high-quality sound. In a development of great future significance, the late 1970s also saw the advent of the personal computer.

American life in these years was not all escapism and technological novelties. The protest mood of the 1960s survived. In sharp contrast to disco were the raw working-class songs of Bruce Springsteen of Asbury Park, New Jersey. His *Darkness at the Edge of Town* (1978) and *Born in the USA* (1984) evoked the stresses of blue-collar life and offered a bleak view of widening class divisions in post-Vietnam, post-Watergate America. *Born in the USA* tells of a young man "sent . . . off to a foreign land to go and kill the yellow man" who now finds himself "in the shadow of the penitentiary" with "[n]owhere to run . . . nowhere to go." Bob Dylan, best-known for his 1960s protest songs, produced some of his best work in the 1970s. His 1974 album *Blood on the Tracks* expressed distrust of authority and the difficulty of personal relationships while celebrating outlaws and outsiders who defied the established order.

Along with escapist fare, directors also produced some brilliant films exploring the darker side of American life in the 1970s. Robert Altman's *Nashville* (1975) offered a disturbing vision of cynical mass-culture producers, manipulative politicians, and lonely, alienated drifters. Roman Polanski's *Chinatown* (1974) probed the personal and political corruption beneath the sunny surface of Southern California life. Such work, too, is part of the cultural legacy of the decade.

The Environmental Movement Gains Support A legacy of the 1960s that grew stronger in the 1970s was the movement to protect the environment against the effects of heedless exploitation. This movement built upon a decade of activism triggered by Rachel Carson's *Silent Spring* of 1962 and including the environmental laws of the 1960s and the inauguration of Earth Day in 1970 (see Chapters 27 and 29).

The heightened environmental consciousness found many outlets. Established groups such as the Sierra Club as well as new organizations won fresh recruits. One of the new organizations, Greenpeace, was founded in 1971 when Canadian activists protested a planned U.S. nuclear test at Amchitka Island in the Bering Sea. The U.S. branch, established soon after, addressed a range of environmental issues, including the preservation of old-growth forests and protection of the world's oceans. By 2000 Greenpeace had 250,000 U.S. members and 2.5 million members worldwide. The Save the Whales campaign, launched by the Animal Welfare Institute in 1971, mobilized opposition to the killing of the world's largest mammals by fleets of floating processing factories to provide dog and cat food for pet owners.

In the later 1970s environmentalists targeted the nuclear-power industry. Reviving protest techniques first used in the civil-rights and antiwar campaigns, activists across America staged rallies at planned nuclear-power plants. The movement crested in 1979 when a partial meltdown crippled the Three Mile Island nuclear-power plant in Pennsylvania. A movie released at the same time, *China Syndrome,* graphically portrayed a fictitious but plausible nuclear-power disaster caused by a California earthquake. *China Syndrome* starred Jane Fonda, an antiwar leader of the 1960s, underscoring both the continuities and the changes of focus in the activism of the two decades.

The Women's Movement: Gains and Uncertainties Of the many legacies of the 1960s, the revitalized women's movement (see Chapter 28) had a particularly lasting effect. As middle-class young women had found themselves marginalized in the civil-rights and antiwar movements, many had begun to examine their own status in society. The National Organization for Women (NOW), founded in 1966, boasted nearly fifty thousand members by 1975. Feminist support groups and Gloria Steinem's *Ms.* magazine (launched in 1972) spread the message. The movement, however, remained mainly white and middle class.

With the movement's growth came political clout. The National Women's Political Caucus (1971) promoted a feminist agenda. By 1972 many states had liberalized their abortion laws and outlawed gender discrimination in hiring. That same year Congress passed an equal rights amendment (ERA) to the Constitution barring discrimination on the basis of sex. When twenty-eight states quickly ratified it, ultimate adoption seemed assured.

In the landmark case *Roe v. Wade* (1973), the Supreme Court proclaimed women's constitutional right to abortion by a 7 to 2 vote. The decision gave women broad abortion rights in the first trimester of pregnancy, in consultation with a physician, while granting states more regulatory authority as the pregnancy progressed. The majority decision, written by Justice Harry Blackmun, relied heavily on the right to privacy grounded in the Fourteenth Amendment's due-process clause. In the wake of *Roe v. Wade,* the number of abortions rose from about 750,000 in 1973 to more than 1.5 million in 1980 and then leveled off.

The women's movement splintered in the late 1970s, as Betty Friedan and other moderates opposed the lesbians who were becoming increasingly assertive (see below). The moderates also deplored the strident rhetoric of some radical feminists and criticized their tendency to downgrade the family while celebrating female autonomy and careerist goals. In *The Second Stage* (1981), Friedan urged feminists to add family-protection issues to their agenda.

While feminist leaders struggled to define the movement, the realities of many women's lives changed dramatically. The proportion of women working outside the home leaped from 35 percent in 1960 to nearly 60 percent in 1992. Not only feminist ideology but also the soaring cost of living encouraged this trend, as many families found they could not manage on a single income.

Despite the gains, working women's earnings still lagged behind those of men, and the workplace remained largely gender segregated. Women were still concentrated in such fields as nursing, teaching, sales, and secretarial work, while men dominated management positions and the professions. But even this was changing as more women entered the ranks of management. (Top management remained a male preserve, however, a phenomenon known as the "glass ceiling.") Even in medicine and the law, change was in the air. By the early 1990s the legal and medical professions were nearly 20 percent female, while the growing ranks of female medical students and law students promised even more dramatic changes in the future.

These changes had broad social effects. As women delayed marriage to pursue higher education or careers, their median age at first marriage rose from twenty in 1960 to twenty-four in 1990. The birthrate fell as well. By 1980 the statistically average U.S. family had 1.6 children, far below the figure in earlier times. Conservatives

Breaking the Gender Barrier *Martha Fransson, the sole female member of the Class of 1970 at the Tuck School of Business at Dartmouth College, poses with her classmates.*

Women in the Work Force, 1950–1992

After 1960 the proportion of American women who were gainfully employed surged upward. As a result, young women coming of age in the 1990s had far different expectations about their lives than had their grand-mothers or even their mothers.

Sources: Statistical Abstract of the United States, 1988 (Washington, D.C.: U.S. Government Printing Office, 1987), 373; World Almanac and Book of Facts, 1989 (New York: Pharos Books, 1988), 152; Statistical Abstract of the United States, 1993 (Washington, D.C.: U.S. Government Printing Office, 1993), 400, 401.

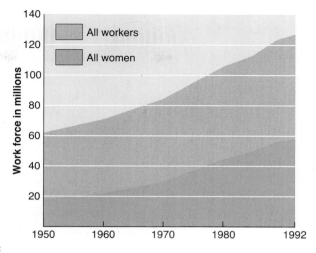

worried that women's changing roles would weaken the family. Working women themselves conceded the stresses of balancing career and family, but few were prepared to return to the era when "women's sphere" had consisted exclusively of child care, housework, and good works. As the 1980s ended, feminists could take satisfaction in many gains achieved. But major challenges still loomed and complex issues remained unresolved.

Changing Patterns of Sexual Behavior; the Looming Specter of AIDS

The long shadow of the 1960s was evident, too, in the realm of sexual behavior. The 1960s counterculture had challenged the prevailing sexual code, and the loosening of old taboos that resulted had long-lasting effects. In 1960 about 30 percent of unwed nineteen-year-old U.S. women had sexual experience. By 1980 more than half did, and the figure soared still higher by 2000. The number of unmarried couples living together jumped from 523,000 in 1970 to 3.5 million by 1993. This trend, too, accelerated as the twentieth century wore on.

Many gay men and lesbians "came out of the closet" in the 1970s and openly avowed their sexual preference. As we saw in Chapter 29, the 1969 Stonewall riot, when patrons at a gay club in Greenwich Village fought back against a police raid, launched an era in which homosexuals became more vocal in asserting their presence and demanding equal rights. This movement continued in the later 1970s and beyond, in a wave of rallies, parades, and protests against job discrimination and harassment. In 1977 "Gay Pride" parades drew seventy-five thousand marchers in New York City and three hundred thousand in San Francisco, a center of gay activism. Two years later the first national gay and lesbian civil-rights

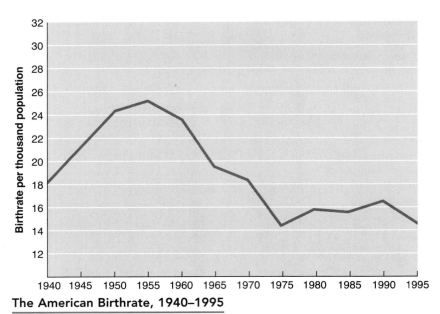

The American Birthrate, 1940–1995

Families of four or five children or even more were once common in the United States. But from 1960 to the mid-1970s, the U.S. birthrate fell by nearly half.

Source: Statistical Abstract of the United States, 1994 (Washington, D.C.: U.S. Government Printing Office, 1994), 76.

parade attracted one hundred thousand to Washington, D.C. Exclaimed one participant later, "It was such a feeling of power, like the storming of the Bastille."

In 1974 Elaine Noble, an avowed lesbian, won a seat in the Massachusetts legislature. Harvey Milk, a proudly gay candidate, was elected to the San Francisco board of supervisors in 1977. In 1987 Massachusetts Congressman Barney Frank acknowledged his homosexuality.

Organizations like the National Gay Task Force, founded in 1973 and later renamed the National Gay and Lesbian Task Force, and a militant New York group called ACT-UP (1987) demanded the repeal of anti-gay laws and passage of legislation protecting the civil rights of homosexuals. Responding to the pressure, many states and cities repealed laws against same-sex relations between consenting adults. Like other reforms of these years, this movement was mainly white and middle class, though black gay and lesbian organizations emerged as well.

The freer attitude toward sex received a setback with the spread of sexually transmitted diseases (STDs), especially the deadly viral infection AIDS (acquired immune deficiency syndrome), first diagnosed in 1981. At first, AIDS spread mainly among sexually active homosexuals and bisexuals, intravenous drug users sharing needles, and persons having sexual intercourse with members of these high-risk groups. (Early in the epidemic some persons, including tennis star Arthur Ashe, contracted AIDS through blood transfusions.) Though the worst of the epidemic still lay ahead, more than thirty-one thousand Americans had died of AIDS by the end of the 1980s.

Medical authorities warned against unprotected sex. The message was driven home when basketball superstar Earvin ("Magic") Johnson and Olympic diver Greg Louganis announced that they carried the HIV virus, a precursor of AIDS. While the AIDS epidemic emboldened some Americans to express their hatred of homosexuality (see below), it also stimulated medical research and an outpouring of concern. Hospices cared for sufferers, and a large AIDS quilt honoring victims toured the nation. Under the shadow of AIDS and other STDs, many Americans grew more cautious in their sexual behavior. The exuberant slogan of the 1960s, "Make Love, Not War," gave way to the more somber message of "Safer Sex."

Conservative Backlash and Evangelical Renaissance

As we saw in Chapter 29, another legacy of the 1960s was a conservative reaction. An early target was *Roe* v. *Wade*. In the wake of the Supreme Court's legalization of abortion, a "Right to Life" movement led by Roman Catholic and conservative Protestant groups pressed for a constitutional amendment outlawing abortion. This practice, they charged, undermined respect for human life; it was "the murder of the unborn." "Pro-life" advocates held rallies, signed petitions, and picketed abortion clinics and pregnancy-counseling centers.

Responding to the pressure, Congress in 1976 cut off Medicaid funding for most abortions, in effect denying this procedure to the poor. Most feminists adopted a "pro-choice" stance, arguing that reproductive decisions should be made by women and their physicians, not by the government. Opinion polls reflected deep divisions, although a majority favored the "pro-choice" position.

The women's movement, too, faced an antifeminist backlash. In 1972 President Nixon vetoed a bill setting up a national network of day-care centers, criticizing its "communal approach to child-rearing." The ERA amendment died in 1982, three states short of the three-fourths required for ratification.

The gay and lesbian movement particularly inflamed conservatives, who saw it as evidence of society's moral collapse. TV evangelist Jerry Falwell thundered, "God . . . destroyed the cities of Sodom and Gomorrah because of this terrible sin." In 1977 singer Anita Bryant led a campaign against a recently passed Miami ordinance protecting the civil rights of homosexuals. "God created Adam and Eve, not Adam and Bruce," she pointed out. Thanks in large part to Bryant's efforts, Miami voters repealed the ordinance by a two-to-one margin. Soon after, readers of *Good Housekeeping* magazine voted Bryant "the most admired woman in America." Other cities, too, reversed earlier measures in favor of gay rights.

In 1978, as the backlash intensified, a conservative member of the San Francisco board of supervisors, Dan White, fatally shot gay board-member Harvey Milk and Milk's ally, Mayor George Moscone. "The city weeps" headlined the *San Francisco Examiner*. When White got off with a light sentence (after claiming that junk food had affected his judgment), riots erupted in the city. In 1980 disco singer Donna Summer, highly popular in the gay community, announced that she had been become a born-again Christian and speculated that AIDS had been "sent by God to punish homosexuals."

Another manifestation of the conservative turn was a revival of religion and spiritual questing. Some young people joined the Reverend Sun Myung Moon's Unification church or the International Society for Krishna Consciousness, whose shaved-head, saffron-robed followers added an exotic note in airports, city streets, and college campuses. More long-lasting was the rapid growth of evangelical Protestant denominations such as the Assemblies of God and the Southern Baptist Convention, which espoused strict morality, the Bible's verbatim truth, and a "born-again" religious conversion.

Evangelical Christians had pursued social reform before the Civil War, including the abolition of slavery, and their modern-day successors also preached reform, but of a conservative variety. As one evangelical observed in 1985, "I always thought that churches should stay out of politics. Now it seems almost a sin not to get involved." Jerry Falwall's Moral Majority, founded in 1979 as a "pro-life, pro-family, pro-moral, and pro-America" crusade, channeled this activism into support for conservative candidates. While battling domestic evils such as abortion, homosexuality, and pornography, many evangelicals also embraced a fiercely militant anticommunism.

A network of Christian bookstores, radio stations, and TV evangelists fueled the revival. Along with Falwell's *Old Time Gospel Hour,* popular broadcasts included Pat Robertson's *700 Club,* Jim and Tammy Bakker's *PTL* (Praise the Lord) program, and Jimmy Swaggart's telecasts from Louisiana. Many of these shows aired on Robertson's CBN (Christian Broadcasting Network). With their constant pleas for money, the televangelists repelled many Americans, but millions embraced their spiritual message. The so-called electronic church suffered after 1987 amid sexual and financial scandals, but the influence of evangelicalism continued. In *The Culture of Disbelief* (1993), law professor Stephen J. Carter called on politicians and the media to cease "trivializing" religion and to recognize its importance for many Americans. In a world of change, evangelicals found certitude, reassurance, and a sense of community in their shared faith. In the process, they profoundly influenced late-twentieth-century American life.

PATTERNS OF SOCIAL CHANGE IN POST-1960S AMERICA

While white, urban, middle-class Americans pursued the good life or embraced various reform causes, other groups grappled with urgent economic worries and struggled to move up the ladder. Family farmers became an endangered species amid the proliferation of giant agribusinesses. Although many African-Americans successfully pursued the academic and professional avenues opened by the civil-rights movement, others remained trapped in poverty. While Native Americans continued to face many hurdles, the 1970s brought brighter economic prospects and a new assertiveness in pursuing long-ignored treaty rights. New patterns of immigration, meanwhile, changed the nation's ethnic and demographic profile, with profound implications for the future.

Decline of the Family Farm

The family farm, historically revered as the backbone of America, continued its long decline in these years. In 1960 about 6 percent of the U.S. labor force worked on farms; by 1994 the figure was 2.5 percent. The farm population was aging, as young people sought opportunities in the cities. The small-farm operators who still hung on often held second jobs to make ends meet.

Total farm production increased, however, thanks to factory farms and agribusinesses. The acreage of the average farm grew from 375 to 430 between 1970 and 1990, and farms of several thousand acres were not unusual. Big operators bought up failing farms, demolished the homes that had sheltered successive generations, and consolidated them into large-scale operations involving major capital investment and heavy-duty equipment. Mass-production factory farms dominated poultry and hog production. Although politicians paid lip service to the family farm, federal crop subsidy programs accelerated the process of consolidation, as they had since the 1930s.

While the family farm disappeared, movies, novels, and songs kept it vivid in the nation's collective memory. In the 1985 film *The Trip to Bountiful,* an aging Texas woman, movingly played by Geraldine Page, living in a cramped city house with her son and his wife, pays a nostalgic final visit to her girlhood farm home, only to find it abandoned and falling to ruin. In that same year, country singer Willie Nelson, combining nostalgia and show-business savvy with a genuine desire to help small farmers, began a popular series of annual concerts he called "Farm Aid." The first, in Champaign, Illinois, featured Nelson, Bob Dylan, Billy Joel, Roy Orbison, and other stars. By 1999 Farm Aid had contributed nearly $15 million to programs designed to help small farmers survive.

Like much else in the 1970s, the movement to recapture a vanishing rural past owed a debt to the 1960s. As the sixties ended, many members of the counterculture formed rural communes to escape the urban-corporate world and live in harmony with nature. As one commented, "We're learning self-sufficiency and rediscovering old technologies . . . and we're doing this, as much as possible, outside the existing structures." Several thousand rural communes soon arose across America. Periodicals like *The Whole Earth Catalog* and *The Mother Earth News* provided guidance on organic farming and sold simple, hand-operated products for rural living.

The Two Worlds of Black America

The story of black America in these years is really two very different stories. On one hand, millions of blacks experienced significant upward mobility thanks to the doors opened by the civil-rights movement. In 1965 black students accounted for under 5 percent of college enrollments; by 1990 the figure had risen to 12 percent, as the proportion of black high-school graduates going on to college nearly matched that of whites. By 1990 some 46 percent of black workers held white-collar jobs. TV's *Cosby Show,* a comedy of the later 1980s in which Bill Cosby played a doctor married to a lawyer, portrayed this upwardly mobile world.

Outside this world lay the inner-city slums, inhabited by perhaps a third of the black population. Here, up to half the young people never finished high school, and the jobless rate soared as high as 60 percent. Inflation, periodic recessions, growing demands for specialized skills, and economic changes that eliminated many of the unskilled jobs once held by the urban poor all wreaked havoc with the black underclass. Black factory workers suffered from job cuts in steel, automaking, and other industries.

Cocaine and other drugs pervaded the inner cities. Some black children recruited as lookouts for drug dealers became dealers themselves when they reached their early teens. With drugs came violence. In the 1980s a young black male was six times as likely to be murdered as a young white male. In Los Angeles two rival gangs, the Bloods and the Crips, accounted for more than four hundred killings in 1987. Warned Jewelle Taylor Gibbs of the University of California at Berkeley, "Young black males in America's inner cities are an endangered species . . . , [the] rejects of our affluent society."

In truth, drug abuse affected all social levels, including yuppies, sports and show-business celebrities, and young corporate executives. Despite the tough Comprehensive Drug Abuse Act of 1970, illegal-substance abuse was widespread and was even glorified in movies, songs, and rock concerts. But the devastating impact of drug use and drug trafficking on entire communities fell most heavily on the inner cities.

Unmarried women—mostly young and poor—accounted for nearly 60 percent of all black births in 1980, and the figure rose still higher thereafter. Scarcely beyond childhood themselves, many of these single mothers depended on welfare payments for survival. Buffeted by complex social and economic forces, the predominantly nonwhite inner-city populations posed a major social challenge. Caught in a cycle of dependence, they were at risk of becoming a permanent underclass, cut off from all hope of bettering their lot.

In one effort to improve conditions, governments extended "affirmative action" programs to groups previously discriminated against. Cities set aside a percentage of building contracts for minority businesses, for example. Some educational institutions reserved a certain number of slots for minority applicants. Such programs faced court challenges, however. In *Bakke* v. *U.S.* (1978) the Supreme Court overthrew the affirmative-action plan of a California medical school. In 1989 the high court invalidated a Richmond, Virginia, requirement that 30 percent of building contracts be awarded to minority businesses.

The conservative backlash affected African-Americans. The Reagan administration, distrusting government, opposed federal action to remedy past injustices. Reagan's appointees to the U.S. Civil Rights Commission, charged with enforcing civil-rights laws, shared his suspicion of federal activism. This governmental foot dragging complicated efforts to address the urgent problems of inner-city jobless-ness and social disorganization.

Brightening Prospects for Native Americans Like other developments discussed in this chapter, the Native American experience in these years was shaped by events of the 1960s. Influenced by the decade's protest cli-mate, members of the militant American Indian Movement (AIM) had occupied Alcatraz Island in San Francisco Bay; the Bureau of Indian Affairs in Washington; and, in 1973, a trading post at Wounded Knee, South Dakota, site of the 1890 Indian massacre by the U.S. army. This militancy spurred yet another shift in federal policy. The Indian Self-Determination Act of 1974 granted tribes control of federal aid programs on the reservations and over-sight of their own schools.

In the 1990 census, more than 1.7 million persons identified themselves as American Indians, in contrast to fewer than eight hundred thousand in 1970. This upsurge reflected not only natural increase and ethnic pride, but also economic advantages associated with tribal membership. Under a 1961 law permitting them to buy or develop land for commercial and industrial projects, tribes launched business ventures ranging from resorts to mining and logging operations. They licensed food-processing plants, electronics firms, and manufacturing enterprises on tribal lands, providing jobs and income. Tribes also opened gambling casinos, although some Native American leaders deplored the casinos as a threat to tradi-tional Indian values.

Indian tribes also reasserted rights granted them in treaties that had long gath-ered dust in government archives. The Indian Claims Commission, a federal agency set up in 1946, worked overtime after 1970. In 1971 the Native peoples of Alaska won 40 million acres of land and nearly $1 billion in settlement of long-standing treaty claims. In 1980 the Sioux were awarded $107 million for South Dakota lands taken from them in violation of treaty agreements. The Penobscot Indians in Maine won claims based on a 1790 federal law. In 1988 the tiny Puyallup tribe of Washington State received $162 million in settlement of their claim that the city of Tacoma occupied land granted them by treaty in the 1850s. Among other projects, the Puyallups laid plans to restore salmon runs on the Puyallup River.

High jobless rates, alcoholism, and disease persisted on the reservations and among urbanized Indians. But the renewal of tribal life, new federal policies, and the courts' willingness to honor legally binding treaties clearly represented an advance. In the popular culture, movies such as *Little Big Man* (1970) and *Dances with Wolves* (1990), while idealizing Indians, represented an improvement over the grotesque stereotypes of earlier cowboy-and-Indian films.

New Patterns of Immigration America's growth from 204 million people in 1970 to 275 million in 2000 reflected a steady influx of immigrants, both legal and illegal. Whereas most immigrants once came from Europe, some 45 percent of the late-twentieth-century arrivals came from the Western Hemisphere and 30 percent from Asia. As in the past, economic need drew these newcomers. In oil-rich Mexico, for example, an oil price collapse in the 1980s worsened the nation's chronic poverty, spurring many to seek jobs in the north. But these immigrants, like their predecessors, faced continued hardships. In 1990 nearly 20 percent of Mexican-Americans and 30 percent of Puerto Ricans lived below the poverty line.

Despite adversity, Hispanic newcomers preserved their language and traditions, influencing U.S. culture in the process. In Los Angeles, with nearly a million Mexican-Americans, Spanish-language businesses, churches, newspapers, and radio stations proliferated. Large parts of Miami seemed wholly Hispanic.

Estimates of the number of illegal aliens in the United States ranged as high as 12 million by the early 1990s. Working long hours with few legal protections, these migrants, mostly Mexicans and Haitians (as well as Puerto Ricans, who are U.S. citizens), sweated in the garment trades, cleaned houses, changed diapers, and labored in agricultural fields. Addressing the problem, the Immigration Reform and Control Act of 1986 outlawed the hiring of illegal aliens, strengthened border controls, and offered legal status to aliens who had lived in the United States for five years.

Immigration from Asia climbed as newcomers arrived from Korea, Vietnam, and the Philippines. Prizing education, many Asian immigrants moved up rapidly. The younger generation, torn between the new and the old, generally retained

Sid Gutierrez, Astronaut
Hispanics entered all arenas of American life in the late twentieth century. Gutierrez, a native of Albuquerque, New Mexico, piloted space shuttle Columbia on a 1991 NASA mission.

strong group loyalties while exploring larger opportunities. All these ethnic trends made contemporary America of the 1970s and 1980s a more diverse and vibrant place than it had been a generation earlier.

YEARS OF MALAISE: POST-WATERGATE POLITICS AND DIPLOMACY, 1974–1980

The Vietnam debacle and the disastrous end of Richard Nixon's presidency had a dispiriting effect on the nation's political culture, as Gerald Ford and Jimmy Carter grappled with a tangle of domestic and foreign problems. As soaring oil prices led to inflation, unemployment, and recession, a sense of the limits of economic growth gripped many Americans. Globally, the later 1970s brought mostly humiliations, from the sorry end of the Vietnam War to Iran's seizure of U.S. hostages. The stark polarities of the Cold War blurred as complex problems in Asia, the Middle East, Latin America, and Africa hinted at the kinds of issues the United States would face in the future.

The confident days of the 1950s and early 1960s, when a prosperous America had savored its role as the Free World's leader, equal to any challenge, now seemed remote. A nation long convinced that it was immune to the historical forces that hedged in other societies seemed buffeted by forces beyond its control. Although the Vietnam failure encouraged isolationist tendencies, the events of the post-1970 era made it clear that America could not evade global involvement. By 1980 the accumulating frustration had generated a strong political revolt.

The Caretaker Presidency of Gerald Ford, 1974–1976 Gerald Ford took the presidential oath on August 9, 1974, following Richard Nixon's forced resignation. A Michigan congressman who had been House minority leader before becoming vice president, Ford conveyed a likeable decency, if little evidence of brilliance. After the trauma of Watergate, he inspired cautious hope. "Our long national nightmare is over," he declared.

Ford's period of grace soon ended, however, when he pardoned Richard Nixon for "any and all crimes" committed while in office, thus shielding him from prosecution for his Watergate role. Ford said he wanted to help heal the body politic, but many Americans reacted with outrage.

On domestic issues Ford proved more conservative than Nixon, vetoing a series of environmental, social-welfare, and public-interest measures, among them a 1974 freedom of information bill granting citizens greater access to government records. The Democratic Congress overrode most of these vetoes.

Economic problems triggered by events abroad occupied Ford's attention. Beginning in 1973, oil prices shot up as a result of an Arab oil embargo (see Chapter 29) and price hikes by the Organization of Petroleum Exporting Countries (OPEC), a thirteen-nation consortium formed in 1960. The effect on the United States, heavily dependent on imported oil, was severe. The soaring cost of gasoline, heating oil, and other petroleum-based products worsened already-serious infla-tion. Consumer prices rose by 23 percent in 1974–1975. In October 1974 Ford unveiled a program of voluntary restraint dubbed "Whip Inflation Now" (WIN), but prices continued to zoom. When the Federal Reserve Board tried to cool the economy by raising interest rates, a severe recession resulted. Unemployment approached 11 percent by 1975. As tax receipts dropped, the federal deficit increased.

In a dramatic turnaround, Americans seriously tried to curb their energy con-sumption for the first time since World War II. As they stopped buying Detroit's gas guzzlers, GM, Ford, and Chrysler laid off more than 225,000 workers. Smaller, fuel-efficient imports increased their market share from 17 to 33 percent in the 1970s. Congress set fuel-efficiency standards for automobiles in 1975 and imposed a national speed limit of fifty-five miles per hour.

The national morale suffered another blow in April 1975 when the South Vietnamese government fell, ending two decades of U.S. effort in Vietnam. The TV networks chronicled desperate helicopter evacuations from the roof of the U.S. embassy in Saigon (soon renamed Ho Chi Minh City) as North Vietnamese troops closed in. A few weeks later, when Cambodia seized a U.S. merchant ship, the *Mayagüez,* a frustrated Ford ordered a military rescue. This hasty show of force freed the thirty-nine *Mayagüez* crew members but cost the lives of forty-one U.S. servicemen.

As the nation entered the election year 1976—also the bicentennial of the Declaration of Independence—Americans found little reason for optimism.

The Outsider as Insider: President Jimmy Carter, 1977–1980

Gerald Ford won the Republican nomination in 1976 despite a challenge from former California Governor Ronald Reagan. On the Democratic side, Jimmy Carter, a Georgia peanut grower and former governor, swept the primaries by stressing themes that appealed to post-Vietnam, post-Watergate America. He emphasized his status as a Washington outsider, pledged never to lie to the American people, and avowed his religious faith as a "born-again" Christian. As his running mate Carter chose Minnesota Senator Walter Mondale, a liberal Democrat.

Carter's early lead eroded as voters sensed a certain vagueness in his program, but he won by a narrow margin. The vote broke sharply along class lines: the well-to-do went for Ford; the poor, overwhelmingly for Carter. The Georgian swept the South and received 90 percent of the black vote. While in the long run the conser-vative backlash against 1960s radicalism would help the Republicans, popular revulsion against Nixon and Watergate temporarily interrupted the Republican advance, providing an opening for the Carter-Mondale ticket.

Underscoring his outsider image, Carter rejected the trappings of what some in Nixon's day had labeled "the imperial presidency." On inauguration day, with his wife and daughter, he walked from the Capitol to the White House. In an echo of Franklin Roosevelt's radio chats, he delivered some of his TV speeches wearing a sweater and seated by a fireplace. To broad public approval, he appointed a number of women and members of minority groups to federal judgeships.

Despite the populist symbolism and gestures of inclusiveness, Carter never framed a clear political philosophy. Liberals and conservatives both claimed him. Intensely private, he relied on young staff members from Georgia and avoided socializing with politicians. "Carter couldn't get the Pledge of Allegiance through Congress," groused one legislator. An intellectual who had worked as a nuclear-submarine engineer after graduating from the U.S. Naval Academy, Carter was at his best when focused on specific problems. His larger political vision, if any, remained unclear. He fought the recession with a tax cut and a modest public-works program, and the unemployment rate dropped to around 5 percent by late 1978. But he sensed the nation's lack of sympathy for large-scale government initiatives, and offered few proposals to deal with inner-city poverty, the family-farm crisis, the plight of unemployed industrial workers, and other major social problems.

Environmental issues did loom large for Carter, however, just as they did for many Americans. In 1980, in a major victory for environmentalists and for the administration, Congress passed the Alaska Lands Act, which set aside more than 100 million acres of public land in Alaska for parks, wildlife refuges, recreational areas, and national forests, and added twenty-six rivers to the nation's Wild and Scenic River System. Energy companies eager to exploit Alaska's oil fields were deeply unhappy, and laid plans to renew the battle at a later time.

A major environmental crisis during Carter's presidency erupted in Niagara Falls, New York, where for years the Hooker Chemical and Plastics Corporation had dumped tons of waste products in a district known as the Love Canal. In 1953, as the landfill reached capacity, Hooker had covered the site with earth and sold it to the city. Schools, single-family houses, and low-income apartments soon sprang up, but residents complained of odors and strange substances oozing from the ground. In the later 1970s tests confirmed that toxic chemicals, including deadly dioxin, were seeping into basements, polluting the air, and discharging into the Niagara River. Medical researchers found elevated levels of cancer, miscarriages, and birth defects among Love Canal inhabitants.

In 1978 New York's health commissioner declared a medical emergency and closed a school directly over the landfill. A few days later, President Carter authorized federal funds to relocate the families most at risk. In 1980 Carter declared the Love Canal a national emergency, freeing more federal money for relocation and clean-up. The fact that Love Canal lay a few miles from Niagara Falls, once a symbol of America's sublime and unspoiled wilderness, added a level of tragic irony to the situation. Viewed together, the Alaska Lands Act, involving long-term wilderness preservation, and the urgent Love Canal crisis illustrate the complexity of the effort to confront the environmental implications of decades of industrialization and corporate pressures for further development.

Overall, Carter's domestic record proved thin. Congress ignored his proposals for administrative reforms in the civil service and the executive branch of government. His calls for a national health-insurance program, an overhaul of the welfare system, and reform of the income-tax laws fell flat. His problems arose from his own political clumsiness, but perhaps even more from the limitations imposed by a conservative electorate in no mood for bold initiatives.

Carter's foreign-policy record was similarly mixed. As a candidate he had urged increased attention to human rights. His secretary of state, Cyrus Vance, worked to combat abuses in Chile, Argentina, Ethiopia, South Africa, and elsewhere. (Human-rights problems in countries allied with the United States, such as South Korea and the Philippines, received less attention.)

In Latin America Carter sought improved relations with Panama. Since 1964, when anti-American riots had rocked Panama, successive administrations had been negotiating a new Panama Canal treaty that would address Panama's grievances. The Carter administration completed negotiations on treaties transferring the Panama Canal and the Canal Zone to Panama by 1999. Although these agreements protected U.S. security interests, conservatives attacked them as proof of America's post-Vietnam loss of nerve, and recalled Teddy Roosevelt's bold maneuvers that had brought the canal into existence. But in a rare congressional success, Carter won Senate ratification of the treaties.

In dealing with America's Cold War adversaries China and the Soviet Union, Carter pursued the Nixon-Kissinger strategy of seeking to normalize relations. After China's long-time leader Mao Zedong died in 1976, his successor, Deng Xiaoping, expressed interest in closer links with the United States. Carter responded by restoring full diplomatic relations with Beijing in 1979, thus opening the door to

President Jimmy Carter with Egypt's Anwar Sadat at Camp David, 1978
Carter's role in brokering a peace accord between Israel and Egypt was the high point of his presidency. This event was cited as one of the reasons that Carter received the Nobel Peace Prize in 2002.

scientific, cultural, and commercial exchanges. Relations with China remained rocky because of that nation's human-rights abuses, but the era of total hostility and diplomatic isolation had ended.

Toward the Soviet Union Carter showed both conciliation and toughness, with toughness ultimately winning out. In a 1979 meeting in Vienna, Carter and the Soviet leader Leonid Brezhnev signed the SALT II treaty, limiting each side's nuclear-weapons arsenals. When Carter sent the treaty to the Senate for ratification, however, advocates of a strong military attacked it for favoring the Soviets. Support for SALT II dissolved entirely in January 1980 when Russia invaded Afghanistan. The reasons for the invasion were complex, but many Americans viewed it as proof of Moscow's expansionist designs. As U.S.-Soviet relations soured, Carter withdrew SALT II from the Senate and adopted a series of anti-Soviet measures, including a boycott of the 1980 Summer Olympics in Moscow. This hard-line Soviet policy reflected the growing influence of Carter's national security adviser, Polish-born Zbigniew Brzezinski, who advocated a tough stance toward Moscow.

The Middle East: Peace Accords and Hostages Carter's proudest achievement and his bitterest setbacks came in the Middle East. Despite Henry Kissinger's efforts, a state of war still prevailed between Israel and Egypt. When Egyptian leader Anwar el-Sadat unexpectedly flew to Israel in 1977 to negotiate with Israeli prime minister Menachem Begin, Carter saw an opening. In September 1978 Carter hosted Sadat and Begin at Camp David, the presidential retreat in Maryland. The Camp David Accords that resulted set a timetable for granting greater autonomy to the Palestinians living in the West Bank and Gaza Strip, occupied by Israel since the 1967 war. In March 1979 the two leaders signed a formal peace treaty at the White House.

Carter's hopes for a comprehensive Middle Eastern settlement came to nothing. Despite the Camp David Accords, Israel continued to build Jewish settlements in the occupied territories. The other Arab states rejected the accords, and in 1981 Islamic fundamentalists assassinated Sadat. Tension in the region remained high, and peace seemed as elusive as ever.

A new Middle Eastern crisis erupted in 1979. For years, Iran had been ruled by Shah Mohammed Reza Pahlavi, who headed a harshly repressive but pro-U.S. regime. Iran's Shiite Muslims, inspired by their exiled spiritual head, Ayatollah Ruhollah Khomeini, bitterly opposed the shah's rule. In January 1979, amid rising Shiite unrest, the shah fled Iran. Khomeini returned in triumph, imposed strict Islamic rule, and preached hatred of the United States.

In November, after Carter admitted the shah to the United States for cancer treatment, Khomeini supporters stormed the U.S. embassy in Tehran and seized more than fifty American hostages. Thus began a 444-day ordeal that nearly paralyzed the Carter administration. TV images of blindfolded hostages, anti-American mobs, and U.S. flags being used as garbage bags rubbed American nerves raw. A botched rescue attempt in April 1980 left eight GIs dead. Secretary of State Vance, who had opposed the rescue effort, resigned. Not until January 20, 1981, the day Carter left office, did the Iranian authorities release the hostages.

Troubles and
Frustration
at the End of
Carter's Term

The decade's second oil crisis hit in 1979. When OPEC again boosted oil prices, U.S. gasoline prices edged toward the then-unheard-of level of $1 a gallon. Tempers flared as long lines formed at gas stations. Driven by repeated oil-price hikes, inflation worsened. Prices rose by more than 13 percent in both 1979 and 1980. In 1979 alone, U.S. consumers paid $16.4 billion in added costs related to the oil-price increases. As the Federal Reserve Board battled inflation by raising interest rates, mortgages and business loans became prohibitively expensive. Economic activity stalled, producing "stagflation"—a combination of business stagnation and price inflation. Once again, events abroad directly affected the American home front.

Pondering the crisis, Carter drew a larger lesson: the nation's wasteful energy consumption must give way to a new ethic of conservation. He recognized that two key factors that had buttressed U.S. economic growth—cheap, unlimited energy and the lack of foreign competition—could no longer be counted on. The era of endless expansion was over, he concluded, and the nation must adopt a philosophy of restraint. In 1977 Carter had created a new Department of Energy and proposed an energy bill involving higher oil and gasoline taxes, tax credits for conservation measures, and research on alternative energy resources. Congress had passed a watered-down version of his plan in 1978, and Carter now decided that tougher energy legislation was needed. But he failed to convince either Congress or the public that he could provide the leadership to resolve either the hostage crisis abroad or the energy crisis at home.

As with Herbert Hoover in the early 1930s, Americans turned against the remote figure in the White House. When Carter's approval rating sagged to 26 percent in the summer of 1979 (lower than Nixon's at the depths of Watergate), he isolated himself at Camp David and then emerged to deliver a TV address that seemed to shift the blame to the American people for their collective "malaise" and "crisis of confidence." A cabinet reshuffle followed, but the whole exercise deepened suspicions that Carter himself was a big part of the problem. In mid-1980, an election year, Carter's approval rating fell to an appalling 23 percent. The Democrats glumly renominated him, but defeat in November loomed.

Carter's sudden emergence in 1976 illustrated how, in the TV era, a relative unknown could bypass party power brokers and win a national following almost overnight. At a moment when Americans longed to see integrity restored to the presidency, he seemed a godsend. Keenly analytical, Carter identified many emerging issues, including the need for environmental protection; energy conservation; and reform of the nation's tax, welfare, and health-care structures.

But in contrast to Franklin Roosevelt and Lyndon Johnson, he lacked the political skills to build a consensus around the solutions he believed necessary. A post-presidential career devoted to humanitarian service and international conflict-resolution restored Carter's reputation, and brought him the Nobel Peace Prize in 2002. But when he left office in January 1981, few expressed regrets.

THE REAGAN REVOLUTION, 1981–1984

In 1980, with the conservative backlash against the 1960s in full swing, voters turned to a candidate who promised to break with the recent past: Ronald Reagan. His unabashed patriotism appealed to a nation still traumatized by Vietnam. His promise to reverse the Democrats' "tax and spend" policies and his attacks on the social-welfare ideology of the New Deal, the Fair Deal, and the Great Society resonated with millions of white middle-class and blue-collar Americans.

As president, Reagan called for a renewal of patriotism. His economic policies at first brought on a recession, but eventually lowered inflation and triggered consumer buying and a stock-market boom. These same policies caused economic difficulties after his departure. In his first term Reagan unleashed blasts of belligerent Cold War rhetoric, pursued the arms race with the Soviets, and financed guerrilla forces in Latin America seeking to overthrow leftist regimes. He also confronted crises in the Middle East and elsewhere that did not readily fit into his Cold War world view.

Background of the Reagan Revolution What underlay Reagan's appeal? First, voters frightened by the prospect of chronic stagflation were drawn to his seemingly painless panacea: a big tax cut that would stimulate the economy. This in turn would boost tax revenues so the budget could be balanced, reducing inflationary pressures. George H. W. Bush, Reagan's rival for the Republican nomination, ridiculed this plan as "voodoo economics," but it impressed many voters. Moreover, Reagan's tributes to self-help and private enterprise appealed to many as an alternative to the New Deal–Great Society ideology of government activism. His uncomplicated patriotism, calls for military strength, and praise of America's greatness soothed the battered national psyche.

Reagan also embraced the cultural conservatism of the so-called New Right, which included millions of religious evangelicals. The social unrest and sexual revolution of the 1960s; the women's movement; rising abortion and divorce rates; the open celebration of homosexuality; the pervasiveness of sex and violence in the media; court rulings against prayer in the classroom; and "secular humanism" in school textbooks all upset Americans who longed for clear-cut moral standards and a return to "traditional values."

Jerry Falwell and others eagerly translated such concerns into political action. Falwell's pro-Reagan Moral Majority registered an estimated 2 million new voters in 1980 and 1984. The organization disbanded after 1984, but Pat Robertson's Christian Coalition took its place, mobilizing conservative Christians to elect candidates to town councils and school boards as a prelude to expanded national influence. Reagan also benefited from the erosion of Democratic strength in the South fostered earlier by George Wallace and Richard Nixon.

Demographics contributed to Reagan's success. While New York City, Chicago, Detroit, and other Democratic strongholds in the Northeast and Midwest lost population in the 1970s, Texas, California, Florida, and other historically conservative Sunbelt states gained population. In 1978 Californians passed Proposition 13, a referendum calling for deep tax cuts. Elsewhere in the West, ranchers and developers demanded a return of federal lands to state control.

Reagan, a skillful actor and seasoned public speaker, combined these themes into a potent message. Belying his sixty-nine years, he conveyed a youthful vigor. At a time of national malaise, he seemed to offer confident, assured leadership. Critics found him superficial and his ideology selfish and mean-spirited, and time would reveal gaps between substance and image in Reagan's appeal, but in 1980 a majority of voters found him irresistible.

Reagan grew up in Dixon, Illinois, the son of an alcoholic father and a pious mother active in a fundamentalist church. After finishing college he announced sports events for a Des Moines radio station and in 1937 moved to Hollywood. His fifty-four films proved forgettable, but he gained political experience as president of the Screen Actors' Guild. A New Dealer in the 1930s, Reagan had moved to the right in the 1950s, and in 1954 he became a corporate spokesman for the General Electric Company. In a 1964 TV speech for presidential candidate Barry Goldwater, he passionately praised American individualism and the free-enterprise system.

Elected governor of California in 1966 with the help of a group of California millionaires, Reagan continued to popularize conservative ideas while taking a tough line against campus demonstrators. He nearly won the Republican presidential nomination in 1976, and in 1980 he easily disposed of his principal opponent, George H. W. Bush, whom he then chose as his running mate. Like his one-time political hero Franklin Roosevelt, Reagan promised the American people a new deal. But unlike FDR, Reagan's new deal meant smaller government, reduced taxes and spending, and untrammeled free enterprise.

Hammering at the question "Are you better off now than you were four years ago?" Reagan garnered 51 percent of the popular vote to Carter's 41 percent.

The Rev. Pat Robertson *Head of the Christian Broadcasting Network (CBN) and founder of the Christian Coalition, Robertson helped mobilize evangelical Christians politically in the 1980s and beyond.*

The Election of 1980

Jimmy Carter's unpopularity and Ronald Reagan's telegenic appeal combined to give Reagan a crushing electoral victory.

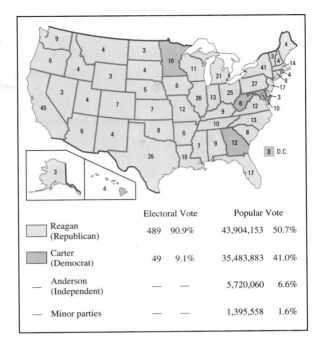

	Electoral Vote		Popular Vote	
Reagan (Republican)	489	90.9%	43,904,153	50.7%
Carter (Democrat)	49	9.1%	35,483,883	41.0%
Anderson (Independent)	—	—	5,720,060	6.6%
Minor parties	—	—	1,395,558	1.6%

(An independent candidate, liberal Republican John Anderson, collected most of the balance.) Republicans gained eleven Senate seats, and with them, for the first time since 1955, a majority. These Senate victories revealed the power of conservative political action committees (PACs), which used computerized mass mailings focusing on emotional issues like abortion and gun control. (PACs were not confined to conservatives; organizations of all ideological stripes used them.)

Reaping the benefits of Nixon's southern strategy, Reagan carried every southern state except Carter's own Georgia as well as every state west of the Mississippi except Minnesota and Hawaii. Over half the nation's blue-collar workers voted Republican. Of FDR's New Deal political alliance, only black voters remained firmly Democratic.

Reaganomics   The new president's economic program, called Reaganomics by the media, boiled down to the belief that U.S. capitalism, if freed from heavy taxes and government regulation, would achieve wonders of productivity. Reagan's first budget message proposed a 30 percent reduction in federal income taxes over three years. Trimming this proposal slightly, Congress voted a 25 percent income-tax cut: 5 percent in 1981 and 10 percent in 1982 and 1983.

To make up the lost revenues, Reagan proposed massive cuts in such programs as school lunches, student loans, job training, and urban mass transit. Congress cut less than Reagan wanted, but it did slash more than $40 billion from domestic spending. Conservative southern Democrats, nicknamed boll weevils, joined

Republicans in voting these cuts. Journalists harked back to FDR's Hundred Days of 1933 to find a time when government had shifted gears so dramatically. Economists warned that the tax cut would produce huge federal deficits, but Reagan insisted that lower tax rates would stimulate business growth and thereby push up total tax revenues.

Reaganomics also involved drastic cutbacks in federal regulation of business. Deregulation had begun under Carter, but Reagan extended it into new areas such as banking, the savings-and-loan industry, transportation, and communications. The head of the Federal Communications Commission hacked away at federal rules governing the broadcast industry. The secretary of transportation cut back on regulations Congress had passed in the 1970s to reduce air pollution and improve vehicle efficiency and safety.

Secretary of the Interior James Watt of Wyoming worked tirelessly to open federal wilderness areas, forest lands, and coastal waters to oil and gas companies and developers; undermine endangered-species programs; and cut programs to protect environmentally threatened regions. Before coming to Washington, Watt had headed the Mountain States Legal Foundation, which spearheaded the so-called Sagebrush Rebellion of western conservatives seeking to open public lands to private development. In response to Watt's extreme anti-environmentalist positions, the Sierra Club, the Wilderness Society, and other environmental organizations grew rapidly. More than a million environmentalists signed petitions demanding Watt's ouster. After a series of public-relations gaffes and comments offensive to various groups, Watt resigned in 1983.

Although the Reagan administration's attack on "big government" affected certain federal functions, particularly in the regulatory and environmental realm, it had little overall effect. The century-long growth of the federal government's budget and bureaucracy continued in the 1980s.

While implementing Reaganomics, the administration also faced the immediate problem of inflation. The Federal Reserve Board led the charge, pushing interest rates ever higher. This harsh medicine, coupled with a drop in oil prices, did its job. Inflation fell to around 4 percent in 1983 and held steady thereafter.

Recession and Boom Times The high interest rates necessary to curb inflation soon brought on a recession. By late 1982 unemployment stood at 10 percent. As funding for social programs dried up, the plight of the poor worsened. Inner-city blacks and Hispanics suffered severely. The Reagan recession also contributed to falling exports. As foreign investors bought dollars to earn high U.S. interest rates, the dollar rose in value vis-à-vis foreign currencies, making U.S. goods more expensive abroad. With exports declining and U.S. consumers buying TVs, stereos, and automobiles made in Japan and other countries, the U.S. trade deficit (the gap between exports and imports) more than tripled in the early 1980s, reaching a whopping $111 billion in 1984.

The industrial heartland reeled under the triple blows of slumping exports, foreign competition, and technological obsolescence. The hard-hit auto plants, aging steel mills, and other industries of the Midwest laid off hordes of workers, and many plants closed. In 1979–1983, 11.5 million U.S. workers lost jobs as a result of plant closings and slack work. Farmers suffered as well. Wheat exports fell 38 percent from 1980 to 1985, and corn exports by 49 percent. In foreclosure sales evocative of the 1930s, still more family farms vanished.

Soaring federal deficits added to the economic muddle. Reagan's tax cuts reduced federal revenues without immediately producing the predicted business boom, while soaring military appropriations far exceeded domestic spending cuts. With the economy sputtering, budget deficits mounting, and critics denouncing him as callous toward the poor, Reagan in 1982–1983 accepted a reduced rate of military spending, a slowing of funding cuts in social programs, new emergency job programs, and various tax increases disguised as "revenue-enhancement measures."

Despite a stock-market upturn, the economy remained worrisome through 1982. In the elections that fall, the Democrats gained twenty-six House seats. Like other recent presidents, Reagan appeared headed for failure. But 1983 brought an economic rebound. Encouraged by tax cuts, falling interest rates, and evidence that inflation had been tamed at last, consumers went on a buying binge; unemployment dropped; and Reagan's popularity revived.

With better times came a wave of stock-market speculation reminiscent of the 1920s. The bull market began in August 1982, and it lasted for five years. Entrepreneurs like Donald Trump, a Manhattan real-estate tycoon, and Ivan Boesky, an apparent genius at stock transactions, became celebrities. E. F. Hutton and other brokerage firms advertised heavily to lure new investors. Corporate mergers proliferated. Chevron bought Gulf for $13 billion in 1984; GE acquired RCA (and its NBC subsidiary) for $6.3 billion in 1986. The stock market roared on. Banks and savings-and-loan companies, newly deregulated and flush with the deposits of eager investors, ladled out billions to developers planning shopping malls, luxury apartments, condominiums, retirement villages, and office buildings.

The Wall Street frenzy had a downside. In 1985 E. F. Hutton officials pled guilty to the illegal manipulation of funds. Ivan Boesky went to prison after a 1986 conviction for insider trading (profiting through advance knowledge of corporate actions). On October 19, 1987, the stock market crashed. The Dow Jones Industrial Average, a leading indicator of stock prices, plunged 508 points as one-fifth of the paper value of the nation's stocks evaporated. Thanks to prompt government action to ease credit, the market soon recovered, but the collapse reminded giddy investors that stocks can go down as well as up.

Even during the great bull market, economic problems persisted. The trade gap widened; the deficit passed $200 billion in 1986; and many farmers, inner-city poor, recent immigrants, and displaced industrial workers suffered through the boom times. But by 1984—just in time for Reagan's reelection campaign—the overall economic picture looked brighter than it had in years.

Reagan Confronts the "Evil Empire" and Crises in the Middle East
The anti-Soviet rhetoric of the late 1970s intensified during Reagan's first term. Addressing a convention of Protestant evangelicals, the president demonized the Soviet Union as "the focus of evil in the modern world." Anti-Soviet fury exploded in September 1983 when the Russians shot down a Korean passenger plane that had strayed into their airspace, killing all 269 aboard. Moscow claimed that the plane had been spying, but later abandoned this excuse.

The administration's anti-Soviet obsession influenced its policy toward El Salvador and Nicaragua, two desperately poor Central American nations caught up in revolutionary turmoil. The Reagan White House backed the Salvadoran military junta in its brutal suppression of a leftist insurgency supported by Fidel Castro's Cuba. A U.S.-backed moderate won the 1984 presidential election in El Salvador, but the killing of the regime's opponents went on.

In Nicaragua, the Carter administration had initially granted aid to the Sandinista revolutionaries who overthrew dictator Anastasio Somoza in 1979. Reagan reversed this policy, claiming that the leftist Sandinistas were turning Nicaragua into a pro-communist state like Castro's Cuba. In 1982 the CIA organized and financed a ten-thousand-man anti-Sandinista guerrilla army, called the contras, based in neighboring Honduras and Costa Rica. The contras, many of whom were linked to the hated Somoza regime, conducted raids, planted mines, and carried out sabotage inside Nicaragua. This U.S.-financed guerrilla campaign took a heavy toll of civilian lives.

For Reagan, the campaign to overthrow the Sandinistas and to control events in Latin America became an obsession. "The national security of all the Americas is at stake," he somberly told a joint session of Congress in May 1983; ". . . if we cannot defend ourselves there, we cannot expect to prevail elsewhere . . . and the safety of our homeland would be put at jeopardy."

Fearing another Vietnam, Americans grew alarmed as details of this U.S.-run "covert" war leaked out. Congress voted a yearlong halt in U.S. military aid to the contras in December 1982 and imposed a two-year ban in 1984. Reagan's enthusiasm for the contras held steady. Despite congressional prohibitions, the White House continued to funnel money contributed by foreign governments and right-wing groups in the United States to the contras. Reagan grudgingly backed a 1988 truce between the Sandinistas and the contras arranged by Central American leaders, but he still hoped for a contra victory.

Reagan's militarization of U.S. foreign policy fell heavily on the tiny West Indian island of Grenada, where a 1983 coup had installed a radical leftist government. In October 1983 two thousand U.S. marines invaded Grenada and set up a pro-U.S. government. Democrats voiced sharp criticism, but most Grenadians, as well as other West Indian governments, approved.

The continuing turmoil and conflict in the Middle East that had so frustrated President Carter also preoccupied the Reagan administration. Hoping to slow the spread of Islamic fundamentalism, the United States tilted toward Saddam Hussein's Iraq in its eight-year war with Iran (1980–1988), which resulted in an estimated 1.5 million casualties, devastated both nations' economies, and created millions of refugees.

Meanwhile, the conflict among Israel, the Palestinians, and Israel's Arab foes dragged on. The United States had vital interests in the region. Many Americans felt a deep emotional bond with Israel, and each year the United States gave Israel large grants in military aid and other assistance. At the same time, the United States also gave extensive aid to Egypt and relied heavily on oil from Saudi Arabia and other Arab states, some of which were violently anti-Israel. Despite or because of these conflicting pressures, successive U.S. administrations proved unable to achieve peace in the region, and the Reagan administration was no more successful than the others.

In 1981 Israel and the Palestine Liberation Organization (PLO) concluded a cease-fire. But the PLO continued building up forces at its base in southern Lebanon. In June 1982, when an extremist faction within the PLO shot and critically wounded Israel's ambassador to Great Britain, Israeli troops under General Ariel Sharon, Israel's defense minister, invaded Lebanon, defeated the PLO, and forced its leaders, including chairman Yasir Arafat, to evacuate Lebanon. The invasion intensified conflicts among Lebanon's various Christian and Muslim factions. With Sharon's approval, a Lebanese Christian militia force entered two Palestinian refugee camps near Beirut to root out armed gunmen. Instead, in revenge for the assassination of Lebanon's Christian president a few days earlier, they massacred as many as 700–800 camp residents, including women and children. An Israeli commission of inquiry found Sharon negligent for permitting the militiamen to enter the camp and recommended his dismissal, but found no evidence that Sharon knew of the planned massacre in advance. Sharon resigned as defense minister, but remained in the government.

After the Beirut massacre, President Reagan ordered two thousand marines to Lebanon as part of a multinational peacekeeping force. The Muslim militias saw the Americans as favoring Israel and the Christian side, and in October 1983 a Shiite Muslim on a suicide mission crashed an explosive-laden truck into a poorly guarded U.S. barracks, killing 239 marines. Reagan had never clearly explained how the deployment served U.S. interests, and the disaster further discredited his policy. In early 1984 he withdrew the surviving marines.

Reagan's efforts to promote a wider Middle East peace settlement proved equally ineffective. In September 1982 he tried to use the Lebanese crisis to jump-start Arab-Israeli peace talks based on the 1978 Camp David Accords. This effort failed, like others before it.

Military Buildup and Antinuclear Protest   Insisting that the United States had grown dangerously weak since the end of the war in Vietnam, Reagan launched a massive military expansion. The Pentagon's budget nearly doubled, reaching more than $300 billion by 1985. Later, after the Cold War ended, Reagan's supporters would claim that Moscow's efforts to match Reagan's military buildup was the final blow to an already faltering Soviet economy.

Others, however, traced the Soviet collapse primarily to structural weaknesses within the U.S.S.R. itself.

The military buildup included nuclear weapons. Secretary of State Alexander Haig spoke of the utility of "nuclear warning shots" in a conventional war, and other administration officials mused about the "winnability" of nuclear war. Despite popular protests across Europe, the administration deployed 572 nuclear-armed missiles in Western Europe in 1983, fulfilling a NATO decision to counter-balance Soviet missiles in Eastern Europe. The Federal Emergency Management Agency issued a nuclear-war defense plan whereby city residents would flee to nearby small towns. A Defense Department official argued that backyard shelters would provide protection in a nuclear war. "With enough shovels," he asserted, "everybody's going to make it."

Such talk, coupled with the military buildup and Reagan's anti-Soviet rhetoric, convinced many Americans that a serious threat of nuclear war existed. A campaign for a freeze on the manufacture and deployment of nuclear weapons won strong support. Antinuclear protesters packed New York's Central Park in June 1982. That November, voters in nine states, including California and Wisconsin, approved nuclear-freeze resolutions.

To counter the freeze campaign, Reagan in March 1983 proposed the Strategic Defense Initiative (SDI), a system of space-based lasers and other high-tech defenses against nuclear missiles that critics quickly dubbed Star Wars. Even though skeptics warned of the project's monumental technical hurdles and the danger that it would further escalate the nuclear-arms race, the Pentagon launched a costly SDI research program.

Reagan Reelected As the 1984 election neared, liberal Democrats and many independents criticized the Reagan presidency for runaway military spending, Cold War belligerence, massive budget deficits, cuts in social programs, and assaults on the government's regulatory powers. To critics, jingoism abroad and selfishness at home summed up the meaning of *Reaganism*.

But many Americans applauded Reagan's attacks on big government and his tough policy toward the Soviets. Rhetoric aside, the administration had some solid achievements to its credit, a booming economy and notably an end to rampant inflation. Reagan's personal popularity remained high. Some dubbed him the Teflon president—nothing seemed to stick to him. Feminists welcomed his 1981 nomination of Sandra Day O'Connor as the first woman justice on the U.S. Supreme Court. Americans admired his jaunty response when a ricocheting bullet fired by a deranged young man struck him in the chest as he left a Washington hotel in March 1981. Rushed to the hospital, Reagan walked in under his own steam, quipping to the physicians, "Please tell me you're all Republicans." (The attack disabled Reagan's press secretary, James Brady, who with his wife Sarah later became leaders of the campaign for stricter gun-control laws.) By 1984 many citizens believed that Reagan had fulfilled his promise to revitalize the free-enterprise system, rebuild U.S. military might, and make America again "stand tall" in the world.

The 1984 Republican convention, staged for TV, accented themes of patriotism, prosperity, and the personality of Ronald Reagan.

The Democratic hopefuls included Gary Hart, a former Colorado senator, and Jesse Jackson, a Chicago black leader who proposed a "rainbow coalition" of African-Americans, Hispanics, displaced workers, and other outsiders. But former vice president Walter Mondale won the nomination with backing from labor unions, party bigwigs, and various interest groups. His vice-presidential choice, New York congresswoman Geraldine Ferraro, became the first woman to run on a major-party presidential ticket.

Reagan and Bush won 59 percent of the popular vote and carried every state but Mondale's Minnesota and the District of Columbia. Many traditionally Democratic voters, especially blue-collar workers, again defected to Reagan. Despite Ferraro's presence on the Democratic ticket, a higher percentage of women voted Republican in 1984 than in 1980. Reagan's ideological appeal and his mastery of TV, combined with prosperity, had carried the day. Though the Democrats retained control of Congress and remained strong at the state and local levels, the Republicans' post-1968 dominance of the White House—interrupted only by Jimmy Carter's single term—continued.

Some frustrated Democrats sought to reverse their image as a "big government" and "tax-and-spend" party dominated by special-interest groups. In 1985 Arkansas governor Bill Clinton and Senators Al Gore of Tennessee, Joseph Lieberman of Connecticut, and John Breaux of Louisiana, along with others, formed the Democratic Leadership Council (DLC) to stake out a more centrist party position. In the early 1990s Clinton would use his chairmanship of the DLC as a springboard for a presidential bid.

A Sea of Problems in Reagan's Second Term, 1985–1989

In his first term, Ronald Reagan had set the political agenda: tax cuts, deregulation, and more military spending. His second term, by contrast, was dominated by economic problems and by events linked to foreign affairs. In 1986 the so-called Iran-contra scandal erupted, caused by Reagan's stubborn determination to pursue his objectives in Latin America by secret means despite congressional prohibitions. Reagan's historic trip to Moscow in 1988 marked a dramatic easing of Cold War tensions, but continued conflict in the Middle East and a wave of terrorist bombings made clear that even if the Cold War ended, the world would remain a dangerous place.

Budget Deficits and Trade Gaps   Reagan's second term brought some legislative achievements, including the Immigration Reform and Control Act of 1986, discussed earlier, and a tax-reform law that made the system fairer by eliminating many deductions and establishing uniform rates for taxpayers at comparable income levels. The law removed some 6 million low-income Americans from the income-tax rolls as well. Reagan also reshaped the Supreme Court and the federal judiciary in his own conservative image.

But sky-high federal deficits—the legacy of Reaganomics—grew worse. The deficit surged to over $200 billion in 1985 and 1986, and hovered at about $150 billion for the next two years. This, coupled with the yawning trade gap, were Reagan's principal economic legacies to his successor.

Issues related to foreign policy dominated Reagan's second term. His domestic record would rest on the tax cuts, deregulation, and other legislative initiatives of his first term.

| The Iran-Contra Affair and Other Scandals | The worst scandal to hit the Reagan presidency arose from the administration's efforts to control events in Latin America, a perennial temptation for U.S. presidents. Late in |

1986 a Beirut newspaper reported the shocking news that in 1985 the United States had shipped, via Israel, 508 antitank missiles to the anti-American government of Iran. Admitting the sale, Reagan claimed that the goal had been to encourage "moderate elements" in Tehran and to gain the release of U.S. hostages held in Lebanon by pro-Iranian groups. In February 1987 a presidentially appointed investigative panel placed heavy blame on Reagan's chief of staff, Donald Regan, who resigned.

More details soon spilled out, including the explosive revelation that Lieutenant Colonel Oliver North, a National Security Council aide in the White House, had secretly diverted the profits from the Iran arms sales to the Nicaraguan contras at a time when Congress had forbidden such aid. In November 1986, a step ahead of FBI agents, North and his secretary had altered and deleted sensitive computer files and destroyed incriminating documents. North implicated CIA Director William Casey in illegalities, but Casey's death thwarted this line of investigation.

In May 1987 a joint House-Senate investigative committee opened televised hearings on the scandal. The nation watched in fascination as "Ollie" North, resplendent in his marine uniform, boasted of his patriotism, and as Reagan's national security adviser, Admiral John Poindexter, testified that he had deliberately concealed the fund-diversion scheme from the president.

In some ways the scandal seemed a sickening replay of the Watergate crisis of 1974. The committee found no positive proof of Reagan's knowledge of illegalities, but roundly criticized the lax management style and contempt for the law that had pervaded the Reagan White House. In 1989, after his indictment by a special prosecutor, North was convicted of obstructing a congressional inquiry and destroying and falsifying official documents. (The conviction was later reversed on the technicality that some testimony used against North had been given under a promise of immunity.) Although less damaging than Watergate, the Iran-contra scandal dogged the Reagan administration's final years as a gross abuse of executive power in a zealous campaign to overthrow a Latin American government the administration found objectionable.

Other unsavory revelations plagued Reagan's second term, including allegations of bribery and conspiracy in military-procurement contracts. Reagan's California friend Edwin Meese resigned as attorney general in 1988 amid charges that he had used his influence to promote ventures in which he had a financial interest. In 1989 came revelations that former Interior Secretary James Watt and other prominent Republicans had been paid hundreds of thousands of dollars for using their influence on behalf of housing developers seeking federal subsidies.

Reagan's personal popularity seemed unaffected by all this dirty linen. Drawing on his training as an actor, he possessed an uncanny ability to communicate warmth and sincerity and to shrug off damaging revelations with a disarming joke. Moreover, Reagan benefited from an unanticipated turn of events abroad that would end his presidency on a note of triumph.

Reagan's Mission to Moscow   A dramatic warming of Soviet-American relations began early in Reagan's second term. At meetings in Switzerland and Iceland in 1985 and 1986, Reagan and Soviet leader Mikhail Gorbachev revived the stalled arms-control process. Beset by economic problems, Gorbachev pursued an easing of superpower tensions to gain breathing space for domestic reform.

In 1987 the two leaders signed the Intermediate-range Nuclear Forces (INF) Treaty, providing for the removal of twenty-five hundred U.S. and Soviet missiles from Europe. This treaty, for the first time, eliminated an entire class of existing nuclear weapons rather than merely limiting the number of future weapons as

President Reagan Visits Red Square *As the Cold War crumbled, President Reagan flew to Moscow in 1988 to sign a nuclear-arms reduction treaty with Soviet premier Mikhail Gorbachev.*

Milestones in Nuclear-Arms Control

Year	Event	Provisions
1963	Limited Test Ban Treaty	Prohibits atmospheric, underwater, and outer-space nuclear testing.
1967	Outer Space Treaty	Prohibits weapons of mass destruction and arms testing in space.
1968	Non-Proliferation Treaty	Promotes peaceful international uses of nuclear energy; aims to stop the global proliferation of nuclear weaponry.
1972	Strategic Arms Limitation Treaty (SALT I)	Limits for five years U.S. and Soviet deployment of strategic weapons systems.
	Anti-Ballistic Missile (ABM) Treaty	Restricts U.S. and Soviet testing and deployment of defensive systems. (Allowed to expire, 2002.)
1974	Threshold Test Ban Treaty	Establishes limits on size of underground tests.
1979	Strategic Arms Limitation Treaty (SALT II)	Limits strategic launch vehicles and delivery craft and restricts the development of new missiles. (The treaty was never ratified, but the United States and the Soviet Union observed its terms.)
1982	Strategic Arms Reduction Talks (START)	Sought a 50 percent reduction in U.S. and Soviet strategic nuclear weapons.
1988	Intermediate-range Nuclear Forces (INF) Treaty	Commits the United States and the Soviet Union to withdraw their intermediate-range nuclear missiles from Eastern and Western Europe and to destroy them.
1991	START Treaty	Provides for a 25 percent cut in U.S. and Soviet strategic nuclear weapons.
2002	Treaty on Strategic Offensive Reduction	Requires deep cuts in number of U.S. and Soviet nuclear warheads by 2012.

SALT I had done. It, in turn, led to Reagan's historic visit to Moscow in May 1988, where the two leaders strolled and chatted in Red Square, in front of the Kremlin.

Some of Reagan's supporters were dismayed as their hero, having denounced the Soviet Union as an "evil empire" five years before, now cozied up to the world's top communist. One conservative paper, *The Manchester* [New Hampshire] *Union-Leader,* called Reagan's trip "a sad week for the free world." Reagan himself, with his usual breezy good humor, pointed to changes in Soviet policy and argued that "the evil empire" was becoming more benign. Most Americans welcomed improved relations with the long-time Cold War enemy.

Historic in themselves, the INF treaty and Reagan's trip to Moscow proved a mere prelude to more dramatic events. They marked, in fact, nothing less than the beginning of the end of the Cold War. That one of America's most dedicated Cold Warriors should be the president to preside over its final phase remains one of the great ironies of recent U.S. history.

The Dangerous Middle East: Continued Tension and Terrorism
As relations with Moscow improved in Reagan's second term, the situation in the Middle East worsened. In 1987 Palestinians in Gaza and the West Bank rose up against Israeli occupation. In response, Secretary of State George Shultz tried to start talks among Israel, the Palestinians, and Jordan on a plan for Palestinian autonomy. Israel refused to negotiate until the uprising ended, and the Palestinians rejected Shultz's proposals as not going far enough toward creating a Palestinian state. Despite U.S. opposition, Israel continued to build settlements in the disputed West Bank region.

A deadly by-product of the Middle East conflict was a series of bombings, kidnappings, assassinations, airplane hijackings, and other attacks linked to Palestinian terrorists (or "freedom fighters," as the Palestinians called them) and their backers in the Arab world. In 1985 terrorists set off deadly bombs in the Vienna and Rome airports and hijacked a TWA flight en route to Rome from Athens, holding the crew and 145 passengers hostage for seventeen days and murdering a U.S. sailor among the passengers. That same year, four heavily armed PLO members demanding the release of Palestinian prisoners held by Israel hijacked an Italian cruise ship, the *Achille Lauro,* dumping a wheelchair-bound Jewish-American tourist into the sea. In 1986 two GIs died and many were injured in the bombing of a Berlin disco club popular with U.S. troops.

Accusing Libyan strongman Muammar el-Qaddafi of masterminding the Berlin bombing and other terrorist attacks, Reagan ordered U.S. bombers to hit Libyan military sites in 1986. But the cycle of large-scale and small-scale terrorist attacks continued, reaching more than one thousand in 1988. In the worst attack, Pan Am flight 103 from London to New York crashed in December 1988 near Lockerbie, Scotland, killing all 259 aboard, including many Americans. Experts quickly identified a concealed bomb as the cause. In 1991 the United States and Great Britain brought formal charges against Libya for the attack. After years of stalling, Qaddafi allowed two accused Libyan officials to be extradited and face trial in 1999. In 2001 a special Scottish court sitting in the Netherlands acquitted one of the men but found the other guilty of murder and imposed a life sentence.

This cycle of terrorism, which would continue well beyond the 1980s, was a by-product of festering tensions in the Middle East. Hatred of Israel, and even the belief that the Jewish state had no right to exist, gripped parts of the Arab world, particularly the Islamic fundamentalists who appeared to be growing in numbers and influence as the century ended. The Palestinian leader Yasir Arafat bore responsibility as well, for repeated failures of leadership and missed opportunities. The continued building of Israeli settlements in the Palestinian territories also contributed to the climate of hopelessness and resentment that helped spawn terrorist attacks.

In a global context, then, Reagan's term ended on a note of deep uncertainty. The easing of Cold War tensions offered hope of a more peaceful and secure future. Yet the rising tempo of surprise attacks by shadowy terrorist groups pointed to a future that, in its way, threatened to be as dangerous and unsettling as the Cold War itself.

Assessing the Reagan Years After Nixon's disgrace, Ford's caretaker presidency, and Carter's rocky tenure, Ronald Reagan's two full terms helped restore a sense of stability and continuity to U.S. politics. Domestically Reagan compiled a mixed record. Inflation was tamed, and the economy turned upward after 1983. But the federal deficit soared, and the administration largely ignored festering social issues, environmental concerns, and long-term economic problems.

Reagan's critics, stressing the Hollywood aspects of his presidency, dismissed his two terms as more an interlude of nostalgia and drift than of positive achievement—a time when self-interest trumped the public good. Critics pointed out how readily Reagan's celebration of individual freedom translated into self-centered materialism and a callous disregard of social injustice. Apart from anticommunism, a military buildup, and flag waving, they contended, Reagan offered few goals around which the nation as a whole could rally.

The critics gained an unexpected ally from the Reagan inner circle in 1988 when former Chief of Staff Donald Regan, still smarting over his forced resignation during the Iran-contra scandal, published a memoir of his White House years that portrayed the president as little more than an automaton: "Every moment of every public appearance was scheduled, every word was scripted, every place where Reagan was expected to stand was chalked with toe marks."

To his admirers, such criticism was beside the point. They felt that Reagan deserved high marks for reasserting traditional values of self-reliance and free enterprise; contributing to America's Cold War victory through his military buildup; and, with his infectious optimism and patriotism, helping restore national pride.

On the international front, Reagan's aggressive anticommunism dragged his administration into the swamp of the Iran-contra scandal. But he had the good fortune to hold office as the Cold War thawed and the Soviet menace eased. By the end of his term, détente, derailed in the late 1970s, was barreling ahead. The shadow world of international terrorism, however, which announced itself with assassinations, exploding bombs, and crashing airplanes, signaled new global challenges ahead. In his post-presidential years, as Reagan himself lived on in a twilight realm darkened by Alzheimer's disease, "the Reagan revolution" continued in some ways to define the terms of contemporary American politics.

IMPORTANT EVENTS, 1974–1989

1970	Comprehensive Drug Abuse Act.
1972	Equal Rights Amendment passed by Congress.
1973	Major rise in OPEC prices; Arab oil boycott. *Roe* v. *Wade.*
1974	Richard Nixon resigns presidency; Gerald Ford sworn in. Indian Self-Determination Act.
1975	South Vietnamese government falls. *Mayagüez* incident.
1976	Jimmy Carter elected president.
1977	Panama Canal treaties ratified. Introduction of Apple II computer. Gay Pride parades in New York and San Francisco.
1978	Carter authorizes federal funds to relocate Love Canal residents.
1979	Menachem Begin and Anwar el-Sadat sign peace treaty at White House. Second round of OPEC price increases. Accident at Three Mile Island nuclear plant. Carter restores full diplomatic relations with the People's Republic of China.
1980	Alaska Lands Act. Soviet invasion of Afghanistan. Iran hostage crisis preoccupies nation. Ronald Reagan elected president.
1981	Major cuts in taxes and domestic spending, coupled with large increases in military budget. AIDS first diagnosed.
1982	Equal Rights Amendment dies. CIA funds contra war against Nicaragua's Sandinistas. Central Park rally for nuclear-weapons freeze.
1983	239 U.S. Marines die in Beirut terrorist attack. U.S. deploys Pershing II and cruise missiles in Europe. Reagan proposes Strategic Defense Initiative (Star Wars).
1984	Reagan defeats Walter Mondale in landslide.
1984–1986	Congress bars military aid to contras.
1985	Rash of airline hijackings and other terrorist acts. First Farm Aid concert.
1986	Congress passes South African sanctions. Immigration Reform and Control Act.
1987	Congressional hearings on Iran-contra scandal. Stock-market crash.
1988	Reagan trip to Moscow.

31

Beyond the Cold War: Charting a New Course, 1988–1995

Tension gripped the gray streets of East Berlin late in 1989, amid rumors that "Die Mauer," the wall that divided the city, might soon be opened. In May Soviet Premier Mikhail Gorbachev had announced that Moscow would no longer use its power to uphold the pro-Soviet governments of Eastern Europe. One by one, these governments fell. On October 18, the East German communist regime run by Erich Honecker collapsed, and a new, more liberal government took its place.

One of the most detested features of the old regimes had been their restrictions on travel, and as these governments disintegrated, travel barriers fell. Thousands of people poured westward in early September, for example, when Hungary opened its border with Austria. Of all the physical barriers preventing free travel, the most notorious was the Berlin Wall. The Russians had built it in 1961, at a time of bitter East-West conflict. Snaking ninety-six miles around the city and ramming through its heart, this concrete and barbed-wire barrier with 302 watchtowers and armed guards had stood for nearly thirty years as a stark emblem of Cold War oppression and divisions.

Passage was permitted only at three closely guarded checkpoints, nicknamed Alpha, Bravo, and Charlie by the U.S. military. Checkpoint Charlie, the most famous of the three, was the scene of several Cold War spy exchanges between the United States and the Soviet Union. Nearly two hundred people had been shot trying to escape across the Wall, and more than three thousand arrested. (An estimated five thousand had succeeded.) On the West Berlin side, the Wall was covered with colorful graffiti that defied its grim expanse.

In 1963 President Kennedy had visited the Wall and uttered his memorable proclamation, "Ich bin ein Berliner" ("I am a Berliner"). In 1987 President Reagan had made the pilgrimage, demanding, "Mr. Gorbachev, tear down this wall!"

Now the end had come. One of the first acts of the new East German government was to remove the restrictions on free movement within Berlin. At a press

End of the Berlin Wall, November 1989 *As East German border guards watch passively, a West Berliner pounds away at the hated symbol of a divided city.*

conference on November 9, 1989, a government official was asked when the travel ban would be lifted. He replied (in German), "Well, as far as I can see . . . , immediately."

This was the news East Berliners had been waiting for. Thousands rushed to the Wall and demanded that the crossing points be opened. At 10:30 P.M. the guards flung open the gates. Pandemonium resulted. As East Berliners joyously poured through, West Berliners greeted them with flowers, tears, and shouts of welcome. Declared one old woman, "Ick glob es erst, wenn icke drüben bin" ("I won't believe it until I'm on the other side"). A blind man made the crossing simply to breathe the air of freedom, he said. Giddy young people danced on the Wall itself. Families divided for years were reunited.

The glare of TV lights, beaming the event worldwide via communications satellites, added a surreal quality to the scene. This was not only a watershed moment in world affairs, but also one of the first truly real-time global media events. Americans sat glued to their sets as CNN and other networks carried the story live.

The celebrations went on for days. Famed Russian cellist Mstislav Rostropovitch gave an impromptu concert at the Wall. East Berliners who visited West Berlin's giant Ka De We department store were given one hundred deutsche marks (the West German currency) as a welcoming gift. Hundreds of Berliners whom the newspapers dubbed "woodpeckers" attacked the Wall with picks, chisels, and hammers to gather chunks of concrete as souvenirs or simply to share in its destruction.

The official demolition began in June 1990. Workers mobilizing bulldozers, cranes, and other heavy equipment worked through the summer and fall. By November, the wall had disappeared, except for a few sections left for commemorative purposes. A hated Cold War symbol had faded into history.

The end of the Cold War and the global events of the immediate post–Cold War era provide the framework of the early parts of this chapter. At first, the Soviet Union's shocking collapse brought an enormous sigh of relief in the United States. An era of great danger was over; surely the future would be safer and more tranquil. As the initial euphoria faded, however, Americans realized that the world remained a threatening and unsettled place. While U.S. leaders struggled to come to terms with the new post–Cold War world order, an immediate crisis arose in the Middle East as Saddam Hussein's Iraq invaded oil-rich Kuwait, forcing Reagan's successor, President George Bush, to respond.

Changes were underway at home as well as abroad. When Bill Clinton replaced George Bush in the White House in 1993, domestic policy moved front and center. This chapter also discusses home-front politics and culture in the 1990s, as well as long-term social and economic trends, the effect of which became particularly visible in this eventful decade. U.S. history has always been a story of change, and the changes came at a dizzying pace as the twentieth century ended.

This chapter focuses on five major questions:

What major events marked the end of the Cold War, and why did the long conflict between the United States and the Soviet Union end so suddenly?

How effectively did George Bush, President Reagan's successor, cope with the "new world order" that emerged with the end of the Cold War?

What key themes dominated Bill Clinton's 1992 presidential campaign and the early years of his presidency?

What long-term social and economic trends had the greatest effect on the United States at the end of the twentieth century?

How did U.S. popular culture reflect the prosperity of the 1990s, and what issues divided Americans in the "culture wars" of these years?

THE BUSH YEARS: GLOBAL RESOLVE, DOMESTIC DRIFT, 1988–1993

Ronald Reagan's vice president, George Bush, elected president in his own right in 1988, was a patrician in politics. The son of a Connecticut senator, he had attended Yale and fought in World War II before entering the Texas oil business. He had served in Congress, lost a Senate race, been U.S. ambassador to the United Nations, and directed the CIA before being tapped as Ronald Reagan's running mate in 1980.

As president, Bush compiled an uneven record. Internationally, his administration responded cautiously but positively to upheavals in the Soviet Union that signaled the end of the Cold War. Bush also reacted decisively when Iraq invaded Kuwait, took positive steps in Latin America, and worked to ease Israeli-Palestinian tensions. Bush's domestic record was thin, however, as he typically substituted platitudes for policy.

The Election of 1988

As the 1988 election approached, Vice President Bush easily won the Republican presidential nomination. A large group of Democratic contenders eventually narrowed to two: Jesse Jackson and Massachusetts Governor Michael Dukakis. Jackson, preaching concern for the poor and urging a full-scale war on drugs, ran well in the primaries. But Dukakis's victories in major primary states like New York and California proved decisive. As his running mate, Dukakis chose Texas Senator Lloyd Bentsen.

Accepting the Republican nomination, Bush called for a "kinder, gentler America" and pledged, "Read my lips: no new taxes." As his running mate he selected Senator Dan Quayle of Indiana, the son of a wealthy newspaper publisher. In the campaign Bush stressed Reagan's achievements while distancing himself from the Iran-contra scandal. Emphasizing peace and prosperity, he pointed to better Soviet relations, low inflation, and the 14 million new jobs created during the 1980s—an achievement unmatched by any other industrial nation.

A TV commercial aired by Bush supporters, playing on racist stereotypes, featured a black man who committed rape and murder after his release under a Massachusetts prisoner-furlough program. Bush assailed Dukakis's veto of a bill requiring Massachusetts schoolchildren to recite the Pledge of Allegiance, even though the Supreme Court had found such laws unconstitutional. In response, Dukakis emphasized his accomplishments as governor. "This election is not about ideology, it's about competence," he insisted. He hammered at the failures of the "Swiss-cheese" Reagan economy and urged "Reagan Democrats" to return to the fold. But Dukakis seemed edgy and defensive, and his dismissal of ideology made it difficult for him to define his vision of America. Even Dukakis supporters wearied of his stock phrases and his repeated boasts of his managerial skills.

Both candidates avoided serious issues in favor of TV-oriented "photo opportunities" and "sound bites." Bush visited flag factories and military plants. Dukakis proved his toughness on defense by posing in a tank. Editorial writers grumbled about the "junk-food" campaign, but fleeting visual images, catchy phrases, and twenty-second spots on the evening news had seemingly become the essence of presidential politics.

On November 8 Bush carried forty states and garnered 54 percent of the vote. Dukakis prevailed in only ten states plus the District of Columbia. The Democrats, however, retained control of both houses of Congress and most state legislatures.

The Cold War Ends

The collapse of Soviet power symbolized by the opening of the Berlin Wall proceeded with breathtaking rapidity. Germany reunited for the first time since 1945. Estonia,

Latvia, and Lithuania, the Baltic republics forcibly annexed by the Soviet Union on the eve of World War II, declared independence. Calls for autonomy resounded within the other Soviet republics as well.

The Cold War was over. In August 1991 President Bush and Mikhail Gorbachev signed a treaty in Moscow reducing their strategic nuclear arsenals by 25 percent. The nuclear-arms race seemed to be over as well. Secretary of Defense Dick Cheney proposed a 25 percent reduction in U.S. military forces over five years. With the Soviet-sponsored Warsaw Pact ended, NATO announced plans for a 50 percent troop reduction.

As the Soviet Communist party's centralized control collapsed, the nation's economy sank into crisis. Soviet reformers called for a market economy on the Western model. In August 1991 hard-line Communist leaders in Moscow tried to overthrow Gorbachev, but thousands of Muscovites, rallied by Boris Yeltsin, president of the Russian Republic, protectively surrounded the Russian parliament, and the coup failed. Yeltsin increasingly assumed a dominant role.

Exuberant crowds toppled statues of Lenin and other communist leaders across the Soviet Union. Leningrad resumed its tsarist name, St. Petersburg. As the various Soviet republics rushed to independence, Gorbachev was overwhelmed by forces he himself had unleashed. The coup attempt thoroughly discredited the Soviet Communist party. Late in 1991 most of the Soviet republics proclaimed the end of the U.S.S.R. Bowing to the inevitable, Gorbachev resigned.

Secretary of State James Baker, a long-time Bush ally who had been chief of staff and Treasury secretary under Reagan, proceeded cautiously as the Soviet empire disintegrated. U.S. influence was limited, in any event, as long-suppressed forces of nationalism and ethnicity burst forth in Eastern Europe and in the former Soviet Union.

One issue of vital concern was the future of the Soviet arsenal of twenty-seven thousand nuclear weapons, based not only in Russia but in newly independent Ukraine, Belarus, and Kazakhstan. Baker worked to ensure the security of these weapons and to prevent nuclear know-how from leaking out to other nations or terrorist groups. As strategic talks with Yeltsin and other leaders went forward, Bush announced further major reductions in the U.S. nuclear arsenal.

For decades the superpowers had backed their client states and rebel insurgencies throughout the Third World. As the Cold War faded, the prospect for resolving some local disputes brightened. In Nicaragua, for example, Bush abandoned Reagan's failed policy of financing the contras' war against the leftist Sandinista government. Instead, Bush and Congress worked out a program aimed at reintegrating the contras into Nicaraguan life and politics. In the 1990 elections in Nicaragua, a multiparty anti-Sandinista coalition emerged victorious.

Poverty, ignorance, and economic exploitation still plagued Latin America, however, and open guerrilla war continued in Peru. The flow of cocaine and heroin to U.S. cities from the region posed a serious problem as well. In December 1989 concern over the drug traffic led to a U.S. invasion of Panama to capture the nation's strongman ruler, General Manuel Noriega. Formerly on the CIA payroll,

Noriega had accepted bribes to permit drugs to pass through Panama on their way north. Convicted of drug trafficking, Noriega received a life prison term.

America's relations with the Philippines, a former colony and long-time U.S. ally, shifted as well. In 1991 the Philippines legislature ended the agreement by which the United States had maintained two naval bases in the islands. With the Cold War over, the Bush administration accepted this decision and closed the bases.

In a key development, U.S. policy helped bring an end to South Africa's policy of racial segregation, called apartheid. In 1986, over a Reagan veto, Congress had imposed economic sanctions against white-ruled South Africa, including a ban on U.S. corporate investment. This action, strongly endorsed by U.S. black leaders, reflected an anti-apartheid campaign led by South African Anglican Bishop Desmond Tutu. Economic sanctions by America and other nations hastened change in South Africa. In 1990 the government released black leader Nelson Mandela after long imprisonment and opened negotiations with Mandela's African National Congress. When South Africa scrapped much of its apartheid policy in 1991, President Bush lifted the economic sanctions.

China proved an exception to the world trend toward greater freedom. Improved relations with China suffered a grievous setback in 1989, when the Chinese army crushed a prodemocracy demonstration by masses of unarmed students in Beijing's Tiananmen Square, killing several hundred young men and women. A wave of repression, arrests, and public executions followed. The Bush administration protested, curtailed diplomatic contacts, and urged international financial institutions to postpone loans to China. But Bush, strongly committed to U.S. trade expansion, did not break diplomatic relations or cancel trade agreements with China.

As the Cold War faded, trade issues loomed large. The U.S. trade deficit with Japan stirred special concern. Although this gap dropped from its 1987 high, it still hovered at $43 billion in 1991. Early in 1992, facing a recession and rising unemployment in an election year, President Bush turned a planned Asian trip into a trade mission. He took along a team of business leaders, including the heads of the "big three" U.S. auto companies, who tried, with little success, to persuade the Japanese to buy more U.S. products. When Bush collapsed and vomited from a sudden attack of flu at a state dinner in Tokyo, some found the mishap unhappily symbolic.

Operation Desert Storm   As the Bush administration cautiously charted a course in the post–Cold War world, one unexpected crisis brought a clear-cut, forceful response. On August 2, 1990, Iraq invaded the neighboring nation of Kuwait. Iraq's dictator, Saddam Hussein, had long dismissed Kuwait's ruling sheiks as puppets of Western imperialists and asserted Iraq's historic claims to Kuwait's vast oil fields.

Under Saddam, Iraq for years had threatened not only Kuwait but also other Arab nations as well as Israel. Iraq's military program, including both chemical- and nuclear-weapons projects, had worried many governments. During the Iran-Iraq war, however, the United States had favored Iraq over Iran, and even assisted Iraq's military buildup (see Chapter 30). But Iran's anti-Americanism eased after the death of Ayatollah Khomeini in 1989, removing this incentive for the United States to tilt toward Iraq. When Iraq invaded Kuwait, Washington reacted quickly.

Avoiding Lyndon Johnson's mistakes in the Vietnam era, Bush built a consensus for a clear military objective—Iraq's withdrawal from Kuwait—in Congress, at the United Nations, and among the American people. He deployed more than four hundred thousand troops in Saudi Arabia to achieve that goal. The U.N. imposed economic sanctions against Iraq and insisted that Saddam withdraw by January 15, 1991. On January 12, on divided votes, the Senate and the House endorsed military action against Iraq. Most Democrats voted against war, favoring continued economic sanctions instead.

The air war began on January 16. For six weeks B-52 and F-16 bombers pounded Iraqi troops, supply depots, and command targets in Iraq's capital, Baghdad. The air forces of other nations participated as well. In retaliation, Saddam fired Soviet-made Scud missiles against Tel Aviv and other Israeli cities, as well as against the Saudi capital, Riyadh. Americans watched transfixed as CNN showed U.S. Patriot missiles streaking off to intercept incoming Scuds. As portrayed on TV, the war seemed a glorified video game. The reality of many thousands of Iraqi deaths, military and civilian, hardly impinged on the national consciousness.

On February 23 two hundred thousand U.S. troops under General H. Norman Schwarzkopf moved across the desert toward Kuwait. Although rain turned the roadless sands to soup, the army pushed on. Iraqi soldiers either fled or surrendered en masse. U.S. forces destroyed thirty-seven hundred Iraqi tanks while losing only three. With Iraqi resistance crushed, President Bush declared a cease-fire, and Kuwait's ruling family returned from various safe havens where they had sat out the war. U.S. casualties numbered 148 dead—including 35 killed inadvertently by U.S. firepower—and 467 wounded.

Despite some campus protests, the war enjoyed broad public support. After the victory celebrations, however, the outcome seemed less than decisive. Saddam still held power. His army brutally suppressed uprisings by Shiite Muslims in the south and ethnic Kurds in the north. Saddam agreed to grant U.N. inspection teams access to his weapons-production facilities, but reneged on this agreement within a few years. Despite the stunning military success of 1991, Iraq remained a thorn in the flesh for the United States and its U.N. allies.

Home-Front Discontents: Economic, Racial, and Environmental Problems

In the early 1990s some of the longer-term effects of the Reagan-era tax cuts, Pentagon spending, and deregulatory fervor began to be felt. As the economy soured, the go-go climate of the 1980s seemed remote, and discontent increased, especially among the middle class.

First came the collapse of the savings-and-loan (S&L) industry, which had long provided home loans to borrowers and a modest but secure return to depositors.

Kuwait, 1991 *Burning oil fields, set ablaze by retreating Iraqis, provide an eerie backdrop to motorized U.S. troops participating in Operation Desert Storm, the high point of the Bush presidency.*

As interest rates rose in the late 1970s because of inflation, the S&Ls had been forced to pay high interest to attract deposits, even though most of their assets were in long-term, fixed-rate mortgages. In the early 1980s money freed up by the Reagan tax cuts flowed into S&Ls that were offering high rates of return. In the fever to deregulate, the rules governing S&Ls were eased. Caught up in the high-flying mood of the decade, S&Ls nationwide made risky loans on speculative real-estate ventures. As the economy cooled, many of these investments went bad. In 1988–1990, nearly six hundred S&Ls failed, especially in the Southwest, wiping out many depositors' savings.

Because the government insures savings-and-loan deposits, the Bush administration in 1989 set up a program to repay depositors and sell hundreds of foreclosed office towers and apartment buildings in a depressed real-estate market. Estimates of the bailout's cost topped $400 billion. " 'Savings and loan,' " wrote a journalist, "had become synonymous with 'bottomless pit.' "

The federal deficit, another problem linked to the Reagan tax cuts and military spending, continued to mount. In 1990 Congress and Bush agreed on a five-year deficit-reduction plan involving spending cuts and tax increases. Bush would pay a high political price for this retreat from his 1988 campaign pledge, "Read my lips: no new taxes." Despite the agreement, the red ink flowed on. The deficit reached $290 billion in 1992. The Gulf War, the S&L bailout, and soaring welfare and Medicare/Medicaid payments combined to undercut the budget-balancing effort.

To make matters worse, recession struck in 1990. Retail sales slumped; housing starts declined. The U.S. auto industry, battered by Japanese imports, fared disastrously. GM cut its work force by more than seventy thousand. Hard times hung on into 1992, with a jobless rate of more than 7 percent. As the states' tax revenues fell, they slashed social-welfare funding. The number of Americans below the poverty line rose by 2.1 million in 1990, to about 34 million. As the economy stumbled, the plight of the poor roused resentment rather than sympathy. Political strategists diagnosed a middle-class phenomenon they called "compassion fatigue." Declared Ohio's governor, "Most Ohioans have had enough welfare, enough poverty, enough drugs, enough crime."

In this bleaker economic climate, many Americans took a second look at Reaganism. If 1984 was "morning in America," wrote a columnist, quoting a Reagan campaign slogan, this was "the morning after."

For middle-class Americans the recession was more anxiety-producing than desperate. For the poor it could be disastrous. In April 1992 an outbreak of arson and looting erupted in a poor black district of Los Angeles. The immediate cause was black rage and incredulity (shared by many others) over a jury's acquittal of four white Los Angeles police officers whose beating of a black motorist, Rodney King, had been filmed on videotape. For several days the explosion of anger and pent-up frustration raged, leaving some forty persons dead and millions in property damage, and again reminding the nation of the desperate conditions in its inner cities.

The Bush administration did little to address these issues. In 1990, when Congress passed a bill broadening federal protection against job discrimination, Bush vetoed it, claiming that it encouraged racial quotas in hiring. (In 1991, announcing that his concerns had been met, Bush signed a similar bill.) When Bush came to Atlanta in 1992 to observe Martin Luther King Day, King's daughter, a minister, asked bitterly, "How dare we celebrate in the midst of a recession, when nobody is sure whether their jobs are secure?"

The recession also stung public-school budgets. Bush proclaimed himself the "education president" but addressed the issue only fitfully. He called for national testing of schoolchildren, supported a voucher system by which parents could enroll their children in private schools at public expense, and urged corporate America to fund experimental schools. Such proposals hardly matched the magnitude of the problems facing the public-school system.

One measure supported by Bush, the Americans with Disabilities Act of 1990, did have significant educational implications. This law, barring discrimination against disabled persons, improved job and educational opportunities for the handicapped. Thanks in part to the measure, the number of physically or cognitively impaired children attending public schools rose from 4.4 million to 5.6 million in the 1990s.

Environmental concerns surged in March 1989 when a giant oil tanker, the *Exxon Valdez*, ran aground in Alaska's Prince William Sound and spilled more than 10 million gallons of crude oil. The accident fouled coastal and marine habitats, killed thousands of sea otters and shore birds, and jeopardized Alaska's herring and salmon industries. That summer the Environmental Protection Agency (EPA) reported that air pollution in more than one hundred U.S. cities exceeded federal standards. A 1991 EPA study found that pollutants were depleting the ozone shield—the layer of the atmosphere that protects human life from cancer-causing solar radiation—at twice the rate scientists had predicted.

Squeezed between public worries and corporate calls for a go-slow policy, Bush compiled a mixed environmental record. He deplored the *Exxon Valdez* spill but defended oil exploration and drilling. In a bipartisan effort, the White House and the Democratic Congress passed a toughened Federal Clean Air Act in 1990. (California and other states enacted even stricter laws, tightening auto-emission standards, for example.) In addition, the government began the costly task of disposing of radioactive wastes and cleaning up nuclear facilities that in some cases had been contaminating the soil and ground water for years.

The Bush administration more often downgraded environmental concerns. It scuttled treaties on global warming and mining in Antarctica, backed oil exploration in Alaskan wilderness preserves, and proposed to open vast tracts of protected wetlands to developers. Vice President Quayle openly ridiculed environmentalists. Bush's defensive, self-serving speech to a U.N.-sponsored environmental conference in Rio de Janeiro in 1992 further alienated environmentalists.

The Supreme Court Moves Right

Like all presidents, Reagan and Bush sought to perpetuate their political ideology through their Supreme Court choices. In addition to the Sandra Day O'Connor appointment (see Chapter 30), Reagan named William Rehnquist as chief justice, replacing Warren Burger, and chose another conservative, Antonin Scalia, to fill the Burger vacancy. When another vacancy opened in 1987, Reagan nominated Robert Bork, a judge and legal scholar whose rigidity and doctrinaire opposition to judicial activism led the Senate to reject him. Reagan's next nominee withdrew after admitting that he had smoked marijuana. Reagan's third choice, Anthony Kennedy, a conservative California jurist, won quick confirmation.

President Bush made two Court nominations: David Souter in 1990 and Clarence Thomas in 1991. Souter, a New Hampshire judge, won easy confirmation, but Thomas proved controversial. Bush nominated him to replace Thurgood Marshall, a black who had fought segregation as an NAACP lawyer. Thomas, also an African-American, was notable mainly for supporting conservative causes and opposing affirmative-action programs. Having risen from poverty to attend Yale Law School and to head the Equal Employment Opportunity Commission (EEOC), Thomas viewed individual effort, not government programs, as the avenue of black progress. Noting his lack of qualifications, critics charged Bush with playing racial politics.

The nomination became even more contentious when a former Thomas associate at EEOC, Anita Hill, accused him of sexual harassment. As the Senate Judiciary Committee probed Hill's accusations, the face-off dominated the nation's

TV screens and heightened awareness of the harassment issue. In the end, Thomas narrowly won confirmation and joined the Court.

These conservative appointments blunted the liberal social-activist thrust of the Court that began in the 1930s and continued in the 1950s and 1960s under Chief Justice Earl Warren and others. In 1990–1991 the Court narrowed the rights of arrested persons and upheld federal regulations barring physicians in federally funded clinics from discussing abortion with their clients. In a 5-to-4 decision in 1992, the Supreme Court upheld a Pennsylvania law further restricting abortion rights. The majority, however, did affirm *Roe* v. *Wade,* the 1973 decision upholding women's constitutional right to an abortion.

The Politics of Frustration   In the afterglow of Operation Desert Storm, George Bush's approval ratings hit an amazing 88 percent, only to fall below 50 percent as the recession hit home. In 1991 the *New York Times* damningly described him as "shrewd and energetic in foreign policy . . . , clumsy and irresolute at home. . . . The domestic Bush flops like a fish, leaving the impression that he doesn't know what he thinks or doesn't much care, apart from the political gains to be extracted from an issue." In January 1992 Bush offered various recession-fighting proposals, including tax breaks for home buyers, lower taxes on capital gains, and tax incentives for business investment. Democrats dismissed this initiative as politically motivated and inadequate to the problem.

Intimidated by Bush's post–Desert Storm popularity, top Democrats had stayed out of the 1992 presidential race. But Governor Bill Clinton of Arkansas took the plunge and, despite rumors of his marital infidelity, defeated other hopefuls in the primaries and won the nomination. As his running mate, Clinton chose Senator Al Gore of Tennessee. In his acceptance speech at the Democratic convention, Clinton pledged an activist government addressing the environment, health care, and the economy. On abortion, he was strongly pro-choice. As he oriented the party toward the middle class and muted its concern with the poor, traditional liberals and black leaders expressed uneasiness.

President Bush easily quashed a primary challenge by conservative columnist Pat Buchanan, but the Republican right dominated the party convention. Buchanan and evangelist Pat Robertson gave divisive speeches urging a GOP crusade for "family values" and denouncing abortion, sexual permissiveness, radical feminism, and gay rights. Delegates who belonged to Robertson's Christian Coalition cheered, but moderate Republicans deplored this rightward turn.

One gauge of voter discontent was the presidential race of political outsider H. Ross Perot. At the peak of "Perotmania," nearly 40 percent of the voters supported the Texan, who had grown rich as founder of a data-processing firm. The nation's economic problems were simple, Perot insisted on TV talk shows; only party politics stood in the way of solving them. As president he would conduct electronic "town meetings" by which voters would judge his proposals. Perot's eccentricities and thin-skinned response to critics turned off many potential supporters, but he remained an unpredictable wild card in the election.

Bush attacked Clinton's character and charged that he had evaded the draft during the Vietnam War. Addressing public concerns about the recession, Bush promised to put James A. Baker in charge of domestic affairs in a second term. Clinton, meanwhile, focused on the stagnant economy and the problems of the middle class. He pledged to work for a national health-care system, welfare reform, and a national industrial policy to promote economic recovery and new technologies.

In the election, 43 percent of the voters chose Clinton. Bush trailed with 38 percent, and Perot amassed 19 percent—the largest share for a third-party candidate since Teddy Roosevelt's Bull Moose campaign in 1912. Clinton, carrying such key states as California, Ohio, and New Jersey, lured back many blue-collar and suburban "Reagan Democrats" and partially reclaimed the South for the Democrats. Younger voters, who had tilted Republican in the 1980s, went for Clinton in 1992.

Most incumbents in Congress won reelection. In Pennsylvania, Republican Senator Arlen Specter, a Judiciary Committee member who had angered women by his harsh questioning of Anita Hill in the Clarence Thomas hearings, narrowly beat back a woman challenger. Congress was becoming less of a white male club. Thirty-eight African-Americans and seventeen Hispanics won election. Colorado elected American Indian Ben Nighthorse Campbell to the Senate, and a California congressional district sent the first Korean-American to Washington.

California became the first state to elect two women senators, Barbara Boxer and Dianne Feinstein. Illinois sent the first African-American woman to the Senate, Carol Moseley Braun. Overall, the new Congress included fifty-three women: six in the Senate and forty-seven in the House. This outcome encouraged feminists who had proclaimed 1992 the "Year of the Woman."

The 1992 election marked a shift of voter attention to domestic issues as the Cold War faded. With Democrats in control of both the legislative and executive branches, the end of the much-deplored Washington "gridlock" seemed possible. In the hopeful beginnings of his term, President Bill Clinton eagerly engaged the formidable challenges facing the nation.

THE CLINTON ERA I: DEBATING DOMESTIC POLICY, 1993–1997

George Bush was of the generation shaped by World War II. William Jefferson Clinton—or Bill, as he preferred—was a baby boomer formed by Vietnam, JFK, and the Beatles. Born in Arkansas in 1946, he admired Elvis Presley, played the saxophone, and thought of becoming a pop musician. Graduation from Georgetown University and Yale Law School, and a stint at Oxford University as a Rhodes scholar, roused an interest in politics. After marrying his law-school classmate Hillary Rodham, he won the Arkansas governorship in 1979, at age thirty-two.

Clinton began his presidency with high energy. But his administration soon encountered rough waters, and the 1994 midterm election produced a Republican landslide. The newly energized congressional Republicans pursued their conservative agenda, including—with Clinton's cooperation—a sweeping welfare-reform law.

Shaping a Domestic Agenda In contrast to Republican predecessors like Nixon and Bush, Clinton preferred domestic issues to foreign policy. Of course, no modern president can wholly neglect world issues, and Clinton and his first secretary of state, Warren Christopher, confronted an array of diplomatic challenges: ethnic conflict in Bosnia and Somalia, trade negotiations with China, an evolving new framework of world trade, and the Israeli-Palestinian conflict. (For a full discussion of Clinton-era foreign-policy issues, see Chapter 32.) For the most part, however, global issues took a back seat to domestic policy in the Clinton era.

Clinton and Vice President Al Gore were leaders of the New Democratic Coalition, the group of moderates who sought to shed the party's reputation for high taxes and heavy spending. Trying to win back middle-class and blue-collar voters, Clinton's campaign stressed Middle America's concerns: the recession, health care, and runaway welfare costs. Clinton also embraced causes that had inspired activists of his generation, including abortion rights, environmental concerns, and feminism.

Clinton named women to head the Departments of Justice, Energy, and Health and Human Services; the Council of Economic Advisers; the Environmental Protection Agency; the United Nations delegation; and (in 1994) the Bureau of the Budget. To fill a Supreme Court vacancy in 1993, he nominated Judge Ruth Bader Ginsberg. (To fill a second vacancy in 1994, Clinton nominated moderate liberal Stephen G. Breyer, a federal judge in Boston.) Clinton appointed his wife Hillary Rodham to head the Task Force on National Health-Care Reform.

Clinton's early weeks in office proved rocky. His effort to fulfill a campaign pledge to end the exclusion of homosexuals from military service provoked much controversy. A study commission eventually crafted a compromise summed up in the phrase "Don't ask, don't tell."

Amid a recession and high budget deficits, Clinton promised to focus "like a laser beam" on the economy. His economic program, offered in February 1993, proposed spending cuts (especially in military appropriations) and tax increases to ease the budget deficit. Clinton also proposed new spending to stimulate job creation and economic growth. In August Congress passed an economic plan that incorporated Clinton's spending cuts and tax increases but not his economic-stimulus package. Enactment of even a modified budget plan spared Clinton a major early embarrassment.

Clinton also endorsed the North American Free Trade Agreement (NAFTA) negotiated by the Bush administration. This pact admitted Mexico to the free-trade zone earlier created by the United States and Canada. While critics warned that low-wage jobs would flee to Mexico, NAFTA backers, including most econo-mists, predicted a net gain in jobs as Mexican markets opened to U.S. products. The House passed NAFTA by a comfortable margin in 1993, handing Clinton another welcome victory.

An improving economy eased pressures on Clinton to devise an economic-stimulus program. By 1994 the unemployment rate fell to the lowest point in more than four years. Inflation remained under control as well, owing to interest-rate increases by the Federal Reserve Board and a weakening of the OPEC oil cartel. In constant dollars, crude oil cost about the same in 1993 as it had in 1973, before the cycle of OPEC price increases. The 1994 federal deficit dropped as well, with fur-ther decline expected.

Meanwhile, Hillary Rodham Clinton's health-care task force, working mainly in secret, devised a sweeping reform plan. Providing universal coverage, the plan mandated that employers pay 80 percent of workers' health-insurance costs. To cover start-up expenses, the plan proposed new taxes on tobacco. The proposal also addressed the serious problem of spiraling health-care costs. From 1980 to 1992 government Medicare and Medicaid payments ballooned from 8 percent to 14 percent of the federal budget. Without controls, analysts calculated, total U.S. health spending would soon consume 20 percent of the Gross Domestic Product. The plan's cost-containment provisions included regional health-care purchasing cooperatives, caps on health-insurance premiums and on Medicare and Medicaid payments, and a national health board to monitor costs.

Lobbyists for doctors, the insurance industry, tobacco companies, retired per-sons, and hospital associations all worked to defeat the plan. Critics also attacked the secretive way the plan had been formulated. By fall 1994 health-care reform was stalled, at a heavy cost to the Clinton presidency. The administration had mis-read public complaints about medical costs and about bureaucratic red tape as support for a radical overhaul of the system. But the problems that had triggered the administration's reform effort persisted, and health care remained on the political agenda.

As the economy improved, crime and welfare reform topped voter concerns. In response, Clinton in 1994 proposed an anticrime bill to fund drug treatment, more prisons and police officers, boot camps for first-time offenders, and a ban on assault weapons. After much partisan maneuvering, Congress enacted a crime bill similar to Clinton's proposal.

Clinton's 1994 welfare-reform bill fulfilled a campaign pledge to "end welfare as we know it." Under Clinton's bill, all able-bodied recipients of payments from the government's major welfare program, Aid to Families with Dependent Children (AFDC), would have to go to work after two years, in a public-service job if necessary. The bill included job training and child-care provisions, as well as measures to force absent fathers ("deadbeat dads") to support their offspring. It also permitted states to deny additional payments to welfare mothers who bore more children. Congress took no action on Clinton's bill, but this issue, too, remained high on the public agenda.

By mid-1994 Clinton's approval ratings had dropped to 42 percent. Many found him too ready to compromise and too inclined to flit from issue to issue. Exploiting the "character issue," critics publicized various questionable dealings from the Clintons' Arkansas days, including their involvement in a shady real-estate speculation, the Whitewater Development Company. The 1993 suicide of assistant White House counsel Vincent Foster, the Clintons' close friend, whetted the interest of conspiracy theorists. Charges of sexual harassment, first aired during the campaign, resurfaced in 1994 when Paula Jones, an Arkansas state employee, alleged in a lawsuit that Clinton had solicited sexual favors when he was governor.

As Clinton proved vulnerable, the political climate turned nasty. Radio commentator Rush Limbaugh won celebrity with his jeering attacks on liberals. Televangelist Jerry Falwell offered a videotape suggesting that Clinton had arranged the murder of political enemies. Pat Robertson's Christian Coalition mobilized voters at the local level. By 1994, with some nine hundred chapters nationwide, the Christian Coalition controlled several state Republican parties. With its passion and organizational energy, the religious Right represented a potent force in American politics of the 1990s.

1994: A Sharp Right Turn   Bill Clinton had won in 1992 as a "new Democrat" offering fresh ideas, but by 1994 many voters saw him as simply an old Democrat of the big-government, "tax-and-spend" variety. His early call for an end to the ban on homosexuals in the military convinced some that special-interest groups controlled the White House agenda. To his critics, Clinton's failed health-care plan epitomized the dead end of a New Deal/Great Society style of top-down reform. The "character issue" further undermined Clinton's standing, as did his reputation as hopelessly indecisive. Commented Jesse Jackson, "When the president comes to a fork in the road, he chooses the fork."

Meanwhile, a movement to downsize government, reform welfare, slash taxes and spending, and shift power to the states gained momentum among the middle class. A bubbling brew of cultural and social issues added to the disaffection. These included such emotional topics as abortion, pornography, school prayer, "radical feminism," affirmative action, and an alleged collapse of "family values."

A network of conservative organizations orchestrated the rightward swing. As the Christian Coalition mobilized evangelicals, the National Rifle Association (NRA) contributed to candidates who opposed restrictions on firearms. Conservative think tanks such as the Heritage Foundation funded studies critiquing liberal policies. Limbaugh and other conservative radio commentators continued to denounce the "liberal elite."

Normally, prosperity helps the party in power, but not in 1994, in part because the recovery did little for ordinary Americans. Adjusted for inflation, the actual buying power of the average worker's paycheck fell from 1986 to 1990, and remained flat through the 1990s. Automation, foreign competition, an influx of immigrants into the labor market, and the weakness of organized labor all combined to keep average wages down. In October 1994 an ominous 58 percent of Americans told pollsters that they felt no better off despite the economic upturn.

Republican Congressman Newt Gingrich of Georgia shrewdly translated the disgruntled mood into Republican votes. In a photogenic ceremony on the Capitol steps, some three hundred Republican candidates signed Gingrich's "Contract with America" pledging tax cuts, congressional term limits, tougher crime laws, a balanced-budget amendment, and other popular reforms.

In a Republican landslide that November, voters gave the GOP control of both houses of Congress for the first time since 1954; increased the number of Republican governors to thirty-one; and cut down such Democratic giants as New York Governor Mario Cuomo and Texas Governor Ann Richards. Only 38 percent of eligible voters went to the polls, so the great shift rightward was actually achieved by about one-fifth of the total electorate. Still, a significant ideological change seemed under way.

Evangelical Christians flocked to the polls, mostly to vote for GOP candidates. Republican strategists hailed the election as the death knell of the activist, big-government tradition, and a further step in a conservative resurgence launched by Barry Goldwater in 1964. Republican governors like Wisconsin's Tommy Thompson, a champion of welfare reform, insisted that the states, not Washington, were now the best source of policy ideas. In the Senate, Republican Robert Dole of Kansas became majority leader; the reactionary Jesse Helms of North Carolina ascended to the chairmanship of the Foreign Relations Committee; and ninety-two-year-old Strom Thurmond of South Carolina, presidential candidate of the States Rights (Dixiecrat) party in 1948, headed the Armed Services Committee.

In the House of Representatives, a jubilant horde of 230 Republicans, 73 of them newly elected, chose Newt Gingrich as Speaker by acclamation, made Rush Limbaugh an "honorary member," and set about enacting the "Contract with America." One early bill forbade unfunded mandates, by which Washington had imposed regulations on the states without providing money to cover the costs. A constitutional amendment requiring a balanced federal budget passed by the House was narrowly rejected by the Senate.

On the cultural front, House Republicans targeted such "liberal elite" institutions as the Public Broadcasting Corporation and the National Endowments for the Arts. Fulfilling pledges to restore morality and uphold family values, Congress passed legislation to increase the government's power to combat obscenity in the mass media and curb pornography on the Internet. Other "Contract with America" issues, including repeal of a 1993 ban on assault weapons (the NRA's top priority), awaited their turn.

GOP leaders also promised tax credits and benefits for the middle class and the wealthy that, if enacted, would have gutted the Tax Reform Act of 1986, which had been designed to eliminate tax breaks and loopholes. As in the Reagan years, the promise of tax cuts coupled with increased defense spending threatened worse budget deficits, but Republican leaders insisted that large savings could be achieved in other parts of the budget. Where these savings would come from was unclear, since the biggest budget items apart from defense were mandatory interest payments on the national debt and two programs sacred to the middle class, social security and Medicare.

The torrent of bills, hearings, and press releases of early 1995 recalled the heady days of Lyndon Johnson's Great Society and even the early years of FDR's New Deal. Now, however, the activist energy came from conservatives, not from liberals.

For a time, House Speaker Newt Gingrich displayed a cockiness that struck many as arrogance. He stumbled early in 1995, however, when he first accepted, and then turned down, a $4.5 million book-royalty advance from a publishing house owned by Rupert Murdoch, a publishing tycoon with vital interests in federal legislation. Journalists also focused on Gingrich's network of political action groups, dubbed "Newt, Inc.," funded by corporate money and conservative foundations. Attacking "left-wing elitists," the Georgia firebrand praised laissez-faire sink-or-swim individualism and challenged the entire structure of social programs and federal-state relations that had evolved since the New Deal.

On the foreign-relations front, the 1994 Republican landslide signaled a turn inward. Newt Gingrich's "Contract with America" largely ignored foreign policy, and key Republican legislators pushed isolationist views. Jesse Helms denounced the United Nations, criticized environmental treaties, and saw little good in U.N. peacekeeping efforts or America's $14 billion foreign-aid program. Congressional Republicans refused to pay America's $1 billion in past U.N. dues. Even the Clinton administration felt the pressure. Yielding to Pentagon objections, Clinton rejected a multinational treaty banning land mines. The isolationist upsurge dismayed those who saw an intimate link between America's long-term well-being and the fate of the world.

Welfare Reform   In the aftermath of the Republican sweep in 1994, welfare reform took on fresh urgency. Newly confident conservatives challenged the underlying premises of the welfare system, whose origins stretched back to the New Deal of the 1930s. The critics offered two principal arguments. The first was cost. AFDC, with 14.2 million women and children on its rolls, cost about $125 billion in 1994, including direct payments, food stamps, and Medicaid benefits, a sharp jump since 1989. Though dwarfed by the benefits that flowed to the middle class through social security, Medicare, farm subsidies, and various tax deductions, this was still a heavy drain on the budget. The second argument for welfare reform was ideological—the belief that the system undermined the work ethic and trapped the poor in a cycle of dependence.

The debate raised serious policy issues and ethical questions. Would cutting welfare penalize children for their parents' actions? Would the government provide public employment to individuals dropped from the welfare rolls if no private-sector jobs were available? In *The Poverty of Welfare Reform* (1995), historian Joel Handler took a skeptical view. Dismissing the welfare-reform campaign as largely symbolic, he argued that without fundamental changes in the labor market

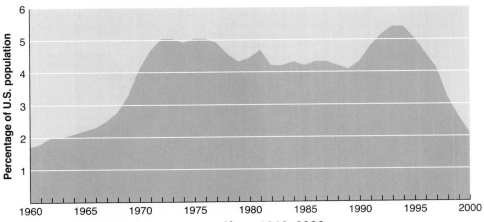

Percentage of U.S. Population on Welfare, 1960–2000

From just 1.7 percent in 1960, the percentage of Americans on welfare crept steadily upward until 1994, when it peaked at 5.5 percent, representing more than 14 million people. The percentage declined sharply thereafter, reflecting both the booming economy of the later 1990s and the impact of the Welfare Reform Act of 1996.

Source: Administration for Children and Families, Department of Health and Human Services. http://www.acf.hss.gov/news/stats/6097rf.htm.

and the political and social climate, changes in welfare policies would mean little: "[F]or the vast majority of mothers and their families, life will go on much as before."

Nevertheless, politicians of both parties jumped aboard the welfare-reform bandwagon. A broad consensus held that the present system had failed and that welfare should be a short-term bridge to gainful employment, not a lifelong entitlement. Many observers also saw a link between a system that paid higher benefits for each child and the soaring rate of out-of-wedlock births. The debate, therefore, was not over whether change was needed, but what changes. While Clinton favored federally funded child-care, job-training, and work programs to ease the transition from welfare to employment, conservative Republicans believed that the labor market and state and local agencies could best handle these problems. Clinton vetoed two welfare bills that lacked the safeguards he thought essential.

At last, in August 1996, Clinton signed a landmark welfare-reform bill. Reversing sixty years of federal welfare policy, the law ended the largest federal program, AFDC. Instead, states were free to develop their own welfare programs with federal block grants while following tough federal rules limiting most welfare recipients to two years of continuous coverage, with a lifetime total of five years. The law also granted states authority to withdraw Medicaid coverage once welfare benefits had been terminated.

Supporters argued that ending welfare as a lifetime entitlement would encourage initiative and personal responsibility. Critics warned of the effects on poor

Welfare to Work *A former welfare recipient in Georgia receives training for a new job.*

children and on ill-educated welfare mothers in inner cities lacking jobs and social services, and cautioned that the real test of the reform would come in times of recession and high unemployment.

Clinton's approval of a Republican welfare bill disappointed liberals, including Senator Edward Kennedy, and such mainstays of the Democratic coalition as women's groups, minority organizations, and advocacy groups for children and the poor. In the election summer of 1996, still smarting from the repudiation of 1994, Clinton had adjusted to the shifting political winds and moved to the right.

In the short run, the law seemed a success. By December 1998 the welfare rolls had dropped by 38 percent to a thirty-year low of 7.6 million people. The reductions came at a time of economic expansion. How the new system would work when the boom ended, as it did in 2000–2001, remained to be seen.

SOCIAL AND CULTURAL TRENDS IN 1990S AMERICA

As the economy expanded through most of the 1990s (see Chapter 32), Americans continued to move to the thriving South and West, and immigrants poured in from Asia and Latin America. Not all Americans prospered. Minorities in the inner cities, including recent immigrants, struggled under harsh conditions to make ends meet. Long-term changes in the economy affected the lives of millions of citizens, benefiting some and creating serious difficulties for others.

U.S. culture of the 1990s reflected the general prosperity, with a heavy emphasis on consumerism, leisure pursuits, and mass-media diversions. But uneasiness stirred beneath the surface, and the good times did not prevent bitter conflicts over issues of morality and belief.

America in the 1990s: A People in Transition   Historically, U.S. society has been marked by rapid growth, geographic mobility, and ethnic diversity, and—as the 2000 census revealed—this remained true as a new century began. The total population in 2000 stood at more than 281 million, some 33 million more than in 1990, the largest ten-year increase ever. The historic shift of population to the South and West continued, reflecting both internal migration and immigration patterns. The West added 10.4 million residents in the 1990s, with California alone increasing by more than 4 million. Maricopa County, Arizona (which includes Phoenix), grew by nearly 1 million. The South expanded by nearly 15 million people in the decade. Georgia, which outpaced Florida as the most rapidly expanding southern state, grew by more than 26 percent.

The graying of the baby-boom generation (those born between 1946 and 1964) pushed the median age from around 33 in 1990 to 35.3 in 2000, the highest since census records began. The 45 to 54 age group (including most baby boomers) grew by nearly 50 percent in the decade. Government planners braced for pressures on the social-security system and old-age facilities as the baby boomers reached retirement age.

The census also revealed changing living arrangements and family patterns. The proportion of "traditional" nuclear-family households headed by a married couple fell from 74 percent in 1960 to 52 percent in 2000. People living alone made up more than one-quarter of all households, while the proportion of households maintained by unmarried partners continued to increase, reaching 5 percent in 2000. Commenting on the census data, the *New York Times* observed, "[T]he nuclear family is not the only kind of family or even the only healthy kind of family. In modern America no type of family can really be recognized to the exclusion of all others."

The overall crime rate fell nearly 20 percent between 1992 and 2000. Experts attributed the decline to a variety of factors, including the decade's prosperity, stricter gun-control laws, a drop in the young male population, the waning crack-cocaine epidemic, and tougher law enforcement and sentencing rules. The U.S. prison population increased sharply throughout the decade, approaching 2 million by 2000.

Despite the falling crime rate, public fears of crime and violence remained high, fed in part by the appalling annual toll of gun deaths, which exceeded thirty thousand in 1998. Multiple shootings drew special notice. In 1999 an Atlanta man distraught by investment losses shot and killed nine employees at a financial firm. A rash of school shootings proved particularly unsettling. In a particularly horrendous 1999 event, two students at Columbine High School near Denver shot and killed twelve students and a teacher before committing suicide. These episodes produced anxious discussions of America's obsession with firearms, of a breakdown of parental authority, and of the influence of mass-media violence. In the aftermath of the school massacre in Colorado, President Clinton intensified his campaign for tougher gun-control laws.

Public-health statistics, by contrast, brought encouraging news. Average life expectancy at birth rose from seventy-four to seventy-seven between 1980 and 1999. (Life expectancy differed by gender, race, and other variables, however.) Total health expenditures hit $1.2 trillion in 2000, up 17 percent from 1990. The decline in cigarette smoking by Americans continued, falling to under 25 percent of the population in 2000.

The U.S. AIDS epidemic peaked at last, thanks to safer-sex practices and advances in drug therapies. After cresting in 1995 AIDS deaths and new HIV/AIDS cases both declined thereafter. Health officials warned against complacency: AIDS remained deadly, producing some forty-one thousand new cases in 2000, with African-Americans and Hispanics especially at risk. New (and expensive) drugs slowed the progression from HIV to full-blown AIDS, but no cure had been found. Wrote a gay journalist in 2001, "[Public-health warnings] may have to start anew with gay America as a whole, since some of us weren't around the first time HIV started killing us."

Globally, the AIDS epidemic raged on, with 22 million deaths and an estimated 36 million HIV/AIDS cases worldwide by 2001. Sub-Saharan Africa, with 25 million cases, was devastated by the disease, and many women and children were among the victims.

The 2000 census underscored the nation's growing racial and ethnic diversity. The U.S. population at century's end was about 13 percent Hispanic, 12 percent African-American, 4 percent Asian, and 1 percent American Indian. Each of these broad categories, of course, included many subgroups. The Asian category included persons whose origins lay in the Philippines, China and Hong Kong, Vietnam, India, Korea, and elsewhere. The Hispanics (who may be of any race, and are linked by a shared language, Spanish) were nearly 60 percent of Mexican origin, with Puerto Ricans, Cubans, and Salvadorans comprising most of the balance. The number of persons with ancestral roots in Haiti (where the languages are Creole and French) increased as well, reaching 385,000 by 2000.

While many Mexicans entered the country legally, others bypassed immigration checkpoints, making dangerous treks across the desert led by guides called "coyotes." In May 2001 fourteen young Mexicans died of dehydration and exposure when their "coyote" abandoned them in the Arizona desert.

Growing immigration from Asia and Latin America reversed a long decline in the proportion of foreign-born persons in the population. From a low of about 5 percent in 1970, the figure rose steadily, reaching more than 10 percent in 2000. As in earlier immigration cycles, the new immigrants mostly settled in cities from Los Angeles, San Francisco, Houston, and Seattle on the West Coast to New York City and Miami in the East. In New York, Catholic priests regularly said mass in thirty-five different languages!

U.S. Population by Race and Hispanic Origin, 2000 and 2050 (Projected)

By 2050, the Census Bureau projects, the Asian-American population will total some 40 million persons, and the number of Hispanics, at around 90 million, will surpass the number of African-Americans. According to these projections, non-Hispanic whites will constitute less than half the total U.S. population at mid-century.

*Hispanics may be of any race

Source: U.S. Census Bureau

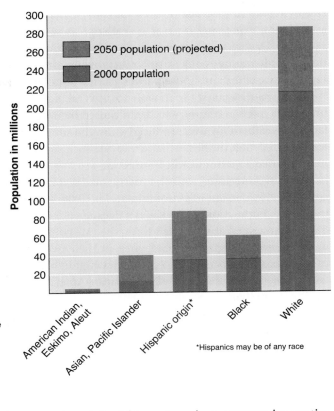

Population in millions

- 2050 population (projected)
- 2000 population

American Indian, Eskimo, Aleut   Asian, Pacific Islander   Hispanic origin*   Black   White

*Hispanics may be of any race

| Challenges and Opportunities in a Multiethnic Society | At century's end the African-American community continued to present diverse social, educational, and economic characteristics. In a decade of prosperity, many African-Americans made significant advances. The black unemployment rate fell from more than 11 percent in 1990 to 6.7 |

percent in 2000, and the proportion of blacks below the government's poverty line dropped from 32 percent to under 24 percent.

By 2000, black families' median income stood at nearly $28,000, a record high, close to that of non-Hispanic white families. The earnings of college-educated blacks was significantly higher, while the number of black-owned businesses, including such giants as TLC Beatrice International, a food company, reached six hundred thousand by mid-decade. Reversing a long trend, some 370,000 blacks moved from North to South in 1990–1995, strengthening the thriving black middle-class and professional communities in Atlanta and other cities. (When recession hit in 2001, some of these encouraging trends slowed or reversed, at least temporarily; see Chapter 32.)

In the inner cities, chronic problems persisted. Movies such as *Boyz 'N the Hood* (1991), set in Los Angeles, portrayed the grim inner-city reality. Drug-related carnage, peaking in the early 1990s, took a fearful toll. In April 1994 James

Darby, a black third-grader in New Orleans, wrote to President Clinton as a school assignment, expressing his fear of violence. A week later, walking home from a Mother's Day picnic, James was shot dead. While the crack-cocaine epidemic diminished, another dangerous hallucinogenic drug called Ecstacy, sold in tablet form at rave clubs and house parties, gained popularity.

In the battle against urban violence, several big cities sued the major gun manufacturers in cases of injury or death caused by unregistered firearms. The manufacturers deliberately overproduced guns, the suits alleged, knowing that many of them would enter the illegal market. In one such suit in 1999, a Brooklyn, New York, jury awarded a victim nearly $4 million.

African-Americans, mostly young males convicted of drug-related crimes, comprised 41 percent of prison inmates in 2000. Although the rapid expansion of the prison population slowed as the decade ended, young black males continued to be incarcerated at nearly ten times the rate of young white males. By 2000, one study found, a third of all black men in their twenties were either in prison, on probation, or on parole. Such statistics highlighted the continuing heavy odds facing this vulnerable sector of the African-American community.

Inner-city black women faced risks as well, particularly drug use and out-of-wedlock pregnancy. In 1970 unmarried women had accounted for some 37 percent of all black births; by the 1990s the figure hovered at around 70 percent. Some 30 percent of these births were to teenagers, reducing the young mothers' opportunities for education and employment and narrowing their children's prospects. (The out-of-wedlock childbirth rate for white women, while far lower, rose as well.) Whether eliminating automatic benefit increases for each new baby would reduce teen pregnancy in the inner cities, as welfare reformers predicted, remained to be seen, particularly as recession hit and job opportunities diminished.

Among Native Americans, the reassertion of tribal pride and activism continued in the 1990s. Citing Article VI of the U.S. Constitution, which describes all treaties approved by Congress as "the supreme law of the land," and assisted by groups like the Indian Law Resource Center of Helena, Montana, tribes pursued the enforcement of the 331 Indian treaties ratified between 1778 and 1871. This movement roused antagonism, as non-Indians, including some western politicians, complained that the treaty-rights movement was going too far.

The growth of Indian-run businesses produced further controversy. In Utah, the tiny Skull Valley Band of Goshute Indians, proclaiming themselves an independent nation, offered to lease the valley for nuclear-waste disposal, alarming environmentalists. The Omaha Indians of Nebraska opened a cigarette factory, dismaying public-health advocates.

Indian gambling casinos, approved by Congress in 1988, stirred intense debate. The giant Foxwoods Casino run by the Mashantucket Pequots in Connecticut earned $6 billion annually. As they competed for casino licenses, Indian tribes became major political contributors, pouring $7 million into the 1996 campaign. While the casinos brought needed capital into Indian communities, many citizens deplored the spread of gambling; states battled to extract more tax revenues from the casinos; and some Indians lamented the internal conflicts and erosion of traditional values the casinos brought in their wake.

Despite new sources of income, alcoholism, joblessness, and poor education persisted in Indian communities. The tribes fought back, supporting tribal colleges and community centers, and using casino earnings to fund alcohol-treatment centers that drew upon such Native American traditions as the sweat lodge and respect for the wisdom of elders.

The Hispanic population, fueled by immigration and high natural increase, grew rapidly in the 1990s. The name most frequently given to male babies in California and Texas in 1999, reported the Social Security Administration, was José. Given a birthrate notably higher than that of either non-Hispanic whites or African-Americans, demographers predicted, Hispanics would comprise 25 percent of the population by 2050.

The diverse Hispanic population, too, resisted easy generalizations. While Mexican-Americans concentrated in the Southwest and West Coast, many lived in other regions as well. Cubans, Puerto Ricans, and other Hispanic groups, as well as Haitians, resided mainly in Florida, New York, New Jersey, and Illinois. Many Hispanics were well educated, prosperous, and upwardly mobile. The median income of Hispanic households rose to more than $30,000 by 2000, and the poverty rate fell. Unemployment among Hispanics dropped from more than 8 percent in 1990 to 5.7 percent in 2000. In the five-year interval between 1993 and 1998, Hispanic-owned businesses nearly doubled in number, with more than two

Americanization, Twenty-first-Century Style *Recent immigrants from Afghanistan join a fitness class in Fremont, California, in 2001.*

hundred thousand in Los Angeles County alone. Miami's Cuban émigré community, with many professionals and benefiting from government aid programs for refugees from communism, was especially prosperous (see A Place in Time: Miami, Florida, 1990s).

As was the case with African-Americans, however, perhaps a quarter of Hispanics lived in inner-city neighborhoods plagued by gangs, addiction, failing schools, and teen pregnancy. Despite the importance of religion and family in Hispanic culture, 25 percent of Hispanic children lived in households with only the mother present in 2000. Ill-educated and unskilled Hispanic newcomers settled in decaying neighborhoods and took the lowest-paid jobs as gardeners, maids, day laborers, and migrant farm workers. Despite the low status of such work, however, the economy depended on it. The British journal *The Economist* wrote in 1998, "Wherever the booming [U.S.] economy cries out for workers, or a place needs regenerating, the ever-arriving and ever-progressing Latinos will move in. Nothing daunts them."

Hispanics, like other immigrant groups, mobilized to address problems, lobby politically, and campaign for community betterment. The largest advocacy group, La Raza, worked to promote Hispanic interests. By the early 1990s, in California alone, more than four thousand Hispanics held public office.

One thing was clear: the burgeoning Hispanic population was changing America. In June 2001 *Time* magazine devoted a special issue to what it called "Amexica," a Southwestern border region of 24 million people, growing at double the national rate. "The border is vanishing before our eyes," declared *Time,* creating a new nation within a nation "where hearts and minds and money and culture merge." *Time* focused on the paired U.S. and Mexican cities dotting this border: from Brownsville, Texas, and Matamoros, Mexico, near the Gulf of Mexico, westward to San Diego and Tijuana on the Pacific. This vast region, the magazine argued, was spawning a vibrant new borderlands culture; new trade and economic ties; and also social problems, including communicable diseases such as tuberculosis, illegal immigration, and drug trafficking.

Asian newcomers also presented a highly variegated picture. Prizing education, supported by close family networks, and often possessing needed skills and entrepreneurial talent, many Asian immigrants moved rapidly up the economic ladder. After passage of the Immigration Reform Act of 1965, for example, Indian doctors, engineers, and academics emigrated to America in large numbers, often joined later by aging parents and other family members, for a total of some 1.7 million by 2000.

Chinese and other Asian immigrant groups often followed a similar pattern of assimilation and upward mobility. In Fremont, California, near San Francisco, the Asian population increased from 19 percent in 1990 to 37 percent in 2000. Many of the newcomers worked as engineers and businesspeople in nearby Silicon Valley. At Fremont's Mission San José High School, the enrollment was 61 percent Asian; a visitor in 2001 found walls plastered with such signs as "Amanda Chan for Class Treasurer" and "Sadaf Gowani for Secretary." The Hmong, a Laotian mountain people who had supported the United States in the Vietnam War, formed a distinct Asian immigrant group. Settling mainly in Wisconsin and Minnesota, their numbers reached about one hundred thousand by 2000. On campuses and in city neighborhoods, Asian-Americans organized to promote their interests, sometimes acting collectively and sometimes in specific national groups.

Rethinking Citizenship in an Era of Diversity
By 2050, demographers calculate, no single racial or ethnic group will be a majority in America. Non-Hispanic whites, in other words, while still a plurality, will simply be another ingredient in the ethnic mix. In a parallel development, many Americans of mixed racial and ethnic origins, like the golfer Tiger Woods, resisted being pigeonholed. The number of interracial married couples in the United States rose tenfold in the years 1960–2000, from 149,000 to 1.5 million. Recognizing these realities, in 2000 the Census Bureau permitted citizens to check more than one racial category.

Many Americans found the new diversity exhilarating and full of promise, but others did not, and the phenomenon of "white flight" continued. As immigrants arrived in the cities, native-born whites tended to move out. Between 1990 and 1995 both Los Angeles and New York lost more than 1 million native-born inhabitants, approximately equal to the new arrivals from Asia and Latin America. Cities such as Las Vegas, Phoenix, Portland, Denver, and Austin attracted non-Hispanic whites departing from larger metropolitan centers with growing immigrant populations.

Amid these swirling demographic changes, what did it mean to be an "American" in a multiethnic, multicultural society? What would bind together such a diverse population? Some observers feared that Americans, at least emotionally and psychologically, would divide into separate camps based on ethnicity, religion, national origin, or skin color. The pressures in this direction seemed strong. At the UCLA law school, for example, blacks, Latinos, and Asians had their own student associations and their own law reviews. Newt Gingrich in 1995 gloomily foresaw "a civilization in danger of simply falling apart."

While countertrends toward a more cosmopolitan culture could be seen, particularly among the professional classes, racial and ethnic loyalties remained strong. This was hardly surprising as long as income and opportunity remained linked to race and ethnicity. Nor was it surprising that Americans disturbed by the anonymity of modern mass society should seek the reassurance of a clear-cut group identity, whether of blood, geography, ancestry, or faith.

Language became a major battleground. While some Anglo politicians campaigned to make English America's "official language," advocates for various immigrant groups called for school instruction in children's native tongue, or at least bilingual classes. However, a 1998 study of immigrant children found that they overwhelmingly wished to learn and speak English in school.

In his 1908 play *The Melting Pot,* Israel Zangwill, a Jewish immigrant from England, foresaw the blending of different immigrant groups into a common

Miami, Florida, 1990s

In the 1990s America's changing ethnic profile was nowhere better illustrated than in Miami, whose sun-drenched beaches, flamboyant skyscrapers, and pastel-tinted Art Deco buildings all proclaim its status as the nation's southernmost major city. Spain, having subdued the local Calusas Indians, claimed the region until 1819, when the Adams-Onís Treaty ceded title to the United States. Florida entered the Union in 1845, but sporadic Indian resistance—the so-called Seminole Wars—persisted into the 1850s. (A small tribe of Native Americans, the Miccosukee, lives on a nearby reservation.)

A 1920s land boom collapsed in the wake of a killer hurricane, but Miami burgeoned after World War II as GIs who had trained in the area returned. Miami Beach proved especially popular with Jewish retirees from New York. The novelist I. B. Singer, recalling his first visit in 1948, wrote, "Miami Beach resembled a small Israel. . . . Yiddish resounded around us in accents as thick as those you would hear in Tel Aviv."

Today's Miami is more Havana than Tel Aviv. In 2000, 57 percent of the 2.3 million residents of Miami-Dade County were Hispanic, and most of them were Cuban-Americans. Cubans fled their island country en masse after Fidel Castro seized power in 1959; by 1973 three hundred thousand had settled in Greater Miami. Thousands more, the so-called Mariel boat people who left with Castro's approval, arrived in 1980.

Far from being a struggling minority, Cuban-Americans compose a confident, fully developed ethnic community. They influence not only Miami's cultural ambience but also its political and economic agenda. Cuban-born Xavier Saurez became mayor in 1985. "Little Havana," the sprawling downtown district centered on Calle Ocho (Eighth Street), boasts not only churches, restaurants, and shops but also banks, medical centers, law offices, insurance companies, and construction firms employing professionals of all kinds.

This community's political clout was displayed in November 1999 when two fishermen rescued six-year-old Elian Gonzales, who was floating in an inner tube off Key Biscayne, Florida. Elian was one of three survivors of a boatload of Cubans, including his mother, who were lost at sea when attempting to reach Florida. Miami's Cuban-Americans rallied around the boy, and for months the story dominated the media. Parades, demonstrations, banners, and Elian T-shirts were mobilized in a campaign to keep him in the United States. (One person wearied by the media saturation launched an Internet website called "The Elian Gonzales Channel—All Elian All the Time," with parody headlines such as "Elian Gains One Pound. Experts Blame McDonalds.") Stories circulated of dolphins that had miraculously watched over the boy during his watery ordeal. Finally, in June 2000, federal officers, enforcing a court order, removed Elian from his Miami relatives and returned him to his father in Cuba.

Jamaicans and other Hispanic groups also call Miami home. The 1980s brought emigrants from troubled Nicaragua, El Salvador, and especially Haiti. Although U.S. immigration officials intercept and repatriate Haitian refugees arriving by sea, this community continues to grow.

Miami's black community, making up some 20 percent of the population, is centered in Liberty City, Richmond Heights, and other enclaves. While Richmond Heights is middle class and well-to-do, overall the black population ranks among the city's poorest. Relations between African-Americans and Hispanics are strained. While many native-born blacks feel alienated and exploited, Hispanic newcomers tend to view the United States more positively. African-Americans generally vote Democratic, while the Cuban-Americans are mostly conservative Republicans.

Ethnic diversity generates a distinctive Miami style. Jewish delis coexist with Hispanic restaurants. Snapper, paella, conch fritters, stone crabs, Haitian curried goat, potent Cuban coffee, and an array of salsas tempt local palates. In prosperous times, ethnic lines blur in a shared pursuit of the good life. A recession in the 1970s drove the jobless rate to 13 percent, but the economy bounced back in the 1980s and 1990s. The city's love of sports finds many outlets: sailing, windsurfing, sports car rallies, horseracing at Hialeah, and avid support for the Miami Dolphins football team, the Miami Heat basketball team, and the University of Miami Hurricanes.

With its round of parades, fairs, and festivals, the city seems dedicated to the pleasure principle. Casual dress and gold jewelry set the tone for both sexes. The beaches encourage what some call Miami's "body culture." Fashion photography is big business. Journalist Patrick May sums up the city this way: "Non-stop entertainment. Over a stage backdropped by fruit salad sunsets and palm tree props, the curtain for 100 years has risen faithfully each dawn. And there it stands, tongue firmly in cheek, hogging the spotlight. The show-off of American cities admiring itself in a full-length mirror."

Behind the façade lie problems. Racial tensions simmer near the surface. Black neighborhoods erupted in violence in 1968 and again in 1980 when a jury acquitted a white police officer in a black man's death. As the Hispanic population has grown, non-Hispanic whites have moved out. Civic leaders bemoan "Anglo flight," and some non-Hispanics flaunt hostile bumper stickers that proclaim, "Will the last American leaving Miami please bring the flag?"

With Spanish the predominant native tongue, language is contested terrain. In many neighborhoods English is rarely heard or seen. Other languages thrive as well. In 1994 a reporter observed a Vietnamese, a Spanish-speaking Colombian, and a French-speaking Haitian vainly trying to communicate at an auto-repair shop. (They eventually diagnosed the problem: a faulty distributor.) In 1980 the Miami-Dade County commissioners proclaimed English the official language for government business. But many Miamians continue to conduct their daily lives without resort to English.

Miami's links with organized crime go far back. Rum-running and gambling proliferated in the 1920s. Mobster Al Capone retired here in the 1930s. Today, a thriving wholesale drug traffic drives up the crime statistics. Fast boats smuggle in cocaine from "mother ships" hovering offshore; commercial aircraft arriving from South America unwittingly transmit drugs. Miami-Dade County's 1981 homicide toll of 621 earned it the dubious title "Murder Capital USA." A popular TV show of 1984–1989, *Miami Vice,* glamorized the city's underside along with its tropical setting, laid-back fashions, and stage-set architecture. While drug wars and domestic disputes account for most of the bloodshed, the killing of several tourists during robbery attempts tarnished the city's appeal in the early 1990s. "Miami wears its crime like cheap perfume," observes a guide-book half boastfully; "it's hard to ignore."

Decades of development have taken a heavy toll on fragile wetlands and unspoiled wilderness areas. The nearby Everglades, once spread over 4 million acres, has dwindled to one-tenth its former size. Of the exotic wildlife that formerly inhabited this fragile ecosystem, only a fraction survives.

Crime, ethnic tensions, environmental degradation, cultural diversity, hedonistic pleasure seeking—for better or worse, Miami has it all. In this vibrant, garish, future-oriented city, the demographic changes as well as the social problems that characterize contemporary America emerge in particularly stark fashion.

national identity. By the century's end, the "melting pot" metaphor had faded, in part because its advocates had usually assumed that as immigrants entered the "melting pot" they would abandon their ethnic roots and cultural traditions and conform to a standard "American" model.

If there was to be no "melting pot," what would unite this diverse society? Americans shared a common identity as consumers of goods and as participants in the mass culture of movies, TV, theme parks, and professional sports. Was this enough? Could the nation's civic culture match its commercial and leisure culture? This question, first posed by social thinkers of the 1920s, remained unresolved at the dawning of a new century.

The "New Economy"

In 1973 sociologist Daniel Bell published a book called *The Coming of Post-Industrial Society: A Venture in Social Forecasting.* Unlike many such works, Bell's proved remarkably accurate. In the late nineteenth and early twentieth centuries, America's farm-based economy had given way to an economy based on factory production and manual labor in cities. As the twentieth century ended, a second major transformation was again reshaping the U.S. economy: the decline of the industrial sector and the rise of a service-based economy. Manufacturing continued, of course, but it faded as a major source of employment. In 1960 about half of the male labor force worked in industry or in related jobs such as truck driving. By the late 1990s this figure had fallen to under 40 percent.

In the same period, the percentage of professional, technical, and service workers continued its century-long upward trend. In 1960 such workers had comprised about 42 percent of the male labor force; by 1998 the figure was 58 percent. The percentage of women workers in the service sector was even higher.

The service economy was highly segmented. At one end were low-paying jobs in fast-food outlets, video rental stores, nursing homes, and chain stores such as

Changing Patterns of Work, 1900–2000

This chart illustrates the sweeping changes in the male U.S. labor force in the twentieth century. The share of the male work force engaged in farming, fishing, forestry, and mining fell dramatically. The percentage of workers in industry and related occupations climbed until about 1960, and then began to decline. The service, technical, managerial, sales, clerical, and professional categories rose steadily throughout the century.

Source: Historical Statistics of the United States, Colonial Times to 1970 (1975); Statistical Abstract of the United States, 2002; Caplow, Hicks, and Wattenberg, The First Measured Century: An Illustrated Guide to Trends in America (Washington, D.C.: The AEI Press, 2001).

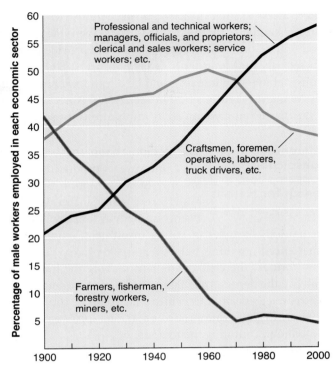

Percentage of male workers employed in each economic sector

Professional and technical workers; managers, officials, and proprietors; clerical and sales workers; service workers; etc.

Craftsmen, foremen, operatives, laborers, truck drivers, etc.

Farmers, fisherman, forestry workers, miners, etc.

Wal-Mart. At the other end were lawyers and physicians; money managers and accountants; and workers in the entertainment and telecommunications fields. The latter category expanded rapidly with the growth of high-speed telecommunications systems and the rise of the personal computer with its Internet-based spinoffs.

This sector of the service economy helped give the economic boom of the later 1990s its aura of sizzle and excitement (see below). As the Web-based *Encyclopedia of the New Economy* proclaimed somewhat breathlessly,

> When we talk about the new economy, we're talking about a world in which people work with their brains instead of their hands. . . . A world in which innovation is more important than mass production. A world in which investment buys new concepts . . . rather than new machines. A world in which rapid change is a constant.

The decline of the industrial economy and the rise of the service economy had different meanings for different groups. Young people with the education, skills, and contacts to enter the new high-tech industries often found exciting challenges and substantial economic rewards. For less-privileged youths, supermarkets, fast-food outlets, or discount superstores could provide entry-level work, but doubtful job security and long-term career prospects. For older workers displaced from industrial jobs, the impact could be devastating both economically and emotionally. Whatever their position in society, few Americans were unaffected by the rise of the new economy with all its implications for social change.

Affluence, Conspicuous Consumption, a Search for Heroes
The economic boom that began in 1992 and roared through the Clinton years produced instant fortunes for some and an orgy of consumption that set the tone of the decade. Wall Street and Silicon Valley spawned thousands of twenty-something millionaires. In 1997, surveying the ostentatious lifestyles of young investment geniuses, most of whom had never experienced anything but rising stock prices, *Vanity Fair* magazine described New York as "the champagne city, making the brash consumption of the 1980s look like the depression." Tales circulated of elegant restaurants offering obscenely expensive cigars and rare wines, and exclusive shops selling $13,000 handbags. In 1999, as the good times rolled on, the nation's top one hundred advertisers spent $43 billion promoting their goods.

The economic boom also encouraged what some considered a smug, hard-edged "winner take all" mentality like that of the Gilded Age, when those at the top turned their backs on the larger society. In *Bowling Alone: The Collapse and Revival of American Community* (2000), political scientist Robert Putnam sharply criticized American public life. Putnam found diminished civic engagement and weakened interest in public issues, as evidenced by declines in voter participation, political activism, and participation in civic organizations. He even found less informal socializing, from dinner with friends to card parties and bowling leagues, as Americans pursued purely personal goals. While some saw the Internet as a new form of community, Putnam viewed it as further evidence of the privatization of life and the erosion of the public sphere.

Anecdotal evidence supported Putnam's conclusions. A 1997 survey of college students found that 77 percent expected to become millionaires. A motivational book called *The Prayer of Jabez,* which became a bestseller in 2000, cited a biblical prayer by a shepherd recorded in I Chronicles ("Bless me indeed, and enlarge my territory") as a key to success. Wrote the author, the Reverend Bruce Wilkinson, "If Jabez had worked on Wall Street, he might have prayed 'Lord, increase the value of my investment portfolio.'"

With the stock market surging, the Cold War over, and other threats only beginning to come into focus, many Americans set out to enjoy themselves. Attendance at the Disney theme parks in Florida and California neared 30 million in 2000. The sales of massive sport-utility vehicles (SUVs) soared, despite environmentalists' laments about their fuel inefficiency. When a White House press secretary was asked in the summer of 2001 if Americans should change their consumption patterns to conserve energy, he replied, "[I]t should be the goal of policy makers to protect the American way of life—the American way of life is a blesséd one."

As in the 1980s, the media offered escapist fare. Popular movies included historical extravaganzas like *Braveheart* (1995) and *Gladiator* (2000). The 1997 blockbuster film *Titanic*, with spectacular special effects, grossed $600 million. In the 1994 hit movie *Forrest Gump*, Tom Hanks played a kindly but simple-minded young man who becomes a wealthy business tycoon by chance. The top-rated TV show of 1999–2000, *Who Wants to Be a Millionaire?*, unabashedly celebrated greed. So-called "reality" TV shows like *Survivor*, popular as the decade ended, offered viewers a risk-free taste of the hazards that American life itself (at least for the affluent) conspicuously lacked.

Millions avidly followed TV coverage of the 1995 trial of O. J. Simpson, a former football star accused of murdering his former wife and her friend. The 1996 murder of a six-year-old Colorado girl whose parents had pushed her into child beauty pageants similarly mesmerized the public. So did the 2001 disappearance of a young federal-government intern from California after an alleged affair with her congressman. (In 2002 the congressman was defeated for reelection, and the young woman's body was found in a remote section of a Washington park.) The sex scandals that swirled around President Clinton and ultimately led to his impeachment (see Chapter 32) often seemed to be no more than another media diversion in a sensation-hungry decade.

Again, as was true of the 1980s, other evidence from the popular culture suggests a more complex picture. Some critics interpreted *Titanic*, which sided with its working-class hero in steerage against the rich snobs in first class, as a subtle comment on a decade when class differences in America were blatantly on display. One even called the movie "an exercise in class hatred." *American Beauty* (1999) explored dark and murderous currents beneath the façade of a comfortable suburban family.

The Clint Eastwood western *Unforgiven*, winner of the 1992 Academy Award for best picture, seemed to express nostalgia for an earlier era when life presented rugged challenges and hard moral choices. The same longings, some suggested, underlay the outpouring of admiring biographies of larger-than-life heroes from the past, such as Stephen Ambrose's *Eisenhower* (1991), A. Scott Berg's *Lindbergh* (1999), and David McCullough's *Truman* (1993) and *John Adams* (2001).

The decade also reveled in the heroic era of World War II, featuring it in a series of TV specials, books such as Ambrose's *Citizen Soldiers* (1997) and Tom Brokaw's *The Greatest Generation* (1998), and movies like *Saving Private Ryan* (1998) and *Pearl Harbor* (2001). Commenting on the latter film, *New York Times* columnist Frank Rich observed,

> *Pearl Harbor* is more about the present than the past. . . . The motivation, in part, is overcompensation . . . for what is missing in our national life: some cause larger than ourselves, whatever it might be. . . . Even those Americans who are . . . foggy about World War II . . . know intuitively that it was fought over something more blessed than the right to guzzle gas.

A Truce in the
Culture Wars?

Elsewhere on the cultural landscape, the 1990s also saw a continuation of the moralistic battles that had begun in the 1970s, which some viewed as nothing less than a struggle for the nation's soul. The Christian Coalition's attempted takeover of the Republican party was only part of a larger campaign to reverse what conservatives saw as America's moral decay. In earlier times, the culture wars had raged along sectarian lines, with native-born Protestants battling Catholic and Jewish immigrants. During the Cold War, the source of evil had been clear: the global communist conspiracy, centered in Moscow. Now many Americans translated the same apocalyptic world view to the home front, and searched for the enemy within.

Some viewed the sexual revolution as the great threat. As gays and lesbians grew more vocal politically (and increasingly visible in the popular culture and in TV programming), a rash of state-level efforts sought to counter their demands for equality. In 1998, amid this climate of reaction, a gay student at the University of Wyoming, Matthew Shepard, was tortured and murdered by two local youths because of his sexual orientation.

As the abortion controversy continued, a small number of "pro-life" advocates turned from peaceful protest to violence. In 1995 an anti-abortion activist fatally shot a physician and his bodyguard outside a Florida abortion clinic, and an unstable young man murdered two people and wounded five others at a clinic near Boston. In 1997 bombers struck abortion clinics in Tulsa and Atlanta. The following year, a Buffalo, New York, physician who performed abortions was shot dead. (In part because of such terror tactics, the abortion rate dropped by some 12 percent between 1992 and 1996.)

On April 19, 1995, in the worst outburst of domestic terrorism up to that time, a bomb demolished an Oklahoma City federal building, killing 168 people. The bomber struck precisely two years after a government raid on the Waco, Texas, compound of the Branch Davidians, an apocalyptic religious sect charged with firearms violations. The 1993 Waco raid ended tragically when fires burst out inside the main building as federal tanks moved in, leaving some eighty Branch Davidians dead. After the Oklahoma City blast, the authorities soon arrested Timothy McVeigh, a Gulf War veteran outraged by the Waco incident. McVeigh and his co-conspirator, Terry Nichols, had vague links to the secretive right-wing militia movement that sprang up in the 1990s. These organizations were often obsessed with conspiracy theories and deeply suspicious of the government. McVeigh, convicted of murder, was executed by lethal injection in June 2001. Nichols received a life sentence.

Adding to the national jitters over violence-prone loners and shadowy antigovernment groups was a series of bombs mailed between 1978 and 1995 to individuals whose business or professional activities could be interpreted as anti-environmental. The bombs killed three people and injured twenty-eight others. In 1996 authorities arrested Theodore Kaczynski, a Harvard-trained mathematician and obsessive opponent of modern technology, in his remote Montana cabin. Kaczynski was convicted but escaped the death penalty by reason of mental incapacity.

The culture wars were fought mainly with words and symbolic gestures, not bullets and bombs. In 1995 the Smithsonian Institution cancelled an exhibit marking the fiftieth anniversary of the atomic bombing of Japan when veterans' organizations and some politicians attacked it for allegedly overemphasizing the bombs' human toll and for presenting historians' differing views of Truman's decision.

The struggle unfolded on many fronts, from televangelists' programs and radio talk shows to school-board protests and boycotts of TV shows deemed morally offensive. Conservatives attacked history textbooks for promoting "multiculturalism," for being insufficiently patriotic, and for pandering to the forces of "political correctness." The cultural measures undertaken by Congress after the 1994 Republican landslide, discussed earlier, were a part of this larger drive to purge American life of the evils that religious and cultural conservatives saw on every hand.

Religious conservatives proposed a constitutional amendment permitting prayer in classrooms and called for a renewal of traditional morality and "family values." The rapidly growing evangelical and charismatic churches continued to denounce society's wickedness and the government's role in the moral decline. In October 1997 some seven hundred thousand men belonging to a conservative Protestant religious movement called Promise Keepers rallied in Washington, D.C., for a day of prayer, hymn singing, and pledges to reclaim the moral and spiritual leadership of their households.

Pat Robertson's *The New World Order* (1991) saw much of U.S. and indeed world history as a vast conspiracy that would soon end in the rule of the Antichrist. As the year 2000 neared, popularizers of Bible prophecy intensified their warnings that history's final crisis was at hand. (Widespread fears of massive computer

Remembering Oklahoma City
Matt Story and Dawn Mahan, whose mother died in the 1995 bombing of the Murrah federal building in Oklahoma City, pause at her memorial in the commemorative park honoring the 168 victims.

failures associated with "Y2K," the shorthand term for the coming of the year 2000, added to the apprehension.) The charges of infidelity levied against President Clinton underscored for conservatives the moral rot they saw eating away at America.

As the 1990s ended, the cultural wars seemed to diminish. The Christian Coalition lost momentum when its politically savvy director, Ralph Reed, resigned in 1997. By 1998 leaders of the Christian Coalition and other groups were expressing open frustration with Republican politicians who courted conservative Christians' votes but failed to fight for their cultural agenda once in power. In *One Nation After All* (1998), sociologist Alan Wolfe reported on his interviews with middle-class Americans, whom he found suspicious of extremist positions and broadly accepting of diversity. The virtues of tolerance and live-and-let-live, Wolfe suggested, were thriving in Middle America. One of Wolfe's interviewees reflected, "I wish more people would recognize [that] we can't just stand back and whine about the ways things are and . . . about how terrible the changes will be. We've got to move forward and trust that we can . . . get to a solution eventually." In its optimism and moderate tone, such a perspective captured a deep-seated American pragmatic approach to social problems, and struck an encouraging note as a new century dawned.

IMPORTANT EVENTS, 1988–1995

1986 William Rehnquist becomes chief justice of the United States.
Antonin Scalia joins Supreme Court.

1988 George Bush elected president.
Anthony Kennedy joins Supreme Court.

1989 Massive Alaskan oil spill by *Exxon Valdez.*
Supreme Court, in several 5 to 4 decisions, restricts civil-rights laws.
U.S. invasion of Panama; Manuel Noriega overthrown.
China's rulers crush prodemocracy movement.
Berlin Wall is opened.

1990 Federal Clean Air Act strengthened.
Americans with Disabilities Act passed.
President Bush and Congress agree on five-year budget-deficit reduction package.
Iraq invades Kuwait.
Recession begins.
Germany reunified; Soviet troops start withdrawal from Eastern Europe.
David H. Souter joins Supreme Court.

1991 Gulf War (Operation Desert Storm).
Clarence Thomas seated on Supreme Court.

1992 Supreme Court approves Pennsylvania restriction on abortion but upholds *Roe* v. *Wade.*
Arkansas Governor Bill Clinton elected president.

1993 Congress enacts modified version of Clinton economic plan.
Congress approves NAFTA treaty.
Recovery begins; economy expands, stock-market surges (1993–2000).
Congress debates health-care reform (1993–1994).
Ruth Bader Ginsberg joins Supreme Court.
Federal forces raid Branch Davidian compound in Waco, Texas.

1994 Christian Coalition gains control of Republican party in several states.
Stephen G. Breyer joins Supreme Court.
Republican candidates proclaim "Contract with America."
Republican victory in 1994 elections; Newt Gingrich becomes Speaker of the House.

1995 AIDS epidemic peaks in the United States; continues worldwide.
Oklahoma City federal building bombed.

1996 Welfare Reform Act passed.

1999 Columbine High School shootings.

2000 Federal census finds population surge in West and South, sharp increases in Hispanic and Asian population, and changing family patterns.

32

New Century, New Challenges, 1996 to the Present

riday, February 26, 1993, began like most other business days at New York's World Trade Center, two 110-story towers soaring over lower Manhattan. But suddenly, at 12:18 P.M., a powerful bomb ripped through the parking garage under the north tower. The blast cut off electricity, plunging the building into darkness. Fifty thousand workers hastily evacuated, and hundreds were trapped in stalled elevators. Six persons died in the blast, and more than one thousand were injured.

The first investigators found an eerie scene: a giant hole extending five stories underground, fires from ruptured automobile gasoline tanks, 124 cars destroyed and others heavily damaged, water and sewage cascading from broken pipes, car alarms wailing in the darkness. The FBI quickly identified the vehicle that had carried the bomb into the garage: a Ford Econoline van rented in Jersey City. Five Islamic militants, including a blind Egyptian sheik, Omar Abdel Rahman, the alleged mastermind, were arrested and convicted of conspiracy and other crimes. Three, including Sheik Omar, were found guilty of murder and received life sentences.

Shocking as it was, the attack could have been far worse: at least the tower had survived, and comparatively few lives had been lost. But this was one of a nightmarish series of attacks that would take a heavy toll in life and property, as the upsurge of terrorist attacks in the 1980s (see Chapter 31) continued. In 1995 a bomb shattered a U.S. military training center in Riyadh, Saudi Arabia, killing seven, including five Americans. In 1996 another bomb ripped through a U.S. military barracks in Saudi Arabia, leaving nineteen U.S. airmen dead. Further deadly attacks in East Africa and the Middle East killed more Americans.

Like distant thunder signaling an approaching storm, the attacks were ominous warnings of worse ahead. On September 11, 2001, terrorists again struck the World Trade Center, as well as the Pentagon, this time with horrendous consequences.

Much of this chapter focuses on the impact of escalating terrorist attacks, particularly the aftermath of September 11, at home and abroad. As Americans faced these dangers, they also coped with domestic political battles and economic turmoil. Amid calls for unity, deep divisions remained. A White House scandal in Clinton's second term, a disputed presidential election in 2000, and the policies of Clinton's successor, George W. Bush, who seemed to favor the privileged and powerful and took the nation into a preemptive war in Iraq, all proved highly divisive. As prosperity gave way to recession, bankruptcies and charges of fraud hit some of the nation's largest companies, undermining investors' confidence and tarnishing the reputation of the corporate world.

This chapter focuses on five key questions:

What domestic initiatives marked Clinton's second term, and how did the scandals that swirled around him in 1998–1999 affect his ability to govern?

On balance, was President Clinton's foreign-policy record a success?

What factors fueled the economic boom of the 1990s, and why did it end?

What key domestic policies did George W. Bush propose early in his presidency?

How did the Bush administration respond to the terrorist attacks of September 2001, domestically and internationally? Was the response appropriate? Was it effective?

THE CLINTON ERA II: DOMESTIC POLITICS, SCANDALS, IMPEACHMENT, 1996–2000

Moving to the political center, Bill Clinton won a second term in 1996. Apart from his support for tough regulation of the tobacco industry, Clinton's second term is remembered mainly for a sex scandal that led to an impeachment effort by his Republican foes. This effort further poisoned an already highly partisan political climate.

Campaign 1996 and After; The Battle to Regulate Big Tobacco

After the Republican landslide in 1994, Clinton's prospects looked bleak. But he had won the nickname "the Comeback Kid" after a long-shot victory in the 1992 New Hampshire presidential primary, and he again hit the comeback trail. Despite the missteps of 1993, he had won good marks for signing the budget-balancing and welfare-reform bills (see Chapter 31). The Republicans suffered a black eye in 1995 when House Speaker Newt Gingrich, battling Clinton over the budget, twice allowed a partial government shutdown.

Clinton got another lucky break: a weak Republican opponent in 1996. When General Colin Powell, the popular former chairman of the Joint Chiefs of Staff, declined to run, Kansas Senator and Majority Leader Bob Dole, a partially disabled World War II hero, won the nomination. A seventy-three-year-old party stalwart, Dole ran a lackluster campaign.

Clinton won with just under 50 percent of the vote, to Dole's 41 percent. (The Texas maverick H. Ross Perot garnered 8 percent.) The Republicans held control of Congress, though Gingrich and other GOP legislators proved less combative than after their 1994 triumph.

The cost of television advertising continued to drive up campaign expenses, and fundraising scandals marked the 1996 contest. One Democratic fundraiser with links to Indonesian and possibly Chinese corporate interests raised $3.4 million, of which nearly half was eventually returned. At a Los Angeles Buddhist event attended by Vice President Al Gore, priests and nuns sworn to poverty contributed over a hundred thousand dollars to the Democratic cause. The money apparently came from Asian business tycoons eager to curry favor with the administration.

Launching his second term, Clinton further distanced himself from his party's activist past. In 1997 he signed a Republican bill cutting taxes and setting a timetable for a balanced budget by 2002. (As prosperity continued, Clinton beat that deadline by three years.) Many Clinton proposals involved no legislation or spending. He urged parents to read to their children, and set up a commission to lead a national dialogue on race.

Clinton cautiously defended affirmative action, but support for such programs was weakening, especially among non-Hispanic whites. The Supreme Court restricted the awarding of federal contracts on the basis of race in 1995, and in 1996 California voters barred racial or ethnic preferences in state agencies, including the universities.

Clinton did act forcefully on one issue: tobacco regulation. In 1997, facing lawsuits by former smokers and by states hit with heavy medical costs related to smoking-related diseases, the tobacco industry agreed to pay some $368 billion in settlement. The agreement limited tobacco advertising, especially when directed at young people.

When this settlement came before Congress for approval, southern legislators close to the tobacco companies opposed it, but Clinton supported an even stronger measure that would have imposed tougher penalties, higher cigarette taxes, and stronger antismoking measures. Supporters of the administration's bill documented the industry's manipulation of nicotine levels and deliberate targeting of children. The industry struck back with a $40 million lobbying campaign and heavy contributions to key legislators, killing the bill. Commented John McCain, Arizona's maverick Republican senator, "Some Republicans might be vulnerable to the charge that their party is in the pocket of the tobacco companies."

In 1998, facing a wave of private lawsuits, the tobacco industry reached a new settlement, scaled back to some $200 billion, with forty-six states. Clinton, however, continued to push for tougher federal regulation and for legal action to recover Medicare costs arising from smoking-related illnesses.

In his January 1998 State of the Union address, Clinton boasted that his 1999 budget would include a modest surplus, the first in thirty years. Most of the surplus, he argued, should go to reduce the national debt and strengthen the social-security system, which faced eventual bankruptcy as the baby boomers retired.

Clinton's call to "Save social security" shrewdly painted Republican tax cutters as irresponsible.

This speech defined Clinton's second-term agenda. After the health-care fiasco, he had abandoned large-scale programs in favor of modest proposals that appealed to progressives without alienating moderates. He offered some initiatives to help the poor, such as enrolling the nation's 3 million uninsured low-income children in Medicaid. But he also introduced proposals attractive to the middle class (college-tuition tax credits; extending Medicare to early retirees) and to fiscal conservatives (reducing the national debt; shoring up social security). Under normal conditions, the speech would have certified Clinton's political comeback.

Scandal Grips the White House   But conditions were not normal. Even as Clinton spoke, scandal enveloped the White House. Adultery charges had long clung to Clinton, and now he faced the Paula Jones sexual-harassment suit, dating from his days as the governor of Arkansas (see Chapter 31). The Supreme Court had helped Jones's case by permitting lawsuits against sitting presidents.

Seeking to show a pattern of sexual harassment, Jones's lawyers subpoenaed Clinton and quizzed him about reports linking him to a young White House intern, Monica Lewinsky. The president denied the story, as did Lewinsky in an affidavit. As the rumors became public (via an Internet website devoted to political gossip), Clinton denounced them as false. Hillary Clinton blamed "a vast right-wing conspiracy." In fact, political conservatives *were* digging for damaging information on Clinton, and he helpfully provided them with ample material.

Clinton settled the Paula Jones suit by paying her $850,000, but more problems awaited. In telephone conversations secretly and illegally taped by Monica Lewinsky's "friend" Linda Tripp, Lewinsky had graphically described an affair with Clinton starting in 1995, when she was twenty-one, and continuing through early 1997. Early in 1998, Tripp passed the tapes to Kenneth Starr, an independent counsel appointed by a three-judge panel to investigate the Whitewater matter. At Starr's request, FBI agents fitted Tripp with a recording device and secured further Lewinsky evidence.

Starr now focused on whether Clinton had committed perjury in his testimony and whether he had persuaded Lewinsky to lie as well. In August, under heavy pressure, Lewinsky admitted the affair in testimony before Starr's grand jury. Soon after, in testimony videotaped at the White House, Clinton admitted "conduct that was wrong" with Lewinsky but denied a "sexual relationship" under his rather narrow definition of the term. In a brief TV address, Clinton admitted to an inappropriate relationship with Lewinsky, but called his testimony in the Jones case "legally accurate" and attacked Starr as politically motivated. The scandal provided grist for late-night television, Internet humor, and conservative radio talk-shows.

Other presidents had pursued extramarital affairs, but by the 1990s the women's movement and sexual-harassment laws had made such behavior

Ken Starr Meets the Press, January 1998 *Independent Counsel Starr's dogged investigations into legal issues arising from President Clinton's affair with a White House intern set off a media frenzy, which in turn ignited a round of hand-wringing about the state of American journalism.*

increasingly objectionable. In a media-saturated age, politicians lived in the glare of public scrutiny. Indeed, politicians themselves had paraded intimate personal details for political advantage. Unsurprisingly, then, the Clinton scandal unfolded on TV and in tabloid headlines.

Impeachment In a September 1998 report to the House Judiciary Committee, Kenneth Starr narrated the Clinton-Lewinsky affair in lurid detail and found "substantial and credible" grounds for impeachment. The president, Starr charged, had committed perjury and influenced others to do the same, and had obstructed justice by retrieving gifts he had given Lewinsky and coaching his secretary on his version of events.

The Judiciary Committee, on a party-line vote, forwarded four articles of impeachment to the House of Representatives. In a similarly partisan vote, the House approved two articles of impeachment charging Clinton with perjury and with obstructing justice. For the first time since Andrew Johnson's day, a president of the United States had been impeached.

Opinion polls sent the Republicans an ominous message: most Americans opposed impeachment. In the 1998 midterm elections, as the House impeachment process went forward, the Democrats gained five House seats. Soon after, Speaker Newt Gingrich abruptly resigned both the speakership and his House seat.

Since removing a president requires a two-thirds Senate vote, and since the Republicans held only a ten-vote Senate majority, the impeachment campaign seemed foredoomed to failure. Nevertheless, early in 1999 the new Senate conducted a trial. As Chief Justice William Rehnquist presided, Republican members of the House Judiciary Committee, acting as the impeachment managers, presented their case. White House lawyers challenged what one called a "witches' brew of speculation."

Paradoxically, as these events unfolded, Clinton's approval ratings soared. While most people deplored Clinton's personal behavior, few believed that it met the "high crimes and misdemeanors" standard set by the Constitution for removal from office. With the economy booming and Clinton adopting popular positions on most issues, the public appeared willing to tolerate his personal flaws. Further, many people concluded that Clinton was the target of Republican zealots determined to drive him from office.

On February 12, 1999, the Senate rejected the impeachment charges and ended the trial. In a brief statement President Clinton again apologized and urged the nation to move on. While some Republicans warned darkly of a double standard of justice, most Americans felt relief that the ordeal was over.

On his last day in office, admitting that he had lied in sworn testimony, Clinton agreed to a $25,000 fine and a five-year suspension of his law license. In March 2002 the special counsel who had succeeded Kenneth Starr in the original Whitewater inquiry found insufficient evidence to convict the Clintons of criminal behavior. The *New York Times* offered a final assessment:

> The nation may never again see a president with Bill Clinton's natural political talents, his instinctive grasp of policy and his breadth of understanding of government issues. He was capable of being an extraordinary leader. The fact that he turned out to be so much less is a tragedy.

While escaping removal, Clinton had suffered grievous damage, mostly self-inflicted. His character flaws, whose consequences he had managed to avoid in a charmed political life, had overtaken him at last, eroding his leadership and tarnishing his historical standing. The Republican party suffered as well, as some of its most extreme and moralistic members took center stage, rubbing raw the partisan differences that threatened to fragment American public life.

CLINTON'S FOREIGN POLICY: BEYOND THE COLD WAR

Bill Clinton preferred domestic issues to foreign policy. Yet the United States, as the world's only remaining superpower, could not escape its global role. Confronting scandal and partisan sniping at home, Clinton turned his attention abroad. He faced two key challenges: using American power wisely in the post–Cold War era and responding to terrorist acts against the United States and the threat of further attacks.

The Balkans, Russia, and Eastern Europe in the Post-Soviet Era

In the region of southeastern Europe known as the Balkans, the Soviet collapse unleashed bitter ethnic conflicts. As Yugoslavia broke apart in 1991, Serbian forces launched a campaign of "ethnic cleansing" in neighboring Bosnia, which meant supporting Bosnia's ethnic Serbs while slaughtering or driving out Muslims and Croats.

Incited by Serbia's president Slobodan Milosevic, Serbian troops overran U.N.-designated "safe havens" and committed brutal atrocities against Muslims.

To stop the slaughter, the United Nations introduced a peacekeeping force. When this effort failed, the NATO command in Europe, in its first joint military operation, launched air strikes against Bosnian Serb targets in August 1995. The Clinton administration reluctantly joined this operation.

Later in 1995 the administration flew the leaders of Bosnia's warring factions to Dayton, Ohio, for talks. The resulting Dayton Accords imposed a cease-fire and created a framework for governing the region. Clinton committed twenty thousand U.S. troops to a NATO force in Bosnia to enforce the cease-fire.

In 1998, Slobodan Milosevic launched a campaign against Muslims in Serbia's southern province of Kosovo. In 1999, as the bloodshed continued, NATO, under U.S. leadership, bombed Serbian facilities in Kosovo and in Serbia itself, including Belgrade, the capital.

President Clinton, eager to avoid U.S. losses and haunted by memories of Vietnam, avoided committing ground forces. American public opinion wavered as well, appalled by the suffering and a growing refugee crisis, but wary of expanding U.S. involvement. In June 1999, however, U.S. troops joined a NATO force that occupied Kosovo. With the Serbian army under control, the refugees trickled back. Milosevic was overthrown in 2001, and a more democratic Yugoslav government, eager for Western aid, delivered him for trial before a war-crimes tribunal at the Hague.

These developments affected U.S. relations with its former Cold War opponent, Russia. Although Russia protested the air attacks on its traditional ally, Serbia, Russian forces joined in NATO's occupation of Kosovo. Facing unrest among its own Muslim population, Russia in 1995–1996 waged war against the breakaway Muslim republic of Chechnya. Some called this unpopular and inconclusive conflict Russia's Vietnam.

Amid these troubles, Russia's hasty conversion to a free-market economy caused a severe economic crisis. Having put together a multi-billion-dollar loan package for Russia, the Clinton administration watched anxiously as chaos threatened. Despite U.S. disapproval of the Chechnya war, and despite President Boris Yeltsin's periodic alcoholic binges, Clinton continued to support him as Russia's best hope. In 1999 the administration backed Russia's admission to the Group of Seven (G-7), the world's leading industrial nations, and the G-7 became the G-8. In the same year, over Russia's protests, NATO admitted three new members from the former Soviet bloc—Hungary, Poland, and the Czech Republic. Yeltsin resigned in 1999, transferring power to Vladimir Putin, a former agent of the KGB, the Soviet secret police.

Symbolic Gestures in Africa; a Modest Success in Haiti Clinton was stirred by conditions in Africa, a continent wracked by poverty, AIDS, tribal conflict, and authoritarian regimes. His engagement, however, proved mainly symbolic.

In 1992 in the East African nation of Somalia, afflicted by civil war and famine, President Bush had committed some twenty-six thousand U.S. troops to a U.N. mission to provide humanitarian aid and end the fighting. As the warring factions battled, forty-four Americans were killed and many injured. President Clinton withdrew the U.S. force in 1994, and the U.N. mission ended a year later. Traumatized by this fiasco, Clinton failed to intervene in other African conflicts, including Rwanda, where as many as half a million people died and thousands more became refugees in intertribal massacres.

During Clinton's presidency South Africa, prodded by U.S. and other nations' economic sanctions, ended apartheid and became a multiracial democracy. In 1994 Nelson Mandela, long imprisoned by South Africa's white government, was elected president. Touring Africa in 1998, President Clinton visited South Africa and greeted Mandela. Calling upon six nations in eleven days, he offered modest aid assistance.

Closer to home, in Haiti, a 1991 military junta overthrew President Jean-Bertrand Aristide and terrorized his supporters. Thousands of Haitians fleeing poverty and repression set out for Florida in small, leaky boats. African-American leaders demanded U.S. action, as did Haitians born in the United States. Clinton assembled an invasion flotilla off Haiti's coast in 1994, and former president Jimmy Carter persuaded the junta's leaders to accept voluntary exile. Backed by a U.S. occupation force, Aristide resumed the presidency, giving Clinton a modest diplomatic success.

The Middle East: Seeking an Elusive Peace, Combating a Wily Foe   In the Middle East, the 1987 Palestinian uprising, or Intifada, against Israel's military occupation of the West Bank and Gaza (see Chapter 30) continued into the 1990s. Prospects for peace brightened in 1993, however, after Israeli and Palestinian negotiators meeting in Norway agreed on a six-year timetable for peace.

The so-called Oslo Accords provided for a Palestinian state, the return of most Israeli-held land in the West Bank and Gaza to the Palestinians, and further talks on the claims of Palestinian refugees and the final status of Jerusalem. In 1994 President Clinton presided as Israeli prime minister Yitzhak Rabin and Yasir Arafat, head of the Palestine Liberation Organization, signed the agreement at the White House.

Rabin was assassinated in 1995, however, by a young Israeli opposed to the Oslo Accords. Israel's next election brought Benjamin Netanyahu of the hard-line Likud party to power. Suicide bombings by Palestinian extremists in 1996–1997 killed some eighty Israelis, triggering retaliatory attacks. More Jewish housing was built in Palestinian territory, and by 2000 an estimated two hundred thousand Israeli settlers were living there. Secretary of State Madeleine K. Albright struggled to return the two sides to the negotiating table. (Albright was named to the post in 1997, thereby becoming the highest-ranking woman in U.S. government history.)

Ehud Barak of Israel's more moderate Labor party became prime minister in 1999. In 2000 Clinton invited Barak and Arafat to Camp David. Barak made

The Mideast Crisis, 1980–Present

With terrorist attacks, the Iran-Iraq War, the Persian Gulf War, Iraq's secretive weapons program, and the ongoing struggle between Israel and the Palestinians, the Middle East was the site of almost unending violence, conflict, and tension in these years.

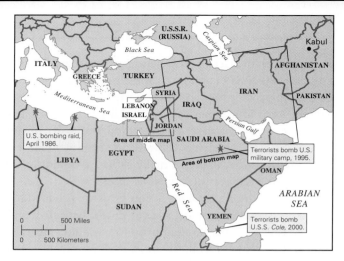

U.S. bombing raid, April 1986.

Area of middle map

Area of bottom map

Terrorists bomb U.S. military camp, 1995.

Terrorists bomb U.S.S. Cole, 2000.

0   500 Miles
0   500 Kilometers

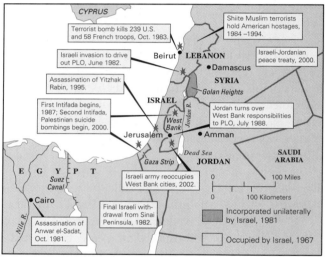

Terrorist bomb kills 239 U.S. and 58 French troops, Oct. 1983.

Shiite Muslim terrorists hold American hostages, 1984–1994.

Israeli invasion to drive out PLO, June 1982.

Israeli-Jordanian peace treaty, 2000.

Assassination of Yitzhak Rabin, 1995.

First Intifada begins, 1987; Second Intifada, Palestinian suicide bombings begin, 2000.

Jordan turns over West Bank responsibilities to PLO, July 1988.

Israeli army reoccupies West Bank cities, 2002.

Final Israeli withdrawal from Sinai Peninsula, 1982.

Assassination of Anwar el-Sadat, Oct. 1981.

0   100 Miles
0   100 Kilometers

Incorporated unilaterally by Israel, 1981

Occupied by Israel, 1967

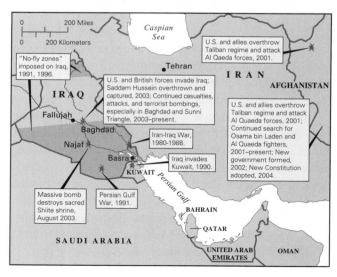

"No-fly zones" imposed on Iraq, 1991, 1996.

U.S. and allies overthrow Taliban regime and attack Al Qaeda forces, 2001.

U.S. and British forces invade Iraq; Saddam Hussein overthrown and captured, 2003; Continued casualties, attacks, and terrorist bombings, especially in Baghdad and Sunni Triangle, 2003–present.

U.S. and allies overthrow Taliban regime and attack Al Quaeda forces, 2001; Continued search for Osama bin Laden and Al Quaeda fighters, 2001–present; New government formed, 2002; New Constitution adopted, 2004.

Iran-Iraq War, 1980-1988.

Iraq invades Kuwait, 1990.

Massive bomb destroys sacred Shiite shrine, August 2003.

Persian Gulf War, 1991.

0   200 Miles
0   200 Kilometers

1192

unprecedented concessions based on the principle of "land for peace." According to press reports, he agreed to Israeli withdrawal from 95 percent of the West Bank and all of Gaza; the creation of a Palestinian state; Palestinian control of East Jerusalem; and the transfer of control over Jerusalem's Temple Mount, sacred to both Muslims and Jews, to a vaguely defined "religious authority." In return, Arafat would declare an end to hostilities and give up further claims on Israel.

Arafat refused Barak's offer, and the summit failed. In September the Likud leader Ariel Sharon with a horde of Israeli soldiers and police made a provocative visit to the site of Al-Aqsa Mosque, an Islamic shrine on Temple Mount. Soon after, Palestinians launched a new Intifada against Israel. Early in 2001, Sharon became Israel's prime minister. Like other presidents before him, Clinton bequeathed the Israeli-Palestinian conflict to his successor.

A renewed crisis in Iraq also demanded Clinton's attention. After the Persian Gulf War, the United Nations had imposed trade sanctions on Iraq and set up an inspection system to prevent Saddam Hussein from building weapons of mass destruction. This system was effective, but late in 1997, when Saddam refused U.N. inspectors access to certain sites, Clinton dispatched ships, bombers, and thirty thousand troops to the Persian Gulf. He sought to rally support for a military strike, as George Bush had done in 1991, but France, Russia, and various Arab states resisted. At home, critics questioned whether bombing would further the goal of unrestricted inspections.

Clinton drew back after the new U.N. secretary general, Kofi Annan of Ghana, secured Saddam's agreement to open inspection. Saddam soon reneged, and the crisis continued. The Iraqi muddle underscored the difficulty of combating potential terrorist threats by military actions whose long-term outcome seemed murky.

Nuclear Proliferation and Terrorism: Confronting Global Security Challenges

Despite the Nuclear Nonproliferation Treaty of 1970, the proliferation threat continued. In 1998 a long-simmering dispute between India and Pakistan over Kashmir escalated sharply when India tested a nuclear bomb. Despite urgent pleas from the United States and other powers, Pakistan followed suit, and fears of nuclear conflict rose.

Proliferation fears also focused on communist North Korea, which, in violation of the 1970 treaty, began a program of nuclear-weapons development and missile testing. In 1994, facing U.N. economic sanctions and the loss of $9 billion in international assistance (and following a visit by Jimmy Carter), North Korea pledged to halt this program. In 1999, confronting famine and economic crisis, North Korea agreed to suspend long-range missile testing in return for an easing of U.S. trade and travel restrictions. North Korea's continued violation of these pledges caused ongoing concern, however.

Nuclear dangers also arose in the former Soviet Union. In the 1993 Strategic Arms Reduction Treaty (START II), the United States and Russia agreed to cut their long-range nuclear arsenals by half. This left many nuclear weapons in Russia and in three nations once part of the Soviet Union: Ukraine, Kazakhstan, and

Belarus. With unrest and economic crisis in the region, Washington feared that foreign powers or terrorist groups might acquire nuclear weapons or know-how through espionage or bribery. The Bush and Clinton administrations expended much money and diplomatic effort to speed the dismantling and secure disposal of nuclear weapons in Russia and elsewhere in the former Soviet Union.

The cycle of terrorism continued in the Clinton years. On August 7, 1998, powerful bombs destroyed the U.S. embassies in Nairobi, Kenya, and Dar-es-Salaam, Tanzania, killing 220 people, including Americans and many Kenyans and Tanzanians. U.S. antiterrorism specialists pinpointed a wealthy Saudi Arabian, Osama bin Laden, who in 1982 had moved to Afghanistan, where he established and financed terrorist training camps. In the 1990s he had spent time in Sudan.

After the embassy bombings, Clinton ordered cruise missile strikes on a suspected chemical-weapons factory in Sudan allegedly financed by bin Laden and on a training camp in Afghanistan. A U.S. grand jury indicted bin Laden on charges of planning the embassy attacks and also of inciting the killing of GIs in Somalia in 1993. Clinton called for new measures to cope with rogue states and terrorist groups that might acquire nuclear, chemical, or biological weapons. Secretary of State Albright, foreseeing "a long-term struggle," declared: "This is, unfortunately, the war of the future."

Underscoring Albright's grim assessment, on October 12, 2000, a bomb aboard a small boat in the harbor of Aden, Yemen, ripped a gaping hole in the U.S. destroyer *Cole*, killing seventeen sailors. The peaceful post–Cold War era that many had anticipated seemed an ever-receding mirage.

A New World Order?

The end of the Cold War had initially brought a wave of relief, but it soon became clear that the world remained dangerous and posed challenges as daunting as those of the Cold War. The Soviet empire had collapsed, and the threat of global nuclear war had subsided, but trouble spots around the world still clamored for attention. Like firefighters battling many small blazes rather than a single conflagration, policy makers now wrestled with a tangle of issues. Somalia, Bosnia, Iraq, Kosovo, North Korea, Pakistan, Afghanistan, Israel and the Palestinians, and terrorists who ignored national boundaries all claimed Washington's attention.

At the same time, many citizens turned away from world affairs. In a 1997 poll only 20 percent of Americans said that they followed foreign news, a sharp decline from the 1980s, with the biggest drop among young people. TV coverage of world news fell by more than 50 percent from 1989 to 1995. Post–Cold War America, commented one observer in 1998, "has no mission other than to keep itself entertained."

Four large-scale developments helped define America's post–Cold War global role. The first was the growing centrality of economic and trade issues. Trade agreements; multinational corporations; and global systems of communications, finance, and marketing loomed large in shaping America's foreign policy.

Second, in contrast to economic globalization, the world saw a turning inward toward various forms of religious fundamentalism. Muslim fundamentalists, reacting against Western secularism, searched for Islamic purity, in some cases concluding that terrorist attacks on America, which they viewed as demonic and threatening, represented a religious duty. In Israel, some Orthodox Jews claimed Palestinian lands on the basis of biblical prophecies. In India, a fundamentalist Hindu party gained power in 1998, replacing the secularist Congress party. America harbored Christian fundamentalists suspicious of international organizations and of the U.S. government itself and dismayed by an array of social and cultural trends. The struggle between fundamentalist and inward-turning impulses, on the one hand, and the globalizing economy and communications system, on the other, posed a major challenge for diplomats.

Third, a growing gulf separated prosperous, industrialized societies with high living standards and stable birthrates, and regions scourged by poverty, disease, illiteracy, explosive population growth, and a dangerous gap between the masses and privileged elites. This vast disparity created conditions ripe for conflict and unrest, including the spreading menace of terrorism.

Finally, the Cold War's end left the future of international organizations uncertain. Some Americans either turned to isolationism or favored unilateralist, go-it-alone approaches. Some even demanded U.S. withdrawal from the United Nations and other world organizations.

Others, however, continued to hope that the United Nations, long a pawn of the superpowers' conflict, could at last function as its founders had envisioned in 1945. Indeed, in 2003 some forty-three thousand U.N. peacekeeping forces and civilian personnel were serving in trouble spots around the world. U.N. agencies also addressed global environmental and public-health issues.

Post–Cold War opinion polls indicated that most Americans supported internationalist approaches to world problems and viewed the United Nations favorably. Despite flagging attention to foreign affairs, Americans could become engaged when they understood an issue in human terms, or grasped how events abroad affected U.S. interests. Clearly, however, Americans of the 1990s were still adjusting to a new era of complex international issues that could not be reduced to simple Cold War slogans.

THE ECONOMIC BOOM OF THE 1990S

The 1990s saw one of the longest periods of sustained economic growth in U.S. history. Productivity increased, unemployment fell, and inflation remained under control. Prosperity helped bring crime rates down and reduce welfare rolls. Federal deficits gave way to surpluses as tax revenues increased.

For some, the surging stock market stimulated the urge to get rich quick and enjoy the good times. But real wages did not keep pace with the stock market, and workers who lacked the skills required by the new economy remained stuck in dead-end jobs. America's participation in the global economy fueled growth, but when foreign economies faltered, Americans felt the effects as well.

Economic Upturn; Surging Stock Market   Although Bill Clinton targeted the sluggish economy in the 1992 campaign, a turnaround had already begun. Economists differ over the reasons, but the new products, efficiencies, and business opportunities associated with the personal computer and the information revolution were certainly crucial (see Chapter 31). Rising international trade and high consumer confidence helped sustain the boom, as did low inflation, the Federal Reserve Board's low interest rates, and a steady flow of immigrants eager to work.

Whatever its sources, the fact of the boom is clear. Unemployment fell from 7.5 percent in 1992 to 4 percent by 2000. Corporate profits soared. Wal-Mart racked up revenues of $193 billion in 2000; General Motors, $185 billion; and on down the list. Houston's Enron Corporation, an energy broker, vaulted into the ranks of corporate giants, reporting revenues of $101 billion. The gross domestic product, a key economic indicator, rose nearly 80 percent in the decade.

The stock market reflected and then outran the economic upturn as the stock of many companies far outpaced their actual value or earnings prospects. From under 3,000 in 1991, the Dow Jones Industrial Average edged toward 12,000 by

The U.S. Economy, 1990–2002

The unemployment rate fell and the gross domestic product (GDP) rose during the boom years of the 1990s. As recession hit in 2001, however, the jobless rate increased.

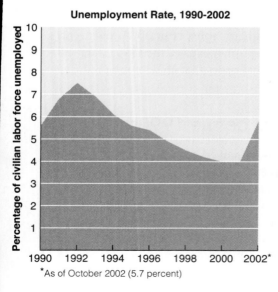

Unemployment Rate, 1990-2002

Percentage of civilian labor force unemployed

1990 1992 1994 1996 1998 2000 2002*

*As of October 2002 (5.7 percent)

Gross Domestic Product, 1990-2002

Billions of dollars

1990 1992 1994 1996 1998 2000 2002*

*Annual estimate based on First Quarter figures

early 2001. New investors flocked into the market. By 1998 nearly 50 percent of American families owned stock directly or through their pension plans.

Information-technology stocks proved especially popular. The NASDAQ composite index, loaded with technology stocks, rose more than tenfold from 1991 to early 2000. Some new stock offerings by Silicon Valley start-up companies surged to fantastic levels, turning young entrepreneurs into paper millionaires. The brokers who managed these offerings (and profited from the rising stock prices) fueled the speculation with glowing assessments of new companies' earning prospects. As early as 1996 Alan Greenspan, chairman of the Federal Reserve Board, warned of "irrational exuberance" in the stock market, but it only surged higher.

Corporate mergers proliferated as companies sought to improve their profitability. In 2000 the communications giant Viacom swallowed CBS for $41 billion, and the pharmaceutical company Pfizer acquired rival Warner-Lambert for $90 billion. In the biggest merger of all, the Internet company America Online (AOL) acquired Time-Warner (itself the product of earlier mergers) for $182 billion.

The stock-market boom stimulated the quest for luxury possessions and leisure pursuits that helped shape the cultural climate of the decade (see Chapter 31). In 2000 Americans spent $105 billion on new cars; $107 billion on video, audio, and computer equipment; and $81 billion on foreign travel. The so-called dot-com millionaires of Silicon Valley and Wall Street seemed living proof that the new economy was the wave of the future. With so many Americans speculating in stocks rather than investing in more secure forms of savings, some economists warned, the inevitable downturn could have severe consequences.

An Uneven Prosperity

The benefits of the boom were unevenly distributed. From 1979 to 1996 the portion of total income going to the wealthiest 20 percent of the population increased by 13 percent, while the share going to the poorest 20 percent dropped by 22 percent. Commented Harvard economist Richard Freeman in 1998, "The U.S. has the most unequal distribution of income among advanced countries—and the degree of inequality has increased more here than in any comparable country." While stockholding was widely diffused by the later 1990s, the top 5 percent of the owners held 80 percent of all stock.

As corporations maintained profits through "downsizing" and cost cutting, job worries increased. Adjusted for inflation, the wages of industrial workers rose only slightly in the 1990s. The rapidly growing service sector included not only high-income positions but also low-paying, low-skilled jobs in sales, fast-food outlets, custodial work, telemarketing, and so forth. While some service workers as well as teachers and other white-collar groups were unionized, overall union membership stood at only 13.5 percent of the labor force by 2000, weakening this means by which workers had historically improved their wages and job conditions. Unions' political clout weakened as well. Congress ratified the 1993 NAFTA treaty, for example, despite protests from organized labor (see Chapter 31).

Job-market success increasingly required special training and skills, posing problems for young people, displaced industrial workers, and welfare recipients thrown into the labor force. Overall employment statistics also concealed racial and ethnic variables. In 2000 the jobless rate for blacks and Hispanics, despite having dropped, remained significantly higher than the rate for whites. In short, the economic boom brought real benefits to many, but also left millions behind.

America and the Global Economy As NAFTA made plain, expanding foreign trade ranked high on Clinton's agenda. At the 1994 meeting of the G-7, Clinton declared, "Trade as much as troops will . . . define the ties that bind nations in the twenty-first century." When the U.S. trade deficit shot up to $133 billion in 1993, after several years of decline, and included a $59 billion trade gap with Japan, Clinton like his predecessor pressured the Japanese to buy more U.S. goods.

Clinton also opted to preserve trading ties with China despite Beijing's human-rights abuses; restrictive trade practices; threats to Taiwan; and pirating of U.S. movies, CDs, and computer software. Brushing aside protests from human-rights activists, Clinton welcomed Chinese president Jiang Zemin in 1997, and returned the visit in 1998. As China's actions stirred growing dissatisfaction, Congress grew skeptical of the administration's policy of "constructive engagement" with Beijing.

Clinton's China policy reflected hard economic realities, however: with U.S. imports from China surpassing $100 billion annually, China was America's fourth largest trading partner, after Canada, Mexico, and Japan. In 2000 Congress permanently granted China the same trading status as America's other trading partners, rather than making trade agreements with China dependent on year-by-year congressional action, as in the past.

Economic calculations also defined U.S. relations with Europe, which became a powerful trading competitor in 1993 when fifteen nations created the European Union (EU) to integrate their economic policies and work toward a common currency, the Euro, adopted in 2001.

In 1994 the Senate ratified a new global trading agreement that created the World Trade Organization (WTO) replacing the old General Agreement on Tariffs and Trade (GATT) established in 1947 (see Chapter 26). The WTO agreement provided for a gradual lowering of trade barriers and set up mechanisms for resolving trade disputes.

Several events underscored the interconnectedness of the new global economy. When the Mexican peso collapsed in 1995, jeopardizing U.S.-Mexican trade and threatening to increase the flow of illegal migrants northward, Clinton quickly granted Mexico $40 billion in loan guarantees. In 1997–1998 the economies of Thailand, South Korea, Indonesia, and other Asian nations weakened as a result of corruption, excessive debt, and other factors. Viewing the crisis as a danger to the United States, the administration took steps to avoid political chaos and regional instability.

Conditions became especially dangerous in Indonesia, the world's fourth-most-populous nation. Working through the International Monetary Fund, the administration sought to bail out Indonesia's faltering economy and to reduce corruption in the regime.

The once-sizzling Japanese economy stumbled as Asia's economic crisis spread. The Tokyo stock market fell and the yen lost value, unsettling the U.S. stock market and further jeopardizing U.S. exports and investments in Asia. Again recognizing the threat to U.S. prosperity, the Clinton administration urged Japan to undertake needed economic reforms. By 1999, as the economies of Brazil, Argentina, and other South American nations sank into recession as well, analysts questioned how long the American boom could continue.

With globalization, foreign investors flocked into the American market. By 2000 foreign investment in the United States totaled a staggering $1.24 trillion. Australian-born tycoon Rupert Murdoch snapped up U.S. entertainment and communications companies. Investment flowed the other way as well. As American fast-food chains, soft drinks, movies, pop music, and TV programs spread globally, other nations fretted about being swamped by U.S. mass culture.

Globalization aroused opposition in other quarters as well. Union leaders and environmentalists warned that multinational corporations could build plants in poor countries, bypassing U.S. environmental and worker-protection laws. Activists pressured companies selling clothing, footwear, and other consumer goods made in poor nations to upgrade labor conditions in their factories. At a 1999 WTO conference in Seattle, opposition exploded in the streets. For several days, demonstrators representing a variety of causes nearly shut down the city.

DISPUTED ELECTION; CONSERVATIVE ADMINISTRATION, 2000–2002

The 2000 election highlighted the acrimony pervading U.S. politics. The disputed election ended the Democrats' hold on the White House, but only after the Supreme Court intervened on behalf of the Republican candidate, George W. Bush. Pursuing his father's unfulfilled agenda, Bush advocated policies supported by corporate America and by religious conservatives. On the military front, Bush pursued a missile-defense system first proposed by Ronald Reagan. In its approach to the world, the administration followed a go-it-alone policy, arousing widespread criticism abroad.

Election 2000: Bush Versus Gore   The 2000 campaign shaped up as a contest of personalities. The Democrats, bouncing back from the impeachment crisis, confidently nominated Al Gore for president. As his running mate, Gore chose Connecticut Senator Joseph Lieberman, making him the first Jewish-American candidate on a major party ticket. The fact that Lieberman had denounced Clinton's extramarital affair and his efforts to cover up the scandal helped insulate Gore from the "sleaze factor" in the Clinton legacy.

The Republican contest pitted Senator John McCain of Arizona, a former prisoner of war in Vietnam, against Texas governor George W. Bush, son of the former president. McCain, a champion of campaign-finance reform and a critic of corporate influences in his party, made a strong bid. Bush, however, with powerful backers and a folksy manner, won the nomination. His running mate Dick Cheney had been defense secretary in the first Bush administration and then head of the Halliburton Corporation, a Dallas-based energy company. Conservative columnist Pat Buchanan won the nomination of Ross Perot's Reform party. The Green party nominated consumer advocate Ralph Nader.

Both Gore and Bush courted the center while trying to hold their bases. For Bush, this meant corporate interests, religious conservatives, and the so-called Reagan Democrats in the white middle and working classes. Gore's base, by contrast, consisted of liberals, academics and professionals, union members, African-Americans, and many Hispanics.

Gore's prospects looked good. He pointed to the nation's prosperity and pledged to extend health-care coverage and protect social security. In televised debates Gore displayed greater mastery of detail than his opponent.

Bush, while projecting a likeable manner, had little national or foreign-policy experience. Many saw him as a lightweight who owed his political success to family influence. As one Texas Democrat quipped, "George Bush was born on third base and thought he had hit a home run." But he campaigned hard, pledging tax cuts, education reform, and a missile-defense system. Calling himself a "compassionate conservative," Bush subtly reminded voters of Clinton's misdeeds by promising to restore dignity to the White House.

Gore had image problems. He had been tainted by fundraising scandals in the 1996 campaign, and many voters found him pompous. The factual mastery he flaunted in the debates struck many as arrogant. Eager to prove his political independence after eight years as vice president, Gore distanced himself from Clinton, despite the president's high approval ratings. Peeved, Clinton played little role in the campaign.

Polls showed that most voters agreed with Gore on the issues, approved the Democrats' economic policies, and conceded Gore's intellectual edge. Ominously for Gore, however, they preferred Bush as a person. The election seemed a toss-up.

Feuding in Florida The intensely partisan politics so vividly on display in the impeachment crisis was further symbolized by a bitter dispute over the election outcome. Gore won the popular vote by a narrow but clear margin of more than 500,000. The electoral college, however, remained up for grabs. Soon the struggle narrowed to Florida, whose 25 electoral votes would give either candidate the presidency.

Flaws in Florida's electoral process quickly became apparent. In Palm Beach County, a poorly designed ballot led several thousand Gore supporters to vote for Buchanan by mistake. In other counties, particularly those with many poor and African-American voters, antiquated vote-counting machines threw out thousands of ballots in which the paper tabs, called "chads," were not fully punched out. Gore

The Election of 2000

For the first time since 1888, the winner of the popular vote, Al Gore, failed to win the presidency. The electoral-college system and the Supreme Court's intervention in the disputed Florida vote put George W. Bush in the White House.

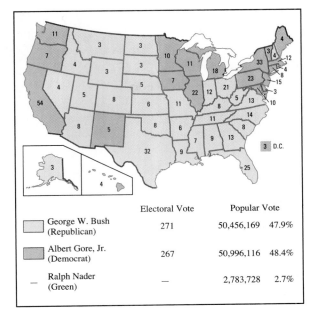

	Electoral Vote	Popular Vote	
George W. Bush (Republican)	271	50,456,169	47.9%
Albert Gore, Jr. (Democrat)	267	50,996,116	48.4%
Ralph Nader (Green)	—	2,783,728	2.7%

supporters demanded a hand count of these rejected ballots. Bush's lawyers filed suit to halt the recounts.

Florida secretary of state Katherine Harris refused to extend the deadline for certifying the Florida vote to allow for a hand recount. Democrats questioned Harris's impartiality, since she had cochaired Bush's Florida campaign and was an ally of Florida Governor Jeb Bush, the candidate's brother.

As various counties conducted hand counts, election officials scrutinized ballots to see whether the chads were detached, dangling, or "pregnant" (partially pushed out). On November 21 the Florida Supreme Court, with a preponderance of Democrats, unanimously held that the hand count should constitute the official results. Bush's legal team appealed to the U.S. Supreme Court, which, despite a well-established precedent of letting state courts decide electoral disputes, accepted the case. Overturning the Florida justices' ruling, the U.S. Supreme Court on December 4 sent the case back to Tallahassee for clarification.

Meanwhile, Secretary of State Harris had certified the Florida vote, awarding Bush the state. But on December 8, the Florida Supreme Court ordered an immediate recount of all ballots thrown out by voting machines. "At this rate," mused a radio commentator, "the Inaugural Ball will be a surprise party." The U.S. Supreme Court again heard an appeal, and on December 12, in a 5 to 4 vote, ordered an end to the recount. Republican appointees to the court generally supported Bush. Five Supreme Court justices had made George W. Bush president.

Ralph Nader, though winning only 3 percent of the vote, also helped put Bush in the White House. Had it not been for the 97,488 Floridians who voted for Nader, Gore would doubtless have won the state.

The election produced an evenly divided Senate, giving Vice President Cheney the deciding vote. (The Republicans narrowly held the House of Representatives.)

The Florida Election Dispute *A Fort Lauderdale judge scrutinizes a partially punched-out ballot in late November 2000.*

Hillary Rodham Clinton won election as senator from New York, becoming the first presidential wife to pursue a political career. Overall, the new Senate included thirteen women, a record number.

To the end, President Clinton continued his mix of statesmanlike and shady behavior. In January 2001, he issued tougher worker-safety regulations, particularly relating to repetitive-motion injuries common among computer users. He also issued an executive order protecting millions of acres of federal forest land from logging and road building.

On his last day in office, however, he pardoned 167 people, including his half-brother, facing drug charges; persons caught up in Clinton-era scandals; and white-collar offenders who were major Democratic contributors, including a commodities trader who had fled to Switzerland to avoid trial for tax evasion and other crimes. Despite Clinton's political skills and good intentions, few Americans expressed regret as he left Washington.

The George W. Bush Administration: A Conservative Turn in Domestic Politics

The election crisis over, Americans focused on the incoming president, fifty-four-year-old George W. Bush. After graduating from Yale, sitting out the Vietnam War in the Texas Air National Guard, and attending Harvard Business School, Bush returned to Texas and entered the oil business. Known for partying and heavy drinking since his college days, he was convicted of drunk driving in 1976, but then experienced a religious conversion and married a schoolteacher, Laura Welch, who helped bring stability to his life. Bush's business ventures did not thrive, but in 1989 he joined a consortium that bought the Texas Rangers baseball team. Frequently appearing at games, he used this visibility, plus his family connections, to win the Texas governorship in 1994.

Attention soon focused on the team Bush assembled. Colin Powell, former head of the Joint Chiefs of Staff, became secretary of state, and the highest ranking African-American ever to serve in a presidential administration. As national security adviser Bush named Condoleezza Rice of Stanford University, also an African-American.

Other Bush appointees were, like Vice President Cheney, veterans of earlier Republican administrations with strong corporate ties. Secretary of Defense Donald Rumsfeld had held the same post under President Ford and later headed a large pharmaceutical company. Treasury Secretary Paul O'Neill had been CEO of Alcoa Corporation. Army Secretary Thomas E. White came from Houston's Enron Corporation. To appease his party's right wing, Bush named ultra-conservative John Ashcroft, who had just lost a bid for reelection to the Senate, as attorney general.

Despite his razor-thin victory, Bush did not move to the center, as many had expected. Rather he tailored his policies to reflect the interests of the wealthy, corporate leaders, and the religious right. His probusiness outlook, combined with the influence of businesspeople in his inner circle and a desire to win favor with religious conservatives (whose alienation had helped defeat his father in 1992), shaped his administration.

Evangelical Protestants had voted overwhelmingly for Bush, and his political adviser Karl Rove and his chief speechwriter, an evangelical, paid close attention to this constituency, as well as to conservative Catholics. Bush's speeches included many religious allusions, and his policy proposals reflected the views of evangelicals and cultural conservatives. He addressed anti-abortion rallies (usually by telephone). Pursuing his so-called faith-based initiative, he set up a White House office to funnel federal funds to religious organizations providing social services. National Park Service officials permitted religious groups to erect mottos containing Bible verses in national parks. When a Massachusetts court in 2003 found no constitutional bar to gay marriage, Bush called for a constitutional amendment banning such unions and urged Congress to appropriate $1.2 billion to promote marriage among heterosexual couples.

Bush's education program, called No Child Left Behind, proposed standardized national basic-skills tests from grades three through eight, with penalties on schools that failed to measure up. He also called for a voucher system by which children could attend private or religious schools at taxpayers' expense. In 2001 Congress mandated annual testing and provided funds for tutors in poorly performing schools, but rejected the controversial voucher provision.

Fulfilling a campaign promise, Bush proposed a bill to cut taxes by $1.6 trillion over a ten-year period. The cuts would stimulate investment, he argued, as the economy faltered (see below). Democrats attacked the bill for giving the greatest tax breaks to the wealthiest taxpayers. Recalling the huge deficits that followed the 1981 Reagan tax cut, they also charged that Bush's plan reflected overly optimistic economic projections. In May Congress passed a $1.35 trillion tax cut—lower than Bush's proposal and somewhat less tilted toward the rich. As the economy worsened, second thoughts about Bush's tax cut increased. The *New York Times*, estimating the lost federal revenue over a twenty-year period at a staggering $4 trillion, warned that the shortfall could be covered only by dipping into social security and Medicare trust funds.

As Bush's conservative program unfolded, moderate Republicans grew restive. In May 2001, Vermont Senator James Jeffords left the Republican party to become an independent. With Jeffords's vote, the Democrats regained control of the Senate. Jeffords's action, observed political commentator Flora Lewis, offered "a sharp reminder that the voters did not choose the clear swing to the right that George W. Bush seems to assume."

Bush's energy bill reflected the industry's influence in the administration. Kenneth Lay, for example, head of Houston's Enron Corporation and a major GOP contributor, enjoyed access to top administration officials and the heads of federal regulatory agencies. The bill was drafted in secret meetings between Dick Cheney and energy-company executives.

Warning of America's dependence on imported oil, Bush proposed two thousand new electric power plants, including more nuclear power plants, and vastly expanded coal, oil, and natural-gas production, including mining and drilling in environmentally fragile regions such as Alaska's Arctic National Wildlife Refuge (ANWR). Energy conservation and research on renewable energy barely figured in the bill.

The Republican House passed a bill favored by the White House. It provided $27 billion in incentives for the domestic oil, gas, and coal industries and permitted drilling in the Arctic National Wildlife Refuge. In April 2002 the Democratic Senate passed a very different bill featuring tax breaks and other incentives to promote energy conservation and the use of renewable fuels, and forbidding drilling in the ANWR. The two bills went to a joint House-Senate conference committee.

The bill that finally emerged late in 2003 closely paralleled Bush's original proposal, without the controversial authorization of drilling in the ANWR. It provided many tax breaks and other incentives to energy companies, with little emphasis on conservation or environmental protection. Despite heavy administration pressure, however, the Senate took no action. The process illustrated the difficulties of governing in a climate of sharp partisan divisions.

Bush's attempt to placate the religious right without alienating moderate voters was illustrated by his maneuvering on the emotional issue of research on stem cells, which are produced during an early stage of human embryo development. Biomedical specialists and many bioethicists argued that the potential medical benefits justified stem-cell research. Some religious organizations as well as anti-abortion groups protested, arguing that such research could lead down a slippery slope of subordinating potential human life to scientific projects. Bush's compromise, announced in August 2001, permitted federal funding of research on stem-cell lines already held by laboratories, but barring funding for research on stem cells taken from embryos in the future.

A Go-It-Alone Foreign Policy; Pursuing Missile Defense   The administration of George W. Bush at first proceeded with scant regard for other nations' views. This contrasted with his father's more internationalist approach. On military matters, the younger Bush pursued programs initiated by his Republican predecessors.

Both these generalizations are illustrated by the administration's determination to build the antimissile system first proposed by President Reagan in 1983. Reagan's "Star Wars" initiative had been criticized as a fantasy, and its strategic rationale seemingly evaporated with the Cold War's end. Clinton had downgraded the program, but George W. Bush gave it high priority. True believers and military contractors argued that the technical problems could be solved. As for its strategic rationale, they now focused on possible missile attacks from "rogue states" such as North Korea.

Bush's enthusiasm for missile defense had diplomatic implications, because such a system would violate the 1972 Anti-Ballistic Missile (ABM) Treaty. Russian president Vladimir Putin, eager for U.S. investment and for a greater role in NATO, agreed to discuss dropping the ABM Treaty if both sides further reduced their remaining nuclear arsenals. The Bush administration valued Russia as an ally in the war against terrorism (see below) and as a potential supplier of oil should imports from the Middle East be disrupted, and accepted Putin's terms. In 2002, despite protests from other nations and arms-control specialists, the United States allowed the ABM Treaty to lapse. Soon after, Bush and Putin signed a treaty pledging to cut their nuclear arsenals by two-thirds within ten years. Fulfilling another of Moscow's objectives, NATO granted Russia a close consultative relationship.

In 2002 work began at Fort Greely, Alaska, on a missile defense facility that planners hoped would be operational by 2004. Alaskans who were worried about the state's economy welcomed the infusion of jobs and federal dollars the project promised. Pentagon planners envisioned a much expanded and extremely costly future system, including warship-based interceptors and modified laser-firing Boeing 747s.

In 2003, despite its concerns about nuclear proliferation, the administration requested funds to research tactical nuclear weapons capable of penetrating hardened underground bunkers. Congress refused to go along, however, at least temporarily sidetracking the project.

Other U.S. actions underscored the administration's go-it-alone approach. In 2001 the United States boycotted a U.N. conference in Bonn, Germany, considering an international treaty aimed at reducing global warming (see "Environmental Issues Persist" below). When most other nations, including the European Union and Japan, agreed to strengthen a 1972 treaty banning biological weapons, the

United States balked. The administration refused to join the International Criminal Court, created by the U.N. in 1998 to prosecute individuals charged with war crimes or crimes against humanity, claiming that U.S. officials might be unjustly prosecuted. The administration also rejected a U.N. agreement to regulate the global trade in handguns, a treaty banning discrimination against women ratified by 169 other nations, and a U.N. effort to reduce smoking worldwide.

The United Nations had long been a target of conservatives skeptical of international commitments. Beginning in 1994, conservatives in Congress led by Republican Jesse Helms of North Carolina had withheld payment of America's U.N. dues. By 2001 the back debt totaled $2.3 billion. Early in 2001 the Senate Foreign Relations Committee agreed to pay part of this sum and to resume payment of future dues at a reduced percentage rate. In 2001, in a symbolic action underscoring the growing resentment of America's strong-arm tactics, the United States was voted off the U.N. Human Rights Commission, on which it had served since 1947.

The Bush administration, like its predecessors, actively promoted U.S. trade interests, a fact underscored by its relations with China. In April 2001 a U.S. spy plane off China's coast collided with a Chinese aircraft monitoring it. The Chinese plane crashed, killing the pilot, and the damaged U.S. plane landed in China. Angry words followed, but $120 billion in annual trade spoke more loudly, and after negotiations China released the U.S. crew. Later that year President Bush attended an Asia-Pacific economic cooperation conference hosted by Beijing, and China formally entered the World Trade Organization.

The global economy remained a focus of protest, however. When the G-8 met at Genoa, Italy, in 2001, violent street protests resulted in one death and many arrests and injuries. To discourage protesters, the 2002 G-8 meeting was held in remote Calgary in the Canadian Rockies.

Despite Bush's commitment to foreign trade, domestic pressures influenced him as well. In 2002, responding to demands from U.S. steel producers and the steelworkers' union, Bush slapped tariffs of up to 30 percent on imported steel products for a three-year period. While the tariffs did not apply to Canada, Mexico, or certain developing nations, they did hit China, Japan, Russia, South Korea, and the EU, which protested this violation of free-trade principles. Whether the U.S. steel industry, with its steadily shrinking labor force and high production costs, could long survive even with tariff protection remained an open question.

RECESSION WOES; CAMPAIGN-FINANCE BATTLES; ENVIRONMENTAL DEBATES

A sharp recession abruptly ended the prosperity of the 1990s and raised questions about the wisdom of the tax cut. Disagreements over economic policy, combined with criticism of Bush's environmental actions and a long-running battle over campaign-finance reform, helped perpetuate the intense political partisanship as the Bush administration began.

End of the Economic Boom

The stock-market boom of the later 1990s barely outlasted the decade. As Asian and Latin American economies faltered, the U.S. economy suffered as well. In March 2001, the stock market recorded its worst week since 1989, falling by 6 percent. Millions of stockholders felt the pain. Consumer confidence fell, corporate profits plunged, and businesses announced layoffs. Ford fired five thousand managers and engineers. The unemployment rate rose from under 4 percent in 2000 to nearly 6 percent by November 2001. In that month alone, three hundred thousand workers lost their jobs.

The bursting of the Internet bubble worsened the downturn. By one calculation, nearly 250 dot-com businesses collapsed in a few months' time. The market value of the companies that did survive fell sharply. Instant millionaires watched their portfolios melt away.

To stimulate the economy, the Federal Reserve Board cut interest rates eleven times in 2001, to a forty-year low. The Bush administration, having based its tax-cut plan on the assumption of continued budget surpluses, now projected years of deficits. Democrats attacked the administration's overly optimistic economic projections and warned about threats to social security and Medicare funds. As an antirecession stimulus package, the administration proposed generous new tax breaks for corporations and the wealthy, and a speeding up of tax cuts already approved.

Few shed tears when the recession hit casinos, luxury boutiques, overpriced restaurants, and dealers in vintage wines and expensive cigars. But retirees with pension plans invested in the stock market and low-paid workers lacking job security also suffered as the recession that began in Silicon Valley and Wall Street spread ominously. Industrial production declined, and every state lost jobs. Service-sector employment fell faster in the last quarter of 2001 than in any three-month period since World War II. Unskilled workers and former welfare recipients seeking entry-level jobs faced problems. Openings for temporary workers dropped precipitously. The long economic boom had ended with a thud, and the impact spread through society. An anemic recovery began in 2002, but it was slowed by business scandals that eroded investor confidence (see below).

The Rocky Path of Campaign-Finance Reform

In Congress, meanwhile, two senators—Arizona Republican John McCain and Wisconsin Democrat Russ Feingold—carried on the battle for campaign-finance reform. They targeted so-called soft-money contributions made to political parties (rather than to specific candidates) by individuals and lobbying organizations seeking to influence legislation. Such lobbies ranged from (mostly pro-Republican) business associations, tobacco companies, anti-abortion groups, and the National Rifle Association to the (mostly pro-Democratic) National Education Association, trial lawyers association, and labor unions. Given the soaring cost of TV advertising, soft money loomed increasingly large in electoral campaigns. In the 1997–1998 electoral cycle the national parties raised more than $190 million in soft money; Wall Street investment companies alone gave $9 million to the Republican party and $6.2 million to the Democratic party.

President Clinton had paid lip service to reform while endlessly appearing at fundraising events, and as scandal gripped the White House, the campaign-finance issue had faded. In the 2000 election, soft-money contributions reached nearly $500 million.

McCain and Feingold persevered, and in April 2001 the Senate passed a version of their bill. In the Republican-controlled House, Christopher Shays, a Connecticut Republican, and Massachusetts Democrat Martin Meehan championed the cause. The Shays-Meehan bill passed in 2002. A committee reconciled the House and Senate versions, and Bush signed the bill. It banned soft-money contributions to national parties by lobbying organizations and phony TV "issue ads" that were really aimed at influencing elections, and included other measures seeking to reduce the torrent of money sloshing through the election system. The law faced legal challenges on free-speech grounds, but in December 2003 the Supreme Court upheld all its major provisions.

Whether the new law would achieve its purpose remained unclear as politicians and special-interest groups searched for ways to circumvent it. As the battle went on, skeptics compared politicians of both parties, dependent on an endless flow of campaign money, to drug addicts facing the agonies of withdrawal.

Environmental Issues Persist   The Three Mile Island and *Exxon Valdez* incidents (see Chapters 30 and 31) underscored modern technology's environmental risks, and a 1984 disaster in Bhopal, India, in which deadly gases from a U.S.-owned chemical plant killed seventeen hundred people highlighted the global scope of these risks. Beyond specific incidents, long-term environmental changes gravely jeopardized human well-being. The late twentieth and early twenty-first centuries brought growing environmental awareness, but a mixed record of environmental action.

With the Cold War over, Americans faced the estimated $150-billion cost of cleaning up nuclear-weapons facilities, including disposing of 70,000 tons of highly radioactive uranium and plutonium from dismantled nuclear weapons and aging nuclear-power plants. The Hanford Nuclear Reservation in Washington State was a vast dump of radioactive waste. The disposal of this material, which will remain lethal for 10,000 years, stirred political disputes and grass-roots protest. In 1997 scientists reported water seepage into the vast cave intended for nuclear-waste storage at Nevada's Yucca Mountain. In 2002, over objections from environmentalists, Nevada politicians, and Las Vegas civic leaders, the Senate approved the Yucca Mountain site for storage beginning in 2010. Lawsuits and controversy continued, however.

Other environmental and health risks arose from atmospheric changes linked to industrial processes. Acid rain carrying sulfur dioxide and other pollutants from U.S. factories and auto exhaust threatened Appalachian forests and Canadian lakes. Fluorocarbons from spray cans, refrigeration equipment, and other sources depleted the upper-atmosphere ozone layer, allowing higher levels of solar radiation to reach Earth's surface, increasing skin-cancer risks and other health hazards.

The threat of global warming seemed especially urgent. As carbon dioxide and other gases produced by fossil-fuel emissions and deforestation (as well as naturally occurring sources) accumulated in the lower atmosphere, the resulting "greenhouse effect" prevented Earth's heat from escaping. Scientists predicted a 40 percent increase in carbon dioxide emissions by 2020. Long-term global warming could disrupt agricultural production and plant and animal ecosystems. In the most dire scenario, rising sea levels from melting polar ice could flood low-lying coastal regions.

Heightening global-warming fears, the ten hottest years of the twentieth century all occurred after 1985. In Alaska, where the average annual temperature rose seven degrees from 1972 to 2002, rising water levels in the Chukchi Sea threatened coastal villages, and a new species of beetle that arrived with the warmer weather devastated spruce forests. Highways buckled as the permafrost melted, and engineers warned that the Alaska pipeline stretching from Prudhoe Bay to Valdez could be destabilized.

Some environmental gains were recorded. U.S. emissions of the principal air pollutants fell more than 60 percent from 1970 to 1999. In 1996–1997, Congress strengthened pesticide regulation and the Environmental Protection Agency (EPA) announced new air-quality standards to reduce soot and ground-level ozone. (In 2001 the Supreme Court unanimously upheld the EPA's right to establish such standards.) In 1997 the EPA created an environmental "superfund" to clean up hazardous-waste sites. By 2001 more than thirteen hundred such sites had been designated, though the pace of cleanup proved slow.

The first three years of the George W. Bush administration dismayed environmentalists. On taking office, Bush announced that he would not implement proposed EPA measures to reduce carbon dioxide emissions from power plants. As noted above, the administration's energy program stressed increased production and less regulation, with little attention to environmental concerns. Conservation might be a "sign of personal virtue," Vice President Cheney suggested, but offered no basis for "a sound, comprehensive energy policy." Some of Bush's environmental actions roused particular opposition. An order permitting higher levels of arsenic in drinking water proved a public-relations nightmare. The proposed oil drilling in the Arctic National Wildlife Reserve and other public lands stirred intense resistance.

The United States under Bush, alone among 178 nations, including 38 industrialized nations, boycotted a U.N.-sponsored effort, launched at a conference in Kyoto, Japan, in 1997, to combat global warming by setting emissions standards for industrialized nations. Bush charged that the treaty threatened America's economic growth and standard of living. The administration refused to participate in an international conference in Bonn, Germany, called specifically to meet U.S. objections to the Kyoto treaty. The treaty was "not in [America's] interests," declared National Security Adviser Condoleezza Rice tersely, offering no alternative proposals for cutting industrial emissions.

These actions came at a time when the United States, with under 5 percent of the world's population, accounted for 25 percent of global energy consumption. In 2001 passenger-vehicle fuel economy (including the popular light trucks and sport-utility vehicles) fell to the lowest level in a decade. Yet the Bush administration appeared to envision no slacking in this rate of consumption.

The administration's environmental insensitivity flew in the face of mounting scientific evidence. A National Science Foundation (NSF) report in 2001 concluded that global warming was real, and likely to become more serious.

Thanks in part to his approach to energy and environmental issues, Bush's approval rating stood at only about 50 percent midway through his first year. But suddenly, politics as usual went out the window, as the nation faced a crisis that would test it to the limit.

September 11 and Beyond

The course of American history changed profoundly in September 2001, when a terrorist attack left thousands dead and the nation in shock. The nation's priorities shifted at home and abroad as President Bush summoned the country to a war on terrorism. At home, the administration took far-reaching measures to enhance security. While all Americans agreed on the objective of these actions, some saw a threat to civil liberties in the vast strengthening of governmental powers of surveillance and detention.

Having shown little concern for world opinion earlier, Bush now called upon all nations to join the United States in a drive to eradicate terrorism. A broad coalition of nations supported the U.S. effort to uproot Osama bin Laden's Al Qaeda organization, the group responsible for the 9/11 attacks, from its base in Afghanistan. However, America's subsequent invasion of Iraq proved far more controversial. Despite the administration's single-minded focus on the antiterrorism campaign, other world issues demanded attention, particularly the Israeli-Palestinian conflict.

Despite the post–September 11 unity impulse, major differences soon arose over Bush's domestic and international policies. Contentiousness deepened as Americans reacted to revelations of greed, deception, and fraud in some of the nation's largest corporations during the boom years of the 1990s.

America Under Attack   Throughout American history, watershed events have marked historic turning points. The Confederates' attack on Fort Sumter in Charleston harbor on April 12, 1861, began the Civil War. The Japanese attack on Pearl Harbor on December 7, 1941, characterized by President Roosevelt as "a day that will live in infamy," drew the United States into World War II.

Another such pivotal moment came on the morning of September 11, 2001. As Americans watched their televisions in horror, the blazing twin towers of New York's World Trade Center crashed to the earth, carrying more than 2,600 men and

America Under Attack *Rescuers remove a flag-draped body from the ruins of the World Trade Center.*

women to their deaths, including nearly 350 firefighters. A simultaneous attack on the Pentagon left 125 dead on the ground, and a plane crash in western Pennsylvania directly related to these events killed still more innocent people. Only the Civil War battle of Antietam, in which 3,650 soldiers died, brought a higher single-day toll of American dead.

Many people trapped by the flames leapt to their death. Father Mychal Judge, a fire department chaplain, was killed by fallling debris after administering last rites to victims. Firemen placed his body on the altar of nearby St. Peter's Catholic church. Businesses with offices in the Twin Towers suffered catastrophic losses. One brokerage firm lost 600 workers.

New York City essentially shut down. Bridges were closed; subway trains stopped running. Commercial aircraft were grounded; incoming flights from abroad were ordered to return or diverted to Canada. Only military fighters patrolled the skies over New York and Washington. President Bush put the military on high alert and mobilized the national guard.

The World Trade Center towers and the Pentagon had been struck by three commercial aircraft piloted by hijackers in a carefully planned assault on these highly visible symbols of U.S. economic and military power. The Pennsylvania crash occurred when heroic passengers prevented terrorists from diverting the plane to another target, possibly the White House.

The destruction of the World Trade Center that terrorists had failed to accomplish eight years before (see chapter introduction) had now tragically been achieved. Along with the dead on the ground, 246 passengers and crew, plus 19 hijackers, died in the four planes. The government soon identified the hijackers, all from the Middle East, and traced their pre-9/11 actions, including enrollment in Florida flight-training schools.

In a few hours of terror, a new and menacing era began. Terrorism—whether assassinations or bombed buildings, buses, ships, and planes—was familiar elsewhere, of course, and many U.S. citizens, civilian and military, had died in earlier terrorist attacks in the 1980s and 1990s. The 1995 bombing of the Oklahoma City federal building had made clear that America was not immune to such attacks. But now terrorism had erupted on U.S. soil on a far vaster and more horrifying scale. For the first time since the War of 1812, a foreign enemy had attacked the American homeland.

A wave of patriotism swept the nation as political divisions were put aside. Flags flew from homes, public buildings, and automobile antennas. Irving Berlin's "God Bless America," a World War II favorite, became the anthem of the moment. "United We Stand" proclaimed banners, billboards, and bumper stickers. President Bush visited a mosque to urge Americans to distinguish between a handful of terrorists and the world's 1.2 billion Muslims, including as many as 6 million in the United States. Nevertheless, many Middle Easterners in America faced hostility and even violence in the post-attack period.

The damaged New York Stock Exchange closed for six days. When it reopened, stock prices plunged. Even after stocks slowly edged upward, retail sales declined and consumer confidence remained fragile. The airline and travel industries reeled as jittery travelers canceled trips or chose ground transportation. A $15 billion bailout of the airlines by Congress helped, but the industry's problems remained. New York's tourist and entertainment industries suffered. "Vacant Rooms, Empty Tables, and Scared Tourists," headlined one New York newspaper.

Post–September 11 anxieties deepened in early October when an editor at the Florida offices of the *National Enquirer,* a tabloid newspaper that had attacked Osama bin Laden, died of anthrax, a rare and deadly bacterial disease contracted from spores sent in a letter. Letters containing high-grade anthrax spores next appeared in the office of NBC news anchor Tom Brokaw and Senators Tom Daschle and Patrick Leahy. The Senate Office Building was closed for decontamination. Four other persons, two of them postal workers, died from anthrax-tainted pieces of mail.

Analysis indicated that the anthrax spores had probably been made in a U.S. research laboratory, and investigators focused on finding a domestic source of the deadly mailings. Fears revived in February 2004 when a letter containing the poison ricin reached the office of Senator Bill Frist, the majority leader.

Battling Terrorist Networks Abroad President Bush, speaking from the White House on September 12, declared the attacks an "act of war." On September 15, the Senate unanimously authorized Bush to use "all necessary and appropriate force" to respond.

On September 20, as had other presidents in times of crisis, a somber Bush addressed a joint session of Congress. He blamed the attack on the Al Qaeda terrorist network headed by Osama bin Laden from headquarters in Afghanistan. Bin Laden, already under indictment for the 1998 attack on U.S. embassies in Africa, had long denounced America for supporting Saudi Arabia's corrupt regime, stationing "infidel" troops on Saudi soil, backing Israel, and spreading wickedness through its sinful mass culture. (Ironically, the United States had aided bin Laden in the 1980s, when he was fighting Russian forces in Afghanistan.) A videotape discovered in Afghanistan in which bin Laden described how he planned the attack and even laughed about the massive damage clinched his guilt. Though bin Laden invoked the name of Allah, and claimed to have acted on behalf of Islam, most Islamic leaders repudiated him and condemned attacks on innocent civilians.

Bush announced a military campaign to uproot Al Qaeda and its protectors, the Pakistan-trained Islamicist group called the Taliban, which had seized power in Afghanistan in 1996. As part of a program to disrupt the terrorists' money supply, Bush froze the assets of organizations with possible terrorist links.

Despite the pro-Taliban sympathies of Muslim fundamentalists in Pakistan, Bush enlisted the cooperation of Pakistan's military government. Complicating U.S. military planning was Afghanistan's forbidding terrain and patchwork of ethnic and tribal groups. The major anti-Taliban force, the Northern Alliance, was an uneasy coalition of rival warlords.

The military phase of the antiterrorist operation, launched on October 7, achieved impressive success. Battered by U.S. bombing and an offensive by Northern Alliance forces, the Taliban soon surrendered Kabul (the Afghan capital) and other strongholds. British, Canadian, Pakistani, and other forces played an important role in this campaign. By mid-December, despite sporadic resistance, the United States claimed victory. More than six hundred captured Al Qaeda fighters, or persons caught up in the fighting, were transferred to prison facilities at the U.S. base in Guantánamo, Cuba. As more U.S. Special Forces arrived, a remnant of Al Qaeda fighters retreated to Pakistan or to fortified caves in the rugged mountains of eastern Afghanistan, between Kabul and the Khyber Pass. The whereabouts of Osama bin Laden remained unknown.

International support for this phase of America's antiterrorist campaign remained strong. British Prime Minister Tony Blair proved a pillar of strength. For the first time, NATO forces fought in defense of a member nation.

The fighting was brutal. Northern Alliance fighters killed some Taliban even after they had surrendered. In November, Taliban prisoners, mostly Pakistanis, among hundreds held at a fortress near Kunduz, seized weapons from their guards. In a wild night of fighting and bombing, most of the prisoners were killed. The civilian population, already devastated by drought, civil war, and Taliban oppression, suffered terribly. Despite U.S. and international relief efforts, including food drops, the refugee situation—worsened by winter weather—remained desperate.

A British-led international force was mobilized to maintain law and order in Kabul, but the diplomatic challenge of welding rival factions into a post-Taliban government proved difficult. In June 2002, with U.S. support, an assembly of

Afghan regional and ethnic leaders called a loya jirga established a new government and chose an interim prime minister, Hamid Karzai. The nation-building effort had the blessing of Afghanistan's eighty-nine-year-old former king, who returned to Kabul after years in exile.

The loya jirga initially bogged down in rancorous debate among Afghanistan's two major ethnic and linguistic groups, the majority Pashtuns and the Tajiks. At times it seemed on the verge of breaking up. But early in 2004, thanks to the negotiating skills of a seasoned U.N. envoy from Algeria, the loya jirga approved a constitution. It protected women's rights, finessed the competing claims of Pashtuns and Tajiks, and established Afghanistan as an Islamic republic with an elected president and assembly and an independent judiciary.

But Afghanistan remained violent and unstable. Al Qaeda and Taliban insurgents carried out periodic bombings and other attacks. Early in 2004, suicide bombers struck in Kabul, and eight GIs died in another town when a possibly booby-trapped Taliban weapons cache exploded. "There is no shortage of volunteers," claimed a Taliban leader ominously. President Karzai and other officials faced assassination attempts, and outside Kabul, regional warlords and their heavily armed followers controlled the countryside.

U.S. efforts to ferret out Al Qaeda and Taliban fighters sometimes had tragic results, stirring bitter resentment. In one incident, U.S. bombs killed at least thirty members of a village wedding party when pilots mistook their celebratory gunfire for hostile attack. Adding to the tension, Arabic TV and radio periodically broadcast video and audio recordings in which Osama bin Laden, still at large, urged more attacks on the United States. Western nations only partially fulfilled pledges of billions in reconstruction and development aid. As Washington's attention turned elsewhere, Afghanistan's future remained uncertain.

Shadowing the post–September 11 strategic debate was a troubling question: would breaking up Al Qaeda's centers of power end the terrorist threat? While most Arab leaders repudiated bin Laden, many among the impoverished, ill-educated Arab masses were receptive to his anti-American harangues. Ending terrorism, clearly, involved not only military operations, but also long-term diplomatic, political, and ideological efforts.

Tightening Home-Front Security
The Bush administration's campaign in Afghanistan enjoyed broad support at home. The administration's domestic antiterrorism campaign proved more controversial, however. Despite Republicans' traditional hostility to big government, the administration and Congress significantly expanded the federal government's role in many aspects of American life.

On September 20, 2001, Bush appointed former Pennsylvania governor Tom Ridge to head a new White House office of homeland security. Ridge and the Congress gave high priority to the newly urgent issue of aviation security. While some urged that the nation's 28,000 airport security workers become federal employees, others opposed this expansion of the federal labor force. Late in 2001,

Congress required all security personnel to be U.S. citizens and to meet rigorous job criteria and performance requirements set by a newly created Transportation Security Administration. As air travelers faced long lines at check-in, armed air marshals accompanied some flights. Other flights were cancelled altogether because of security threats.

The USA-Patriot Act, the administration's sweeping antiterrorist law, was overwhelmingly passed by Congress in October 2001. This law extended the government's powers to monitor telephone and e-mail communications, including conversations between prisoners and their lawyers. It also authorized authorities to seize suspects' financial, medical, computer, and even library records. Some conservatives who had applauded John Ashcroft's appointment as attorney general were troubled by his calls for vastly expanded federal powers after September 11.

In May 2002 news media reported disturbing evidence of missed clues before the terrorist attack. In August 2001, for example, a flight school in Minnesota warned the FBI of a suspicious person named Zacarias Moussaoui who had tried to enroll. Moussaoui had been arrested on immigration charges, but the Justice Department had denied a request by the Minneapolis FBI office for permission to check his computer. (After September 11 Moussaoui's link to bin Laden was discovered, and in 2002 he went on trial in Virginia.) Late in 2002 Congress created a bipartisan national commission, chaired by former New Jersey governor Thomas Kean, to investigate intelligence failures and other circumstances relevant to the 9/11 attacks, including a lack of communication among and within various government agencies, notably the FBI and the CIA.

Diverting attention from these potentially damaging inquiries, President Bush seized the moment to propose a new cabinet-level Department of Homeland Security to coordinate the domestic antiterrorism effort. The new department, with 170,000 employees, approved by Congress in November 2002, absorbed twenty-two government agencies, including the Coast Guard, the Customs Service, the Immigration and Naturalization Service, and the Federal Emergency Management Agency. It did not, however, include the FBI or the CIA.

The new department's most visible public face was a color-coded security-alert system reflecting the government's assessment of the current risk level. On the second anniversary of 9/11, and again in December 2003, apparently responding to heightened security threats, Ridge raised the alert level from yellow to orange, the next-most dangerous.

After September 11, the Justice Department detained more than one thousand Middle Easterners living in the United States, some for visa violations, and held them for questioning without filing charges or, in most cases, revealing their names. In an Orwellian touch, Attorney General Ashcroft claimed that to identify the detainees would violate their civil rights. Some local police officials refused to cooperate in the wholesale roundup of persons not accused of crimes simply on the basis of their ethnicity or national origin.

In November, without consulting Congress, Bush signed an executive order empowering the government to try noncitizens accused of fomenting terrorism in secret military tribunals rather than in the civilian justice system. While precedent existed for such tribunals in wartime, this proposal roused opposition from civil libertarians and others. Opinion polls found Americans divided on the use of military tribunals, but strongly at odds with Bush's failure to consult Congress.

While few questioned the need for heightened security, the civil-liberties implications of all these measures raised growing concern. Over 150 cities and towns passed resolutions criticizing the Patriot Act for infringing citizens' rights. Addressing the New York Bar Association early in 2003, Supreme Court justice Stephen Breyer noted pointedly: "The Constitution always matters, perhaps particularly so in times of emergency." That July, Congress repealed a Patriot Act provision that allowed the FBI to search suspects' homes without informing them.

In December 2003, a New York federal appeals court heard a case involving José Padilla, a U.S. citizen arrested in May 2002 on suspicion of planning a bombing and imprisoned him as an "enemy combatant" with no access to a lawyer or to family members. The court ruled that the government had violated Padilla's Fifth Amendment right to due process of law. The Justice Department appealed, and in April 2004 the Supreme Court heard arguments in the case, setting the stage for a ruling on the civil-liberties issues raised by the antiterrorism campaign. With key provisions of the Patriot Act scheduled to expire in 2005, President Bush in his 2004 State of the Union address called on Congress to extend the law. Opponents mobilized to insist on modifications.

Meanwhile, despite protests by the International Red Cross, Amnesty International, and civil-liberties organizations, the U.S. military continued to hold at Guantánamo around 650 prisoners, some in their early teens, most captured in Afghanistan or Pakistan, with no legal representation or outside contact. In December 2003, in a case involving three Guantánamo prisoners, a California federal appeals court ordered their release or transfer to the civil-court system. The Justice Department appealed this ruling, too, to the Supreme Court.

WAR IN IRAQ AND ITS PAINFUL AFTERMATH

While the military action against Al Qaeda and its Taliban protectors in Afghanistan enjoyed broad support, the next front in Bush's war on terrorism proved highly controversial. In his 2002 State of the Union address, Bush had identified three nations as an "Axis of Evil" that menaced U.S. security: Iraq, Iran, and North Korea. Of these, Iraq topped the list. Iraqi strongman Saddam Hussein had been a thorn in America's flesh since the Persian Gulf War, which had left him weakened but still in power. Even before 9/11, some prominent conservatives had called for his overthrow to complete the "unfinished business" of the Gulf War.

In a barrage of speeches in 2002–2003, Bush, Cheney, and other administration officials accused Saddam of complicity in the 9/11 attacks. They further insisted that Saddam possessed chemical and biological weapons and was actively pursuing a nuclear-weapons capability. U.N. weapons inspectors, sent to Iraq after

Saddam Hussein
The Iraqi strongman following his arrest in December 2003, after eight months in hiding.

the Persian Gulf War to monitor Iraq's weapons programs, had departed in 1998 when the Iraqis denied them access to Saddam's presidential palaces. Clearly, the administration insisted, Saddam posed a terrible and imminent threat to American security. Further, they suggested, overthrowing Saddam could lead to other regime changes in the Middle East and promote peace and democracy in the region. They also noted Saddam's well-documented brutality against his opponents, including restive Kurds in the north and Islamic Shiites in the south. In short, the administration insisted, Saddam's ouster would not only advance the war on terrorism but also transform the entire Middle East. Most Iraqis would welcome American troops with open arms, Cheney predicted.

Some prominent Democrats and even a few Republican leaders, as well as religious groups and organizations committed to conflict-resolution through diplomacy, opposed the administration position. Charging that a preemptive war would violate U.S. principles, the critics challenged the administration to produce firm evidence that Saddam posed an immediate threat to the United States, and warned that such a war could unleash turmoil across the Arab world and bog down U.S. forces for years. Critics also cautioned that the preoccupation with Saddam could undermine the larger antiterrorist campaign.

British Prime Minister Tony Blair backed the administration, as did Italy, Spain, Poland, and other smaller nations. France, Germany, other European nations, as well as Canada, Mexico, and most Arab leaders objected. To counter the rush to war, they called for a U.N. resolution demanding that Iraq grant complete and unrestricted access to U.N. weapons inspectors.

Under pressure to secure U.N. backing, President Bush in September 2002 presented the case against Saddam in a U.N. address. Despite deep divisions in U.S. public opinion, the House and Senate in October passed resolutions authorizing U.S. military action against Iraq. Republican lawmakers embraced the resolutions while Democrats divided, fearful of opposing Bush as an election neared but concerned about a unilateral, preemptive war with no clear plan for dealing with a post-Saddam Iraq. On November 8, the U.N. Security Council unanimously adopted a resolution imposing tough new weapons inspections on Iraq. Baghdad agreed and U.N. inspectors returned.

The U.S. administration continued the buildup for war, however, unleashing protests at home and abroad. As antiwar marchers rallied in London, Paris, Rome, and other cities, the level of anti-American sentiment reached alarming proportions. In a February 2003 U.N. address, Secretary of State Powell again insisted that Iraq possessed weapons of mass destruction. Again, however, the U.N. Security Council refused to authorize an attack, calling instead for continued pressure on Iraq to cooperate with the weapons-inspection process.

Nevertheless, on March 20, 2003, after an extended military buildup, a U.S. force in excess of 100,000, supplemented by 10,000 British troops, invaded southern Iraq. While the British seized the southern city of Basra, a center of Iraq's oil industry, the Americans moved north toward Baghdad, the capital, which fell on April 5. Saddam Hussein eluded capture until December, however, when he was found hiding near Tikrit, his birthplace and center of power. Two of his sons had earlier died in a gun battle as they resisted capture.

The Americans occupied Iraqi government buildings and pulled down a huge statue of Saddam that dominated Baghdad. Except for officials and supporters of Saddam's Baath party, most Iraqis, particularly the Shiites and Kurds, welcomed Saddam's overthrow. On May 1, aboard the aircraft carrier *Abraham Lincoln* anchored off San Diego, before a banner proclaiming "Mission Accomplished," President Bush declared the end of major hostilities in Iraq. Signaling trouble ahead, however, looters in liberated Baghdad had invaded the national museum and the national library, stealing a vast hoard of cultural treasures.

President Bush named L. Paul Bremer III to administer postwar Iraq. Bremer set up a Governing Council representing Iraq's religious and ethnic groups, but it initially exercised little authority. Bremer also worked to restore Iraq's electric power, communications, transportation, educational system, and medical services, as well as the nation's vital oil industry, its main source of income, all suffering from the effects of war and neglect. Multimillion-dollar reconstruction contracts went to large U.S. businesses, some of which, such as the Halliburton Corporation, formerly headed by Vice President Cheney, had close ties to the administration and were major Republican contributors.

In September 2003, President Bush requested $87 billion for expenses connected with Iraq's occupation and reconstruction. With budget deficits mushrooming, this sum shocked legislators, but Congress appropriated the money. The long-range cost of the Iraq operation, warned Paul Bremer, was "almost impossible to exaggerate."

The monumental task was complicated by continued violence in Iraq carried out by Saddam loyalists and others unhappy with the American occupation, possibly reinforced by outside terrorists. Bombings, sniper attacks, and land mines planted on roadways took a steady toll of GIs and innocent bystanders. Surface-to-air missiles brought down several U.S. helicopters. British, Spanish, and Italian occupation forces suffered casualties as well. Much of the violence erupted in the so-called "Sunni Triangle" north of Baghdad, a center of pro-Saddam sentiment. U.S. authorities claimed steady progress against the insurgents, but the attacks continued. As GIs conducted raids and searched houses for insurgents and weapons, Iraqi resentment deepened.

The insurgents' campaign of disruption also targeted international organizations and Iraqis cooperating with the Americans. A woman member of the U.S.-appointed Governing Council was assassinated. In August 2003, a lethal truck bomb destroyed the U.N.'s Baghdad headquarters, killing seventeen, including the U.N.'s chief envoy in Iraq. Soon after, a massive car bomb in the sacred Shiite city of Najaf killed 125, including a leading Shiite cleric whose brother served on the Governing Council. In October, terrorists bombed the International Red Cross's Baghdad office.

As conditions deteriorated, President Bush in November 2003 instructed Bremer to transfer governing power to Iraqis by June 30, 2004. Complicating this task, Iraq's leading Shiite cleric, Grand Ayatollah Ali al-Sistani, rejected a U.S. plan for choosing the new government by regional caucuses, and instead demanded direct national elections—a procedure that would assure the Shiite majority a leading role. In response to a U.S. request, U.N. Secretary General Kofi Annan agreed to send a team to Iraq to help prepare election procedures. Observed a leading German newspaper, *Die Zeit:* "With the Bush administration politely asking the U.N. for help in Iraq, Gulliver now realizes that . . . the most important interests require legitimacy and cooperation, especially in Iraq."

As the casualties and costs mounted in Iraq, so did home-front uneasiness. Many criticized Washington's inadequate planning for the postwar phase. The administration's arguments for starting the war faced heavy scrutiny. No evidence proved Saddam's involvement in the 9/11 attacks. Indeed, Islamic fundamentalists like Osama bin Laden and his followers hated Saddam's secular Baath party.

The claim that Saddam possessed weapons of mass destruction (WMD) proved similarly unfounded. After the war, the Bush administration sent 1,200 weapons inspectors to Iraq, but early in 2004 the head of the inspection team, David Kay, reported that no WMD had been found. While some administration officials insisted that the search go on, President Bush retreated to the more general claim that the world was better off without Saddam. In the 2004 State of the Union address, the president spoke vaguely of "weapons-of-mass-destruction-related program activities." Bush reluctantly agreed to demands for an inquiry into the entire WMD fiasco. Debate centered on whether prewar intelligence had been faulty or Bush, Cheney, and the others had exaggerated the WMD danger to build support for a war they were determined to wage.

More broadly, the critics argued that the United States should have supported strengthened U.N. inspections, which had successfully monitored Iraq's weapons programs in 1991–1998, and again briefly in 2003, rather than launching a war that exacted a heavy toll in U.S. lives and treasure and squandered the world sympathy extended to America after 9/11. The administration's defenders responded that despite the problems, the Iraq war was worthwhile and a legitimate extension of the war on terrorism.

Adding to the administration's woes, the bipartisan commission investigating the 9/11 attacks held open hearings early in spring 2004 in which Richard Clark, a top government counter-terrorism advisor, testified that the Bush administration had failed to give urgent priority to pre-9/11 intelligence warning of a likely Al Qaeda terrorist attack in the United States. After 9/11, Clark further asserted, administration officials seemed obsessed with Iraq, even thoough Al Qaeda was based in Afghanistan. Clark elaborated his charges in TV interviews and a best-selling book, *Against All Enemies*. National Security Advisor Condoleezza Rice, after initially refusing to testify in open hearings, eventually appeared before the commission to deny Clark's charges. Deepening the controversy, Washington journalist Bob Woodward of Watergate fame suggested in his 2004 book *Plan of Attack* that Secretary of State Colin Powell, critical of the Iraq invasion plan, had been marginalized in the decisionmaking process.

Meanwhile, the situation in Iraq further deteriorated. When American authorities shut down the newspaper of a violently anti-American young Shiite cleric, Moqtada Sadr, in March 2004, his militant supporters unleashed a bloody anti-American uprising as Sadr took refuge in the holy city of Najaf. Further north, in the Sunni Triangle, insurgents in Fallujah ambushed four American civilian contract workers in late March, burned their truck, and brutalized their charred bodies. As fighting raged around Najaf and Fallujah, and attacks continued in Baghdad and elsewhere, the situation looked grim. Comparisons to Vietnam were heard with increasing frequency. A total of 153 soldiers died in Iraq in April 2004, the bloodiest month of the conflict, bringing the total since the war began to nearly 750 GIs dead and more than 4000 wounded, many seriously.

As conditions worsened, the fragile coalition of governments with troops in Iraq weakened. On March 11, 2004, bombs planted on crowded commuter trains in Madrid killed 191 and injured 1800. Spanish authorities soon arrested suspects belonging to a Morocco-based Islamic extremist group. On March 14, Spanish voters defeated the pro-U.S. government and elected a socialist government that proceeded to withdraw all Spanish troops from Iraq.

Meanwhile, the Bush administration pressed forward with plans to turn over power to an Iraqi authority on June 30. To facilitate the process, the United States turned to a special U.N. envoy, Lakhdar Brahimi, who proposed a plan for an interim authority to exercise limited powers until elections could be held. Having earlier dismissed the U.N., the administration now called upon the world body to help resolve the crisis.

U.S. aurhtories made clear that American forces would remain in Iraq for the indefinite future, however, and that the U.S. military would continue to control security matters. A fresh crisis for the administration arose in May 2004 with the release of graphic photographs of the abuse and sexual humiliation of Iraqi prisoners held in U.S. custody at Baghdad's notorious Abu Ghraib prison, scene of earlier torture and killings by Saddam Hussein's regime. As the International Red Cross confirmed reprts of more widespread abuses of prisoners, Americans reacted in disgust and disbelief, anti-Americanism in the Arab world and in Europe intensified, and Iraqis demanded ever more vehemently that the Americans leave the country. Leading Democrats and even some Republicans called for the resignation of Secretary of Defense Donald Rumsfeld. President Bush defended Rumsfeld and insisted that the goal of installing a free and democratic regime in Iraq remained unchanged, but the final outcome of his venture into Iraq, launched with such bravado in March 2003, seemed increasingly uncertain.

Meanwhile, as the terrorist threat erupted elsewhere in the world, the campaign to contain it widened as well. The CIA and other security agencies tracked Middle Eastern terrorist cells in various European nations. In Pakistan, President Pervez Musharraf, who allied himself with the United States after 9/11, survived two assassination attempts by Islamic fundamentalists. Early in 2004, Pakistan's leading nuclear scientist confessed to having sold nuclear-weapons technology to North Korea, Libya, and Iran.

Indonesia, another predominantly Muslim country, was also a hotbed of Islamic fundamentalism. A nightclub bombing on the resort island of Bali in October 2002 killed more than 200, including many young Australian visitors. The bomber, an Islamic extremist, was tried and sentenced to death. A top Al Qaeda operative implicated in the bombing of the *U.S.S. Cole* in 2000 and other terrorist attacks was also seized in Indonesia. Post- 9/11 terrorist bombings in Morocco, Saudi Arabia, Turkey, and Spain further underscored the global scope of the threat.

The antiterrorist campaign did record some gains. After Saddam's overthrow, Iran agreed to U.N. inspections to verify that it did not possess WMD. So, too, did Libya, a nation long identified with terrorism, including the 1998 bombing of Pan Am flight 103 over Scotland. North Korea, the isolated and impoverished communist nation ruled by the unpredictable Kim Jong Il, posed special dangers. Despite its pledges to the contrary, North Korea flaunted its nuclear-weapons program and rattled its Asian neighbors with missile tests. Administration officials feared that North Korea might pass nuclear materials or know-how to Al Qaeda or other terrorist organizations. Although President Bush had included North Korea in his "axis of evil," the administration, in cooperation with China, South Korea, and Japan, pursued a diplomatic approach, offering aid and security guarantees if North Korea would halt its nuclear program and admit inspectors.

The Israeli-Palestinian Conflict Worsens   The war on terrorism diverted American attention from the ongoing conflict between Israel, backed by the United States, and the Palestinians, supported by the Arab world and many Europeans. The issues were linked, however, since a major grievance of the terrorists was U.S. economic and military support of Israel and Israel's occupation of, and promotion of Jewish settlements in, the Palestinian territories of Gaza and the West Bank.

With Yasir Arafat's rejection of Israel's peace plan at Camp David and the launching of a second Intifada in 2000, violence in the region exploded. Suicide bombings took many Israeli lives as the bombers deliberately chose crowded targets such as buses and restaurants.

Israel retaliated, using U.S.-supplied tanks and military aircraft to attack Palestinian targets in the West Bank and Gaza, and assassinated leaders of Hamas, a violently anti-Israel organization responsible for many of the bombings. The Israelis periodically closed border crossings for security reasons, keeping Palestinian laborers from jobs in Israel and deepening Palestinian anger. None of these measures stopped the suicide attacks; indeed, they increased.

Prime Minister Ariel Sharon demanded an end to violence before peace talks could resume, and denounced Arafat's failure to stop the terrorists or end corruption in the Palestinian Authority. Arafat, in turn, insisted that as long as Israel fostered Jewish settlements in the West Bank and Gaza; dominated the region militarily; controlled water rights and highway access; and in other ways behaved as a colonial power, the anger that fueled the violence would continue. A fact-finding mission headed by former Senator George Mitchell concluded that peace was unlikely until Israel halted construction of new West Bank settlements.

Since Israel depended upon economic and military aid from the United States, America was implicated in the events in the region. Nevertheless, the Bush administration initially stood apart from the worsening conflict.

In March 2002, after a devastating round of suicide bombings, including a deadly attack on a Passover seder at a restaurant, Israel launched a major assault in the West Bank. Parts of the city of Jenin, a center of terrorist activity, were reduced to rubble. A standoff between armed Palestinians and Israeli troops unfolded around Bethlehem's Church of the Nativity. The Israelis besieged Arafat's compound in Ramallah, confining him in a single building for days. Eventually the Israelis withdrew, but conditions remained tense.

In a June 2002 speech offering a "road map" for peace, President Bush called for creation of a Palestinian state, Israeli withdrawal from the occupied Palestinian territories, and the resolution of other disputed issues. He also demanded an end to terrorism and recognition of Israel's right to exist secure within its borders, and he embraced the Israeli position that Arafat must go.

In June 2003 Bush met with Israeli and Palestinian leaders in Jordan to promote the "road map," but a brief truce collapsed after a deadly bus bombing in Jerusalem. From September 2000 to late 2003, the conflict had killed 800 Israelis and 2,300 Palestinians.

As violence continued, Israel began construction of a massive security fence separating Israel from the West Bank and Gaza. In places this fence extended into Palestinian territory and divided Palestinian communities from their lands, deepening Palestinian anger. In 2004, while pursuing construction of the wall, Sharon proposed withdrawing Jewish settlements and outposts from Gaza and a few from the West Bank, angering settlers and the hard-line expansionists in his own governing coalition.

At the same time, Sharon insisted that the largest Jewish settlements in the West Bank must remain, thereby angering the Palestinians, who argued that this should be a matter of negotiation, not unilateral action. Sharon also authorized the assassination of two successive heads of Hamas, accusing them of being nothing but terrorists. When President Bush endorsed Sharon's West Bank plan, Arab leaders reacted wth fury, accusing him of siding with Israel and abandoning America's role as an honest broker between the two sides.

Settlement of the Israeli-Palestinian conflict seemed essential to any comprehensive plan to combat terrorism by Islamic extremists, yet, that goal seemed more distant than ever. Since 1948 the United States, as Israel's principal ally, had tried without success to broker an enduring peace in the region. The familiar pattern of fresh initiatives by each new administration followed by frustration and defeat appeared to be repeating itself.

Bankruptcies and Scandals in Corporate America   Despite the distractions of tightened home-front security and a war in Iraq, economic matters also vied for attention as the recession led to a series of high-profile bankruptcies among energy and telecommunications companies that had thrived in the high-flying 1990s. Accusations of accounting fraud and other criminal behavior soon followed, producing a crisis of confidence in the integrity of corporate America.

First to fall was Houston's Enron Corporation, with close ties to the Bush administration. Selling electric power in advance at guaranteed rates, Enron flourished in the freewheeling climate of the 1990s and expanded into utilities and telecommunications. Hailed as a model of the new economy, the company charmed investors. In 2000, claiming assets of $62 billion, it ranked seventh in *Fortune* magazine's list of America's top corporations.

Late in 2001, Enron filed for bankruptcy and admitted to vastly overstating profits. Thousands of Enron workers lost both their jobs and their retirement funds, which consisted mostly of Enron stock. Like the 1980s savings-and-loan scandal and the disgrace of traders like Michael Milkin and Ivan Boesky (see Chapter 30), Enron's demise highlighted the risks of obsession with instant riches and ever-rising stock prices.

Enron was only the beginning. The overbuilt fiber-optics industry, having laid 100 million miles of optical fiber worldwide in 1999–2001, suffered staggering blows. Lucent Technologies, a telecommunications giant, cut nearly one hundred thousand jobs in 2001. Global Crossing, a high-speed voice and data carrier, declared bankruptcy in 2002, the fourth largest in U.S. history. In June 2002 WorldCom, America's second-largest telecommunications company and long-distance carrier, with 85,000 employees in 65 countries, announced that its chief financial officer had overstated profits by $3.8 billion. As WorldCom stock dropped to nine cents a share, the company fired seventeen thousand employees and filed for bankruptcy.

The Securities and Exchange Commission launched criminal proceedings; congressional committees held hearings; and President Bush called the WorldCom deception "outrageous."

In 2002 the Justice Department brought criminal charges, including the deliberate destruction of incriminating files and e-mail, against Arthur Andersen, a giant Chicago accounting firm that had certified the accuracy of the financial reports of Enron, WorldCom, and other troubled companies. A grand jury found the firm guilty, and it faced dissolution. The integrity of the accounting industry as a whole, so crucial to investor confidence, fell under suspicion.

Investment companies faced scrutiny as well, amid evidence that to generate business and keep profits high during the boom years, analysts at Merrill Lynch and other Wall Street firms had advised investors to buy stocks they knew to be vastly overpriced. Under pressure from the New York State attorney general, Merrill Lynch agreed to pay $100 million in fines.

In July 2002, in the first of what promised to be a series of criminal prosecutions, John J. Rigas and two of his sons, who had allegedly looted the family-owned TV-cable business, bankrupt Adelphia Communications, of $1 billion, were arrested and held for trial.

Public outrage deepened amid reports of corporate executives who made millions selling their own stock holdings just before their companies collapsed. Attention focused, too, on the stratospheric salaries and stock benefits these CEOs had earned. In his 2002 book *Wealth and Democracy*, Kevin Phillips reported that America's top ten CEOs earned an average of $154 million each in 2000. The greed at the upper levels of capitalist America seemed boundless.

The bankruptcies of seemingly healthy companies and the disclosures of deception in the business world slowed the economic recovery. Despite positive economic news, the stock market sank through much of 2002, as distrustful investors stayed away.

At a deeper level, the escalating scandals eroded the standing of corporate America. Executives who had been celebrities in the 1990s now faced deep public skepticism if not criminal charges. University of Maryland business students took field trips to penitentiaries where white-collar criminals warned them to be honest. Declared the chairman of Goldman Sachs, a major Wall Street investment bank, "I cannot think of a time when business . . . has been held in less repute."

Politicians and government agencies scrambled to respond to mounting public anger. President Bush delivered a stern speech about the need for business morality. The head of the Securities and Exchange Commission, the watchdog agency created in the 1930s, pledged to pursue wrongdoers, but he himself resigned in November 2002 amid conflict-of-interest charges.

To reassure investors, Congress passed a new regulatory law imposing stricter accounting rules, tightening procedures for corporate financial reporting, and toughening criminal penalties for business fraud. But the wave of scandals rolled on. In 2003, the head of the New York Stock Exchange resigned after revelations

| Martha Stewart outside of Courthouse

that his hand-picked board had given him a $187 million pay package. Martha Stewart, a famed home-decorating guru, was convicted in March 2004 of obstructing justice and lying to officials investigating charges that she had profited from insider trading in the stock of a pharmaceutical company whose head was a personal friend. Top officials at Enron faced criminal charges as well.

All these scandals were nurtured by the get-rich-quick mood of the booming 1990s, when investors came to expect stock prices to move ever higher, pressuring corporations to issue glowing reports of endless growth and soaring profits. The scandals also arose in a laissez-faire political climate that left regulatory agencies like the SEC understaffed, underfunded, and vulnerable to politicians and corporate leaders hostile to the entire notion of government regulation.

The widespread disgust with big business evoked memories of the Progressive Era, when reformers had denounced corporate greed and ruthlessness. It also recalled the early 1930s, when once-admired business leaders faced public hostility as hard times sank in. The pendulum would no doubt swing again, but for the moment the status of corporate America could hardly have been lower.

Elections of 2002 and 2004   The corporate scandals posed dangers for the Bush administration, with its close ties to big business. Bush's tax, energy, and environmental policies all served the interests of corporate America. His original tax-cut proposal (later scaled back by Congress) would have given lucrative tax breaks to America's biggest corporations, including a $254 million windfall to Enron. Bush's own well-timed and highly profitable 1990 sale of his stock in a failing Texas energy company of which he was a director came up for fresh examination.

As the business scandals unfolded, the 2002 election approached. Would Bush be seen as the bold leader of the just war on terrorism, or as a president who did the bidding of a powerful corporate elite whose reputation lay in tatters?

November 5, 2002, brought the answer, as Republicans regained control of the Senate and increased their House majority. President Bush, enjoying popularity ratings close to 70 percent, had campaigned tirelessly, stressing the antiterrorism campaign. The Democrats proved unable to shift focus to the economy and corporate scandals. In the wake of the defeat, Representative Richard Gephardt of Missouri resigned as House Democratic leader. He was replaced by Nancy Pelosi of California, who became the first woman of either party to hold such a major leadership position in Congress.

By early 2004, with another presidential election looming, Bush's approval ratings had sunk to around 50 percent, presaging another close contest. An improving economy helped the president's cause. The stock market had recovered most of its losses and other economic indicators looked good. Unemployment in March 2004 stood at 5.7 percent, down from 6.5 percent in January 2003, and the jobs picture looked brighter. Bush took credit for the recovery, pointing to the stimulus effect of his tax cuts. But many jobs had been lost in the recession, including 2.8 million in manufacturing, as corporations shifted production to foreign countries with lower wage scales and fewer employee benefits. The southern textile industry was especially hard-hit. The shift of manufacturing overseas emerged as a major campaign issue. "America's greatest export is jobs," went one Democratic campaign slogan. Supporters of NAFTA and the WTO vigorously insisted that despite job losses in some sectors, globalization and lower trade barriers benefited the U.S. economy overall.

Bush continued to hammer on security issues and to defend the Iraq war. His 2004 State of the Union address mentioned "war" twelve times and "terror," "terrorism," or "terrorists" twenty times. Offering a variant of the Cold War charge that Democrats were "soft on communism," Bush came close to suggesting that Democrats were "soft on terrorism." The administration's 2005 budget proposed a 7 percent increase in military spending (not including upwards of $50 billion more for the continuing Iraq operations), and a 10 percent increase for homeland security. (On the cost-cutting side, Bush proposed to slash the Environmental Protection Agency's budget by 7 percent.)

Bush gained some support among senior citizens in 2003 when Congress passed his Medicare reform bill providing limited prescription-drug benefits beginning in 2006. Hispanics and many employers welcomed his 2004 proposal to issue temporary work permits to some 8 million illegal immigrants, mostly from Mexico, working for low wages and no job security in the shadow economy.

As Democrats moved into election mode, they charged the administration with favoritism to big business, a needlessly belligerent and unilateralist foreign policy, and an unwise rush to war in Iraq. Pointing to a record federal deficit of $521 billion in 2004, they portrayed Bush as a profligate spender concerned only with short-term political calculations. Challenging the Republicans' reputation for fiscal restraint, the senior Democrat on the Senate Budget Committee, Kent Conrad of North Dakota, attacked Bush as "the most fiscally irresponsible [president] in the nation's history." (Many Republican leaders, while not attacking Bush so openly, shared this view as well.)

As for the president's Medicare reform, Democrats charged that the massive cost of the new drug coverage ($540 billion in the first ten years) would worsen the federal deficit, and noted that the law placed no restraints on drug-company prices and prevented seniors from buying less-expensive prescription drugs from Canada. Democrats especially criticized a provision that permitted seniors to opt out of Medicare and join private for-profit health-maintenance organizations, arguing that this could potentially destroy the Medicare system.

In the race for the Democratic presidential nomination, former Vermont governor Howard Dean, an outspoken opponent of the Iraq war who appealed to young voters and raised millions through the Internet, surged to an early lead. Dean faded after he placed third in the Iowa caucuses in January 2004, however. Two other contenders also dropped out as the primary season continued: North Carolina senator John Edwards, a wealthy trial lawyer, and retired general Wesley Clark, a former NATO commander and Iraq War critic. By April the unchallenged frontrunner was Senator John Kerry of Massachusetts, a Yale graduate (like George W. Bush) and decorated Vietnam War veteran who later opposed the war and then in 1982 won election to the U.S. Senate. Some early straw polls put Kerry slightly ahead of Bush. But the president, amassing a campaign war chest expected to reach $150 million and presenting himself as a leader committed to protecting the nation in perilous times, remained a formidable foe as he sought a second term.

CONCLUSION

Brief as it was, the interval spanning Bill Clinton's second term and George W. Bush's first term brought many changes. The Republican administration that emerged from the disputed 2000 election pursued a conservative, probusiness domestic agenda, advocating fiscal and environmental policies that many critics denounced as irresponsible, and a go-it-alone approach to foreign policy. The humming economy of the 1990s stalled in 2000–2001, leading to a recession and, indirectly, to a wave of business failures and corporate scandals. And, as we saw in Chapter 31, America's social and demographic profile continued to change as the population grew older, the surging growth of the Sunbelt continued, and the Hispanic and Asian populations increased at a rapid pace.

On September 11, 2001, a shocking act of mass terrorism transformed America. Like Pearl Harbor sixty years before, the shattering events of that day opened a new chapter in U.S. history. The 9/11 attacks initially produced a world outpouring of sympathy and a spirit of unity at home. However, as the Bush administration pursued security measures that many believed jeopardized civil liberties and launched a preemptive war in Iraq without a clear international mandate, controversy arose at home and abroad.

A post–Cold War future that had looked so promising only a few years earlier had suddenly become more menacing, adding a dark strand of apprehension to Americans' traditional optimism and confidence. Coping with the complex new realities of a post-9/11 world would clearly challenge the tolerance and wisdom of all citizens. Yet the enduring vision of what America at its best might become, despite the dangers stalking an uncertain world, remained strong.

As 2001 ended, Norway awarded the Nobel Peace Prize to Kofi Annan, secretary general of the United Nations. Accepting the award in Oslo, Annan acknowledged the irony of celebrating peace amidst rampant war and terrorism. "We have entered the third millennium through a gate of fire," he said. Annan went on to call for a rededication to the vision that had inspired the U.N.'s founders fifty-six years earlier. Despite the hatred and vast inequalities dividing nations and peoples, he insisted, the fate of all Earth's inhabitants was interconnected. "In the 21st century," he said, ". . . [h]umanity is indivisible."

IMPORTANT EVENTS, 1996 TO THE PRESENT

1994 Oslo Accords establish framework for peace between Israel and Palestinians.

1995 World Trade Organization (WTO) replaces GATT as regulator of world trade.
Dayton Accords establish cease-fire in Bosnia.

1996 Clinton reelected.

1997 Kyoto Accords on emission standards.

1998 Terrorist bombings of U.S. embassies in Kenya and Tanzania.
House of Representatives impeaches Clinton.

1999 NATO offensive drives Yugoslav forces out of Kosovo.
Senate trial acquits Clinton.

2000 Congress normalizes trade relations with China.
End of economic boom.
Yasir Arafat rejects Israeli peace plan; second Intifada begins.
U.S.S. Cole bombed in Aden harbor, Yemen.
Presidential election: Al Gore wins popular vote; George W. Bush chosen by electoral college after Supreme Court intervenes to resolve disputed Florida vote.
Republicans retain slim majorities in both houses of Congress.

2001 Bush administration repudiates Kyoto protocol on emission standards.
Congress passes $1.35 trillion tax-cut bill.
Senator Jeffords becomes an independent; Democrats regain control of Senate.
September 11 terrorist attacks on World Trade Center, Pentagon.
U.S. and allied forces defeat Taliban regime in Afghanistan and attack Al Qaeda terrorist network.

U.S. withdraws from ABM (Anti-Ballistic Missile) Treaty and begins construction of missile defense system.

Collapse of Enron Corporation; wave of corporate bankruptcies and accounting scandals.

2002 Bipartisan Campaign Reform Act.
Department of Homeland Security created
Palestinian suicide bombings; Israeli invasion of West Bank.
Republicans regain Senate in midterm elections.

2003 U.S. and British forces invade Iraq (March).
Bush declares end of major hostilities (May).
Bush requests $87 billion for Iraq occupation and reconstruction.
Continued insurgent attacks on U.S. troops and Iraqi supporters.
U.N. headquarters and major Shiite shrine in Iraq bombed.
Saddam Hussein captured (December).
Medicare reform provides prescription drug benefits for seniors.
Federal courts challenge government treatment of security suspects.

2004 Heavy losses in Iraq as insurgency continues
Loya Jirga in Afghanistan approves new constitution.
Scheduled turnover of authority to new Iraqi government (June 30).
Martha Stewart convicted in insider-trading case.
Federal deficit reaches $521 billion.
John Kerry emerges as front-runner for Democratic nomination.
Bush amasses large campaign war chest for 2004 election.

Credits

Photo Credits

CHAPTER 16 *p. 577: Harper's Weekly*, 1866. *p. 585:* Schlesinger Library, Radcliffe Institute / Harvard University. *p. 588:* Museum of the Confederacy. *p. 593:* William Gladstone. *p. 598:* ID 50819 © Collection of the New-York Historical Society.

CHAPTER 17 *p. 618 (left):* National Anthropological Archives, Smithsonian Institution, Washington, D.C. *p. 618 (right):* Library of Congress. *p. 628:* Denver Public Library, Western History Division. *p. 633:* Museum of New Mexico. *p. 639:* Denver Public Library, Western History Division.

CHAPTER 18 *p. 652:* Hagley Museum and Library. *p. 667: Harper's Weekly*, March 26, 1877. *p. 670:* Library of Congress. *p. 678:* Museum of American Political Life, University of Hartford, West Hartford, Connecticut.

CHAPTER 19 *p. 689:* Granger Collection. *p. 693:* Library of Congress. *p. 695:* California Historical Society. *p. 701:* Copyright © John Grossman, the John Grossman Collection of Antique Images *p. 711:* Henry Ford Museum and Greenfield Village.

CHAPTER 20 *p. 733:* Granger Collection. *p. 745:* Library of Congress. *p. 753:* Smithsonian Institution, Washington, D.C. *p. 761:* National Archives.

CHAPTER 21 *p. 765:* Brown Brothers. *p. 779:* Brown Brothers. *p. 786:* Library of Congress. *p. 788:* Library of Congress. *p. 796:* © Bettmann – Corbis.

CHAPTER 22 *p. 811:* Naval Historical Foundation. *p. 824:* U.S. Army Military History Institute. *p. 839: The Brooklyn Eagle*, 1919. *p. 842:* Collection of David J. and Janice L. Frent.

CHAPTER 23 *p. 851:* Walter P. Reuther Library / Wayne State University. *p. 858:* Courtesy of the Arizona Historical Society, Tucson AHS #62669. *p. 864 (left):* Picture Research Consultants and Archives. *p. 865 (right):* Stock Montage. *p. 867:* National Portrait Gallery, Smithsonian Institution, Washington, D.C. / Art Resource, NY.

CHAPTER 24 *p. 891:* © Bettmann – Corbis. *p. 901:* Smithsonian American Art Museum, Washington, D.C. / Art Resource, NY. *p. 911:* Library of Congress. *p. 919:* Library of Congress.

CHAPTER 25 *p. 932:* Thomas McAvoy / TIMEPIX – Getty Images. *p. 944:* Library of Congress. *p. 946:* National Archives. *p. 961:* Library of Congress. *p. 964:* U.S. Army / Franklin D. Roosevelt Library.

CHAPTER 26 *p. 975:* Indiana University. *p. 983:* Bettmann – Corbis. *p. 988:* Bettmann – Corbis 4EP.799. *p. 993:* Hy Peskin / TIMEPIX – Getty Images. *p. 1000:* "I Have Here in My Hand ..." from HERBLOCK: *A Cartoonist's Life* (Macmillan Publishing Company, 1993).

CHAPTER 27 *p. 1013:* Wide World Photos, Inc. *p. 1017:* Wide World Photos, Inc. *p. 1023:* Alfred Eisenstaedt / Life Magazine, TIMEPIX – Getty Images. *p. 1032:* Gaslight Advertising Archives. *p. 1037:* Bettmann – Corbis.

CHAPTER 28 *p. 1046:* Wide World Photos, Inc. *p. 1048:* © Bettmann – Corbis. *p. 1054:* Lyndon B. Johnson Presidential Library. *p. 1067:* Bettmann – Corbis. *p. 1078:* Bettmann – Corbis.

CHAPTER 29 *p. 1085:* John Filo. *p. 1091:* Wide World Photos, Inc. *p. 1092:* Elliot Landy / Magnum Photos, Inc. Wide World Photos, Inc. *p. 1105:* Flip Schulke / Black Star / Stock Photo. *p. 1110:* Illustration by Jack Davis for *Time* cover, April 30, 1973 / TIMEPIX – Getty Images.

CHAPTER 30 *p. 1118:* Courtesy Tuck School of Business Archives, Dartmouth College, Hanover, New Hampshire. *p. 1126:* NASA / Johnson Space Center. *p. 1130:* Jimmy Carter Presidential Library. *p. 1134:* © Wally McNamee / Bettmann – Corbis. *p. 1143:* Wide World Photos, Inc.

CHAPTER 31 *p. 1149:* © Bettmann – Corbis, Seth Resnick / Stock Boston. *p. 1155:* Bruno Barbey / Magnum Photos, Inc. *p. 1166:* Brooks Kraft / Sygma – Corbis. *p. 1171:* M. Almeida / *The New York Times.* *p. 1181:* R. Fremson / *The New York Times.*

CHAPTER 32 *p. 1188:* Richard Ellis / Sygma – Corbis. *p. 1202:* Reuters – Corbis. *p. 1211:* Don Tellock / Gamma Press, USA, Inc. *p. 1217:* Handout – Corbis. *p. 1224:* Chip East / Reuters – Corbis.

Text Credits

CHAPTER 23 *p. 846 Figure:* From *The First Measured Century: An Illustrated Guide to Trends in America, 1900–2000,* by Theodore Caplow, et al., 2000. Reprinted with the permission of The American Enterprise Institute for Public Policy Research, Washington, D.C.

CHAPTER 26 *p. 987 Figure:* Copyright © 2000 by Bedford/St. Martin's. From *America's History,* Volume II, Fourth Edition by James A. Henretta et al. Reprinted with permission of Bedford/St. Martin's.

Index